Oracle Case Management Solutions

Oracle Case Management Solutions

Léon Smiers
Manas Deb
Joop Koster
Prasen Palvankar

CRC Press
Taylor & Francis Group
Boca Raton London New York

CRC Press is an imprint of the
Taylor & Francis Group, an **informa** business
AN AUERBACH BOOK

CRC Press
Taylor & Francis Group
6000 Broken Sound Parkway NW, Suite 300
Boca Raton, FL 33487-2742

Printed on acid-free paper
Version Date: 20150813

International Standard Book Number-13: 978-1-4822-2382-8 (Hardback)

Visit the Taylor & Francis Web site at
http://www.taylorandfrancis.com

and the CRC Press Web site at
http://www.crcpress.com

Printed and bound by CPI Group (UK) Ltd, Croydon, CR0 4YY

Contents

Foreword xvii
List of Acronyms xxi
Preface xxv
Acknowledgments xxix
Authors xxxi

SECTION I THE CASE FOR CASE MANAGEMENT **1**

1 Basics of Case Management **3**
1.1 Introduction 3
1.2 Unexpected Surprises (or Shocks) 4
1.2.1 "Are You Being Served?" 4
1.2.2 "Doctor, I Have a Headache…" 5
1.2.3 "Look! There's a Dead Man in the Closet!" 7
1.2.4 Goal-Driven, Knowledge Work Freedom, On-Demand Collaboration 9
1.3 Handling of Credit Card Rewards Disputes 10
1.4 Case Management: Basics 14
1.4.1 What Is Case Management? What Is Adaptive Case Management? 14
1.4.2 Case Management Ecosystem 18
1.4.3 Brief History of Case Management 20
1.4.4 Formal Definition of (Adaptive) Case Management 21
1.4.5 Application of Case Management Solutions 24
1.5 Creating Case Management Solutions 27
1.5.1 High-Level Solution Architectures 27
1.5.2 Build or Buy? 30
1.5.3 Building a Fit-for-Purpose Case Management Solution 33
1.6 ACM and Business Agility 40
1.7 Summary 45

2 Adaptive Case Management (ACM)–Related Topics **47**
2.1 Introduction 47
2.2 Adaptive Systems and ACM 48
2.2.1 Nile Crocodiles and Cuttlefish 48
2.2.2 Sense-and-Respond, Anticipate-and-Preempt, and Complex Adaptive Systems (CAS) 49
2.2.3 ACM Solutions as Sense-and-Respond (Complex) Adaptive Systems (SR-CAS) 55

2.3 Dynamic, Production, and Adaptive Case Management (DCM, PCM, and ACM) 61
2.3.1 Basic Debates 61
2.3.2 Digging Deeper into DCM, PCM, and ACM 63
2.4 Process Management and Case Management: Friends or Foes? 70
2.4.1 Anatomy of a Journey 70
2.4.2 Process Management vis-à-vis Case Management 71
2.4.3 Case Management as Part of a BPMS? 76
2.5 Adoption of Case Management: Capability Maturity Considerations 79
2.5.1 "Generalized" BPM 80
2.5.2 Maturity Levels 81
2.5.3 Maturity Model Capabilities 82
2.5.4 Adoption of Case Management: A Case Study 88
2.5.5 Maturity Is More Than Technology 91
2.6 Making the Business Case for Case Management 92
2.6.1 General Considerations for Creating and Presenting a Business Case 92
2.6.2 Specific Considerations for a Case Management Business Case 94
2.7 Summary 97

SECTION II CASE MANAGEMENT SOLUTION FRAMEWORK 99

3 Case Management Functional Design 101
3.1 Introduction 101
3.2 Principles for the Solution Design Components 101
3.3 Design Components 102
3.3.1 Design Components Overview 102
3.3.2 Case Lifecycle Design Category 103
3.3.2.1 Aim 103
3.3.2.2 Relation with the Principles 104
3.3.2.3 Case Management Lifecycle Design Components 104
3.3.3 Case Information Design Category 108
3.3.3.1 Aim 108
3.3.3.2 Relation with the Principles 108
3.3.3.3 Case Management Information Design Components 108
3.3.4 Case Interaction Design Category 112
3.3.4.1 Aim 112
3.3.4.2 Relation with the Principles 112
3.3.4.3 Case Management Interaction Design Components 113
3.3.5 Case Cross-Functional Design Category 114
3.3.5.1 Aim 114
3.3.5.2 Relation with the Principles 114
3.3.5.3 Case Management Cross-Functional Design Components 114
3.4 Design Template 116
3.5 Conclusion 116

4 Case Management Classifications 119
4.1 Introduction 119
4.2 Forrester Case Management Classifications 119
4.3 Common Principles for the Classifications 120
4.4 Service Request Classification 120
4.4.1 Context 120
4.4.2 Determination 120
4.4.3 Alignment with Industry Processes 121
4.4.4 Business Challenges 122
4.4.5 Principles for the Solution 123
4.4.6 Case Management Design Components 123
4.4.6.1 Service Request Design Category Overview 124
4.4.6.2 Case Lifecycle Design Category 124
4.5 Incident Management Case Classification 133
4.5.1 Context 133
4.5.2 Determination 134
4.5.3 Alignment with Industry Processes 134
4.5.4 Business Challenges 134
4.5.5 Principles for the Solution 135
4.5.6 Case Management Design Components 135
4.5.6.1 Incident Management Design Category Overview 135
4.5.6.2 Case Lifecycle Design Category 135
4.6 Investigative Case Classification 143
4.6.1 Context 143
4.6.2 Determination 145
4.6.3 Alignment with Industry Processes 145
4.6.4 Business Challenges 145
4.6.5 Principles for the Solution 145
4.6.6 Case Management Design Components 146
4.6.6.1 Investigative Handling Design Category Overview 146
4.6.6.2 Case Lifecycle Design Category 146
4.7 Conclusion 153

5 Determine Solution Mapping 155
5.1 Introduction 155
5.2 Techniques Used to Determine the Impact of Functionality onto the IT Landscape 155
5.2.1 Common Reference Architecture Model 155
5.2.2 CORA Model Layering and Capabilities 156
5.2.3 Delivering a Solution with the CORA Model 157
5.3 Perform a Functional Decomposition Using CORA Application Layers 158
5.3.1 How to Map the Case Management Design Areas onto the CORA Application Layers 158
5.3.1.1 Case Lifecycle Design 159
5.3.1.2 Case Interaction Design 161

5.3.1.3 Case Management Information Design....162
5.3.1.4 Cross-Functional Design Areas....162
5.4 Determine Required Technology Capabilities....165
5.4.1 Case Flows and Processes Capabilities....165
5.4.2 Event Handling Capabilities....165
5.4.3 Business Rules Capabilities....165
5.5 Decide What Technologies to Use....168
5.6 Conclusion....168

6 Concluding Remarks....171

SECTION III ORACLE CASE MANAGEMENT TECHNOLOGIES 173

7 Oracle BPM/ACM....177
7.1 Introduction....177
7.2 Oracle BPM/ACM/SOA Suite Overview....177
7.3 Oracle BPM/ACM Usage Characteristics....179
7.4 Case Management Lifecycle Functionality with Oracle BPM/ACM....179
7.4.1 Case Flow and Process Design....180
7.4.1.1 Case Flow Design with Oracle Adaptive Case Management....180
7.4.1.2 Process Modeling....181
7.4.2 Event Design....182
7.4.3 Rules Design....182
7.4.4 Life Cycle Design Product Mapping to Oracle BPM/ACM/SOA Suite....183
7.4.4.1 Case Flow and Process Mapping....183
7.4.4.2 Event Handling Mapping....185
7.5 Case Management Interaction Functionality with Oracle SOA Suite....185
7.5.1 Portal Design: 360-Degree View of the Case....186
7.5.1.1 Out-of-the Box Functionality via the Oracle BPM/ ACM Portal....186
7.5.1.2 ADF, Customized Functionality with the Aid of the Case Management/BPM and Human Task APIs....186
7.5.2 Channel Design....187
7.6 Case Management Information Functionality with Oracle BPM/ACM/ SOA Suite....187
7.6.1 Case Execution Data: Detailed Audit Trail....188
7.6.2 Document and Media Design....189
7.7 Cross-Functional Case Management Capabilities....189
7.7.1 Case Management Integration Functionality with Oracle SOA Suite....190
7.7.2 Case Management Security Functionality with Oracle....190
7.7.2.1 Case Stakeholders....190
7.7.2.1 Permissions....190
7.8 Conclusion....191

8 Siebel....193
8.1 Introduction....193
8.2 Oracle Siebel Overview....193

8.2.1 History 193
8.2.2 Horizontal and Verticals 194
8.2.3 Configuration versus Customization 194
8.2.4 Extensions of Functionality 194
8.2.5 Siebel Specific Terminology 194
8.2.6 Market Example: Law Enforcement and Policing Operations Solution 195
8.3 Oracle Siebel Usage Characteristics 195
8.4 Case Management Information Functionality with Oracle Siebel 198
8.4.1 People Relationship Design and Data Design 198
8.4.2 Document and Media Design 200
8.5 Case Management Life Cycle Functionality with Oracle Siebel 200
8.5.1 Case Flow and Process Design with Oracle Siebel 200
8.5.1.1 State Model 201
8.5.1.2 Workflow Management 202
8.5.1.3 Assignment Management 202
8.5.1.4 Extending the Life Cycle Management, with the Law Enforcement and Policing Operations Example 202
8.5.2 Rules Design 203
8.5.3 Event Design 203
8.5.4 Life Cycle Design Product Mapping to Oracle Siebel and Related Products 203
8.6 Case Management Interaction Functionality with Oracle Siebel 205
8.6.1 Portal and Channel Design 205
8.7 Cross-Functional Case Management Capabilities 206
8.7.1 Case Management Integration Functionality with Oracle SOA Suite 206
8.7.2 Case Management Roles and Authorization Functionality with Oracle Siebel 206
8.8 Conclusion 207

9 Oracle Service Cloud 209
9.1 Introduction 209
9.2 Oracle Service Cloud Overview 209
9.2.1 History 209
9.2.2 Basic Functionality 210
9.2.3 Cloud-Based Management and Usage 210
9.2.4 Extensions of Functionality 210
9.3 Oracle Service Cloud Usage Characteristics 211
9.4 Case Management Interaction Functionality with Oracle Service Cloud 212
9.4.1 Portal Design 212
9.4.2 Channel Design 213
9.4.3 Dashboard Design 214
9.5 Case Management Information Functionality with the Oracle Service Cloud 214
9.5.1 Data Design 215
9.5.2 People Relationship Design 217
9.5.3 Document and Media Design 217

9.6 Case Management Life Cycle Functionality with Oracle Service Cloud 217
9.6.1 Case Flow and Process Design 218
9.6.2 Rules Design 219
9.6.3 Event Design 219
9.6.4 Life Cycle Design Product Mapping to Oracle Service Cloud 220
9.7 Cross-Functional Case Management Capabilities 220
9.7.1 Integration 220
9.7.2 Case Management Roles and Authorization Functionality 220
9.8 Conclusion 222

10 Intelligence in Relation to the Case Execution 223
10.1 Introduction 223
10.2 Case Intelligence Design 223
10.2.1 Intelligence Determined by Rules Design 224
10.2.2 Intelligence Determined by Event Design 224
10.2.3 Intelligence Determined by Dashboard Design 225
10.2.4 Intelligence Information Levels 225
10.3 Oracle Intelligence Products 225
10.3.1 Oracle Business Analytic Monitoring 225
10.3.1.1 Functionality 227
10.3.1.2 How Does BAM Relate to Case Management? 228
10.3.1.3 Technical Architecture 229
10.3.2 Oracle Event Processing 230
10.3.2.1 Functionality 230
10.3.2.2 How Does CEP Relate to Case Management? 231
10.3.3 Oracle Policy Automation 232
10.3.3.1 Functionality 232
10.3.3.2 How Does OPA Relate to Case Management? 233
10.3.4 Oracle Endeca Information Discovery 234
10.3.4.1 Functionality 234
10.3.4.2 How Does Endeca Information Discovery Relate to Case Management? 235
10.3.5 Oracle Real-Time Decisions 236
10.3.5.1 Functionality 236
10.4 Summary 237

11 Concluding Remarks 239

SECTION IV CASE MANAGEMENT EXAMPLES 243

12 Mortgage Request Handling 245
12.1 Introduction 245
12.2 Reading Guide 245
12.3 Mortgage Request and Business Challenges 245
12.3.1 Mortgage Request 245
12.3.2 Business Challenges 246

12.3.2.1 Serving the Customers 246
12.3.2.2 New Regulations 246
12.3.2.3 Minimizing the Probability of Default 247
12.4 Deriving a Solution Based upon the Case Management Solution Framework 247
12.4.1 Introduction 247
12.4.2 Determine Case Management Classification 247
12.4.3 Determine Functional Components and Needs 247
12.4.3.1 Case Flow and Process Design 248
12.4.3.2 Case Information Design 251
12.4.3.3 Case Interaction Design 254
12.4.4 Determine Solution Mapping 255
12.4.4.1 Impact of a Mortgage Request Operating Model on Solution Capabilities 255
12.4.4.2 Mapping Mortgage Request Operating Models to Oracle Products 258
12.5 Conclusion 262

13 Citizen Services in the Public Sector 263
13.1 Introduction 263
13.2 Reading Guide 263
13.3 Welfare Request and Business Challenges 264
13.3.1 Welfare Request Handling 264
13.3.2 Business Challenges 264
13.4 Deriving a Solution Based upon the Case Management Solution Framework 265
13.4.1 Introduction 265
13.4.2 Determine Case Management Classification 265
13.4.3 Determine Functional Components/Needs 265
13.4.3.1 Case Life Cycle Design 265
13.4.4 Determine Solution Mapping 271
13.4.4.1 Determine Solution Capabilities 271
13.4.4.2 Mapping the Welfare Request to Oracle Products 273
13.5 Conclusion 276

14 From Crime to Court 277
14.1 Introduction 277
14.2 Reading Guide 277
14.3 Police Investigation and Business Challenges 278
14.3.1 Police Investigation 278
14.3.2 Business Challenges for the Police Force Related to Crime Investigation 279
14.3.2.1 Globalization 279
14.3.2.2 Effectiveness of the Police Organization 280
14.3.2.3 Technology 280
14.3.2.4 Social Values Are Changing Rapidly 280
14.3.2.5 Adaption to Social and Crime Patterns 280
14.3.2.6 National Budgets Are Being Reduced 281

14.4 Solution Design Aspects 281
14.4.1 Introduction 281
14.4.2 Determine Case Management Classification 281
14.4.3 Determine Functional Components/Needs 281
14.4.3.1 Case Life Cycle Design 281
14.4.3.2 Case Information Design 284
14.4.3.3 Case Interaction Design 285
14.4.4 Deriving a Solution Based upon the Case Management Solution Framework 288
14.4.4.1 Full-Blown or Umbrella Type of Solution 288
14.4.4.2 Solution Mapping 290
14.4.4.3 Mapping Police Investigation to Oracle Products 292
14.5 Conclusion 294

15 End-to-End Insurance Claim Management 297
15.1 Introduction 297
15.2 Reading Guide 297
15.3 Insurance Claims and Challenges 298
15.3.1 Insurance Claims 298
15.3.2 Business Challenges Related to Insurance Claims 298
15.3.2.1 Financial 298
15.3.2.2 Customer Facing 299
15.3.2.3 Supporting IT Landscape 299
15.4 Deriving a Solution Based upon the Case Management Solution Framework 299
15.4.1 Introduction 299
15.4.2 Case Management Classification 299
15.4.3 Determine Functional Components and Needs 300
15.4.3.1 Case Life Cycle Design 300
15.4.3.2 Rules Design 301
15.4.3.3 Case User Interface Design 301
15.4.4 Determine Solution Mapping 303
15.4.4.1 Determine Solution Capabilities 303
15.4.4.2 Mapping the End-to-End Insurance Claim Handling to Oracle Products 304
15.5 Conclusion 307

16 Concluding Remarks 309

SECTION V TUTORIAL 311

17 Oracle BPM/ACM Tutorial 313
17.1 Introduction 313
17.2 Credit Card Charge Dispute: Use Case 313
17.2.1 Use Case Design Topics 313
17.2.2 Use Case Description 313
17.2.3 Credit Card Charge Dispute Life Cycle Design 317

17.2.3.1 Case Flow and Process Design 317
17.2.3.2 Rules Design 319
17.2.3.3 Event Design 321
17.2.4 Credit Card Charge Dispute Information Design 322
17.2.4.1 People Relationship Design 322
17.2.4.2 Data Design and Document Management Design 323
17.3 Installation and Tutorial Files 324
17.4 Key Elements of Oracle Adaptive Case Management 325
17.4.1 Case 325
17.4.2 Case Activities 326
17.4.2.1 Activity Implementation 326
17.4.2.2 Activity Properties 326
17.4.3 Case Data 326
17.4.3.1 Data Definition 326
17.4.3.2 External Case Data 327
17.4.4 Case Stakeholders 328
17.4.5 Case Documents 328
17.4.6 Rules and Policies 328
17.4.7 Case Events 329
17.5 Implement the Case with Oracle ACM 329
17.5.1 Create the Case Management Project 331
17.5.2 Define the Case Properties 333
17.5.2.1 Title 333
17.5.2.2 Summary 333
17.5.2.3 Priority 334
17.5.2.4 Category 334
17.5.2.5 Due Time 334
17.5.2.6 Milestones 334
17.5.2.7 Outcomes 334
17.5.3 Define the Data Model 335
17.5.3.1 Identify the Case Data Objects 335
17.5.3.2 Define the Case Data Objects 336
17.5.3.3 Create Data Forms 340
17.5.3.4 Define Flex Fields 341
17.5.4 Content Configuration 343
17.5.5 Define User Events 344
17.5.6 Define the Stakeholders and Permissions 344
17.5.6.1 Application Roles 344
17.5.6.2 Application Policies 345
17.5.6.3 Stakeholders 345
17.5.6.4 Permission Labels 345
17.5.6.5 Define Roles 345
17.5.6.6 Define Stakeholders 346
17.5.6.7 Define Permissions 347
17.5.7 Define Case Activities 348
17.5.7.1 Create a BPMN-Based Activity 350
17.5.7.2 Create a Human Task–Based Case Activity 354

17.5.8 Define the Rules 356
17.5.8.1 Activity Event Rules 358
17.5.8.2 Milestone Event Rules 361
17.5.8.3 User Event Rules 362
17.5.9 Resulting Application 363
17.6 Deploy and Test 364
17.6.1 Prepare Server for Deployment and Test 364
17.6.1.1 Start the Integrated WebLogic Server 364
17.6.1.2 Enable Development Mode 365
17.6.1.3 Create Test Users 365
17.6.2 Deploy Case Application 366
17.6.2.1 Deploy the Case Composite 366
17.6.2.2 Deploy Case Data Forms Application 366
17.6.2.3 Deploy Task Form Applications 367
17.6.3 Create a Case Instance 367
17.6.4 Working on the Case 368
17.6.4.1 Case Workspace 369
17.6.4.2 Update Process Roles 370
17.6.4.3 Grant Investigator Access Permission 371
17.6.4.4 Scenario #1 373
17.6.4.5 Scenario #2 374
17.7 Summary 374
17.A Appendix 375

18 Siebel Tutorial 379
18.1 Introduction 379
18.2 Siebel Implementation Approach 379
18.2.1 Choosing the Siebel Solution Type 380
18.2.2 Familiarization 380
18.2.3 Design 381
18.2.3.1 Functional Design 381
18.2.3.2 Solution Mapping 385
18.2.4 Implementation 385
18.3 Using the Police Investigation Application 386
18.3.1 Storyline 387
18.3.2 Recording a Lead 387
18.3.2.1 Creating the Lead and Entering the Generic Lead Information 387
18.3.2.2 Entering the Person, Object Location, and Event Information 390
18.3.2.3 Recording the Operational Information 390
18.3.2.4 Adding More Lead Details 391
18.3.2.5 Provide All Relevant Lead Information in the Lead 360° Overview 392
18.3.2.6 Sharing the Lead Information via Lead Export 392

18.3.3 Recording an Incident....393
18.3.3.1 Creating an Incident....393
18.3.3.2 Working on an Incident....393
18.3.3.3 Offence Management.... 394
18.3.3.4 Coercive Measures....395
18.3.3.5 Incident Overview....395
18.3.4 Recording a Case.... 396
18.3.4.1 Information Held as Part of the Case File.... 397
18.3.4.2 Assignment of Cases and Ownership.... 397
18.3.4.3 Case Serialization.... 398
18.3.4.4 Evidence Management.... 399
18.3.4.5 Involved Persons.... 400
18.3.4.6 Report Out.... 400
18.4 Conclusion....401

19 Concluding Remarks....403

Appendix A: CORA Model Capabilities.... 407

Appendix B: A Solution Characteristic.... 413

Index....419

Foreword

There were many lessons I learned while doing my MBA in the beginning of the twenty-first century. Two of the topics we learned kept puzzling me for a long time:

1. The importance of operational excellence by measuring and then optimizing the individual elements of a process.
2. The X and Y theory: Can you trust your employees and should you give unlimited freedom or are employees per definition not to trust and should you therefore install fixed procedures to support and control them.

Working in the services industry, it seemed that creating operational excellence was not really applicable since it all depends on the knowledge of the individual, of course supported by frameworks and best practices. Would it be useful and possible to break up the processes in a consulting engagement and optimize them accordingly?

In the later case you would also apply more control to the consultant workforce. Would that bring the best value to the customer, or should one apply the X theory and give full trust and freedom to the individual consultant in the hope they will act on the best behalf of the customer with the highest impact and productivity?

After several years managing P&Ls within our organization, I became convinced that probably a combination of both theories should apply. On the one hand, industrialize the way of working, meanwhile preserving the creativity of the individual. As once somebody told, each tailor uses the same procedures to create a suit; it is the fabric and the elegant touches that make him/her unique.

For me the big question is how can you facilitate the decision process of the individual, making sure he or she has all the information required to make the best decision for the company.

Current technology has finally come to maturity to deal with these questions. Case management allows you to gather information, industrialized or from creativity to guide knowledge workers in their decision-making. Not only in guiding but also allowing us to capture the Case in a structured way, making it possible to learn and adapt our decision making for future cases. In other words, to really make us a learning organization.

Case management is too often seen as a toolset to allow document handling in the public space. Case management can bring so much more.

The authors demonstrate in this book that if you want to be leading the digital space, if you want to provide the best customer experience, you need to start with facilitating the decision making process. This is what case management is all about. It is not about registering the transaction—it is to allow a better interaction with the end user.

With some great examples, this book will give you a better perspective of the art of the possible. How you can achieve a superior customer experience. How you can allow your employees to leverage their creativity to the max, based on thorough information and analysis. Yes, that can go hand in hand!

In other words, this book gave me the answer to the questions that puzzled me since the beginning of 2000. Can we further industrialize and optimize the services business while giving employees the maximum freedom to use their intellect? Yes we can; we call it case management.

Frank Wammes
CTO Application Services Continental Europe
Capgemini, the Netherlands

In 1959, Peter Drucker, an American management consultant whose work contributed to the foundations of the modern business, coined the term "knowledge worker" to refer to "employees such as data analysts, product developers, planners, programmers, and researchers who are engaged primarily in the acquisition, analysis, and manipulation of information as opposed to in the production of goods or services."

Fast-forward to today's modern IT landscapes, case management solutions aim to support the knowledge worker in his decision-making process and find the way into software vendor product portfolios. In fact, a business process management (BPM) product is not considered complete without some support for case management. BPMN 2.0 very well addresses the requirements for structured and human-centric business processes and has become quite successful for both process analysis and execution.

However, in situations with a large degree of process variance (a number of channels to consider, product groups, regions, etc.) and where new situations must be considered while the process is running, it has turned out to be quite hard or even impossible to implement in Business Process Modeling Notation (BPMN). The combinatorial explosion considering all variants of a process typically ends in bloated process diagrams with many decision gateways and/or event subprocesses with the process engine in full control of the execution. For an optimal support of the knowledge worker, the user should be in the driver seat of the business process though.

The upcoming Object Management Group (OMG) standard for case management model and notation (CMMN) addresses those requirements by providing the ability to "plan" work and in general follows an event and condition (considering the case data) paradigm rather than a strict sequence flow model.

This book is a "must read" for people who want to learn more about the area of case management and how case management functionality is supported in various Oracle products, including Oracle BPM Suite. It motivates with real-world examples and goes into details all the way to concrete implementation. The case management solution framework (CMSF) carved out in the book is technology agnostic and applicable in general. The case diagrams of the CMSF are modeled on CMMN, which makes this book a good complement to the CMMN specification and, thus, is among the first books using CMMN.

In our roles of Oracle BPM Suite product development and as contributors to the OMG BPMN 2.0, CMMN 1.0, and DMN 1.0 standards, we welcome this book as it nicely introduces the field of case management and then shows how the Oracle BPM Suite with its comprehensive set of functionality from low-level service orchestration and mediation to business processes with BPMN 2.0 and case management components can be used to implement adaptive case management solutions.

Ralf Mueller
Architect
Oracle BPM Suite

Vaishnavi Sashikanth
Vice President
Oracle Product Development

Presently, as machines and software are providing all the necessary means to automate routine work to their maximum possible extent, automation efficiency is receding in value as a competitive differentiator. Instead, a company's ability to use its organizational knowledge and experience to solve customer problems effectively is becoming more and more a favored strategy for excellence and competitiveness. Knowledge workers, those who actually translate the organizational knowledge to problem-solving tricks and techniques, need highly flexible work tools that traditional BPM, with rigid process models, do not provide; event-based adaptive case management (ACM) approach fills this gap. Of course, the world is typically not black-and-white, and, as we also see in my own company's work, most solutions aimed at organizing business activities naturally demand that there be a combination of case management and traditional BPM to deliver the right balance of effectiveness and efficiency. This book calls this combination "Generalized BPM."

Oracle provides a wide range of software tools to create Generalized BPM solutions, the most notable being the Oracle Unified BPM Suite, which uses essential features of SOA Suite as its foundation. ACM, BPM, and SOA are a natural match. Together, they facilitate the next phase in the evolution of digitization and automation of the next-generation business process management and derive higher value from SOA services, including better reuse, composability, and manageability. With this combined approach, business process management will no longer be about hard coding functions in a rigid process model but will rather become an agile platform helping to cope with continuous business changes and operations improvements.

However, having only the tools does not help with the whole process of taking user requirements and building solutions. Adequate and practical guidance on solution design philosophy as well as solution architecture and the implementation of best practices are necessary for the realization of a quality solution. This book, the first of its kind, provides this guidance starting at high-level considerations through appropriate technology choices from Oracle's big basket of products right up to solution design details, thus making the dream of creating business applications to manage structured and unstructured business activities an achievable one.

Geoffroy de Lamalle
CEO
eProseed

In the early years of web services and service-oriented architecture (SOA), I had the pleasure to work in my role at Oracle with some key architects at leading system integration companies. Across companies, we started to exchange information and best practices to deliver successful SOA customer projects, for example, one of the first European Oracle Service Bus or one of the first Oracle BPEL projects. This group of experts became the "masons of SOA." Based on the mission to share knowledge, leading industry experts like Thomas Erl invited us to speak at conferences, for example, the SOA Symposium. We also contribute to *SOA Design Patterns* or *Next Generation SOA* and the *SOA Magazine* with the Industrial SOA series.

From the early days of web services, we were part of the SOA journey and became more mature by adopting the service bus technology, orchestration like BPEL, business activity monitoring, pattern matching, and API management—all the solutions that became Oracle SOA Suite. The next step for Oracle was to adopt BPMN as an executable engine in the middleware portfolio. In 2013, it was obvious to extend BPM Suite with adaptive case management (ACM) functionality. ACM benefits from the whole Oracle middleware technology stack, including SOA, traditional BPM, document management, business intelligence, and identity management solutions.

In my role in Oracle, where I am responsible for Fusion Middleware Partner Adoption in Europe, Middleast, and Africa, I have the privilege to talk to industry experts as well as to Oracle product management and product development teams. It is wonderful to see that many of them contributed to this book. Oracle is organized by key product areas like database, middleware, and applications. Since more than 10 years, I have focused on the middleware technology set and this book is an eye opener for me to leverage this technology set as well as a few other Oracle application products for different case management solutions. It defines the starting point of an ACM journey. The solutions framework helps customers to design and classify your project. Based on the solution characteristics and the functional design, the technology capabilities are determined. The CORA framework is an excellent tool to determine an ACM solution that fits the use case. Customers benefit from selecting the right case management solution based on their need from the broad Oracle portfolio.

Like SOA, ACM, as we can see, continues to evolve. With the rise of the Internet of Things (IoT), the amount of information explodes. Big data make this information available. Knowledge workers can leverage ACM systems to make better decision. My daily work and the huge success of the Oracle Middleware Partner Community is an excellent example for knowledge workers working on cases—I would like to congratulate all the writers of this book to have achieved another milestone in our case.

Jürgen Kress
Fusion Middleware Partner Adoption EMEA

List of Acronyms

A2A	Application to application
ABC	Activity-based costing
ACM	Adaptive case management
ADF	Application development framework
AIIM	Association for Information and Image Management
AP	Accounts payable
API	Application programming interface
AR	Accounts receivables
B2B	Business to business
BAM	Business activity management
BI	Business intelligence
BO	Business object
BPEL	Business Process Execution Language
BPM	Business processes management
BPM Suite	Oracle Middleware Suite delivering BPM on top of the SOA Suite (containing ACM functionality)
BPM/ACM	Combination of business processes management and adaptive case management
BPMN	Business Process Modelling Notation
BPMN 2.0	Business Process Modelling Notation version as defined by OMG
CAS	Complex adaptive systems
CDO	Case data object
CEP	Complex event processing
CES	Complex evolving system
CM	Case management
CM L1, L2, L3	Case management design levels
CMM	Capability maturity model
CMMN	Case management model and notation
CMS	Content management system
CMSA	Case Management Society of America
CMSF	Case management solution framework
CORA	COmmon Reference Architecture
CQL	Continuous Query Language
CQS	Continuous query service
CRM	Customer relationship management

CRP	Conference room pilot
CSR	Customer service representative
CSS	Cascading style sheets
CX	Customer experience
DCM	Dynamic case management
DILO	Day in the life of
DO	Data object
EAI	Enterprise application integration
EDA	Event-driven architecture
EDN	Event delivery network
ERP	Enterprise resource planning
Four-Cs	Context, capabilities, collaboration, and coordination
GIS	Geographic information system
GPS	Global positioning system
H2A	Human to application
H2H	Human to human
HCM	Human capital management
IDE	Integrated development environment
INSEAD	Business school
J2EE	Java 2 Enterprise Edition
JSF	Java server faces
KPI	Key performance indicators
KRI	Key risk indicators
LDAP	Lightweight Directory Access Protocol
LOB	Line of business
LOV	List of values
M&A	Mergers and acquisitions
MAF	Mobile application framework
MDS	Meta data store
MQ	Magic Quadrant
MS	Microsoft
OA&M	Operations, administration, and management
OASIS	Organization for the Advancement of Structured Information Standards
OEP	Oracle event processing
OLAP	Online Analytical Processing
OMG	Object management group
OOTB	Out of the box
OPA	Oracle policy automation
Open UI	(Siebel related) Open user interface
OPSS	Oracle platform security services
Oracle SOA Suite	Oracle Middleware Suite delivering service-oriented architecture capabilities
PCM	Production case management
PDF	Acrobat portable document format (PDF)
PoC	Proof of concept
POLE	Person, object location, event
PoV	Point of view
PWT	Package walkthrough

REST	Representational state transfer
RFID	Radio frequency identification
RTD	Real-time decisions
SAAS	Software as a Service
SCA	Service composite architecture
SCM	Supply chain management
SI	System integrator
SLA	Service level agreement
SOA	Service-oriented architecture
SOAP	Simple object access protocol
SQL	Sequential Query Language
SR	Sense and respond
SR-CAS	Sense and respond complex adaptive systems
STP	Straight through processing
T&Cs	Terms and conditions
TCO	Total cost of ownership
TEI	Total elemental interactions
UI	User interface
VIP	Very important person
WF	Workflow
XLS	Microsoft Excel
XML	EXtensible Markup Language

Preface

"A crop farmer, motivated by the success of his friend's chicken farm, decided to 'grow' chickens himself. He tilled and fertilized his land nicely and 'planted' eggs in the soil. When no chickens emerged from the ground, utterly frustrated, he sent some soil sample to his regional agricultural office who promptly tested the soil and advised the farmer to increase the watering frequency…". I (Manas Deb) had once read a little narrative along these lines where the author was trying to illustrate (albeit using an absurd example) the difference between "doing the right thing" and "doing things right"—the difference between "effectiveness" (the former) and "efficiency" (the latter). Effectiveness is related to how useful some work is while efficiency is a measure of how well a "given task" is done. It is conceivable that a given task is not very useful for the ultimate goal; this was the case with the actions of this crop farmer or the regional agricultural office. At their simplest definition, effectiveness and efficiency may be seen as "perpendicular" concepts; that is, one can be achieved without worrying about the other and that one does not necessarily lead to the other. However, it should be immediately obvious to a sane mind that a simultaneous achievement of both effectiveness and efficiency would be highly desirable in most situations. The real question then is "How difficult is it to attain high effectiveness at high efficiency simultaneously?"—this is an "optimization" problem.

Tempted by the efficiency of machines that resulted from the various chapters of the Industrial Revolution and due to the fact that efficiency is relatively easy to measure and improve in most situations, we are often inclined to exclusively focus on it especially when trying to boost organizational performance. Is this enough? Say, we are trying to improve customer service. Rapid access to customer care representative (CSRs) or some helpful information is surely a good thing, but will they relieve the customer's agony when he or she is faced with a complex issue? Probably not. On the other hand, if the CSR is able to quickly navigate through the details of the customer complaint and is able to come up with creative solutions to resolve the issue, then that would certainly be a rewarding experience for the customer resulting in customer loyalty and competitive advantage for the company. Such actions (of the CSR) require the benefit of their experience and knowledge. Peter Drucker, one of the most notable management gurus of modern time, had been discussing the nature and importance of "knowledge work" since 1954. In his 1999 book, *Management Challenges for the 21st Century*, Drucker notes, "The most valuable assets of a 20th-century company were its production equipment. The most valuable asset of a 21st-century institution, whether business or nonbusiness, will be its knowledge workers and their productivity." So, how can we help knowledge workers do their jobs better?

Knowledge work is typically directed toward the nonroutine, that is, where not all work activities are preordained and require the use of human experience either acquired through formal education or on-the-job learning. Often, collaboration of peers or consultation with subject matter experts features as one of the ways to resolve complex issues. A knowledge worker requires more flexibility in the way work activities are selected and sequenced. Timely and proactive supply of helpful information can guide and facilitate a knowledge worker's performance. A traditional business process management (BPM)–based application has a fully predefined process model that captures the details of all work activities, logic for their sequencing, information about process worker assignments to specific tasks, and the necessary business rules. Such applications handle routine work very well but fall short in supporting knowledge work. In fact, even small deviations from the routine path are treated as "exceptions," that is, singled out as special cases typically dealt with by human experts at relatively higher costs; this strategy may be workable when the number of exceptions are small, however, from the description of knowledge work that we just provided, knowledge work modeled via traditional BPM is guaranteed to generate excessive amount of exceptions. Clearly, we need another approach to handle nonroutine knowledge-based work. This is where the idea of case management comes in.

In case management, instead of a fully predefined process model, work is organized more loosely under the umbrella of a "case" (as opposed to a "process") using "events," "phases," "milestones," and "activity lists" where some of these may be "mandatory" and the rest are selected by the case workers (who are essentially playing the roles of knowledge workers). Details of case progression are recorded in a "case folder" and case workers refer to this folder to learn about the history of the case progression and to decide what actions to undertake next. In certain implementations of case management, case workers can also add new activities or invite additional participants for contribution in the middle of a case progression—this is often termed as "adaptive" case management (ACM). One the other hand, if the case worker's flexibility to choose activities to be executed in a given case is limited to preset lists of available activities, then this variant is termed as "production" case management (PCM). Of course, it is conceivable that some of the case activities can be well described by processes (as in traditional BPM); conversely, starting from a process, we may find that certain process activities are better handled as cases; these hybrid solutions, which are likely to be quite common, is what we have termed here as "Generalized BPM."

While the idea of case management has been around for a long time and case workers have utilized things like paper trails, phone calls, and e-mails to manage the case progression, in recent years, with the increasing maturity of event-based application architecture, content management, real-time decision management, and supporting technology platforms, it is now possible to create comprehensive case management applications. Since a large portion of business activities contain some level of unpredictability and knowledge work, especially in the high-value-add situations, this technical feasibility of creating case management solutions has now pushed the interest in case management to a significantly high level. As can be expected, where case management is applicable, it brings higher efficacy, but how do we maintain high efficiency as well? Also, how do we continue to benefit from our knowledge of traditional BPM even in the presence of unpredictable knowledge work? In other words, how do we conceptualize, architect, and build Generalized BPM solutions that achieve the right balance of flexibility and efficiency and evolution and transformation of human behavior and expectations? The book is dedicated to this exploration, both from theoretical and practical points of view, starting with key concepts and observed examples to solution architectures and specific implementation strategies. While we have chosen a set of

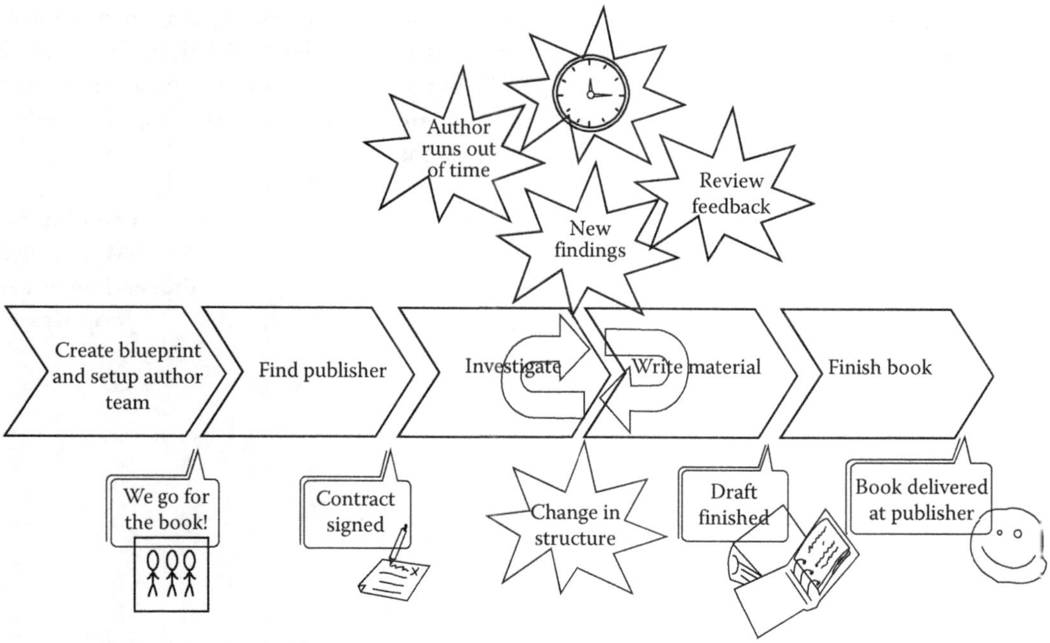

Figure P.1 The writing process of case management with Oracle Technologies.

Oracle technology products for the implementation examples, the rest of the book is technology platform–agnostic and, thus, should be helpful for anyone interested in going deeper into case management applications.

Looking back in retrospect, now that the book is finished, we realized that the writing process of our book was actually a case on its own. Figure P.1 gives a high-level overview of the activities, milestones, and events that formed the process of writing this book. The overall process is predictable: A set of high-level activities aimed at delivering a book. The process of writing this book started with creating a blueprint and finding authors. Once the team was composed, we all decided to go for it. This was the first milestone in the process. Then we started looking at where to publish our book. We were supported by the Oracle Publishers Program, which brought us in contact with different publishers. Different proposals were sent to the recommended publishers. Taylor & Francis Group were enthusiastic about the proposal and the contract was signed with them, marking the next milestone. A continuous loop of investigations, discussions with experts, writing, and reviewing took place followed by a one-and-a-half-year-long quest. Some unpredictable events occurred during this period that made us deviate from the desired path. *New findings* during the investigation and some of the *review feedback* from our esteemed reviewers made us change the content and the structure of the script. As this book was written next to our day-to-day busy jobs and in different time zones, our jobs required us to rearrange the writing priorities. At the same time we also had an arrangement with our publisher to deliver the book within a certain timeframe. The *investigate* and *write material* phases were the milestones accomplished next, in which the draft material was delivered. The last set of activities dealt with finishing the book, aligning the different book parts, getting all the pictures together, and reviewing the language. The final milestone was reached where the book was delivered to the publisher, and the case was closed.

In order to support this book a website has been created, see: http://oraclecasemanagement-solutions.com/. At this website code examples that are used in this book and errata on the book material are provided. From time-to-time insightful blogs on the topic of Case Management with Oracle technologies will also be posted at this site. If an error is found in the book or more information is needed, we request the reader to contact us via the website.

Léon Smiers
Manas Deb
Prasen Palvanker
Joop Koster

Acknowledgments

This book required a lot of insight and energy from many of our learned colleagues. Our sincere thanks to all those who were involved in reviewing, discussing, challenging, cowriting, and testing the book material even if we somehow missed to list them here explicitly. Since the book covers knowledge from three areas—architecture, industry, and Oracle technology—we needed support from a variety of people in different phases of the book writing process. We are especially indebted to them for giving us their tremendous support despite us being grumpy at times!

In the architecture area, we would like to thank Joost van der Vlies (think about meta-model!!) and Theo Elzinga for extensive (typically nightly) discussions on the case management solution framework. We thank Danilo Smiedel for collaboration on the generalized BPM maturity model and the ACM adoption case study. We gratefully acknowledge Tom Barrett for doing a very thorough review of the case management solution framework! We also enjoyed our discussions with Sybren de Hartog and Tim Arkin around the patterns. Last, but not the least, it was always a pleasure discussing with Roeland Loggen different aspects of case management.

In the example area in the book, we required specific industry knowledge in mortgage, public sector, police and insurance area. We thank Onur Balcak and Nicholas Kitson for numerous discussions around case management and the mortgage and insurance industry. Special thanks go to Hans Telgen for all the knowledge he brought in for the police and the public sector cases. Jeroen van Essen did a tremendous job contributing to the police case information! We thank Peter Kuijvenhoven and Maurice Vuijk for enriching our insurance knowledge.

In the Oracle technology area, we thank Ruben Spekle for collaborating on Oracle Service Cloud. We thank Hans Telgen, again, for his Siebel knowledge and for his help with the tutorial material. We also thank Martijn van der Kamp, Steven Boon, Jon Petter Hjulstad, and Alexander van der Woude for discussing and reviewing the material.

Thanks to Joost Smiers and Roeland Jansen for checking the book contract.

In the writing and finalization phase a special thanks goes out to Hiske van Haren for reviewing all the material and removing all the Denglish (Dutch-English) in the work.

We would like to thank the publishing team at Taylor & Francis Group, specifically John Wyzalek and Jessica Vakili, for their patience, cooperation, and help with the book delivery.

A last thanks is for all the coffee places in Cape Town, Shanghai, Rotterdam, Utrecht, Terschelling, Leeds, London, Sao Paulo, Singapore, Saigon, Hanoi, San Francisco, Santa Cruz, Sydney, Osaka, and Tokyo for providing the right amount of caffeine and atmosphere to write this book.

Acknowledgments

Authors

Léon Smiers works as a solution architect for Capgemini, The Netherlands, in the area of Oracle technology and architecture, where he is one of the leading Oracle specialists. He has done a lot of work and research in the field of integration and new technologies, like RFID, SOA, EDA, BPM, and case management, on which he wrote articles and presented in international conferences. Currently Léon is setting up Solution Architectures for large Oracle-based projects and is Oracle BPM Thought Leader for Capgemini. Léon is coinventor of the Common Reference Architecture mode or CORA model (www.coramodel.com), which helps in getting control over the IT landscape in hybrid environments and delivers a predictable, repeatable, and risk-aware solution design. Based upon his close cooperation with Oracle product management and field experiences, Léon was awarded the Oracle ACE title in 2010.

Dr. Manas Deb is president and COO of eProseed, a well-recognized Oracle technology partner. Previously he was a senior director in the Fusion Middleware/SOA and BPM Suite products group at Oracle HQ, where he had been leading outbound product management globally with a special focus on strategic customer engagements. Dr. Deb has worked in the software industry for more than 25 years, most of which was spent in business development, sales enablement, product development and management, and on architecting and leading many enterprise-level application development and business integration projects in a wide variety of industries. Dr. Deb has coauthored three other books on SOA and BPM and has been a speaker in many industry conferences. Dr. Deb attended postgraduate studies at The University of Texas at Austin. He has a PhD in computer science and applied mathematics, and an MBA.

Joop Koster is an experienced Oracle solution architect, CRM, and front-office consultant. He is one of the founding fathers of the Capgemini t-Police solution (https://www.capgemini.com/public-sector/transform-police-t-police), which entails a standardized solution for the police force. He has 15 years of IT consulting experience and more than 10 years of (management) experience in the printing industry. He is familiar with front-office and contact center, multichannel customer interaction, and CRM technologies. He has a broad experience in marketing, sales and services processes and technologies, and has worked in both B2B and B2C environments.

Prasen Palvankar is a director of product management at Oracle and currently leads development of industry solutions using Oracle's various PaaS offerings. Prior to taking on this role in February 2015, he was the product manager for Oracle Adaptive Case Management, Business Activity Monitoring, and Oracle Business Rules products in the Oracle BPM Suite product family. Prasen has more than 20 years of work experience in all aspects of software application development such as consulting, solution and enterprise architecture, business integration and process management, and advanced training development and delivery.

THE CASE FOR CASE MANAGEMENT

I

Introduction

Case management is a particular style of business activity management that has attracted significant attention in recent years. In the traditional business process management (BPM) discipline, all work activities, their execution sequences, and the rules governing them are predesigned via a "process model." A "process worker" interacts with an executable form of the process model and is mainly concerned with handling a subset of these work activities, and the process model guarantees the desired outcome of the whole process when the relevant activities are completed. All situations, known or unknown, that are not covered by the process model are tagged as "exceptions" and are handled in a special manner, typically outside the main process and often by humans.

In case management, where a case is some problem to be solved or a transaction to be completed, the primary goal is to reach a resolution for the case. The actual (case) work activities, their execution sequences and the involvement of case participants (i.e., the "case workers"), etc., while kept within what is permissible and reasonable, are secondary to the ultimate goal attainment (i.e., resolution of the case). Thus, case management provides a more flexible work activity management framework than traditional BPM; in its "adaptive" variation, adaptive case management (ACM) even provides the ability to modify work lists and case participant lists. In many instances, for example, those involving unstructured and knowledge work, turns out to be a better paradigm to manage business activities.

In the first section of this book, we provide a general treatise on case management, using mostly nontechnical verbiage, to cultivate an appreciation for case management philosophy and discipline. Chapter 1, titled "Basics of Case Management," establishes the usefulness of the case management discipline through a series of day-to-day work examples and sketches out what a basic case management system would look like, and then provides a historical background, discusses formal definitions, and illustrates typical industry applications of case management. The chapter concludes with a short discourse on how case management helps with increasing business agility.

Chapter 2, titled "Adaptive Case Management (ACM)–Related Topics," explores several concepts that are interesting when considering the "adaptive" aspect of ACM. These concepts include sense-and-respond, anticipate-and-preempt, and the characteristics of complex adaptive systems (CAS), and indicate how case management style of problem solving in fact mimics the way humans solve problems on a day-to-day basis. Often a bit philosophical, these discussions are aimed at helping case management system solution architects better imagine the overall solution characteristics in a manner best suitable for target unstructured and knowledge work. A small discussion on the case management system classifications like dynamic case management (DCM) and production case management (PCM) along with ACM is presented here as well with the goal to help solution architects pick the most appropriate style of case management system for their problem at hand. Next, case management is compared and contrasted with essentials of BPM. A notion of "Generalized BPM" that combines capabilities of both is then introduced as an approach likely to find broader usefulness in capturing business activities that display both structured and unstructured aspects. A "capability maturity model" for Generalized BPM is also discussed. The chapter ends with a short discourse on considerations relevant to the creation of business cases for case management.

Chapter 1

Basics of Case Management

1.1 Introduction

Home proponit, sed Deus disponit (or in English: Man proposes, but God disposes) first appeared in a published work in the collection named *Die Imitaione Christi* (or *The Imitation of Christ*) by Thomas Kempis in the early 1400s. The *Imitation of Christ* is claimed to be the second most read Christian text after The Bible, and the quote itself is well known and well appreciated by all regardless of their religious beliefs. A secular interpretation of the quote would simply state that we (the humans) cannot foresee it all. Hence, the wiser among us must "plan for the unplanned"! The fact that uncertainty could hit our otherwise planned activities is not limited to our personal lives—the same is true in many business situations. Clearly, some suitable strategy has to be in place if organizations want to track and improve business activities that include unplanned actions.

Uncertainty is not the only variable introducing complexity in managing business activities. We can be certain that there has always been a standing struggle between two distinct work patterns: those that can be done by preset "routine" activities requiring relatively low skills typically perfected by mere practice and those that require "knowledge work" performed by experienced personnel requiring some level of freedom in a way how the activities are chosen and executed. Routine work can be made highly efficient and often automated, thus speeding up the work and driving down the cost. Routine work is also more easily managed, monitored, and improved than knowledge work since knowledge work involves a variety of "loosely connected" tasks undertaken in sequences that depend on the evolving context of the business problem. Thus, predetermined routine work patterns are simpler and preferred in many ways; however, they have limited capability of handling complex contextual variation and emergent events—knowledge work pattern is much better suited in these situations.

If we took a close look at the nature of work that businesses perform, we would find that a significant portion of the business activities are not of routine and deterministic type; instead, they are either done by knowledge workers or contain some nondeterministic characteristics. Work flow (WF) and business process management (BPM) have been traditionally used as the chosen disciplines to handle preset deterministic routine work. The necessary technology, solution, architecture, and practices supporting WF and BPM are now quite mature. Unfortunately, they do not provide a suitable approach to design, implement, and execute business applications that are knowledge work driven and need to handle uncertainties due to emergent events. This is the job of "case management" where work is done (i.e., the case is progressed) primarily to achieve a set of goals for the ultimate benefactors, for example, customers. A customer may contact a business with a request for resolution of a complaint that he or she may have about a product or a service, which may lead to starting of a "case" with the goal of delivering the requested resolution satisfactorily. The "case owners" and "case workers" will progress the case via completing certain milestones by arranging their activities best suited for achieving the goal of the case. We will be delving into more details of what a case is made of, how it is progressed, how work during the case progression is "adapted" when necessary, etc., later in this chapter and throughout the rest of the book as opportunities arise. First, let us look at a few real-life problems where it should be obvious that the solutions to the problems involve dealing with unpredictable or knowledge work.

1.2 Unexpected Surprises (or Shocks)

1.2.1 "Are You Being Served?"

Sometime in the 1970s a customer in Fairbanks, Alaska, walked into a Nordstrom store, returned a tire, and got some refund. Ordinarily this would sound like nothing special unless of course the store, in this case, Nordstrom, was an "apparel and shoes" store and did not sell tires! Founded in 1901, Nordstrom is now a large fashion retail chain and prides itself in providing extraordinary customer care and experience; "A relentless drive to exceed expectation" is a quote from the "About Us" page at their website (shop.nordstrom.com). While there are many variations that exist as to the exact details of the aforementioned tire incident (and the curious reader is welcome to do some fun research). The "tire refund" tale has become legendary in the realm of high-quality customer service. In fact, there is a well-established perception in the buyer community that Nordstrom staff is knowledgeable and is keen on providing a lasting positive buying experience to their customers whether it is to find the right product, arrange custom orders, or provide insight into latest fashion trends. Corporate resolve to serve customers excellently must be matched by the knowledge and freedom of action of the customer care people that are needed in order to handle tricky customer situations. Exceeding customer expectation is generally not trivial. However, a pleasantly surprised customer often becomes a loyal follower of the brand, providing the company a strong source of competitive advantage. In fact, a company's reputation as a bad customer service provider can cost them dearly in many ways and really fast with today's customers constantly posting reviews online, which prospects almost always look into before making buying decisions; bad reviews are posted and shared much more frequently compared to good reviews. Companies serious about healthy growth and margin therefore take the delivery of good customer service very seriously and sometimes employ interesting and creative means to recover from bad service delivery. Take, for example, the Canadian health care company "Nurse Next Door." As reported in an online article by Justin Martin accessed at cnn.com in January/2014 (http://money.cnn.com/galleries/2007/fsb/0709/gallery.where_customers_come_first.fsb/) when this company fails to deliver good service it delivers a "humble pie," which is a real fresh-baked apple pie, to the affected customer with an apology note. The company estimated that the value of customer retention via this innovative and proactive is the range of 60–70 times the cost of apology.

Are you being served? was a highly popular (and remains popular to date to select audiences) British sitcom (http://www.bbc.co.uk/comedy/areyoubeingserved/; accessed December/2013) that ran from 1972 to 1985. Set in the early-twentieth-century culture and etiquette and the day-to-day on goings at Grace Brothers, a fictional department store in London, the episodes of this sitcom humored viewers by parodying customer service and innuendo filled exchanges among the shop floor workers across gender and class lines. Often, the customers in this sitcom were put in awkward and unpleasant situations by the doings of the shop floor employees and the customer would vow never to come back to the store. This was fine since it was a sitcom and the only goal there was is to provide entertainment to the viewing audience. Had this been a real store, it would have had to close its doors rather rapidly with such bad customer service.

In fact, in the real world the task of acquiring and retaining customers is a very big deal to companies. It is rather expensive to acquire new customers, and companies spend significant resources to marketing their products and services. By certain accounts (http://economicsofadvertising.com/?page_id=44; accessed January/2014) in the United States, advertising alone could range between 2% and 5% of GDP (depending on whether nontraditional advertising is included in the estimate) with top spenders such as financial and health care industries spending above 30% of their sales in ads (http://www.econlib.org/library/Enc/Advertising.html; accessed January/2014). Thus, once acquired, sensible companies that aspire to continue to sell to the existing customer base would put in the extra effort by providing quality customer service to retain the customers.

Business dictionary (http://www.businessdictionary.com/definition/customer-capital.html; accessed January/2014) defines "customer capital" as "the value of relationship that a firm holds with its customers, and which is reflected in their loyalty to the firm and/or its products." Customer capital is one of the three components of intellectual capital (the other two being human capital and structural capital) and is a measure of customer intimacy that a firm develops in its customer base and is a major contributor to firm's sustained competitive advantage (Jan Duffy, Measuring customer capital, *Strategy and Leadership*, 28(5), 10–15, 2000). If you have ever received a fair and smooth claims settlement from an insurance company, you are likely to stay with that company even if their premiums are higher; if you have had a pleasant experience at a clinic, you are far more likely to stick to them even if the charges there are higher; if you have felt that one of your investment bankers is going the extra mile to protect and grow your investment, you will probably channel all your life savings to him/her—examples of customer satisfaction as a result of superior customer service and the obvious benefits to the firms delivering those services are easy to find in all walks of life. Figure 1.1 provides a qualitative relationship between the ability to provide superior customer service, customer capital, and sustained competitiveness of firms stating essentially that the better the customer service the higher the competitive advantage generating customer loyalty. Superior customer service is particularly important and often a positive differentiator in mature markets. As we had remarked earlier in this chapter, in order to exceed the customer's expectation on the customer service front all those that are involved in providing the service must have the required knowledge and adequate freedom to exercise their judgment (based on their knowledge) to take a few nonstandard steps, if necessary.

1.2.2 "Doctor, I Have a Headache…"

A middle-aged man shows up at a hospital with severe headache due to high blood pressure. The check-in clerk does the necessary paperwork, and the patient sees the doctor in due course. In many instances, such a visit would end in the doctor conducting some basic investigations, asking a few pertinent questions, and prescribing a set of common medicines, and all will be well. However, in this particular instance, during the basic investigation phase, the assisting nurse reports to the doctor that while the patient's blood pressure is little high it seems unlikely that the headache might have been caused by it (typically, high blood pressure may cause some headaches in situations of hypertensive crisis, i.e., systolic pressure higher than 180 and/or diastolic pressure higher than 110 but not when the blood pressure is only mildly high; ref.heart.org).

Figure 1.1 Customer capital, customer service, and competitiveness of firms.

This information causes the doctor to look for other symptoms. She notices, among other things, that the patient is exhibiting occasional speech disability. Using her years of education and work experience, the doctor suspects a possible brain tumor and proceeds with the diagnosis activities and treatments accordingly. What could have been a common case of headache suddenly involves sophisticated tests like CT scans and MRI, and upon confirmation of the existence of a tumor requires complicated chemotherapy, radiation, or surgery as part of the treatment. From a general practitioner adequate in dealing with most common headache complaints, a headache due to brain tumor will now involve a group of collaborating radiation experts, specialized oncologists, and neurosurgeons that are now required to handle the treatment of this patient.

More than 10% of the overall human population complain about headaches and in the majority of the cases they are the "vanilla-type" that are easily diagnosed and are generally treatable by common medicines. However, on occasions, there are situations that are similar to the aforementioned one and require vast amounts of specialized knowledge and myriads of activities including cross-discipline collaboration that need to be adjusted based on the result of a previous diagnosis or the reaction of the patient to a particular treatment regimen. Being experts in their trade, these collaborators are also granted a lot of freedom as they pick the next best action during the diagnosis or treatment phases. Coordination of such a wide variety of activities is not easy, and given the large number of participants, many and possibly large financial transactions, and potential liability issues and activities must also be tracked for immediate and future reference. It is not hard to imagine that management of the complexity of such activities will grow rapidly as the amount of collaboration increase and as the level of freedom granted to the collaborators gets high unless, of course, a suitable framework is put in place to enable and track these activities; Figure 1.2 states this concern graphically.

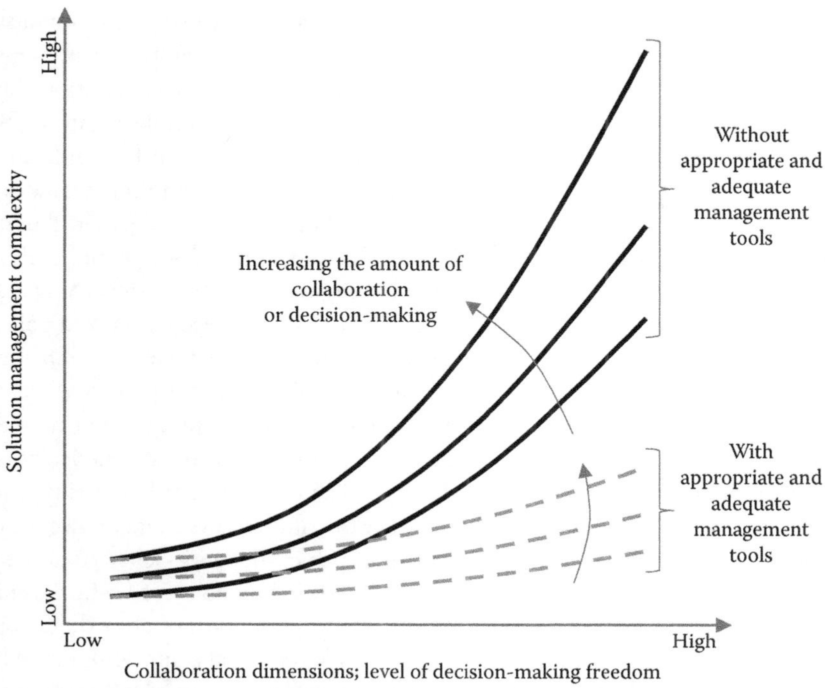

Figure 1.2 Collaboration, work freedom, and management complexity.

1.2.3 "Look! There's a Dead Man in the Closet!"

"You may succeed in silencing me but that silence comes at a price. You have shown yourself to be as barbaric and ruthless as your most hostile critics have claimed." Reported in a *New York Times* article in 2006 (http://www.nytimes.com/2006/11/24/world/europe/25spycnd.html; accessed January/2014), these remarks aimed at the then Russian President Vladimir Putin were made by Alexander V. Litvinenko, a 43-year-old former Russian K.G.B. officer, in his death-bed in London. Litvinenko died of poisoning from Polonium 210, a rare and highly radioactive isotope—the poisoning is alleged to have been carried out by the Kremlin since Litvinenko was apparently considered an enemy of the Kremlin due to his anti-Russian government activities after he left the K.G.B. The British authorities called the circumstances unprecedented and launched an investigation. One can only imagine how complicated such investigations must have been for the police—so many facts to uncover, so many allegations to weed through, and so many geopolitical aspects to consider. Who can foresee or preplan all activities in such investigations, or for that matter predict as to how long it will last? In fact, given the involvement of multiple governments who are not the best of friends and possible unveiling of government secrets during investigative activities, making progress in the Litvinenko has proven to be difficult—to our knowledge, as of summer of 2013 a satisfactory resolution was still pending.

One does not have to look for a Litvinenko-type situation to appreciate how a police investigation can get easily complicated real fast. Finding a dead body unexpectedly in the clothing closet when a police visits a residence following a neighbor's complaint due to loud music, correlating signals from multiple channels to pursue a bomb threat investigation, or discovering an international drug cartel while chasing a few counterfeit notes are the type of things that are not at all uncommon in police work. In this type of work, often there is a great distance between where the investigation starts and where it ends with the middle riddled with steps continuously adapting to the situation at hand. In fact, police investigations involving substantial detective work would often be characterized by disjoint spells of high activity, many creative explorations by the detectives where keeping within legal bound the detectives are likely to undertake whatever investigation activity that would seem appropriate, some of these activities may be ad hoc and some would be well formulated like collecting evidence and running forensic tests, and there would be plenty on demand information exchanges among many connected organizations. Further, the investigation may be suspended one or more times if pertinent information flow dries up and will be reopened again on receipt of new information and the whole thing could take months or years to complete.

In Figure 1.3, for a fictitious yet realistic nontrivial criminal investigation by a police organization, we chart a time-lapse evolution of four related but distinct entities relevant to the investigation. Going from bottom to top in the chart, the first entity "number of events processed" represents sum of the number of interviews the police conducts, the tips they received, the testimonies that they collected, the forensic reports that are generated, etc., with each of these generically representing an "event," as a function of time after the police investigation begins. While it is typical that such events would be high as the investigation starts, their distribution over time, however, depends on how the case progresses and it is generally nondeterministic. The entity charted above number of events processed termed "impact of processed events" shows the impact or usefulness of the events and indicates that the impact or usefulness is not necessarily proportional to the amount of such events processed. For example, the police might receive a lot of tips at some point (i.e., a lot of events processed as per our terminology here) but these tips may not be very useful (i.e., may not have much

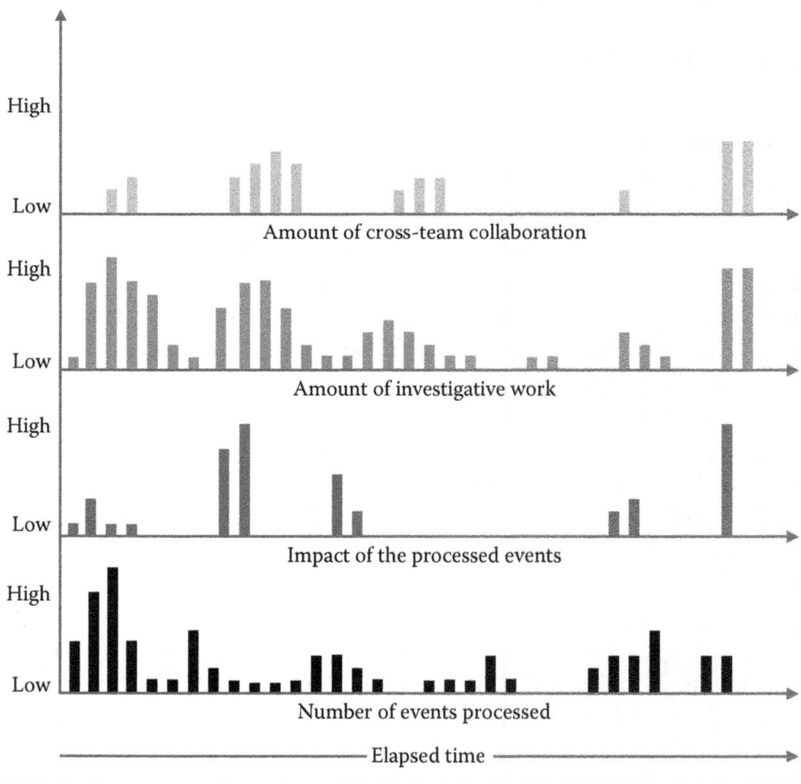

Figure 1.3 Time-scale variations of events and work in a criminal investigation.

impact on the case being pursued) while an isolated event, for example, receipt of some key information, may suddenly provide a deep insight into the case and thus trigger a lot of follow-up action from the police. The entity next up is "amount of investigative work" that quantifies the amount of activities the police is undertaking, which is a complex function of the events that they are processing and the impact of those events on the case. The topmost entity, "amount of cross-team collaboration," indicates the amount of activities where collaboration among many individuals, teams, and departments is needed for reasons like leveraging of knowledge or geographical proximity for on-site investigations. The main observations that we want to make here, with the current example, is that in situations like a police investigation there are many internal and external factors that introduce lack of predictability in the course of actions that are undertaken to solve the case. Thus, software solutions intended for helping with police investigations need a framework that has great access to all related current information, relevant knowledge from the past, and can process and adapt to a large variety and volume of intrinsic and extrinsic events; a framework that provides broad freedom yet enforces law and governs extremes; a framework that keeps strong audit trail.

1.2.4 Goal-Driven, Knowledge Work Freedom, On-Demand Collaboration

In the three distinctly different situations we just explored, and it is very easy to think of many such situations in all types industries, we notice a common set of characteristics in the purpose of the work and the way work gets done. First, we see that the work is motivated by some end goal that has the primary importance and the actual actions and the sequence in which they are executed are of lesser importance. High customer satisfaction is the real goal of superior customer service and not the specific actions by the customer service representatives; alleviation of ailment is the ultimate goal for health care givers and not the dispensing of diagnostic tests or medicines; a police investigation will have achieved its goal when the alleged crime situation is resolved and the perpetrators have been brought to justice, if indeed there was a crime committed. These types of work are identified as "goal-driven" work. Given that there could be many variations in work planning, scheduling, and execution, such goal-driven work generally has an "owner" (this is a role) assigned to it and it is the owner's responsibility to make sure that work activities contribute to the goal. This goal-driven notion of work is different than a series of activities done as part of traditional WFs or BPM where the "goal" for a given process worker is to properly (and repeatedly) execute one or more activities assigned to him/her, and it is the process model that ensures that the ultimate purpose is achieved.

Second, we note that the goal achievement relies on the workers being able to use their knowledge and experience to make decisions. In a complicated customer service request, the servicing representative may request from his/her supervisor special considerations in order to meet customer expectation; in treatment of complex diseases or injuries, the medical team members are expected to use their experience to adapt the course of treatment; police investigators will undertake the necessary investigation activities depending on emerging leads and facts. In other words, to benefit from the knowledge and experience of the workers they cannot always be restricted to follow preset directions in every step and must be allowed to decide on what next best action to be taken; judgment of these knowledge workers is also relied upon to create the next step when there are no preset directions available.

Finally, we see that the workers tend to or need to collaborate among themselves in order to reach the ultimate goal. While the workers may generally know what they may be collaborating on, the exact instances, amount, and details of the collaboration are usually dependent on the specific situation. Hence, we term this as "on demand" collaboration. The idea is to provide the participating knowledge workers the ability to bring their knowledge and experience to solve the problem at hand as a team, all contributing to reaching the target goal.

The real questions can now be asked: What type of solution framework would best facilitate goal-driven work by knowledge workers who may want to engage in just-in-time collaboration? Most of the work our businesses do today is made more efficient and effective by information technology. What flavor of information technology would enable this type of knowledge work? Historically WF, either embedded in packaged applications or implemented independently in middleware, and more recently BPM solutions have been utilized to organize and execute business activities. However, WF or BPM disciplines assume that we are able to "model" the work, i.e., prescribe how the work activities will be sequenced and how the "agents" will perform those activities before the work begins. As per WF or BPM models, simply by knowing which activities have been executed at a given time, we are able to state the exact status of the overall work and how close we are to completion. While WF and BPM strategy are obviously well suited for many classes of business work patterns, for the three types of situations we described earlier in this chapter, i.e., complex customer service, critical patient care, and police investigation, and many more similar to them, these (WF and BPM) approaches will clearly not be suitable. A different paradigm called "case management" where the "case" represents the overall problem to be solved, engaging case owner and case workers (aka the knowledge workers) endowed with the necessary flexibility to "work the case" so as to reach the goal of resolving the problem is much better suited for the problem classes we explored earlier in this chapter. Given that this book is about case management, we will get much deeper into the nitty-gritty of case management from many different points of view as we progress through the book. To begin with, in the next section, we will use a relatively simple business situation to illustrate how predefined business process (BP) models can quickly turn inadequate when a bit of real-life deviation gets added to mix of preplanned work; this example will also show some preliminary attributes and capabilities of case management solutions.

1.3 Handling of Credit Card Rewards Disputes

A customer of Diamond Credit Card Company has been a member of that company's credit card loyalty program for some time. When reviewing his last credit card statement, he suspected some error in the reward points—even though he had been charged more in the last billing cycle than in the previous ones he had received fewer reward points. So, he promptly called a customer service representative (CSR) at the Diamond Credit Card Company and filed a reward dispute claim. The CSR collected some basic information from the customer and told him that their reward dispute claims processors will look into the situation and get back to him as soon as possible. Using the information collected, the CSR opened a "ticket" for this case and the dispute resolution activities got kicked off; a case owner or manager got assigned to the ticket or the case who would be ultimately responsible for a proper and fair resolution of the case so that the customer is satisfied with the handling of the dispute by the credit card company.

The major activities that can be expected in such a dispute resolution at the Diamond Credit Card Company, as may be with most credit card companies, are collection of necessary information from the customer, a quick analysis of the situation to assess whether the reported claim has any merit, an investigation into what caused the alleged error and identification of possible remedies, and finally deciding on a resolution that could be handed back to the customer. The roles that would perform these activities could be: "CSR" mainly communicating with the customer, "case owner" making a preliminary check that enough information has been obtained (by the CSR) to start an assessment, "analyst" doing the initial assessment, "investigator" doing a deeper analysis and suggesting recommendations, and the case owner then taking the final decision regarding the resolution. Here we assumed these roles and responsibilities just to keep the situation simple—in reality, there may be multiple roles that could share a given responsibility, for example, under certain circumstances a CSR may be permitted to close such a case. Figure 1.4 shows a traditional BPM model sketched using BPMN (Business Process Modelling Notation, see: omg.org for details on BPMN) involving around 10 activities (rectangular boxes with rounded corners) and the flow controls or gates (crossed circles) and transition lines. The swim lanes are used to indicate primary assignment of activities to the roles participating in the dispute resolution. The highlighted trace over this process model diagram shows the "happy path" where information collected at the start was adequate for the analyst to validate the merit of the claim, the investigator did not need any more information to conduct the necessary deep dive into the situation, and the case owner ended the dispute resolution activities with concrete and unambiguous decision about the remedy that the credit card company would offer the customer.

Of course, a few small real-life variations can easily make the planned progression challenging. For example, let's say that when the case owner gets his assignment (of the dispute resolution) and does a quick review of the customer information collected and entered by the CSR, he (the case owner) notices that the customer has multiple credit cards from the Diamond Credit Card company and suspects a mixup of credit card numbers. He requests the CSR to confirm the details; the CSR contacts the customer back for some information updates and verification (and this could take more than one iteration). When a deeper investigation is undertaken, the investigator may feel the need to double check some of the transactions within the scope of the dispute. Thus, additional contacts are made with the customer and more documents are obtained or more information is collected. In the meantime, the anxious customer may call the CSR to get an update on the resolution or the CSR may proactively contact the customer to give him an update on the progress, and these could also happen more than once. The investigator's recommendation on the resolution may turn out to be not so pleasing to the customer and the case owner may override that with a more favorable conclusion since he notices that the customer has been with the credit card company for a long time and has always been in good standing.

Thus, a few little deviations from what is expected to happen in the "happy path" (per the process in Figure 1.4) introduces a good lot of criss-cross conversations and out-of-sequence activities among the involved parties, frequent updates to information attached to the work, and requires some allowance in decision making be granted to those trying to resolve the dispute. The progression of the dispute resolution in the presence of the deviations mentioned in the last paragraph is shown with the highlighted segments and dotted arrows in Figure 1.5. Note that even though parts of the process in Figure 1.4 are still used, these parts are now disjointed. Also, the dotted lines only indicate logical connections or activity initiations and are not intended to show a directed activity to activity transition (as in traditional process flow diagrams). What would be a good way to treat such interactions in a digital solution? How would we ensure that the participants have easy and timely access to data and documents they need in order to complete their work? Further, good visibility into the progress of the resolution, archiving of information, and activity audit trails for future reference is also necessary.

Could BPM models, nowadays most popularly created using the modeling language BPMN 2.0 (ref.omg.org), adequately handle the requirements for a suitable solution? BPMN 2.0 is quite rich in the number and variety of modeling elements and perhaps it would be possible to create a model to handle the scenario with the real-life variations described. Of course, the BP model

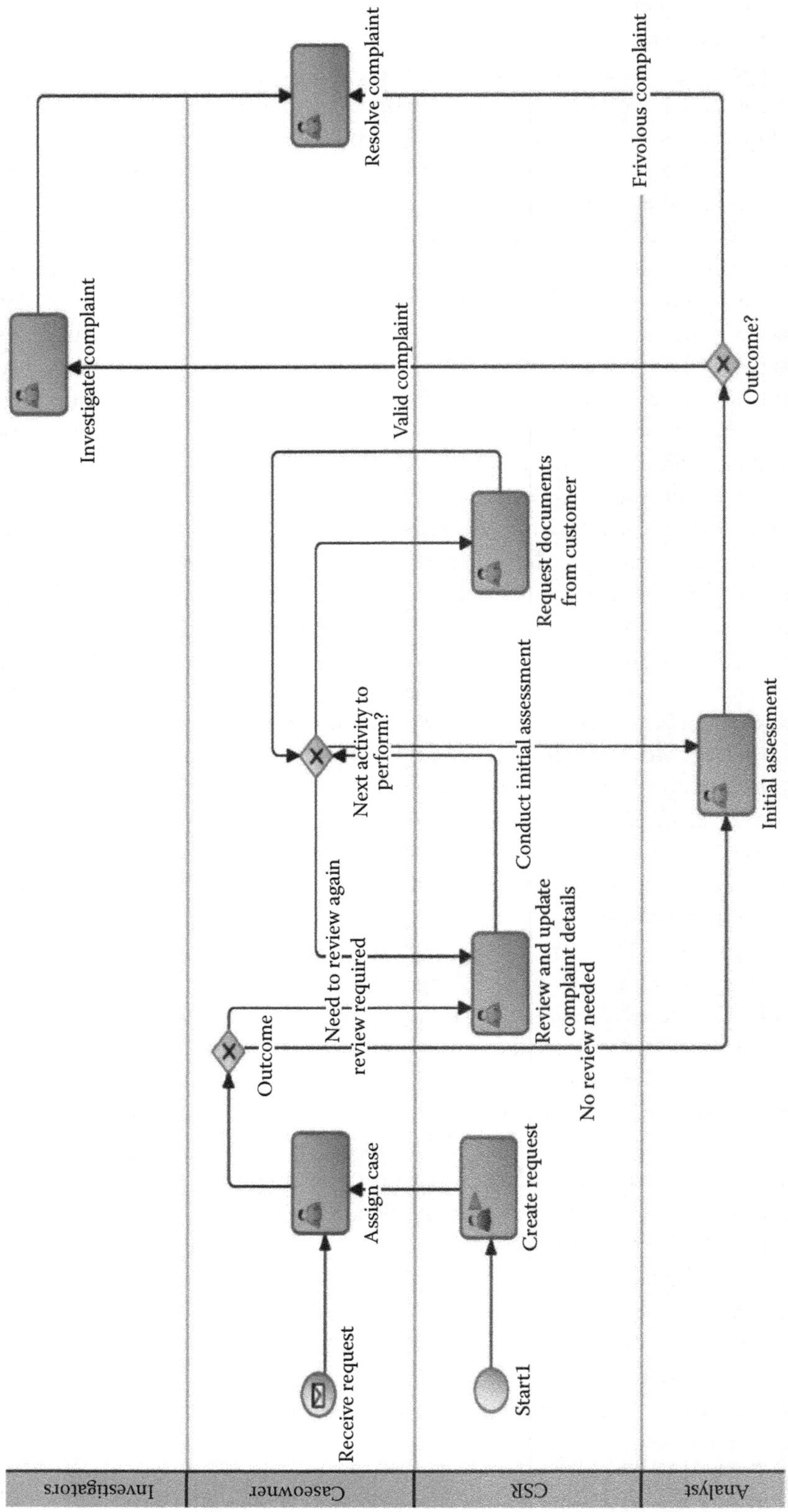

Figure 1.4 A traditional BPM model for credit card reward dispute resolution.

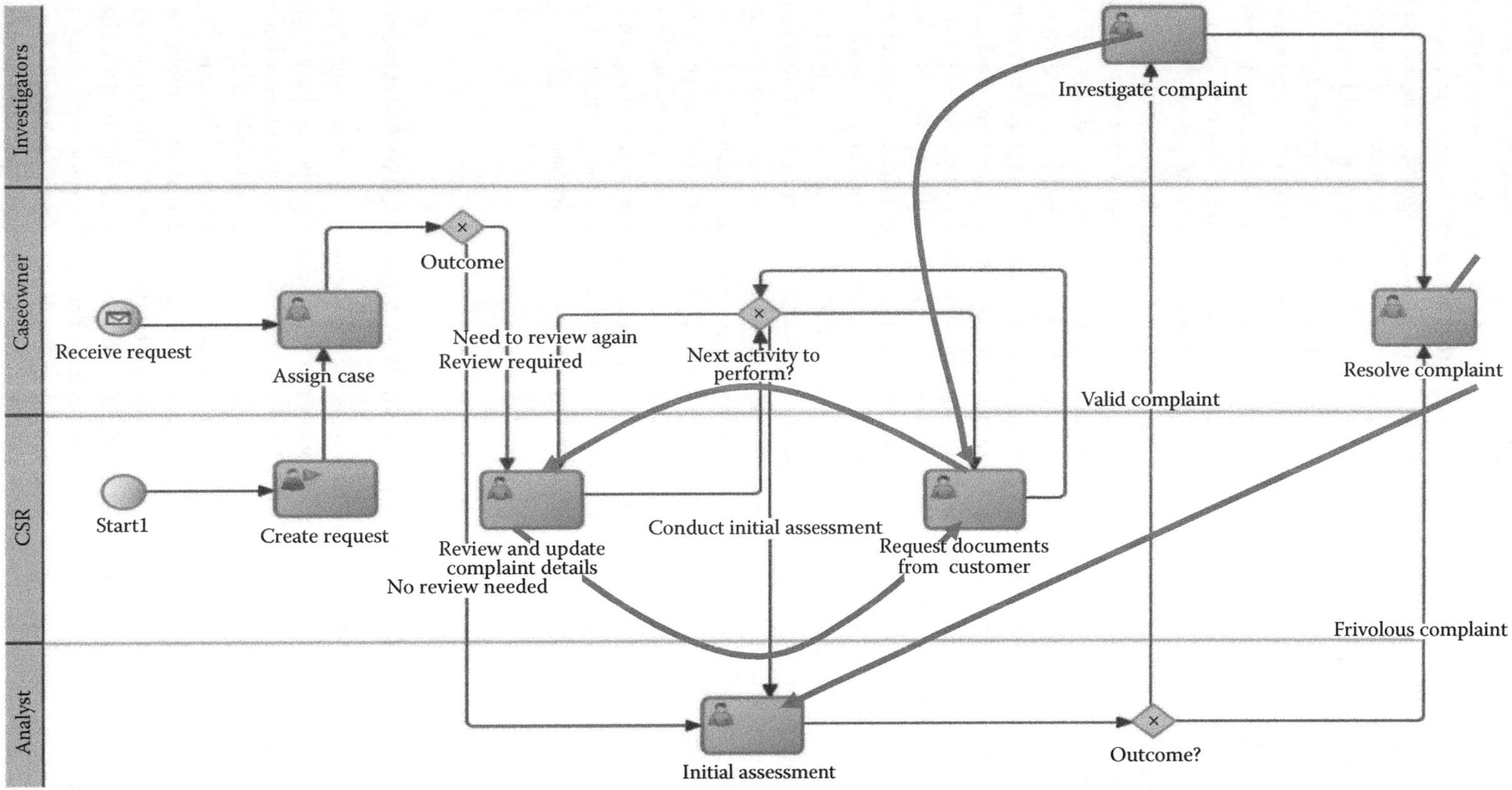

Figure 1.5 Credit card reward dispute resolution with real-life variations (#1).

would look quite different than the "happy path" BPMN process model depicted in Figure 1.4, and it will be a significantly more complicated model due to the presence of interaction loops with dynamic counters, participants reaching out to each other as and when necessary, new (or newer versions of existing) documents being uploaded as the resolution progresses, and the ability of the case owner to override the standard progression of activities and enforce a decision, if necessary. To make matters further challenging, we can anticipate that the next dispute could easily introduce or generate a different set of variations. For example, after the initial assessment by the analyst, the case owner may feel that he/she has seen several similar situations before and may conclude the dispute resolution process abruptly (with a decision, of course) bypassing the investigation phase and simply inform all the participants about the decision (Figure 1.6 provides a visual for this variation). This will require yet another version of a traditional BPM process. Continuing in this manner, we can conclude that in order to take care of all possible variations we will need an inordinate number of (complicated) business processes, thus making the prospect of solving such a business problem using traditional BPM technique quite daunting; and, this is clearly not the most difficult business problem that we can imagine. Using traditional BPM approach of creating a software solution to this problem would be highly tedious, expensive, and difficult to manage at best and thus would be generally impractical; any of the readers who may have tried to use traditional process models in these types of problem situations will readily agree with this statement.

Just to be clear, the aforementioned conundrum is not a shortcoming of BPMN or any similar process modeling language or a specific BPM practice—it is the set of solution requirements where the solution goals are of primary importance and the specific activities are, generally speaking, less important, where the progress of the solution is difficult to measure by simply observing the status of the activities, where content often plays a significant role and in those situations actions and content are closely related, where internal and external events can influence the actions and outcomes easily and significantly, and where knowledge workers are granted freedom to make decisions that are not already preordained, that make an approach based only on traditional BPM inadequate. Clearly, there has to be another approach that is capable of handling such challenges. The answer, of course, is "yes," and as we describe the art and science of designing and building solutions using case management (or in some cases a hybrid approach using traditional BPM and case management) in rest of the book, this affirmation will become clearer.

1.4 Case Management: Basics

1.4.1 What Is Case Management? What Is Adaptive Case Management?

From all the examples and introductory remarks so far, it should be apparent that even though BPM and Case Management (CM) are both ways to solve business problems, they approach the problem and the solution very differently. BPM relies on predefined process models where activities are connected together using a set of activity to activity transition rules. In BPM, a given business problem is captured in an "instance" of the process model that "executes." The (business) process workers are typically engaged in completing one or more activities that they might be assigned and are not generally responsible for the outcome of the total process; it is the process model that progresses the solution. All the necessary knowledge and experience needed to drive the solution is captured at designtime (i.e., when the process model is designed)—sometimes small variations from the most likely paths through the process are handled by an exception handling strategy. In case of CM, the problem to be solved is captured in the notion of "case" (we will describe the key

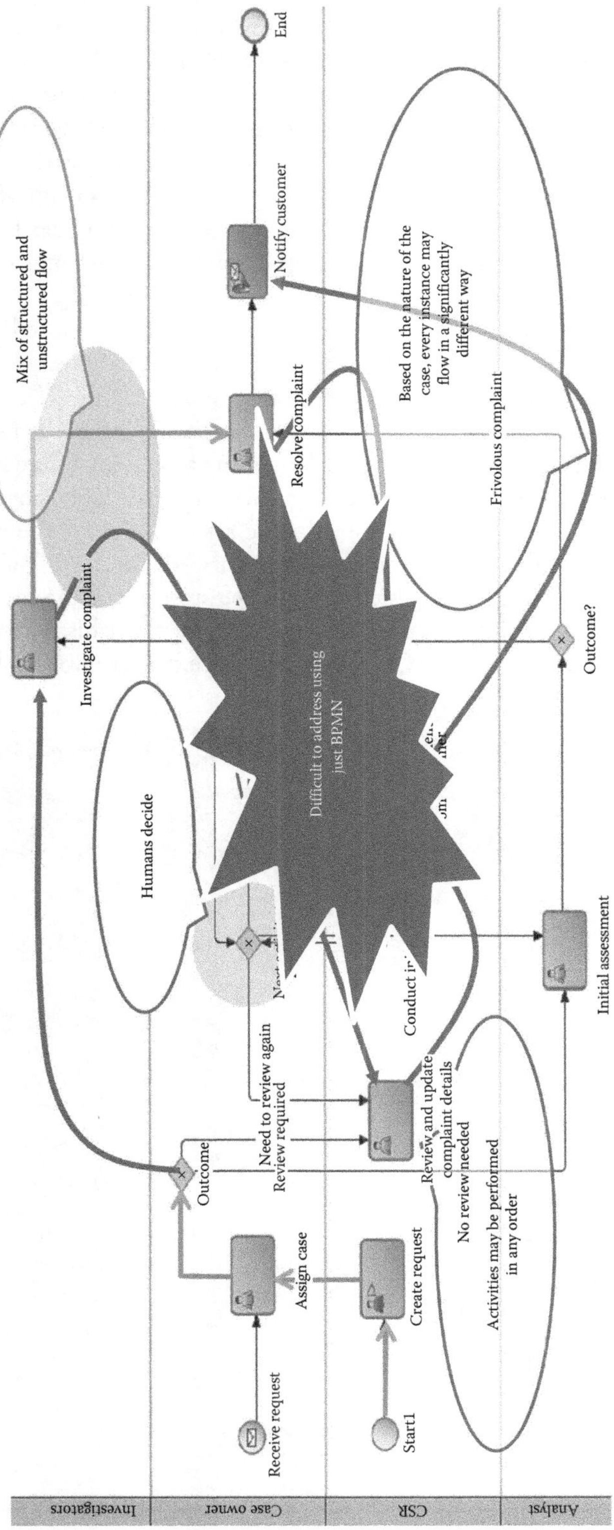

Figure 1.6 Credit card reward dispute resolution with real-life variations (#2).

attributes of a typical case later) as opposed to a process, and a case manager or a case owner role is made responsible for ensuring a closure of the case that usually corresponds to achieving a set of end goals signifying solution to the original business problem. Besides the case owner there may be many others (aka "case workers") who may put in effort and contribute toward the closure of the case through their actions, i.e., by performing "tasks." In order to keep track of the progress of the case, a set of "milestones," spread over the collection of tasks, are used—milestones typically correspond to start or end of something significant to the case. A set of "phases" grouping closely related tasks and milestones are used to provide a logical flow of activities from start (or "opening") of the case to its closure. A logical "case file" or "case folder" concept is used to keep track of information and status related to the case.

Figure 1.7 displays the essential CM concepts described in the preceding paragraph. It is important to note that phases in a case are not necessarily connected to each other as activities in processes and that, when necessary and permitted, case workers can jump from tasks to tasks, forward and backward, crossing milestones and phases. Also, the notion of the task in the context of CM is quite generic—it can be a simple phone call, making a decision, following a process (which could be predetermined) or even physically creating a new task. The tasks may be done by humans or could be automated, i.e., executed by the software system once all the necessary preconditions have been met. The tasks could be either "mandatory" or "optional" (aka "discretionary"). The tasks could be "planned," i.e., suggested prior to the start of the case or could be added by the case owner or a case worker during the progression of the case (this is an important qualifier for "Adaptive Case Management" or "ACM"—we will delve deeper into this later). The concepts

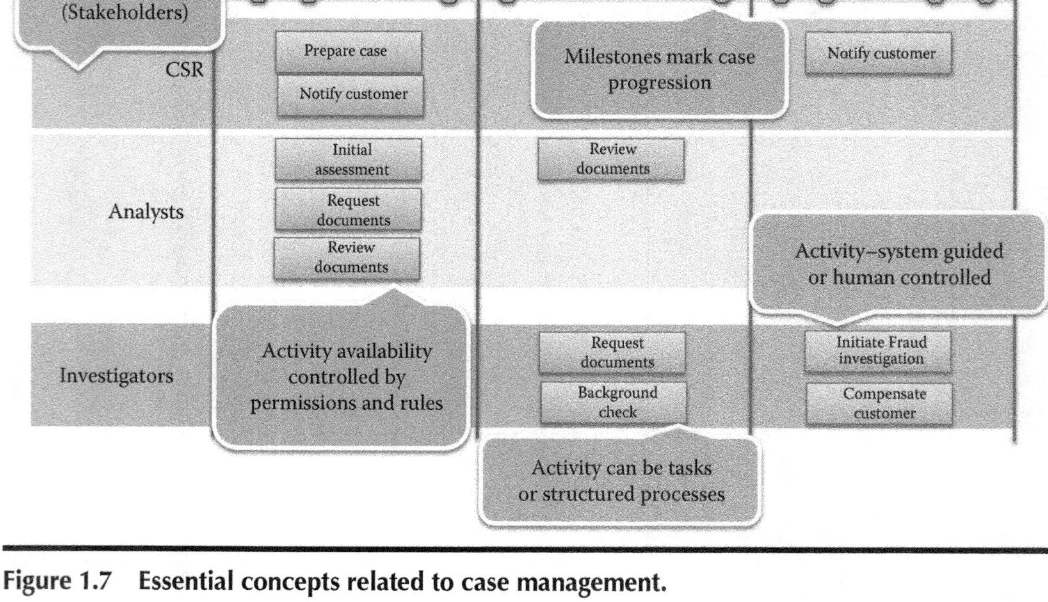

Figure 1.7 Essential concepts related to case management.

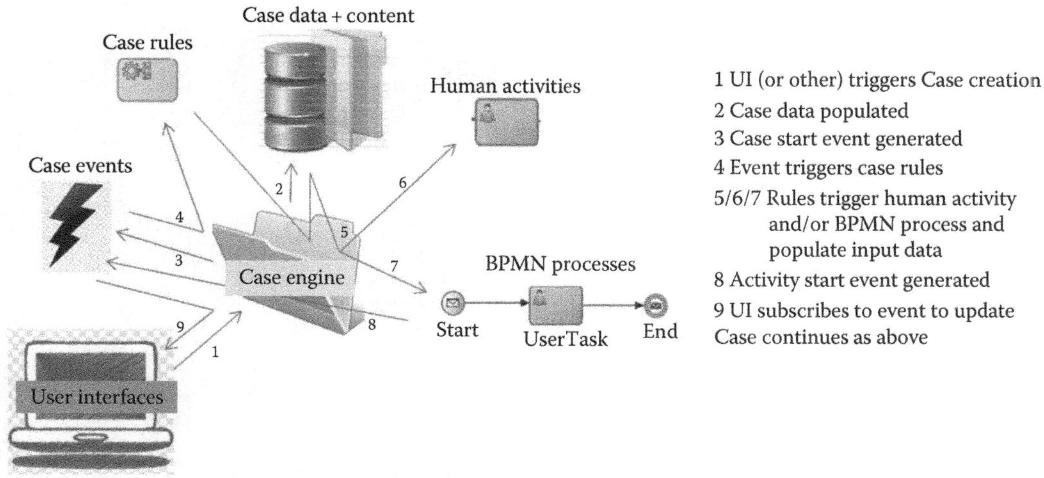

Figure 1.8 Start and progression of a case in a case management system.

of "events" i.e., signature of something that happened and "event handling," i.e., sensing and responding to events, and "rules" that guide how to handle events are used to manage the loose coupling of all the case tasks. As an example, using the mechanism employed in Oracle's Case Management (a comprehensive set of functionalities packaged in Oracle Unified BPM Suite) in Figure 1.8 we present a simple chronology of how a case management (software) system could handle the start and progression of a case; this is only to demystify the basic working of such systems, and more general situations will be dealt with in later chapters.

As we just indicated that ACM furthers the flexibilities and the capabilities of simple case management solutions by letting case workers and owners modify the tasks to be executed as well as their execution sequence at runtime without the need of solution developers to change the design of the solution and then having to redeploy the solution (as would be the case for most other software application including traditional BPM). Thus, in principle, ACM includes CM and in this book we will use CM and ACM interchangeably and will point out if we specifically mean one or the other when the situation demands that.

Let's revisit the issue of knowledge workers needing to have adequate freedom to take actions that they deem most fitting at a given point in the progression of a case. Note that case management is after all a strategy to solve business problems. This means that knowledge worker freedom will still have some boundaries that are defined by prevailing organizational and industry business practices and government rules and regulations and any applicable laws. For example, in case of a police investigation involving a lot of detective work (i.e., a lot of knowledge work) will generally start with some guidance as to what the investigation needs to accomplish and how such investigations are usually approached by the concerned police organization. As the investigation is launched the detectives, within these high-level guidelines, will have reasonably high amount of freedom to undertake a variety of activities many of which will be determined depending on how the investigation evolves. From time to time, there will be activities such as gathering and recording evidences or testimonies or running forensic tests that would have to follow strict discipline for the results of such activities to be admissible in the court of law, eventually. Similarly, we can consider the situation of credit insurance processing for businesses where large (often in tens and hundreds of millions of dollars' worth) credit applications from businesses are vetted and decisions regarding credit eligibility, terms and conditions (T&Cs) and premiums are taken.

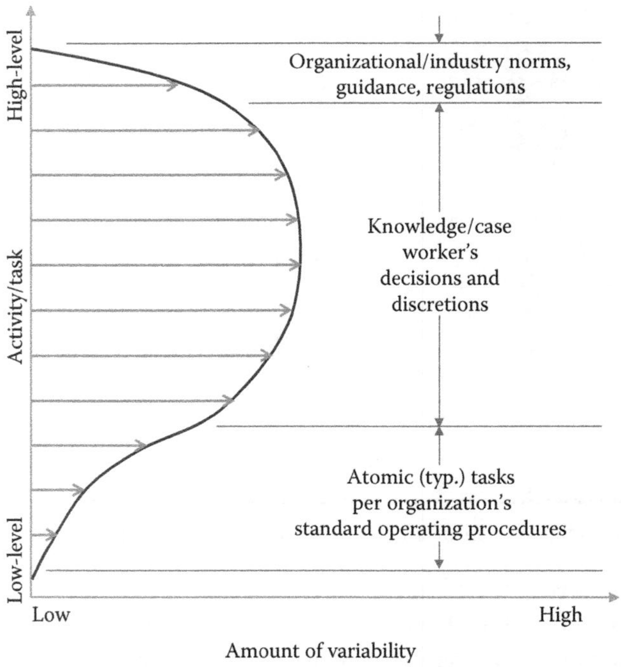

Figure 1.9 Knowledge work freedom and case activity levels.

The basic review of the credit application, the key phases and milestones that need to be covered before approving the requested credit, the formal contracting during the credit grant, etc., are all tightly regulated yet the risk analysts and the underwriters will typically be expected to and will have the necessary freedom to exercise their knowledge and experience in order to dig deeper into the supplied and related information and to hold negotiations with the customer. Generalizing these observations, we can state that in case management involving knowledge work restriction will commonly apply when case activities are "high level," i.e., those activities that help enforce overall guidance for handling the case or when the activities are "low level," i.e., where they are usually governed by the organization's standard operating practices, and that most of the freedom for the knowledge workers will be needed when the activities are between high-level and low-level ones (see Figure 1.9); such realizations are helpful for solution architects as they go about designing case management solutions.

1.4.2 Case Management Ecosystem

Figure 1.10 shows the core and supporting systems of a full-featured general purpose case management platform. As this figure indicates, the core system contains those features that are deemed essential to provide all the standard capabilities and expected flexibilities of a case management platform. Typically, case activities that can range from a simple task to firing of a business process are governed by a set of rules and policies associated with a particular "case type" or "model." These activities are triggered by internal or external events where the internal events could be generated either by the case engine or by a case worker. Thus, rules engine, and event handling needs to be an integral part of the core of case management platform. Concept of a "case folder" is commonly used by the case engine to keep track of various activities as the

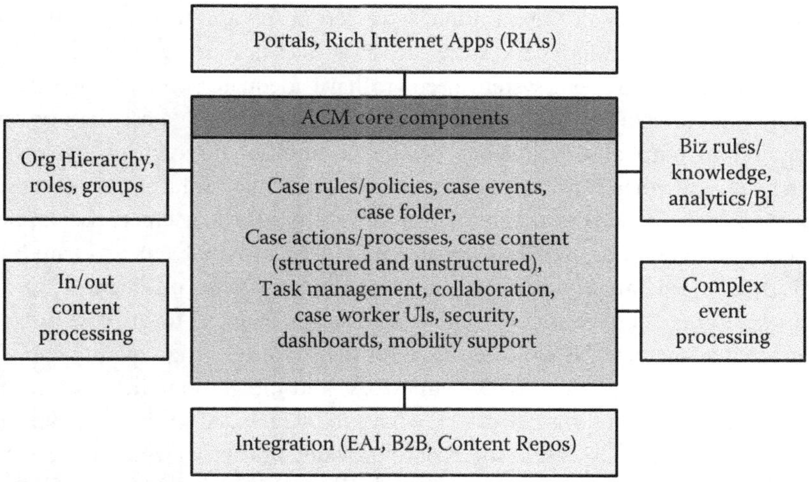

Figure 1.10 Core and supporting components of a case management system.

case progresses. The case folder can either be a concrete one or could be a virtual one, and this should not be of material importance on the usability of the case engine. Cases also frequently deal with some case specific content which can be either structured (as in formatted documents) or unstructured (such as emails or notes from a phone call). The core functionality of a case management platform must be able to handle at least the case specific content. Since case workers may choose to alter the tasks to be done or the sequence in which they are done, some task management capability that includes task presentment and audit is necessary. In many complex case resolutions, team collaboration is highly beneficial and the case management platform has to facilitate that. Basic security features are also mandatory for case management platforms as with most other platforms targeted for business solutions. Certain amount of dashboard capability is essential for visibility into tasks and their status. These dashboards can have a "case worker view" that gives the details of the cases a particular case worker is involved in and a "manager" view that provides higher level summaries such as how many cases are in the system, how many have been completed, how many are in progression, how many are in the queue, how many are (potentially) in jeopardy, statistics on completion and wait times, and on case worker load distribution. Case management generally involves significant amount of human work and thus the case management platform must provide the ability to create and manage appropriate user interfaces (UIs) on desktops and on mobile devices.

A full-featured enterprise-grade general purpose case management platform needs more capabilities than what we just listed for the core system. It needs to be able to handle a large variety of inbound and outbound content that could be either structured or unstructured including (at least in some cases) the ability to automatically derive and use information embedded in such content, for example, deciphering identifying information from the scan of an invoice via image processing, or extracting routing information from a PDF form, or outputting formatted communications based on case resolution. Besides the set of rules that govern the basic progression of case activities, the system needs to facilitate access to various context and industry specific "expert systems" or at least to knowledge capturing rule bases should the knowledge workers need such support. Analytics and business intelligence (BI) are special types of knowledge that can be also helpful in certain case progression, for example, a case manager may want to quickly check the historical and current level of underwriting risks before deciding on a high-risk loan. Since case management often involves dealing with humans who, in an organization, have certain organizational privileges due to their assigned position and responsibilities and since such privileges need to be referred to when assigning or sharing work, case management system needs to have adequate access to organizational structure (often stored in "directories"). Information being handled within a case can be sensitive from privacy or regulation compliance points of view; hence, additional security considerations beyond the basics can be critical when putting together a case management solution. As the case progresses, information typically held under the supervision of an organizations enterprise applications such as ERP, financial, inventory, or even HR systems may need to be referenced or updated; in some situations information exchange could extend beyond the boundaries of the organization; also case management system may need to access content repositories external to the case management system. Thus, a case management system often requires the support of high quality application (EAI) and business to business integration (B2B) framework, and integration with content management systems (CMS). Finally, a portal framework may have to be included in the case management solution either for convenience of the case workers or to provide information about the cases to a broader set of stakeholders including periodic updates to and self-servicing of certain steps in the case by the ultimate customer. How much of these additional capabilities beyond the core (as we have described earlier) are integrated and packaged as part of the case management platform offering or what needs to integrated on a case-by-case basis varies from software vendor to vendor; what is optimal for the buyer of course depends on the actual scope of the case management solution.

1.4.3 Brief History of Case Management

While there is a lot of buzz these days about case management, and some project that the market for case management to be 5–10 times as large as that of BPM, we can say quite confidently that there is a high chance that you have heard of case management prior to this latest round of excitement. In fact, by some accounts the concepts of case management were already in action over a century ago in countries like England and the United States (see, for example, the 1989 book *Case Management: Historical, Current and Future Perspectives* edited by Mary Hubbard Linz, Patricia McAnally, and Colleen Wieck from Brookline Books, and the 2002 article "Towards a Typology of Case Management" by Philip Fleisher and Mark Henrickson accessible at ftp://ftp.hrsa.gov/hab/Typology.pdf; accessed January/2014). Most of the early case management like activities were around church and social workers trying to help the poor in need. These caregivers had to be aware of what services were available via public and private sources and coordinate them for the benefit of the recipient. In the beginning, such work was organized in intuitive and commonsensical fashion; there was no real methodology, framework, or training that would help prepare these caregivers and consequently these caregiver actions often lacked efficiency and efficacy. In early twentieth century, Western governments started organizing social care via federal programs (e.g., the Social Securities Act of 1932 in the United States, and the like) and naturally there were efforts to evaluate how effective these programs were and how efficiently they could be run.

While government funding surely helped the social service cause, many organizations, public and private, emerged controlling or specializing in specific services and roles. Situations that needed more than one service became harder to deal with. The concept of "service integration" emerged whose goal was to treat the problems more comprehensively (like a "case"), increase the ability of the caregivers to address the problems wholesomely by giving them appropriate training (i.e., making them sort of knowledge workers), and organize the necessary service components in a manner that they would be easily accessible to the caregivers. In some ways, the discipline of case management was taking root through the need for meeting higher standard of efficiency and effectiveness in relatively complex service offering. Outside of social work, this case management discipline was first visible in nursing and other medical care operations. The case management approach had other benefits as well—it organized information in a manner that facilitated collaboration among multiple participants (i.e., managed shareable information via case folders and content repositories accessible by the participants) and it kept track of "who did what and when" (i.e., audit trails). These characteristics made case management concept welcome in conducting police investigations and in organizing legal work. Over time, case management techniques spread into wider varieties of problem solving work, typically done by knowledge workers, and often by several of them on a given case, sharing experience and best practices.

As noted by Keith Swenson in "Historical perspectives" in the book *Mastering the Unpredictable* (Meghan-Kiffer Press, 2010), one of the early applications of computers was in the area of office work automation and related information sharing. Use of emails instead of handwritten memos passed around from desk to desk for coordination of work is now taken for granted. However, organizing and tracking more complex work needed something more than emails. Thus, the concept of "workflow" emerged and became popular as a paradigm to specify work that human "agents" did toward achieving some target outcome. The so-called middleware-based WF software systems helped create and execute digital models. In the meantime, packaged enterprise applications (like ERP, HCM, SCM, etc.) that had emerged and had become popular as systems of record also offered specific WFs embedded in them. About a decade ago, BPM emerged as a more generalized version of this WF concept and combined human and machine work including handling of documents where necessary. WF or BPM approached the problem to be solved as the end result of a preset sequence of predefined activities and proved to be quite efficient in delivering expected results when the work indeed followed a planned path; using a mechanism called "exception handling" deviations (i.e., exceptions) from the planned path were dealt with. Such exceptions typically handled relatively small deviations efficiently and effectively, in some cases used automated alternatives but often diverting the work to capable human workers. Work like complex service deliveries, complicated investigative work, monitoring and reacting to emerging threats, and overseeing compliance activities needed human knowledge and experience to figure out the next set of actions as events emerged during the execution of such work. Often such actions or their execution sequences could not be planned conveniently beforehand, thus making the WF or BPM approach less useful as applicable paradigms to construct software systems to handle such work. Case management, by definition, is designed to handle these types of work. In recent years, advances in construction of software systems have made it possible to design and implement efficient and effective case management systems.

1.4.4 Formal Definition of (Adaptive) Case Management

The pursuit of case management today is quite general, spans applications in many industries, and is supported by all applicable technical advancements. Here we need to recognize two things: (1) as briefly discussed in the preceding section, case management originated and spread its roots in a variety of organizations (albeit the biggest emphasis had been in the social and healthcare arenas) and these organizations have "customized" the meaning of case management as best suited for their purposes and (2) the flexibility afforded by case management is in part due to fewer solution design constraints imposed on it (as compared to say, WFs or traditional BPM). These two aspects of case management make it difficult for all to agree on a common definition that is unambiguous and sufficient to preserve all the intended characteristics of case management. To appreciate what we are talking about here, let us look at a few definitions put forth by industry analysts and different types of organizations or industries.

The analysts firm Forrester, in their 2009 report on dynamic case management or DCM (and Forrester has clarified that by DCM they mean the same thing as what others mean by ACM), put forth this definition: *A highly structured, but also collaborative, dynamic, and information-intensive process that is driven by outside events and requires incremental and progressive responses from the business domain handling the case. Examples of case folders include a patient record, a lawsuit, an insurance claim, or a contract, and the case folder would include all the documents, data, collaboration artifacts, policies, rules, analytics, and other information needed to process and manage the case.*

A couple of years later, another prominent analyst firm, Gartner, offered this definition in their 2011 BPM Conference: *Case management is the optimization of long-lived collaborative processes that require secure coordination of knowledge, content, correspondence, and human resources and require adherence to corporate and regulatory policies and rules to achieve decisions about rights, entitlements, or settlements. The path of execution cannot be completely pre-defined; human judgment and external events and interactions will alter the flow.*

Association for Information and Image Management (AIIM, www.aiim.org/what-is-case-management) offers the following definition: *A "case" is any project, transaction, service or response that is "opened" and "closed" over a period of time to achieve resolution of a problem, claim, request, proposal, development or other complex activity. It is likely to involve multiple persons inside and outside of the organization, with varying relationships to each other, as well as multiple documents and messages.*

CMSA or the Case Management Society of America focused on healthcare sector defines case management as (http://www.cmsa.org/Home/CMSA/WhatisaCaseManager/tabid/224/Default.Aspx; accessed January/2014): *Case management is a collaborative process of assessment, planning, facilitation, care coordination, evaluation, and advocacy for options and services to meet an individual's and family's comprehensive health needs through communication and available resources to promote quality, cost-effective outcomes.*

In a September 23, 2009, post at the site http://social-biz.org/2009/09/23/what-is-casemanagement/ (accessed January/2014), Keith Swenson, a contemporary and big proponent of case management, also collected case management definitions from a variety of sources that can be used do some contrast and compare exercise. Below are a few excerpts from his post on the definition of case management:

From a legal site: *Techniques used to process cases from one stage of the proceeding to another, such as setting deadlines for discovery or scheduling a series of pretrial conferences. Case management calls for different approaches from one case to the next and is the primary responsibility of judges, assisted by lawyers and clerks' office personnel.*

One from the healthcare sector: *Coordination of services to help meet a patient's healthcare needs, usually when the patient has a condition which requires multiple services from multiple providers.*

Another one from the healthcare sector: *Offers a single point of entry to the aging services network. Managers assess clients' needs, create care plans, and coordinate and monitor services. They may operate privately or may be employed by social service agencies or public programs. Typically, case managers are nurses or social workers.*

A constructive definition that utilizes the what and the how of a "broker type" case management model: *The linking of a consumer to the service system and coordinating the various system components in order to achieve a successful outcome. The five case management activities are: (1) assessment, (2) planning, (3) linking, (4) monitoring, and (5) advocacy. Case management's primary goal is service provision for the consumer, not management of the system or its resources.*

While there are many common elements in the aforementioned definitions of case management, there are also notable variations. Besides, the style and scope of the definitions are focused on the specific needs of the industry that produced it. In an attempt to both simplify the definition and to make it more generic, Keith, in the same post (as noted earlier), offered his own version: *Case management is the handling of non-routine work processes.* He explained his proposed definition further as: "One might argue that this is too broad and not precise enough, but it is hard to find examples of work that fit this definition and could not be considered case management. Patient care, in general, is not routine. Legal cases are in general not routine. Law enforcement investigations are not routine. The types of work that executives and knowledge workers perform are not routine either. It is a useful definition for that conversation in the elevator."

Indeed, the definitions are either too specific or too broad, and in some instances deficient in a set of high level and precise constructs that could be expanded on to make the definition actionable. Also, some definitions, at least in our opinion, have added restrictions that are not helpful. For example, we do not believe "highly structured" in Forrester's definition is a useful requirement for case management. Of course, in this book we are not aiming to settle the debate around the definition of case management nor do we expect that the definition we will adopt will be universally accepted. Here our goal is to work with a definition that will adequately cover a broad set of case management use cases that can be well tackled by the set of technologies and approaches that this book will be focusing on. Keeping these goals in mind, we adopt the January 2013 conceptual explanation of a "case" from the ongoing efforts of the standards organization OMG (the Object Management Group) to define a standard for "Case Management Model & Notation" aka CMMN (see http://www.omg.org/spec/CMMN/1.0; accessed January/2014) as the working definition for the purpose of this book. It stated:

> *A* `case` is a proceeding that involves actions taken regarding a subject in a particular situation to achieve a desired outcome. Traditional examples come from the legal and medical worlds, where a legal `Case` involves the application of the law to a subject in a certain fact situation, and a medical `Case` involves the care of a patient in the context of a medical history and current medical problems. The subject of a `Case` may be a person, a legal action, a business transaction, or some other focal point around which actions are taken to achieve an objective. The situation commonly includes data that inform and drive the actions taken in a `Case`.

Accordingly, we can define case management as the overall handling of cases (per above definition). Drawing a parallel from the relationship between business processes and BPM, we can then characterize case management as *a discipline that guides the activities related to solution conception and design, deployment, management, and improvement of handling of cases.*

The definition uses "proceeding" (which taken in a general sense just means "a course of actions," see, for example, http://www.thefreedictionary.com/proceedings), which does not impose any restriction of a process (it does not exclude it either). Also, since a reference to "process" is eliminated we do not need to distinguish between the so-called "structured" and "unstructured" processes. As we will see later in the book, in order to offer adequate flexibility during case management solution design we need to free the designer of such restrictions as starting from a process framework. Of course, it is quite likely that some of the case activities or tasks may actually be fulfilled by the execution of processes, structured or not. In most proceedings, actions are documented as they happen—this is a desirable quality in case management solutions that need to produce audit trails for retrospection. The broadness of the ultimate beneficiary, i.e., the "subject" in the OMG definition is also quite appropriate since in application of case management the ultimate beneficiary, generally speaking, can be something or someone different than an individual customer in the traditional sense such as a patient or a plaintiff, and can be something broader or more abstract such as a business (as in company litigations) or a whole country (as in a terror threat resolution case). This definition also identifies the importance of "data" as an important component of case management that coincides well with the solutions required in real-life situations. In our view, data in case management need to be interpreted more generally to include events, messages, content, and knowledge-bearing information.

While our adopted definition does not highlight it nor it is essential to include this in a basic definition, analysis of typical case management requirements shows that on demand collaboration among the "actors" in a case (i.e., the case workers or the knowledge workers engaged in the case) is of critical importance if we want to ensure higher levels of efficacy and efficiency in the solution. Another aspect our definition is silent about is whether the case workers have the freedom to choose the actions and the sequence in which these actions are executed during the proceedings of a case are to be necessarily defined at design time (i.e., predefined) or can also be created at runtime (i.e., adaptive). As we will see later, many case management solutions will require that certain activities be created by the case workers at run time, hence, they (the case workers) will need the freedom to either alter predefined sequence of activities or create their own actions in order to best serve the resolution of the case. As we have already mentioned, the abilities to handle runtime changes in case worker actions are some of the key aspects of what are known as "adaptive" case management (ACM) solutions. We will embark on a detailed discussion about "adaptivity" in the context of case management later in the book.

1.4.5 Application of Case Management Solutions

Work done by employees of an organization, whether it is designing and manufacturing products or providing services, is the essential mechanism that ultimately delivers value for its customers; it is the payments for this delivered value to the customer that translates to the revenue for the organization. For public sector organizations, the revenue is replaced by government allocated budget, which is apportioned from taxes and other income that the government generates typically from citizens and businesses. Since work costs money and resources, optimization of work has always been a key goal of organizational improvement efforts. Due to significant progress made to date in work design, it has been possible to make a large portion of work fairly "routine" (i.e., predictive and repetitive) that often requires low skill (or at least skills that can be learned via simple trainings and applied without much variation). Much of the routine work has also been automated and this automation is well supported by a wide variety of technology currently available to solution designers. With most of the routine work is automated, the remaining work required to fulfil an organization's promise to its customers has now become increasingly more "knowledge"-oriented, i.e., require expertise of the workers and in many cases information from external sources. Given that a lot of the customer care has been steadily moving to self-service models, when a customer does need to get hold of a (human) CSR the problem that needs to be solved is usually more complex than what could already have been handled by the self-service model (e.g., via a self-service web portal). Thus, a CSR, faced with an anxious and troubled customer, needs to quickly assess the problem, do some research into possible solutions, get help from others if necessary, override a few of the rules of organization's standard operating practices (within reason, of course), etc., to deliver a high-quality response back to the complaining customer. Moreover, for legitimate reasons, the complaint may not be resolvable in one interaction, hence, it is important that proper record of what went on in each of the interactions be kept and utilized in subsequent contacts to expedite the resolution process, as well as to maintain an audit trail. Such CSR activities are clearly not routine. And, then there are activities that naturally tend to be nonroutine such as investigations looking to validate or uncover facts or masterminding a threat response. Solutions based on ACM, as we have already mentioned (and more details will follow), have the necessary capabilities to handle all these types of work that cannot be preplanned, nonroutine, or cannot be automated. Since the need for such unpredictable collaborative knowledge work is present across industries, ACM-based solutions are now spreading well beyond the social work, healthcare, and legal sectors.

From the point of view of value that is delivered, ACM solutions can be distinguished by the type of services that are delivered, the nature and expectation of the ultimate beneficiary (i.e., the "subject" in OMG's case management definition), and the type of end goals that are to be met. For example, in the social and healthcare realm there exist case management solutions where the case worker's responsibility is largely consultative, i.e., the case manager analyzes the assistance required, locates appropriate services, informs the care recipient of the options, and in some cases coordinates the recipient's efforts to avail the necessary services. This is called a "Broker Model" (see, for example, US National Institutes of Health or NIH manuscript "Effectiveness of different models of case management for substance-abusing populations" at http://www.ncbi.nlm.nih.gov/pmc/articles/PMC1986794/ as applied to helping substance-abusers; website accessed January/2014)—these are light-touch and relatively cheap service models. On the other hand, there are more comprehensive and more expensive case management models also directed to helping substance abusers such as "assertive community treatment and intensive case management," "strength-based case management" and "clinical case management," which are high-touch and the case workers not only recommend remedial services but also help with access and administration of the same. Clearly the applicability of any of these models would depend on the acuteness of the need of the substance abuser and availability of budget for such care operations. It should be apparent that the case management software systems targeted to serve the lighter-touch models can be a lot simpler than the higher-touch models. Although we cited these case management models for a very specific type of care giving, one can imagine usefulness of similar models in other industries as well.

As we mentioned, case management solutions can also differ vastly in terms who they are serving (i.e., the end customer, the ultimate beneficiary, or the subject) and what type of end goal will signify a successful closure of the case. When a customer contacts a business with a complaint about a product or service, a case may be opened in order to pursue the activities that would collect, review, analyze, and remedy the complaint; here both the ultimate beneficiary, i.e., the customer who complained and the end goal, i.e., a remedy of the complaint is well defined and easily understood. However, for example, when a case is opened by a regulatory agency in order to either monitor or investigate some regulatory compliance of certain prevailing practices of a business, say, accuracy of financial record keeping or use of gifts during promotion of products. In this case, the subject of the case is compliance and not any particular individual and in some sense all stakeholders of that business may be impacted by the outcome. In certain situations, the goal of a particular case may be defined only very broadly. For example, if an incident is reported to the antiterrorist agency of a government and the agency suspects a possible terror threat, it may open a case to keep track of all the follow-up investigations. Such investigative actions may or may not be able to confirm the actual threat even if it were to exist; however, prompt investigative actions like these are in general beneficial to all concerned citizens; here we notice the difficulty in specifying some concrete end goals or in identifying a set of individuals who would be the ultimate beneficiary of the investigations every time a case is opened following an incident reporting. The type and amount of interactions between the case workers and the rest of stakeholders of the case, and the kind of information that is expected to be exchanged between those who trigger the opening of the case and those who pursue the case are clearly quite different in these examples and these differences must be adequately considered when designing the software systems for handling each of these types of cases.

In a December 2009 report by Craig Le Clair and Connie Moore of the analyst firm Forrester titled "Dynamic Case Management—An Old Idea Catches New Fire," the authors classified case management solutions as "dynamic business applications" for a new generation of people-driven processes that would offer all the flexibilities that we have been discussing thus far. The report provided several examples of business problems where case management was either being used or could potentially be used. The examples had a broad range and included applications for high-quality customer experience, multichannel customer support, overseeing audit processes, fraud investigations, dealing with request for sensitive information from government agencies, adverse incident reporting during medical trials, handling of potential terror threats, and the like. Several case management "case studies" contributed by customers, technology vendors, and system integrators have been compiled in the books *Taming the Unpredictable* and *How Knowledge Workers Get Things Done* published by Future Strategies, Inc. in collaboration with Workflow Management Coalition in 2011 and 2012, respectively, and both edited by Layna Fischer. These case studies briefly described the business problems they solved, technologies that were used, benefits that were obtained, and the challenges that were encountered and handled. While most of these case studies focused on the traditionally popular areas of application case management such as advanced customer care and patient care, claims processing for insurance and social benefits and handling of legal proceedings albeit powered by modern technology platforms there were also somewhat nontraditional use cases like handling of investments, collection of biometric information by police, airport operations tracking landing to takeoff of aircrafts, and driving brand and product promotions. Almost in all cases some level of runtime flexibility in selection of case worker tasks and execution sequence based on human judgment, on-demand collaboration among various stakeholders of the case, and appropriate handling of content and events were important. The primary benefits were increased effectiveness of the solutions driving customer satisfaction while maintaining good efficiency and providing comprehensive visibility into case progression.

In the 2009 Forrester report already cited, based on functional and operational goals targeted by specific implementations, the authors predicted emergence of three broad categories of case management solutions (see Figure 1.11): *investigative, incident management,* and *service requests.* Investigative use cases include activities to find and disseminate facts and could range from criminal and fraud investigations to handling requests (e.g., researching, selecting, complying with provisions of the law, etc.) for release of information from government agencies critical to public policy and economy. Management of incidents typically starts with one or a few triggering events (or the incidents) that may be received by agencies, organizations, or businesses, and often the responses to these incidents would involve timely notifications to all concerned, sometimes a very select set of people (e.g., covertly informing the local police of a possible bank heist, formally informing regulatory authorities of adverse drug reactions during a drug trial) or a broad population (e.g., all travelers in certain regions about a possible terrorist attack, broadcasting possible danger due to contaminated food supply or spread of an emerging epidemic). Communication and sharing of vital information among all stakeholders is critical to handling incident management type of cases. In case management problems involving complex customer service situations, whether the service is sought from a government agency or from a commercial business, exchanges between the customer and the case workers and the ability of the case workers to select and provide the components of the service necessary to satisfy the customer are critical to successful closing of the cases.

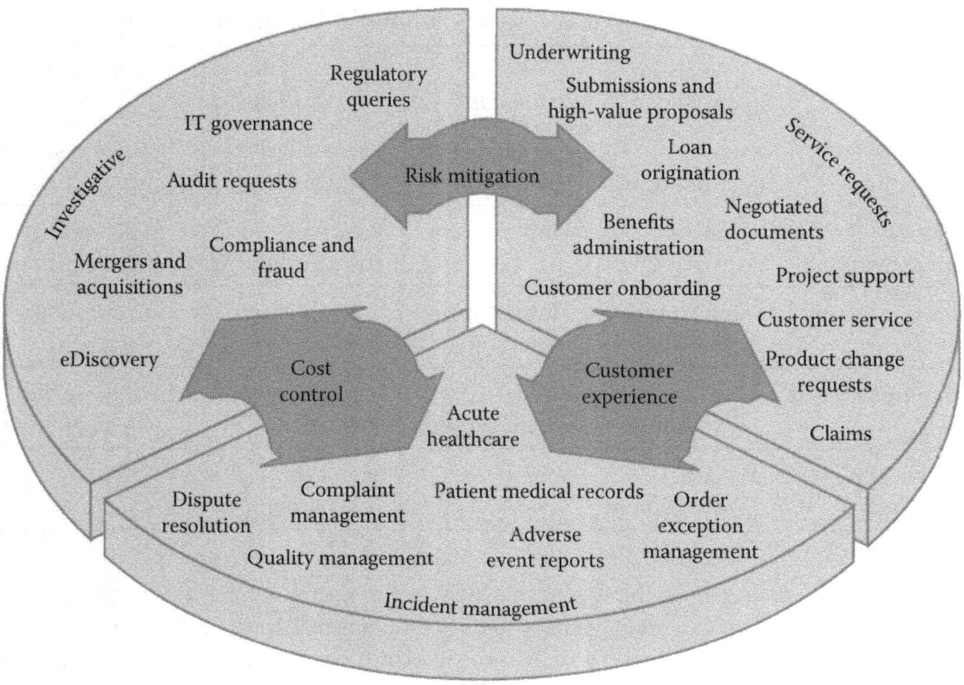

Figure 1.11 Forrester's classification of case management solutions (2009).

While these three categories of case management solutions display many distinct characteristics, we should not be surprised by overlaps of certain common functionalities that are at the core of each of these case management solutions such as work flexibility, on demand collaboration, content and event management, and overall visibility to case progression, as we have already pointed out earlier. Also, many case management solutions may embody characteristics from more than one of these three solution categories. In Table 1.1, we provide a list of case management applications for several industries and indicate how their primary characteristics are aligned with one or more of the three categories we have just discussed. This table is a shorter version of a bigger collection that we have analyzed; we present the longer version in the Appendix. Please note that the case management solutions listed for any given industry are only just examples and are not meant to be exhaustive, and through the information in Table 1.1 (or the table in the Appendix) we are also not saying that the industries not listed there do not have use cases where case management solutions are applicable; in fact, with the broad capabilities included in the case management paradigm, there are likely applications in practically all industry sectors.

1.5 Creating Case Management Solutions

1.5.1 High-Level Solution Architectures

In an exercise to typify ACM solutions, especially in the context of this book where one of the primary goals is to assist the readers gain insight into ACM solution design, besides understanding the business problems that ACM is capable of solving as described in the last section, we must also

Table 1.1 Examples of Case Management Solutions in Various Industries

Public Sector	*Financial Services*	*Insurance*	*Healthcare*	*Energy and Utility*
Benefits eligibility	Loan origination	P&C claims processing	Payer claim processing	Process safety management
Grants management	Investor servicing	Underwriting	Policy and procedure mgmt	FERC eTariff
Tax processing	New account opening	New account opening	Virtual patient record	Transmittals process
Unemployment	Dispute resolution	Policy management	Legal contracts mgmt	Well log file management
Welfare services	Wealth management		Member enrollment	

look into the main construction blocks of the ACM solutions. We present core and supporting technology components of case management solutions in Figure 1.10. As should be expected, not all components are important in every ACM solution. In order to focus on the design considerations and to identify relative importance of such technology components in a particular ACM solution, a pattern's approach that relates to high-level solution architecture can be helpful. The key question that follows is "what are the distinct solution architecture patterns that we should analyze and understand" so as to make knowledgeable choices during a solution design exercise. One option and the one that we have chosen to pursue here is to start with the three ACM solution types enumerated by Forrester. These types, as already described earlier in this chapter, are service request, incident management, and investigative. Of course, there are many pertinent questions that still need to be addressed before settling down on these three types of ACM solutions as targets for high-level solution architecture patterns. For example, how useful are these types in characterizing any given ACM solution? Are these types sufficiently distinct to warrant a solution architecture pattern? Does a given ACM solution fall purely under one of these solution types? To answer such questions, we analyzed over 50 ACM solutions across more than six industries and observed the following:

1. Most real-life ACM solutions would display characteristics that would be found in a combination of two or more of the three types (i.e., service request, incident management, and investigative) although in some instances one of these three types may assume a dominant role. For example, a new bank account opening case is predominantly a service request type solution while a loan origination case can include, besides the characteristics of service request–type solutions, some flavors, and amount of investigation-type activities.
2. Investigative type of case work is typically triggered by either a service request or an incident reporting. Examples include sorting through causes of an insurance claim as a result of filing of a claim (a service request–type ACM solution) and searching for the culprits after receiving a report of a murder (an incident management type ACM solution). Even though investigative case types may be triggered by other case types, we feel that it is distinct enough that it can be treated as a high-level solution architecture pattern just as service request or incident management types.

3. There are wider variations in the types of case work (i.e., activities) that could be associated with incident management and investigation while service request type of case work would typically have narrower variation. This is mainly because in service request type of solutions use cases where most of the actors (i.e., the participants) are usually well defined and the activities to be undertaken are generally known. On the other hand, a fraud investigation or handling of sudden epidemic can easily require many unexpected steps that only reveal themselves as the cases progress.
4. A significant portion of case work tends to require human touch and these could vary between a simple human task like a phone call to complex approval chains or fact finding missions. Of course, wherever possible routine work tends to get automated and executed by machines. Work that requires a lot of conversation, substantial exchange of information and ideas, subjective decision making or consultations with topical experts are best done by humans or under human supervision.
5. Use of rules plays a big part in construction of ACM solutions. Rules (along with case worker knowledge) typically determine triggering of case activities, either human tasks or automated machine tasks, as events emerge during case progression. For example, in a loan origination use case upon receipt of all the necessary application material a rule may cause notifications to be fired in order to inform the loan processor and the underwriter to take the next steps toward closing the loan application. In addition, many business logics such as risk indices associated with a credit application and calculation of insurance premiums can also be conveniently encoded in rules.
6. Many ACM solutions need to adhere to regulations or stipulations imposed by governmental authorities or by prevailing industry practices. This fact adds a stronger requirement of capturing detailed audit trails of actions and the corresponding actors associated with the case activities. Examples of such situations can be easily visualized in complex financial, legal, or medical cases.
7. Handling of documents and content is an integral part of most ACM solutions; however, large variations exist in terms of type of documents handled, i.e., whether they are structured such as a form or unstructured such as emails or scanned images, and in their role, i.e., either driving or supporting, in the progress of the case. Take, for example, a case that may be dealing with a contract dispute. As the case workers try to resolve the case, they may have to reference all the related contract and the terms and condition documents, and in this situation documents mainly support the case activities. On the other hand, imagine a case to handle possible terror threat–case-related information may be gleaned from all sorts of sources including postings on the Internet, news, and social media, etc., none of which are well structured and a lot of the case activities are likely to be driven by such information. There are also certain cases management problems where extensive pre- or post-processing of documents is needed either to trigger the case or to disseminate the case resolutions. Deciphering of information in an invoice scan, verifying a signature on a contract or creating notifications in multiple formats for multiple recipients are examples of pre- or post-processing of case-related documents.
8. Application integration shows up as a major component where information exchanges are needed between the case solution system and other systems of record such as ERP, HCM, or SCM. In some situations, information may have to be exchanged between companies or relatively independent business units and there B2B-type integrations between private (i.e., within the company or business unit) and public (i.e., shared among the companies or business units) processes are needed.

9. While case management systems are built around the concept of sensing and responding to emerging events, in some special cases, more specific treatment for handling events may be necessary. Commonly termed as complex event processing (CEP) where through a variety of techniques such as filtering, aggregation, and pattern matching important insights are derived out of a large number of events and the ultimate actions or responses reflect these insights or conclusions. For example, during a communication network or a power grid outage many monitoring devices could generate large number of events even if the outage is caused by failure of a single network element—CEP can be used to sort through the collection of all such events to identify the root cause and initiate or assist a case to help resolve the problem.
10. While standard access control and security requirements are relevant in most case management solutions, these requirements are quite similar to typical enterprise software solutions. In situations where the solution involves sensitive information, for example, in financial transactions or adverse incident reporting, access to information needs higher levels of control and more complicated policies.

In Figure 1.12 for the three types of ACM solution types, i.e., service request, incident management, and investigative, we present a summary highlighting the similarities and differences among them of the technology or enabling components that are likely to be needed to construct them. In Part 3, we discuss these solution types in more technical detail and address implications of some of the observations listed earlier.

1.5.2 Build or Buy?

Whenever there would be a need for a case management solution, it would be natural to ask the question: "Build or buy?" How should we answer this? Of course, there are organizations that simply prefer, for whatever reason, one option versus the other, i.e., either choose one of "build" or "buy" as part of their standard operating procedure, no matter what the consequences are. However, if instead we sought to find some rationale for our choice, then how should we go about it? First of all let us consider the three basic approaches that we can take to realize a case management solution: *bespoke* (i.e., custom developed or tailor-made software), *packaged application*, or a *middleware-based application*. Bespoke approach by definition has the advantage of being able to deliver a solution that exactly fits the requirements and this is a positive. However, often bespoke approach leads to a large collection of handwritten code typically utilizing low-level programming languages and scripts that are difficult to understand, maintain, debug, and enhance, thus incurring high cost and long project times. If the business problem is truly unique and the solution is really critical to the business, a bespoke approach may be justified, at least to start with.

Use of packaged applications sit on the other end of the spectrum from bespoke approach. The vendors of such applications package functionalities that serve most common use cases, provide some ability for customization, and generally carry the responsibility for bug fixing and regular upgrades to the software. As will be discussed later in this book, one packaged application from Oracle called Siebel provides a set of out-of-the-box (OOTB) case management functionalities for some of the public sector use cases. If the solution requirements are such that OOTB functionalities of a packaged application, perhaps with light customization (say, changes in configuration), are good enough to solve the problem at an acceptable level of satisfaction, and if the business has already invested in and is familiar with the packaged application (for example, a company already

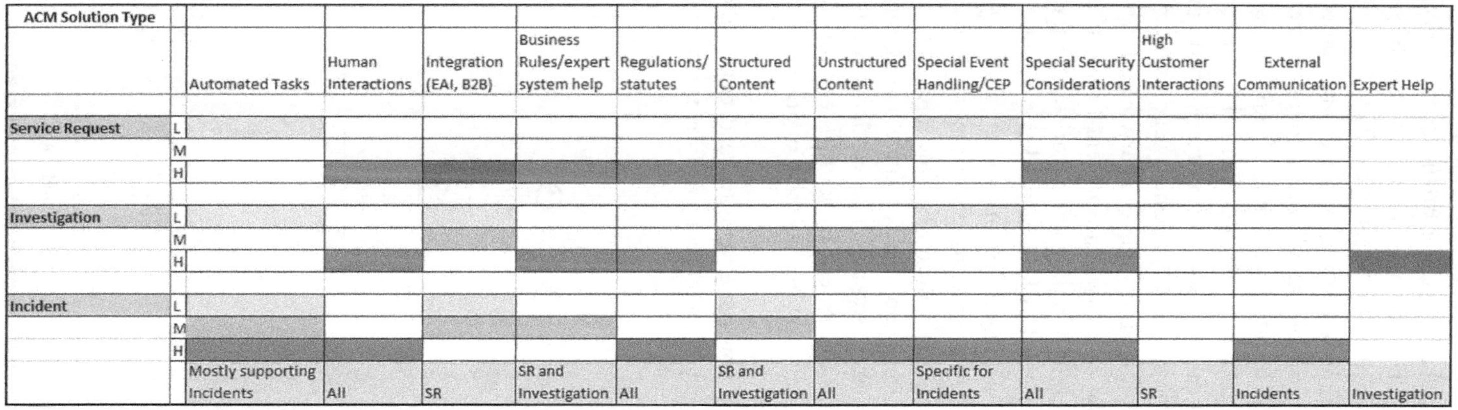

Figure 1.12 High-level solution patterns—dominant components.

using Siebel for CRM) or the initial license and implementation costs of the target packaged application are acceptable, then this (i.e., the packaged application approach) is quite viable. It should be noted that if heavy and invasive customization are needed in order to make a package application fit the requirements adequately, then one can expect very high maintenance and upgrade costs for that application down the line—in fact, these difficulties can sometimes surpass those of bespoke software, hence in such situations use of packaged applications should be avoided.

The third approach uses a suitable middleware, for example, Oracle BPM Suite Case Management from Oracle Fusion Middleware family of products, as the basis for creating case management solutions. This approach mostly involves visual programming, can connect to packaged applications if needed, and can be also made as exactly fitting to requirements as bespoke software. In fact, most of the leading case management vendors offering that are targeted as general case management platforms fall under this category. Middleware-based case management platforms essentially combine the core case management functionalities (see Figure 1.10) such as case rules and policies, basic event handling and security, management of case activities (i.e., tasks and processes) and case content, UIs for case worker collaboration and task execution over multiple channels (including mobile where appropriate), and management dashboards. In addition, these platforms provide ways to connect to other supporting components such as integration backbone, analytics, and organizational directories. Due to componentized architecture of these platforms and the visual programming approach, change management solution creation is usually cheaper and can be done faster. It should be noted that handling of middleware platforms does require some specific training and expertise and in absence of adequate middleware competency any middleware-based solution, case management or otherwise, faces possible unsatisfactory delivery of functionalities and benefits.

Figure 1.13 provides a visual of how these three approaches would generally fare when we consider how well they deliver on functional requirements, time taken for initial deployment, and cost

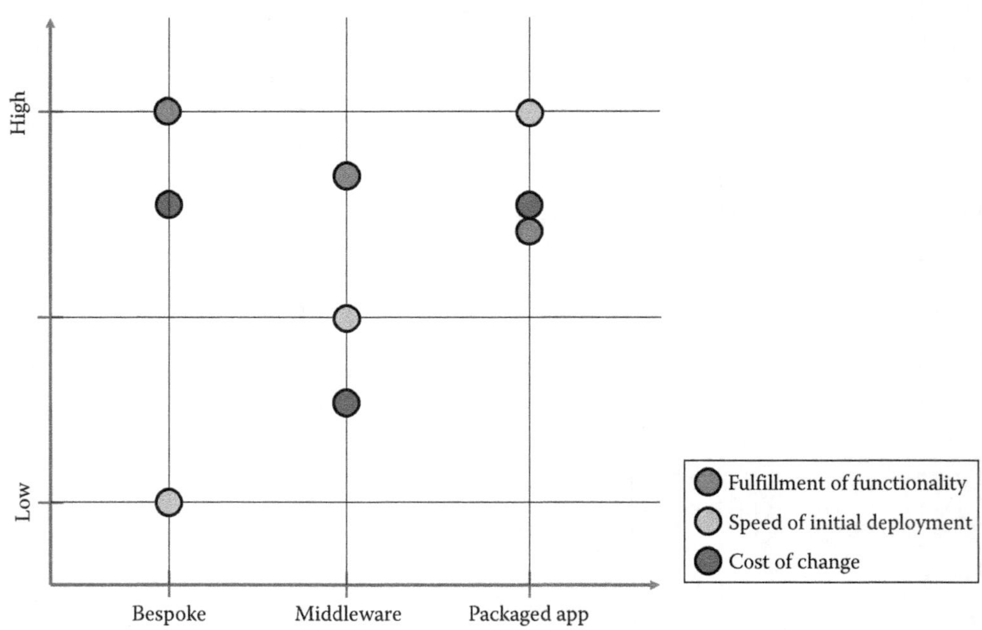

Figure 1.13 Comparison of bespoke, middleware-based and packaged application choices for ACM.

of ongoing change management (either for bug fixes or enhancements). This depiction assumes that we are applying each of the approach using its best practices and not stretching reasonable limits of its as designed capabilities such as undertaking massive invasive customization for a packaged application in order to meet solution requirements adequately or resorting to large and complex code plug-ins in a middleware-based solution to achieve fulfillment of not so important requirements. In some situations, a hybrid approach such as using a combination of packaged and middleware-based application may also be useful. As an example, we can envision extending the base case management capabilities of Oracle Siebel with Oracle BPM Suite Case Management in order to accommodate a set of special processing or tasks or to enhance the overall adaptiveness of the solution.

1.5.3 Building a Fit-for-Purpose Case Management Solution

So, how does one go about building an ACM solution? Where does one begin? Is there something characteristically different about creating an ACM solution as compared to other traditional software solutions, e.g., a standard BPM-based application? In this section, our goal is to discuss the essential methodology concepts related to creation of an ACM solution, in particular using a middleware product (e.g., Oracle BPM Suite or similar). We will defer the finer and more technical details till later in the book after prebuilt case management solutions in Siebel and ACM-related features of BPM Suite have been presented and discussed. A pertinent question at this point of course is what type of information we need to collect and sort through as we embark on designing an ACM solution—the mind map in Figure 1.14 displays a set of information dimensions that can be conceptually handy in answering this question. Also, such mind maps can provide a flexible format to record notes and highlights as we collect input from various parties during the solution design process. Before proceeding further, we would like to note that unlike traditional BPM projects, methodology for ACM projects are still being developed by concerned vendors and SIs, hence, a universally agreed approach is not yet available; what we are discussing in this book are based on our experiences working with customers.

As with most software application development project, an ACM project will start with a "project discovery and requirements gathering" phase. Of course, when using iterative or agile

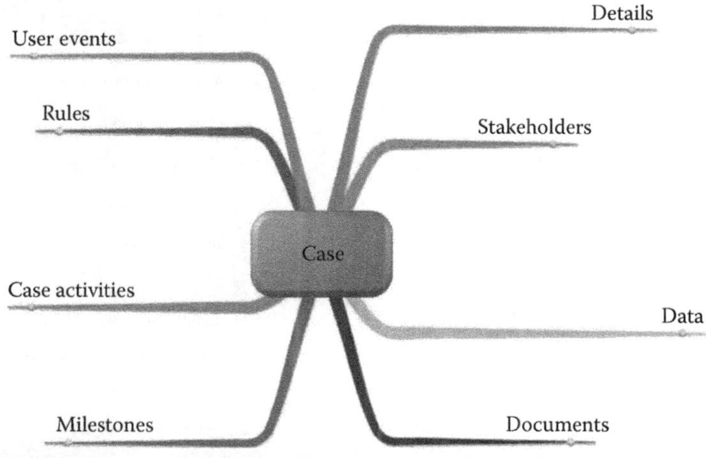

Figure 1.14 Key information required to construct a case model (in Oracle BPM Suite).

methods of project delivery additional requirements are gathered, whether to capture newer capabilities or to modify existing ones, in each cycle of the iteration. These phases are vital since majority of large defects or shortcomings of software applications can generally be traced to not having done a good job in these phases. In fact, much of the differences in handling of an ACM project compared to a traditional BPM project will show up in these phases. Let us recall that ACM solutions are aimed at providing much greater flexibility to the stakeholders of the case by conceptualizing the solution as a composite of events and the response to those events via rules and case activities. This means that as we go through the discovery process we need to have the discussions free from constraints that, for example, a traditional BPM approach may impose. We will also need to use more free formatted documentation styles to capture the information that we would collect during the discovery phase; in our experience, simple mind maps and suitably organized spreadsheets serve well for this purpose. The main idea is to capture enough information to be able to construct a "case model" that would be used to instantiate individual cases and will guide the progression of those case instances. In this context, we evaluated the proposed CMMN standard (ref. omg.org) and concluded that it was too technical for many typical case management solution stakeholders and thus may pose unnecessary burden during the discovery phase.

With a goal to decompose the business problem so as to identify the necessary solution components, we start with very loosely coupled events that describe the high-level interaction among the case stakeholders and the information that they interact with which may involve external sources like the customer or internal supporting systems (e.g., packaged applications like ERP, HCM, or CRM). Then we delve into the case activity details and we start to recognize pieces of the solution that display familiar solution component patterns, e.g., human tasks like uploading or reviewing a document or an approval, BPM processes like making payments or settling credits, etc. As shown in Figure 1.15, we have arranged the progression of the project discovery and requirements gathering activities in three levels, "CM L1" through "CM L3", and have listed the type of information that should be collected at each level. These have been designed in a manner that by CM L2 it should be possible to grasp how the target case model would look like, and by CM L3 there would be enough information to complete the construction of the case model along

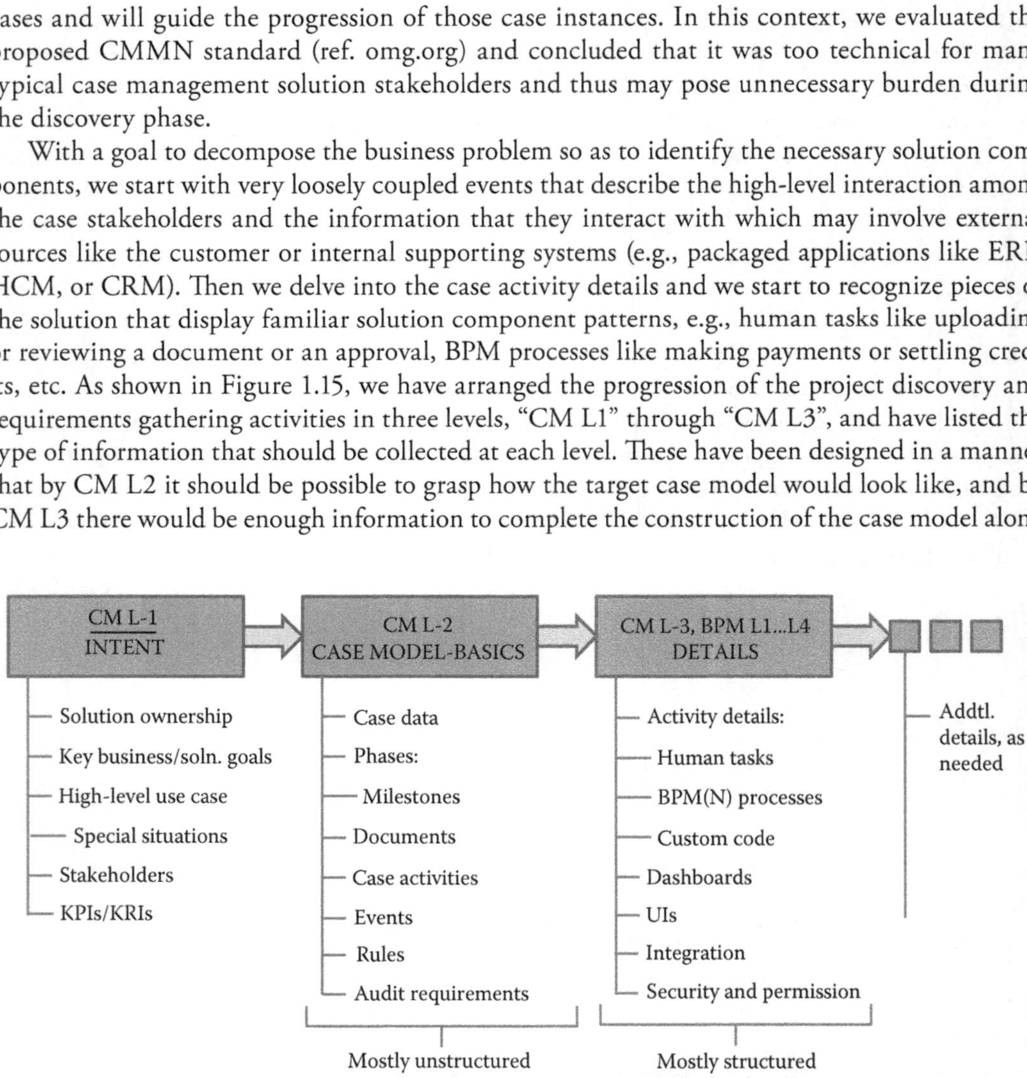

Figure 1.15 Case management solution creation and discovery phase and CM levels.

with some level completion of the associated case activities and UIs. Next we present a high-level description of information that needs to be collected in each of these levels and the reasons for doing that.

1. *Case Management Level 1* (*CM L1*): In CM L1, our goal is to collect enough high-level information such that completion of CM L1 will provide adequate contextual information about the target ACM solution that would be normally sufficient for the solution owner to feel satisfied about the expected outcome and for the solution designers and developers to grasp the "big picture." As we have stated before, case management paradigm is result or goal oriented and the ultimate result or the goal that would characterize the resolution of the case is a key input under the entity "key business and solution goals." In addition, key business and solution goals should also include the overall capabilities of the solution as well as any major performance considerations including any service-level agreement (SLA) information. The "use case" along with "special situations" is meant to capture the essential business problem, the expected solutions strategy, and the possible known exceptions.
   The "stakeholders" (aka case participants) are the main "actors" (in use case terminology)—these are roles that are interested in the resolution of the case and some of these roles are also the ones that perform the case activities. As an example, for a loan origination case it is quite common that there will be a loan officer (often this is the person that provides the quotes and T&Cs), a loan processor (who does most of the document checks and some of the calculations), an underwriter (who accepts the risk associated with the loan, i.e., has the final say on the approval of the loan) and a closing agent (someone who does the title checks, gets the buyer and the seller to sign-off on their paper work, and collects or disburses funds from or to all parties). Case stakeholders interact with the case through human activities (e.g., review, approve, etc.). A variety of computer applications may also execute case activities—such activities are usually termed automatic activities (as they are automatically fired when all the preconditions for the activities are met). "KPIs or KRIs," i.e., the key performance indicators or key risk indicators, would be the measures that the "solution owner" and any concerned management and stakeholders would inspect in order to gain knowledge about how the solution is performing against expectations.
2. *Case Management Level 2* (*CM L2*): Having captured the overall solution context in CM L1, next we proceed to gather information required to create the structure of the case that we have been referring to as the case model (aka case type or case template). A solution designer, through the process of discovery and requirements gathering, will collect the necessary information about the attributes described under CM L2 column and, using the facilities of the case management tool that he/she is using, will create the case model. While ACM provides great flexibilities in terms of what activity to undertake when and by whom, often leveraging the knowledge and experience of the participants, some sort of a structure like a case model is still needed to kickoff a case instance. The level of detail for this case model could of course vary from solution to solution depending on the nature of the problem being solved and the amount of *a priori* knowledge about the paths the solution is likely to take. At one end of the spectrum of required case model detail, when the *a priori* knowledge about the solution cannot be established, the case model may have just a name and one stakeholder, and everything else could be added as the case progresses. On the other end of this spectrum where everything about the solution is known *a priori*, the case model will have many attributes and will be endowed with a lot of detail; in fact, in this situation an ACM solution and a traditional BPM solution will become functionally equivalent

(although the solution complexities of the two approaches may not be the same). As always in real life typical ACM solutions will fall somewhere in between; as per our experience, the list of attributes given in column "CM L2" in Figure 1.16 would be a set of information that would be required to create most case models.

A typical case progresses by going through a set of phases and by completing a set of milestones within those phases (see Figure 1.7 for a schematic). A phase is a coarse-grain group of activities and all the phases taken together should provide a fairly good idea of what all things, at least at a high level, that need to get done in completing the case. For example, if a loan origination for home mortgage is modeled as a case, it may have phases like document collection for eligibility, quotation of interest rate and other T&Cs, underwriting of the loan, and the closing. Each of such phases may contain, besides a start and an end (of the phase), intermediate milestones to signify important activity completion points in the case progression. For example, the document collection phase may have intermediate milestones like completion of loan application, collection of income documents, etc., as intermediate milestones. We want to point out that phases and milestones do not have to be *necessarily* traversed in a fixed sequence; after completion of a milestone or a phase, if the need arises and based on either machine analysis or human judgment, case workers should be able to revisit some of the activities summing up to that milestone or contained in that or another phase unless prohibited by some company rules or government regulations. This ability to move back and forth between activities depending on case status is an important difference

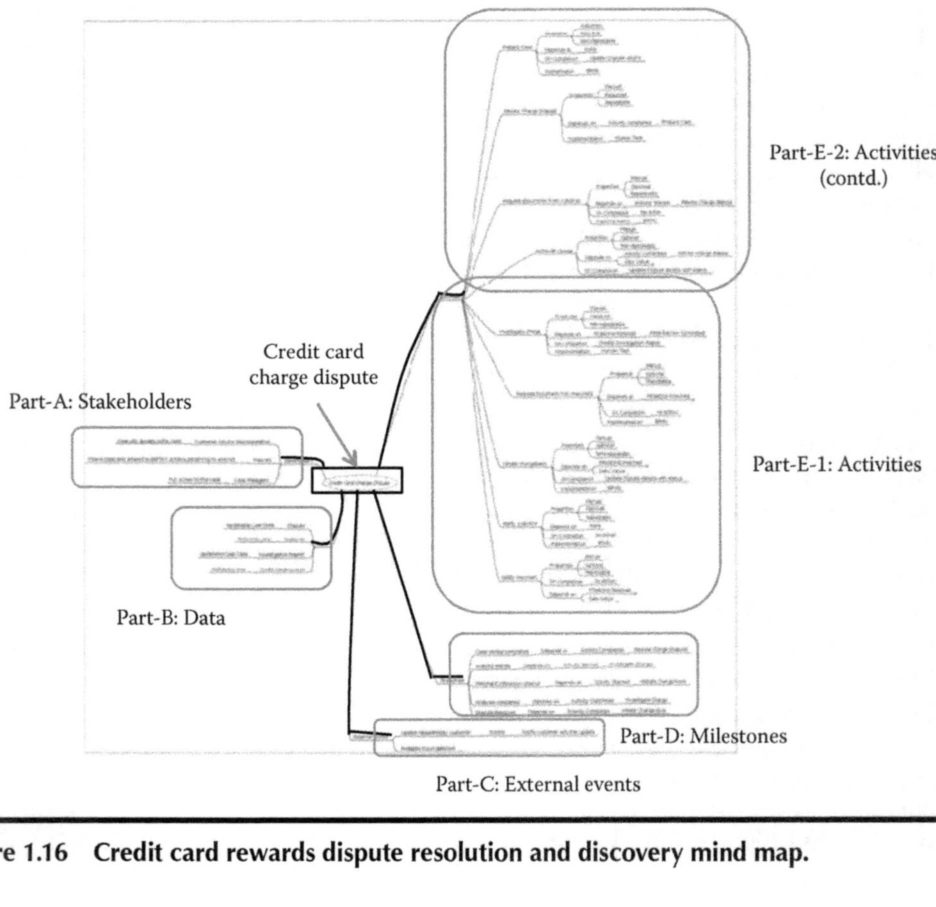

Figure 1.16 Credit card rewards dispute resolution and discovery mind map.

between the natural flow of activities in ACM solutions compared to that in traditional BPM where activity flows are fixed at design time.

"Events" in a case signify occurrence (or nonoccurrence) of something of interest, e.g., uploading of required documents needed for the case or reporting of an accident by a rental car customer or an excessive delay in making a particular decision. Using case "activities" that are typically triggered by a set of "rules" upon receipt of pertinent events, a case model provides the necessary response to such events. Case activities are either completed by case workers (i.e., human tasks) or by machines (i.e., automated tasks); case activities may be mandatory or optional and rules can be specified to indicate this fact.

Case "data" normally refers to the basic information that triggers the start of case and then supports the case progression, possibly getting modified or enriched through the life of the case. Case data is mostly structured information. In case of loan origination, the loan application could be a key part of the case data. Case "documents," on the other hand, can be an arbitrary mix of structured and unstructured data; involvement of such documents in a case can range from a purely support role to a driving force. In case of loan origination, images of recent tax returns may be one of supporting documents while the scan of the contract signature page could trigger, i.e., drive, the next suitable case activity. Note that besides the events and the activities that the solution designer may include in the case model, during the execution of a case, case workers may add events and activities at run time and may alter the sequence in which these activities are completed (as pointed out before these runtime modification capabilities make a case management solution adaptive).

Generally speaking, all ACM solutions should be able to provide, for intermediate and postmortem reviews, an audit trail of all the events that occurred and actions taken (as a result of those event occurrences) as the case progresses. However, certain types of cases, for example, those dealing with law enforcement or critical patient care or adverse incident management may have special regulatory audit or compliance requirements—such concerns should be recorded under the "audit requirements."

3. *Case Management Level 3* (*CM L3*): CM L3, as shown Figure 1.15, continues with additional discovery and requirements gathering process mainly to make the case activities and UIs more concrete. Requirements like security and permission that tend to be more technical in nature can also be handled at this level. At CM L3, the case activities should be sufficiently detailed for us to recognize if they are simple or complex tasks, if they are business processes, or perhaps they are something so unique that special supporting applications may have to be custom developed. Once we have identified the exact nature of a case activity, we can then use any suitable existing methodology to further develop the design and eventually implement that activity. For example, if a case activity turns out be, say, standard credit check, we can use an appropriate business process to model and implement this activity. Similar comments can be made for simple human tasks or complex human approval chains. CM L3 can be seen as a level where hand-offs from ACM to a variety of standard modeling techniques can take place. As an example, in situations where a case activity has been identified to be a business process, as we have indicated in Figure 1.15, it would correspond, depending on the granularity of the activity, to some generally accepted process decomposition level (BPM L1, L2, L3, or L4). And, once we have recognized the case activity to be a business process at some level, we can then simply follow an appropriate process modeling technique (see, for example, http://www.oracle.com/technetwork/topics/entarch/oracle-pg-bpm-bus-proc-eng-r3-0-292099.pdf; accessed January/2014) to realize that activity.

Recall the credit card rewards dispute resolution case that we had mentioned in Section 1.3 when discussing the consequence of the occurrence of even a small amount of real-life variation in an otherwise simple business process. From that discussion, a general conclusion is that such situations are better modeled with the ACM approach. As a constructive example of some of the preliminary outputs of ACM discovery and requirements gathering process, in Figures 1.16 through 1.20 we present the mind map capturing the essential outcomes from the discovery interviews and the spreadsheet listing the key case activities highlighting whether an activity is automatic (i.e., executed by machines) or knowledge driven (i.e., handled by humans). Of course, in order to create an ACM solution one will have to get to much finer nitty-gritty of all the attributes in various CM levels. We defer such finer details later in the book, keeping this early chapter focused more on familiarization of the key concepts.

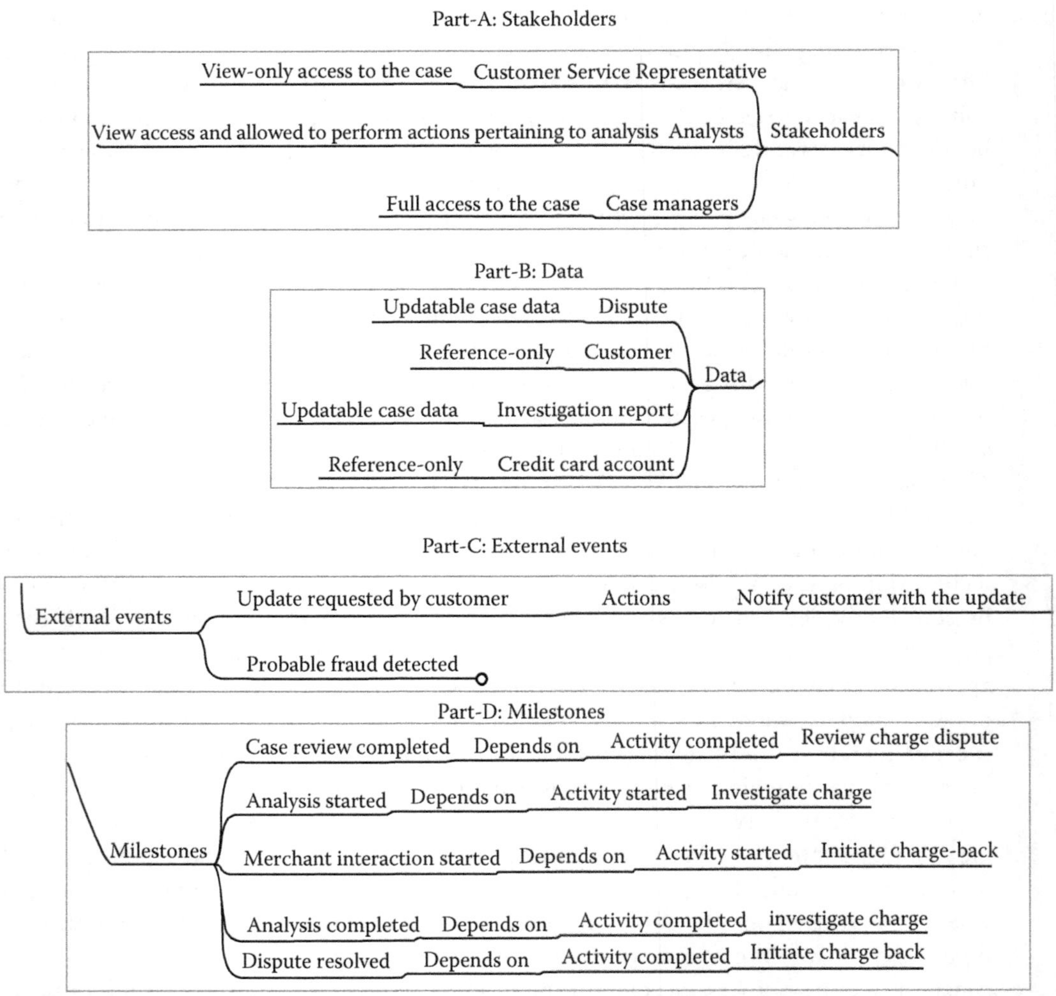

Figure 1.17 Credit card rewards dispute resolution and discovery mind map (detail #1).

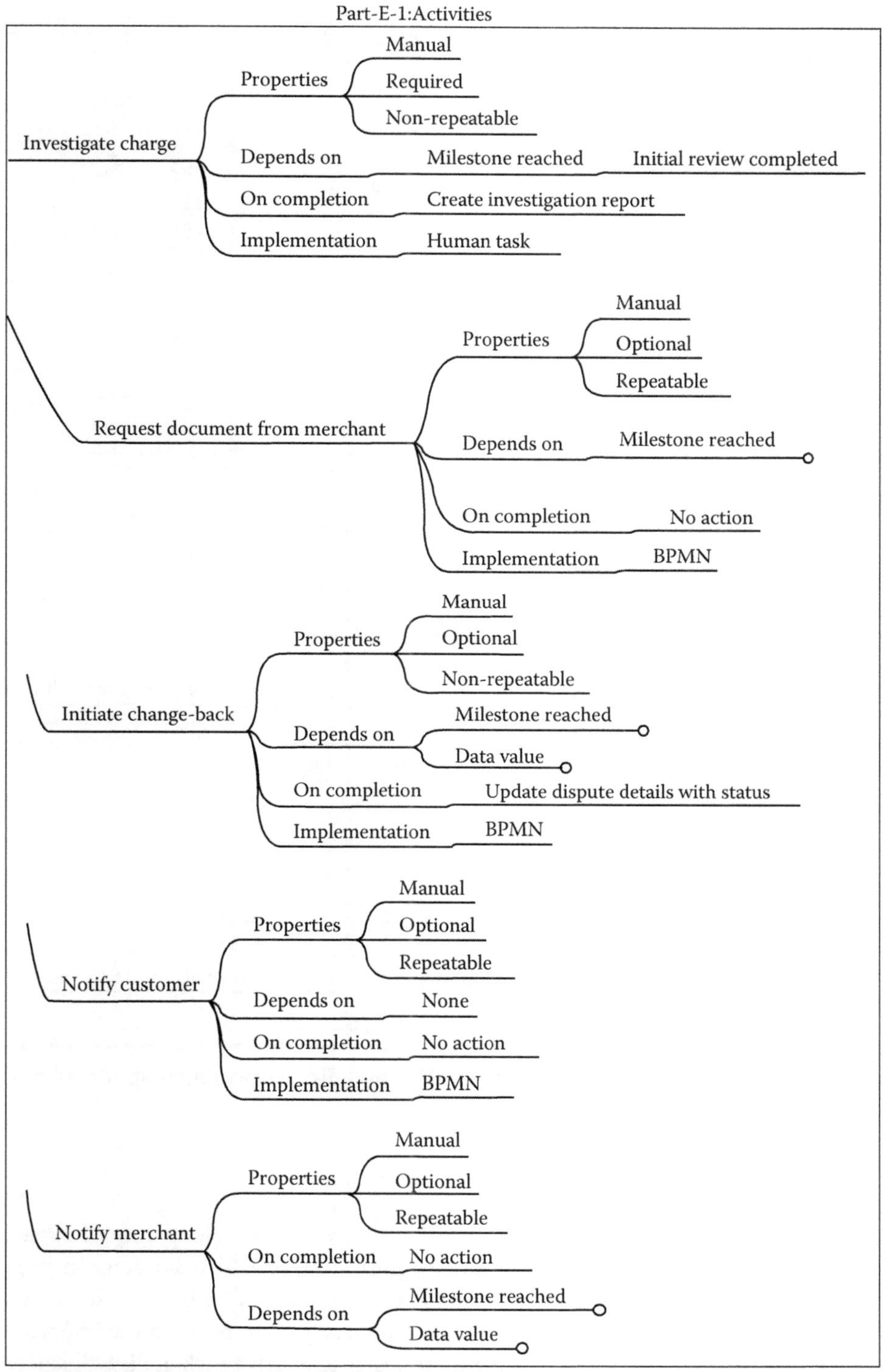

Figure 1.18 Credit card rewards dispute resolution and discovery mind map (detail #2).

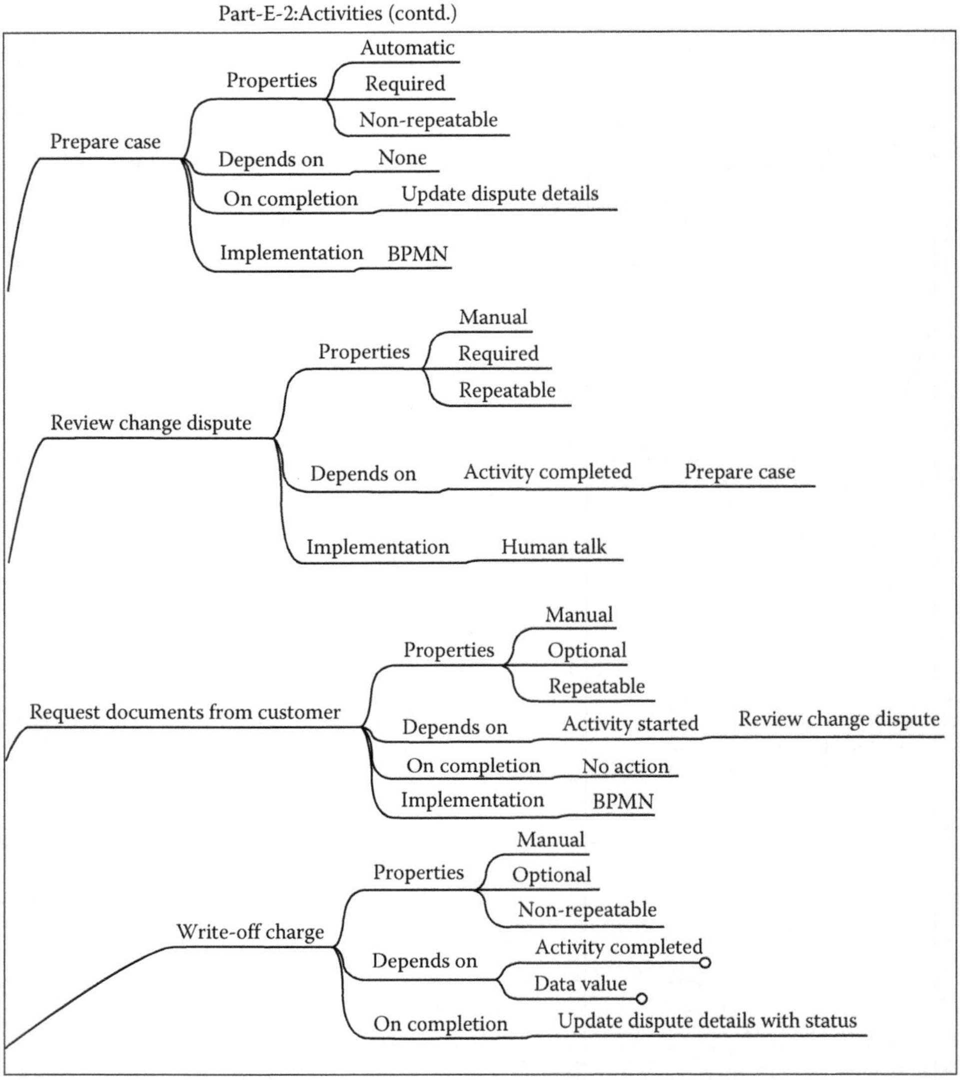

Figure 1.19 Credit card rewards dispute resolution and discovery mind map (detail #3).

1.6 ACM and Business Agility

In today's highly competitive environment, "agility" is a very desirable quality of all successful businesses, and consequently, the phrase "business agility" receives a lot of coverage in many ranks of organizations; there are often many initiatives to improve agility of businesses, and management consultants and industry analysts enthusiastically play their part in pushing the importance and urgency of businesses being agile offering many strategies to achieve such agility. Business agility can mean different things to different people: at the highest level, say, at an LOB or higher level, speed at which new or variants of existing products or services are delivered or customer disputes resolved can be critical; operational divisions would be more interested in speed of execution in particular when work activities are added or modified; faster speed of application implementation,

Phase	Milestone	Pre-condition	Activities	Predefined Execution	Knowledge Worker Driven
Assessment phase	Initial assessment started	Case owner claims the case for processing	Update complaint details		X
			Conduct assessment/review		X
			Send email		X
			Create and assign ad-hoc task		X
			Prepare case	X	
	Initial assessment completed	Conduct assessment completed			
Investigation phase	Investigation started	Initial assessment completed and complaint deemed to be a valid complaint	Ad-hoc task for expert analysis		X
			Investigate complaint		X
			Notify customer that the complaint is being Investigated	X	
			Request more information from customer		X
			Review received documents	X	
			Send Email		
	Investigation completed	Investigation activity completed	Catalog uploaded documents	X	
Resolution phase	Complaint resolution started	Investigation completed or initial assessment found that the complaint had no merit	Notify customer		X
			Initiate process to credit missing rewards (If type if of complaint is rewards related)		X
			Initiate process to revert finance charges (If type of complaining is finance charge related)		X
			Initiate process to send a gift card to address a loyal customer's dissatisfaction due to this complaint		X
			Initiate fraud investigation		X
			Blacklist a merchant (if type of complaint is merchant experience related)		X
			Close the case		X
	Complaint resolved		Notify customer regarding the final resolution	X	

Some activities are added, execution sequences changed, and ad-hoc collaborations utilized at RUN-TIME

Figure 1.20 Credit card rewards dispute resolution and case activities and their classification.

improvement, and maintenance would be of primary importance of IT groups. Business capabilities that would provide such agilities would be enabled by better business and IT solution architectures, ability to quickly understand signals of change and make fast decisions with respect to appropriate responses, end to end visibility and control of business activities, easier access to right information at the right time, higher productivity, and so on. Given that ACM advocates certain departures from the traditional management of business activities, (i.e., via predefined business processes or BPM paradigm) it may be worthwhile to understand how the adoption of ACM influences business agility. However, before we can address ACM's role in business agility, it would be useful to embark on a short discourse on key characteristics of agile businesses.

As per its basic definition, agility of an organism or an organization or a system indicates its ability to react or move fast and with ease. Often the ability to be "adaptive," i.e., the ability to incorporate change efficiently and effectively and on demand, is also seen as an essential characteristic of being agile. An organization may need to react quickly to a wide variety of emerging events caused by changes internally to the organization or by the external business environment. A company may need to offer different types or quality of products and services due to changing customer expectation; it may need to adjust its internal working leading to a different way it delivers value to the end customers. Any combination of drivers like cost optimization, market penetration and product or service leadership can demand agile reactions from an enterprise. Citing work done by Kishore Sengupta from INSEAD and Andrea Masini of the London Business School a November 2007, a report by Henry Peyret of Forrester points out that organizations need to manage two types of agilities based on the nature of the change imperatives: *Range* and *Time*. As explained in this report, range agility refers to an organization's ability to react adequately to expected change events, for example, fast assimilation of merging organizations in an M&A (mergers and acquisitions) situation; such change-forces can be anticipated reasonably well in advance although considerable organizational capabilities are needed to effect such changes efficiently. Time agility, on the other hand, concerns an organization's ability to respond quickly to a single or perhaps a few events, such as a sudden price drop or a sharp demand for a new feature, where the organization may need to fast modify its current way of working to accommodate reactions to such challenges. For example, if car buyers start to strongly favor built-in GPS systems, an automaker would have to find ways to make quick design and production changes to respond to this customer demand. As we will see later in this section, the ACM paradigm can help with both these kinds of agility.

While essentially an organization must be able to quickly and accurately "sense" the applicable change imperatives and then effectively "respond" faster than competition in order to demonstrate a beneficial level of agility, a little more detailed structure to capture the key characteristics of agile enterprises is helpful in judging whether a given paradigm would promote agility. For example, in 2012 a blog article (http://strategicfrontier.wordpress.com/2012/01/05/business-agility-defined/; accessed January/2014), Eric Jansen, a VP at ThoughtWorks (a software consulting company), describes business agility with six key components (see Figure 1.21): "Adaptive planning," i.e., not restricted to sequential planning but embracing frequent adjustments to the original plan, "focus on time-to-value," i.e., adopting a strong focus on frequent and on-demand deliveries of products and services, "decoupling," i.e., practicing loosely coupled business processes where departmental or functional processes are designed to be relatively independent from each other, "low latency," i.e., faster execution, "economic efficiency," i.e., promoting "lean" style of execution, and "rapid adaptation" i.e., allowing for fast course correcting of execution whenever necessary. In September 2013, Craig Le Clair et al. of the analyst firm Forrester Research published a report titled "The 10 Dimensions of Business Agility" (http://www.forrester.com/The+10+Dimensions+Of+Business+Agility/fulltext/-/E-RES98503; accessed January/2014) that follows a similar approach to

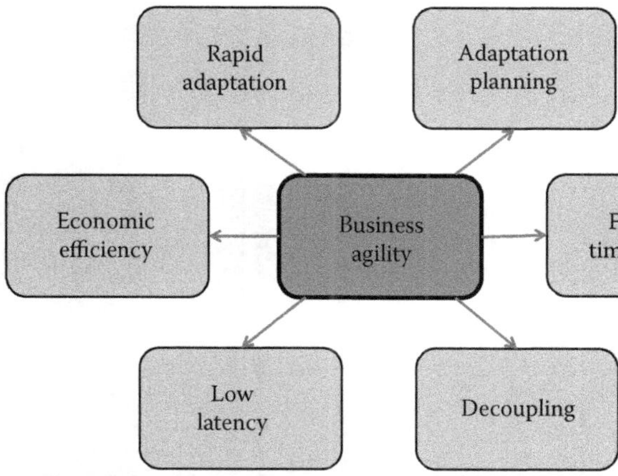

Figure 1.21 Six key components of business agility. (Adapted from Eric Jansen, 2012, http://strategicfrontier.wordpress.com/2012/01/05/business-agility-defined/. Accessed on January 2014.)

Jansen's and defines 10 key dimensions as yard-sticks for an enterprise to measure and grow agility. Forrester report grouped these 10 dimensions under three major categories: market, organizational, and process; for market, the dimensions are channel integration and market responsiveness; for organizational, they are knowledge dissemination, digital psychology, and change management; and for process, they are business intelligence, infrastructure elasticity, process architecture, software innovation, and sourcing and supply chain. These key components or dimensions of business agility cover activities and capabilities spanning from planning to execution; the ACM paradigm, as we will soon see, impacts favorably a similar spread of activities and capabilities.

In a quest to provide a system-theoretic approach to identification of the key characteristics of agile enterprises, one may look for similarities between such enterprises and complex systems; work of P. Cilliers ("What Can We Learn From a Theory of Complexity?" published in Emergence, Vol. 2, Issue 1, 2000) provides such a comparison. Cilliers uses concepts from complex systems like "interactions," "self-organizing," "co-evolution," and the "edge of chaos" to characterize agile enterprises. Easy and meaningful interactions among all concerned participants with a common goal to achieve, as Cilliers observes, is the most important attribute of complex systems that can enhance enterprise agility. The self-organizing characteristic refers to the feedback-driven governance that a participating set of individuals would naturally adopt and leads to faster delivery of products and services leveraging experience and creativity of the individuals yet staying within the guard rails of applicable rules and norms. Organizational learning and adaptations based on such learning to improve organizational performance are captured in the coevolution attribute and are important for an agile enterprise as they the enterprise stay aligned with (or sometimes even ahead of) the market trends and demands. The edge of chaos is an organizational behavioral notion that relaxes rigid rules of traditional bureaucracy so that the agility enablers like self-organization and coevolution can be sustained and fostered. This system-theoretic view of the key components of an agile enterprise turns out to be the most helpful approach to investigate and establish how the ACM paradigm impacts business agility.

As we have described previously in the context of case model, ACM approach decomposes the problem in terms of very loosely coupled phases, milestones, and activities that are triggered by events and controlled by associated rules. This approach of solution construction is inherently rapid and allows easy modifications. Thus, solution development time can be significantly reduced, release of frequent versions of the solution can be handled easily, and evolving solution capabilities

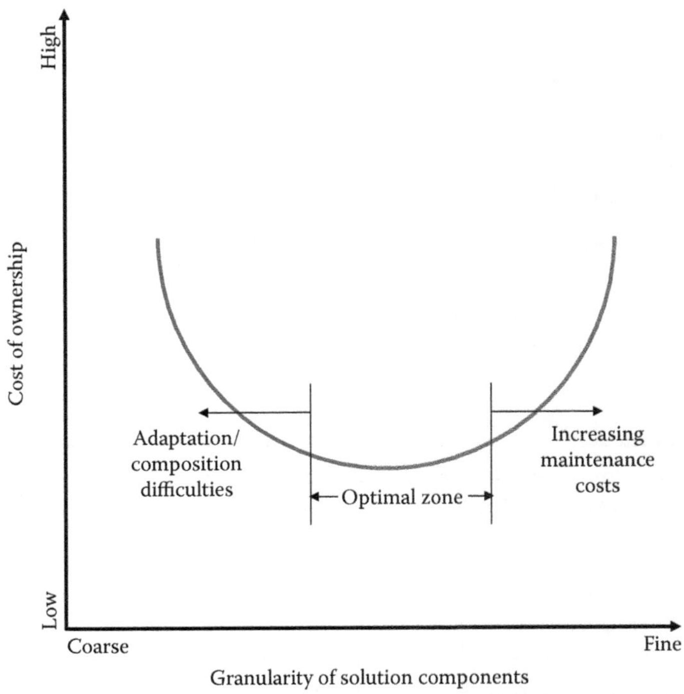

Figure 1.22 Solution management complexity versus solution component granularity.

can be promptly incorporated. In other words, the ACM approach to implementing solution is naturally amenable to agile style of software development. Throughout the life of software solutions, often significant costs are incurred in trying to keep the solution up to date as the problem definition continues to evolve over time. Optimal componentization (see Figure 1.22) is a strategy, first well studied within the purview of component based development (CBD) and then later through the practice of service oriented architecture (SOA), that can be utilized to reduce the time and effort costs for ongoing changes in ACM-based solutions since they are inherently composed (via events and rules) of solution components whose granularities are easier to control. Due to the inherent event-driven design of ACM solutions they are also suitable for rapid and agile extension of packaged applications or for quickly creating umbrella applications that facilitate collaboration between disparate business processes as may be the case in M&A situations. Thus, we see that the ACM approach of creating and maintaining software solutions can boost both range and time agility of an enterprise in the context of handling business activities while maintaining economic efficiencies.

Next we examine the working styles associated with ACM. As we have indicated before, ACM targets unstructured and unpredictable business activities that often require involvement of multiple individuals (aka participants or stakeholders) and need to leverage their collective experience and knowledge to attain the goal of solving business problems. Case models are designed such that they can handle expected and unexpected events, and are endowed with rules that can provide the necessary checks and balances while still affording high degree of autonomy of action by the participants. The adaptive aspect of ACM allows the list of activities and participants to be modified at runtime depending on the need of the case as it progresses. In ACM-based solutions, these runtime modifications can be done by the participants themselves without having to create and deploying a new version of the solution as would be the case, for example, in a traditional

BPM-based solution or legacy or packaged applications. In earlier sections, we also noted that an ACM solutions can (and ideally should) include solution components which lend themselves well to predefined (i.e., predictable) models, for example, case activities that can be modeled via routine human tasks or well-known business processes. As ACM solutions are developed, in early stages, many of the case proceedings can be treated as unpredictable and nonroutine some of which could be converted or reimplemented later as predefined tasks and processes as the organization learns from handling many cases. Learnings from handling of past cases can also be used to provide better guidance to case workers as they tackle new instances of cases, thus improving case resolution speed and reducing the amount of work needed to do so. While the event-based structure of ACM solutions provide great flexibility as to what activities can be used to achieve the final goals and who should execute those activities, rules that are inherent part of a case model can be utilized to keep the required level of order as the case progresses so that the whole process does not turn unmanageably chaotic. Good management and visibility of information related to the case, whether these are documents or messages or status of the progress, are also strengths of ACM solutions, and thus reduces delays associated with access to right information. It should be clear by now that indeed ACM paradigm is capable of providing products and services quickly to the end customers (i.e., organizational agility as seen by the end customers) and is well aligned with the necessary key elements of an agile enterprise as we have stated earlier (i.e., boosting organizational agility systematically); in fact, there is almost a one-to-one correspondence between the key characteristics of ACM and those of an agile enterprise when viewed through the system-theoretic lens.

1.7 Summary

Our key goals for this chapter were to provide adequate motivation behind pursuing the ACM approach and to familiarize you with some of the basic but important concepts involved in ACM. Traditional ways of handling business activities in organizations have largely focused on predictable and often routine actions. Over the years, packaged applications like enterprise resource planning (ERM), human capital management (HCM), supply chain management (SCM), and workforce management (WFM) have captured and streamlined the essential record keeping and repetitive tasks. Customer relationship management (CRM) systems, nowadays quite a popular type of packaged applications, tended to go beyond the routine flavors of packaged applications in trying to match idiosyncrasies of customer behavior. While all packaged applications provide some capability for customization, customizability of CRM applications is usually broader. Also, most packaged applications embed a set of business processes that define and execute sequences of automated and human tasks in order to complete information queries or business transactions for internal and external customers. When the work set spans multiple applications or the capabilities of packaged applications need substantial extensions, use of external business processes that are typically realized in middleware type of software platforms (e.g., in BPMS) is usually the common practice. Both packaged applications and external (to packaged applications) business processes have well-defined models and thus are easy to monitor and optimize, which has led to their pervasive adoption. Unfortunately, and as we have illustrated in this chapter, a significant amount and variety of business activities do not lend themselves well to such predefined approach that do not allow runtime modification to the definition of the solution; work patterns that need to deal with lack of predictability or need to facilitate knowledge work are all examples of such business activities and this is where ACM approach shines.

Case management paradigm is goal-driven; it is the attainment of desired results that is of primary importance and the actual activities performed are of secondary consideration. Often cases are strongly driven by data and documents, and collaboration and knowledge sharing are frequently leveraged in resolving a case. We should note that a select set of packaged application such as Oracle Siebel do offer some prebuilt case management solutions, which, when these solutions fit the requirements well, should be duly considered as opposed to building solutions from scratch in middleware; we discussed this topic in the context of build versus buy decisions for case management solution. Even if case management functionalities of packaged solutions are used, it may be beneficial to handle the customizations and extensions of such packaged applications either for enhancing their functionality or for making them adaptive at run time, using middleware-based ACM capabilities and hence should also be duly considered during solution architecture creation. Additionally, as we have explained in this chapter, fundamental characteristics of ACM paradigm and solution are natural agility boosters; when packaged applications are customized or extended with agile ACM, the agility of the end-to-end solution increases as well.

As we have also mentioned in this chapter, the idea of viewing a business problem as a case has been around for a long time and its application by social workers predates even the emergence any type of modern technology. Today, with all the advancements of software technologies, in particular the loosely coupled event-driven type, case management is seen as a highly applicable computer-aided business problem solving strategy across many industries. At a high level, we cited three types of case management flavors: service request, investigative and incident management; in reality, many case management solutions turn out to be some mix of these three types. Through simple examples, we have touched upon the nature of things, the attributes of a case model, that need to be discovered as the ACM solution design starts; in fact, we have introduced a three-level methodology to help with organization of discoveries needed for ACM solution design. While the building blocks of case management solutions across industries tend to be similar, it is the details, the types of events that are of importance, the activities that need to be performed as response to the events, the type and amount of documents that are involved in the solution, and the breadth and depth of collaboration among the case participants that can be quite different from industry to industry. As the book progresses, we will systematically visit many finer aspects of designing and building ACM solutions.

Chapter 2

Adaptive Case Management (ACM)–Related Topics

2.1 Introduction

If we reflect on the relationship between human behavior and technology, we are certain to agree on at least one thing: they influence each other, bidirectionally. Need for a better quality of life is often a major driver for emergence of new technologies. On the other hand, technology can make new things possible or old things easier and better, and through use of such technology we allow changes to our behavior. If we consider technology in a broad sense, examples supporting this bidirectional relationship would require a very long list; even if we restrict ourselves to information and computing technologies, the list of such examples would still be quite long. Just consider technologies or systems like the Internet, the worldwide web, and social media—these continue to evolve and improve as we adopt them more and more in our lives, and as we realize things we can do with these we continue to change our socio economic behavior in order to derive bigger benefit and higher gratification from these technologies. Interestingly, adaptive case management (ACM) turns out to be a great example of this two-way human-technology coevolution. "Interactionism" (see, for example, http://www.slideshare.net/jquemada/socialprotocolbaseddesign; accessed February/2014 for some basic information on interactionism) is a currently popular sociological theory about the drivers and modes of interaction that is used to explain a variety of human behavior. In interactionism, actors have the ability to alter their behavior to best suit the needs of the environment they are in. These notions have immediate relevance in today's social media–dominated world—digitally sharing of knowledge and experiences in our private lives has become a daily habit of most of us. With easy and up-to-date information readily available, we tend to take decisions quickly and accordingly adjust our actions. Such habits in private life invariably influence the way we conduct our work day; often, we find it easier to solve difficult problems collaboratively, and we desire such abilities from the tools that we use at work. ACM solutions nicely fill this need. On the flip side, on demand collaboration tools with great flexibility to arrange work activities in real time, as offered by ACM solutions, also strongly encourage knowledge workers to engage in team collaboration and in finding individualized solutions to tough customer problems. Thus, ACM and emergent human needs are nicely aligned.

When faced with a complex problem, we typically tend to devise a high-level strategy to solve the problem and then as we work on the problem we evaluate the progress and course-correct our actions in the direction that would provide a higher, better, or faster chance of resolution. Besides facilitating spontaneous on demand collaboration, it is the adaptive nature of ACM solutions where the case workers are able to make choices about what next steps to take that make them (the ACM solution) a more natural fit for the way we humans solve complex problems. In fact without the ability for the case workers to enjoy the freedom of choosing a context-appropriate activity, whether it is already made available as part of the packaged solution or needs to be created at run time, how would the added benefit of on-demand collaboration and expert advice be incorporated into the problem resolution exercise? Given the importance of adaptivity of ACM systems, it is fitting that we delve a little deeper into the essential properties and considerations for adaptive systems. This will be one of the key topics we will discuss in this chapter, and our expectation is that such a discussion will strengthen our grasp of the fundamentals about designing ACM solutions. Additionally, in this chapter, we will take up short discussions on a few other topics related to either the concept or the implementation of ACM. In the literature, there has been a fair amount of discussion around different types of case management solutions—we will compare and contrast ACM, dynamic case management (DCM) and production case management (PCM). Since traditional BPM is another dominant way of designing and managing business activities, we will extend the comments we have already made regarding the differences and similarities between BPM and ACM paradigms.

2.2 Adaptive Systems and ACM

2.2.1 Nile Crocodiles and Cuttlefish

"It is not the most intellectual of the species that survives; it is not the strongest that survives; but the species that survives is the one that is able best to adapt and adjust to the changing environment in which it finds itself."—Leon Megginson, a management professor at Louisiana State University, made this remark (see: http://www.darwinproject.ac.uk/one-thing-darwin-didnt-say; accessed February/2015) in 1963 when reflecting on Darwin's work on evolution in *Origin of Species*. Darwin or Megginson are not the only ones upholding the importance of the ability to adapt. Famous scientists like Albert Einstein and Stephen Hawking have proclaimed this ability as a sign of intelligence; the well-known playwright and essayist, George Bernard Shaw, had remarked that all reasonable people adapt to their environment; notable writer H.G. Wells has also alerted, "adapt or perish." The word "adapt" means to "change something" so that it functions better in or is better suited for a given situation or environment (ref. *Merriam-Webster dictionary*). Conceptually it seems easy to understand the meaning of and the reason for adaption; however, it may not be as easy to create adaptive capabilities or systems. Evolution of life forms provides us abundant example of adaptivity, most of which have occurred over a really long time and the end results show a wide range of variations. The crocodiles of the Nile, one of the most ferocious and predatory animals of Africa or the thousand pounds plus sea turtles, appear to have essentially retained their image and characteristics from prehistoric times yet they have had to adapt to changes in climate and environment; in a sense these creatures have adapted to stay "the same." Evolution of land animals (e.g., tetrapods) from aquatic creatures or *cetaceans* (i.e., whales, dolphins, porpoises) from land mammals introduced significant amount of very slow morphological changes, ultimately resulting in large differences in their forms and structures. It is theorized that these evolutions were triggered by a desire for the concerned animals to have a better survival. And, then there are creatures like the cuttlefish—it can alter its body shape, color, and skin texture in the blink of an eye to make itself essentially indistinguishable from its surrounding whether that is a smoothly patterned sandy sea bottom or highly rough coral reef (if interested search for cuttlefish camouflage videos on the Internet to see cuttlefish in action), and thus can easily fool a predator or a prey. Cuttlefish's adaptation demonstrates very high agility—if we were to wish a type of adaptiveness for a modern business or a business application, we are sure to favor the cuttlefish type of adaptivity over the resilience of the Nile crocodile or the slow adjustments that the land mammal made on its way to becoming a whale.

Cuttlefish is a special breed of creature—it is a mollusk with three hearts and greenish-blue blood. It displays its mastery in active camouflage with the help of a large brain that manipulates its tens of millions of color and reflector cells. How many camouflages can a cuttlefish do? For an external observer, it may seem uncountably large. However, as Dr. Roger Hanlon of the acclaimed Marine Biology Laboratory in Woods Hole, Massachusetts, explained in a 2008 interview in *New York Times* (see: http://www.youtube.com/watch?v=mW4PbW893ik; accessed February/2014), cuttlefish and most other animals that display active camouflage to adapt to their environment rely on three basic camouflage templates, namely *uniform*, *mottled*, and *disruptive*, to rapidly construct the shapes and colors needed for adaption. Reflecting on cuttlefish's strategy and ability to adapt in the context of a business or business system, we can note the following:

1. In order to adapt, we must first decide when to adapt, i.e., recognize the triggers that demand adaption.
2. Given an adaption imperative, we must identify what aspects of the system, i.e., structure or behavior, need to change.
3. We must be prepared, prior to the instance when we need to adapt, with the necessary modular building blocks or capabilities that we could manipulate or derive from in order to adapt.
4. The central ability to adapt is intrinsic, i.e., an inherent property of the system and result of adaption can change the system itself even if that change is temporary.
5. We need to adapt in an agile fashion, i.e., the system response times need to be adequately fast as the system adapts.

So, what model or at least the key structural and behavioral characteristics of a business system should we focus on in order to evaluate and improve its ability to adapt in an agile way? How would we translate these observations from a general adaptive and agile system to an ACM solution? We will explore answers to these questions in the next two sections.

2.2.2 Sense-and-Respond, Anticipate-and-Preempt, and Complex Adaptive Systems (CAS)

As we concluded in the previous section, the type of business systems we are focused on here needs to have properties that are a union of those from adaptiveness and agility, i.e., we are shooting for systems with "agile adaptivity" or for "adaptively agile" systems. In particular, solutions we would like to design and build through ACM paradigm need to be capable of responding to the emerging and often unpredictable case events; they need to provide a good balance between case worker freedom and overall governance; they need to have mechanisms to learn from the past to be better functioning in the future. In a quest to better define the philosophy and the underlying structure and mechanism of such systems, we can start by visiting the work published by Stephan Haeckel (*Adaptive Enterprise*, Harvard Business School Press, 1999). Haeckel's work targeted the

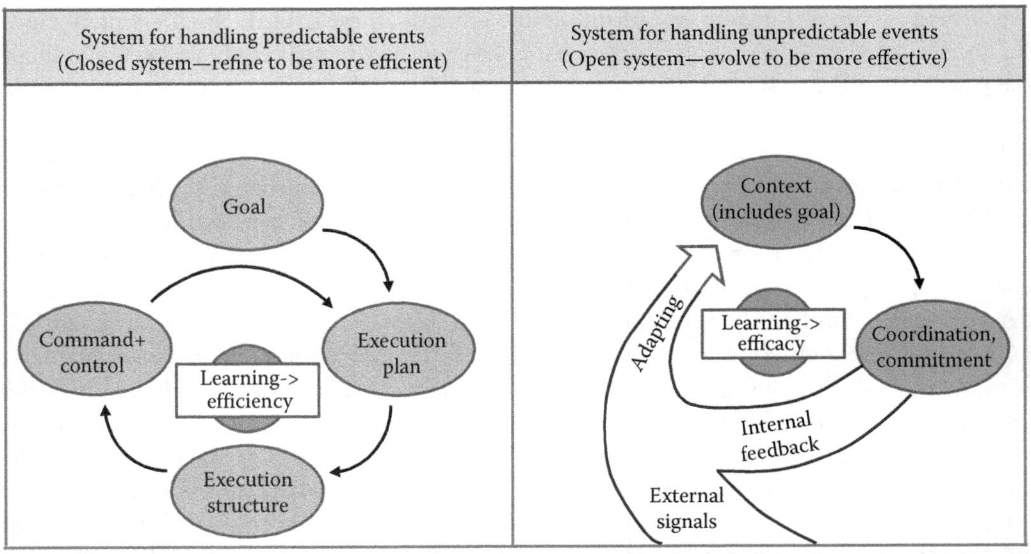

Figure 2.1 System characteristics for handling of predictable and unpredictable events.

topic of adaptive enterprise, which we have reinterpreted here in the context of adaptive systems as may be relevant to ACM solutions. Accordingly, given our current system requirements, we would conclude that our solution would include, as necessary, properties an "open and adaptive" system (see Figure 2.1—this is a slightly modified version of what Haeckel presented in his book) capable of handling unpredictable events. Such a system would recognize the goals to be achieved within a broader context; it would have built-in capability to both assess external signals (i.e., events) as they arise and evaluate (and correct, when necessary) its own actions via feedback (i.e., adapt); various subsystems would collaborate within a framework of commitment and coordination so as to deliver the overall system capabilities; the system (and its subsystems) would learn from its own actions and evolve to become more effective (i.e., "open" definition of the system). We can compare these characteristics with those of standard closed systems (e.g., packaged applications like ERP or HCM, or solutions built using traditional BPM) designed to handle at most predictable change (shown in the left part of Figure 2.1), where the system is focused on achieving its immediate goals via a set of predefined steps monitored closely by a "command and control" management framework. Effectiveness of such closed systems is limited by their preplanned structure and behavior and working of such systems is analyzed typically to identify opportunities to enhance operational efficiency (e.g., higher throughput, faster response time, lesser resource need, etc.).

An adaptive system interacts with its environment in a *sense-and-respond* manner, i.e., the system dynamically senses external signals and using its capabilities provides a response back. A four-phase adaptive loop (Haeckel, 1999) of *sense*, *interpret*, *decide*, and *act* captures the internal mechanism of such a system (see Figure 2.2 where we present a slightly enhanced depiction of Haeckel's adaptive loop diagram). These four phases are as such quite intuitive: in *sense* phase, the system captures external (or even internal) signals or stimuli, does the necessary filtering and classification so as to make a preliminary decision whether to process or reject these triggers; in *interpret* phase, using collective experience of its subsystems the triggers selected for further processing are analyzed to gain insight; in *decide* phase, possible system responses are explored and choices are made to select a final action plan that is what is executed in *act* phase. One can argue that (at least in a broad sense) most systems go through these four phases in order to display their capabilities.

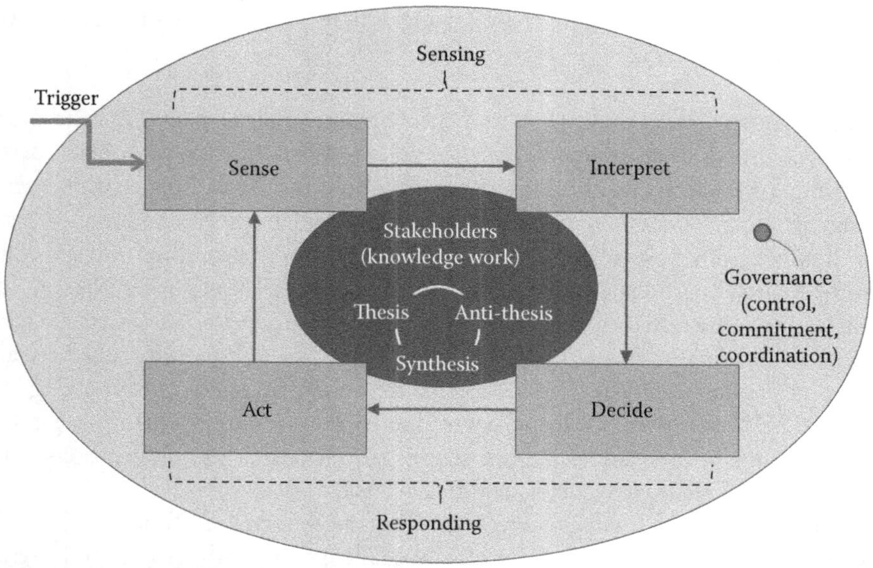

Figure 2.2 Essentials of sense-and-respond mechanism of an adaptive system.

However, it should be noted that for traditional closed systems where external signals and internal behaviors are predictable much of the sense, interpret, and decide activities are already done in the design phase and the system simply acts, using one of the prespecified actions plans that best fits the triggering event; in the event the situation at hand does not have a corresponding prespecified action plan, a closed nonadaptive system will classify that as an "exception" and rely on some type of special handling, often outside the system, to find and execute the appropriate actions. Exception handling typically is very expensive, and depending on the situation a transaction with one or more exceptions can easily incur several times to several orders of magnitude higher time and cost than a normal transaction. Hence, exceptions are a killer of efficiency and can adversely impact quality of service. Adaptive systems are designed to handle variations and unpredictability as a rule instead of as exceptions, and using the assets of its subsystems and suitably adapting its structure and behavior construct appropriate actions plans at run time to meet the demands of the situation at hand, i.e., create unique solutions to unique problems. Thus, adaptivity helps reduce exceptions. In fact, adaptive systems can go a step further than sense-and-respond, which has the connotation of being reactive—it is possible to design adaptive systems that can interact with their environment proactively, i.e., *anticipate-and-preempt*, as Haeckel points out in his earlier cited book referring to a comment made by Adrian Slywotzky in the preface of the book. The system stakeholders, those who have *bona fide* interest in proper functioning of the system, play a major role in enabling the adaptivity of these systems. Given all available input using their experience and applicable policies, they may form many conclusions, stakeholders evaluate merits and demerits of possible for and against arguments and construct suitable action plans (some readers may find it interesting to note that such actions of the stakeholders parallels the dialectic triad, *thesis-antithesis-synthesis*, usually associated with the philosophical school of *German Idealism* promoted by Hegel, Kant and Fichte). Such knowledge work by the stakeholders endows a key property that distinguishes adaptive systems (of the type we are interested in here) from static systems.

Since ACM, the central theme of this book, aims to deal with unpredictability and knowledge work leading the requirement of the ability to provide runtime change in work activities and participating workers, we want to note the following with respect to the desirable properties of our typical target adaptive system:

1. It will "empower" the system users and their organizations to not only handle unpredictability but also to leverage it whenever possible in order to derive or provide better value, for example, handling of difficult customer situations makes the service team better at rendering customer service or solving a hard design problem pushes an engineering team to innovate, etc. This property of a system that turns unpredictability into an opportunity to provide better than expected system performance is essentially what Nassim Taleb calls "antifragility" (interested readers can access a healthy discussion on antifragility in Taleb's 2012 book *Antifragile: Things That Gain from Disorder* from Random House; see also Keith Swenson's presentation "Antifragile Systems for Innovation and Learning Organizations" at *2013 BPMNext Conference*, http://www.bpmnext.com/bpmnext-2013-presentations/antifragile-systems-for-innovation-and-learning-organizations/ where he mentions antifragility in the context of adaptive systems including ACM).
2. It will be "robust" (i.e., will not break down or be rendered dysfunctional) so as to provide enough resilience when faced with the challenge of handling change in structure or behavior.
3. It will "eliminate" or at least significantly reduce bottlenecks that lead to delays either in making decisions or in taking actions.

Complex systems theory has been used to better understand adaptive system (Haeckel also refers to this fact). Our interest here in exploring the properties of appropriate variant of complex systems is to recognize the underlying structure and mechanisms of systems that, in our opinion, most ACM solutions do or will represent. With such understanding, it is our belief that solution architects would be able to better focus on and design the right elements of the solution so as to endow it with the aforementioned qualities (we will deliberate on this aspect in the next section).

While humans have been dabbling in exploration of complex systems for quite some time, organized scientific quests for modeling and analysis of complex systems are relatively recent (see, for example, http://www.health.org.uk/public/cms/75/76/313/2590/jIq8CP.pdf for a quick review; webpage accessed Februray/2014). The scope of this book will not allow us to present a detailed description of complex systems and their variants; instead, we will be content with just enough information about them so as to achieve our ultimate goal here, i.e., developing a better understanding of systems represented by ACM solution. At a basic level, complex systems can be defined as a set of interacting parts (or agents) where behavior of the system cannot be fully deduced by simply aggregating the behavior of the individual parts, i.e., there is always some level of unpredictability and nonlinearity in the overall behavior of such systems. Such agent-based interpretation of complex systems is usually attributed to J.H. Holland (ref. *Hidden Order*, Addison-Wesley, 1995). Figure 2.3 shows a schematic depicting the essentials of a complex system. The system exists within an environment and through system facades or interfaces it interacts with that environment, i.e., receives input from and provides output to that environment. The components inside the system are indicated as agents who interact with each other in any manner that may be necessary. These interactions result in summary responses from the system to the outside environment and the reaction of the environment due the system responses are fed back to the agents who in turn react to such feedback, and the cycle goes on. Generally speaking the inter agent interactions are more spontaneous and less regular than the "system to environment"

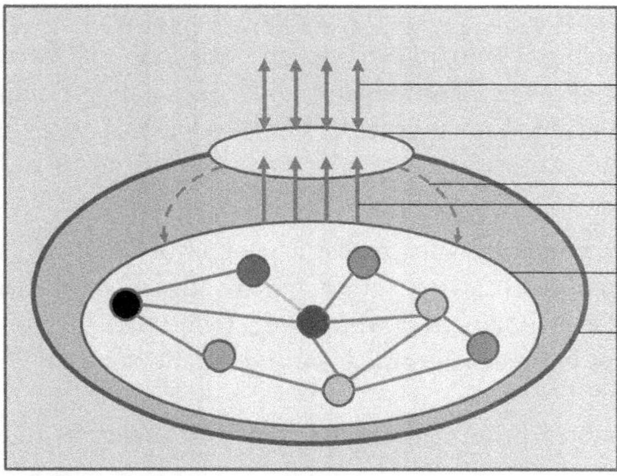

Figure 2.3 Simple schematic of complex adaptive systems. (Adapted from ref. http://www.trojanmice.com/articles/complexadaptivesystems.htm.)

interactions. As a simple example consider a system consisting of a family and their real estate agent and the internal and external behavior of this system during the process of making offers to a seller of a property; in this case, the seller will represent the external environment with which the system will interact. Various members of the family and the real estate agent will engage in several brainstorming sessions and discussions (i.e., nearly ad hoc agent interactions in our parlance) in order to decide on the details of the offer to be made to seller. Once these decisions are made, an appropriate interface of this system, most likely the real estate agent, will respond to the seller with the offer using proper protocol and terms and conditions (i.e., following a more disciplined interaction style than the brainstorming style used by the system agents to come up with the offer). The seller may or may not accept the offer. The system interface will receive seller's decision and relay it back to the concerned agents (i.e., the family members) who, depending on the feedback received (i.e., acceptance or rejection of offer by the seller), will either move towards finalization of a sales contract or consider a revision of the offer.

Complex systems must not be confused with complicated systems where the latter can always (at least theoretically) be reduced to a combination of simple (linear) systems for analysis purposes and where cause and effect relationships always hold. Most things in nature are actually nonlinear complex systems even though often many of them are approximated as (at most complicated) linear systems for modeling, analysis, and prediction exercises. Complex systems that have the ability to adapt, i.e., change their behavior due to internal and external stimuli or feedback are termed "Complex Adaptive Systems" (CAS). In fact, most naturally occurring complex systems are of CAS type and hence the motivation for the study of CAS. Currently there is rising interest in applying CAS ideas to problem solving in many industries including IT (see, for example, http://emergentpublications.com/(S(gkhrfo5szaqgz0waagkcfjig))/ECO/submissions/manuscript_85.pdf, ftp://ftp.cordis.europa.eu/pub/ist/docs/directorate_d/st-ds/emitleton.pdf, etc.; accessed February/2014). It should be noted that although CAS have a lot of flexibility in the way they act and react, in real world they are ultimately bound by some higher order laws; in case of natural systems, these higher order laws can include speed of light, laws of thermodynamics, etc., and for business systems similar disciplines may be imposed by industry practices and applicable regulations. Some CAS may also have the capability to evolve, i.e., become different in structure or behavior as these systems or their parts interact with their ecosystem. Some researchers simply include this capability to evolve as part of CAS properties, wherever applicable, while some others refer to such CAS as Complex Evolving System; in this book, we will adopt the former strategy.

The work of Paul Cilliers (Complexity and Postmodernism: Understanding Complex Systems, Routledge, 1998) discusses a set of major characteristics for CAS—some that are of direct interest to us are paraphrased as follows:

1. Multiple agents—These are the interacting parts that make up the CAS.
2. Rich interactions—Elements of the subsystem affect and are affected by elements of many, the system as a whole, and the environment in which the system exists.
3. Nonlinearity—Small changes in input can cause large and nonproportional changes in the output.
4. Openness—CAS are open systems, i.e., defining exact system boundaries are not always easy.
5. Nonequilibrium operation—CAS often operate away from equilibrium (or average) conditions.
6. History—Present behavior of CAS is affected by the past.

CAS can have multiple levels of subsystems. CAS are "emergent" (i.e., display spontaneity) and "self-organized" (i.e., loosely connected seemly chaotic actions governed or guided by higher level order and goals). Typically the interaction rules between CAS are relatively simple. Many CAS can learn from the past and evolve to something of better quality or more suitable to its environment. In some situations, CAS can also anticipate possibilities using its endowed and acquired knowledge. Given these characteristics of CAS and the ACM discussions, we have already had so far we should start noticing strong similarities between them. A pertinent question at this point would be: Can CAS be modeled, and if yes, what modeling artifacts would be needed? In general, thorough modeling of nontrivial CAS can be difficult although representative structures with elements, subsystems, and guiding rules for interaction and evolution can be assembled and simulations of CAS can be done to gain reasonable understanding of the overall system. It is therefore important that whenever a CAS is designed the construction of the necessary building blocks is given proper attention. In their book, *Harnessing Complexity* (Basic Books, 2001), Robert Axelrod and Michael Cohen have discussed a set of modeling components for CAS that could be summarised as follows:

1. Strategy—A conditional action pattern that indicates what to do in which circumstance.
2. Artifact—A material resource that has a definite location and can respond to the action of agents.
3. Agent—A collection of properties, strategies, and capabilities for interacting with artifacts and other agents.
4. Population—A collection of agents, or in some situations, collection of strategies.
5. Type—All the agents (or strategies) in a population that have some characteristics in common.
6. Variety—The diversity of types within a population or system.
7. Interaction pattern—The recurring regularities of contact among the types within a system.
8. Space (physical)—"Location" in a geographical space and time of agents and artifacts.
9. Space (conceptual)—"Location" in a set of categories structured so that "nearby" agents will tend to interact.

10. Selection—Processes that lead to an increase or decrease in the frequency of various types of agents and strategies.
11. Success criteria or performance measures—A "score" used by an agent or designer in attributing credit in the selection of relatively successful (or unsuccessful) strategies or agent.

While some of the items in the list may seem a bit theoretical, we have retained them for the sake of completeness.

As we have discussed already, the type of business systems that we would like to design and build through ACM paradigm needs to be capable of responding to the emerging needs of cases in a *sense-and-respond* (and possibly even in an anticipate-preempt) manner; they need to provide a good balance between case worker freedom and overall governance; they need to have mechanisms to learn from the past to be better functioning in the future. Will the set of goals and modeling components be enough for the type of CAS we are interested in here? Haeckel's book (see citation earlier in this section) points out that while CAS characterizations as given here do provide a lot of insight and guidance for building our target CAS, they either miss or do not emphasize enough a few key properties: *intentionality* and *purposefulness*, i.e., desire of the system to reach certain goals that also in turn influences the behavior of the agents, and the fact that agents working within the system can redefine (or evolve) the system itself (this is a defining aspect of *social* systems). As we compare ACM solutions with CAS more closely in the next section, we will keep Haeckel's observation in mind.

2.2.3 ACM Solutions as Sense-and-Respond (Complex) Adaptive Systems (SR-CAS)

Having discussed various types and aspects of complex systems so far in this section, we would now like to investigate how that knowledge relates to ACM solution, and if indeed the notion of complex systems is relevant to ACM then how that knowledge could help us derive some design philosophies for ACM solutions. In this section, we first introduced complex systems where multiple agents or subsystems interact with each other with high level of freedom and spontaneity to bring about the overall response characteristics of the system, which is a nonlinear complex function of the individual agent or subsystem characteristics. Next we focused on those complex systems that can adapt, i.e., change their structure and behavior due to internal or external forces—these were termed complex adaptive system (CAS). We then explored the key concepts behind adaptive organizations that behave like CAS and in that context deliberated on the sense-and-respond (SR) behavior of such organizations. It turns out that ACM systems have strong similarities with SR adaptive organizations when we view these organizations as systems and thus we will pay closer attention to the properties of SR adaptive organizations that henceforth we will term "SR-CAS." We can establish these similarities if we can validate a strong correspondence between constructive elements of SR-CAS and a typical ACM solution. While we have made occasional remarks about ACM while discussing SR-CAS earlier in this section, in Table 2.1 we present a more thorough comparison by noting relevance of key SR-CAS elements (referring to work of Cilliers, Axelrod and Cohen, and Haeckel, as discussed earlier in this section) with the elements of typical ACM solutions.

The remarks in Table 2.1 should easily convince the reader that the structure and essential properties of SR-CAS are highly relevant to ACM solutions. This means that knowledge of how we can construct or influence the behavior or functioning of SR-CAS should provide us useful clues as to how to design ACM solutions as well. Comparing properties that have high influence

Table 2.1 Relevance of Elements of Sense-and-Respond i.e., SR-CAS in ACM Solutions

Sense-and-Respond CAS Attribute	*Relevance in ACM Solutions*
Cilliers (1998)	
Multiple agents	Typical ACM solution system will have more than one stakeholder
Rich interactions	Collaborations among stakeholders
Nonlinearity	A single or few events can potentially change the case progression significantly
Openness	An ACM system can evolve with learning
Nonequilibrium operation	Flexibilities to move away from an "average" execution path, when necessary
History	Often the next best step depends on the case progression thus far
Axelrod and Cohen (2001)	
Strategy	Org. procedures, industry norms, and regulations guiding stakeholder actions
Artifact	Case data, documents, information
Agent	Stakeholders; software applications
Population	A typical ACM solution involves multiple agents
Type	Roles and responsibilities of the stakeholders
Variety	A typical ACM solution involves multiple roles and responsibilities
Space (physical)	Organizational affiliation of individual stakeholders
Space (conceptual)	Expertise of individual stakeholders
Selection	Periodic evaluation and consequential modification of case models
Success criteria/performance measures	KPIs/KRIs; goal achievement
Haeckel (1999)	
Sense-and-respond	This is the style for inter participant collaboration and customer interactions
Intentionality and purposefulness	Goal-driven nature of ACM solutions
Evolution	Progressive improvement in system strategy and structure due to past learning

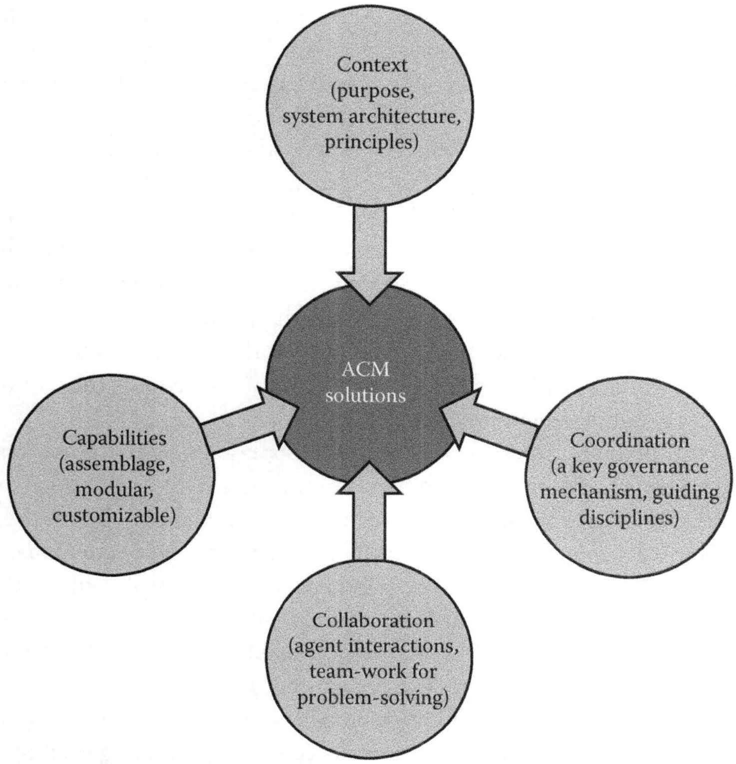

Figure 2.4 The "Four-Cs" of ACM solutions.

on the behavior of SR-CAS and the key functionalities of typical ACM solutions, we have identified four high-level considerations, "*context*," "*capabilities*," "*collaboration*," and "*coordination*," that we feel are critical for conception and design of ACM solutions (we would term these as the "Four-Cs" of ACM—see Figure 2.4). We would like to point out that at some level most of these Four-Cs considerations are also generally relevant to the process of designing many other systems; however, in our opinion, these are fundamental considerations for typical ACM solutions. The meaning and relevance of these Four-Cs are as follows:

1. *Context*: For a SR-CAS like an ACM, solution context is the highest-level description of the system. Following Haeckel (1999) we can define this to be a combination of purpose of the system, i.e., why does it exist, essential governing principles, i.e., the guard rails that define what must or must not be done, and the architecture, i.e., a prescription of the system components and their interaction styles and protocols. Of course, during the design of any system the designer considers the goals of the system and the means to achieve them through his/her design. So, why is this special for ACM? The answer lies in the realization that the systems where the execution path is fully predefined and the activities are prescheduled and assigned, the workers who use the system to resolve a business problem are primarily (if not solely) focused on completing their tasks; these workers may be aware of the design goals and context of the system but those facts are not generally essential for completion of their tasks.

   Take, for example, the processing of a typical employee expense report. Once an expense report is submitted via an ERP or financials application (this is quite a common approach) a manager approves or rejects it; if approved the expense reports proceeds to the next step and if rejected it is sent back to the employee for revision and resubmission. Next, the approved expense report is accessed by an accounts payable person who checks every line item in the report for its legitimacy following all applicable rules, verifies the reported amounts against expenditure receipts, and finally clears the expended sum for payment. These fixed steps of expense verification, the set of applicable rules, and any additional supervisory checks on the proceedings were all put into the design of the expense payment application part of the ERP by some application designer starting from a higher level context. However, for the accounts payable person processing a particular expense report that high-level context is not pertinent. In fact, by limiting the scope of what the worker does in this example, the work activity can be tuned to be as simple as possible and the required skill level of the worker as low as possible, both of which enhances the efficiency and reduces the cost of the execution of the expense reimbursement process.

Things can be quite different in case of a transaction going through an ACM system. For example, let us consider a case representing the processing of a high-value and high-risk credit application from a business by a credit insurance company. From the time that such an application is accepted (for processing) by the credit insurance company, several workers with a variety of expertise (e.g., analysts who analyze viability of companies, risk assessors, underwriters, lawyers, etc.) will undertake many predetermined tasks and many case specific tasks not necessarily preordained, sometimes individually and in some instances in collaboration with others, in order to come to a conclusion for the case.

Clearly, these proceedings of high-value and high-risk of credit insurance application processing are lot more complex than the expense report processing example and from time to time case workers, given some unique characteristics of the case, may find themselves with questions like "What should be done next?" or "Who could help with the next step?" or "Will the next step violate some rules or regulations?"; resolving questions like these at runtime (i.e., when the case is being executed and not when the ACM system was being designed) require the case workers to be aware of the full system context as formulated above. In other words, for ACM knowledge of context is not a "good to know" thing, it is essential to proper working of the system.

Contextual statements can be described at a high-level however must be done without ambiguity as the context becomes the ultimate reference for the SR-CAS agents and subsystems when they need guidance or inspiration as to what action to take in a given situation. In Chapter 1 as part of the discussion of CM Level-1 discovery phase for ACM solutions, we have recommended a set of attributes that should be included as the solution designers create the necessary context for their solutions.

2. *Capabilities*: In multiagent systems like SR-CAS, the system capabilities are a fairly complex function of agent or subsystem capabilities. One of the key mechanisms via which the overall system delivers its functionality is by on-demand composition of appropriate component capabilities, i.e., the capabilities of its agents or subsystems. This means that the capability components have to be modular and composable. Haeckel (1999) uses modular and composable capabilities as the foundation for the design of the underlying structure and strategy creation of sense-and-respond adaptive enterprises, and the same philosophy is also valid for ACM solutions. Again, creating larger and complex systems from more manageable smaller and less complex modules is a fairly standard design strategy for most systems, whether we are talking about a software system or an automobile. In these cases, however, the users of the systems deal primarily with the overall system capabilities and are not concerned with

the modules that were used to create the system. If there are two versions of a software system to handle bank transactions providing the same user experience and performance, one written as a million lines of code and the other assembled from several hundred subroutines or methods, from the point of view of the bank and its users the two systems are equivalent even though the time and cost of developing and maintaining the systems may be quite different. In ACM solutions, however, the agents utilize subsystem capabilities and ultimately deliver the system capability, at least in part, through inter-agent interactions. Hence, the design of the capability modules is a critical consideration as the inter-agent interactions tied together selects subsystem capabilities at runtime shape the behavior of the overall system. Since ACM solutions must be capable of handling unique situations on a case-by-case basis, and since these variations cannot always be predicted upfront, the solution designer cannot aim to program the complete problem solving strategy along with its execution steps that would be sufficient for all situations; at least a part of the problem solving strategy will evolve along with the progression of the case. Instead, the agents responsible for executing the emerging parts of the problem-solving strategy will combine suitable capability components at run time. This consideration has a direct implication on how individual tasks in ACM solution are designed from modularity and composability points of view, i.e., what granularity they should have and what kind of functional independence they should possess; readers conversant with the key concepts related to design of "services" with a goal to create agile application building foundation in the context of Service-Oriented Architecture (SOA) should find these granularity, functional independence, and composability concerns as familiar topics.

3. *Collaboration*: As we have already noticed, a key aspect of SR-CAS is the interaction among the individual agents that is central to capability composition and ultimately results in the overall system behavior observed externally. Whenever there are human agents (i.e., workers) engaged in solving a problem, some collaboration among the workers is likely. In fixed nonadaptive systems dealing with routine work, activities are either designed to be performed by individual workers or through some fixed collaboration pattern of a set of workers—this leads to increased efficiency. In adaptive systems like an ACM solution, runtime collaboration is seen as one of the primary enablers and hence not an optional design consideration. In ACM solutions, participants engaged in knowledge work are expected to collaborate with their peers and subject matter experts to resolve case related issues quickly and satisfactorily. A good ACM solution design, therefore, must facilitate easy and quality collaboration among its participants; as a corollary it must also adequately integrate required information sources and applications as timely access to right information is a key factor in to quality collaboration.
4. *Coordination*: Since agents and subsystems of SR-CAS enjoy high levels of freedom in the way they behave, surely some mechanism needs to be in place that would prevent the system from becoming awry. The trick is to adopt a governance style that would provide the right balance of level of freedom and control over agent actions. In traditional nonadaptive systems, a *command-and-control* style of governance is commonly employed. Such governance structures are typically hierarchical, upper levels specifying to lower levels what to do and what not to do for all anticipated situations; a department head giving specific instructions to his/her managers, the managers in turn instructing the workers, and so on. This hierarchy of commands also provides the basis for a mechanism by which the superior members of the organization aim to control the overall behavior of the organization; performances measures are usually aggregated upwards level by level to reflect the overall performance

of the organization or the system. While command and control governance style has been around for a long time, is easily understood and implementable, and thus has been quite popular, such governance styles restrict the freedom of action as would be required by agents of adaptive systems. Some CAS researchers have pointed to *self-organization*, a type of endogenous discipline, as the paradigm that maintains the higher level order of adaptive systems. However, as Haeckel (1999) illustrated for CAS with higher levels of complexity and multiple levels of agents only self-organization is not enough to guarantee purposefulness of the system, i.e., the requirement that the system ultimately achieve some stated goal. While command-and-control style of governance works for closed systems where the execution strategies are completely predefined, for multiagent adaptive systems dealing with unpredictability and knowledge work a governance strategy based on "*coordination of commitments*" is a better model (Haeckel, 1999), one that would provide the required balance between freedom and control of agent actions. For a sense-and-respond governance system, Haeckel defines commitment as "an agreement between two parties to produce a defined outcome and to accept that outcome if it meets the agreed-to conditions"; the governance structure then is set as a coordination of such commitments, i.e., specifying a set of norms and protocols as to how different parties should interact with each other. Thus, coordination of commitments essentially articulates the expected behavior of the agents, i.e., how agents of the adaptive system will react to a given stimulus, and the rules for inter-agent interactions. In ACM systems, this strategy and style of governance translates to appropriately specifying privileges, tasks and interaction protocols for various stakeholder within the high-level context of the solution; typically a case owner assigned to the case has the responsibility of making sure that this coordination of commitment properly happens and the case ultimately advances to a resolution.

As we have indicated earlier, case models embody most of the essential structure of an ACM solution; solution architects can help ensure proper adherence to most of the mentioned Four-Cs principles by appropriate design of the case models. The mentioned four are not the only considerations when designing ACM solutions; however, in our opinion this is an important set of considerations that need special attention so as to build in the desired adaptive characteristics. As we have already explained when discussing the basics of case management, adaptivity is neither required nor desired in every level or every component of an ACM solution. This is due to the fact that as we decompose the ACM problem some of the tasks and processes emerge as deterministic where either due to efficiency or regulatory reasons prefixed optimized designs that are best governed in the traditional command-and-control manner. In other words, a complete ACM solution is likely to be a hybrid (see Figure 2.5) sitting somewhere between rigid closed systems and flexible adaptive ones.

We would like to close this section by revisiting the three primary characteristics that we had stated in Section 2.2.2 as essential for the type of adaptive systems we are after: our system needed to be robust, empowering, and would have means to eliminate (or at least significantly reduce) bottlenecks that hinder its agility. A rigid system tends to be fragile, i.e., malfunctions when impacted by out of design forces; systems that are malleable, i.e., have the flexibility to adjust to such forces avoid frequent breakdowns and thus are more robust than rigid systems. The adaptive nature of ACM solutions provides the desired robustness in our target solutions. Emphasis on knowledge work and provisions to exercise freedom to do the right thing at the right time encourages ACM system stakeholders to think out-of-the-box when necessary and deliver better solutions than would be possible via a rigid solution framework. As we had illustrated in Chapter 1, the way ACM solutions are built and operated is well aligned with key agility enablers. Since agility

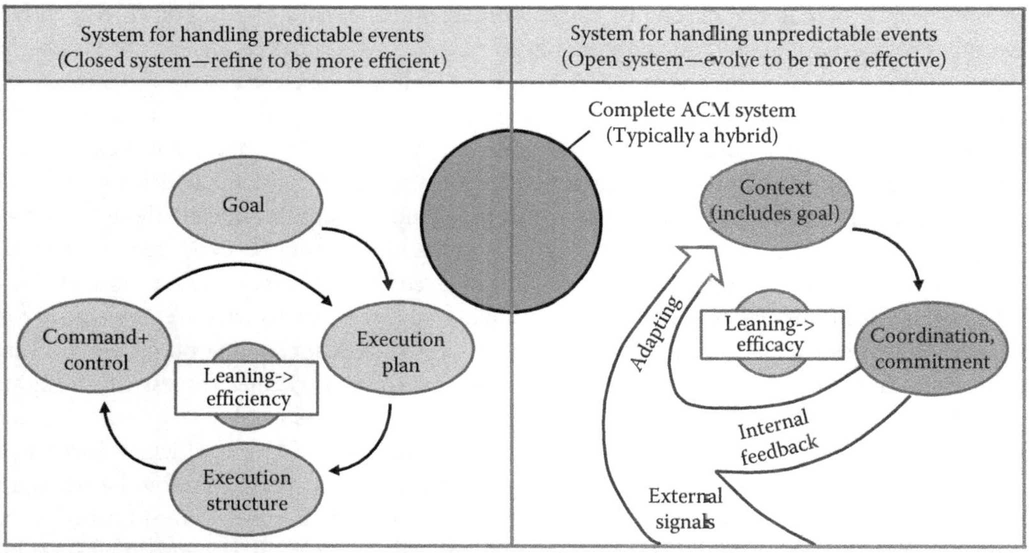

Figure 2.5 Hybrid nature of real-life ACM solutions.

requires a system to demonstrate faster response, particularly in unpredictable situations, it would be useful for us to consider aspects of an ACM solution that, if proper care is not taken, could slow down the system response. From a customer point of view, as they raise unique requirements in a case, the ACM solution, along with the actions of its participants, needs to be able to respond quickly and correctly—the adaptive nature of the solution is at the heart of ACM's fast response capability. However, there are many other aspects of the solution that influence the speed of system response. For example, if the information or documents needed by the case participants are hard to find, or the participants do not have comprehensive visibility into the progression of the case including relevant KPIs or KRIs, their ability to act quickly will be hindered. If the inter-participant interaction protocols or the dos and don'ts are ambiguous, then collaboration among participants, one of the key enablers of ACM solutions, will be poor and slow. Automated tasks, i.e., those executed by machines are typically much faster than if they are done by humans (of course, not all tasks are doable by machines). This means that if we fail to recognize opportunities for task automation we will slow down the system response of ACM solutions along with possible degradation in operational efficiency.

2.3 Dynamic, Production, and Adaptive Case Management (DCM, PCM, and ACM)

2.3.1 Basic Debates

"Better, cheaper, faster—pick any two," sometimes also called the designer's "Holy Triangle" or "Iron Triangle," is commonly taken as a guiding principle when scoping a product or service offering. Although there are those like Daniel Goldin (http://history.nasa.gov/dan_goldin.html; accessed February/2014) who ran NASA between 1992 and 2001 and famously promised to achieve all three simultaneously. Conclusions like "picking better and cheaper will typically slow you down," "combination of better and faster will generally be more expensive," and "doing things fast and cheaply will cut into the quality of the ultimate outcome" surely sound intuitively correct. Two types of questions should be asked at this point: when we say better, cheaper, or faster what we are comparing these with, and would it indeed be foolish to "have it all," i.e., aim to achieve success on all three measures? Firstly, better, cheaper, or faster are relative either to status quo or to what the competition is doing. This assumes of course that the one that is not picked (i.e., as part of the "pick any two" premise) is at least adequate for the purpose for which the system is being designed. The second question, unfortunately, is much harder to answer although anecdotally "pick any two" mantra seems to get a fair amount support from "experienced" project and product managers and developers. The problem is that even though these three measures are fairly well understood in our day-to-day lives, for complex projects these metrics are not always easy to assess. We know that Goldin (of NASA) made the promise of succeeding on all the measures at the same time—did he succeed? It really depends on how one defines success (for a slightly pro-Goldin summary of successes and failures of Goldin's initiatives see: http://www.nationaldefensemagazine.org/archive/2012/April/Pages/Faster,Better,CheaperWhyNotPickAllThree.aspx; accessed February/2014). The facts are that many of Goldin's initiatives did fail but he attempted really ambitious goals and as a result surely pushed the frontier of contemporary knowledge and experience. So did Goldin deliver on his promise? Clearly, the answer will depend on whether one would measure success by the fraction of successful projects or by advancement of science and technology. Regardless of whether this "pick any two" is indeed some unbreakable law of projects, a good solution design must settle the debate of how much to focus on for each of the quality, time, and cost dimensions (see Figure 2.6) as clearly and as "early in the game" as possible; design of a case management solution will not be an exception!

Another equally important question that is pertinent when laying out the plan for creating a solution is "where to start from"? Should one start from "a clean palette" or leverage some existing solutions possibly through modifications and extensions. In the case management solution arena, we see both approaches being used by software vendors and end customers. "Pure play" vendors as well as some customer projects have created their case management offering or solutions "from scratch" that have had the benefit of having fewer restrictions in the way the products or solutions could be designed and implemented—this strategy gave them opportunities for easier innovation. However, these products or solutions generally faced the challenge of having to create a lot of infrastructure either to provide the basic case management capabilities or to make the outcome full-featured and mature. On the other side of the spectrum, established software vendors in related fields, such as those in BPM or content management arena, recognized that they already had much of the necessary infrastructure and created their offering by expanding on such base lines.

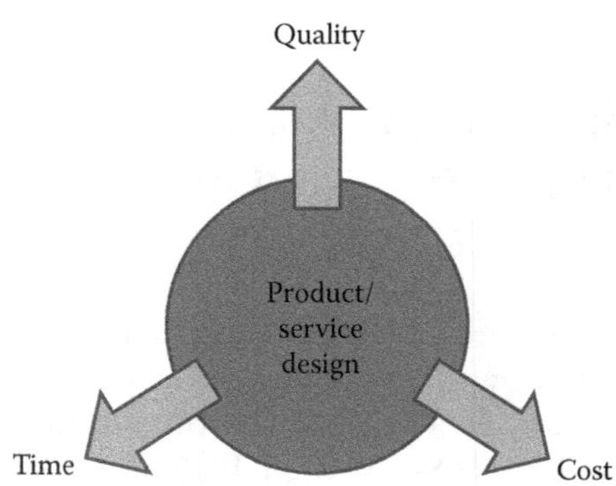

Figure 2.6 Competing design considerations.

Customers with existing projects like CRM or document management felt similarly and extended such implementations with added features to handle case management. Such efforts by established ISVs or by existing application teams have had varied levels of success in matching the innovative features of the pure play efforts. For example, case management solutions, particularly ACM, relies heavily on an event-based engagement and on-demand collaboration of stakeholders that requires the software application to have a strong event handling and collaboration foundation—this is not something that can be easily inserted into existing products or applications unless of course the necessary foundations for event handing were already present in them. Practically all industrial grade software dealing with business activities and transactions need management and monitoring tools, dashboards and altering capabilities, security and other policy enforcements, broad integration support, high performance and reliability standards, and so on—an innovative "built from scratch" case management solution can relatively easily demonstrate advanced functional features yet can find itself to be inadequate in supporting the necessary qualities needed for industrial deployment. Fortunately, over time, consolidation of ideas and technologies from both camps are producing enriched and robust capabilities for the end customer and case management solutions are currently benefiting from such consolidations.

These "quality-cost-time" considerations and the choice of the starting point of a particular case management solution (i.e., whether pure play or legacy extension) have resulted in meaningful distinctions between certain categories of case management solutions like production case management (PCM) and adpative case management (ACM) that would be useful for us understand in the context of case management solution design (see: Keith Swenson's 2012 post at http://social-biz.org/2012/09/12/case-management-contrasting-production-vs-adaptive/; accessed February/2014). Mainly triggered by Forrester's coinage ("Dynamic Case Management—An Old Idea Catches New Fire," Craig Le Clair and Connie Moore, Forrester report, December 2009) there is also the meaning of DCM to be considered. Although it is remarked that DCM is the same as ACM, it would be worthwhile to closely inspect this statement; for a discussion on DCM versus ACM by Max Putcher (see: http://acmisis.wordpress.com/2010/11/18/the-difference-between-dynamic-and-adaptive/; accessed February/2014). In an expanded blog article posted in 2012, Michael Poulin suggested an umbrella category called "Purpose Case Management" where he proposed that the overall purpose of the system be broken down in subpurposes (i.e., subgoals), which would then dictate what type modeling paradigm, i.e., the type of case management or process management would be the most suitable. While this was an interesting proposal and Poulin's analysis as presented in the article is a good read, there has not been much uptake of this purpose case management framework (interested reader can access Poulin's article at http://www.infoq.com/articles/purpose-case-management; accessed February/2014). We should note that "static versus dynamic" or "deterministic versus nondeterministic," or "production versus adaptive" case management is essentially a system "classification" strategy—the universe of case management solutions are being grouped into disjoint sets as per some given points of view. Given a business problem to be solved by case management, which class of solution would be the most appropriate? The motivation and characteristics of such system classifications are generally useful as background knowledge for designers to make the right choice for picking the solution class, and we delve into more details on these next.

2.3.2 Digging Deeper into DCM, PCM, and ACM

Our main goal in this section is to understand better the meanings of and motivations behind labels like DCM, PCM, and ACM as these phrases are currently in active circulation in the case management practitioner circles. Our hope is that with a clearer understanding of these phrases

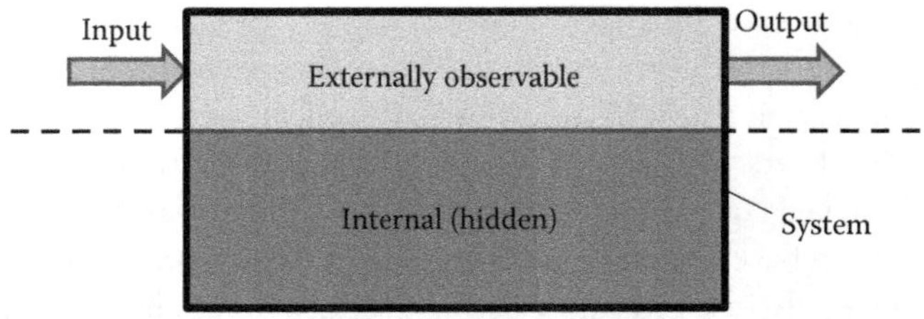

Figure 2.7 A generic system.

we will avoid confusion as we try to absorb industry literature and also will be able to make better choices for our case management solution architectures. Per our earlier remarks, such labels can be identified as system classifications treating case management solutions as systems. We, therefore, will take a small digression into standard notions of system classification in order to lay the basic foundation for the exercise to explore case management system classifications.

Starting at the very basic, a system is simply an encapsulation of a set of interacting components with a visible interface to the world outside the system, which is essentially the environment where the system exists. Most systems interact with their environment by an input-output mechanism: when the system receives some input or trigger from the environment, it responds by exhibiting a corresponding output (see Figure 2.7). When we select a particular point of view (PoV) and observe the universal set of systems from a particular PoV, we create "classification," i.e., nonoverlapping subsets of systems that provide further detail with respect to the chosen PoV. Accordingly, and as shown in Figure 2.8, we have chosen three different PoVs resulting in three different system classifications:

1. *Static or dynamic*: A system is "static" if the system components and their assigned behaviors stay fixed over time, and if the system response at any given time is independent of what may have happened in the past i.e., it is "memory-less." A system that is not static is "dynamic."
2. *Deterministic or nondeterministic*: A system is "deterministic" if it always produces the same output for a given input set, i.e., the system response is fully predictable. Accordingly, "nondeterministic" systems may exhibit different behaviors corresponding to identical input sets applied at different times.

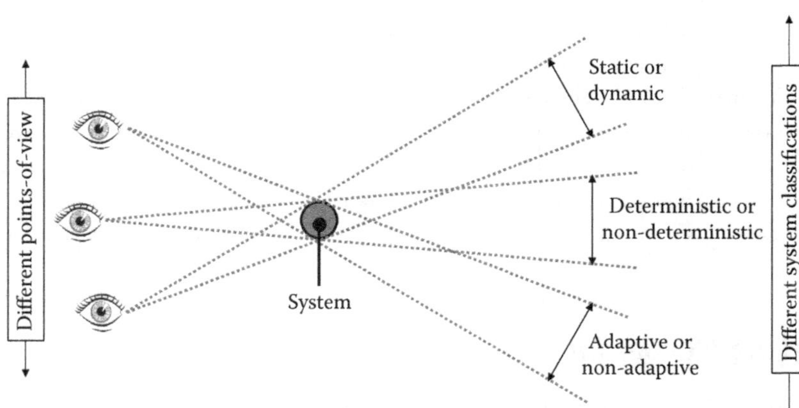

Figure 2.8 Different classifications of a system.

3. *Adaptive or nonadaptive*: A system is "adaptive" if it is able to change its composition or behavior as a result of external stimuli. In software systems, this would mean changes in the system at "runtime," i.e., such changes will not require "design-time" decisions, reimplementation or redeployment of the system. "Nonadaptive" systems belong to the complement subset of adaptive systems and their composition and ability to respond to external stimuli remain fixed over time.

Note that since these classifications correspond to different and independent PoVs, i.e., there is a clear separation of concern for each of the PoVs leading up to the classifications, a system can be simultaneously characterized by as many classifications as necessary. For example, a system can be qualified as "static, nondeterministic and nonadaptive" or "dynamic, nondeterministic and adaptive," and so on. We should also point out that a system can be classified in many more ways than the three we have chosen here—our choice is based simply on the characteristics; we will need to continue with the explanations later in this section and elsewhere in the book.

Let us consider a few simple examples to make the above system classifications more concrete. Take the behavior of an ideal metal spring—when we pull (aka "load") the spring it extends and the extension diminishes as we let go of the pull (aka "unload"). The extension of a metal spring is simply proportional to the force on the spring at any given time as Figure 2.9a depicts; it is immaterial as to how we arrive at that force. If we load or unload a piece of rubber, however, the behavior is quite different. As Figure 2.9b indicates, the extension for rubber does depend on whether we are loading or unloading and how fast we are doing so. Thus, for rubber, unlike the metal spring, the deformation at some load will depend on how we arrived at that load. In other words, a metal spring is not affected by loading history, i.e., it is memoryless and hence it is a static system while response from rubber depends on the loading history and thus it is a dynamic system. Both the metal spring and the rubber are also deterministic systems since their behavior is fully predictable at all times as long as we know the input or the input history. The "throw value" from rolling of dice is an outcome of a memoryless, i.e., static system as every roll is independent from all previous

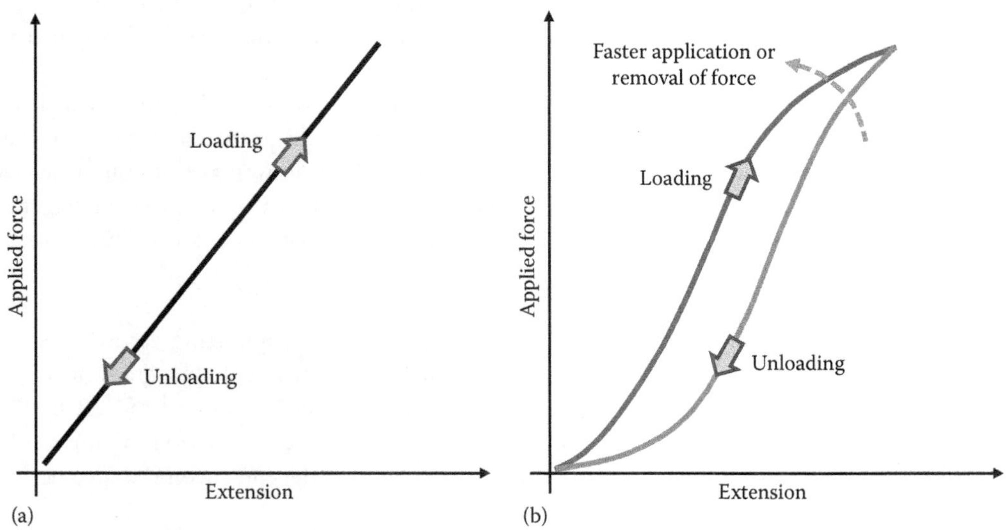

Figure 2.9 Load and deformation characteristics of metal springs (a) and rubber (b).

rolls; however, we cannot predict with certainty the value of the throw—this makes it a nondeterministic static system. Similarly, a pendulum is a deterministic dynamic system while weather system is both dynamic and nondeterministic. Adaptive and nonadaptive systems differ in the way they handle intrinsic and extrinsic stimuli—adaptive systems are capable of changing their constitution and response protocols while in nonadaptive systems these stay fixed. The pendulum is a nonadaptive system and so is a simple pencil sharpener. Of course, nonadaptive systems do not have to be "simple"; in his 2010 book *Management 3.0: Leading Agile Developers, Developing Agile Leaders* published by Addison-Wesley Professional, author Juergen Appelo mentions a whirlpool in a bath tub as an example of a complex nonadaptive systems. Presence of feedback loops is an important characteristic of adaptive systems. Most biological systems, human organizations, and some robots with feedback controls are examples of adaptive systems.

We can easily draw similar examples in software systems as well. A service that, upon receipt of a query, selects and retrieves information from a fixed knowledge base is a deterministic static system. Google's (or similar) search engine learns from the searches that it handles in order to find content with higher relevance faster from an ever increasing pool of information and thus will produce different outputs, both in terms of content and their order, at different time instances even if the exactly same search parameters are used at the input. This is a nondeterministic dynamic system. Consider an online portal that presents catalogs of a fixed set of products and their prices that a customer can browse and choose from, provide the necessary payment and shipping information, and close the buying part of the transaction by executing the "check out" step. Here the customer interaction with the portal provides the input to the system, which in turn provides output responses by displaying prices and shipping confirmations, the portal's response only depends on the customer's order at that instance. As per definitions stated earlier, this portal would correspond to a static system. However, if functionalities like promotional pricing based on the purchase history of the customer are added to this sales portal it will become a dynamic system supporting dynamic pricing. If, based on the customer profile and past purchase history, the portal modifies the content it displays so as to present customized pages to the customer i.e., changes one or some of its constituent parts then the portal system becomes an adaptive dynamical system. We may also note here that while all adaptive systems are dynamic systems not all dynamic systems are adaptive as we just illustrated in the portal example; when specifying the type of system that we are aiming for; it is therefore clearer to state "adaptive" explicitly if that is indeed the intent.

Having refreshed ourselves on a set of system classifications in general terms, we will now turn our focus back to classification of case management systems. In particular, we are interested in exploring PCM, ACM and DCM further. From our experience as well as from published case studies and from discussions in industry circles, we see that PCM is a style of case management that has been and likely to be in broad use. Quoting from Keith Swenson's work (2012), we can define PCM as:

> Production Case Management (PCM) is an approach to supporting knowledge workers which is programmed by specially-trained technical people (programmers) to produce a case management application. That application is deployed for use by knowledge workers to get their work done. The application offers collections of operations that the knowledge worker can select to use or not use depending on the specific needs of the case.

In the same article, Swenson defines ACM as:

> Adaptive Case Management (ACM) is an approach to support knowledge workers who need the most flexibility to handle their cases. ACM allows the knowledge workers themselves to create and modify all aspects of a case at any time. There is no distinction between design time and run time: the designing and running are done at the same time by the same people.

While these definitions nicely capture the essence of PCM and ACM, in our view, Swenson takes a purist approach to ACM—in real projects we find the case management solutions, even the ones that are being termed as "adaptive," are rarely as adaptive as Swenson envisions them to be via his definition.

PCM and ACM are both designed to provide higher degree of flexibility of task execution by case workers than what traditional ERP-like or BPM-based solutions would. They are both goal-driven solution paradigms and share the idea of case folder as a key artifact for collecting the progression of a case. Both approaches facilitate a certain amount of knowledge work for case resolution although in ACM, where the work freedom for knowledge workers is much higher than in PCM, knowledge workers bear a higher level of responsibility for their judgments and actions. As Swenson (2012) points out, PCM systems are targeted for situations where level of unpredictability is significantly less than those where ACM approach is strongly required. We can envision that at one end of the PCM spectrum where essentially all work steps and their execution sequences are fully predefined the solution would correspond to a deterministic case management system. Even though PCM systems are less flexible than ACM systems, activity execution sequences in PCM do not need to be completely preordained, i.e., the execution path can move around through the steps as necessary. Also, in PCM, case workers can be presented with lists of possible actions at each step so that at a given step the case workers, using their knowledge and experience, can pick the right subset of actions based on the case goals and the case progression till that step. Thus, the PCM solution spectrum can stretch from deterministic into the realm of nondeterministic case management as judgments of two humans can sometimes differ even when all the other parameters are the same. The main difference between PCM and ACM though is that in the former the system composition, i.e., the structure and the assigned behavior of the subsystems stay fixed through the case progression. Let us consider an example where a case is being used to coordinate the work by a communications service provider for designing a network service for a business involving a fairly complicated set of steps requiring several different types of expertise. At some given step, as might be the situation with most of the steps, the expert (case) worker is presented with a set of possible actions. The expert worker is expected to review the overall design goals and the status of the design thus far and select a suitable subset of the actions from the possible actions list that he/she is provided. Once the actions at this step are completed, the design status is updated and the case progresses. It is possible that during the review the expert worker at a particular step detects possible errors done in some previous step—the case progress could then be regressed back to that faulty step and reworked. A PCM system would be fine for implementing a solution that would handle case progression through these steps. Now suppose that during this case progression at some step the assigned case worker feels the need for conducting a special survey or pursuing a special permit and he/she desires to accomplish this by adding a new activity and a new participant with the required expertise as the case is progressing then we would need the capabilities of ACM; here we would not only be changing the execution options but will also be altering the definition of the case management system itself by adding new activities and participants at runtime.

In Table 2.2, we have listed some of the key characteristics of PCM and ACM solutions that could be used as a starting point when deciding which style of solution would fit better for a

Table 2.2 Applicability of PCM and ACM-Type Solutions: Key Characteristics

	PCM	*ACM*
Type of work	Largely routine and repetitive	High knowledge and creative problem-solving work
Decision making	Usually from predesign sets	Can go beyond the anticipated
Type of collaboration	Mostly known ahead of time	Special enterprise/services may be needed
Work ownership	Adequate involvement	Sense of responsibility
Case volume	Typically large	Typically moderate

given business problem. If we were to consider systems involving human workflows, implemented either via traditional BPM or delivered as part of a packaged application and ACM at two ends of a spectrum, PCM systems would fall somewhere in between. PCM systems would be targeted towards higher volume transactions where knowledge work is not too deep so that much of the activities can be predefined at design time; essentially repetitive work requiring somewhat special skills like that of an appliance repair person or a benefits administrator would be examples of such work. Many of the building blocks of PCM systems are often found in existing packaged solutions or are easily created using full-featured BPM systems—this allows vendors and customers to put together a PCM style case management solution quickly. It is relatively easy to train workers on repeatable deterministic activities; such activities are also easier to tune for efficiency and monitor for visibility and management purposes. As we noted before, although limited, there is some opportunity in PCM solutions for exercising human judgment for resolving certain unique issues related to a case rendering PCM solutions the ability to handle somewhat nondeterministic i.e., unpredictable situations. These properties make PCM systems an attractive solution proposition in many case management problems; we need to be careful though that in the zeal of landing on a quick solution we do not force ACM used cases into a PCM framework as that would guarantee highly suboptimal system performance and efficacy.

Let us take a closer look at "deterministic versus nondeterministic" system classification in the context of case management systems. If the activities are routine, required demand on human judgment is low, and the available decision options are quite limited, a case management system will behave deterministically. In the presence of high levels of knowledge work, human discretions and ad hoc collaborations a case management system will show nondeterministic characteristics. For example, an engineering design process handled as a case will be lot more deterministic than processing of a case dealing with an application for immigration into a country. How does it help us to know if a particular case management system is likely to be more deterministic or otherwise? Deterministic systems are easier to manage and improve especially from an efficiency point-of-view. Hence, a solution designer should consider keeping the solution as deterministic as possible so long as the effectiveness of the system is not driven below what may have been set by the goals of the system.

By following standard definitions of static and dynamic systems, a typical case management system will be classified as a dynamics system since an evolving case history and dependence of case worker actions on the case history are part and parcel of the case management way of working. In other words, the "dynamic" qualifier in DCM coinage seems superfluous in the sense that it does not add more information to what we might glean by the simply saying "case management," and hence we will not use the DCM abbreviation further in this book. We do want to remind the reader though that since the Forrester report in 2009 on DCM where they described several use cases that would tantamount to a combination of PCM and ACM as we have described here, the acronym DCM has been in circulation—we do see it occasionally appearing in customer specifications and in communications from a few system integrators and ISVs.

In Figure 2.10, we have graphically summarized the case management solution classifications we have been discussing so far. The figure essentially states that all case management solutions fall under the class of dynamic systems but can be either deterministic or nondeterministic; PCM and ACM together cover the spectrum of case management solutions; PCM solutions lean more towards deterministic systems; and, ACM solutions are specifically designed to handle unpredictable situations. We should reiterate that from our experience with customer projects we often see the need of creating solutions that combine features from PCM and ACM styles of case management. For example, a service request type of case management is likely to be dominated by PCM features while handling of incident management cases are likely to demand significant amount of ACM features. Of course, it is ultimately the solution designer's responsibility balance the "cost-quality-time" considerations, select the appropriate features from the relevant classes of solution, and choose the right starting point, i.e., opt for a fresh new development project or modify or extend existing systems.

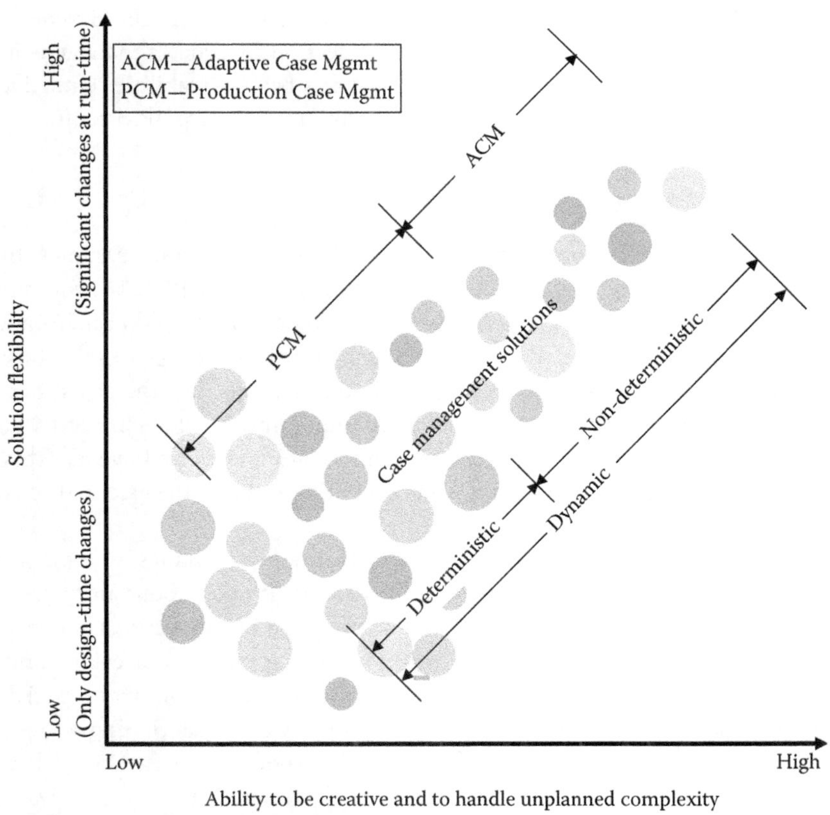

Figure 2.10 Cross-mapping of PCM, ACM, and dynamic systems.

2.4 Process Management and Case Management: Friends or Foes?

In Chapter 1, while discussing the history of case management, we remarked that the basic idea of case management is over a hundred years old—church-affiliated social workers were already using similar strategies trying to keep track of diverse activities as they tried to help the poor and the needy. Since then case management has evolved significantly gaining a formal recognition as a paradigm of organizing, executing, and managing work activities; application of case management has been spreading across diverse industries and organizations as an enabler of knowledge work that can in some situations be even unpredictable; with advances in applications that are capable of handling a wide variety of events and content interest in case management is increasing very rapidly. In the meantime, BPM, a discipline to structure and optimize work activities with the promise of providing great efficiency and competitive advantages to businesses, has also risen to a high popularity level—we will be referring to this as "process management" in this section. As can be expected, there are strong proponents of each of process and case management paradigms. We would not be surprised if you either read articles or saw presentations by leading industry practitioners discussing the strengths and future development outlook of process and case management and concluding that we just need one of process or case management—you may be confused as to which paradigm to put your bet on. Our goal in this section is to compare and contrast process management with case management paradigms, to seek answers to questions like "do we in fact need both process and case management?" and "must we have to choose one or the other, or is there a meaningful middle ground?," and to explore how such answers could benefit concerned solution architects. We want to point out that in this section by process management solutions, unless otherwise mentioned, we would mean both process-based capabilities embedded in packaged solutions or traditional BPM applications built using middleware BPM tools.

2.4.1 Anatomy of a Journey

"Life is a journey not a destination," a phrase that is often part of popular quotes, first used by theologian Lynn Hough in the *The Christian Advocate* periodicals in 1920 but commonly misappropriated to the nineteenth century American essayist and poet Ralf Waldo Emerson, encourages us not to rush through life but to savor every moment of it. Proceedings to solve business problems are also well comparable to journeys except that destinations, i.e., the goals that need to be achieved as part of solving the business problem, are important. Journeys are often planned and sometimes such plans need to be modified to accommodate unexpected events. This "journey" metaphor seems quite suitable for capturing and comparing some of the essentials characteristics of process and case management.

A few years ago on an early winter afternoon in Germany, I (Manas, one of the authors of this book) was scheduled to fly from Munich to Dusseldorf. It takes about an hour in a nonstop flight to reach Dusseldorf from Munch, there are some 25 daily connections between these two cities, and a large volume of passengers travel in this route that include a sizeable number of daily commuters. Flying from Munich to Dusseldorf normally is a routine activity especially for business travelers like me. Ordinarily there would be nothing worth mentioning about such a trip except that on that day due to heavy snowfall Munich airport had been closed! It was all well planned—my travel agent had booked and confirmed my flight many days in advance, I was at the airport well before the scheduled departure with a boarding pass that I had obtained the night before via mobile check-in and I was just looking to go through the rather mechanical process of passing through security checks, boarding the plane and hitting Dusseldorf as planned—there wasn't anything that I was to do specially for this trip—then the airport closed! It was important for me to accomplish my goal of reaching Dusseldorf that evening so undeterred by happenings at Munich airport I started exploring other options. I found out that some of the trains were still running, that I could get to Frankfurt by train and then could reuse the value of my original ticket to fly from Frankfurt to Dusseldorf. A bit more investigation told me that while Frankfurt airport was still operating there could be flight cancellations there as well if the snow continued to fall heavily. I decided to take the chance of traveling via Frankfurt and catching a flight from there, however just to have another option I also booked myself a rental car at Frankfurt. By the time my train arrived in Frankfurt, as feared, flights out of Frankfurt were cancelled due to snow but then I had my rental car booked already that I could use to drive to Dusseldorf. It was not an easy drive and I reached Dusseldorf several hours later than I had originally hoped but I achieved my goal as good as it could be achieved under the circumstances. If we analyze my travel from Munich to Dusseldorf, the planned version would correspond to executing a traditional BPM process—I was to execute a fixed set of routine activities and the plan would have taken me to my goal of reaching Dusseldorf. However, the actual travel corresponds to what happens in a typical case management scenario. Due to unexpected events I had to improvise; I used my knowledge and experience of traveling in Germany to change my plans several times, setting a different set of subgoals and finally achieving my target goal. Interestingly, for each subgoal I was picking from options that already existed, hence, this modified travel would correspond to a PCM style case management (Figure 2.11).

Now, consider a little more exotic travel experience—the one that "Pi" Patel, a 16-year-old boy from Pondicherry, India, experienced as he drifted across the Pacific Ocean in a lifeboat with a bunch of zoo animals after the ship he was traveling on from Philippines to North America sank. This is described in a now famous fictional novel by the Canadian author, Yan Martel, in the book *Life of Pi* whose adaptation directed by Ang Lee won several awards in 2012 including four Academy Awards. In short, Pi Patel escaped the sinking ship in a lifeboat where he found himself sharing the tiny vessel with a hyena, a zebra, an orangutan, and a tiger—these were some of the zoo animals that were also on board the ship that sank. Through a series of events including the hyena eating the zebra and the orangutan only to be finally devoured by the tiger, Pi was left to find ways to deal with a tiger in a lifeboat while fighting extremely harsh elements of the ocean. Pi had no experience in survival at sea or taming a tiger but using his basic knowledge and experience, and some trial and error, he figured out many strategies to beat the odds to keep him alive until circumstances led to his rescue, and he was ultimately able to reach Canada. Clearly, in this journey while the final goal, i.e., that of Pi reaching North America was ultimately achieved, the path to that goal bore little similarities to the original plan. Pi had to set many new subgoals and learn or discover new tricks to achieve them before being able to arrive at the final and target destination. This is in the same spirit as what knowledge workers would do in ACM-style case management.

2.4.2 Process Management vis-à-vis Case Management

"Plans are worthless, but planning is everything"—this was a statement that Dwight D. Eisenhower, 34th president of the United States had made in 1957 in a speech to the *National Defense Executive Reserve Conference* in Washington, DC; Eisenhower made this statement in the context of preparing war strategies where one is expected to encounter many unexpected events. This statement essentially points out that, unlike predictable situations where well-designed plans work great, in the face unpredictability holding onto a predesigned plan is not useful instead

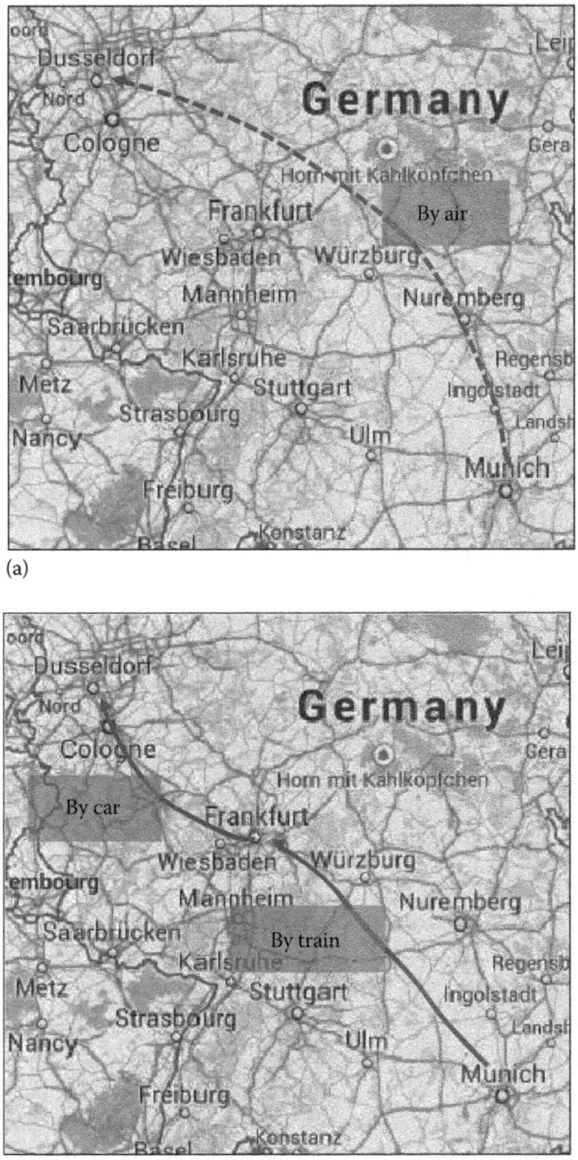

Figure 2.11 (a) Planned versus (b) actual trip (after airport closures).

focus must be given to the ability to plan based on the evolution of events. Interestingly, this comment is also quite relevant in the context of a comparison between process management and case management. Process management excels in implementing a "plan" to execute business activities efficiently; case management facilitates knowledge workers to make or alter work plans depending on how the case evolves. Of course, as we have discussed earlier, the degree to which knowledge workers will able to or will be allowed to modify their work plan depends on whether we restrict ourselves to PCM or embrace all that ACM can offer.

While comparing process management with case management solution, we have already mentioned that they differ greatly in the flexibility of work execution that they offer—traditional BPM being quite rigid and ACM being the most flexible. In fact, Michael Poulin's 2012 article (http:// www.infoq.com/articles/purpose-case-management, 2012) goes through a little logic exercise to establish that "flexible process" is an oxymoron—the "structured" process model that is at the heart of process management and the one that is the key to the efficiency that process management offers is too restrictive to provide work flexibility. Of course, this is a relevant concern if we indeed need that kind of flexibility. Here, we want to explore the modeling implications of another important aspect of knowledge work—"collaboration." Collaboration among case participants is critical in many case management applications, and collaboration implies interaction among these case participants. If we want to keep track of the details of such collaborations, then the solution platform needs have a mechanism that can follow the interactions that underlie these collaborations. In case of a traditional process-based solutions, whether embedded in a packaged solution or built using a middleware BPM tool, this would mean creating additional explicit traces, i.e., paths in the graph that govern the flow of execution of activities to mirror these interactions. Will this be an issue? Let us consider a situation where there are three interacting parties, "A," "B," and "C" (see Figure 2.12). If we explicitly count the possible ways basic interactions can take place amongst these parties, what we have denoted as "Elemental Interactions" in Figure 2.12, we get a count of "15." In fact as the figure shows, we can come up with a general formula for "Total Elemental Interactions" (TEI) using permutation formulas as a function of "N," where N is the number of interacting parties. It is not important for us to derive the stated TEI formula (although readers with a bit of math inclination should find this easy to do); instead, what is important is for us to appreciate how fast TEI grows with N (see the chart at lower right-hand corner of Figure 2.12); the TEI count is already 64 for $N = 4$! What we are trying to show through these calculations is that if we use a directed graph to model all these interactions, as would be the case with traditional process-based solutions, the process graph would become exceedingly complicated. While TEI count reflects the complexity of possible interactions in a particular instance, only a few of these interactions would be required during the resolution of a specific instance of the business problem. If, however, we cannot predict which few interactions would be required or if the set of required interactions vary from instance to instance, in a process-based solution we will have to model all or most of the interactions *a priori*, i.e., we have to carry the burden of this complexity. Now, if we construct the solution in such a way that it will have the ability to create the necessary connections between interacting parties at run time, then we will avoid this interaction complexity and, in particular, the rapid growth of this complexity as the number of interacting parties grows. Case management solutions are based on an event-driven paradigm and the interactions are triggered by

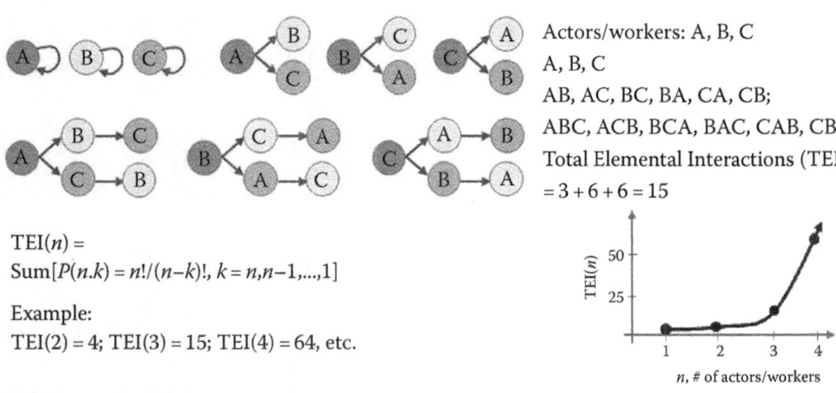

Figure 2.12 Rapid growth of interaction complexity.

and result in events. Thus, case management style of solutions are much better suited for tracking collaboration activities where the interaction ability is inherent in the solution and explicit design-time modeling of all possible interactions are not necessary.

The radar chart in Figure 2.13 compares traditional BPM with case management along eight dimensions. In this figure, by case management we mean the combined features of both PCM and ACM styles of case management solution—this is not unreasonable since many real-life case management solutions will end up combining features from both PCM and ACM styles. Essentially this figure depicts the following:

1. In process management, generally speaking, runtime changes to the system definition are not allowed, unlike as may be typical for case management especially the adaptive variety. Whenever the process needs to be changed, it will have to be done as a design revision and a new version of the solution will have to be created and deployed. In some BPM tools, for example Oracle's BPM Suite, certain amount of change in business rules are allowed on the runtime version of the process model that can take effect without an IT-level project deployment—this adds a limited amount of runtime modification within an otherwise traditional BPM environment. Of course, and as we have discussed before, an ACM implementation will be expected to handle run time changes to many more solution features besides the business rules.
2. Case management solutions are designed to handle nonroutine and unpredictable work that can become necessary due to some emergent events as the case progresses while process management solutions specialize in routine work that are all fixed at design time with worker roles pretty rigidly assigned.
3. In process management, all critical decisions about work flow and work assignment are taken during the design phase and are captured in the process model via different types of activities and their sequence augmented by business rules. In business problems targeted by

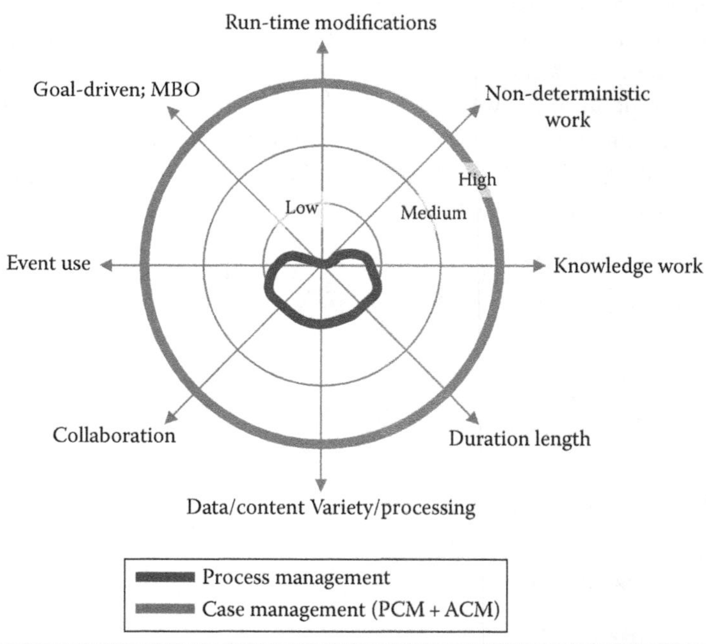

Figure 2.13 Differences between process and case management (PCM+ACM) solutions.

case management, case workers are expected to utilize their knowledge (hence the coinage "knowledge worker") to decide what actions to take next and who would be best candidates to execute them.

4. While some use cases require somewhat long running processes, most process management solutions are designed to provide fast responses; case management use cases, on the other hand, generally span relatively longer time spans typically in the order of days and weeks, and in some special cases like in immigration or legal cases could also be in the order of months and years.
5. Data and content are important to both process and case management solutions; however, in process management these are mostly structured, are "tagged along" with the process, and generally provide supporting role. On the other hand, in case management data and content have much wider variety and often drive the case progression.
6. Collaboration enablement is an essential feature of case management solutions and case workers are expected to utilize collaboration to resolve complex issues at runtime. In process management, such runtime collaboration is usually not needed since process workers are mainly focused on completing their assigned activities.
7. Case management solutions are fundamentally based on event-driven framework and are equipped to handle a wide variety of events including the "emergent" ones, i.e., events that appear as a consequence of peculiarities of the case some of which may even be unexpected. Advanced process management solutions do handle a limited variety of events, which are typically provisioned for at design time.
8. The problem-solving style employed in case management solutions are "goal-driven," i.e., the activities that the case workers execute and the decisions that they take are aimed at reaching some goals set by the type of case they are working on—goal achievement thus becomes the thing of primary importance with the activities playing supporting role. Process management solutions are "activity driven" and the process model ensures that target goals are achieved as long as the activities are completed correctly in a timely manner.

While the previous transcript has identified many categorical differences between process management and case management solutions, there are also many similarities between the two styles of solution paradigms (see Figure 2.14)—this is what we will focus on next.

The ultimate purpose of both process management and case management solutions is to solve business problems, albeit targeting different problem domains and solving them in different styles. Regardless of the actual mechanism used in solving a problem, businesses have certain generic

Similarities
• Task/process modeling
• Rules and policies
• UIs and dashboards
• Analytics
• Governance and audits
• System integration

Figure 2.14 Common features and capabilities in process and case management solutions.

requirements that they expect out of enterprise-grade software applications. Visibility into status and activity-level details of the problems that are being solved or have been solved in the past, for example, is the key to a business making sure that the business is functioning at the right level of efficacy and efficiency. Thus, a variety of dashboards and analytics appropriate for workers and managers are just as essential in case management as they are in process management. The requirement of maintaining adequate traceability is also common in both styles of problem solution. Audit trails to provide traceability are created as work activities steer a problem to a solution—this is done either for regulatory compliance purposes or as reference should someone, and this can be an employee or a customer, need to revisit work done up to a certain instance. Business rules are an easy way to capture organizational knowledge and mandates, and whether they are used for providing guidance or for enforcing policies, rules are considered important and essential components of both process and case management solutions. Typically, case management solutions involve higher amount of human work than process management solution, however, high-quality user interfaces (UIs) and easy to understand modeling of tasks are desirable in either solutions whenever human work is involved. As we have discussed earlier in this book, often a case management activity may turn out to be a process (in the traditional sense) leading to the same requirements as would be with process modeling for process management solutions. System integration is another area of commonality between process management and case management solution styles. Adequate integration of information sources is needed to provide users of both process and case management solutions with access to right information at the right time. Additionally, from time to time as a result of activities being performed in either type of solution, information in systems of record applications (e.g., applications like ERP, HCM, SCM and CRM that are custodians of business records) need to be updated in a timely manner—application integration capabilities are essential in such situations as well.

While we see many categorical differences between process and case management solution styles, we also note a large overlap in functionalities between them. So, how would we answer one of the key questions that we asked ourselves in the beginning of this section: Which one of these two do we really need? In a 2012 blog post (see: http://isismjpucher.wordpress.com/2012/01/04/acm-and-bpm-a-battle-of-hemispheres/; accessed February/2014) titled "ACM and BPM: A Battle of the Hemispheres?" Max Putcher used the contrast of analytical versus creative traits of left and right brains to compare BPM and ACM finally remarking that we need both. Putcher's conclusion seems almost obvious, even intuitively. The real question for a solution designer is how much of each style to include in a solution to create the right balance of efficiency and effectiveness while keeping in mind all the applicable quality-cost-time constraints. Another related question we need to consider is whether process management and case management styles are so different that separate software platforms are needed to support these solutions. Case management purists strongly support separation of platforms proclaiming that any attempt to create platforms that would support both styles could only do so poorly. What would pragmatists say? We will explore this question next.

2.4.3 Case Management as Part of a BPMS?

Ever since there have been profit or growth motivations and competitive pressures, businesses have been after strategies and technologies that could help with their chores more efficiently and effectively. Process management solutions in the form of workflows embedded in ERP, HCM, SCM, or CRM like packaged applications focused on making routine business work faster and less error prone have been in use now for more than four decades. Process-based applications using middleware BPM tools have been enjoying increasing interest and adoption for the last 15 or so years—these solutions targeted cross application, cross departmental, and "white-space" (i.e., functionalities not covered by packaged apps) activities. Occasionally middleware-based process management solutions compete with workflows in packaged solution but mostly they are complementary; they have also strengthened each other in terms of evolution of their functionalities. Case management is the current surge in technology paradigms aimed at handling business activities that are goal driven, involve substantial amount of content handling, collaboration, and knowledge work that can sometimes be unpredictable. Given the shared focus of both process and case management on handling business activities, it would be a natural question to ask if traditional process management tools and platforms are relevant for building out case management platforms. The way of working with case management has many differences compared to process management but does this mean we have to create brand new software platforms for case management or could we suitably extend process management platforms to handle these differences? After all there are also many similarities in requirements and functionalities of these two solutions as we have described earlier. Will existing process management platforms provide a better start for case management platforms? This is where the "purists," i.e., those who believe that case management solutions especially ACM are so different that they must have their own platforms, and the "pragmatists," i.e., those who are more reconciliatory in their approach are at severe odds with each other (Figure 2.15). The purists point at poor attempts of creating ACM solution using existing platforms to bolster their conclusions. However, good understanding about ACM is still immature in the industry and most tools are in their early versions begging the question if these conclusions by the purists would bear out even a few years from now. There is a popular idiomatic expression that says "a bad workman always blames his tools"—could it be that the way these "poor" case management solutions were conceived and used were faulty to begin with and no tooling should take the full blame for the ill outcomes? Besides is there a strong craving for pure ACM solutions in the marketplace? Surely there are some situations where the complete case management solution

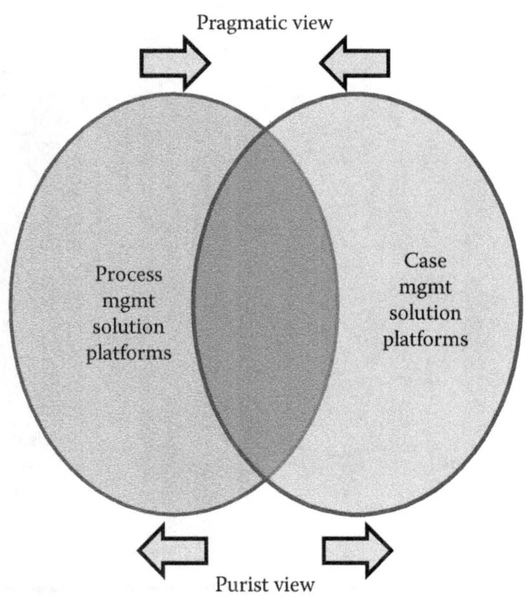

Figure 2.15 Process and case management platforms: Merging and separating forces.

is fully adaptive. However, from our experience in working with customers majority of the case management solutions that we will view as mainstream at this time require a relatively small amount of adaptivity, almost as extensions to the rest of nonadaptive parts of the solution—should the functionalities of software platforms used to build these case management solutions not reflect a similar mix of adaptive and nonadaptive functionalities.

If we were to consider starting a platform for adding case management features, a full-featured Business Management Suite (BPMS) would be a good choice. BPMS is a coinage by the analyst firm Gartner popularized during 2009 and 2010 in the context of their Magic Quadrant (MQ) reports for BPM vendors. A BPMS is an integrated environment with broad capabilities to model and manage all aspects of BPM. Figure 2.16, excerpted from a 2010 post by Janelle Hill of Gartner (see: http://blogs.gartner.com/janelle-hill/2010/04/22/do-you-understand-the-difference-between-workflow-and-bpm/; accessed February/2014), lays out the key components of a BPMS; clearly the capabilities of a BPMS as depicted exceeds what are needed to support "traditional BPM." Regardless of whether it is for faring better in Gartner's MQ or in response to customer needs, leading BPM software vendors have been pushing their BPM platforms along the lines of what is expected of a BPMS that has resulted in pretty rich offering for BPM platforms. How relevant are the BPMS components to case management platform that would include both PCM and ACM capabilities? If we recall the description in Chapter 1 regarding core and auxiliary system components for case management as well as reflect on various discussions so far about what is important for successful case management solutions, project the support necessary from a software platform for case management, and compare the result with the BPMS components in Figure 2.16, we would conclude that a full-featured BPMS will provide nearly every feature that case management solution would require. We would like to point out that content management requirement in case management solution is usually much stronger than process management.

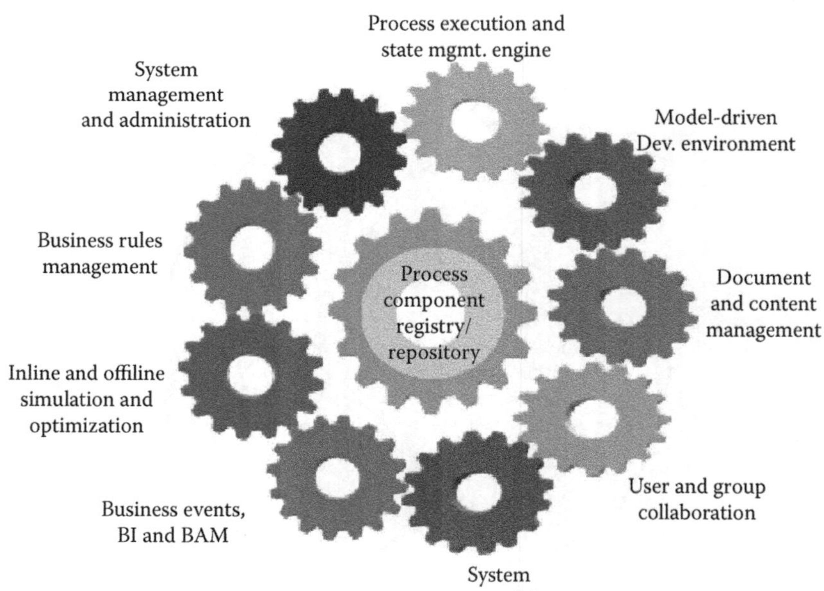

Figure 2.16 Key components of a Business Process Management Suite (BPMS). (Courtesy of Gartner, 2010.)

In fact, a good lot of the features of enterprise content management systems including cataloging, check-in/check-out and revision management facilities, content sharing, access control management and archiving frequently show up as critical requirements in case management solution. This would mean that if we were to use a BPMS as a foundation for case management solutions, then it needs to either include or be seamlessly integrated with a full-feature content management system. We would also like to note the criticality of event handling, rules and collaboration in case management especially in the ACM realm. As opposed to a graph-based sequencing for activities as in process management, in ACM activities are usually triggered by emergent events and rules are used, besides encoding business logic, to guide case worker involvement such as which activities are possible at a given instance and who are allowed to execute them. Knowledge work at times needs the capability of on demand collaboration, for example, a case worker reaching out to a subject matter expert to resolve a unique issue related to the case. Thus, a BPMS targeted for building out a case management platform needs to have an event-handling infrastructure at its core, an integrated rules engine, and adequate facility for on demand collaboration.

From a pragmatist PoV, there are additional benefits of being able to extend a BPMS to handle case management. As we have already, seen there is a lot of overlap of functionalities between process and case management solutions. Also, a complete case management solution is likely to need a certain amount of human tasks and prebuilt processes as well as will require a mix of PCM and ACM capabilities. In certain cases, we may even include case management features of packaged applications like CRM for part of the overall solution. A case management platform that is part of a BPMS will natively handle most of these challenges. In addition, many of the BPMS platforms are now quite mature from a deployment perspective, i.e., they are able to handle large loads with high reliability and good performance characteristics—these properties will directly benefit case management solutions as well if the case management platform is built on top of an established BPMS. Some of the purists have feared an ACM platform built on BPMS would cause the resulting solutions to be too complex. This is a valid concern; however, it is the tooling environment of a particular BPMS and the design of a specific ACM solution that will dictate how easy and useful the solution will be for its end users. Considering all of these arguments, we can see that with proper strategy it is possible to create a quality case management platform on top of a full-featured BPMS; later in the book we will be discussing how this has been accomplished in Oracle's BPM Suite platform.

2.5 Adoption of Case Management: Capability Maturity Considerations

Let us say that you are a good swimmer and do impressive laps in the biggest pool in your city. Would you set out to swim across the English Channel? And, if you are contemplating on doing so, you would surely ask yourself if your swimming "capabilities" like skill and endurance are "mature" enough to give it a shot. You will ask such questions to eliminate (or at least greatly reduce) the chances of you drowning in the English Channel. Successful adoption of a technology or solution paradigm demands that we ask similar capability maturity questions relevant to the specific technology or solution else we run up the risk of failure much like the (naive) swimmer drowning in the English Channel. In the software engineering realm, work done at the Software Engineering Institute (SEI) at Carnegie-Mellon University in Pittsburg, Pennsylvania since 1980s supported by U.S. Department of Defense focused on improvement of software quality. This work has resulted in the development of a five-level Capability Maturity Model (CMM) followed by the more recent Capability Maturity Model Integration (CMMi) aimed at articulating the ability of an organization to develop, deliver, maintain, and improve software applications and platforms; these have been commonly at the heart of most (capability) maturity models in the context of SOA and BPM including those from Oracle. These maturity levels are designed in such a way that the higher the maturity level the more complex projects an organization is capable of handling and yielding higher benefits from them with better certainty.

In the context of technology adoption, maturity models are useful for an organization to assess their "as is" and "to be" competencies in the required capabilities, identify the gaps between the two (i.e., as is and to be states), and plan activities in order to close those gaps. The understanding of maturity levels and the associated capabilities are also useful in analyzing the competencies needed to execute projects successfully and within accepted risk levels. For example, it is conceivable that an organization is, on an average, at level 2 of an applicable maturity model yet an important project requires certain features that demand a few of the capabilities to be at higher levels in order to assure project success. Such information if available in the early stages of a project can be immensely helpful to plan appropriate contingencies in a timely manner and prevent project failures. The idea and use of maturity models are now fairly common in more mature technology areas such SOA or traditional BPM. For case management, however, this is an area of active research. Given the scope of this book, we are not going to critique ongoing efforts in this area instead we will use Oracle's five-level BPM Maturity Model (see: http://www.oracle.com/technetwork/topics/entarch/oracle-pg-bpm-roadmap-r3-0-176693.pdf; accessed February/2014) along with the individual capabilities that have been identified for this model to explore how it can be leveraged for case management. At this point, we also want to thankfully acknowledge significant benefits relevant to content of this section that accrued from extensive discussions and collaboration between one of the authors of this book (Manas) and Danilo Schmiedel of Opitz Consulting, an Oracle partner in Germany.

2.5.1 "Generalized" BPM

As we have discussed earlier in this book, both traditional BPM and case management are strategies to organize, execute, and improve business activities in an organization. We have also seen that while these two strategies have certain clear differences in the way solutions are designed and used they do have a lot of similarities. This consideration leads us to approach case management maturity model as something that could leverage established knowledge assets of traditional BPM maturity models. To start with we want to restate the fact that the collection of business activities fall under two distinct categories (see Figure 2.17):

1. Routine work—done well with structured and completely predefined process models
2. Knowledge work—requires handling of unstructured and unpredictable tasks

In order to capture both of the varieties of business work, we introduced here the notion of "Generalized BPM" that is meant to include both the styles. (Ideally we would have liked to call this "Business Activity Management;" however, the resultant acronym, "BAM," would conflict with the prevailing notion of BAM that describes the monitoring of business activities, hence, the suggestion of Generalized BPM.) This Generalized BPM is both an approach and a formula for designing and implementing business solutions; in this context the word "process" is used loosely, i.e., we do not impose any restriction of structure or predictability as would be the case in traditional BPM rather it simply indicates all the "proceedings" required to solve the business

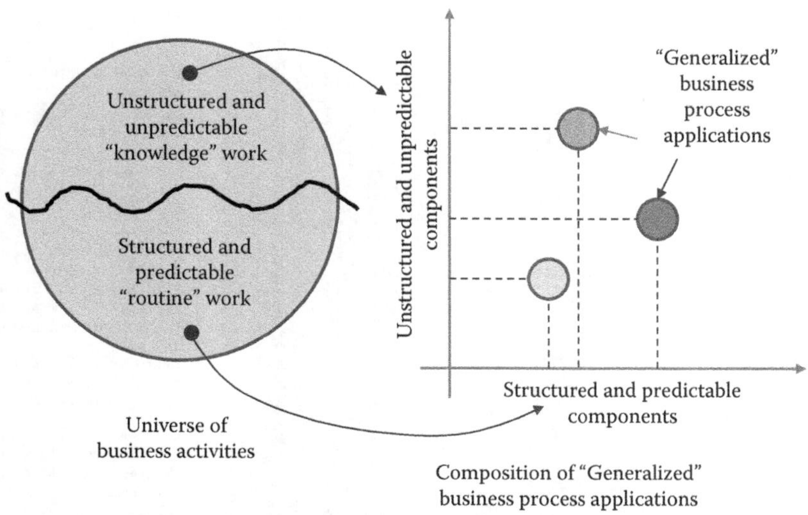

Figure 2.17 Generalized BPM to cover traditional BPM and case management.

problem. Thus, as an approach Generalized BPM will explore a given problem without any preconception as to whether the solution would be a traditional BPM one or a case management one and will let the discovery process answer this question. As a solution paradigm Generalized BPM will facilitate design and implementation of applications that would combine features of traditional BPM and case management, as necessary (see Figure 2.17). With this background, we are now ready to investigate capabilities and maturity levels for case management as a component of Generalized BPM.

2.5.2 Maturity Levels

Capability maturity levels are meant to indicate a measure of competency—the higher the level the higher the competency, i.e., the ability to do something well. Figure 2.18 is a slightly modified version of Oracle's BPM maturity levels that was developed following CMMi's maturity model. Keeping the "strategic goals" essentially the same as in the original version we have introduced small changes, mostly additive, in the tactical plans' column to reflect some of the important case management adoption goals, thus turning these maturity levels appropriate for Generalized BPM. Maturity levels are additive with respect to competencies in individual capabilities—a given level will include all the competencies in the lower levels. The five levels of maturity reflect:

1. *Ad Hoc*—Suitable for doing small or pilot projects this level indicates mainly exploratory activities, often done mainly by small IT initiatives, to "kick the tires," i.e., to "get a feel" for the BPM technologies. At this level of maturity, there is no established or generally agreed methodology or approach for BPM adoption.
2. *Opportunistic*—At this level an organization looks for a few real projects, selected in an opportunistic manner, to prove delivery of business value. Typically both IT and business groups are involved in selecting the projects however approach and methodologies to plan and execute such projects are not fully standardized.
3. *Systematic*—By this level an organization has selected and standardized their approach and methodologies for planning and executing projects that are generally followed in all projects.

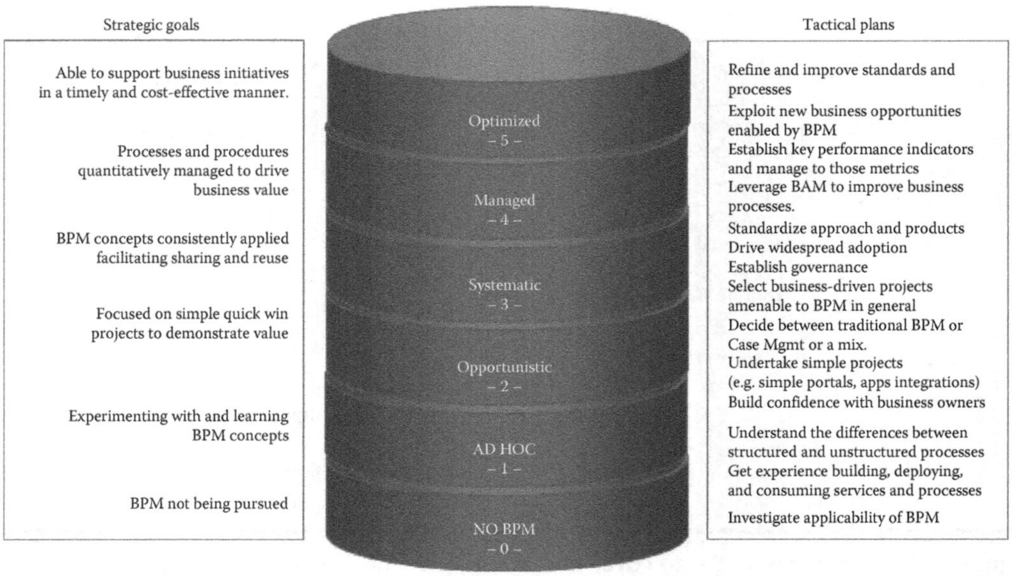

Figure 2.18 Generalized BPM maturity model (based on Oracle's standard BPM Maturity Model).

Technology adoption is on a successful growth path by this level and complex and mission critical projects can be safely undertaken within acceptable risk limits.

4. *Managed*—At this level, capabilities are measured via a set of agreed metrics so as to evaluate how they compare with expected efficacy and efficiency so that any improvement can be systematically planned and executed. Technology adoption is quite significant at this level.
5. *Optimized*—This is the final level of maturity where appropriate balance of effectiveness and efficiency in approach and methodologies for planning and execution have been achieved and are stable. All assets related to technology adoption are proactively monitored, kept current and improved, as needed. At this level, an organization does not worry about technology adoption instead is focused on deriving strong competitive advantages from it.

As we have already alluded to, it is of course conceivable and in fact quite likely that an organization may want or need to undertake projects where certain activities demand a higher level of maturity than the current maturity level of the organization for the relevant technologies. For example, a case management project that from a basic functionality PoV may fit well at the opportunistic maturity level yet may require monitoring of a few system characteristics and KPIs that may correspond to a managed maturity level—this would imply a special attention for those higher level capabilities within the scope of the project.

2.5.3 Maturity Model Capabilities

Besides maturity levels a maturity model covers a set of capabilities that enable the organization gather competencies to accomplish its goals, say, technology adoption in this case. In fact, it is the maturity of these capabilities that aggregate up to the overall maturity level. Here we will adapt Oracle's traditional BPM maturity model capabilities—we will extend them as necessary to account for case management and thus making the enhanced set valid for Generalized BPM (in fact in this section all references to BPM pertain to Generalized BPM unless otherwise stated).

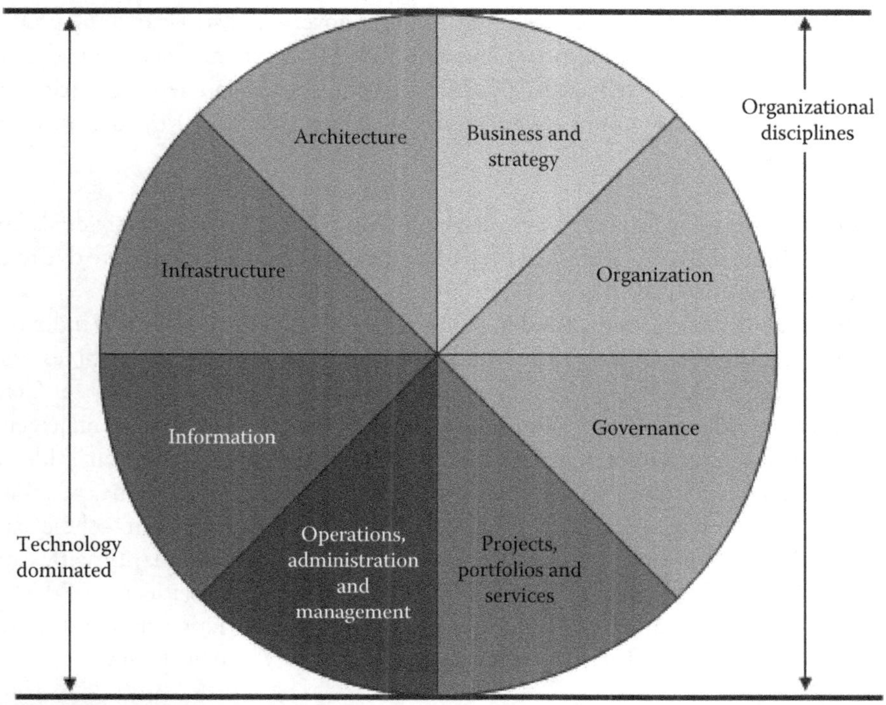

Figure 2.19 Generalized BPM capability domains. (Adapted from Oracle BPM Maturity Model.)

These capabilities can be grouped together using their thematic similarities. In the Oracle BPM maturity model, such a grouping is done by creating eight capability domains half of which are technology dominated and the other half concerns organizational disciplines (see Figure 2.19). These capability domains address

1. *Business & strategy*—contains capabilities that provide the high-level constructs that allow the BPM initiative to proceed. This includes such things as business motivation, expected benefits, guiding principles, expected costs, funding model, etc.
2. *Architecture*—contains capabilities concerning the definitions of the overall architecture and guidelines for various practitioners to ensure adherence to relevant architectural principles.
3. *Infrastructure*—contains capabilities related to the service infrastructure and tools that provide the technical foundation for the BPM initiative.
4. *Information*—contains capabilities focused on the information aspects of BPM, e.g., providing Information as a Service (IAAS). This includes shared data models, message formats and schemas, master data management, content management, etc.
5. *Projects, portfolios & services*—Contains capabilities concerning the planning and building of BPM applications and required services, and the service usage guidelines of service consumers.
6. *Operations, administration, and management* (*OA&M*)—Contains capabilities relevant to post deployment aspects of solutions based on a service-oriented architecture, i.e., the operations, administration, and management aspects of Generalized BPM solutions.
7. *Organization*—Contains capabilities required for the development of corporate competency around BPM including the organizational structure and its evolution (for example, from siloed to integrated and collaborative organization), and skills development.

8. *Governance*—Contains capabilities concerning the governance structures and processes that support and guide the BPM efforts. Generalized BPM governance includes end-to-end process/case owner roles as well as goal/KPI-driven solution development. Maturity and adoption of an adequate amount of governance is a leading indicator of the overall Generalized BPM success.

Even though these capability domains were originally constructed from the individual capabilities applicable to traditional BPM adoption, we have left the domains unchanged here due to their full applicability to Generalized BPM.

The eight capability domains depicted in Figure 2.19 have included around 70 individual capabilities in Oracle's original BPM maturity model. Since Generalized BPM combines both traditional BPM and case management, all of these capabilities remain equally relevant for Generalized BPM. However, in order to address competency requirements unique to case management, we have added a few more capabilities to the original list—the final list is displayed in Table 2.3; these additions are pointed out with a "**." Besides these new additions, there are some capabilities from the original list that need special attention in the context of case management—these capabilities are marked with a "*" in Table 2.3. Assuming the reader's general familiarity with capabilities related to traditional BPM, we will skip explaining those instead we will visit each of the capability domains and devote some comments regarding capabilities that are either new additions or have been marked as needing special attention due to inclusion of case management.

1. *Business & strategy*—In this domain, we have added three new capabilities: "Guiding Principles," "Process Mining," and "Pattern Detection and Template Definition." The *Guiding Principles* competency feeds case management solutions with rules and helpful tips that knowledge workers may need in order to pursue case resolutions; generally speaking these are a mix of mandated and suggested actions that the case participants will have to act on or will choose to act on to drive cases to completion. *Process Mining* is a capability that is useful in the discovery phase of Generalized BPM solutions where, in absence of complete and coherent knowledge of exactly how an organization solves business problems, prevailing activities are "mined," i.e., collected and analyzed in order to trace actual execution paths that are typically used (see www.processmining.org for some more description and links to the underlying philosophies are techniques of process mining); these traces are then used as input to the solution design process. In *Pattern Detection and Template Definition*, an organization matures its ability to extract solution patterns at various levels (of the solution) that is helpful in deciding what mix of traditional BPM and case management a solution should contain plus additional details that need to modeled or provided for in the solution. In this domain, we have also marked "Business Process Analysis" and "Process Improvement Approach" as those needing special attention in a case management solution setting. In case of Generalized BPM, Business Process Analysis capabilities need to approach business problems first without any preconceived bias towards either traditional BPM or case management and should allow for the naturally existing balance of the two to emerge. In Process Improvement Approach, in order to cater for case management, besides traditional BPM improvements of attributes like levels of automation, elapsed time or resource requirements, improvements in decision making and stakeholder collaboration need to be included.
2. *Architecture*—This domain is concerned about various architectural issues including usage of patterns and standards (see examples of case management patterns later in the book) and modularity and style of solution construction (in the context of case management this

Table 2.3 Generalized BPM Capabilities (Extended from Oracle BPM Maturity Model)

Business and Strategy	*Architecture*	*Infrastructure*	*Information*	*Projects, Portfolios, and Services*	*Operations, Admin, and Management*	*Organization*	*Governance*
Business driven	Diverse process types*	Access to enterprise functionality	Process data*	Enterprise functionality portfolio mgmt	Activity monitoring*	Business and IT collaboration	Enterprise functionality
Business process analysis*	Expose enterprise functionality	Service discovery	Message exchange data	Coordinated modeling	Process control*	Business and technical modeling skills	Business rules governance
Business justification	Process participants interaction*	Unified repository	Business process performance management	Business rules abstraction	BPM infrastructure dependency tracking	Executive sponsorship	Business process change management
Business architecture linked	Closed loop	Human interaction	Process definition storage*	Business process identification	Business process release mgmt practices	BPM competency center	Standards vitality
Business automation	Versioning strategy*	Document management*	Process content management*	Business process change mgmt*	Business process exception handling*	Education and training	BPM Infrastructure governance
Process improvement approach*	Accessability of business functionality	Process modeling*	Data permission management**	Process portfolio mgmt		Work structure	Business process lifecycle governance

(*Continued*)

Table 2.3 (*Continued*) Generalized BPM Capabilities (Extended from Oracle BPM Maturity Model)

Business and Strategy	*Architecture*	*Infrastructure*	*Information*	*Projects, Portfolios, and Services*	*Operations, Admin, and Management*	*Organization*	*Governance*
Value chain	BPM security architecture	Process execution*	Case documents**	Process-centric approach		Process change authority	Knowledge (data) governance**
Measurement	System integration and collaboration**	Process views and round-tripping*		Process capture		Process change delivery	Stakeholder governance**
Innovation	Event architecture**	Modeling tools*				Process worker collaboration protocols**	Activity governance**
SOA	Decision management	Business rules**					Policy governance**
Guiding principles**	Stakeholder change mgmt**	Event processing**					
Process mining**	Rules and policy management**	Identity management**					
Pattern detection and template definition**	Data change management**	Predictive analytics**					
	Dynamic activity configuration**						

would also mean moving from large complex processes to simpler "atomic" and "reusable" processlets that are invoked as guided by case progression). In this domain, we have added "System Integration and Collaboration" and "Event Architecture," "Decision Management," "Stakeholder Change Management," "Rules and Policy Management," "Data Change Management," and "Dynamic Activity Configuration" to traditional BPM capabilities. Typical case management systems need to facilitate much higher levels of collaboration among case participants and provide them access to higher varieties and sources of information—this makes the System Integration and Collaboration a necessary capability. Ability to conceive and implement event-based solution architecture is critical for case management since most of the case management activities are usually responses to some internal or external business event—typically events trigger execution of rules, which result in initiation of case activities that in turn generate further events, and so on. Suggestions like "next best action" are provided by a "Decision Management" capability. In adaptive variety of case management, case participants are given the flexibility to dynamically modify stakeholder list, some of the rules and policies, selected data elements, and the list of activities—these are provided by the "Stakeholder Change Management," "Rules and Policy Management," "Data Change Management" and "Dynamic Activity Configuration" capabilities. "Diverse Process Types" and "Process Participant Interaction" capabilities from the original list are marked here for special attention since in Generalized BPM processes, unlike traditional BPM, can be unstructured, process activities can be unpredictable, and participant interactions can be more significant and on demand. Case management solutions, especially in the initial stages, may undergo frequent revisions to reflect rapid learning that would take place from the feedback from actual case resolutions—this makes the "Versioning Strategy" capability especially important in case management situations.

3. *Infrastructure*—Here the word infrastructure encompasses both hardware and generic software capabilities, i.e., the computation enablers. "Business Rules," "Event Processing," "Identify Management," and "Predictive Analytics" are the new capabilities that we have added to this capability domain on account of case management. Business rules are a way to change the behavior of a business application based on a set of preconditions. While business rules are being used increasingly more and more to alter flow control logic for traditional BPM, for case management these have an even greater importance—they practically control "who is doing what and when." These rules are "fired" as certain events occur during case progression; thus, "Event Processing" capability becomes a necessary component of the infrastructure supporting case management solutions. As more experience is gathered around how to solve typical cases, a case management system can suggest "next best action" to case participants—this is supported, in part, by the "Predictive Analytics" capability. We have also marked "Document Management," "Process Modeling," "Process Execution," "Process Views," and "Modeling Tools" capabilities in this domain as "special attention" items. As we have described before, in case management solutions a wide variety of documents, typically much more than traditional BPM, are often involved in supporting and driving case participant activities. In case management, the modeling takes the form of specifying phases, milestones, and activities along with events and rules, at least at the higher levels of solution construction. This requires special support of modeling paradigm, tooling, and visualization. In presence of case management, process execution engine needs to handle execution of case activities and handling of all applicable milestone status.

4. *Information*—Since case management typically involves a significant amount, source, and variety of data and structured and unstructured content (includes traditional formatted and scanned documents, messages, etc.) handling along with management of privileges that case participants need to have as they interact with such data and documents, we have added "Data Permission Management" and "Case Document" capabilities in this domain. It is in the same spirit we have flagged "Process Data" and "Process Content Management" from the original capability list for special attention. We also want to note here that the capability "Process Definition Storage" in the original list now needs to also contain case definitions (aka case templates or case models).
5. *Projects, portfolios & services*—Capabilities in this domain remain generally valid for case management. We have marked "Business Process Change Management" capability mainly to indicate that in case management change management will also include changes in decision making rules and protocols.
6. *Operations, administration, and management (OA&M)*—All the capabilities in this domain are generally valid for case management as well. We have marked "Activity Monitoring," "Process Control" and "Business Process Exception Handling" particularly to remind us that in case management we are required to pay extra attention to human activities or human interaction aspects.
7. *Organization*—All capabilities in this domain are also applicable to case management. Additionally, we have added "Process Worker Collaboration Protocols" capability here since in case management often worker collaboration is important and organizations need to set the necessary guidelines as to the boundaries and expectations in such collaborations.
8. *Governance*—Case management requires all the governance capabilities of traditional BPM. However, since knowledge work and ability to modify stakeholder and activity lists and update certain rules and policies are also important to case management, we have added "Knowledge Governance," "Stakeholder Governance," "Activity Governance," and "Policy Governance" to the original capability list of this domain.

As per our definition, Generalized BPM is a union of traditional BPM and case management functionalities. By augmenting the traditional BPM capabilities with those needed especially for case management, we have created here a capability list that would now be able to support the maturity model for Generalized BPM and would be helpful in guiding related technology adoption.

2.5.4 Adoption of Case Management: A Case Study

Here we will briefly describe the ACM adoption journey at a midsize insurance company in Europe (henceforth labeled the "Company"). This Company has been in existence for a fairly long time, provides nearly a dozen different types of insurance coverage ranging from auto to life, and over time has amassed a sizeable customer base. The Company, until recently, relied on use of a set of "siloed" legacy applications to capture and process insurance claims and to handle associated customer interactions. These legacy applications had grown in complexity due to addition of features catering to emerging business functionalities and changes in rules and regulations. While some of the "old timers" who grew up with the legacy systems had reasonable proficiency in using these systems it was becoming quite difficult to train newer employees on them. These legacy applications were not integrated, thus forcing repeated manual data entry. Collaboration among workers handling claims was done over emails, phone calls, and hallway conversations that were very hard to trace back. Lack of information integration and poor collaboration led to frequent data errors, prolific and expensive exceptions, service delays, and consequent customer dissatisfaction. Also, continual and often ad hoc modifications to large code bases of these systems had rendered them vulnerable to hard to discover coding errors as well as were difficult to change. The Company was hurting in terms of agility and quality in providing new and improved services—it was concerned about losing current and new business to competition. This concern led to explorations into possible technology adoptions that could drastically improve the current situation with their business supporting software systems.

The Company first did a set of experiments with traditional BPM tools and methodologies and found it to be generally difficult and often impossible to capture their claims management activities in a "BPM model." Through such experimentations, they realized that there were two main root causes that limited their success with traditional BPM approach:

1. *Lack of complete knowledge*—Claims management, generally speaking, can be fairly complex and can involve many activities that need to abide by all applicable contract policies, business rules, and relevant government regulations. A fair amount of these policies, rules, and regulations were "hard coded" in their legacy applications. When queried about the execution sequences or paths followed by a set of business activities needed to resolve a claim, different claims processors provided different articulations. It was thus impossible to "sketch" a traditional BPM model with activities, flows, and rules with great confidence.
2. *High variability*—The Company offered insurance for a large variety of risks like home, auto, life, boats, travel, and precious stones and artifacts. For a given risk, they also offered many options with regards to claims admissibility criteria, deductibles, and so on; these choices were introduced to help the customers fine-tune their insurance policies. While the wide range of offers was certainly helpful to the customers, and in fact, contributed to the Company's attractiveness, they also created over a hundred sufficiently distinct types of claims to be processed. Within each such claim type, the actual actions taken by the claims processors and their managers varied, sometimes significantly, due to unique situations associated with the claim instances. Claims processors and their managers made many decisions based on their judgment and experience bypassing or ignoring what the standard operating procedures and the outcomes from their legacy applications would dictate—this made their work activities somewhat unpredictable. Thus even in situations where the Company employees could fully articulate all the actions that were ever taken to process claims the details were too overwhelming to model using standard BPM syntax and tools within reasonable modeling efforts and complexity.

In looking for suitable strategies to cope with these challenges, the Company decided to adopt process mining and ACM, the former to gain more comprehensive knowledge about the actual activities by analyzing past activity logs and the latter to handle the high variability and unpredictability in work activities.

Given that the Company already had a whole set of legacy applications and a "way of working," albeit not satisfactory anymore, many stakeholders, ranging from technical development teams to business owners started wondering ways a different paradigm such as ACM should be adopted. In trying to minimize significant interruptions to day-to-day business and to have the work force ease into a different technology and work style, a "phased" approach of technology adoption made the most sense. Besides, it was felt that a phased approach would allow the Company to become steadily "mature" in the capabilities needed for a successful ACM adoption. Partnering with a trusted implementation partner well conversant with Oracle SOA, BPM, ACM and UI

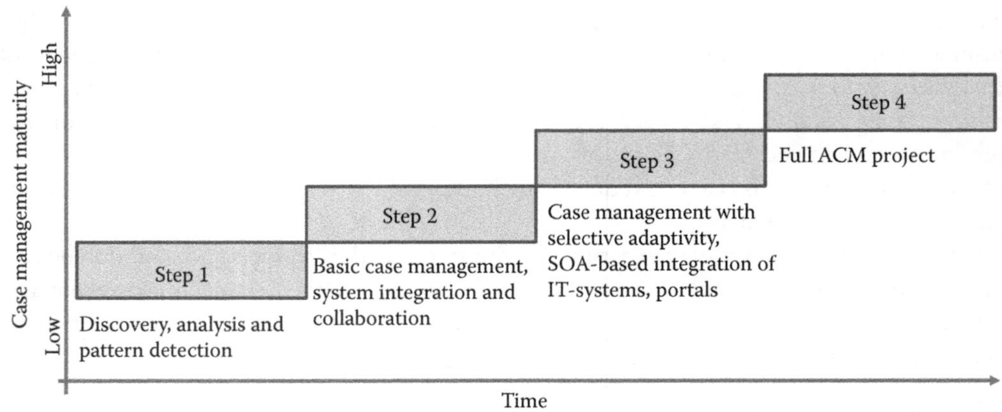

Figure 2.20 An ACM adoption example—from application silos to ACM in four steps.

technologies, the Company put together a phased adoption plan with four steps (Figure 2.20). Major work activities and technology adoption targets for these steps or phases were:

1. *Step #1*—this was a preparatory step. The Company wanted to understand better and create a knowledge base of how they actually performed their day to day work, how much variability in work actually did exist, and how often there were exceptions and special attention was needed. This was done by a variety of methods of process mining such as interviews, analyzing application logs, and monitoring pertinent events and their handling; they also used a process mining tool. Once they were sufficiently comfortable with the "as is" knowledge level, a round of analyses were done to identify groups of work activities that could be fully predefined and thus could be easily and efficiently handled by traditional BPM, and the rest. A high-level case management style discovery was then undertaken to make a tentative roadmap as to how functionalities should be moved from either packaged or legacy applications to more middleware-based BPM and ACM; a cost–benefit estimate for such moves was also done. The outcome of this discovery along with the cost–benefit estimates helped the Company to identify the "low hanging fruits" that could be undertaken in the near term deferring the rest to be distributed over future phases when the Company expected to gain higher levels of maturity. The Company also got a taste of event-based problem decomposition and case management solution formulation by conducting a few simple PoCs with the help of their implementation partner. Comparing with the Generalized BPM maturity model this step or phase would correspond closely to a "Level 1" maturity.
2. *Step #2*—In this step, the Company selected a small group of activities where the notion of case management was deemed to be helpful. These were not PoCs as in the previous step but represented real business problems; business users were involved along with the technical teams to articulate the problems and designing the key features of the end solutions. The activities typically represented some of the "white spaces," i.e., activities there were not (fully) covered by the Company's current applications and required ad hoc actions by the claims processors or their managers. The focus in this step was mainly on organization of work activities around the concept of case folders and to provide a new set of UIs to the claims processors to better access work items and supporting documents, and to have better visibility of the overall progress of claim resolutions. Certain levels of application and UI integrations were needed in order to achieve these goals. The Company chose a "service oriented"

integration strategy keeping in view possible reuse of the integration services in later phases. The key benefits of activities in this step were incremental improvement of work efficiency that could be demonstrated by using simple KPIs and the Company was now getting closer to a "Level 2" maturity as discussed in the Generalized BPM maturity model.

3. *Step #3*—While some of the key concepts of case management were already in place, the projects in the previous step did not include provisions for any runtime adaptivity, i.e., the abilities to either alter the work activities, their sequences or the work assignees. This was done on purpose since the Company wanted to limit the amount of change in the tools and work practices to a level that would not be outright uncomfortable for their existing workforce. In this step, however, the Company started extending the scope of work activity groups to include facilitation of some knowledge work, i.e., started providing ACM-style flexibilities so that in some situations the claims processors could use their experience or expert advice to choose work activities that would resolve their cases better or faster. Additional information and UI integrations were needed in this phase to provide the claims processors with broader and timely access to a variety of documents, work-in-progress reports as well as up-to-date case resolution status, and a more easy-to-use work environment. This phase also introduced collaboration portals to facilitate better team resolution of difficult problems. In addition to extending existing application capabilities, the Company was also targeting a few of the small and new projects using ACM; these projects helped the Company gain deeper experience in conducting case management discoveries and planning and executing case management projects using iterative and agile methods, and in training claims processors in using the runtime adaptivity and on demand collaboration to their advantage. By the end of this step the Company was climbing into "Level 3" of the Generalized BPM maturity model.
4. *Step #4*—Having successfully conquered the key challenges of adoption of case management technology and practices, the Company was now ready to undertake more complex and mission critical projects using ACM. In fact, they were now creating hybrid solutions that employed a mix of traditional BPM and ACM to achieve optimal level of efficiency and flexibility for business problems in scope, i.e., they were using the Generalized BPM approach. The Company started putting in more detailed measures and KPIs to monitor and improve the process of creating and using Generalized BPM solutions. Per Generalized BPM maturity model described earlier, at this phase the Company was operating somewhere between "Level 3" and "Level 4."

It should be pointed out that a maturity model is only a guiding framework to help an organization arrange development and fine-tuning of relevant competencies related to adoption of a paradigm. This sense also applies to Generalized BPM maturity model where required competencies for adoption of case management are included. As was the case with the company we discussed here, project requirements often drives the technology adoption scope and pace; however, being cognizant of required competencies to wholesomely raise organizational maturity can be very helpful in merging the tactical and the strategic goals.

2.5.5 Maturity Is More Than Technology

Since after all we are considering overall organizational maturity, in this case for adoption of Generalized BPM, becoming experts in relevant technologies only is not enough to raise the maturity—behaviors of participating humans individually and the relevant sectors of the organization must also evolve to embrace the associated practices. This concern is reflected in the spread of the capability domains in our maturity model where about half the focus is technology driven and the rest involves organizational and business concerns. For example, when adopting case management, the participants need to change the way they assess and progress a resolution as compared to traditional BPM—in case management progression of the resolution is deciphered from information collected in case folders along with status of milestones (that collectively lead to the end goal) whereas in traditional BPM the process model and the current state is enough to indicate progress of the business transaction. Since some level of knowledge work is involved in case management, a typical participant, i.e., a case worker needs a relatively deeper understanding of the overall problem being solved and the organizational practices for solving them as compared to a typical participant, i.e., a process worker in traditional BPM setting where the process worker specializes in executing the types of (individual) tasks that he/she is normally assigned to. Typically, case management also assigns a "case owner" role that is responsible overall coordination of participant activities, interventions when necessary, and ultimately for a successful resolution of the case instance. In adaptive version of case management implementations, there can be a lot of on-demand team collaboration and just in time expert decisioning—these activities along with their governance cannot be automatically assumed to be present in a traditional BPM driven organizational culture and must be systematically developed through enablement, rewards, and control. Thus, alongside tools and applications, a set of human and organizational capabilities need to be also developed in order to reap higher benefits from case management or Generalized BPM paradigm.

2.6 Making the Business Case for Case Management

"There is no such thing as a free lunch"—a quote often attributed to the late Nobel Prize–winning economist Milton Friedman well captures the sense that everything that we do has a cost, whether direct or indirect. Why should the adoption of case management be any different? In fact, and like any other nontrivial initiative, adoption of case management has to be well justified in all but obvious situations. Since traditional BPM has now been a popular efficiency strategy for some time that is aimed at improving organization and execution, "Why should we adopt yet another paradigm such as case management to manage business activities?" is a legitimate question. The answer, of course, has two parts: technical enablement and business case. So far we have discussed many of the essentials behind technical construction and capabilities of case management; in this section, we will briefly visit the key considerations for creating a business case for case management.

2.6.1 General Considerations for Creating and Presenting a Business Case

Adoption of some new (or newer) paradigm to create capabilities in an organization will always partition people into groups who "like," those who "dislike," and those who are "indifferent" to the idea. Some of these people are likely to be the ones making the decisions about policies and resource allocation that would control whether the initiatives leading to the adoption will be undertaken. A well-composed business case is often critical to obtain a positive decision towards adoption commitments. Figure 2.21 shows the interplay of the dominant forces or the key considerations that directly impact the creation of business case that justify the necessary organizational commitment to initiate and execute an adoption journey. The capabilities resulting from the target adoption are motivated by a set of business requirements and hold the promise of delivering a set

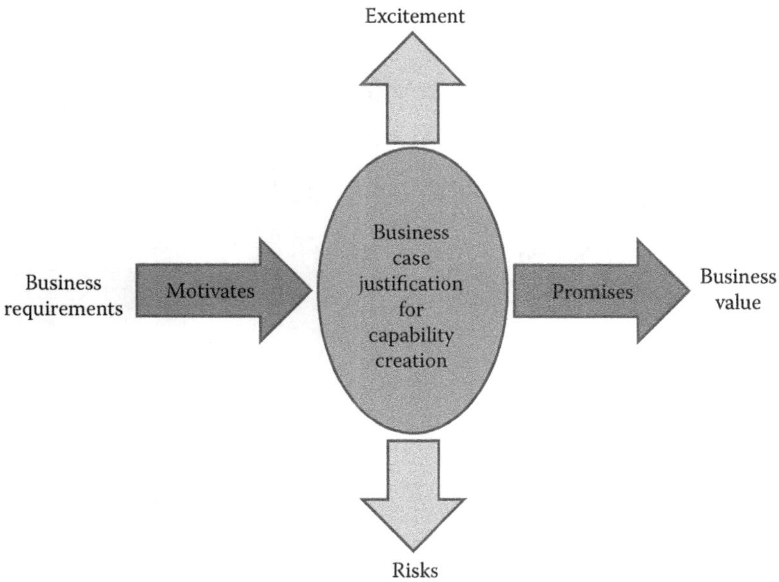

Figure 2.21 Business case justification for capability creation and the key forces.

of business values that could include cost reduction, cost avoidance, revenue growth, compliance management, or creation of a better image for the organization. Those who propose or like the idea of creating such capabilities are usually excited about getting on with the related initiatives as quickly as possible and may sometimes not pay enough attention to the possible risks of failure of such initiatives; the naysayers are, of course, mostly focused on the risks ignoring the possible positive implications of the initiatives if the risks are managed adequately. A well-formed business case aims to rationalize the adoption decision process using objective arguments related to costs, benefits, and potential risks.

Effective creation and presentation of a business case should follow a well-understood format and must contain succinct information useful for deriving conclusions easily. While there are many formats that can be adopted for putting together a business case, the following topics are commonly included:

1. A description of the initiatives and their final goals
2. Business needs served by the proposed initiatives
3. The consequences of staying with the *status quo*
4. Key business benefits of the initiatives, both tangible and intangible, direct and indirect
5. Resource requirements including type, amount, and duration of resources
6. Financial metrics such as payback period, ROI, IRR, or NPV calculations
7. A comparison of merits and demerits of possible alternatives
8. Key assumptions and their impact on the analysis and arguments presented
9. Possible risks, their sources, and impact along with recommendations for their remedies
10. A list of critical success factors (CSFs) that would help ensure better success rate
11. A list of key performance indicators (KPIs) that can be used to measure and tune progress
12. A list of key risk indicators (KRIs) that could help tune or abandon execution, if necessary

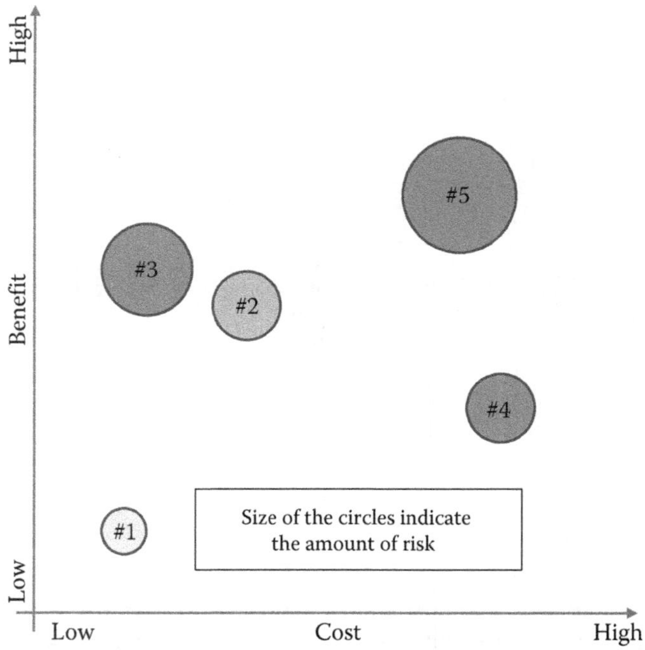

Figure 2.22 A cost–benefit-risk representation of possible options.

In the event there is more than one option that needs to be considered, a cost–benefit risk representation of these options provides a helpful visual for decision making process. As shown in Figure 2.22, options 3, 4 and 5 are not desirable either due to high cost, low benefit, or higher than acceptable risk; option 2 represents a good balance of high benefit, moderate cost, and relatively low risk; option 1 indicates a low level of risk and cost but also provides low benefit—such options may be useful when an organization is starting to climb the learning curve of competencies required to plan and execution adoption initiatives.

2.6.2 Specific Considerations for a Case Management Business Case

With the outline of general considerations for creating and presenting a business case just presented, let us turn our attention back to case management, including the production and adaptive variations, to see what type of business problem indicators, expected outcomes for the business, and likely risk factors that may exist or should be considered for adoption of case management initiatives. Since we have already had several discussions around the technology-related concepts underlying case management, our focus here would be more from a business and organizational angle; we will focus mainly on business needs and financial benefits, costs and risk aspects of case management adoption since the rest of the items required for creating a business case for case management will follow naturally from these:

1. *Business needs and financial benefits*: Here we need to map a set of business imperatives against the capabilities afforded by adoption of case management and then translate the fulfilment of these business needs to changes in the top-line (i.e., revenue) or bottom-line (i.e. revenue–cost) of the organizations that can be reasonably attributed to case management adoption. We have already discussed how production and ACM solutions provide

significantly higher work flexibility than traditional BPM and facilitate knowledge work; PCM solutions will typically allow case workers to choose the right subset of activities, their execution sequence and work assignee from broader predefined sets while ACM will additionally allow the case workers to modify the work list and introduce stakeholders on demand. As mentioned already, it should be expected that many solutions will benefit from a combination of traditional BPM and case management (recall "Generalized BPM") and that with the right solution architecture and technology platform such hybrid solutions are quite feasible. The types of business problems that these case management or Generalized BPM will solve depend on the type of industry the business is in and further the type of product or services it offers.

For example, in financial services industry and in regulatory agencies most of the supervision of compliance adherence, fraud investigations, and special services for high net-worth investors are great candidates for case management. In insurance companies, complex claims management are better dealt with using case management. In utilities industry, while some of the activities in the area of outage and work order management can be handled by traditional BPM, more complicated situations, say, involving damage claims are more suitable for case management based solutions. With relatively higher familiarity with traditional BPM that currently exist solution designers may have high temptation to somehow fit business activities into traditional BPM framework and hope that a seemingly well structured workflow will provide business excellence even for these use cases. However, inherent rigidity in traditional BPM does restrict the ability for knowledge workers to exercise their experience and solve difficult problems creatively. Trying to adhere to fully predefined activities of traditional BPM can lead to solutions that are not effective thus leading to proliferation of exceptions, expensive rework, long delays in resolution of issues and loss of customer satisfaction. Also, in situations where the process definition evolves rapidly, an event-based decomposition of the business problem, as would be in case management paradigm makes it much easier to change the solution definition rapidly. For the purpose of creating a business case for case management, one needs to estimate, using any suitable calculation method, the financial benefits of being able to do work more effectively, being able to handle rapid change in business need or raising customer satisfaction for applicable use cases like the ones we just mentioned. Of course, translation of some of the case management benefits to financial gains like cost reduction due to more accurate and effective issue resolution would be easier to calculate while the financial value of generating long-term customer loyalty would be trickier to compute. In Section 1.4.5, we have presented a discussion on application of case management across many industries—this could be a good starting point when looking for the types of operational benefits that case management can provide and then use the relevant ones for financial benefit calculation.

2. *Costs*: The process of adoption of case management, like other technology adoptions, can and will incur a variety of costs, some of which can be calculated in a straight forward manner while the others may be more nebulous. Generally speaking, costs can be separated into fixed and variable categories, and some of these costs can be directly attributable to specific activities while the others will be more general in nature, i.e., would be associated with many activities.

   In the context of case management adoption, costs would arise from acquisition of needed software, hardware, and training to get technology platforms operational and personnel knowledgeable about using such platforms and following suitable methodologies. There will also be the compensations of the personnel involved in pushing the adoption.

Depending on the scope of various phases of adoption, the shares of fixed and variable costs will vary. For example, if the early phases of adoption are designed as exploratory, it may be possible to construct initiatives with mostly fixed cost. For the purposes of cost estimation, "activity-based costing" (aka "ABC", see: http://www.accountingcoach.com/activity-based-costing/explanation for a primer; website accessed February/2014) can be generally used for the concrete activities. To these costs overall management and support costs plus any relevant opportunity cost should be added to reflect the overall cost. It should be noted that other than activities like well-established manufacturing of products, cost estimates will always carry a decent amount of uncertainty; the level of uncertainty should reduce as additional information becomes available with progression of activities in the initiatives (see: Figure 2.23, courtsey of the US General Accountability Office aka GAO). Sometimes three cost estimate figures, "likely," "pessimistic" (i.e., upper bound) and "optimistic" (i.e., lower bound) are presented in order to provide an idea of the level of uncertainty—these estimates tend to converge as estimation uncertainties reduce. A strategy for measuring costs and course correcting (if necessary) should be in place to guide the adoption process.

3. *Risks*: All real-life activities have some level of risk associated with them—adequate upfront planning along with strategies to adjust the planned course in response to evolving situations is the key to successful navigation through risks. In order to plan for handling risks, we have to first recognize that risks may arise either from "known unknowns" or "unknown unknowns." For the first category, we will typically know the sources of risks but may not be able to fully assess the timing or the impact of their occurrence while in the second category, we would be "caught off guard." Generally speaking, we can be better prepared for the first type of risks with specific remedies already identified while for the second category we have to be "agile" and "adaptive," i.e., rely on the organization's ability to quickly sense and analyze the risks and come up with a suitable remedy on demand. It may be sensible to set some acceptable risk criteria of a given adoption, which when exceeded the adoption may be abandoned in the spirit of "cutting losses" in a timely manner so as to prevent more damage

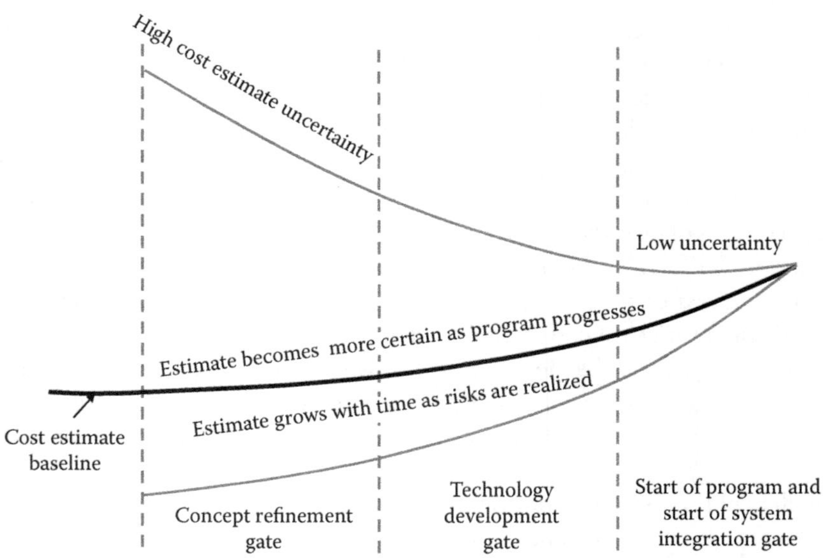

Figure 2.23 Cone of uncertainty in cost estimation. (Adapted from US GAO.)

downstream. Specifically for case management, adoption risks are likely to arise from things like incorrect use case or adoption roadmap (i.e., wrong scope or pace for projects undertaken), inadequate competency, inability to effect required change in work culture, out of balance and noncomprehensive governance, lack of suitable KPIs and KRIs, and inability to appropriately course-correct when necessary. The Generalized BPM maturity model and capability domains that we have previously discussed can provide useful guidance in identifying major sources of risks as well in planning for their remedies.

There is no argument that business cases are generally important for "go" or "no go" decision making for projects; they are even more important when new a type of undertaking has to be initiated due to higher levels of associated uncertainty. Here lies an apparent paradox: just when facts and arguments of a business case are most important and useful to combat uncertainty the difficulty in creating such facts and arguments are the highest due to the same uncertainty. Thus, creating a good business case for adoption of a newer technology adoption like case management will certainly involve both "art" and "science"; proposer's knowledge of current state of the art of case management and of conducting projects of similar complexity in his/her organization would be invaluable assets in creating credible business cases for case management.

2.7 Summary

In this chapter, we have covered a variety of topics that are mutually distinct but are directly related to either better understanding of case management concepts or its adoption in an organization. We started with comparing adaptive aspects of case management with characteristics of complex adaptive systems; this led to a method for identification of key attributes of adaptive case management. We then described different variations of case management solutions; specifically, we focused into the details of production and adaptive varieties of case management and their applicability in solving business problems. Next, we compared and contrasted traditional BPM with case management and noted that many solutions will require a suitable mix of both these paradigms. We introduced the notion of "Generalized BPM" to capture the combined problem solving strategy of using both traditional BPM and case management. From an adoption point of view, we defined a capability maturity model, its associated capability domains and individual capabilities in those domains for Generalized BPM. We advocated the practice of creating strategic adoption framework based on such a maturity model and building up of capabilities through proper scoping and design of case management projects. Finally, we discussed the challenges associated with and strategies for creating business cases for adoption of case management and suggested a "cost benefit risk" framework for evaluating such business cases. We are now ready to take up a set of real-life case studies of case management solutions and then get into the technical details of how to design and implement case management solution both from a solution architecture PoV and using case management features of relevant Oracle technologies, in particular, Siebel and Oracle BPM Suite—these are the discussion topics for the rest of the book.

CASE MANAGEMENT SOLUTION FRAMEWORK

II

Introduction

In this section, we introduce the case management solution framework. This framework enables the functional and technical design of a case management solution with a set of *case management design components*, *three case management classifications*, and the *case management solution mapping*.

Chapter 3 shows the case management functional design describing its functionality in three functional categories and one cross-functional category. The functional categories look at the life cycle of the case, information related to the case, and the interaction with stakeholders. The cross-functional category supports the three functional categories with a security and integration design.

Chapter 4 details the *case management classifications* from a functional perspective. "Forrester's Classification of Case Management Solutions" is introduced earlier (Section I—Chapter 1), where the three classifications are described: *service request*, *incident management*, and *investigative handling*. Case management design components are used to describe the functionality of the three classifications with special emphasis on the life cycle design category.

Chapter 5 shows how functionality is mapped toward solution layers and technical capabilities with the help of the vendor-agnostic architecture model, the Common Reference Architecture (CORA) model, and how Oracle products can be mapped against these technical capabilities.

Chapter 3

Case Management Functional Design

3.1 Introduction

The first part in the case management solution framework is the identification of the design components needed to describe the case management functionality. We will use a design model that contains three functional and one cross-functional design categories. The functional categories describe the *lifecycle* of the case, *information* related to the case, and *interaction* with stakeholders. The cross-functional category supports the three functional categories with *roles and authorization* and *integration* design. For each design component, we will describe the high-level design functionalities.

The goals of this chapter are as follows:

- Describe the principles for the case management design components
- Describe the three functional design components; the *lifecycle* of the case, *information* related to the case, and *interaction* with stakeholders
- Describe the cross-functional category contains the *roles and authorization* and *integration* design
- Provide a design template for the determination of the required, high-level case management functionality

3.2 Principles for the Solution Design Components

In Chapters 1 and 2, we discussed the motivation, concepts, and the characteristics of a case management solution.

The principles for the case management design components are derived from these chapters and summarized in Table 3.1.

Table 3.1 Principles for Case Management Design

Principle	*Statement*	*Rationale*
Goal-driven	The case management paradigm is goal-driven	Reaching the desired result is of primary importance. The actual activities performed, and the order in which these are executed, are of secondary consideration
Generalized BPM	The business activities during case work fall under two distinct categories: routine work and knowledge work	The concept of Generalized BPM combines these two categories
Special situation handling	Interventions interact with the flow of a case	During a case, interventions can originate from different sources that interact with the flow of the case
Adaptable	Adaptive systems are designed to handle variations and unpredictability as a rule instead of as exceptions	Adaptivity helps reduce exceptions
Driven by data and documents	Case management is strongly driven by data and documents	(Un)structured document and data are key components during the flow of a case
Collaboration and knowledge sharing	High level of collaboration and knowledge sharing are required during case work	Collaboration and knowledge sharing are frequently leveraged in resolving a case
One centralized view of the case	Direct insight into what activities are done, which activities are in progress, who are involved, and what incident information is available	Be able to make decisions based on case progress
Spanning multiple applications	Case management work often spans multiple applications	Case work often spans different departments and/or companies and, as such, needs to integrate with multiple applications

3.3 Design Components

3.3.1 Design Components Overview

The functional design of a case management solution contains three main *functional design categories* and two *cross-functional design components* as shown in Figure 3.1.

The *functional categories* each contain three design components and look at

- The *case lifecycle design category* with support for the coordination of activities in reaching one of the end goals.

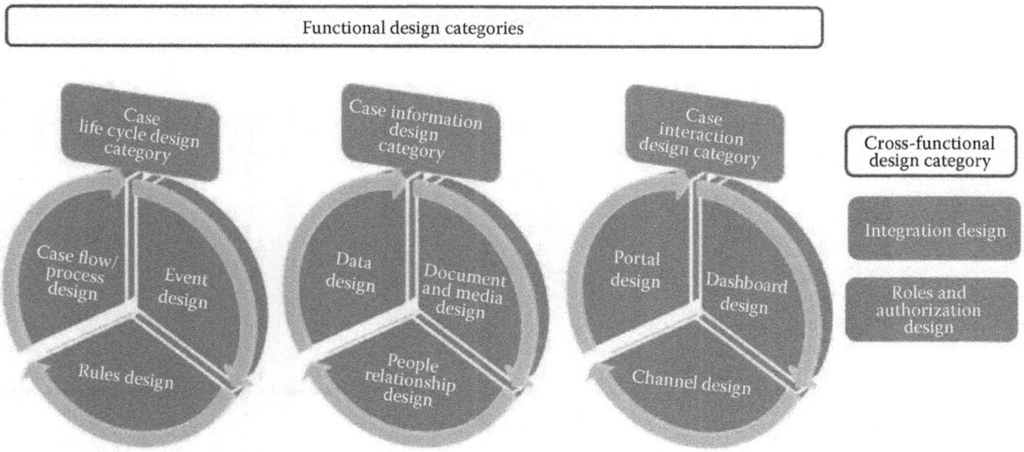

Figure 3.1 Case management design categories and components.

- The *case information design category* dealing with all sorts of data and documentation flowing through the case, and gives insight into the stakeholders and their relations.
- The *case interaction design category* maximizing the support for the case work force.

The *cross-functional design category* supports the functional design components integration and roles and authorization:

- The *case integration design* related to the delivery of functionality and information across all participating applications and stakeholders.
- The *case roles and authorization design* ensures the execution responsibilities, visibility of data, and tracking and tracing across the case execution.

In the following sections, the case management design categories and components are described in more detail and contain the following:

- Aim of the design category/components
- Relation with the principles
- Description of the design components part of the design category
- A modeling notation for lifecycle design

In the description of the design components, topics are described that should be analyzed during the case design. The design component sections do not intend to describe how the design is executed. We touched on this topic in Section 1.5.3 and will show design methods later in the Oracle Adaptive Management tutorial description in Section 17.2.

3.3.2 Case Lifecycle Design Category

3.3.2.1 Aim

The case lifecycle design category describes the coordination of activities in reaching one of the end goals of a case and consists of three design components: *case flow/process design*, *rules design*, and *event design* (Figure 3.2).

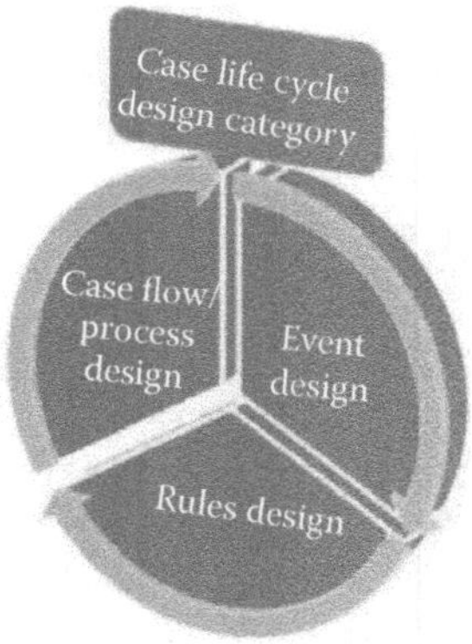

Figure 3.2 Case management lifecycle design category.

3.3.2.2 Relation with the Principles

This design category relates to the following principles:

- Goal driven—The case flow is focused on reaching one of the end goals and also focuses on intermediate goals.
- Generalized BPM—The case can consist of both routine work and knowledge work
- Special situation handling—Interventions can enter at any point in the case flow and these interventions have the potential to alter the case flow
- Adaptable—The case model needs to be adaptable at both designtime and at runtime

3.3.2.3 Case Management Lifecycle Design Components

3.3.2.3.1 Case/Process Flows Design

The design of the case execution can be based upon two types of work:

1. Knowledge work—Requires handling of unstructured and unpredictable tasks.
2. Routine work—Based upon structured and completely predefined process models.

In order to support the design of the case flow, process and events, two modeling notations are used for the description of the architectural patterns in this section: a high-level, case flow model, and a case state model. The *case flow model* gives insight into the interaction of stakeholders and an (high-level) activity flow. The *case state model* focuses on state changes.

The *case flow model* is used to model the case lifecycle from an activity flow perspective and is used to give a high-level overview of the stakeholders, the flow of activities, and the events intervening in the execution of the case flow.

Every activity in the case flow, as shown in Figure 3.3, consists of more detailed work and can be a simple workflow or a complex case functionality involving investigation activities. Lines show the flow of activities and the interaction among the stakeholders. The *stakeholders* are modeled in this diagram as horizontal swim lanes. The stakeholders relate to the roles as will be described in Section 3.3.5 where the stakeholders related to a case and their responsibilities are described. During the design phase, these roles need to be specified further, and related to the more detailed

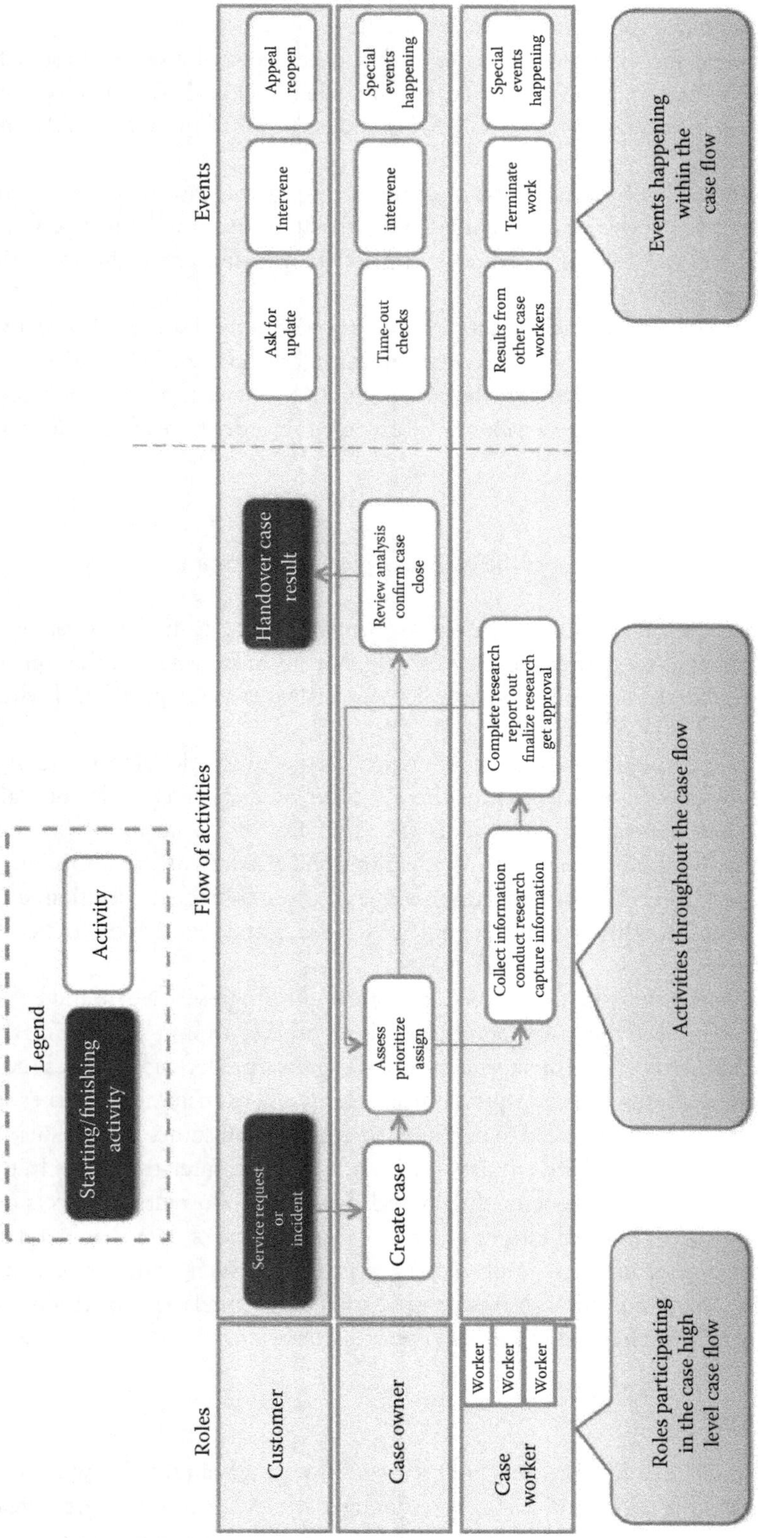

Figure 3.3 Case flow model example.

work in the activities. *Events* are shown in the right hand side of the case flow diagram and represent manual or automated interventions in the case flow.

The *case state model* shows the case lifecycle from another viewpoint related to state flow, activities, and events (Figure 3.4). Stakeholders are not included in this view. This view is based upon the *case management model and notation* (CMMN) and is described in more detail at http://www.omg.org/spec/CMMN/.

The CMMN model is focused on state changes during the case lifecycle. Each case state change determines what activities can be used at a particular moment. This model describes the different activities or groupings of activities and gives insight into entry and exit criteria of the different phases in the state.

The entry criteria determine when activities or a set of activities are allowed to start. Exit criteria determine when a phase or activity can be considered closed. Milestones, which signify important activity completion points in the case progression, determine when a business goal or target is met. Typically, a set of tasks needs to be executed in order to reach a milestone.

3.3.2.3.2 Rules Design

The following rules types can support the case management execution:

- Case lifecycle decision-making—This relates to the ability to make decisions based on a change that happened in the lifecycle of a case. For instance, when a milestone is reached a decision is needed to determine what follow-up activities are required and which ones are optional.
- Entitlement determination—This functionality relates to the decision made in a customer related case, where the entitlement of the customer on a specific service or claim is determined. The entitlement decision entails the eligibility of the customer on the service or claim, and can contain money involved, duration, restrictions, and specific treatments. Examples are the decision in a mortgage request, a welfare request decision, and an insurance claim decision. This typically is guided by policies and regulations, and can change on a regular basis.
- Progress measurement—In order to be able to show the progress of a case and be able to make decisions in relation to the case progress, a decision process around "measuring the progress" is needed. This involves measuring the case state against predefined progress indicators.
- Data entry validation—This is required in situations where customers or other stakeholders enter data into the case that need to be validated against for instance regulations and policies.
- Information discovery—Different data types and sources can relate to case. In the information design of a case, all predefined data and document information objects are designed that determine the input and output of a case. Another type of data that can determine the output and behavior of a case is unstructured in nature, such as data streams, video, and social media. Searching through this unstructured data, in relation to structured data, can deliver some new or changed insights in the case execution.

3.3.2.3.3 Event Design

Events intervene in the case activities in a nonpredictable way and can interact with the case at any moment in the case lifecycle. Summarizing the characteristics from events found in real life cases, events can be interrupting in nature or noninterrupting. Interrupting events have the potential to

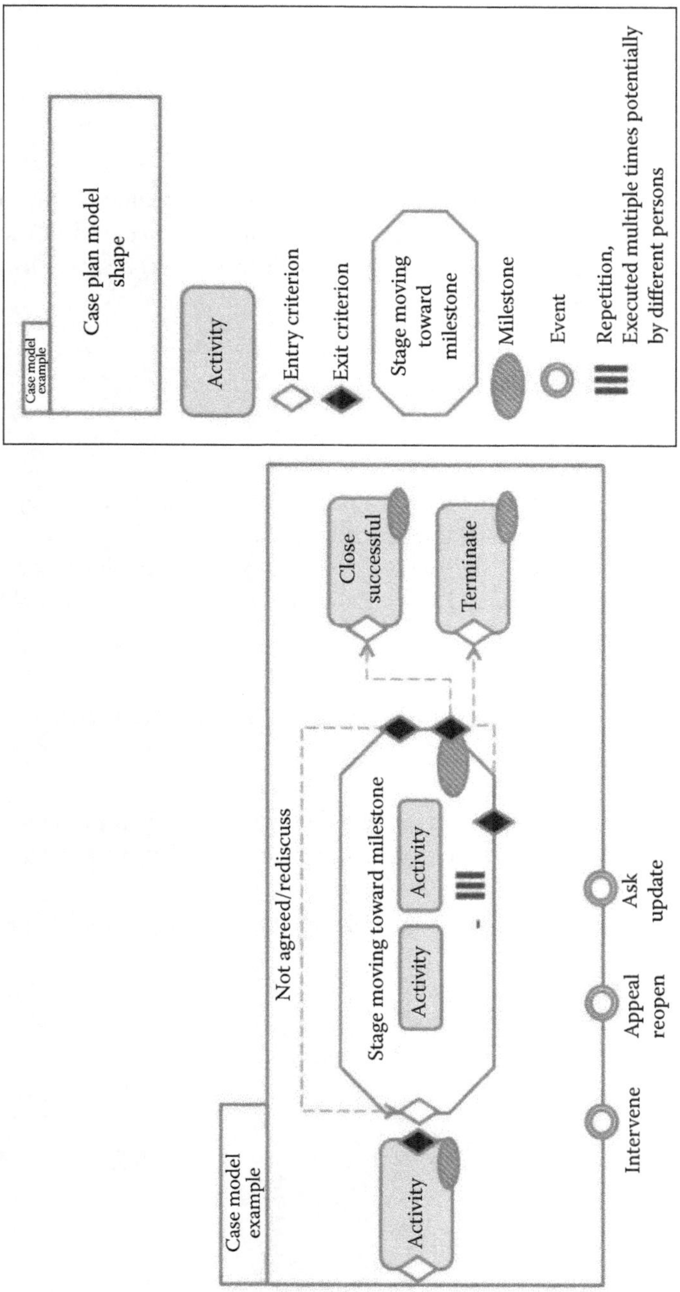

Figure 3.4 Case state model: notation and example.

alter the flow of activities; for instance when in a police investigation new evidence is found at the crime scene the investigation can change into a new direction. A noninterrupting event starts some activities parallel to the case flow, but does not interrupt the flow itself. A request for an update during an insurance claim assessment starts activities to gather the update information and present the update to the customer.

3.3.3 Case Information Design Category

3.3.3.1 Aim

The case information design deals with all sorts of data and documentation flowing through the case and maps the relationships between all persons and/or assets involved in the case. The case information design category contains three design components—*data design*, *document and media design*, and *people relationship design* (Figure 3.5).

3.3.3.2 Relation with the Principles

This design category relates to the following principles:

- Driven by data and documents—Case management is strongly driven by data and documents which can be of structured and unstructured nature.
- Collaboration and knowledge sharing—In order to support collaboration and knowledge sharing, the involved persons and the relation between all case stakeholders need to be understood.

3.3.3.3 Case Management Information Design Components

3.3.3.3.1 Data Design

Case management supports a large group of stakeholders within an organization with the execution of case related activities, all with different intelligence needs related to different information levels:

- At an *operational* level in real time, supporting the work on a single case with the right knowledge.

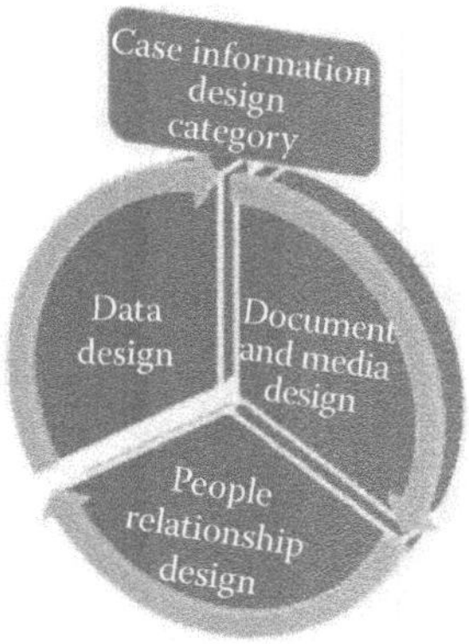

Figure 3.5 Case management information design category.

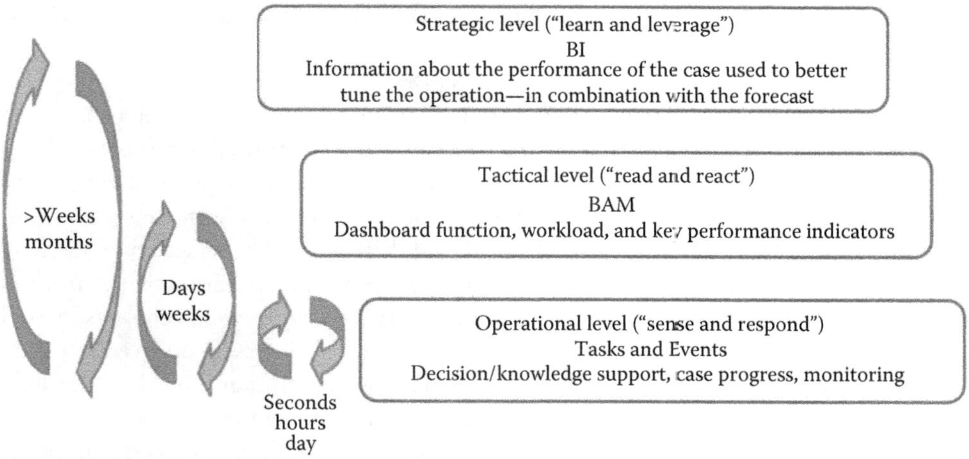

Figure 3.6 Case management information levels. (Courtesy of Ard Jan Vethman.)

- At a *tactical* level aimed at improving the efficiency, customer satisfaction, and controlling case related key performance indicators (KPIs).
- At a *strategic* level looking back in time and investigate process and product improvements and forecasts.

The different information levels for a case supporting the different stakeholders are summarized in Figure 3.6. In this figure additional indicative timing levels are added. These time levels only need to be seen in relation to one another; actual time amounts depend on the case situation and duration.

3.3.3.3.1.1 Operational Level The operational level is where the actual work on the case is done. The execution is lead by the cases owners and executed by the case workers. In the *service request* type of cases, see Chapter 4 for details, also customers have a large stake in what decisions are made and in what direction the case is going. In order to support a case from an operational perspective, the following data functionalities are required:

- Case execution data—This includes all data related to the case execution, such as the case status, activities, decisions, and the history of the case execution.
- Case supporting data—The case execution is supported with details of the case, history of all cases and insight in laws, regulations and policies to which the case must abide. The history in both the case execution and case supporting data area is used for the actual case execution and could be of help for future cases as a reference or a source of investigation.
- Risk parameters for monitoring—In Section 4.5, *the monitoring characteristics* of the incident management case classification are described. The likelihood of an incident can be predicted by monitoring certain risk parameters. These risk parameters are re-evaluated on a regular basis.

3.3.3.3.1.2 Tactical Level Multiple cases can be open and be worked on at the same time. The activities that are related to these cases are distributed by the case owners among the case workers. In environments with hundreds, thousands, or more cases, an overview is needed to check the state of all these cases and related tasks and be able to drill in to the level at which operation activities can be executed. In this area, the following information functionalities are needed:

- *Workload information—This level of information* is aimed at delivering intelligence to ensure *efficiency* in the case *execution*. The case owners and stakeholders need to be able to act upon a changing workload. This can be due to campaigns being executed, a problem with a product, which raises the amount of complaints, or a problem with the workforce such as multiple persons getting flu at the same time. The workload then needs to be relocated to different case workers, extra people being called in, or customers informed that certain activities are deferred.
- *Key performance indicator (KPIs)—Case owners and departmental* stakeholders have KPIs assigned to the case and the related processes. The case owners have KPIs on an end-to-end level. Departmental stakeholders have KPIs more on a micro level, for instance at a departmental level. Case management activities are for a larger part driven by human interactions, which in time and money can make the execution of the case expensive. Both the case owners and the departmental stakeholders have KPIs related to the result and efficiency of (sub) results of the case.
- *Customer satisfaction information—In some industries, the way a case* is handled for a customer can make or break the relation with that customer. In these situations, thorough measurement of the customer satisfaction after (or during) the case execution is crucial.
- *Audit trails—For compliance*, regulatory, or contractual reasons activities, decisions and/or discussions need to be tracked during the execution of a case.

3.3.3.3.1.3 Strategic Level Strategic data involves gathering data in the long run, and identify what happened in all the case executions over the last months and years. This is a "good old" business intelligence (BI) and helps in identifying finding improvement areas, trends, and supports in making forecasts. The result of this intelligence is fed back into the operations level, from which either the case and/or the process lifecycle is adjusted, or the decision support is improved.

In the *improvement* areas, three main topics can be identified, case/process improvement, product improvement, and decision support improvement.

Case/Process Improvement The BPM lifecycle describes the various phases of a case and its related processes during its lifetime, as shown in Figure 3.7. It starts with the design and implementation after which the process "goes live" where it will be executed by the different participants. By measuring the execution time and the behavior of a case/process, we are able to optimize these case/processes. In the last phase of the lifecycle, a case/process can be retired or we can execute another cycle in the lifetime of the case/process. Up until the time that the process is retired the BPM lifecycle will be rerun in various cycles:

- Design—In the design phase, business analysts and participants design the solution.
- Modeling—In the modeling phase, business analysts and developers create the solution.
- Execution—In this phase, case and related processes are executed by participants.
- Monitoring—Monitoring delivers insight in the status and whereabouts of processes.
- Optimization—With the information from the monitoring phase, processes can be adjusted and new simulations can be created and tested.

Product Improvement Case handling is goal driven and deals with the execution of a certain product. This can be a customer supporting product such as a mortgage, or a more abstract product such as a police investigation. The behavior of the case handling for these products is determined

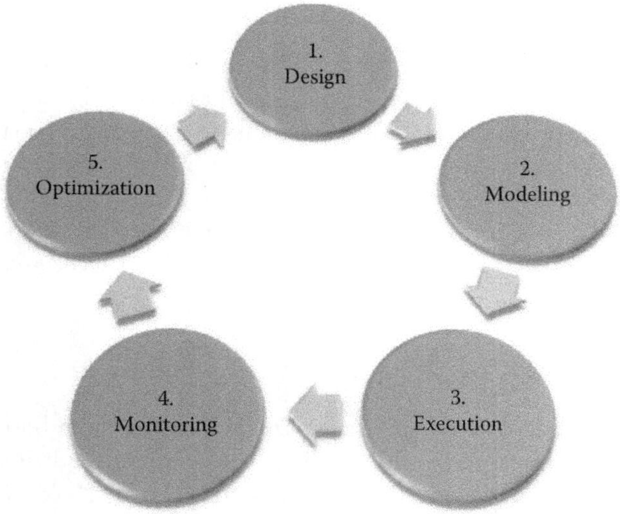

Figure 3.7 BPM process lifecycle.

by product features and policies and can be guided by internal rules and by laws, regulations, and policies. Recording the actual behavior of the case execution in relation to the way the product is dealt with gives insight in where to improve the product.

Forecasts, Trend Analysis, and Customer Behavior Strategic data supports the creation of forecasts, trend analyses, and insight in customer behavior.

Summarizing all the needs described earlier gives the following functionality overview related to the three information levels, as shown in Figure 3.8.

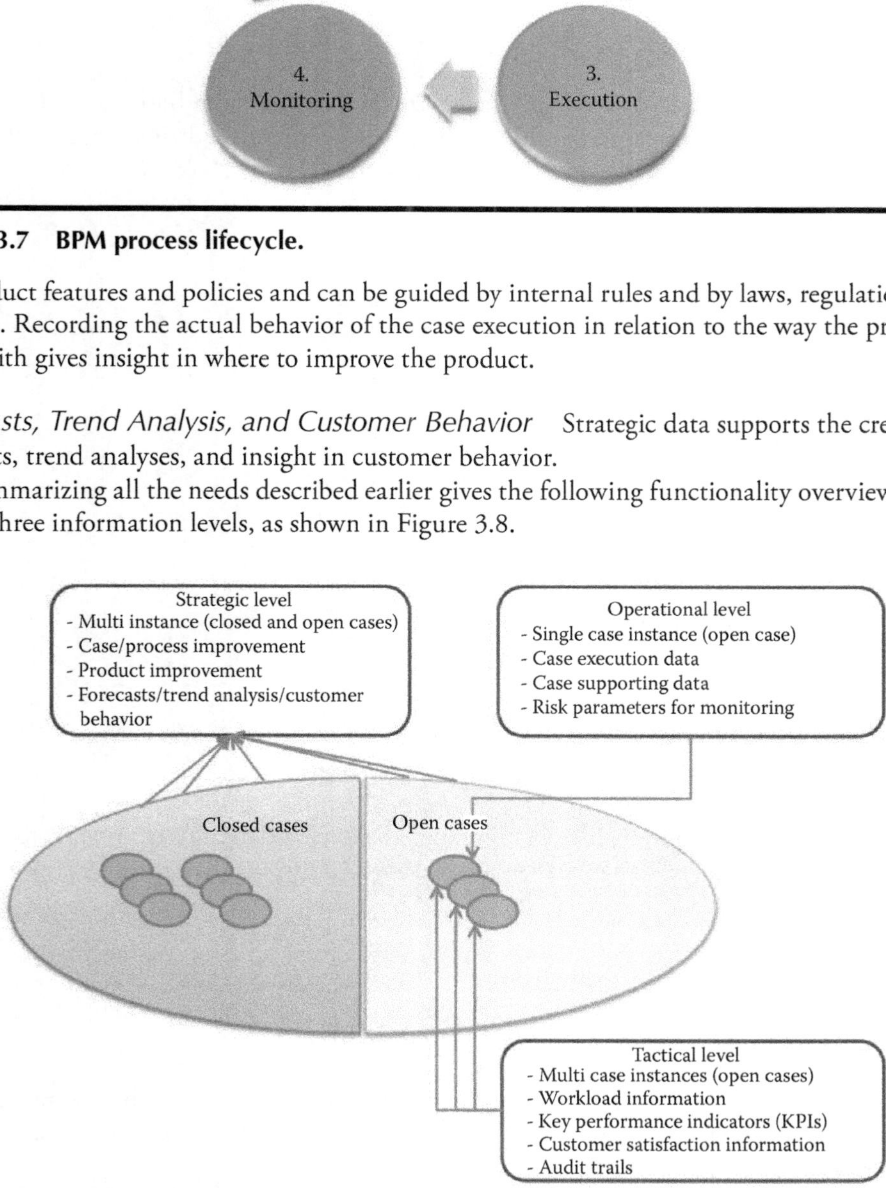

Figure 3.8 Information level–related case functionality.

3.3.3.3.2 Document and Media Design

Case workers can use a variety of documents and media during the case execution delivered as input to the case, and at the same time deliver documents as output. The input for a case is usually supported by a combination of structured and unstructured data such as social media input, video, or sound. The output of a case, as delivered by the case workers, is mostly of structured format, such as standardized documents.

The document and media design investigates the different forms and formats of the input and output material. Additionally, the sources of the input material and the amount of material that can be brought into the case needs to be analyzed.

3.3.3.3.3 People Relationship Design

During the execution of a case, multiple persons can be involved from both internal within the organization as well as external stakeholders. The people relationship design maps all the stakeholders involved in the case and enables interactions among the stakeholders.

Internal stakeholders:

- Case workers/owners
- Front/mid/back office
- Risk department
- Management

External stakeholders:

- Customers (and/or representatives)
- External specialists (such as fraud check specialists)
- Related companies and/or departments
- Victims, witnesses, culprits
- Press

3.3.4 Case Interaction Design Category

3.3.4.1 Aim

The case interaction design enables maximizing the support for the case work force. This design area contains three design parts: *portal design*, *dashboard design*, and *channel design* (Figure 3.9).

3.3.4.2 Relation with the Principles

This design category relates to the following principles:

- One centralized view of the case—Multiple activities can be executed by different persons, involving different data types during the execution of a case. A centralized overview is essential for the execution of a case.
- Collaboration and knowledge sharing—This encompasses the collaboration and knowledge needs to be supported by an interaction platform.

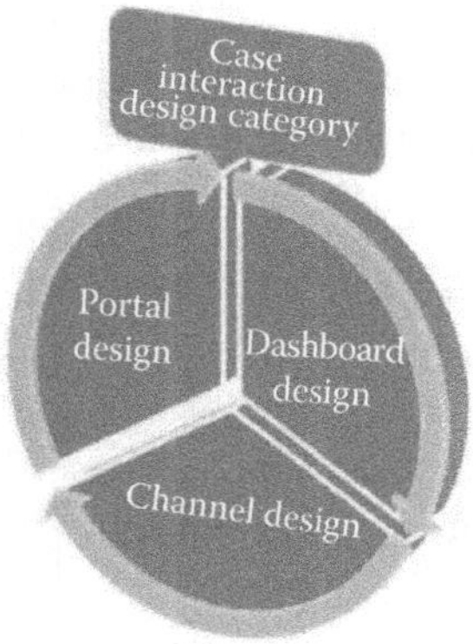

Figure 3.9 Case management interaction design category.

3.3.4.3 Case Management Interaction Design Components

3.3.4.3.1 Portal Functionality

The portal design supports all stakeholders in the case execution with a centralized view on case handling in two areas. The "one central view of the case" gives a complete overview of case details, activities, involved persons, history, decisions, and media. Depending on the role of the stakeholders, the full view or a subset of the case view is presented. Cases that contain customer interactions also need to have a "one overview of the customer" that provides the customer details, related parties, history of activities with the customer, and (optionally) a risk profile. Both the central view of the case and the central view of the customer can be partially shared with the customers.

3.3.4.3.2 Dashboard Functionality

Two types of dashboards are used in case management execution, the tactical related dashboards and strategic dashboards:

Tactical dashboards look at case progress and execution data from all running cases and test this data against predefined KPIs, check the operational performance management, and investigate the customer satisfaction related to the case execution. This functionality relates to the tactical related data as explained in Section 3.3.3.3.1. Dashboards give an insight in all these KPIs and workload related checks. Intelligence behind the dashboards combines data together and, based upon rules, visualize this data and provide insight when thresholds are exceeded.

Strategic dashboards sample data from all finished and still running cases and look at trend analysis, forecast predictions, and for improvement areas in the case execution. This functionality relates to the strategic-related data as explained in Section 3.3.3.3.1.

3.3.4.3.3 Channel Functionality

The case information and functionality can be exposed to the stakeholders via different channels, such as via browsers and mobiles apps. The channel design should be aimed at two communication types, internal and external communication. Internal communication specifically is necessary in cases where direct communication is needed to improve the quality of case work, and could be supported for instances by (secured) mobile access and messenger type of applications. External communication is aimed providing customers and other external stakeholders with case progress information and the ability to intervene with and deliver information to the case.

3.3.5 Case Cross-Functional Design Category

3.3.5.1 Aim

The cross-functionality design category contains the *integration design* and the *roles and authorization design* that both support the other functional design categories (Figure 3.10).

3.3.5.2 Relation with the Principles

This design category relates to the following principles:

- One centralized view of the case—*Roles and authorization*: *Different persons interact with* the centralized view. A security regime is needed to ensure that case participants can only perform activities and have access to information they are allowed to see based upon their role.
  Integration: Supports the delivery of the data needed in the centralized views.
- Collaboration and knowledge sharing—Collaboration and knowledge sharing is restricted according to a roles and authorization model.
- Spanning multiple applications—Integration enables the sharing of information and functionality across applications within the scope of a case.

3.3.5.3 Case Management Cross-Functional Design Components

3.3.5.3.1 Roles and Authorization

Stakeholders who participate in the case have different responsibilities, ranging from working on the case, completing intermediate results, closing the case, auditing the case, and owning the case. In order to ensure that every stakeholder is working within the limits of his responsibilities and has only access to the information tailored for him, a security model is needed.

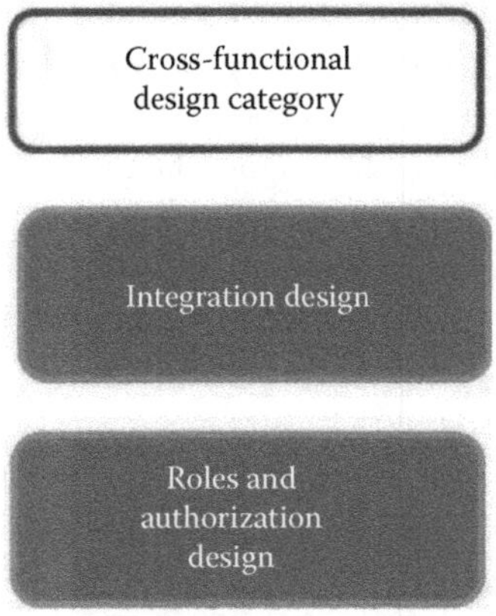

Figure 3.10 Case management cross-functional design category.

On a high level, the following stakeholder profiles can be identified in the context of a case:

- *Case owners* have the responsibility over the case or parts of the case. They are responsible for bringing the case, or parts of it, to a successful end. The ownership ranges from groupings on a case overarching level down to lower level process activity groupings and levels in between such as related to milestones.
- *Case workers* are the specialists in the field executing the work in case activity level. The case workers work in the different departments across the organizational structure of the companies involved, and are chosen because of their responsibilities and knowledge.
- *Customers*, the case is always aimed at delivering an end result for a customer. The customer can be an actual person, such as in a complaint case, another organization, or another case/process needing extra context for a research.
- *Management* is interested in the outcome and the performance of the case. They have their KPIs related to costs, efficiency, and result, which are defined upfront and measured during the execution of the case. Another operational task of management is the allocation of the case workers to the cases.
- *Auditor*, the role description of an auditor encompasses many aspects of financial, organizational and IT related areas. The activities that need to be done in the context of a case are assuring that all tactical related controls (amongst others compliance with regulations, customer agreements, and contracts with third parties) are implemented. Once implemented these controls need to be tested to assure that these are operating with sufficient effectiveness.
- *Risk officer*, in the context of a case the activities of the risk officer are making a risk profile of the cases and keeping track of these case risk parameters. When a case enters a high-risk state, the risk officer is allowed to intervene in the case activity.

The stakeholder interaction can be summarized in a case stakeholder interaction overview as shown in Figure 3.11. Cases where work is executed are in an open state. Cases that have completed in an end result are in a closed state. Case owners, case workers, customers, and risk officers work on cases with an open status. Auditors and management want to measure results on open and closed cases. Management is involved in allocating persons for cases in an open status.

3.3.5.3.2 Integration

Case management usually operates in a hybrid landscape and communicates with other applications to exchange information and manage activities. Three main areas can be identified where integration is needed in the scope of a case:

- Application integration—Relates to the interactions between the case system and other applications, where information is exchanged and functionality is started, and managed to support the case execution.
- Case integration—Relates to all integration activities that interact with the case lifecycle. A case can start and manage external or internal processes. These processes can be a short-lived series of activities or a long-running process, externalized to a separate internal system or to an external provider. A special type of application integration is on event entry initiated from an external application. An event can have direct impact on the case lifecycle or an interrupting event. An event can activate some activities that do not interrupt the current

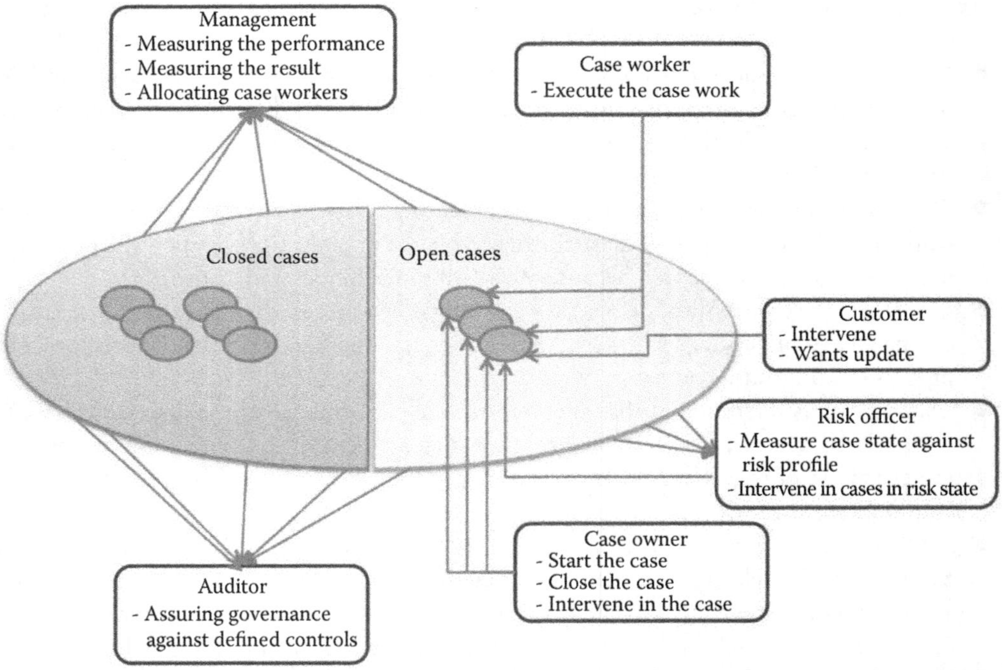

Figure 3.11 Case–stakeholder interaction overview.

case situation. Another topic related to case integration is interaction management between a case and an investigation started as part of a case.

- Portal and channel integration—Relates to the data provisioning for the portals needed to support the case workers, such as the one centralized view on the case, the one centralized view on the customer, and the KPI dashboards. All communication and interaction with the channels, such as internal communication, application support, web support relates to another integration topic for which support is needed.

3.4 Design Template

In this chapter, the different case management design components are described by looking at the high-level functionalities. In Table 3.2, the high-level requirements for a case management solution are summarized. This table will be used as a template in the upcoming chapters (Chapter 4) and Part IV to give an insight into the nature of the case management solution.

3.5 Conclusion

In this chapter, the *case management design components,* as part of the *case management solution framework*, are described. This framework enables the functional and technical designs of a case management solution. The design components form the first step in this framework.

In the previous chapters, we described the motivation, concepts, and the characteristics of a case management solution. With this knowledge of a case management solution, we derived principles

Table 3.2 Summary of Case Management Design Components

Case Design Category	*Case Design Component*	*High-Level Functionalities*
Case lifecycle design	Case flow and process design	The case flow specific for a case
	Rules design	Case lifecycle decision making Entitlement determination Progress measurement Data entry validation Information discovery
	Event design	Interrupting events Noninterrupting events
Case information design	Data design	Case execution data Case supporting data Tactical-related information Strategic data
	Document and Media design	Case input management Case output management
	People relationship design	Internal stakeholders External stakeholders
Case user interface design	Portal design	One central view on the case One overview of the customer
	Channel design	Internal communication External communication
	Dashboard design	KPI management Performance management Customer satisfaction determination
Cross-functional design	Integration design	Application integration Case integration Portal/channel integration
	Roles and Authorization	Internal profiles External profiles Compliance

for the case management design. In this chapter, we use three functional design categories and two cross-functional design categories to describe the case management functional requirements.

The *functional categories* each contain three design components:

- The *case lifecycle design category* with support for the coordination of activities in reaching one of the end goals
- The *case information design category* dealing with all sorts of data and documentation flowing through the case, and gives insight to the stakeholders and their relations
- The *case interaction design* maximizing the support for the case work force

The *cross-functional design components* support the functional design categories:

- The *case integration design* related to the delivery of functionality and information across all participating applications and stakeholders
- The *case roles and authorization design* ensures the execution responsibilities, visibility of data, and tracking and tracing across the case execution

We finished this chapter with a summary of the design components in a table format where a high-level overview of the functionalities is provided. This table will be used as a template in the upcoming chapters to give an insight in the nature of the case management solution.

Chapter 4

Case Management Classifications

4.1 Introduction

In this chapter of the case management solution framework, the case management classifications are discussed. The classifications are based upon the "Forrester's Classification of Case Management Solutions" that is introduced earlier in the book in Chapter 1 and contain the service request, incident management, and investigative solution.

The goals of this chapter are as follows:

- Provide characteristics for classification determination
- Provide alignment of the classifications with industry processes
- Determine principles for the classifications to guide the solution
- Use the case manage management design template to provide a high-level overview of the classifications
- Use the case flow and case state models to detail the case lifecycle design

4.2 Forrester Case Management Classifications

The "Forrester's Classification of Case Management Solutions" is introduced earlier in Section 1.4.5. In 2009, Forrester predicted the appearance of three broad categories of case management solutions: Service requests, incident management, and investigative solution. Looking through multiple industry processes, we identified alignment of the characteristics of these processes with the three Forrester classifications (Section 1.5.1). We will use the Forrester case management classifications as one of the key elements in the case management solution framework. These classifications are elaborated in the rest of this chapter. The observations we identified in Section 1.5.1 are used as input:

- Most real-life solutions display characteristics that could be found in a combination of two or more of the three types (i.e., service request, incident management and investigative).
- Investigative type of case work is typically triggered by either a service request or an incident reporting.
- There are wider variations in the types of case work (i.e., activities) that could be associated with incident management compared with service requests.
- A significant portion of case work tends to require human touch.
- Use of rules play a big part in construction of case management solutions.
- Many case management solutions need to adhere to laws and regulations.
- Handling of documents and content is an integral part of most case management solutions.
- Application integration shows up as a major solution component.
- Event handling is an integral part of most case management solutions.
- Security has high relevance in the solution.

4.3 Common Principles for the Classifications

Principles are used to guide the determination of the solution for the three case management classifications: service request, incident management, and investigative handling. Some of these principles are shared across all three classifications and are summarized in Table 4.1.

4.4 Service Request Classification

4.4.1 Context

Service requests deal with the process of delivering a service that a customer requested from a commercial organization or government agency. These service requests include complex interactions between the customer and the service provider and often contain investigations to reach the end result. The ability of the case workers to select and provide the components of the service necessary to satisfy the customer is critical to successful closure of the cases. In the interaction with the customer, different channels are used such as mail, Internet, mobile, direct communication, and letter. Processing the request within the organization is completed with a variety of processes and actions that require support from different departments and applications.

4.4.2 Determination

The following characteristics can be used to decide when a case is a service request:

- A customer requests a service.
- The service provider is a commercial organization or government agency.
- Complex interactions exist between the customer and the service provider.
- Customer satisfaction is crucial.

Table 4.1 Common Principles for the Case Management Classifications

Principle	*Statement*	*Rationale*	*Implications*
Standardize the process	Standardize the process flow to a reference model	Best practice in the market Improvement of time to market of new products	Every process with the same classification is handled in the same way The information model for every classification product is identical Insight in the efficiency of departments is available A standardized overview of outstanding requests is available
One centralized view of the case	Direct insight in what activities are done and which are in progress, who are involved, and what information is available	Be able to make decisions in relation to the case progress	Case steering is centralized Integration is key
Measuring the progress	Be able to show progress of the case	Be able to make decisions in relation to the case progress	Case progress indicators should be known Case real time state comparison against case progress indicators should be possible
Automate where possible	Automate the parts that speed up the efficiency of a service request product handling process via straight through processing (STP)	Lowering costs Standardized handling of a case classification process	Automation enables faster handling of a case product Integration is key Automation of complex rule verification avoids human errors
End-to-end auditing	All decisions and communication with the customer are recorded	Regulatory requirement Enables playback scenarios	Playback of why decisions are made is possible

- In many situations, the process is predictable.
- (Optionally) Complex policies and/or regulations determine service request entitlement.
- (Optionally) Regulatory requirements are important.

4.4.3 Alignment with Industry Processes

In Section 1.5.1, we analyzed a nonexhaustive list of standard processes across the different industries. In this analysis, we cross-checked these industry processes against the determination characteristics for a service request type of case. These processes are summarized in Table 4.2.

Table 4.2 Service Request Usage across Industry Processes

Horizontal/Common	Employee onboarding Customer onboarding AP and AR processing Facilities management Order/complaint/service exception management Trade and contracts management Complaints
PS + Social Services	Benefits eligibility Grants management Unemployment/welfare services Patent application processing Permits and operator licenses Child protection/substance abuser help/HIV advisory
Financial Services	New account opening Loan origination Investor servicing Regulatory reporting
Insurance	New account opening Policy management
Healthcare	Member enrollment
Legal + Police	Legal practice management, time tracking and billing
Energy & Utilities	Project and transmittals management Work order management

It is clear from this overview that service requests can be found across many industries. For two service request-related examples, more detail is provided in Chapter 12, for the *loan origination* and the *benefits eligibility* in Chapter 13.

4.4.4 Business Challenges

For all the service request industry processes, similar business challenges can be identified. These business challenges are related to *cost, customer handling, regulations and policies,* and *risk management.*

- *Customers* want to be serviced better and faster. Case workers dealing with the service request need to have all customer information available to avoid making errors during the service request handling. Specifically for the commercial organizations the way the companies position themselves to meet the customer needs impacts their operating model. More information on this topic can be found in the book *The Discipline of Market Leaders* by Wiersema (http://www.basicbooks.com/full-details?isbn=9780201407198):
  - Should they focus on *operational excellence* and deliver a standardized product for a low price?
  - Should they go for *customer intimacy* and deliver customized products?
  - Should they aim at *product leadership* in which they provide state-of-the art products?

  Making a choice among these operating strategies has an impact on the solution requirements.

- Stricter *regulations and policies* require end-to-end auditing for all service interactions. At the same time, these stricter regulations and policies need to be implemented at a faster pace by the service request supporting systems. This can be a challenge in the current system landscape.
- *Cost reduction* is an important driver for changes as a result of the financial crisis.
- More attention for fraud and financial risks requires improved *risk management* supporting for the case workers.

4.4.5 Principles for the Solution

The principles for a service request classification are based on the business challenges as defined in the previous section and the common principles described earlier in Section 4.3. Table 4.3 shows the service request-specific principles.

4.4.6 Case Management Design Components

In the first part of the case management solution framework in Chapter 3, we introduced the design components, three functional categories and two cross-functional categories that help describe the case management functionality. In the following sections, we will use the categories to describe the service request functionality. Specific focus will be given to the case lifecycle design category since this contains the core functionality of service request handling.

Table 4.3 Principles for the Service Request Classification

Principle	*Statement*	*Rationale*	*Implications*
One customer view	Provide a complete overview of the customer, personal information, and history of provided citizen services	No mistakes in handling the service request for the customer All case workers have the same understanding of the customer situation	Systems containing (and owning) customer information must be able to deliver customer information The ownership of customer details is clear Integration is key
End-to-end auditing	All decisions and communication with the customer are recorded	Regulatory requirement. Enables playback scenarios	Playback of why decisions are made and what options are offered to the customer is possible
Separation of know and flow	Keep the implementation of the process flow (the flow) and the decision management (the know) separate	Rules are related to laws and regulations and tend to change with a higher frequency than the case/process flow activities	Separate the implementation of decision management from the process flow

4.4.6.1 Service Request Design Category Overview

In Table 3.2, a design template is presented that will be used here. This template contains

- The case management design categories
- The design components that are related to the categories
- The high-level functional areas that are introduced

Table 4.4 is used to the provide an insight into the required functionalities for a service request, two extra columns are added to the original design template:

- The importance of a high-level functionality for the service request design
- The specific usage for a service request.

4.4.6.2 Case Lifecycle Design Category

The service request process can be broken down into two main parts, the triage and the case execution, as shown in Figure 4.1. In the triage, which is the first interaction with the customer, an assessment of the need for a service is investigated. When both parties have reached a decision that follow-up work is needed, the service request continues as a case containing investigations and complex interactions between the service provider and the customer. The triage and the service request handling have different characteristics; the triage is workflow-based and short-lived. The service request handling is case-oriented, containing investigations and customer interactions, and has a longer life span.

4.4.6.2.1 First Interaction with the Customer—The Triage

The customer raises a request for a specific product such as a request for a welfare service or a mortgage. In the first interaction with the customer, the actual need and priority for the service is investigated. When a customer wants to buy a house, without having made an offer on a house, the first interaction only involves providing information on the mortgage products and the mortgage loan amount that can be provided based upon salary and no follow-up activities are executed. In the situation where the customer actually has found a house that fulfills their needs, the assessment evaluates if the mortgage product is aligned with the needs of the customer. When the customer and the mortgage provider decide to continue, this stage is closed and follow-up work will be started.

Figure 4.2 shows the case flow model of the interaction during the triage. The case flow model is introduced earlier in Chapter 3.

In the triage phase, the following stakeholders participate:

- The customer who entered the service request
- The first line of contact who is responsible for all activities in this phase
- The case owner who registers the case after the decision is made to continue the service request

Table 4.4 Service Request Design Overview

Case Design Category	*Case Design Component*	*High Level Functionalities*	*Service Request-Specific Usage*
Case lifecycle design	Case flow/process design	The case flow specific for a case	See Section 4.4.6.2 and Figures 4.2 and 4.3
	Rules design	Case lifecycle decision making	See Sections 4.4.6.2.1 and 4.4.6.2.2
		Entitlement determination	Determine the service request entitlement Agree/not agree Related value Periodicity Terms for which the decisions applies
		Progress measurement	Related to agreements with and expectancy of customers, regulatory demand, and/or internal performance management
		Data entry validation	Validating entry data for the request
		Information discovery	This relates to any investigation where the quality of the service request can be improved or the service request is checked against fraudulent behavior. This often includes verification against large combined (un) structured data sources
	Event design	Interrupting events	See Section 4.4.6.2
		Noninterrupting events	See Section 4.4.6.2
Case information design	Data design	Case execution data	Be able to follow the case execution across the various stakeholders and activities
		Case supporting data	Service request related data

(Continued)

Table 4.4 (*Continued*) Service Request Design Overview

Case Design Category	*Case Design Component*	*High Level Functionalities*	*Service Request-Specific Usage*
	Document and media design	Case input management	Service request input, structured data
		Case output management	Service Request output, mostly documents
	People relationship design	Internal stakeholders	Case owner/workers, front, middle, back office, management
		External stakeholders	Customers External specialists Related companies/departments
Case user interface design	Portal design	One central view on the case	A centralized overview of the service request proceedings is required by all stakeholders
		One overview of the customer	One of the key elements in the determination of the service request is a full overview of the customer
	Channel design	Internal communication	Interaction between case workers and first line of contact
		External communication	Customer interaction
	Dashboard design	KPI management	Cost driven
		Performance management	Cost driven
		Customer satisfaction determination	Avoid potential loss of the customer

(*Continued*)

Table 4.4 (*Continued*) Service Request Design Overview

Case Design Category	*Case Design Component*	*High Level Functionalities*	*Service Request-Specific Usage*
Cross-functional design	Integration design	Application integration	Depends on the service request related IT landscape
		Case integration	During the entitlement, determination processes in different departments/systems can be started. For instance in the entitlement process for a welfare request the tax department is cross-checked for taxation history and behavior
		Portal/Channel integration	Delivering information for the portals and for determination of service request entitlement
	Roles and authorization	Internal profiles	Depends on the sensitivity of the service request case
		External profiles	Profiles determine the amount of information that is shared with the customer via different channels: Direct interaction with the first line of contact One central view on the case One central view of the customer

Figure 4.1 The service request classification—two interactions.

The service request triage contains the following activities:

- Create service request: The customer requests the service via a channel such as online, via a letter, or via direct contact with the service provider.
- Receive customer information: In this step, all information coming from the customer is received. This information is stored for later reference and routed to a person who can perform the first assessment.
- Assess and assign: After receiving the service request, the actual need and priority for the service is investigated by the "first line of contact" and, if needed, rerouted to another person.
- Create result: From the received information and the first assessment, preliminary results can be created for discussion with the customer.
- Share results–discuss results: In this two-step interaction, the first line of contact and the customer discuss the result of the first assessment.
- Create case and finalize: These two steps are the final steps in the triage activity. The customer and the service provider decide to continue working on the service request. Afterward, the service is registered as a case or the work done so far is deemed sufficient and no follow-on work is required. In this situation, the work is finalized.

The triage workflow can be interrupted by two events originating from the customer. These include interrupting and noninterrupting events:

Interrupting events:

- Intervene
  The customer can intervene in the activities when they want to stop the service request or extra information can be delivered that might change the assessment decision.

Noninterrupting events:

- Ask for update
  The customer can ask for an update if the triage assessment takes longer than expected. This is a noninterrupting event.

4.4.6.2.2 The Second Interaction with the Customer—Service Request Handling

Once the decision has been made in the triage stage to continue working on the service request, a case is created and a series of assessments, investigations, and discussions with the customer are executed until a result is reached that meets both the customer and the service provider expectations. One of the characteristic features of the service request pattern is that it has a predictable lifecycle. The service request case lifecycle contains one or more phases each of which ends in a milestone. A milestone signifies important activity completion points in the case progression and determines when a business goal or target is met.

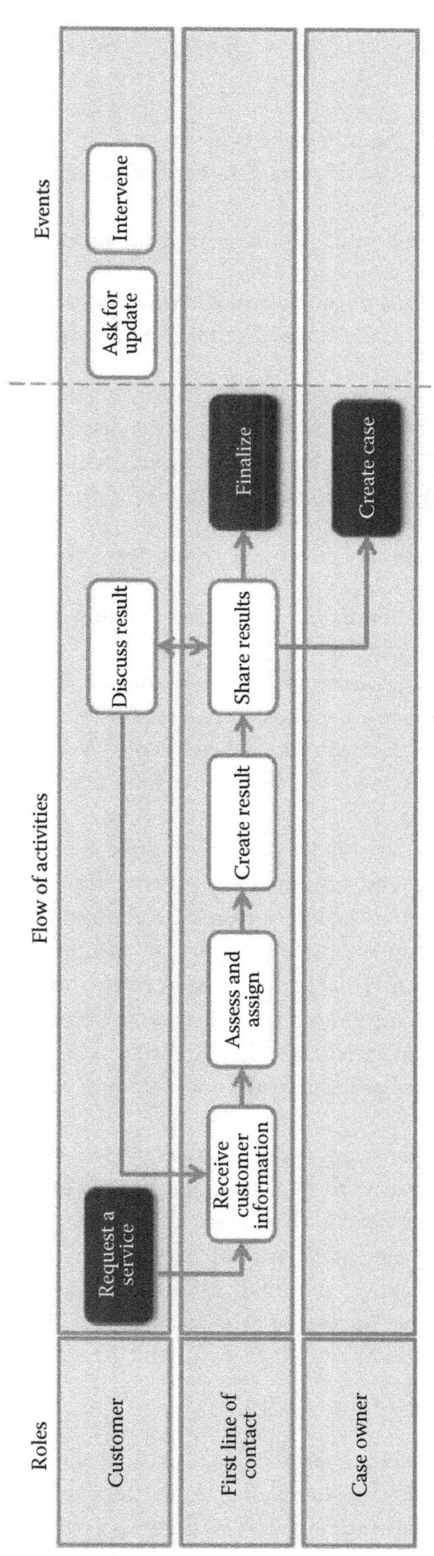

Figure 4.2 The service request triage—case flow model.

When looking at the mortgage example (Chapter 12), three phases can be distinguished: *loan application* (*sales*), *mortgage origination,* and *mortgage fulfillment*. Each of these phases has the same high-level structure:

- An assessment to see if the milestone is met.
- Follow-up investigations working out the service request details.
- Discussions with the customer.
- The phase can be iterated multiple times until the milestone is met.

Figure 4.3 shows the details of the flow of activities in the service request case handling.
In the case handling phase, the following stakeholders participate:

- The customer, who now is engaged in discussions related to the (in-between) results
- The first line of contact who is now acting as the discussion partner with the customer
- The case owner who is actively leading the service request case
- The case workers who are responsible for handling the service request details

The case handling work of the service request contains the following activities:

- *Create case*: If the triage results in a decision that follow-up work for the service request needs to be done, a case is created by the case owner.
- *Loop of investigation and discussion for different milestones*: This is a continuous loop of investigation and involves interactions with the customer until one of the (intermediate) goals is met.
  - *Assess and assign*: After each loop, the case owner makes an assessment if the milestone (or end result) is reached. When another loop is required, the case owner decides what activities need to be done.
  - *Start investigation*: In this stage, one or more investigations are executed in order to reach the required end result. These investigations are started as a separate case and can contain work such as determining the allowed mortgage amount for the customer, deciding the entitlement for a customer based upon laws and regulation, or executing a fraud investigation. This work can be done by internal case workers or by outsourced specialists. The output of each investigation is a report that is used by the case owner to determine follow-up activities in in the execution of the service request.
  - *Create result*: All in-between results and decisions are stored for later reference and end-to-end auditing.
  - *Share results, discuss result, receive customer information*: The (in-between) results are shared and discussed with the customer. This is followed by a decision from the customer on how to proceed with the service request.
- *Finalize*: Once an agreement is reached between the customer and the service provider, whether positive or negative, the final activities are executed. These include activities such as signing of the contract, delivery of products, and setting payment schedules in motion.

4.4.6.2.3 Service Request State Model

The state model of the service request pattern is a predictable flow of activities ordered by one or more phases as shown in Figure 4.4. This state model shows the significance of customer interactions during the case execution. The closure of every phase depends on the agreement with the customer. If no agreement is reached at the end of a phase, the phase is repeated or the case is terminated.

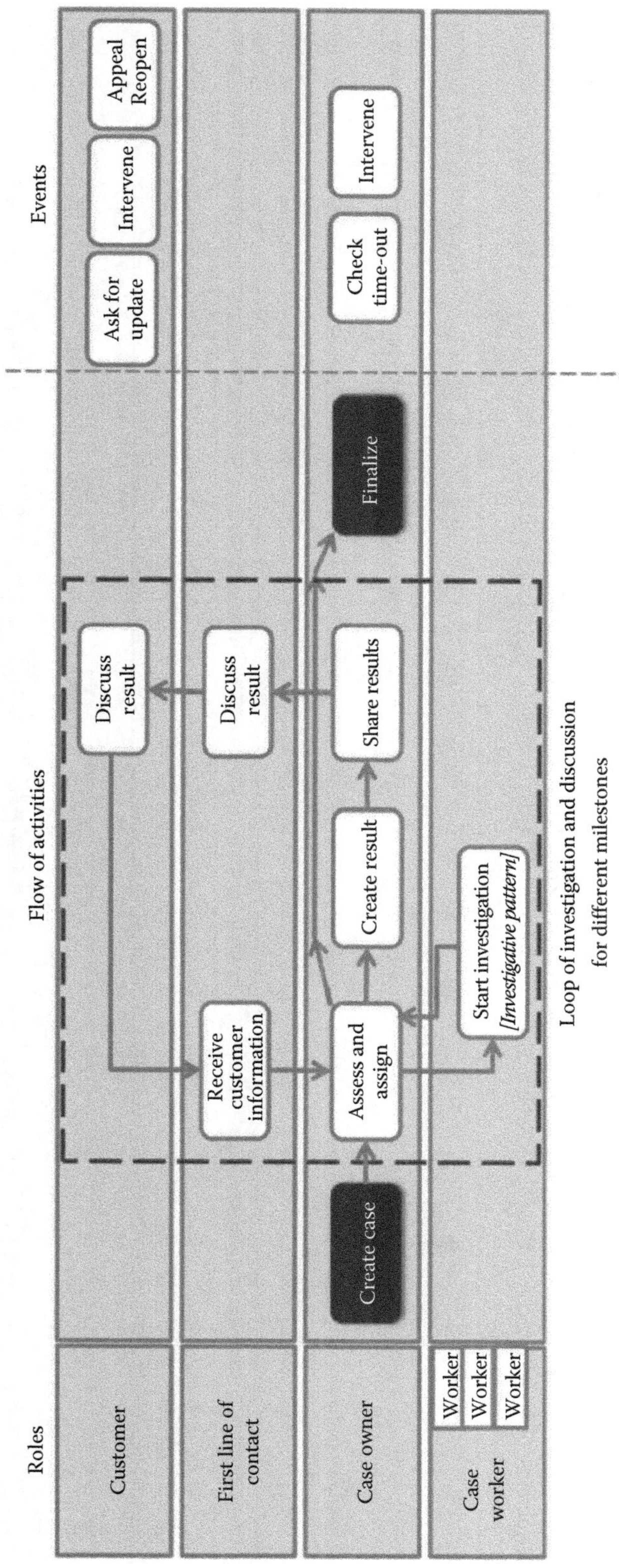

Figure 4.3 The service request case handling work—case flow model.

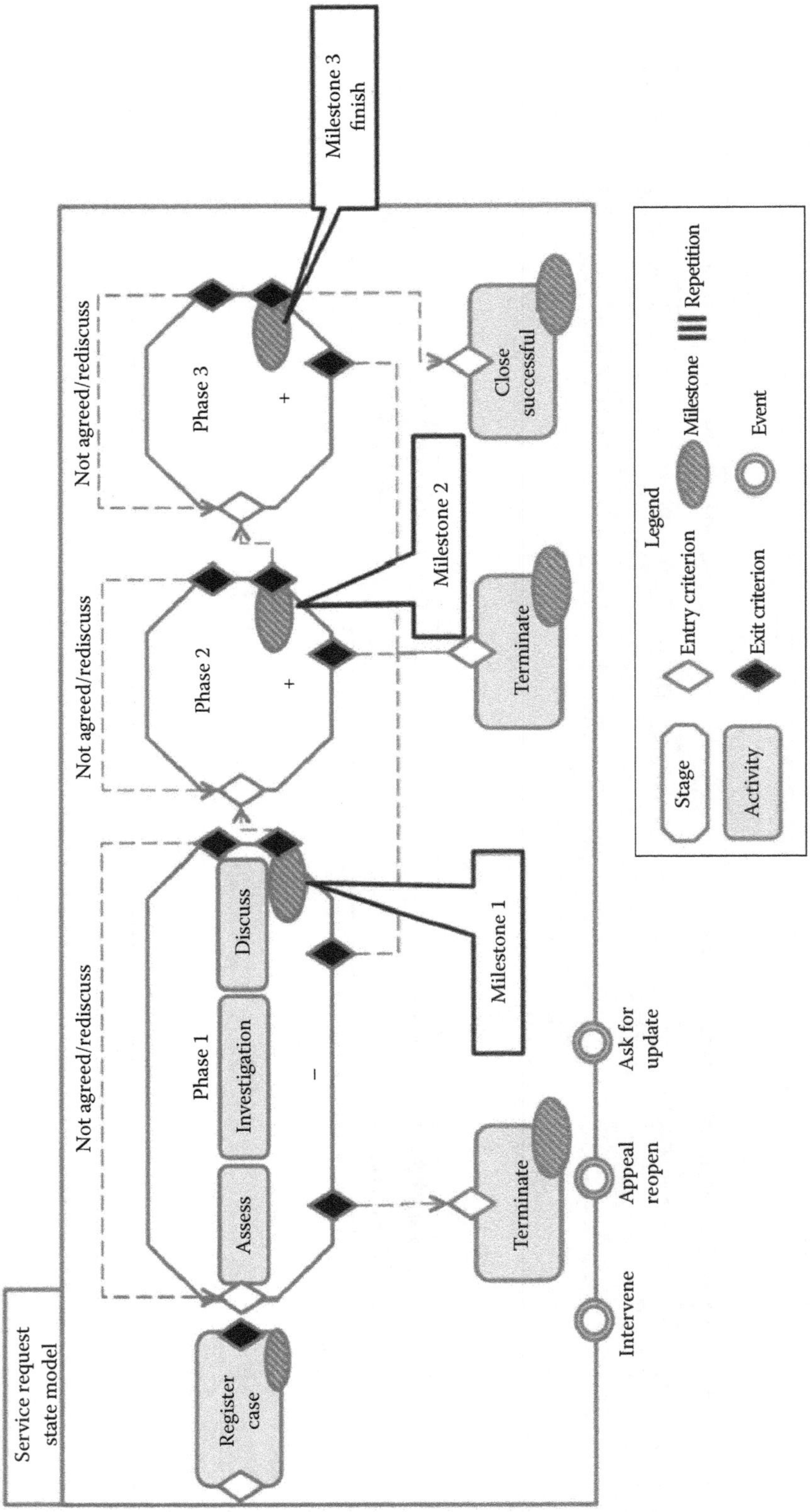

Figure 4.4 Case-state model for service request.

For figurative reasons in Figure 4.4, three phases and related (intermediate) milestones are shown. Real-life cases can have different amounts of phases and milestones.

A phase is a series of activities leading toward a (in-between) result. It is closed when a milestone is reached or when the activities are terminated. The activities within the phase align with the "loop of investigation and discussion for different milestones" in Figure 4.3. In Figure 4.4, these activities are summarized by the three main activities: *assess*, *investigate*, and *discuss*.

Events play a more important role in the case handling part than in the initial assessment workflow phase. This case handling part can be interrupted by events originating from the customer and the case owner.

Interrupting events

- Intervene:
  - This can be the same interrupting event for the customer as in the triage.
  - The case owner can intervene in the case execution when a situation occurs where the execution of activities of the case needs to be altered. For example, at one point in the mortgage service request handling, a suspicion of fraud is raised. The case owner makes a decision to suspend all activities, start a fraud investigation, contact the legal department, and send a formal statement to the customer describing the proceedings.
- Time-out checks:
  The case owner is responsible for timely handling of all activities in the case. Every activity can have requirements around execution and/or communication timings. These may be related to regulatory requirements, agreements with customers, or internal performance agreements. Some of these timing requirements are translated into KPIs for the case owners or one of the other stakeholders. On an operational level, performance dashboards give an insight into the progress of these timing related KPIs.
- Appeal and/or reopen:
  Closing the case is the final stage for a service request handling. However, there are situations that require reopening the case after it is closed. The customer may not be satisfied with the result of the service request handling and may want to reopen the case for further investigation or better service. This can be escalated until the point that the customer files an appeal in court against the service provider.

Noninterrupting events

- Ask for update:
  This may be the same noninterrupting event for the customer as in the triage.

4.5 Incident Management Case Classification

4.5.1 Context

"Expect the unexpected" is a good way to describe incident management. We need to be prepared, but hope that the unexpected will not happen. Most of the time the connotation with incident management is not positive. The aim of an incident-related case is to alleviate a problem that occurred and includes providing help to persons and/or bringing situations to justice.

4.5.2 Determination

The following characteristics can be used to determine the case management classification for an incident management type of case:

- Incident handling is aimed at solving the problem and finding the root cause.
- Initiation of an incident may be unpredictable.
- The high-level execution of an incident is predictable, but certain parts of the execution are highly influenced by events.
- Both internal and external communication is key.
- Data related to an incident is both structured and unstructured by nature.
- Intelligence is needed to solve the case.
- (Optionally) Incident may be started by a customer.
- (Optionally) Regulatory requirements are often important.

4.5.3 Alignment with Industry Processes

The nonexhaustive list of industry processes that relate to incident management, as we analyzed in Section 1.5.1, is presented in Table 4.5. This list is much smaller then what was presented in the previous chapter for service requests. Two incident-related examples are detailed in Chapters 14 and 15.

4.5.4 Business Challenges

Three main business challenge areas can be identified that impact the way the incident management pattern is defined: the *effectiveness of the organization*, *costs reduction*, and *improved external facing communication*.

- Effectiveness of the organization:
  - Better effective internal communication is needed.
  - Improved supporting IT landscape for efficient and effective operation is required.
- Cost reduction can be an important driver for change as a result of the financial crisis. In both the public and financial market budgets are under pressure that impacts the way processes are executed.
- Improved external facing communication.
- The communication with all external stakeholders needs to be improved and formalized.

Table 4.5 Incident Management Usage across Industry Processes

Public + Social Services	Environmental safety monitoring Disaster relief Terror/Epidemic threat handling
Financial Services	Dispute resolution Corporate communications Fraud and money laundering investigations
Insurance	Property and Casualty claims processing
Legal + Police	Crime recording
Energy and Utilities	Process safety management

Table 4.6 Principles for the Incident management classification

Principle	*Statement*	*Rationale*	*Implications*
Communication	Formalize the communication between internal and external stakeholders	Improved internal communication leads to more efficient and effective operation. In some incident cases, the external communication needs to be formalized, for example, to avoid premature coverage in the press, that might disrupt the investigation. When the incident relates to a customer problem, the communication should be brought to the level the customer accepts as fair.	Technology needed to support the internal communication All external communication is redirected to a specific department.

4.5.5 Principles for the Solution

The principles for an incident management classification are based on the business challenges as defined in the previous section and the common principles described earlier in Section 4.3. In Table 4.6, an additional incident management specific principle is added:

4.5.6 Case Management Design Components

4.5.6.1 Incident Management Design Category Overview

Table 4.7 provides an overview of the functionalities need for an Incident management design.

4.5.6.2 Case Lifecycle Design Category

The incident case pattern can be broken down into different phases, each with their own characteristics and behavior, as shown in Figure 4.5. These phases include *being prepared, monitoring the incident risk parameters, acting upon the incident,* and *evaluate.* The work done in the "being prepared" phase is used to prepare the workers what to do when an incident happens. This phase has a short duration. The "monitoring the risk parameters" phase checks, on a regular basis, the likelihood of an incident happening in the near future. The duration of this phase is infinite since this is a continuous activity. When an incident happens, the workers use the templates prepared earlier and can process the information gathered during the monitoring phase, depending on the incident type and severity. This phase can be of short, medium, or long duration. After the work is finished, an evaluation can be used to improve the template and preparation work and also to help adjust the risk parameters used in the monitoring phase.

We start with a short description of the *being prepared, monitoring the incident risk parameters,* and *evaluate* phases. For the *acting upon the incident* phase, a case flow model and case state model will be provided.

Being prepared: This phase ensures that the preparation is done in case an incident occurs. The team is ready to react directly in an organized way with checklists, work templates, activity lists, responsibility schemes, communication schemes (for both internal and external),

Table 4.7 Incident Management Design Overview

Case Design Category	*Case Design Component*	*High Level Functionalities*	*Incident Management Specific Usage*
Case lifecycle design	Case flow/ process design	The case flow specific for a case	See Section 4.5.6.2
	Rules design	Case lifecycle decision-making	See Section 4.5.6.2
		Entitlement determination	Only in Incident cases where customers are involved
		Progress measurement	In order to reach the end goals in a timely fashion, progress measurement is key in an incident where a variety of persons can be involved. Certain parts of the incident process are influenced highly by events and investigations that are started as part of an incident handling
		Data entry validation	Only in incident cases where customers are involved
		Information discovery	The monitoring part in the incident process relies on information discovery. See Section 4.5.6.2
	Event design	Interrupting events	See Section 4.5.6.2
		Non-interrupting events	See Section 4.5.6.2

(Continued)

Table 4.7 (*Continued*) Incident Management Design Overview

Case Design Category	*Case Design Component*	*High Level Functionalities*	*Incident Management Specific Usage*
Case information design	Data design	Case execution data	Be able to follow the case execution across the various stakeholders
		Case supporting data	Incident management-related data
		Tactical related information	Compliance-related
		Strategic data	Forecasts, trend analysis, improvement of incident related predication models
	Document and media design	Case input management	Incident Management input, structured and unstructured data
		Case output management	Incident Management output, mostly documents
	People relationship design	Internal stakeholders	Case owner/workers, front-mid-back office, management, risk department
		External stakeholders	Customers External specialists Related companies/departments Victims, witnesses, culprits Press
Case user interface design	Portal design	One central view on the case	A centralized overview of the incident management proceedings is required by all stakeholders
		One overview of the customer	Only in Incident cases where customers are involved

(*Continued*)

Table 4.7 (*Continued*) Incident Management Design Overview

Case Design Category	*Case Design Component*	*High Level Functionalities*	*Incident Management Specific Usage*
	Channel design	Internal communication	Internal communication between the case workers is key
		External communication	The communication with all external stakeholders needs to be improved and formalized.
	Dashboard design	KPI management	Cost driven
		Performance management	Cost driven
		Customer satisfaction determination	Only in incident cases where customers are involved
Cross-functional design	Integration design	Application integration	It depends on the Incident Management-related IT landscape. Often, an Incident is operated in a hybrid application landscape
		Case integration	All events that intervene with the incident are entered here. In the context of an Incident, case many investigation can be started that interact with the case lifecycle
		Portal/Channel integration	Combine data from disparate sources to provision the portals
	Roles and authorization	Internal profiles	It depends on the sensitivity of the Incident management case. Often incidents handle sensitive situations
		External profiles	Profiles determine the amount of information that is shared with the external stakeholders via different channels

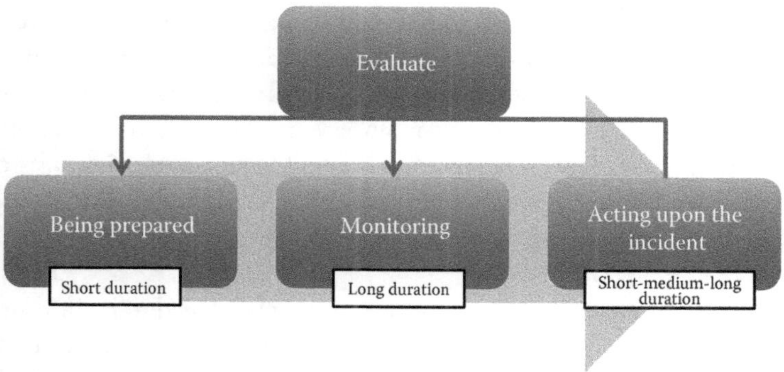

Figure 4.5 Incident management classification—phases.

and access to the information sources. This phase is very structured and predictable and contains milestones aimed at delivering checklists, templates, monitoring preparation, team setup, and training. The preparation phase also includes determination of the risk parameters for the monitoring phase. The duration of this phase is relatively short.

Monitoring the incident risk parameters: In this phase, the risk parameters related to the incident are monitored against "live" data. This information helps predicting the likelihood of an incident in the near future. This, in turn, helps lowering the impact of the incident by early ramp-up of the incident workers. The monitoring measurements are based upon both structured and unstructured information and are enriched with existing information to execute the analysis. All information gathered in this phase is stored for later usage in incident investigations. Business intelligence analysis of the monitored information can also be used to discern trends and improve what needs to be measured. The monitoring process can be implemented as an automated "sleeper" process that gathers and analyzes the information. When the "sleeper" process notices a deviation from the risk parameters, an event is raised and an incident case can be started. Examples range from monitoring the bank payments for getting an insight in fraud and money laundering incidents to monitoring the tectonic movement for an earthquake incident.

Evaluate: Feedback and experiences from incidents are used to improve incident handling and monitoring. These experiences help improve the incident execution in four areas:

- Incident handling, by adding or changing activities, adjusting the work force, and/or outsourcing some activities to external specialist organizations.
- Monitoring, by improving the risk parameters, measurement, and monitoring calculation
- Improving intelligence that helps to drive decisions in the incident handling, by including new data sources, better intelligence methods, or tooling
- Performance management for driving down the costs by improving the workload of the incident workforce.

4.5.6.2.1 Acting upon the Incident—Process Flow

When an incident happens, an incident case is created and the case workers start processing according to the checklists and templates developed in the preparation phase. This work includes investigation of the incident, helping people or groups who are inflicted by the incident, finding potential culprits (depending on the industry process), and preparing work after the incident is closed. Communication, both internally and externally, during the incident resolution, can be crucial depending on the incident case. This phase is guided by the templates and checklists that are created earlier in the *prepare* phase. Events are a main driver for altering the flow of activities. Both structured content and unstructured content are used for the investigation.

Figure 4.6 shows the case flow for an incident where four main activity areas can be seen: the *loop of incident activities*, *close case*, *communication* (both internal and external), and *events*.

In the case handling phase, the following stakeholders participate:

- External stakeholders. Generally, these stakeholders want/need to be informed on the progress of the incident. In a police investigation, this can be the press and in a fraud investigation, this can be the central bank and/or shareholders.
- Depending on the incident industry process, external communication offers a formalized channel with the external stakeholders as needed.
- The incident reporter role depends on the incident triggering event and the incident industry process. In an insurance claim case, the incident is reported by the customer. In a criminal case, the incident can be started by a police officer. Incidents can also be started as a result of (automated) monitoring, for instance, by a bank payment monitoring process that initiated a potential fraud incident.
- The case owner is actively leading the incident case and assesses/prioritizes the current situation and assigns work to case workers. When the incident can be closed, they initiate the closing activities.
- The case workers are responsible for the investigations and/or execution of the high-level incident work.

The case handling work of an incident consists of the following activities:

- *Register case*: An incident is created as a result of it being reported by either an incident reporter or an automated event.
- *Loop of incident handling activities*: This is a continuous loop of investigation and high-level incident work.
  - *Assess and assign*: After each loop, the case owner makes an assessment if the end result is reached. When another loop is required, the case owner makes a decision on which follow-up activities need to be done, how these are prioritized and who is going to execute these activities. The case owner is also responsible for initiating external communication via the external communication role.
  - *Investigate*: Part of the incident handling is investigating root causes, responsible persons, and ways to solve the incident problem. The output of each investigation is used by the case owner to determine follow-up activities in the execution of the incident. It is also used by (other) case workers to decide how to execute the work in the incident work activities (amend and aid). The investigations are started as separate cases and can be executed by internal case workers or outsourced specialists.
  - *Amend and aid*: Depending on the incident industry processes, incidents might cause damages to property, personal belongings, financial situations of persons or companies, or personal (health) situations. The incident "amend and aid" activities are aimed at alleviating these problems, for example, by providing insurance compensation or direct aid to persons.
  - *Create result*: All in-between results and decisions are stored for later reference and end-to-end auditing.

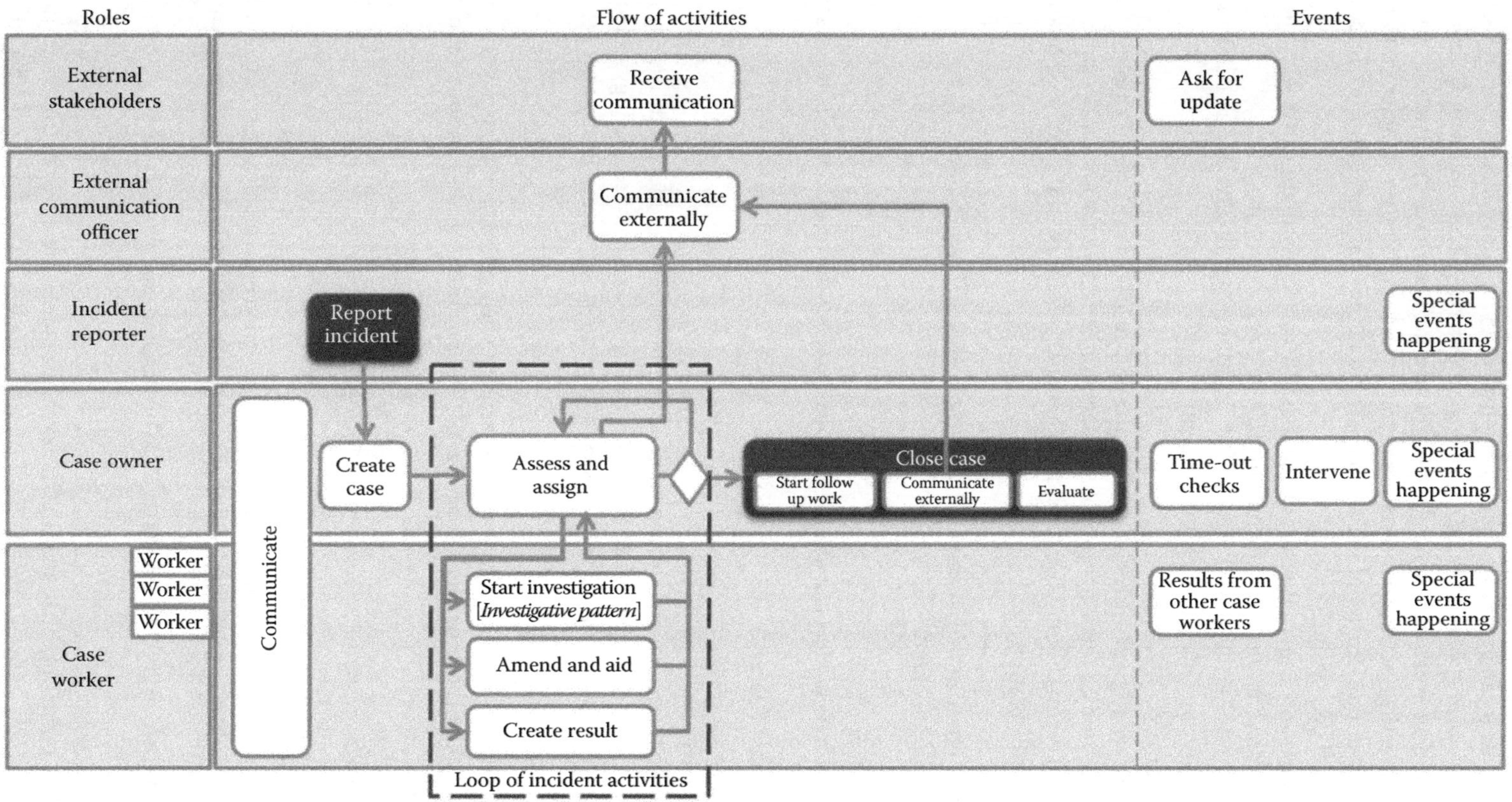

Figure 4.6 Incident management classification—case flow model.

- *Close the case*: In the assessment phase, the case owner decides, based upon predefined exit criteria, if the incident can be closed. The closing phase of an incident contains three main activities:
  - *Start follow up work*: Depending on the industry, process follow-up work might be needed. This work might not be part of the incident handling itself. For instance, a fraud investigation in a bank results in fraud case against one customer that needs to be brought to trial. The fraud incident case initiates the trial case, but is not responsible for the actual proceeding of the fraud case.
  - *Communicate*: The final result of the incident case is communicated with the external stakeholders via the external communication role.
  - *Evaluate*: An evaluation of the incident handling (optionally) is started. This helps in improving the incident handling process.
- Communicate:
  This activity is aligned with the communication principle and specifically to "improved internal communication leads to more efficient and effective operation." Faster insight into (in-between) results among the different teams helps improve the speed and quality of the incident handling work.

This incident case flow can be interrupted by multiple events. These include

external stakeholder–related events:

- Ask for update:
  The external stakeholders can ask for an update to get informed about the latest status.

Case owner–related events:

- Time-out checks:
  The case owner is responsible for the timely handling of all activities in the case. Every activity can have requirements around execution and/or communication timings and are related to regulatory requirements, agreements with external stakeholders, or internal performance agreements.
- Intervene:
  The case owner can intervene in the case execution when a situation occurs where the execution activities of the case need to be altered. Intervention can also include termination of the work.

Case worker–related events:

- Results from other case workers:
  Internal communication is the key for the good operation of an incident case. Any (in-between) results from other case workers can influence the work others in the team are executing.

For all three stakeholders, incident reporter, case owner, and case worker:

- Special events:
  A situation occurring that has the potential to alter the flow of the case drastically. For instance, in a police investigation, a special situation such as new evidence or witnesses giving new information can influence the course of the investigations.

4.5.6.2.2 The Incident Handling Case State Flow

The state model of the incident handling contains two main work phases: *handle incident* and *close incident*, as presented in Figure 4.7. A phase is a series of activities leading toward a (in-between) result and closes when a milestone is reached or when the activities are terminated.

The *handle incident phase* contains three internal phases. The *lead incident* activities, assess, prioritize, assign, and communicate, are executed by the case owner. In this phase, the case owner determines if the end result is met, if follow-up work needs to be done. In addition, they determine what type of work needs to be done. This work comes in two flavors: *investigate* and *amend and aid*. These flavors are described in more detail in the incident case flow. The lead incident phase has three milestones through which this phase can be finished:

- *Incident handling ended*: where the incident handling exit criteria are met. This closes the main phase *handle incident*.
- *Continue work*: where the incident handling exit criteria are not met and more work needs to be done. Based upon the decision of the case owner, more investigation work, and/or amend and aid work is needed.
- *Terminate*: where the incident handling exit criteria are not met and the decision is taken to stop the incident handling work.

Both the *investigate* and *amend and aid* end with the same milestones:

- *Work is finished*, after which the result is handed over to the case owner, who uses this result in a next iteration of the lead incident phase.
- *Terminate,* where the work is terminated by the case workers. For instance, when the case owner terminates the case, all investigation, and/or amend and aid work needs to be stopped as well.

The *close incident* phase contains three activities: start follow-up work, communicate, and evaluate already discussed in the previous section.

Different events intervene in the lifecycle of the incident lifecycle. These are attached to main case level and to the different phases. On the main case level, four events can be identified: *intervene, reopen, ask update,* and *special events*. Attached to the *investigate* and *amend and aid* phases, three events are attached. These include *results from other case workers, terminate,* and *special events*.

4.6 Investigative Case Classification

4.6.1 Context

In Section 1.5.1, we analyzed industry patterns for the Forrester case management classifications and identified that the investigative type of case work is typically triggered by either a service request or an incident handling case in order to deliver intelligence needed in the case flow.

In the case flow models for service request and incident management, we added investigation activities as part of the case flow, as shown in Figures 5.3 and 5.6. These investigations are executed by the case workers as part of the service request provider or incident handling party, but they can also be outsourced to external specialists and/or (partially) automated. The characteristics

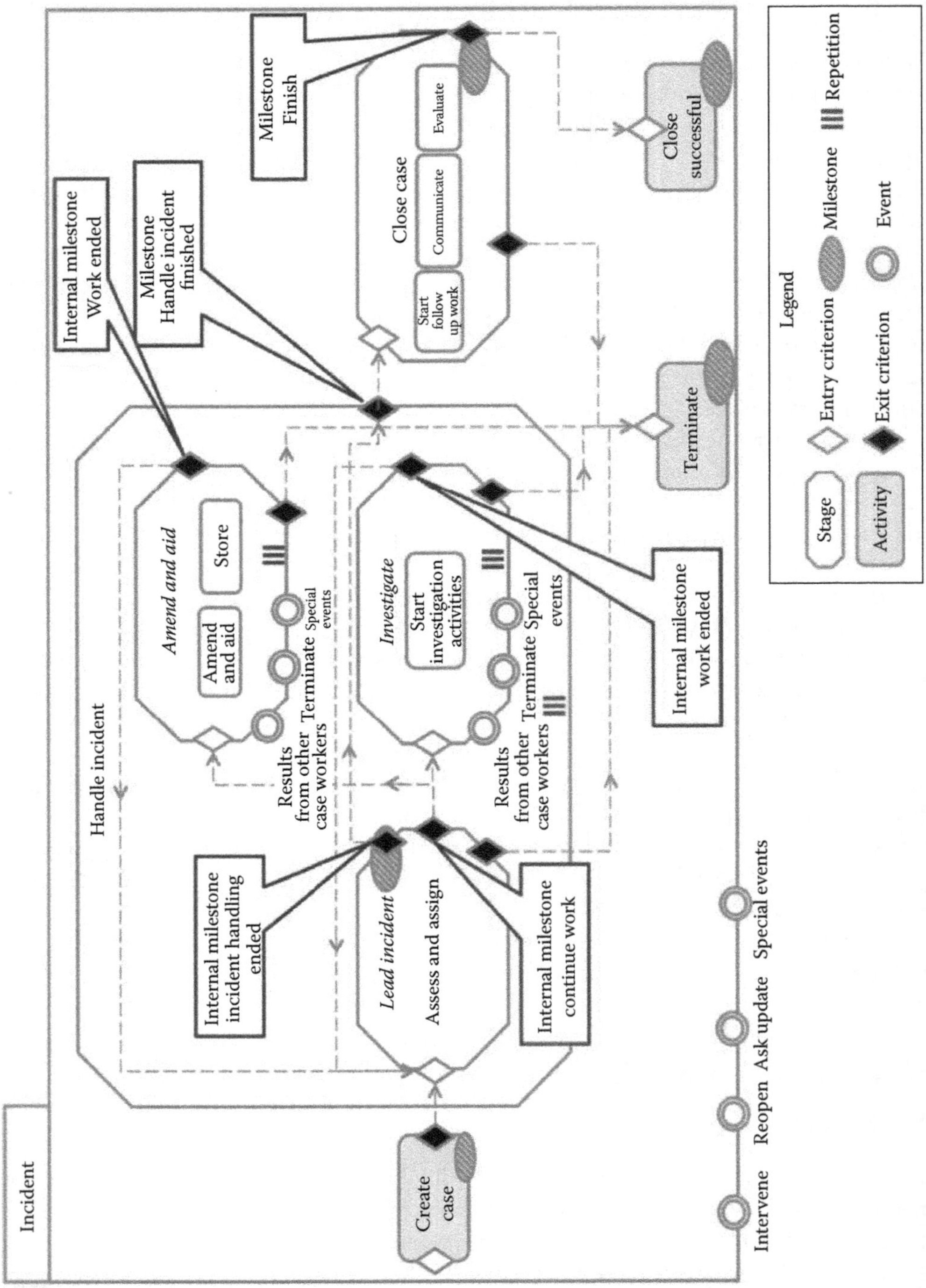

Figure 4.7 Case state model for incident management.

of these investigations range from a predictable set of activities to an event-driven case execution supported by data originating from both structured and unstructured data sources.

4.6.2 Determination

The following characteristics can be used to determine the case management classification for an investigative handling type of case:

- They are started as part of a service request or an incident.
- Investigative cases are aimed at delivering intelligence.
- The high-level execution of an investigation is predictable.
- Certain parts of the execution are highly influenced by events.
- Internal communication is the key.
- Data related to an investigation can be both structured and unstructured.
- An investigation can also initiate new investigative cases.
- (Optionally) Regulatory requirements may play a role.

4.6.3 Alignment with Industry Processes

All industry processes mentioned in Sections 4.4 and 4.5 can include investigations in the case flow.

4.6.4 Business Challenges

Investigative cases are started from a service request or an incident case as discussed earlier. The business challenges related to these classifications also impact the investigative type of cases. Here, we will use the business challenges that are needed in both the service request and the incident management cases:

- Better effective internal communication is needed in order to improve the effectiveness of the organization.
- Cost reduction is an important driver for changes as a result of the financial crisis.
- Stricter regulations and policies require end-to-end auditing.

4.6.5 Principles for the Solution

The principles for an investigative handling classification are based on the business challenges as defined in the previous section and the common principles described earlier in Section 4.3. In Table 4.8, an additional incident management specific principle is added:

Table 4.8 Principles for the Investigative Handling Classification

Principle	*Statement*	*Rationale*	*Implications*
Communication	Formalize the internal communication	Improved internal communication leads to more efficient and effective operation	Technology needed to support the internal communication

4.6.6 Case Management Design Components

4.6.6.1 Investigative Handling Design Category Overview

In Table 3.2, a design template is presented that will be used here to give an insight into required functionalities for incident management.

4.6.6.2 Case Lifecycle Design Category

During the execution of a service request or incident types of cases, intelligence is needed to drive decisions. This intelligence is obtained by starting separate investigation activities from the service request or incident case flow. Multiple investigations can be started from a single service request or incident. Each investigation case is started as a separate case with its own control and responsibilities and has loosely coupled interactions with the service request or incident case. Figure 4.8 shows the relationship between service request or incident cases and investigation cases. This figure also shows that investigation cases themselves can initiate follow-up investigations.

The flow of the investigative case is targeted at delivering intelligence needed by the initiating service request of incident. The main part of an investigation flow is based upon a loop of investigation activities, as shown in Figure 4.9. After every loop, the resulting research information is checked for completeness and quality. The investigation loop continues if more information is needed and the resulting information is handed back to the service request or incident when enough information is available enabling a decision in the calling of service request or incident case (Table 4.9).

In the case handling phase, the following stakeholders participate:

- Service request or incident is the investigation initiating parties.
- The case owner is actively leading the investigative case and assesses/prioritizes the current situation and assigns work to case workers. When the investigation can be closed, the case worker initiates the closing activities.
- The case workers are responsible for the investigation work.

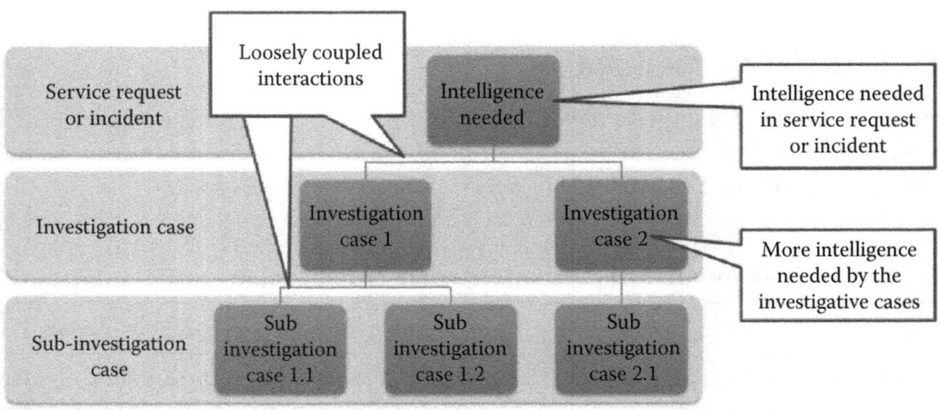

Figure 4.8 Loosely coupled multilayered investigations.

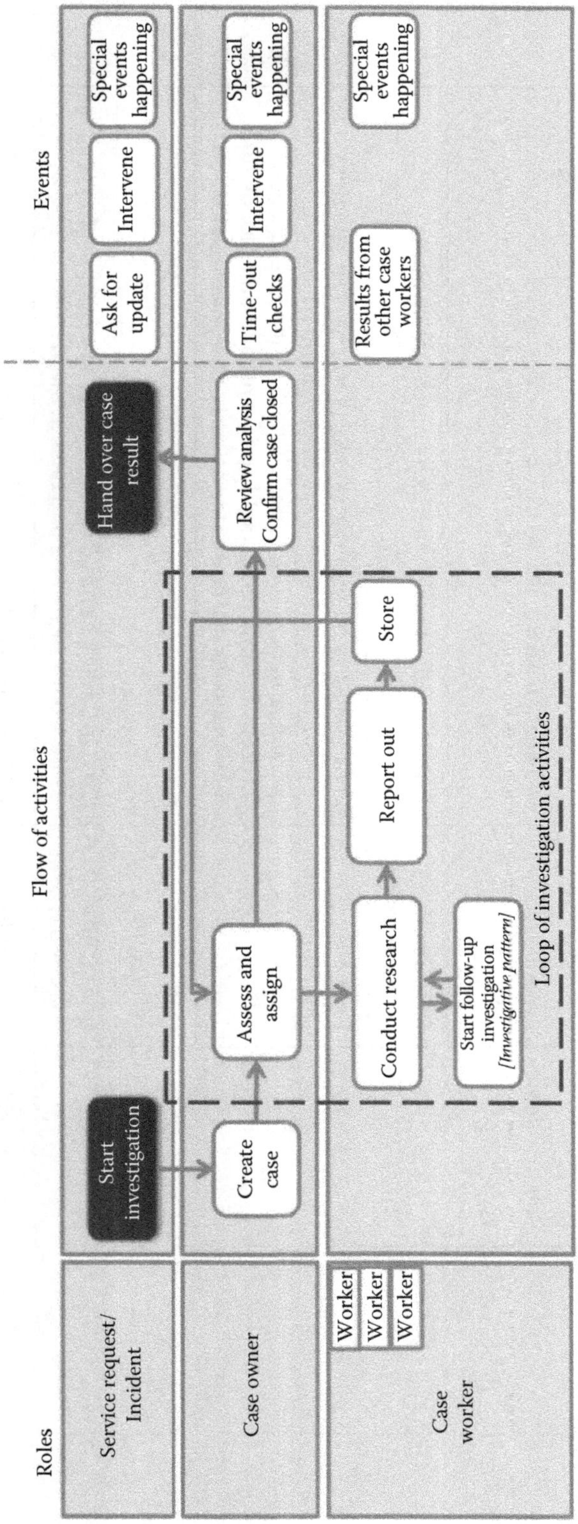

Figure 4.9 The investigative case flow model.

Table 4.9 Investigative Handling Design Overview

Case Design Category	*Case Design Component*	*High Level Functionalities*	*Investigative Handling Specific Usage*
Case lifecycle design	Case flow/ process design	The case flow specific for a case	See Section 4.6.6.2
	Rules design	Case lifecycle decision-making	See Section 4.6.6.2
		Entitlement determination	Only in incident cases where customers are involved
		Progress measurement	In order to reach the end goals in a timely fashion, progress measurement is the key to an investigation where a variety of persons can be involved, certain parts of the investigation process are influenced highly by events and other follow-up investigations can be started as part of the investigation
		Data entry validation	Not used in investigation
		Information discovery	Used in finding trends, evidence, clues in a combination of data stored, both structured and unstructured data
	Event design	Interrupting events	See Section 4.6.6.2
		Noninterrupting events	See Section 4.6.6.2

(Continued)

Table 4.9 (*Continued*) Investigative Handling Design Overview

Case Design Category	*Case Design Component*	*High Level Functionalities*	*Investigative Handling Specific Usage*
Case information design	Data design	Case execution data	Be able to follow the case execution across the various stakeholders
		Case supporting data	Investigative handling related data
		Tactical related information	Compliance related
		Strategic data	Case process improvement
	Document and media design	Case input management	Investigative handling input, structured, and unstructured data
		Case output management	Investigative handling output, mostly documents
	People relationship design	Internal stakeholders	Case owner/workers
		External stakeholders	Stakeholder that started the investigation, originating from the service request, incident management, or another investigation
Case user interface design	Portal design	One central view on the case	A centralized overview of the investigation proceedings is required by all stakeholders.
		One overview of the customer	Only in investigative cases where customers are involved

(*Continued*)

Table 4.9 (*Continued*) Investigative Handling Design Overview

Case Design Category	*Case Design Component*	*High Level Functionalities*	*Investigative Handling Specific Usage*
	Channel design	Internal communication	Internal communication between the case workers is the key
		External communication	Standardized communication with the service request/incident or investigation case that started this investigation
	Dashboard design	KPI management	Cost driven
		Performance management	Cost driven
		Customer satisfaction determination	Not used in investigation
Cross-functional design	Integration design	Application integration	Depends on the investigation-related IT landscape.
		Case integration	This is the entry point for all events that intervene with the investigation In the context of an investigation case other investigations can be started that interact with the case lifecycle
		Portal/channel integration	Combine data from disparate sources to provision the portals
	Roles and authorization	Internal profiles	Depends on the sensitivity of the investigative case
		External profiles	Profiles determine the amount of information that is shared with the external stakeholders via different channels

The case handling work of an investigation consists of the following activities:

- *Create case*: An investigative case is created when a service request or incident requests intelligence.
- *Loop of investigation activities*: This is a continuous loop of investigation work.
  - *Assess and assign*: After each loop, the case owner makes an assessment if the end result is reached. When another loop of investigation work is required, the case owner makes a decision, which follow-up activities need to be done, how these are prioritized, and who is going to execute these activities. The case owner is also responsible for communicating status updates to the initiating service request or incident case.
  - *Conduct research*: This activity is the core activity for the investigation case. Here, all needed information is collected to conduct the research needed to draw conclusions. During this activity, follow-up investigations can be started. The collected information used in this research activities can be based upon a variety of (un)structured data sources.
  - *Report out*: After the research activity is concluded and conclusions are drawn, a report is created and approval/sign off is requested. The resulting information is stored for later reference and auditing purposes.
- *Review analysis and confirm case closed*: When the investigation loop is finished, the resulting work is reviewed and handed over to the service request or incident.

The investigative case flow can be interrupted by multiple events.

Service request or incident-related events:

- Ask for update: The service request or incident case owner or case workers can ask for an update to get informed about the latest status.

Case owner–related events:

- Time-out checks: The case owner is responsible for timely handling of all activities in the case. Every activity can have requirements around execution and/or communication timings, and is related to regulatory requirements, agreements with external stakeholders, or internal performance agreements.

Case worker–related events:

- Results from other case workers: internal communication is the key for the good functioning of an investigation case embedded in a service request or incident cases. Any (in-between) results from other case workers, participating in both the service request or incident and other investigation cases, can influence the work somebody else in the team is executing.

Intervention events relate to both service request or incident and the case owner:

- Intervene: The service request/incident or case owner can intervene in the case execution when a situation occurs where the execution activities of the case needs to be altered. Intervention can also include termination of the work.

For all three stakeholders, service request/incident, case owner, and case worker:

- Special events: A situation can occur that has the potential to alter the flow of the case drastically.

4.6.6.2.1 The Investigative Handling Case State Flow

The state model of the investigative handling contains two main work phases: *investigate* and *close case*, as presented in Figure 4.10.

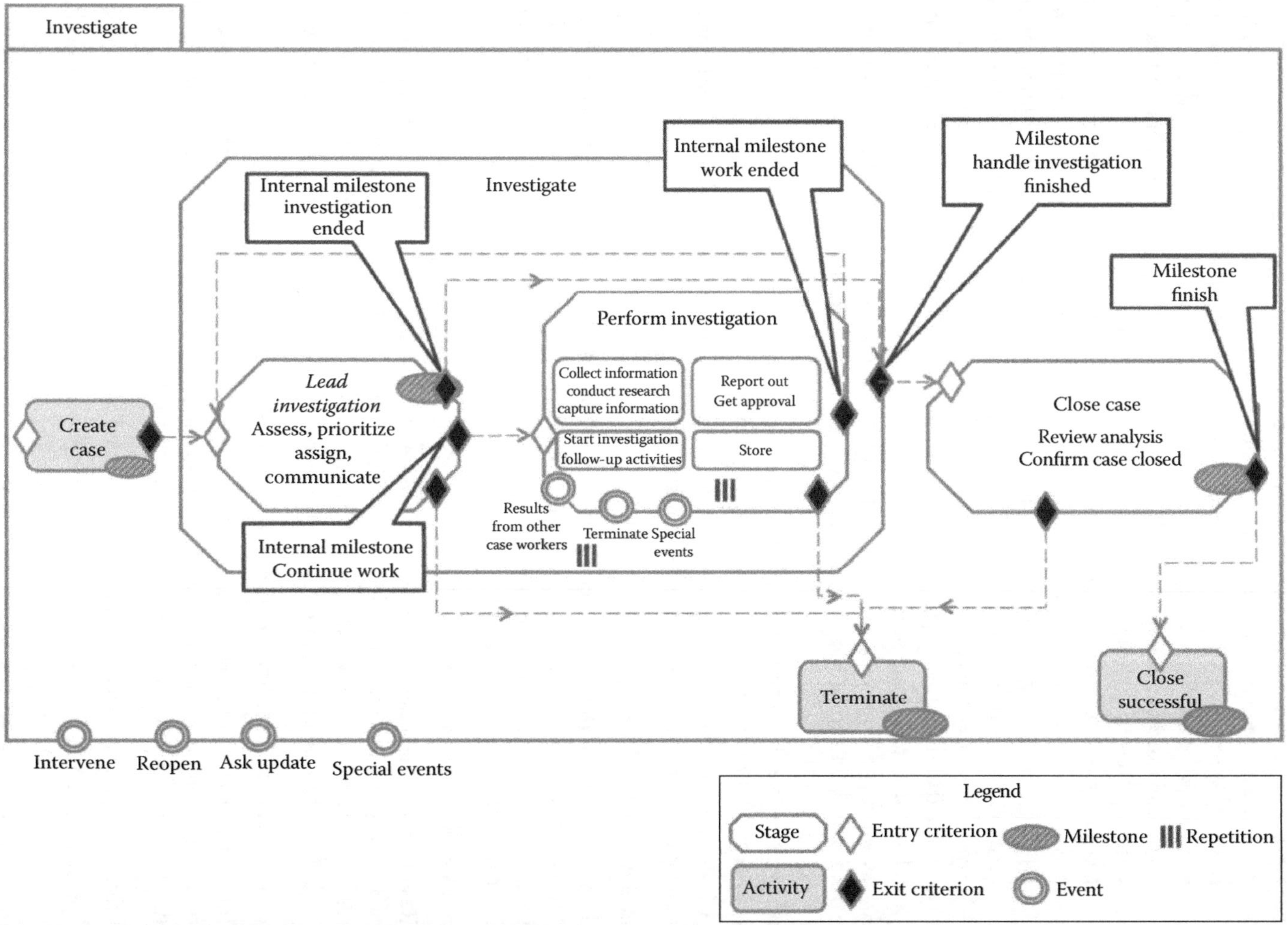

Figure 4.10 Case state model for investigative handling.

The *investigate* phase contains two internal phases. The *lead investigation* activities, assess, prioritize, assign, and communicate are executed by the case owner. In this phase, the case owner determines if the end result is met and if follow-up work needs to be done. They also determine what type of work needs to be done. The *perform investigation* activities related to the work done by the case workers as described in the investigation case flow model.

The lead investigation phase has three milestones through which this phase can be finished:

- *Investigation finished* where the investigation exit criteria are met. This closes the main phase *investigate*.
- *Continue work* where the investigation exit criteria are not met and more work needs to be done. Based upon the decision of the case owner, more investigation work is needed.
- *Terminate* where the investigative exit criteria are not met and the decision is taken to stop the incident handling work.

The *perform investigation* phase has the following milestones:

- *Work ended* in which the result is handed over to the case owner who uses this result for assessment in the next iteration of the lead investigation phase.
- *Terminate* in which the work is terminated by the case workers. For example, when the case owner terminates the case, all investigation work needs to be stopped as well.

The *close case* phase contains two activities: *review analysis* and *confirm case closed.* These are already discussed in the investigation case flow description. Different events intervene in the lifecycle of the investigative lifecycle. These are attached to main case levels and to the different phases. On the main case level, four events can be identified, *intervene, reopen, ask update,* and *special events.* Attached to the *perform investigate* phase are three events: *results from other case workers, terminate,* and *special events.*

4.7 Conclusion

In this chapter, the case management classifications as part of the case management solution framework are described; the service request, incident management, and investigative handling. These three case management classifications have different characteristics that determine what components the case management solution should contain. In the description of all three classifications, a checklist and a list of aligned industry processes is provided that help determine the classification type of a case.

Service requests deal with the process of delivering a service that a customer requested, and contain complex interactions with the customer. The case flow for service requests is predictable, and contains two main parts; the initial interaction with the customer (the triage) that is workflow based, and the service request handling that is case oriented. Interventions in the case originate from the customer or the case owner.

Incidents are aimed at solving a problem and include providing help to persons and finding the root causes. The high-level flow of an incident is predictable, and contains four phases; *being prepared, monitoring, acting upon the incident,* and an *evaluation.*

The actual incident handling, *acting upon the incident* is highly influenced by special events. Internal communication is the key to the operation of an incident since multiple case workers can work on an incident simultaneously. Communication to all external stakeholders needs to be formalized.

Investigations are started by either a service request or an incident and deliver intelligence needed by these cases. Just like in incident handling, this flow is highly influenced by special events and internal communication is the key for success in the operation.

Chapter 5

Determine Solution Mapping

5.1 Introduction

In the third part of the management solution framework, we will determine which technical capabilities are needed to implement a case management solution and how these can be mapped onto an Oracle solution. To apply this in a structured way, the common reference architecture (CORA) model is used.*

The goals of this chapter are as follows:

- Show how to structure a solution with the CORA mode
- Show how the case management design components relate to the CORA application layers
- Show how functionality can be mapped to application layers and technical capabilities
- Show how to derive a decision what Oracle products to use based upon technical capabilities

5.2 Techniques Used to Determine the Impact of Functionality onto the IT Landscape

5.2.1 Common Reference Architecture Model

Current IT landscapes are getting more complex and contain multiple technologies supporting all the functionalities required by the business. The business demands more flexibility, agility, and faster time to delivery. Every change required by the business has an impact on the IT landscape. In order to be able to determine the impact of a business change on the landscape and identify the risks a vendor, neutral reference architecture is required. The CORA delivers a reference model based upon a set of application layers and capabilities. This way it provides an insight into the way an IT landscape can support business functionality, flexibility, and compliance simultaneously.

* http://www.coramodel.com/

The model can be used at both the enterprise architecture level and at the project implementation level to design and implement functions with a mixture of "architecture styles" on the best-fitted platform available (or planned).

5.2.2 CORA Model Layering and Capabilities

The CORA model uses a stacked solution layer to break down the complexity and define a clear separation of duties as shown in Figure 5.1. The definition of the layers and capabilities described in this chapter are obtained from the CORA model (www.coramodel.com).

The layering used in the CORA model to structure functionality is based upon six horizontally stacked layers: channel access, presentation, composition, integration, application, and data. Vertically, next to these stacked layers, are security and compliance and IT governance. Although the layering is stacked, individual layers can be skipped if not required. Here is a short description of the various layers:

- The *channel access layer* groups client specific capabilities to enable access to information systems.
- The *presentation layer* groups presentation specific capabilities for displaying information to the user and handling of user-initiated events.
- The *composition layer* groups composition specific capabilities clustered in Orchestrated and Composed elements.
- The *integration layer* groups integration specific capabilities clustered in "synchronous communication," asynchronous communication, and common elements.
- The *application layer* groups core business capabilities.
- The *data layer* groups data specific capabilities clustered in data access and data storage elements.
- For all horizontal layers, the security and IT governance layers and capabilities may apply.

Every layer within the CORA model contains technical capabilities that can be used within a solution. Groupings of related capabilities within these layers can help in identifying specific functionality required for a solution. In Figure 5.2, an example of the composition layer is used to show the usage of groupings and capabilities.

The following main groups can be identified:

- *Orchestrated capabilities* contain the execution of a predefined, multistep business process models and lifecycle management supporting case management.

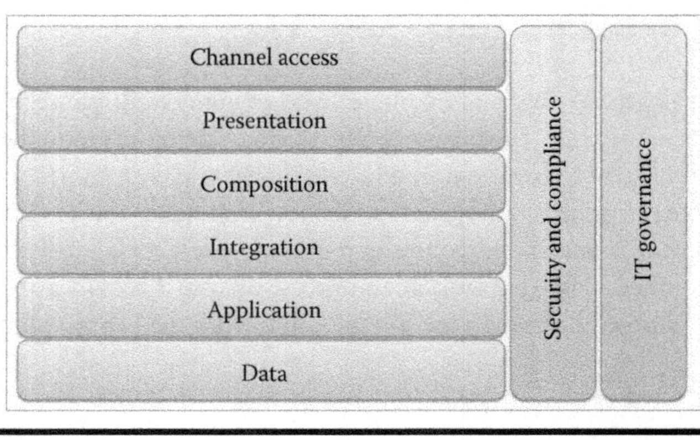

Figure 5.1 The CORA model layers.

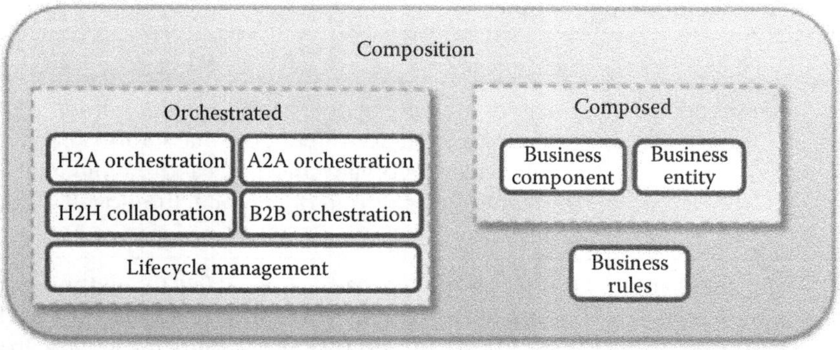

Figure 5.2 CORA model composition technical capabilities.

- *Composed capabilities* contain the composition of existing application logic to create additional logic with specific business value, such as composition of data from different sources to be used within a business rules engine.
- *Business rule capabilities* relate to the business rules used in cross domain processes.

The CORA technical capabilities are summarized in Appendix – CORA capabilities.

5.2.3 Delivering a Solution with the CORA Model

The goal of this chapter is to discuss the determination of the required technical capabilities for the implementation of a case management type of solution. These technical capabilities will be used in Part III to determine which Oracle products are best suited for a specific set of required functionalities. The way a solution is determined using the CORA model is explained in the blog http://www.coramodel.com/cora-methodology-project-level/. In this blog, an overview of the activities describing how to determine a solution based upon the CORA model is shown. We will use a tailored version of the CORA methodology in this chapter to determine the solution mapping and the technical capabilities for the case management solution as shown in Figure 5.3 and Table 5.1.

The activities described in this chapter, as shown in Figure 5.3, help derive the solution architecture for every case management solution and then map this to Oracle products. How to make

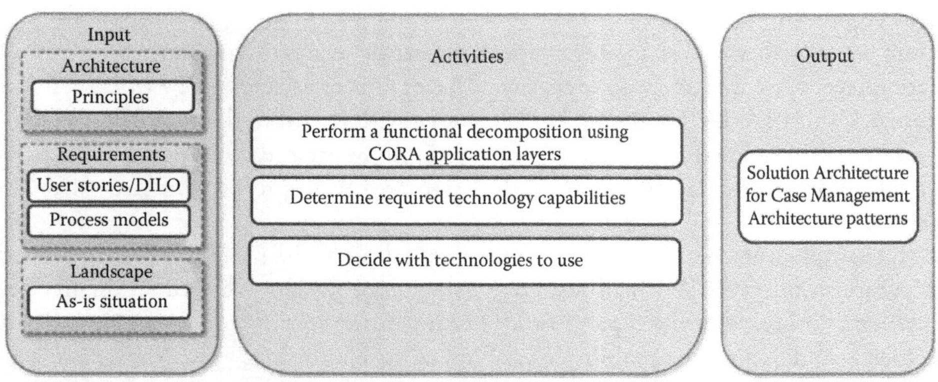

Figure 5.3 Working toward a solution architecture with the CORA mapping.

Table 5.1 CORA Methodology Input

Input	*Provided by*	*Description*
Principles	Architecture	Principles are general rules and guidelines, intended to be enduring and seldom amended, that inform and support the way in which an organization sets about fulfilling its mission. (http://pubs.opengroup.org/architecture/togaf8-doc/arch/chap29.html)
User stories/ DILO	Business and end-users	User stories or *The Day in a Life of* (DILO) method gives insight in the current situation and the business challenges. The objective of the DILO is to walk through the process and experience the day in the life of an "an invoice" for example
Process models	Business analysts	The process models for this chapter are based upon the three case management architecture patterns: service request, incident management, and investigative handling
AS-IS situation	IT	The as-is situation describes the current system landscape, which usually contains different categories of application types: package-based systems, custom made, legacy systems, and SAAS applications

a mapping toward a technology will be explained in further detail in Sections 5.3 through 5.5. The actual mapping to different Oracle products will be done in Part III.

The left-hand side of Figure 5.3 shows that initial input is needed before going through the activities. These inputs originate from different groups within the organization.

5.3 Perform a Functional Decomposition Using CORA Application Layers

5.3.1 How to Map the Case Management Design Areas onto the CORA Application Layers

In Chapter 3, the design categories and components for case management were introduced, as shown in Figure 5.4.

Before we look at the case management design areas in detail (and how they relate to the application layers), we first show an overview of the design areas across the entire CORA model. In Figure 5.5, this high-level mapping has been done with regard to the case management functional and cross-functional categories. This mapping shows that each design area maps to only a few application layers, meaning that every design area relates to a specific set of technology capabilities.

As an example, the core of the case management design, the *case lifecycle design* is mapped to the composition layer. We will see later in Section 5.4 that this functionality requires *orchestration* and *business rules* capabilities. Looking at the specific orchestration/rules related requirements and required capabilities enables us to choose between the Oracle products BPM/ACM, Siebel, Service Cloud, business rules, Oracle policy automation (OPA), and/or Endeca (as will be explained in Section 3).

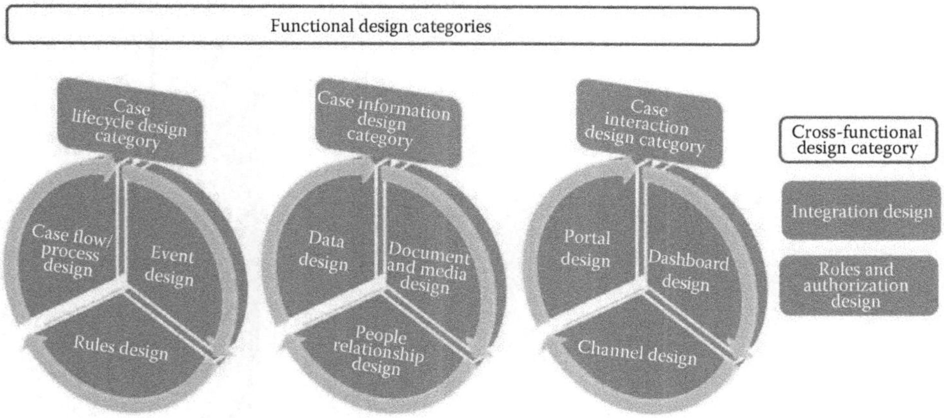

Figure 5.4 Case management design categories and components.

5.3.1.1 Case Lifecycle Design

The case lifecycle design category describes the coordination of activities in reaching one of the end goals of a case and consists of three design components: Case flow/process design, rules design, and event design.

Most of the case lifecycle functionalities are mapped against the composition layer, as shown in Figure 5.6. The case flows and processes for the three architecture patterns, service request, incident management and investigative handling, are each mapped in a separate group

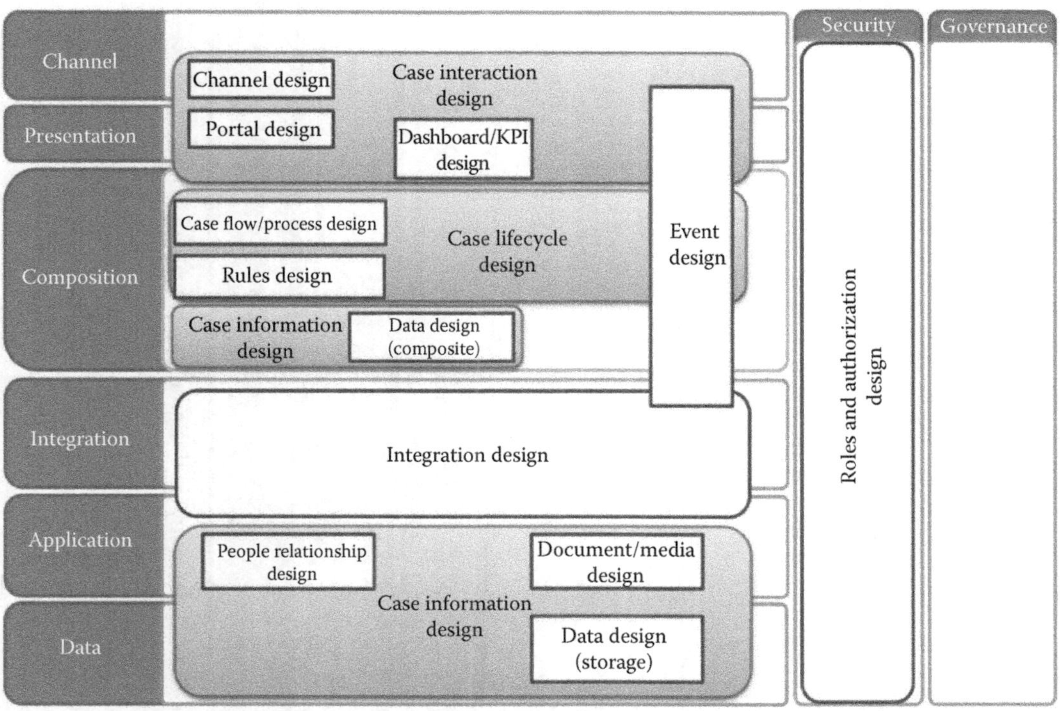

Figure 5.5 Case management design areas mapped onto CORA.

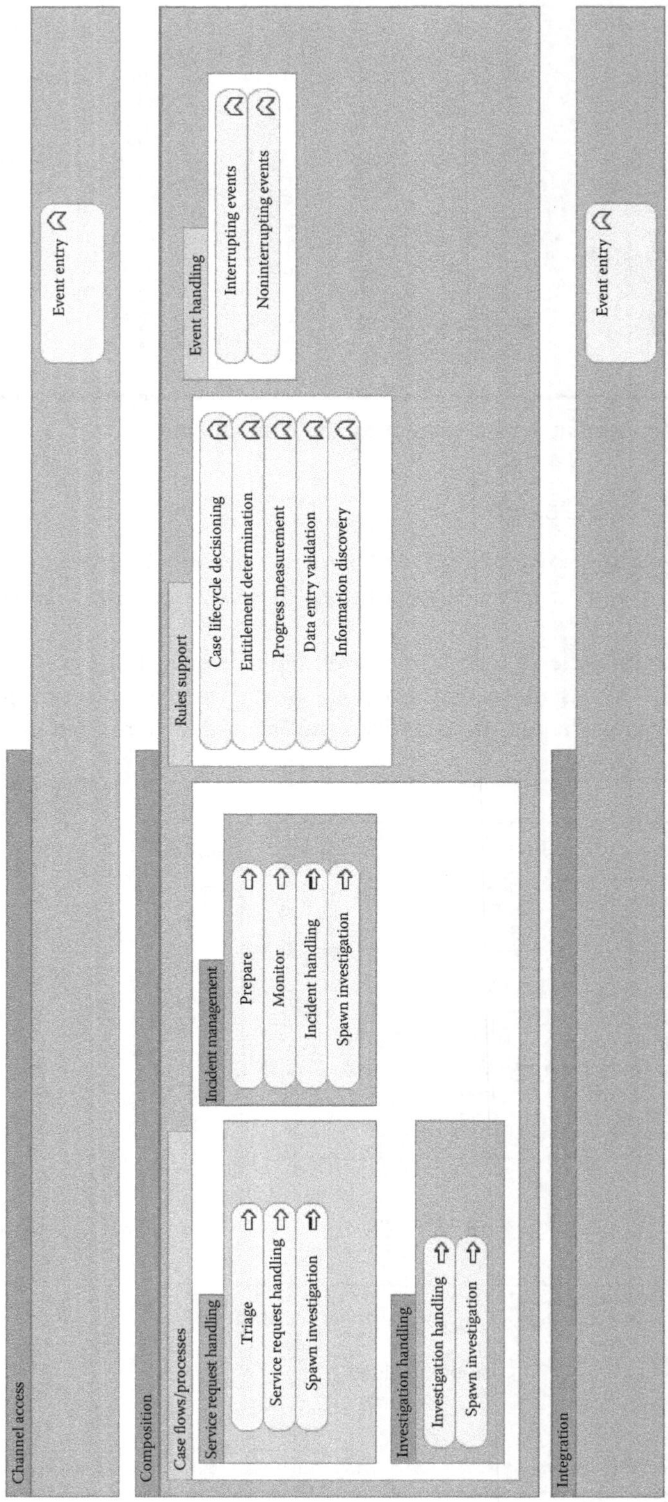

Figure 5.6 Case lifecycle design mapping against CORA layers.

inside the composition layer. The rules functionalities, such as case lifecycle, decision-making, and information discovery, are placed inside the rules support group in the composition layer. The only functionality that is mapped against three layers is the handling of events. While the actual *event handling* is placed in the composition layer, the event entry originates from two layers:

- When an event is entered via human interaction, the event entry is placed in the channel layer.
- An event originating from an application is automatically entered via the integration layer.

5.3.1.2 Case Interaction Design

The case interaction design enables maximizing support for the case work force. This design area contains three design parts: portal design, dashboard design, and channel design.

The *case interaction design* category is mapped on three layers: the channel, the presentation, and the composition layer as shown in Figure 5.7.

- The *case management portal design components* are mapped onto the presentation layer. This contains the user interface functionality supporting the case owner/workers, customers, and management.

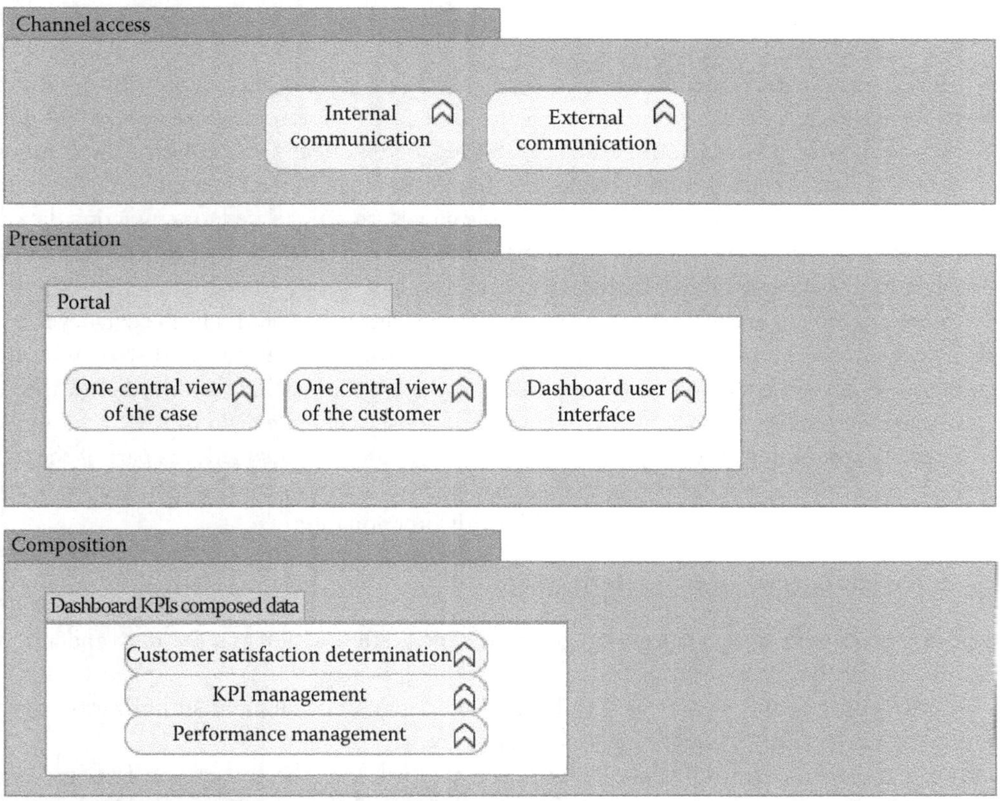

Figure 5.7 Case interaction design mapping onto the CORA layers.

- The *case management channel design components* relate to how the case supporting application is accessed, and contains the *internal and external communication*. The channel design is mapped onto the channel layer.
- The *case management dashboard design components* support the KPI management, performance management, and customer satisfaction measurement. It is mapped toward two layers: the dashboard data determination is part of the composition layer while the user interface part of the dashboard design is part of the presentation layer.

5.3.1.3 Case Management Information Design

The case information design deals with all sorts of data and documentation flowing through the case and maps the relationships between all persons and/or assets involved in the case. The case information design category contains three design components, data design, document and media design, and people relationship design.

The *case management information design* category is mapped onto the composition, application, and data layers, as shown in Figure 5.8:

- Data residing in the *composition* layer
- The case is supported with information originating from a composition of data from three different areas, as described earlier in Section 3.3.3.
  - Case execution data
  - Case supporting data
  - Strategic related information
  - Tactical related information
- This data originates from different sources, including the supporting case or BPM application.
- In the *data* layer, the access and storage capabilities are described that are needed to support the case management solution. These capabilities are described in Appendix. The composed case data that is plotted in the composition application has a direct relation with the storage capabilities. The case execution and supporting data is strongly related to transaction data and master data. Additionally, the decision management, as part of the case execution data, can relate to unstructured data. Tactical/Strategic data look at aggregated data. The supporting case management and BPM application require repository capabilities in the data layer.
- The *application* layer is the place where applications, such as package-based systems, custom made, legacy systems, and SAAS applications, deliver the specific data needed in the case management solution. Specifically customer relationship management (CRM) type applications are required for the people relationship design. Documents/media as part of the input and output management for the case management solution is placed within the application layer since specific products are tailored for this functionality.

5.3.1.4 Cross-Functional Design Areas

The cross-functionality design category contains the integration design and the roles and authorization design that both support the other functional design categories.

The cross-functional design areas (i.e., integration design and roles and authorization design) map directly to the CORA integration and security layers.

The three main integration functionalities are mapped onto the Integration layer as shown in Figure 5.9. All communication is based upon a canonical data model that is the key in the exchange of all information in all integration functionalities.

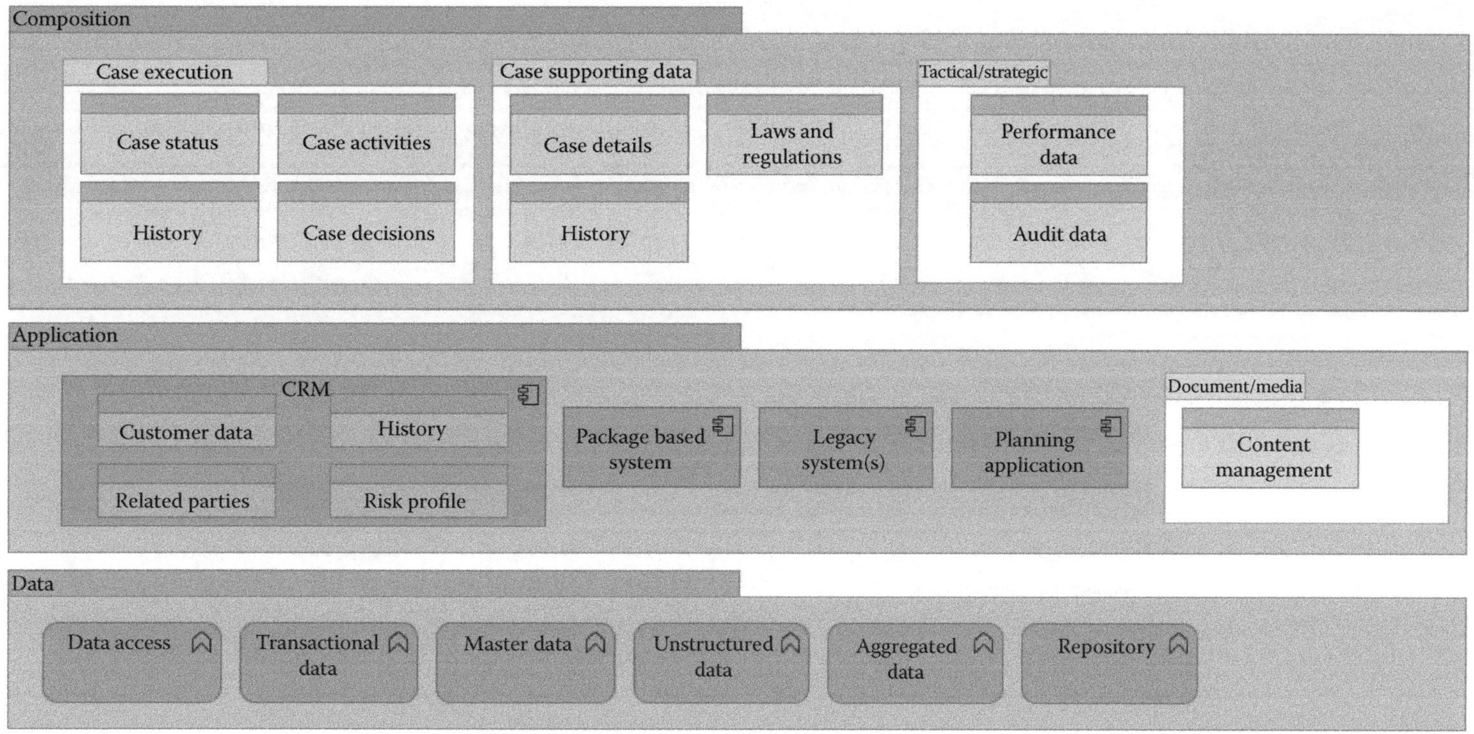

Figure 5.8 Case information design mapping to application layers.

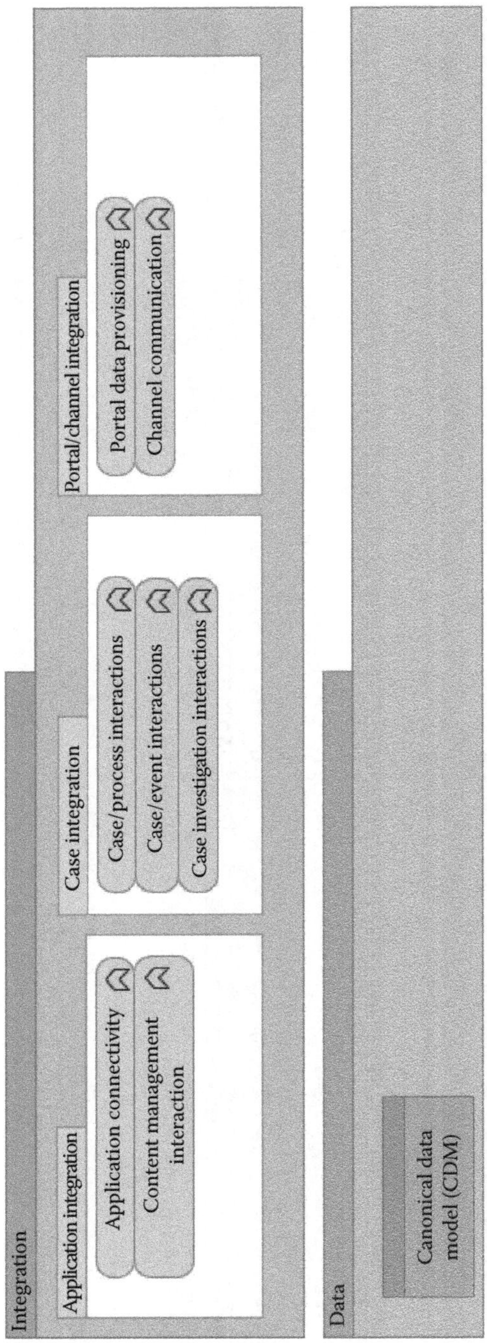

Figure 5.9 Case integration design mapping to application layers.

5.4 Determine Required Technology Capabilities

Every case management solution has its own specific characteristics and can be described with the help of the case management design categories and components. In the previous section, we have shown the relationship between the case management design categories and the CORA layers. The knowledge of the relationship between the design categories and these layers help identifying what technical capabilities could be used to determine the solution. And subsequently, understanding the need for a set of technical capabilities supports the identification of the need for a specific technology, such as making a decision between the Oracle BPM/ACM and Siebel products.

In this section, we will look at what technical capabilities relate to the case management *lifecycle* design category, and under what conditions these capabilities should be included in the solution. The lifecycle design is supported by "core" capabilities and "supporting" capabilities. The "core" capabilities for the case management lifecycle design originate from the composition layer, as we have seen in Figure 5.6. The "supporting" capabilities are additional to the solution, and help in the decision process what (Oracle) products to use. Figure 5.10 shows the mapping of the lifecycle functionalities toward the technical capabilities. On the left-hand side of the picture, the lifecycle design functionalities are shown. The right-hand side contains the capabilities, with a distinction between the "core" capabilities and the "supporting" capabilities. Groupings of related capabilities are denoted by white rectangles.

5.4.1 Case Flows and Processes Capabilities

The *case flows and processes* are mapped onto the composition *orchestration* capabilities. The orchestration capabilities facilitate the case management lifecycle with (automated) support for predefined multistep business process models. Table 5.2 gives an overview of the orchestration capabilities and the usage in a case management solution.

5.4.2 Event Handling Capabilities

The *event handling* function is related to multiple capabilities. First of all, the event handling interferes with the *lifecycle management* of the case:

- *Interrupting* events might impact the lifecycle execution of the case. From within the lifecycle management, new activities can be started or existing activities can be closed.
- *Noninterrupting* events do not impact the lifecycle execution of the case, but can trigger some human and/or automated activities.

Events originate from both human and automated interactions. Human interactions originate from within the channel layer (electronic channel capability). Automated events enter via the integration layer (message capability).

5.4.3 Business Rules Capabilities

As described in Section 3.3.2.3.2, different rule functionalities can be distinguished in a case management solution. These rule functionalities require different data types:

- Transactional data that relates to all dynamic data entered in the case.
- Aggregated data that is an assembly of transactional data often used in progress measurement and key performance indicator (KPI) monitoring.
- Unstructured data that relates to input data often used in investigations and can take any form, such as documents, media, and data streams.

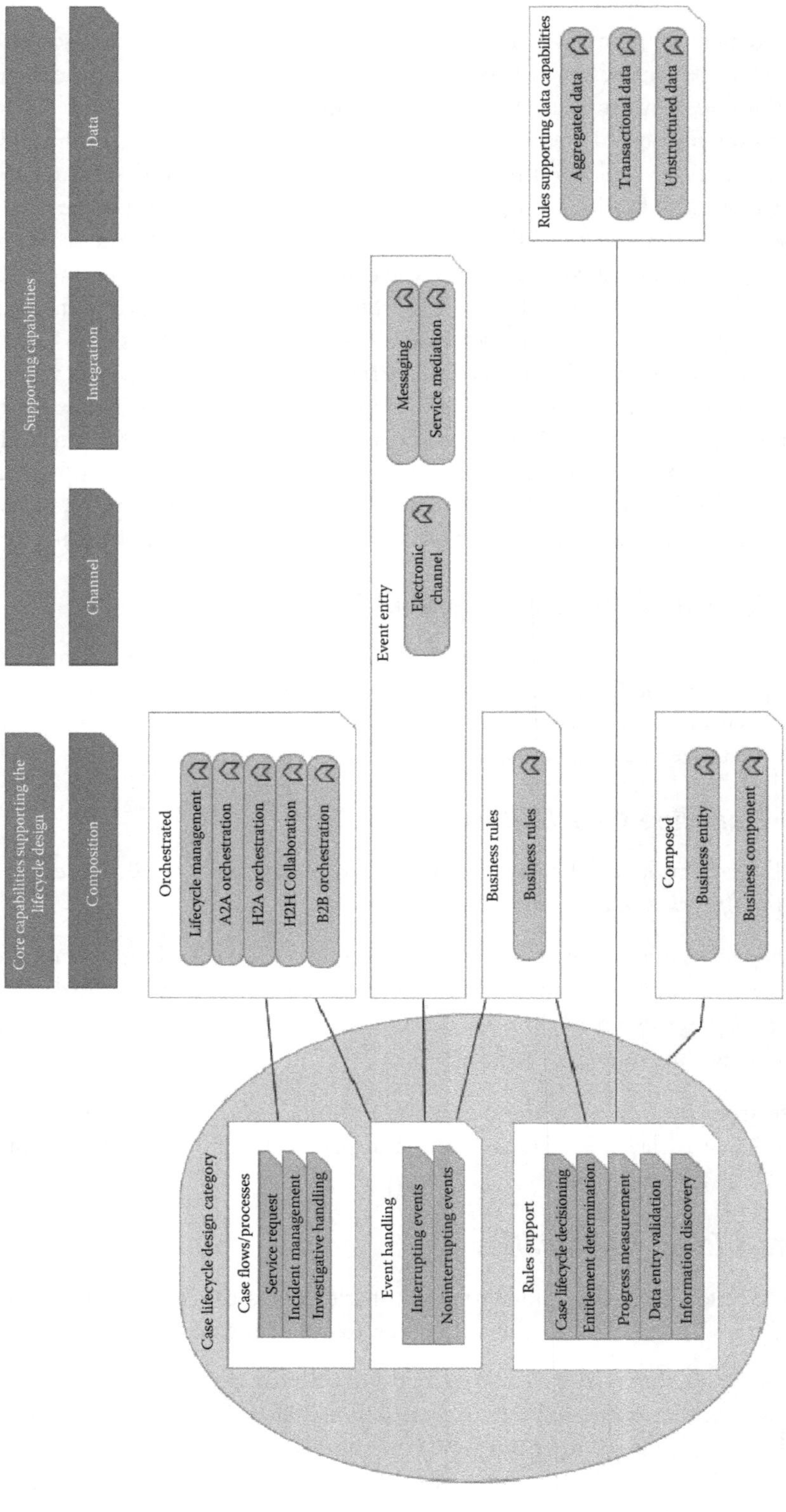

Figure 5.10 CORA technical capability mapping explained for the lifecycle design.

Table 5.2 Orchestration Capability Usage in the Case Lifecycle Design

Orchestration Capability	*CORA Definition*	*Usage in Case Management*
Lifecycle management	The end-to-end management of all activities in a business process and case and monitoring of the progress against predefined parameters. There is a close interaction between the lifecycle management and the orchestration capabilities A2A, H2A, H2H and B2B	This is the core functionality for the orchestration of all activities in a case. The case management paradigm is goal-driven. The lifecycle management supports the case execution with the management of activities and the monitoring of progress in order to reach one of the end goals
Application-to-application (A2A)	Capability to allocate tasks to applications within an organization and control the required routing of these tasks	All automated activities in a case relate to the A2A capability. The automated activity can be either a call to an external application or part of the case management solution itself In Section 4.4.4, the operating models are discussed for a service request classification. The operating model *operational excellence* is aimed at delivering a standardized product for a low price. The A2A capability enables the standardized delivery of tasks through automated handling of activities
Human-to-application (H2A)	Capability to allocate tasks to users and control the required routing of these tasks	Interactions between the case application and different stakeholders can be part of the case execution. When the interactions are predefined, these are modeled as standard BPM processes In situations where ad hoc interaction is required, these interactions need to be modeled at runtime
Human-to-human (H2H)	Capability to collaboratively use the same resource by different users	In Chapter 4, the three case classifications are described, the service request, incident management, and investigative. Each classification has specific needs for human to human interactions *Service request*: When the operating model is customer centric, direct interaction with the customer is a prerequisite for success *Incident management*: Both internal and external communication are the keys in the execution of an incident case *Investigations*: Internal communication between all the case workers is crucial in the execution of the investigation
Business to business (B2B)	Capability to allocate tasks to applications between organizations and control the required routing of these tasks	Both the service request and the incident handling classifications can have requirements for the inclusion of B2B activities. Outsourced work that falls under control of a case is a good candidate of a B2B interaction

In Table 5.3, an overview is provided of the business rule functionalities, the relationship with the different data types, and an explanation of the usage in a case management context.

5.5 Decide What Technologies to Use

The first step in deciding what technology to use is choosing the required functionalities and the supporting technical capabilities. In the previous section, we described the relation between the functional areas and the technical capabilities for the case management life cycle design. Adding a functional area into the requirements can result in the addition of a certain set of technical capabilities needed in the solution.

After we have decided what functionality is included in the case management solution, and what technical capabilities are needed, we can choose the technology based upon the required capabilities. Every technology product has specific product features that relate to a specific capability. In Section III, we will show when to use one of the three main Oracle case management products: Siebel, Oracle BPM/ACM, and Oracle service cloud.

The diagram type as provided in Figure 5.10 will be extended to show the relation between the required functionalities, technical capabilities, and products to use in the case management solution in the remainder of the book. Figure 5.11 shows an example of the technology inclusion for Oracle BPM/ACM:

- On the left-hand side the required functionalities are shown.
- The next column shows the required technical capabilities.
- The remaining columns to the right show the products to use.

In Figure 5.11 the capabilities are shown for the case life cycle design category. This category contains functionality for case flows/processes, events, and rules support.

In the example, we left out the event functionality and all the rules support except for case management decision-making. This remaining functionality is the bare bones of the case management life cycle design and contains all the orchestration features that a case management solution requires. In Section III, an explanation is given for the product choices shown in Figure 5.11.

5.6 Conclusion

Determining the *solution mapping* is the third and last part of the *case management solution framework*. In this chapter, we used a vendor-agnostic reference architecture model, the CORA model to make the translation from requirements toward a decision as to what technology to use:

- Perform a functional decomposition onto the CORA layers.
  This shows the impact of a set of requirements on the application landscape.
- Determine the required technology capabilities.
  Based upon the required functionality a decision can be made what technical capabilities to include in the solution.
- Decide what technologies to use.
  The technical capabilities help make the choice for specific technologies to implement the solution.

We showed a mapping technology with related diagrams that enables us to translate the case management requirements toward a technical solution. In Parts III and IV, we will use these solution diagrams to show what Oracle products support specific functionalities.

Table 5.3 Business Rule Data Usage

Functionality	*Usage in Case Management*	*Transactional Data*	*Aggregated Data*	*Unstructured Data*
Case lifecycle decision making	This rule functionality guides the lifecycle management in the decision process. Any change happening in the status of a case can result in changed behavior of the case lifecycle. The ability to make decisions on a change that happened in the lifecycle of a case is supported by business rules Examples of changes in the context of a case are: a milestone reached, an activity finished, a document entered, a person interacting with the case, an automated event informing the case about a changed situation, or a data object changed	X	X	
Entitlement determination	The determination of an entitlement is based upon regulations and policies and contains complex rules The data contained in the supporting business entities originates from transactional and aggregated data types	X	X	
Progress measurement	During the execution of a case insight is needed in the progress of the case and is calculated via business rules. The data contained in the supporting business entities originates from aggregated data types		X	
Data entry validation	Data entry validation is required in situations where customers or other stakeholders enter data into the case. This data needs to be validated for instance against regulations and policies The data contained in the supporting business entities originates from transactional data types	X		
Information discovery	Information discovery is needed in areas where large datasets of (un) structured data needs to be investigated for trends of direct impact on a case under investigation. The data contained in the supporting business entities originate from unstructured, transactional and aggregated data types	X	X	X

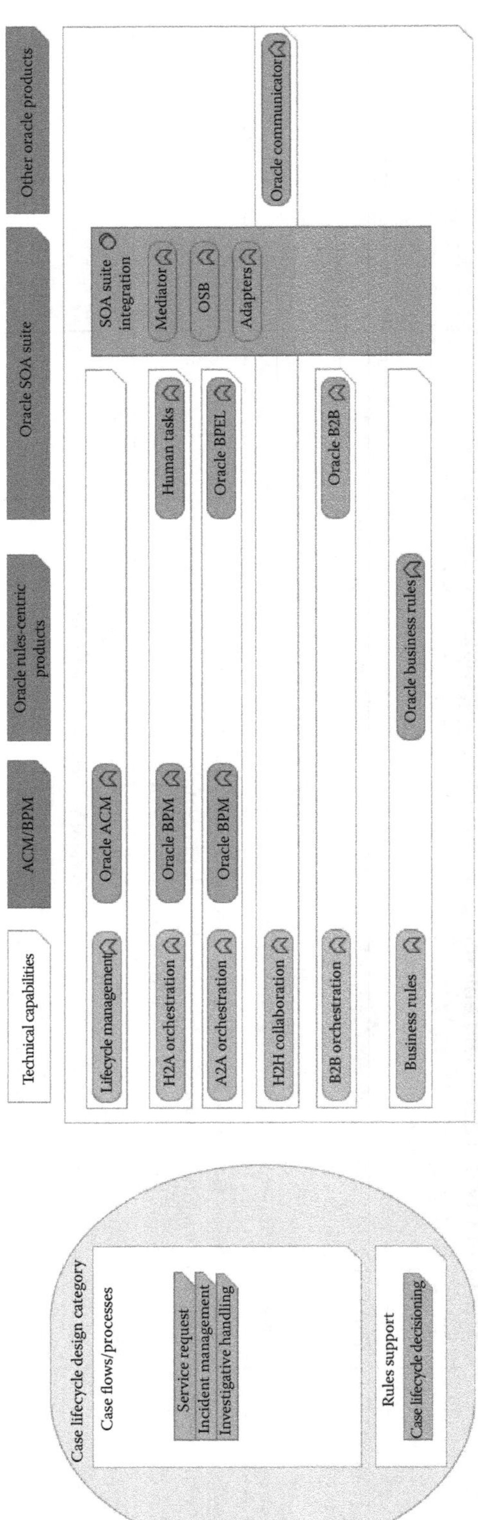

Figure 5.11 Combining functionality, capabilities, and technology in one overview.

Chapter 6

Concluding Remarks

We introduced the case management solution framework in this part. This framework enables the functional and technical designs of a case management solution with a set of *case management design components*, *three case management classifications*, and the *case management solution mapping*.

The *case management functional design components* and the *solution mapping* provide a means to create the functional design and the technical mapping for a case management solution. The *case management classification* gives an understanding of what functionalities are needed for a specific case management solution.

Figure 6.1 gives insight into the way the case management solution framework is used to determine a solution for a specific case. In the process of determining the solution architecture for a case management solution, the *case management solution framework* is used as follows:

- Determine the *case management classification*, service request, incident management, or investigative handling. This gives an insight into what functional requirements are needed. Specifically, insight is provided in the case lifecycle design category.
- Determine the *case management functional design*, based upon the chosen case management classification, and discover the high-level functional needs for the three functional categories and one cross-functional category.
- Determine the *case management technical solution* including the technical capabilities and mapping toward Oracle products based upon the required functionalities.

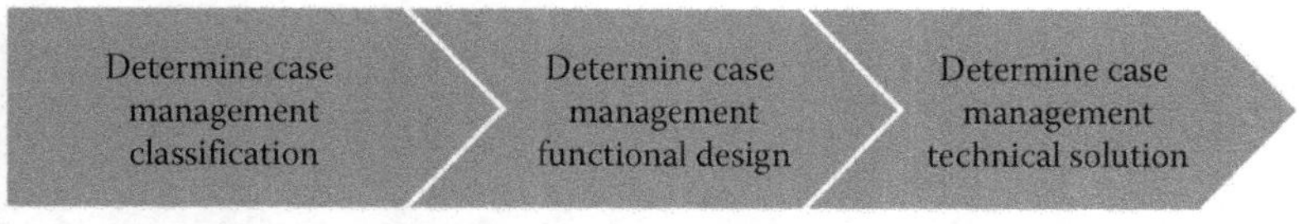

Figure 6.1 Creating a solution with the case management solution framework.

ORACLE CASE MANAGEMENT TECHNOLOGIES

III

Introduction

In the following chapters we introduce the three main products within the Oracle stack that support the case management functionality, Oracle BPM/ACM, Oracle Siebel, and Oracle Service Cloud. Each of these products has different characteristics that determine how it is (best) used in a case management scenario. Integration capabilities can be delivered additionally via the Oracle SOA Suite for all three scenarios. Intelligence in relation to case execution, the Oracle products that support the delivery, and the usage of intelligence will be discussed in Chapter 10.

Product Chapters

The product chapters will be structured according to the case management functional design presented earlier in (Section II—Chapter 1—Case Management Functional Design). Figure S.1 shows the functional design areas that will be used to describe the main features of a product.

Additionally for each technology we will map the life cycle design toward the technology capabilities according to the technique we defined in (Chapter 5 - Determine Solution Mapping), as shown in the example in Figure S.2.

In the usage characteristics description for the products we will look at the main characteristics of the product:

1. Main focus on the functionality in the product:
   a. What is the focus of the design of the product?—Life cycle design, information design, and/or interaction design.
   b. What classifications does the technology support?—service request, incident management, and/or investigative solution.

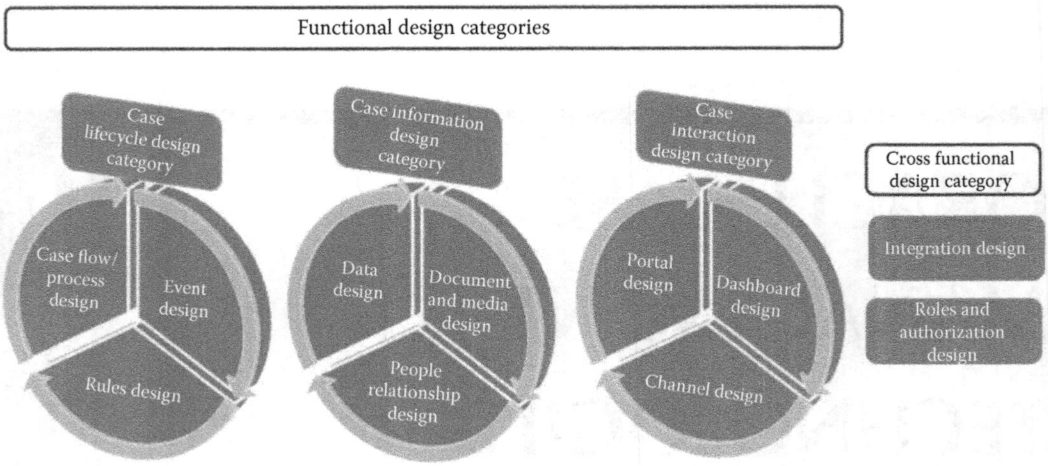

Figure S.1 Case management design categories and components.

2. *Delivery type*: The implementation type determines how the product is delivered: as a single entity that contains the full case management solution or an umbrella type of solution, an end-to-end control that interacts with other applications in the landscape.
3. *Product type*: Is the product package based, middleware based, or cloud based?
4. *Agility at run-time*: In (Chapter 2 - Adaptive Case Management (ACM)–Related Topics) we discussed the case management types, production case management (PCM) and adaptive case management (ACM). Both types are an approach for supporting knowledge workers with the case execution. As was concluded in that section, the main difference between PCM and ACM is that in the ACM type of systems, all aspects of the case can be changed by the case worker at run-time, while in the PCM type the structure and the assigned behavior of the subsystems stay the same throughout the case progression. In summary, ACM systems offer more agility at run-time than PCM systems (Table S.1).

Intelligence in Relation to the Case Execution

In the chapter, the usage of intelligence within the context of case execution is described. Intelligence functionalities are related to three intelligence information levels—operational, tactical, and strategic—and are supported by different Oracle products. Oracle intelligence products support all three case products: Oracle BPM/ACM, Oracle Siebel, and Oracle Service Cloud.

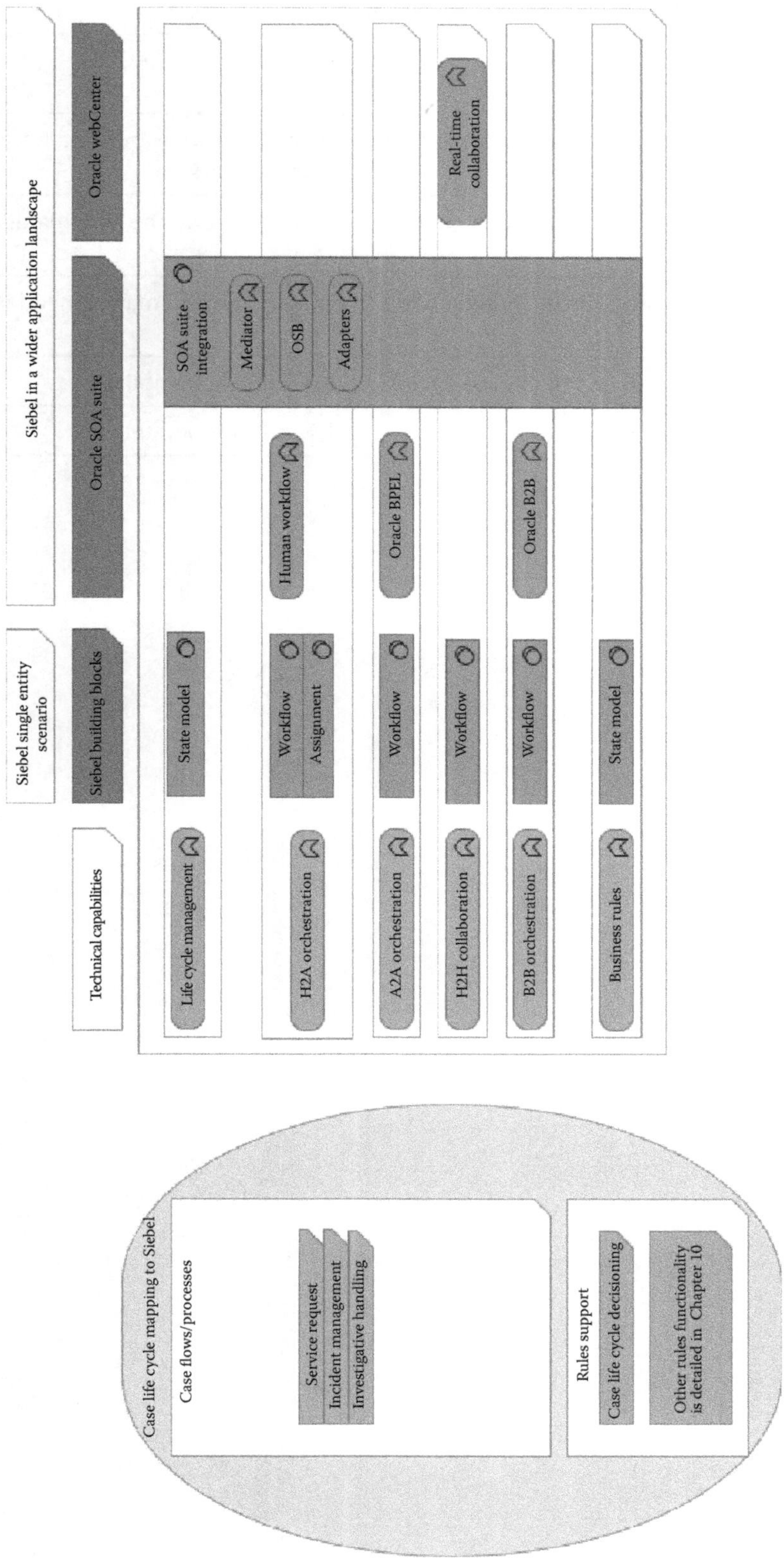

Figure S.2 Lifecycle management Siebel mapping.

Table S.1 Key Characteristics of a PCM and an ACM Type of Case

Key Characteristics	*PCM*	*ACM*
Type of work	Largely routine and repetitive	High knowledge and creative problem-solving work
Decision making	Usually from predesigned sets	Can go beyond the anticipated
Type of collaboration	Mostly known ahead of time	Special services may be needed
Work ownership	Adequate involvement	Send of responsibility
Case volume	Typically large	Typically moderate

Chapter 7

Oracle BPM/ACM

7.1 Introduction

In this chapter, we will describe the Oracle Adaptive Case Management (ACM) product as part of the Oracle Business Process Management (BPM) suite. The combination of Oracle ACM and BPM is built on top of the Oracle SOA Suite, which is a middleware product with a strong set of integration and interaction capabilities.

The goals of this chapter are as follows:

- Give a high-level overview of Oracle BPM/ACM and the SOA Suite
- Describe the usage characteristics of Oracle BPM/ACM
- Describe how Oracle BPM/ACM product supports the case management lifecycle functionality
- Show how the Oracle SOA Suite supports Oracle BPM/ACM with integration and interaction capabilities
- Give an overview of supporting Oracle products

We start this chapter with an overview and usage characteristics of the Oracle BPM/ACM and related SOA Suite products. Then we describe the product features of Oracle BPM/ACM/SOA Suite according to the case management functional design as presented earlier in Chapter 3, with the main focus on the lifecycle functionality.

In Chapter 17, a tutorial is presented on Oracle BPM/ACM where the product will be discussed extensively.

7.2 Oracle BPM/ACM/SOA Suite Overview

The Oracle SOA Suite is the middleware product within the Oracle architecture to support all integration in an enterprise wide landscape and is based upon a service-oriented (SOA) and event-driven architecture (EDA). The strong capabilities of the SOA Suite are in the area of integration and interaction, and can nowadays be delivered on premise and in the cloud. The Oracle SOA

Suite is created based on the principles complete, open, integrated, and reuse to the max. The last principle enables simplification and fast delivery of a new functionality in the SOA Suite:

Reuse of components across the Oracle SOA Suite stack, for instance a database adapter, is essential. It improves stability and predictability of the solution. BPM and ACM are just one of the components plugging into the stack and both reuse all other components.

Many books have already been written on the Oracle SOA Suite, so we will not dive in detail in the behavior of the Oracle SOA Suite.

Oracle BPM was added to the Fusion Middleware 11g stack with the Oracle SOA Suite 11.1.1.3 release in 2010. With this release, Oracle BPM provided a BPMN 2.0 compliant process execution engine complemented with a complete process modeling and development environment that addressed both developers and business analysts. Oracle BPM is layered on top of Oracle SOA Suite and hence benefits from the powerful integration infrastructure; which is seamlessly available to a BPM process.

Customers of Oracle BPM have been effectively using the product to manage a large part of their business processes. They have been able to derive a number of benefits from having successfully automated and streamlined core business processes, such as real-time insight into their processes, quick response to changes in business conditions, reduced costs due to processes optimization, etc.

Although Oracle BPM with its BPMN-based engine has successfully addressed a large part of routine and structured processes such as invoice processing, order processing, etc., there still remain areas of a business that have not been automated using BPM.

In Chapter 2, we discussed the need for "adaptively agile" systems. Solutions in such a system have to dynamically sense external events and respond appropriately. Variations and unpredictability are key attributes of such solutions. Traditional BPMN can be used to build solutions that can interact in a sense-and-respond manner but the responses are based on predefined actions plans. Any unforeseen variations cannot be handled by these applications without having to go back and modify the process models. We also discussed the important role stakeholders play in enabling adaptive behavior of such systems. Oracle BPM Suite extends the scope of BPM to address these highly variable, event driven, knowledge-work based processes.

You may wonder why should we use the Oracle BPM Suite to handle adaptive case management?

We have seen that the nature of work addressed by adaptive case management is quite variable in nature and depends significantly on the case workers' knowledge and expertise to progress the case. The individual tasks that case workers perform could be routine in nature. For instance, a task may be a simple approval workflow or an automated process to complete a set of actions. This means even in an adaptive case-based application there is a need to handle routine tasks.

As we have mentioned, Oracle BPM Suite already handles routine processes, with all levels of complexity, very well. By extending this offering to include the notion of a "case" and a case event model, you can now build adaptive case management applications that can leverage BPM for routine tasks within a case. Since it is layered on top of BPM, ACM is able to enjoy the same benefits as BPM and provide case analytics, opportunities for optimization, and automation, all this without constraining the knowledge worker with predefined structured processes.

As you will see in the following chapters, Oracle ACM builds on Oracle BPM and therefore fully leverages BPM and SOA stacks to provide a powerful case management framework. This allows for creating case management applications that span enterprise business applications. This is possible because of the powerful adapter framework available in the BPM stack with over 200 connectivity options to a large variety of business applications.

7.3 Oracle BPM/ACM Usage Characteristics

With the strong support of the Oracle SOA Suite integration capabilities, Oracle BPM/ACM is a good candidate to use in an enterprise wide, cross application scenario, where work and information are shared across a group of case workers. Oracle ACM takes care of the end-to-end management and monitoring of all activities, where the activities could be shared across tasks defined in Oracle BPM or in external applications. One of the strong capabilities of Oracle ACM is the ability to act upon events; any change in the lifecycle of a case can result in a new chain of activities to be spawned off.

Oracle BPM/ACM is a middleware product and based upon composition of components via visual programming as will be described later in this chapter and shown in Chapter 17. This product feature, combined with the ability to deliver in an agile way, enables the delivery of (partial) solutions in short cycles. This helps in managing the end-to-end case process and getting a better understanding of the complexity in a gradual way.

Oracle ACM offers different aspects of flexibility at runtime. Adhoc tasks provide the case workers with the ability to start tasks that are not part of the predefined case model. The flexible stakeholder model allows (re)assignment of tasks and responsibilities at runtime. Another level of flexibility is the event-driven capability of BPM/ACM. Rules-based event handlers can be used to alter and adapt the case by making activities available, withdrawing existing activities, change milestone states, etc. Oracle ACM also allows adding on new activities from a library of predefined activities.

Table 7.1 summarizes the usage characteristics of the lifecycle design functionalities for Oracle BPM/ACM.

7.4 Case Management Lifecycle Functionality with Oracle BPM/ACM

In Chapter 3, we introduced the various aspects for the design of a case management solution. Oracle ACM and BPM directly relate to the case lifecycle design category, shown in Figure 7.1.

Table 7.1 Usage Characteristics of Oracle BPM/ACM

Focus Area	*Product Characteristics*
Case management design area	Life cycle design
Classification support	All three case management classifications are supported: service request, incident management, and/or investigative solution
Delivery type: Full implementation or umbrella type	Umbrella type
Product type	Middleware
Agility at runtime: ACM or PCM	ACM type: Ad hoc processes as part of a case can be started Flexible stakeholder model Ability to add new event publishing sources

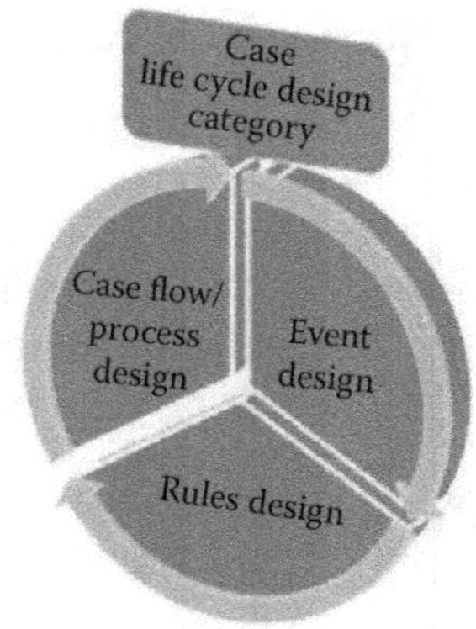

Figure 7.1 Case management lifecycle design category. The case lifecycle design category describes the coordination of activities in reaching one of the end goals and consists of three design components: Case flow and process design, rules design, and event design.

When implementing the lifecycle design for a case management solution with Oracle ACM, three products form the core of the solution: ACM, BPM and Oracle Business Rules. Additionally specific Oracle SOA Suite products, such as human tasks and BPEL, will complete the lifecycle area functionality.

7.4.1 Case Flow and Process Design

7.4.1.1 Case Flow Design with Oracle Adaptive Case Management

ACM was introduced in April 2013 as a feature set on top of Oracle BPM. With this release Oracle BPM Suite can now be used not only for structured BPMN-based processes but also for unstructured and adhoc processes. When using Oracle BPM with ACM, it is now possible to create knowledge-worker driven, event-based and content-focused processes, with the focus on reaching an end goal by acting on events instead following a predefined path.

7.4.1.1.1 Support for Structured and Unstructured Work

Actions performed by case workers to progress the case are represented by activities. An activity can be modeled as a structured process, a task, or as a custom implementation. The ability to define activities using these different implementations makes it possible to provide case workers with a catalog of activities to perform. These activities, some of which could be structured processes, can be performed in any order and any number of times as the case worker deems appropriate, allowing a mix of structured and adhoc or unstructured work.

7.4.1.1.2 Key Features

At a high level, Oracle ACM contains the following key features:

- The case is driven by events, originating from both internal and external origin.
- The case is a container for data, content, and relationships with other cases.
- Activities are the predictable part of the case.
- Audit trails capture every event that occurs and actions that are taken during the lifetime of a case.

- Case policies allow putting in controls to help guide the case worker through the case progression.
- A flexible stakeholder model that can be changed at runtime.

7.4.1.1.3 Key Concepts

Following are key concepts in ACM:

- *Case*: A case is the logical container of data, content, history of events, and actions taken,
- *Case model*: Defines the structure of a case type. This includes case attributes such as name, category, priority, due date, etc. It also includes definitions of case milestones, stakeholders, and structured and unstructured content that the case depends on.
- *Case instance*: A specific instance of a case type and is a collection of documents, data, and case activities that are used to process the case and audit the progress of the case.
- *Case folder*: Case folders are specific locations in the configured content management system where all documents are stored. These folders can either be generic or instance specific.
- *Case data*: the data objects used by the case instance during the case progression. Case data can either be internal (stored in line with the case instance and managed by Oracle ACM) or external (managed by external applications, referenced by Oracle ACM).
- *Case lifecycle*: Case lifecycle tracks the progression of a case instance from start to close and can have states such as active, suspended, aborted or closed,
- *Milestones*: Milestones help track the progression of the case and are used to mark a specific point in the case progression.
- *Case activity*: Case activities allow case workers to perform work in the context of a case. These activities can be BPM processes, workflow tasks, or any custom processing using Java.
- *Case event*: Case events are events that are raised as a consequence of changes to the case. Events are raised for case state changes, activity changes, milestone changes, stakeholder changes, data changes, and document changes.

7.4.1.2 Process Modeling

Oracle BPM features a comprehensive, browser-based composer that business analysts can use to model business processes. The composer provides all the aspects of modeling functions, which allows a process modeler to not only draw out a process model that reflects the real-world business process but also adds implementation artifacts to it, which means right from the browser, depending on appropriate privileges, one can model, simulate, test, and deploy a process to the process engine.

The web-based composer, as shown in Figure 7.2, is complemented by the *BPM Studio* and is part of the *Oracle JDeveloper* IDE. This provides a development environment more suitable for technical developers. A typical BPM application is modeled by business analysts and includes enough details for the developer to take over. The developers then add technical details such as service invocation, complex data mapping, etc., and move the project to a standard code promotion cycle. A key aspect of the BPM project development lifecycle is that both the business analysts and developers work on the same project through a shared repository that is part of a fully collaborative business IT development environment.

Oracle BPM implements BPMN 2.0 standard; which not only defines the notations but also execution semantics. Oracle BPMN engine executes these BPMN 2.0 models directly without having to generate any Java or other intermediate execution code. This means that what you have modeled is what is executed, "what you see is what you execute."

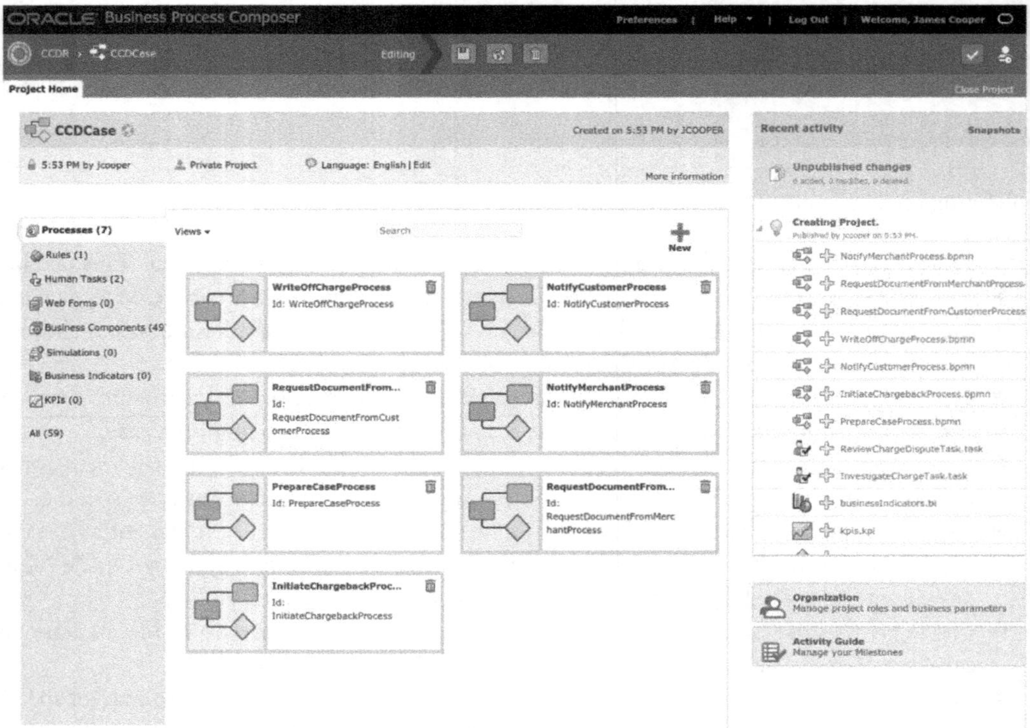

Figure 7.2 Oracle BPM composer.

7.4.1.2.1 Work Management

The human workflow service engine handles all aspects of human work assignment within a BPM process. Oracle BPM provides commonly used workflow patterns as first-class activities in the BPM modeling palette. Hierarchy-based approval workflow and group voting are some examples of these workflow patterns. Using Oracle Business Rules with human workflow rule-based dynamic work assignment can be defined.

7.4.2 Event Design

Case progression in Oracle ACM is event driven. Every change to any of the key elements of a case such as data, documents, activities, milestones, and stakeholders generates appropriate events. Case events are also generated for any case state changes such as the start of a case, close of a case, suspension of a case, etc. In addition to these events generated by the case engine, Oracle ACM also supports user-defined events that can be used to register external events in the case.

7.4.3 Rules Design

As we have seen in Section 3.3.2.3.2, different rule types support the case management execution:

- Case lifecycle decision-making
- Entitlement determination

- Progress measurement
- Data entry validation
- Information discovery

We focus in this chapter on the first rule type, case lifecycle decision-making, since this relates directly to the execution of a case in the Oracle ACM/BPM products. The other rule type functionality is handled in Chapter 10.

Oracle Business Rules is a service component in Oracle BPM Suite that provides decision services to the BPMN process for flow control, task assignment, determination of participants, etc. The rules engine is an inference-based rules engine that allows definition of complex rules using easy-to-use decision tables, verbal rules, and if-then pattern matching.

7.4.4 Life Cycle Design Product Mapping to Oracle BPM/ACM/SOA Suite

We finish the lifecycle design section with a product mapping of the case management lifecycle functionality toward the Oracle BPM/ACM/SOA Suite product sets. In Chapter 5, a drawing technique was introduced that enables us to make a translation from required functionalities towards Oracle products.

The case lifecycle design category contains three main design components:

- Case flows and processes
- Event handling
- Rules support

In the mapping, we include the case lifecycle decision-making rule type. The remaining rule types are described in more detail in Chapter 10.

7.4.4.1 Case Flow and Process Mapping

In Figure 7.3, we summarize the capability mapping toward Oracle BPM/ACM and SOA Suite products. All capabilities in the case flow and process design components relate to only a few Oracle products. Most products in Figure 7.3 have been introduced already earlier in this chapter. Products that have not been introduced will be summarized in the following description.

7.4.4.1.1 Lifecycle Management and Rules Support Case Lifecycle Decision-Making

Both the Oracle ACM and BPM products support the lifecycle management, with Oracle ACM having a more event-based approach and Oracle BPM following a structured predefined path. This functionality is strongly supported by Oracle Business Rules for all decisions to be made during the lifecycle of the case.

7.4.4.1.2 Human-to-Application (H2A)

As part of the case execution, human activities can be initiated. Both ACM and BPM can be the initiating actor for human activities. The human workflow component of Oracle BPMN Suite takes care of the actual execution of the human activity.

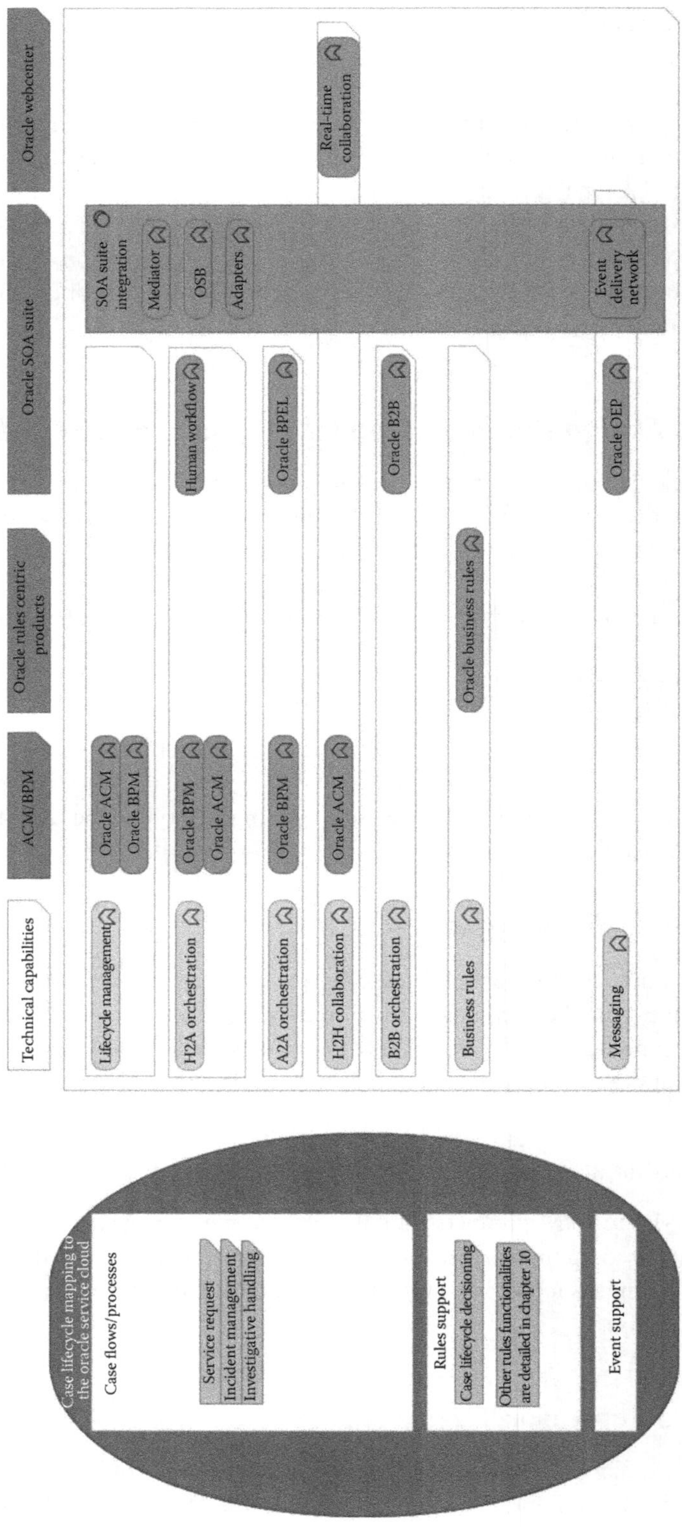

Figure 7.3 Oracle Lifecycle mapping to Oracle BPM/ACM/SOA Suite products.

7.4.4.1.3 Application-to-Application (A2A)

From within the case execution, automated tasks can also be initiated. This is handled by either the SOA Suite Business Process Execution Language (BPEL) product or by BPM.

BPEL was created in an effort to standardize process execution, just like web services helped in standardizing communication between applications. The standard is defined as part of the OASIS standard group.

Both BPM and BPEL can be used to define processes and both can contain automated and human activities. BPEL is a block-structured, top-down process model that is ideal for straight-through processing (STP), which is a typical A2A integration flow. When the process also includes H2A capabilities or cannot be easily modeled as top-down flow and requires more of a directed flow graph, BPMN is a better choice. Mixing both BPM and BPEL is a good way to separate pure technical flows from business-aimed processes.

7.4.4.1.4 Human-to-Human H2H Collaboration (H2H)

Oracle WebCenter Real-Time Collaboration supplies the end users with direct interaction capabilities. The main functionalities of this product are instant messaging, presence, chat rooms, and web and voice conferencing.

Oracle ACM supports simple H2H capabilities with the commenting feature on the case level, this enables users to share insights and thoughts around the case execution.

7.4.4.1.5 Business-to-Business Orchestration (B2B)

The Oracle B2B adapter handles complex automated business transactions with business partners.

7.4.4.2 Event Handling Mapping

Event handling is one of the key features in Oracle ACM. As described earlier in the key features for ACM, the case execution is driven by events, originating from both internal and external origin. The *event delivery network* (EDN) is responsible for delivering events within the BPM/ACM/SOA application. Each application component in the BPM/ACM/SOA application can both start events and listen to events that are delivered via the EDN. The ACM product listens and acts upon these events via the business rules application component. *Oracle Event Processing* (*OEP*) listens to data streams, and has the ability to identify specific situations that require follow-up action, for instance initiate activities in ACM and BPM. In Section 10.3.2, more detail is provided for the OEP product.

7.5 Case Management Interaction Functionality with Oracle SOA Suite

In Chapter 3, we introduced the case management interaction design category, shown in Figure 7.4. We will look here at the portal and channel functionalities the SOA Suite offers. The dashboard functionality will be described later in Chapter 10.

In this section, we will focus on what Oracle products support the portal and the channel design for an Oracle BPM/ACM solution. The dashboard functionality will be described later in Chapter 10.

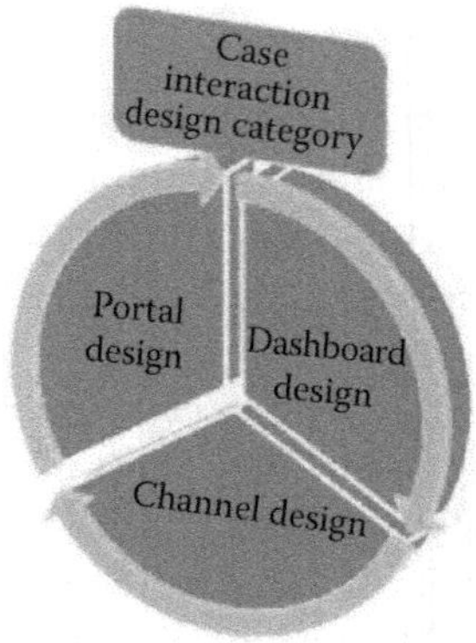

Figure 7.4 Case management interaction design category. The case interaction design enables maximizing the support for the case work force. This design area contains three design parts: Portal design, dashboard design, and channel design.

7.5.1 Portal Design: 360-Degree View of the Case

For a case worker to effectively process the case to completion with the desired outcome, he needs to have all the information—both data-based and content-based information in one integrated workspace.

For the portal functionality, the following options exist to create a 360-degree view of the case with Oracle products:

- Out-of-the-box functionality via the Oracle BPM/ACM portal
- Application Development Framework (ADF), customized functionality with the aid of the case management/BPM and human task application programming interface (API)

7.5.1.1 Out-of-the Box Functionality via the Oracle BPM/ACM Portal

Oracle ACM provides through a web-based, easy-to-use user interface that gives, at a glance, the complete state of the case—from available and completed activities, state of case data, audit trail to current state of the milestones, shown in Figure 7.5.

7.5.1.2 ADF, Customized Functionality with the Aid of the Case Management/BPM and Human Task APIs

Oracle BPM suite provides a comprehensive set of APIs that can be used to build customized user interface that either complements or replaces the out-of-the-box BPM workspace application. These APIs are available as Java APIs, SOAP/HTTP Web services and REST. The Java API is the full set of APIs, which lets you interact with and manage cases, processes, and tasks. This same Java API set is also exposed as SOAP/HTTP web services. A smaller subset, but complete from the perspective of building next generation mobile applications, is available as REST services.

The out-of-the-box BPM workspace is built using these same sets of APIs. Similarly the new Oracle BPM task management mobile application is built using these same REST services based upon the Oracle Mobile Application Framework.

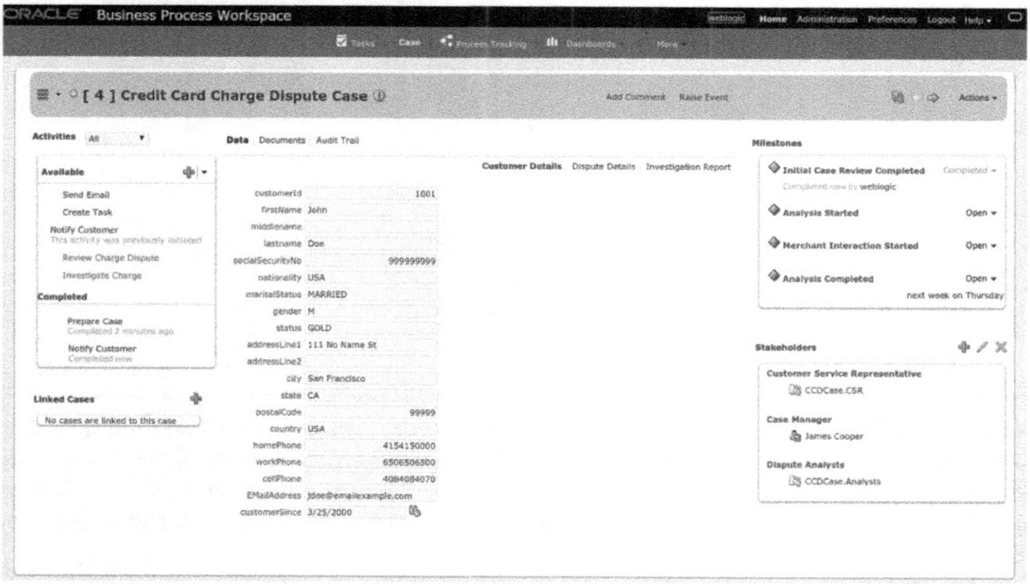

Figure 7.5 Case management portal with the Oracle BPM/ACM workspace.

7.5.2 Channel Design

The Oracle BPM/ACM and SOA Suite provide support for access via different channels.

Oracle ADF delivers the standardized user interface functionality within the Oracle SOA Suite. ADF is based upon the Java Server Faces (JSF) specifications and contains a visual and declarative development. ADF delivers support for usage in multiple channel environments, such as browsers and mobiles. Oracle BPM/ACM delivers presentation of human task forms via ADF technology.

Mobile Application Framework (MAF) is the device-independent development framework used for creating mobile applications using standard development tools. Developers use Java, HTML5, and declarative components that are part of the MAF to design and build mobile applications that can run on both iOS and Android devices. An integral part of MAF is the built-in security for authentication, authorization, and encryption support. With MAF you only develop your mobile application once and run it on leading device platforms without any change.

Oracle BPM uses MAF to provide a task management application on iOS and Android devices. With this application users can act on their assigned tasks on their mobile devices. The application is designed to work offline in case the BPM server is not accessible.

7.6 Case Management Information Functionality with Oracle BPM/ACM/SOA Suite

The last functional category from Chapter 3 is the case information design (Figure 7.6).

Oracle BPM/ACM delivers limited support for the information design, as can be seen in Table 7.2. Oracle BPM/ACM is aimed at delivering a flexible case management solution in an enterprise wide, cross-application scenario. Oracle BPM/ACM is not aimed at a specific market and therefore does not include case supporting and people relationship data models.

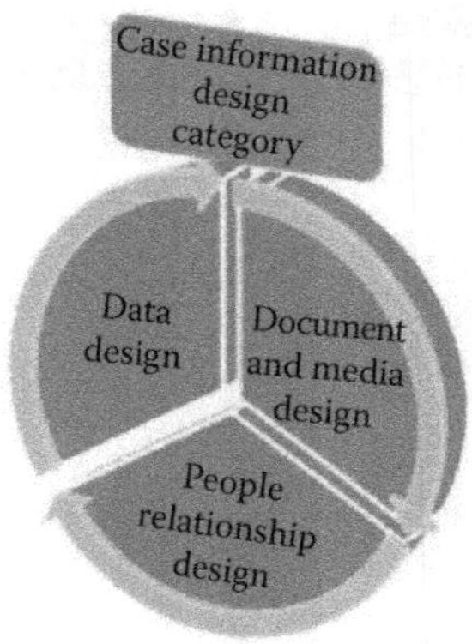

Figure 7.6 Case management information design category. The case information design deals with all sorts of data and documentation flowing through the case and maps the relationships between all persons and/or assets involved in the case. The case information design category contains three design components, data design, document and media design, and people relationship design.

Table 7.2 Information Support for Case Management with Oracle BPM/ACM

Information Design	*Functionality*	*Supported by BPM/ACM/SOA*	*More Information in Section*
Data design	Case execution data	Yes	7.6.1
	Case supporting data	No	—
	Tactical related information	Yes	7.6.1
Document and media design	Case input management	Yes	7.6.2
	Case output management	Yes	7.6.2
People relationship design	Internal stakeholders	No	—
	External stakeholders	No	—

7.6.1 Case Execution Data: Detailed Audit Trail

Oracle ACM tracks every event that occurs in the context of a case and provides a detailed audit trail of these events from the point the case is started, as shown in Figure 7.7.

The audit trail can be protected using permission labels, and allows control of who is allowed to see which events in the audit trail. For instance, the case owner may decide to allow only case participants with "confidential" clearance to view that a particular "document added…" event has occurred. Oracle ACM provides fine-grained access control over different elements of a case. Access control is managed by using permission labels, for instance "confidential" can be a permission label. This label can be attached to any of the elements (data, activities, milestones, documents, and audit trail events). So, if a case worker decides to protect an audit entry and allow only those that have confidential access, he/she can attach the "confidential" label to that particular event in the audit trail. Any stakeholder other than the ones having "confidential" access is not able to see that entry in the audit trail. You can find more details on using permission labels in Chapter 17.

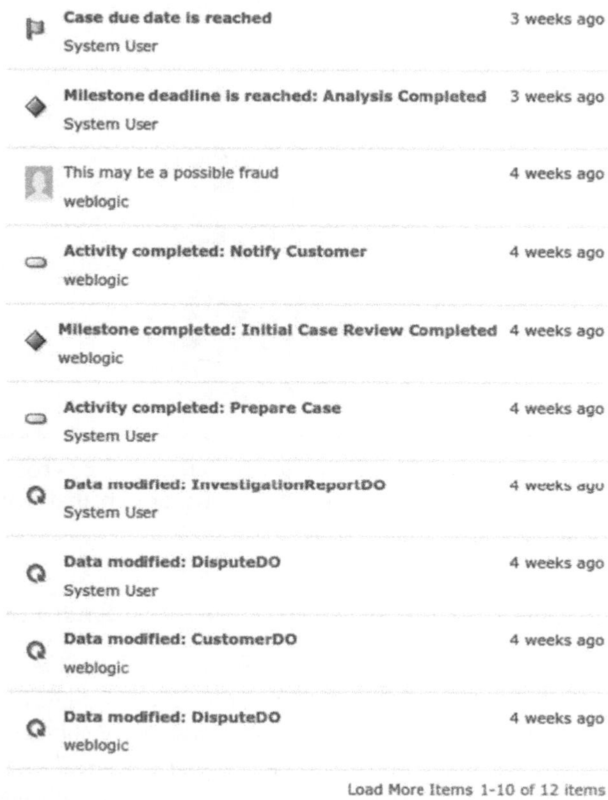

Figure 7.7 Case audit trail.

7.6.2 Document and Media Design

Oracle BPM/ACM deliver support for content management out-of-the-box. Oracle BPM uses Oracle WebCenter Content for storing task attachments. Oracle ACM uses WebCenter Content as its primary content store for all case documents.

Oracle WebCenter Content is an enterprise grade content management system. It provides a web-based interface for managing all types of content such as documents and media content. It also provides plug-ins for desktop applications such as Microsoft Office, which allow you to contribute content directly from these applications.

With WebCenter Content, searching across different types of content is easy and access to content can be secured using a comprehensive security model consisting of security groups, accounts, roles, and permissions.

WebCenter Content comes with conversion services that can be used to convert supported content to various formats. For instance, you can configure that all MS Word documents have a web-viewable version of the document generated as a PDF file.

7.7 Cross-Functional Case Management Capabilities

Functionality shared across all other functional areas is contained in the case management cross-functional category, as shown in Figure 7.8.

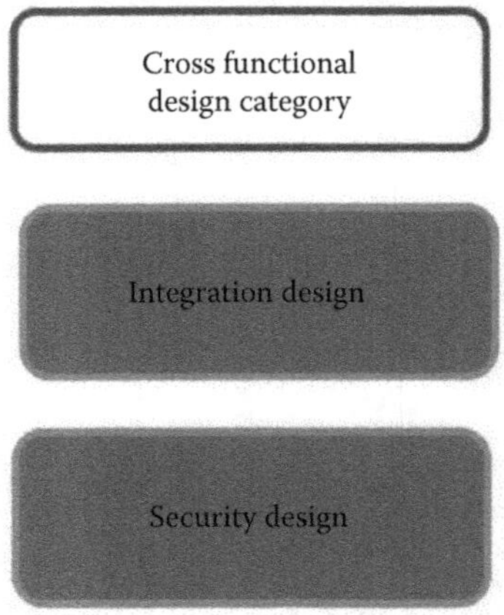

Figure 7.8 Case management cross-functional design category. The cross-functionality design category contains the integration design and the security design that both support the other functional design categories.

7.7.1 Case Management Integration Functionality with Oracle SOA Suite

The BPM/ACM product is built on top of the Oracle SOA Suite. The SOA integration capabilities enable the BPM/ACM applications to act in an enterprise wide, cross application scenario. In Figure 7.3, the Oracle SOA Suite integration product is mapped across all capabilities. Different integration technologies are used to enable integration both internally and externally. The *Oracle Service Bus (OSB)* delivers integration capabilities with external sources, and contains all standard service bus functionalities like transformation, routing, secured, and reliable delivery with high performance.

The *mediator* is the internal service bus used between the application components that are part of the BPM/ACM/SOA application. *Adapters* support both the OSB and the mediator with standardized connections to external applications, such as databases, ERP systems, and cloud applications.

7.7.2 Case Management Security Functionality with Oracle

Oracle ACM defines a notion of a "stakeholder" who has access to the case and can perform various actions to progress the case. Stakeholders' access to the case can be controlled via user-defined permission labels.

7.7.2.1 Case Stakeholders

A case stakeholder is defined as a role with one or more users, groups, or other roles as members of this special stakeholder role. The stakeholder-based user model can be defined during design as part of the case model. It can be changed at runtime, for a specific case instance, by adding new stakeholder roles or changing the composition of an existing stakeholder model.

7.7.2.1 Permissions

Case permissions are defined as permission tags that can be attached to different elements of a case such as data, documents, activities, and audit-trail entries. Permission tags are user-defined strings such as "public," "top secret," etc. Access control policies are defined for each of these tags by the case administrator or security administrator using Oracle Platform Security Services framework to control what each permission label means.

7.8 Conclusion

Oracle ACM is built on top of the already existing Oracle BPM/SOA product stack and is a middleware based product. The combination of Oracle products SOA, BPM, and ACM brings together integration capabilities, predictable BPM based processes and event based case management capabilities. These product features make Oracle ACM a good candidate for usage in an enterprise wide and cross application scenario. In this scenario, ACM takes responsibility for the end-to-end management and monitoring of all activities within the context of a case. These activities can be BPM processes, workflow tasks, and even other cases. Since ACM is layered on top of the SOA infrastructure, these case activities can also easily interact with external applications using the powerful adapter framework. All other functionalities, interaction, and information design can be delivered from other products that reside in the Oracle SOA Suite and database product sets.

Chapter 8

Siebel

8.1 Introduction

In this chapter, we will describe the Oracle Siebel product in relation to case management.

The goals of this chapter are as follows:

- Give a high-level overview of Oracle Siebel
- Describe the usage characteristics of Oracle Siebel for case management functionality
- Describe how Oracle Siebel has strong support for case management information and the case management lifecycle design
- Show how the Siebel case management solution can be extended into different industry verticals
- Give an example of an industry vertical with the public sector case management solution
- Give an overview of supporting Oracle products

We start this chapter with an overview and usage characteristics of the Oracle Siebel product. Then we describe the product feature of Oracle Siebel according to the case management functional design as presented earlier in Chapter 3, with the main focus on the lifecycle and information functionality.

In Chapter 18, a tutorial is presented on Oracle Siebel where the product implementation steps will be extensively discussed.

8.2 Oracle Siebel Overview

8.2.1 History

Siebel started in 1993 as a system for sales force automation, from which it expanded into the customer relationship management (CRM) area. It is now one of the market leaders in this area. The aim of CRM systems is to organize, automate, and synchronize sales efforts and customer support for companies. Siebel extended the CRM capabilities with case management functionality, which will be the focus in this chapter.

8.2.2 Horizontal and Verticals

In the Siebel product, a distinction is made between functionality used in every industry domain, also known as horizontal functionality, and functionality specifically tailored for a specific industry domain, these are known as verticals.

Examples of *horizontal* functionality are sales, marketing, and analytics-related functionality.

Siebel made specializations for different industries to accommodate the differences in the way these industries deliver services to their customers. These industry solutions are called *verticals*, which use the Siebel's standard CRM capabilities as the base functionality and are based on best practices within each industry. Here is a subset of the industries for which Siebel delivers *vertical* solutions:

- Public sector
- Communications and utilities
- Banking and capital markets
- Insurance and healthcare
- Financial services

8.2.3 Configuration versus Customization

The Oracle Siebel product is a package-based solution. The design and the implementation of the product are based upon *configuration* and *customization*.

Configuration is adjusting the package toward the needs of the business without changing the package. This involves determining what data objects and elements are needed, setting up process models and state models toward the business requirements, determining what fields are needed on a specific user interfaces, and setting up the security model. This activity will not change the behavior of the package; it only composes the package toward the business requirements.

Customization is done when the business requirements do not align with the abilities of the package, and the package behavior needs to be changed. This activity should be kept to a minimum since customization poses extra risks to the maintainability of the application, such as the risk of noncompatibility during upgrades. Another factor favoring for keeping the customization to a minimum is the cost of operation. "Plain vanilla" implementation, with no customization, is the preferred option from a maintainability perspective, since this implementation has the lowest cost of operation and less dependency of specific personnel.

8.2.4 Extensions of Functionality

Every solution in Siebel, whether horizontal or vertical, can be extended to adjust to the specific customer situation. These extensions can be done in every level of the application, to name a few, in the data model, the preconfigured processes, approvals and assessments, and the state models. As shown in Figure 8.1 the extensions built on top of the existing CRM functionality and the horizontals and verticals inherit all the functionalities from the lower levels.

8.2.5 Siebel Specific Terminology

The Siebel product contains a set of building blocks that determine the behavior of the application, as shown in Figure 8.2. Each building block can be configured and extended during the design and implementation of the application.

Table 8.1 lists the building block groupings, to which case management design area this relates and in which section more detail is given of the design of these components.

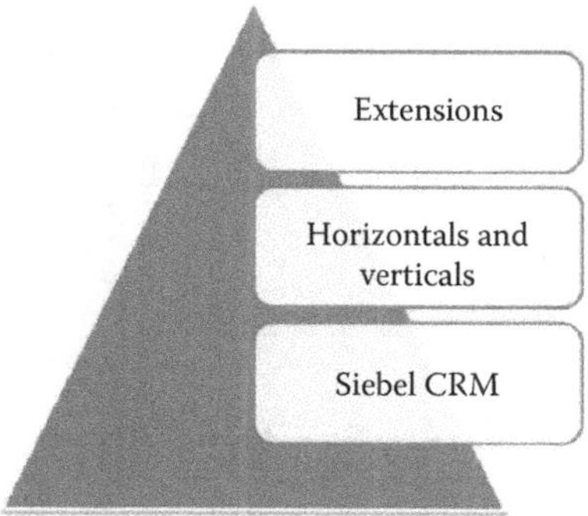

Figure 8.1 Siebel extension model.

8.2.6 Market Example: Law Enforcement and Policing Operations Solution

Throughout this chapter, we will use the law enforcement and policing operations solutions as examples to show how the different functional design areas can be extended to accommodate a specific tailored industry solution.

The Siebel Public Sector vertical is one of the most sophisticated verticals within the Siebel CRM stack. Capgemini extended the public sector case management functionality into an integrated policing solution reflecting the different types of cases that are known within law enforcement organizations (https://www.capgemini.com/public-sector/transform-police-t-police). The extended solution contains a case management environment specialized for the law enforcement and policing operations and contains preconfigured functionalities that are based on best practices of law enforcement organizations from around the world. These extended features will speed up the realization and roll out of leading Oracle technology and reduce operational costs. In the case management, design descriptions for the Siebel product details from this extension solution will be used to give an insight to the usage of the Siebel product.

8.3 Oracle Siebel Usage Characteristics

Siebel case management is a package-based solution and delivers an end-to-end case management solution tailored at a large variety of industries. The Siebel product delivers a full solution stack, containing data, processes, and user interfaces.

The focus of the Siebel solution is primarily on delivering services to customers and is based upon the case management classification service request. In some industries, such as insurance and the solution for justice and public safety the case management solution has a focus toward the incident management classifications. Both classifications, service request and incident management, are supported in Siebel by investigation handling functionality. The Siebel CRM-based case management solution has two key features, the preconfigured CRM based data model and the extensibility of the solution in all design areas.

Within the Siebel case management solution, all scenarios for the case are defined upfront in the data model, the preconfigured processes, approvals and assessments, and the state models, with all its complexities. The Siebel product aligns mostly with the production case management (PCM) type of case management. Some aspects could be changed at runtime, such as changing the state model, but most design components are fixed.

Table 8.2 summarizes the usage characteristics for Oracle Siebel.

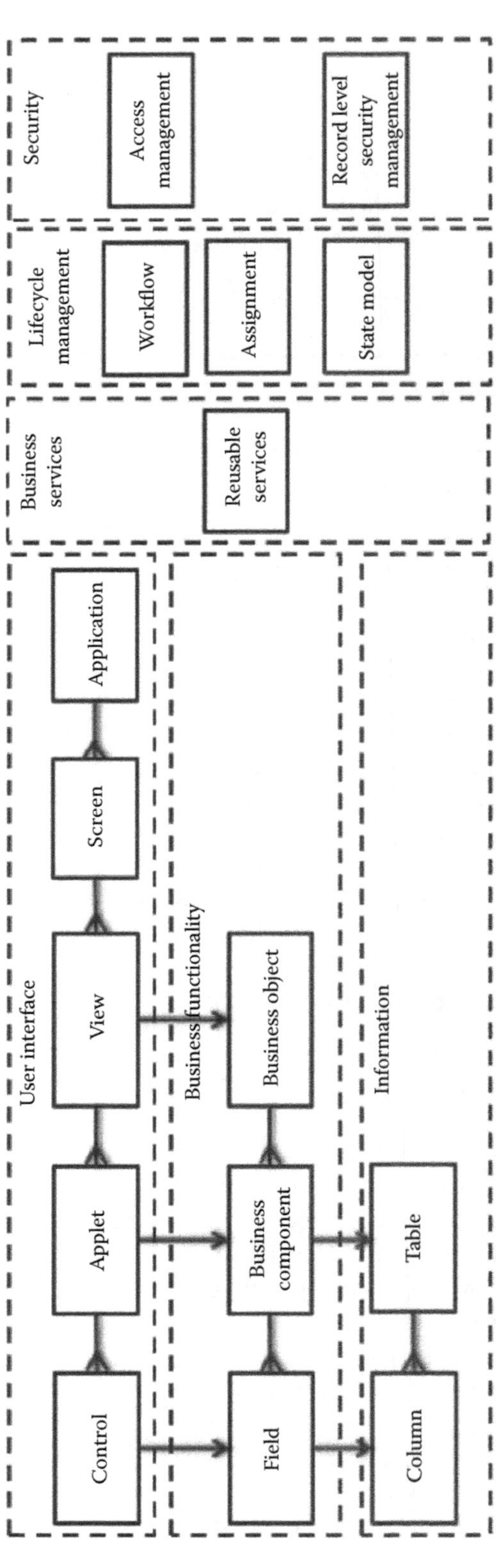

Figure 8.2 Siebel technical overview.

Table 8.1 Siebel Building Blocks

Building Block Grouping	*Description*	*Case Management Design Area*	*More Information in Section*
User interface	The user interface contains the end-user interaction functionality	Case interaction design	8.6.1
Business functionality	This area contains the information objects determining the CRM and case management data model	Case information design	8.4.1
Information	This is the core Siebel repository	Case information design	8.4.1
Business services	A business service is a reusable component within Siebel that combines functionality within the system to simplify and minimize the amount of duplicated codes. It can be used as part of the integration with external systems, but also internally to standardize functionality such as calculations	Case lifecycle Design and case integration design	8.5.2
Lifecycle management	This contains the main functionality used to determine the lifecycle of a Siebel case	Case lifecycle Design	8.5.1
Security	This area contains access and record level security	Case roles and authorization design	8.7.1

Table 8.2 Siebel Usage Characteristics

Focus Area	*Product Characteristics*
Case management design area	Information and life cycle design
Classification support	All three case management classifications are supported: service request, incident management, and/or investigative solution
Delivery type: Full implementation or umbrella type	Full implementation
Product type	Package based
Agility at runtime: ACM or PCM	PCM type: The solution with all its aspects is defined upfront. Flexibility at runtime of the state model is possible

8.4 Case Management Information Functionality with Oracle Siebel

Since the data model is one of the key features in the Siebel product, we start the functional description for Siebel with the case information design. The design components for the information design category are shown in Figure 8.3. For a full description of the case information design category, see Chapter 3.

The Siebel product gives full support for all case management information design components as shown in Table 8.3.

8.4.1 People Relationship Design and Data Design

The key component of Siebel is the CRM-based data model. This CRM model is based upon the party model, which is a generic data model that links together person-related information such

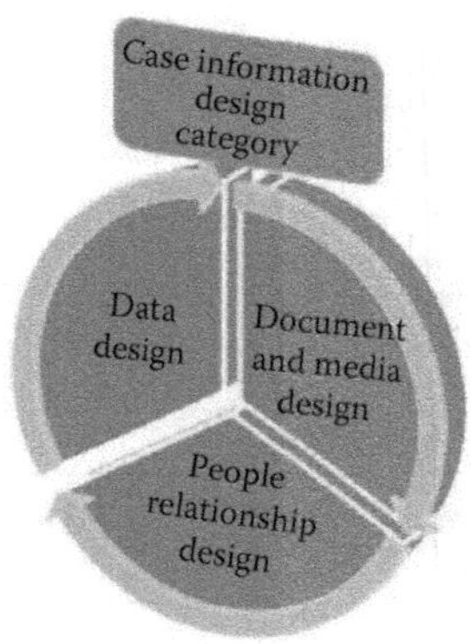

Figure 8.3 Case management information design category. The case information design deals with all sorts of data and documentation flowing through the case and maps the relationships between all persons and/or assets involved in the case. The case information design category contains three design components, data design, document and media design and people relationship design.

Table 8.3 Information Design Support for Case Management with Oracle Siebel

Information Design	*Functionality*	*Supported by Siebel*	*More Information in Section*
Data design	Case execution data	Yes	8.4.1
	Case supporting data	Yes	8.4.1
	Tactical-related information	Yes	8.4.1
Document and media design	Case input management	Yes	8.4.2
	Case output management	Yes	8.4.2
People relationship design	Internal stakeholders	Yes	8.4.1
	External stakeholders	Yes	8.4.1

as personal details, organization structures, and security profiles. With its open extension-based structure, the Siebel CRM data model is designed for structuring and linking additional information, such as individuals with events, agreements, goods, and services. This enables Siebel to act as a CRM-based case management system for a broad variety of tasks where the purpose is to establish links between different information items.

The design of this part requires mapping the business-required information toward the Siebel CRM data model, where specific attention is given to the building blocks contained in the *business functionality* as shown in Figure 8.2.

- *Business Object*: A business object corresponds to the main concepts dealing with the context of the application. In case management, this corresponds to concepts such as "person," "suspect," "offence," or "coercive measure." A business object is used to manage the information related to the specific composed information that is needed for a specific vertical or extension, and is mainly designed via configuration.
- *Business Component* (*Fields*): A business component (and related fields) is used to combine several of the underlying data tables for retrieval and managing of the information. Usually design in this area is done via configuration.
- *Information*: The *information* grouping contains the Siebel building blocks table and columns and is part of the core Siebel repository. Tables (and columns) are used to store all *case execution data* and the *tactical-related information*. Design in this area usually relates to providing access to audit trails.

Extending the Data Model, an example based upon the Law Enforcement and Policing Operations use case:
As mentioned in Section 8.2.6, the police case extends the Siebel Public Sector vertical. The data model for the Siebel Public Sector vertical is known as the public party model. To deal with police cases, specific information needs to be added to the already existing public party model. The Siebel Public Sector vertical is enriched with the following new information objects: Offenses, offenders, victims, witnesses, suspects, locations, properties and evidence, and coercive measures. From an audit perspective, besides an audit trail, it is crucial that the usage of data is also stored. For instance, for a sensitive crime case data related to a VIP it needs to be logged as to who requested this data and what was done with this data.

One specific important characteristic of the police information model relates to the fact that three different police case types, incidents, leads, and cases need to be kept in the information model:

- *Incidents* deal with violations of the law, for which no investigation needs to be set up. Examples of incidents are traffic accidents, traffic offenses, and asocial behavior.
- A *lead* gives an indication of possible crime activities. At the time a lead is brought in, no crime activity has been measured yet. Leads might turn into police cases at a later point in time.
- A *case* deals with the investigation related to a crime that has been committed. In order to get a complete picture of the situation, cases, leads, and incidents can be combined together. This helps in finding and arresting the suspects and enables a successful handover to the prosecutor.

These three main information entities (incidents, cases, and leads) of the solution are the pillars of the law enforcement and policing operations capabilities of the solution. They interact with

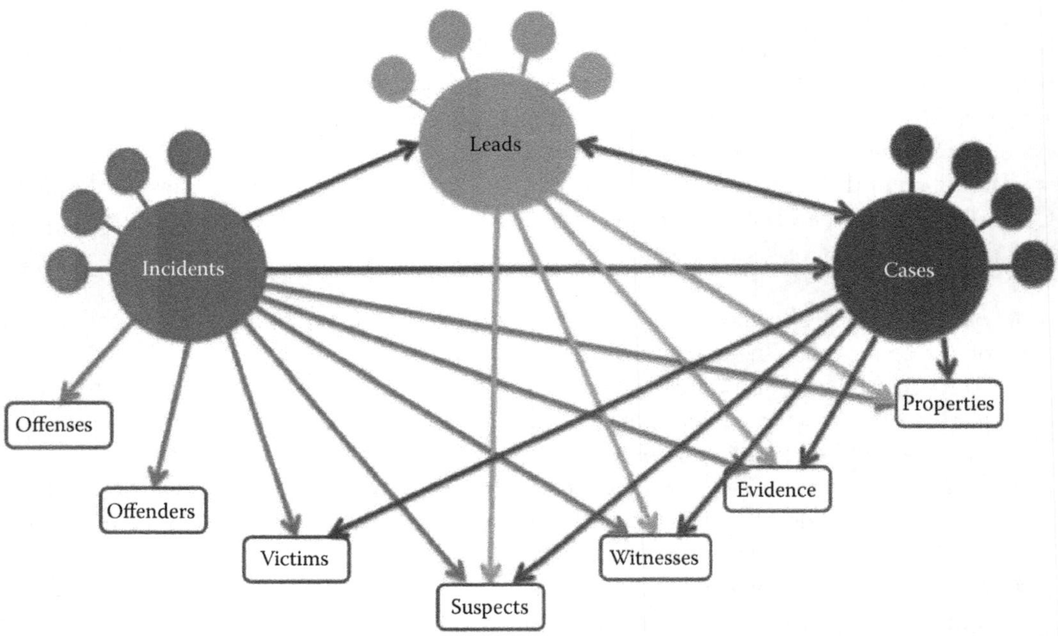

Figure 8.4 Shared information model for cases, leads, and incidents.

each other to support the law enforcement organizations to combat crime and terrorism as well as enhance the public safety and service, and emergency management. The information models for the police case types, incidents, cases, and leads, each have separate aspects but also partially overlap one another, as can be seen in Figure 8.4.

8.4.2 Document and Media Design

Out of the box Siebel offers attachment functionality to add more detail to a case record by adding relevant documents and other external media. This information is stored as part of the Siebel application or via an external document management system. In both options, Siebel offers the functionality to add metadata and unique identifications for later search and easy retrieval.

8.5 Case Management Life Cycle Functionality with Oracle Siebel

In Chapter 3, we introduced the various aspects for the design of a case management solution. We will look here at the case lifecycle design category for the Siebel product, as shown in Figure 8.5.

Specifically we will look at the case flow and process design functionality within Siebel, as this is the main lifecycle supporting area.

8.5.1 Case Flow and Process Design with Oracle Siebel

Siebel supports the case flow and processes design with three main functionalities: the state model, workflow management, and the assignment management.

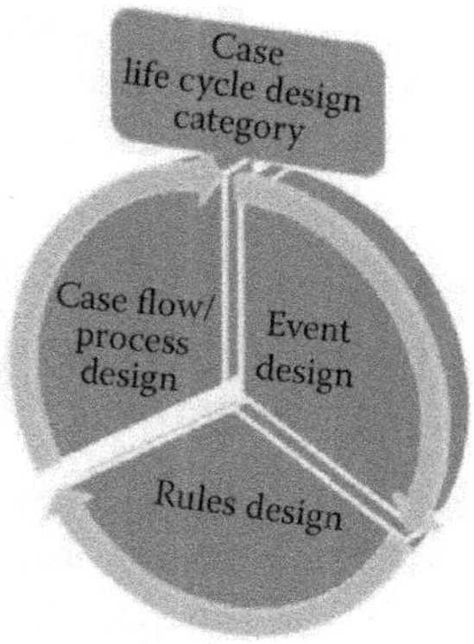

Figure 8.5 Case management lifecycle design category. The case lifecycle design category describes the coordination of activities in reaching one of the end goals and consists of three design components: Case flow and process design, rules design and event design.

8.5.1.1 State Model

The state model is one of the key elements in the lifecycle of a case in Siebel. This model describes the allowed states that can exist in the lifetime of the case and the possible transitions between the different case states, also known as the case flow. The state model can also be more complex with detailed subcase states and state flows going back and forward. An example of a complex state flow is shown in Figure 8.7. Changing a case state may be subject to certain conditions, such as data values. Siebel supports defining constraints on case state changes as part of the state model. For instance, in Figure 8.6 going from *active* to *submitted* is an allowed state transition, whereas going from *rejected* to *submitted* is not an allowed state transition.

8.5.1.2 Workflow Management

The Siebel Workflow Management helps defining the different workflows required in the lifecycle of a case. Workflow models can be bound to a specific state or can be started regardless of any state value. This makes it possible to activate (or deactivate) certain activities based upon a moment in the case lifecycle.

The workflow contains all functionalities required to define a process:

- Orchestration of tasks
- Task management, both automated and human oriented
- Routing and assignment management
- Escalation
- Input/output management
- Policy management
- Tasks user interfaces

8.5.1.3 Assignment Management

Assignment management supports routing the work activities to the most appropriate case workers. Business rules support in the determination of this work activity assignment. The assignment management does this by matching candidates, such as employees, positions, or organizations, to predefined and user-configurable assignment objects like a case, an incident, or a lead. To assign the most qualified candidate to each object, the assignment manager applies assignment rules that are specifically defined for each candidate

8.5.1.4 Extending the Life Cycle Management, with the Law Enforcement and Policing Operations Example

The law enforcement and policing operations extend the Siebel Public Sector vertical, and contain three different types of functionalities, incidents, cases, and leads, as discussed earlier in the extension example for the data model. Even though these functionalities are different, commonalities such as information objects and some processes and activities are shared, as shown in Figure 8.6.

As an example of extending the activities in Siebel, we will look here at investigative lead management. Leads are used to capture all kinds of clues, hints, and tips gathered by the public and agents in the field. Most of this information, in relation to a committed or foreseen crime, can often not be used as evidence. As a result of these leads, follow-up investigations might be started, which may result in evidences that can be used to start a new case and/or may be linked to already existing cases. Leads are handled as "information cases" in which the process of validating, analyzing, enriching, and proofing of information is managed. The ultimate goal of a lead is to promote it as evidence to support a case. Investigative lead management supports processes like an approval process and a sophisticated state model to manage its own process. It can hold information in itself or be linked to information in cases, incidents, or other leads. This requires new and/or extended processes, related to the lead management information objects.

Supporting the crime investigation process different state models are detailed, of which an example is presented in Figure 8.7. These state models define the possible routes a police case can encounter and guide the team through a series of steps that might lead to a solution. The case

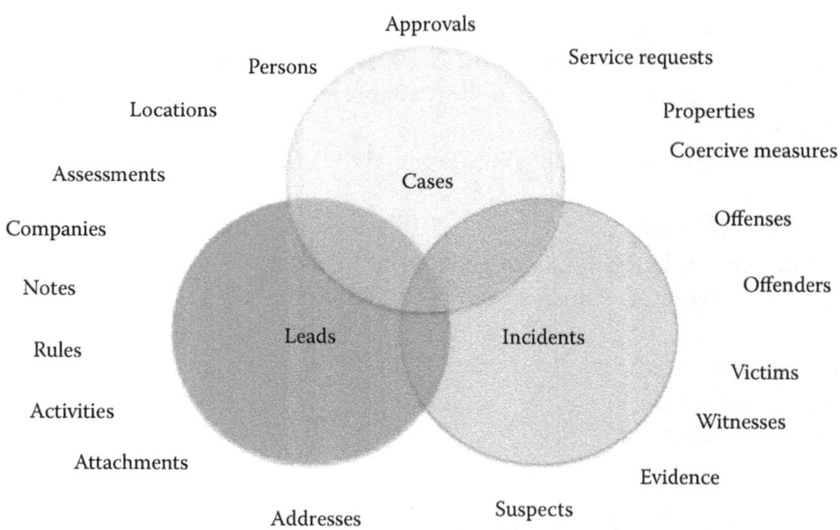

Figure 8.6 Linking cases, leads, and incidents together.

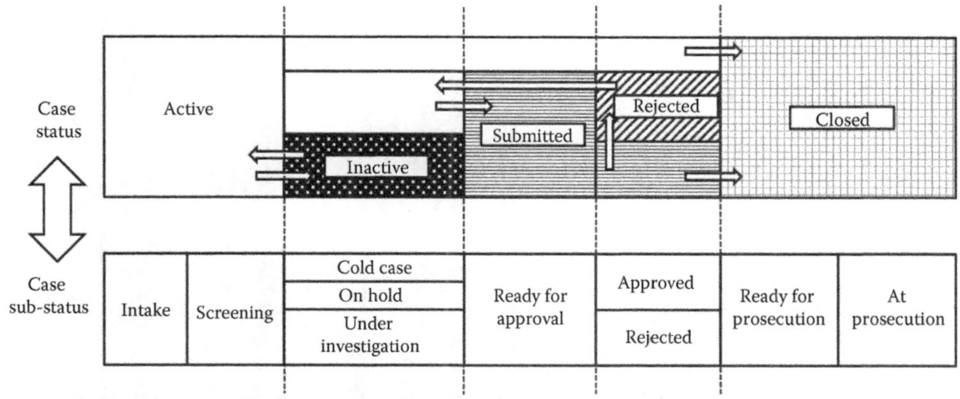

Figure 8.7 Police investigation state model.

owner, i.e., the police officer leading an investigation, can alter the state model, and consequently change the flow of activities. These state models are customizable in which the handling of a case can be tailored in a specific situation.

8.5.2 Rules Design

We identified in Chapter 3 different types of rules functionalities. The case lifecycle decision-making rule type is part of the state model functionality, as described in the previous paragraph. The remaining rule types are described in more detail in Chapter 10. Out of the box Siebel gives rule support for the remaining rule types; however when rules tend to get more complex, an external rule engine or product is a more preferred option.

8.5.3 Event Design

Events can be detected within Siebel on application, applet or business component object level. For details, see the topics mentioned in Section 8.2.6. The Siebel event model is user event based. The event originates from the browser-based application and passes the event toward the applet. The applet in turn passes on the event toward the business component. From these event points functionalities, such as business service or a workflow, can be called.

8.5.4 Life Cycle Design Product Mapping to Oracle Siebel and Related Products

We finish the lifecycle design section with a product mapping of the case management lifecycle functionality toward the Oracle Siebel product sets, based upon the drawing technique presented earlier in Chapter 5. Here we will make a distinction between the "Siebel single entity" scenario and the "Siebel in a wider application landscape" scenario. In the first scenario, the "Siebel single entity" scenario solution is fully covered by the Siebel product. In the second scenario, the Siebel scenario is either part of a larger, end-to-end process, or additional system support needs to be delivered for which Siebel does not offer the required functionality. The product capability mapping for both scenarios is presented in Figure 8.8.

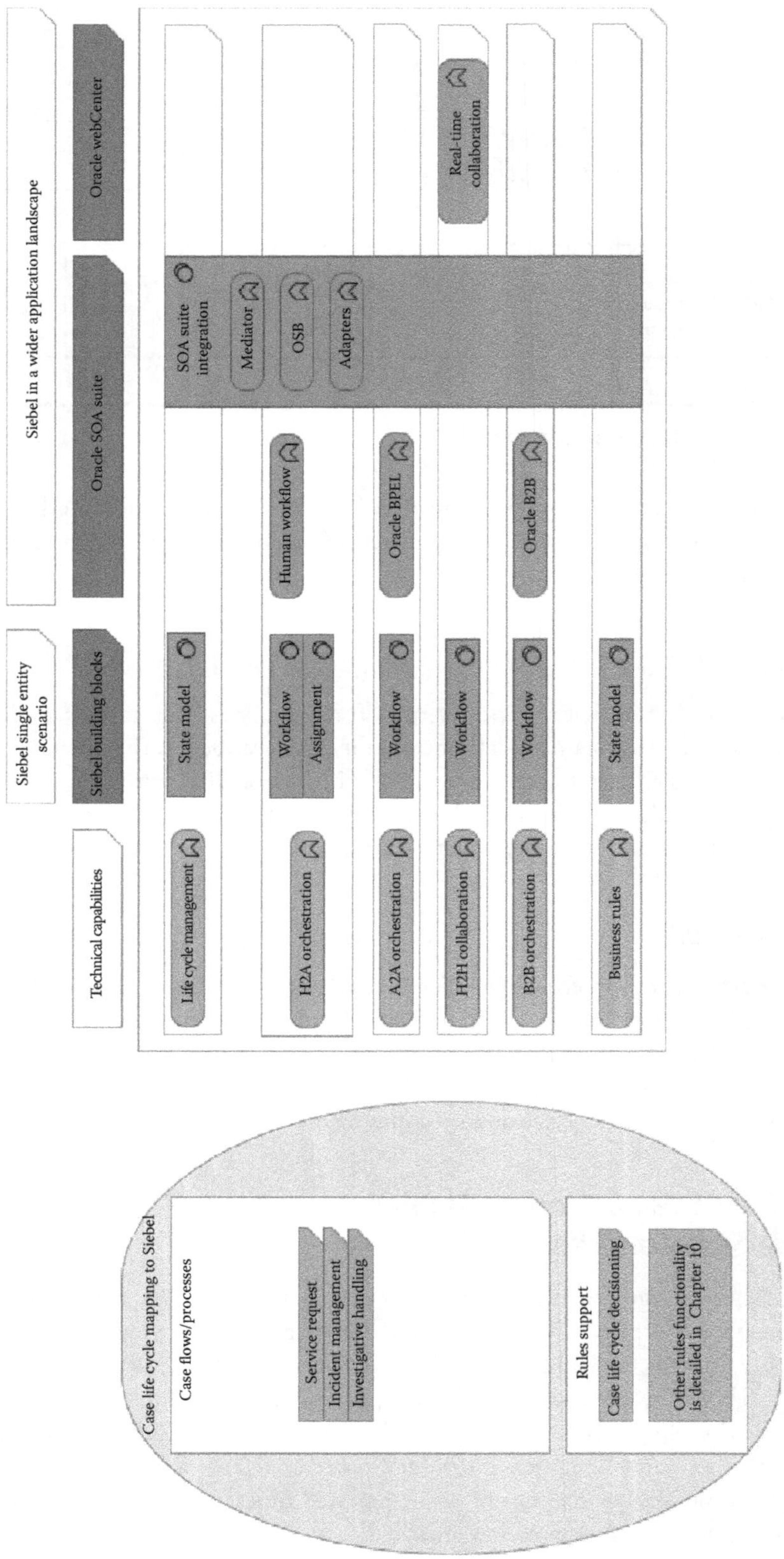

Figure 8.8 Lifecycle management Siebel mapping.

In Figure 8.2, we presented the Siebel building blocks. The lifecycle management functionalities, workflow, assignment, and the state models are mapped toward the case management lifecycle capabilities in Figure 8.8.

The "Siebel in a wider application landscape" scenario covers a (noncomplete) list of scenarios that could be encountered in an IT landscape:

- Integration with external applications is required to call functionality or to share information.
- Application-to-Application (A2A) capabilities are required across applications.
- A workflow is started in an external application.
- Complex rules management is required to support the Siebel functionality.

In the "Siebel in a wider application landscape," the Oracle SOA Suite is an important addition for connecting Siebel and the "wider application landscape" and providing the additional functionality in areas that are not the core functionality of the Siebel product. Examples are the SOA Suite integration capabilities and the addition of BPEL for situations where straight through processing (STP) is required.

8.6 Case Management Interaction Functionality with Oracle Siebel

In Chapter 3, we introduced the case management interaction design category, as shown in Figure 8.9. We will explain here briefly the portal and channel functionalities Siebel offers in this area. The dashboard functionality will be described later in Chapter 10.

8.6.1 Portal and Channel Design

As explained earlier in this chapter, the key component of Siebel is the CRM-based data model. All functionality in the Siebel data model can be made available in the Siebel portal overview for the users. This functionality is out of the box, available, and can be tailored toward usage and role

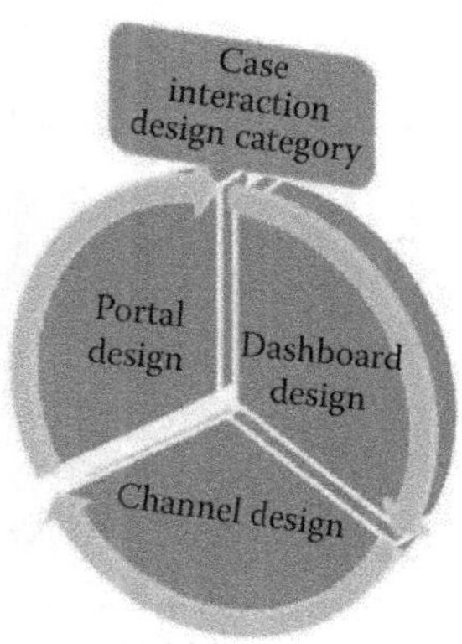

Figure 8.9 Case management interaction design category. The case interaction design enables maximizing the support for the case work force. This design area contains three design parts: Portal design, dashboard design and channel design.

based access. As with other functionalities within Siebel, the user interface part can be extended in order to meet the requirements of the business.

As can be seen in Figure 8.2, the user interface is based upon a composition of applet-based building blocks that directly relate to the business functionality grouping containing the CRM and case management information objects.

Only recently in the Siebel stack a new user interface technology is added, open UI, which is based upon open standards and technologies such as HTML, CSS, jQuery, and AJAX.

Out of the box Siebel supports browser-based access. When more channel types are required for access with the application, functionality can be exposed via the Siebel integration framework as web services that can be picked up by other channels such as mobile.

8.7 Cross-Functional Case Management Capabilities

Functionality shared across all other functional areas is contained in the case management cross-functional category as shown in Figure 8.10.

8.7.1 Case Management Integration Functionality with Oracle SOA Suite

As described in Section 8.4.4, in the "Siebel in a wider application landscape" scenario integration with external applications is required. The Oracle SOA Suite integration capabilities, BPEL, human workflow, and B2B products support Siebel with functionality that is not the core in the Siebel product. A short description of these products is given in Chapter 7.

8.7.2 Case Management Roles and Authorization Functionality with Oracle Siebel

Within the Siebel product, two main functionalities can be configured in relation to roles and authorization; access management on the user interface level and on data level.

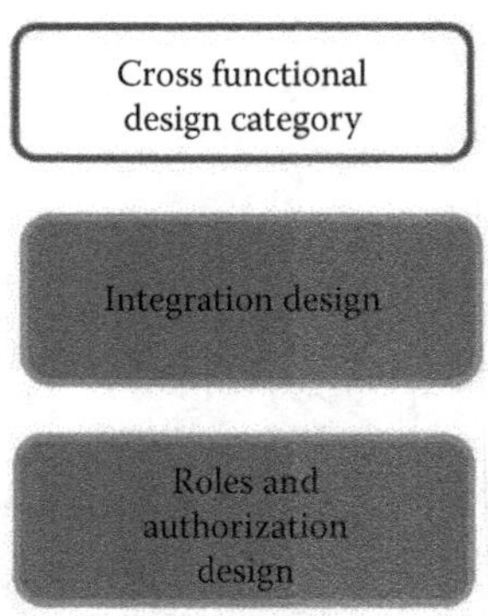

Figure 8.10 Case management cross-functional design category. The cross-functionality design category contains the integration design and the roles and authorization design that both support the other functional design categories.

User interfaces access management and responsibilities:
View-level access control determines which parts of the case management solution a user can access, based on the responsibilities assigned to that user. In Siebel, these responsibilities are known as functions. Based upon defined responsibilities, a user gets access to a specific set of data. An employee assigned to one responsibility might not have access to parts of the case management solution associated with another set of responsibilities. Each user's primary responsibility also controls the user's default screen tab layout and tasks.

Data-related record level access management:
Record-level access control assigns permissions to individual data items within the case management solution. This enables for instance administrators to authorize specific authenticated users who have "view-only access" to particular sensitive data records.

Siebel uses three types of record-level access: *position*, *organization*, and *access group*. When a particular position, organization, or access group is assigned to a data record, only employees within that position, organization, or access group are authorized to view that record:

- A *position* represents a place in the organizational structure, e.g., a specific job. Typically, a single employee occupies a position; however, it is possible for multiple employees to share a position. Position access allows Siebel customers to classify users based on hierarchy, which can be used for dedicated access to data. For example, a unit chief would have access to data that one of his officers can also access; the same applies to other users who report to the same unit chief.
- Similarly, an *organization*, such as a division or department of an organization, is a grouping of positions that maps to the physical hierarchy of an organization. Employees assigned to a position within a certain organization are granted access to data that has been given to this specific organization. Restrictions can be placed on data to avoid data being accessed from outside the organization.
- An *access group* is a less structured collection of users or group of users, such as a task force. Groups can be based on some common attributes of users, or created on a temporary basis, pulling together users from different organizations and granting them access to the same data.

8.8 Conclusion

Siebel is a package based solution with the emphasis on CRM. One of the key features of Siebel is the preconfigured CRM-based data model and the extensibility of the solution in all design areas. Siebel extended the CRM capabilities with case management functionality into different industry and cross-industry specific solutions, known as verticals and horizontals. We showed in this chapter how the industry solution public sector case management could be extended into the law enforcement and policing operations solution. Siebel delivers a complete full solution stack, containing data, processes, and user interfaces. The solution can be used in isolation, the "Siebel single entity" scenario and can be used in collaboration with other applications, the "Siebel in a wider application landscape" scenario.

Siebel delivers all solution components in the "Siebel single entity" scenario. The Oracle Suite delivers additional integration capabilities in the "Siebel in a wider application landscape" scenario.

Chapter 9

Oracle Service Cloud

9.1 Introduction

In this chapter, we will describe the Oracle Service cloud in relation to case management.

The goals of this chapter are as follows:

- Give a high-level overview of Oracle Service cloud
- Describe the usage characteristics of Oracle Service cloud for case management functionality
- Describe how Oracle Service Cloud strongly supports the case management interaction functionality

We start this chapter with an overview and usage characteristics of the Oracle Service Cloud. Subsequently, we describe its product features according to the case management functional design as presented earlier in Chapter 3, starting with interaction functionality.

9.2 Oracle Service Cloud Overview

9.2.1 History

The relationship between the customer and a product company has always been dominated by questions and issues around the products delivered by these companies. These questions can be asked before a product is acquired and will help the customer during the decision process toward the purchase of the product. If the product has been bought, the customer can have questions about product characteristics or wants to report and discuss issues regarding the product. During the early 1990s, a large part of this communication was done via e-mail. RightNow jumped into this market by delivering customer services via a software-as-a-service (SAAS) platform aimed at lowering the amount of e-mail inquiries for a company. In this solution RightNow delivered websites with strong knowledge capabilities in order to deliver customers services via a self-service model. This platform helped to accelerate winning new customers, maximize customer retention, and improve operational efficiency. Oracle acquired RightNow technologies in 2011, for its cloud-based customer service capabilities.

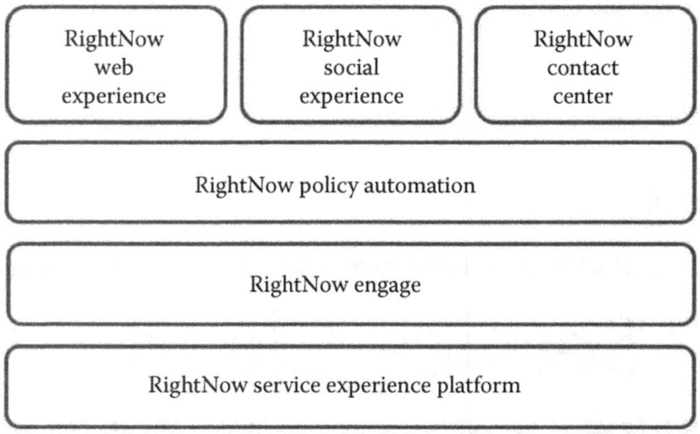

Figure 9.1 Oracle Service Cloud overview.

9.2.2 Basic Functionality

The product stack evolved into a customer experience (CX) stack and contains the products shown in Figure 9.1.

Oracle RightNow Web Experience provides rich user interface where customers can research, purchase, and solve issues for the products they are interested in. This is delivered to any device.

Oracle RightNow Social Experience provides support for social interactions, for example, via Facebook.

Oracle RightNow Contact Center Experience delivers support for call centers improving and standardizing the interaction with customers.

Oracle RightNow Policy Automation is also known as Oracle Policy Automation (OPA) and supports the self-service with complex rules capabilities, for instance, for the determination of eligibilities. OPA will be described in more detail in Chapter 10.

Oracle RightNow Engage delivers the analytics of all customer interactions in order to improve the customer interactions. This product also delivers the knowledge base and is the heart of the RightNow solution. It enables all service request–related information requests.

Oracle Rightnow Service Experience Platform is the cloud-based platform that integrates the aforementioned service cloud functionalities.

9.2.3 Cloud-Based Management and Usage

The Oracle Service Cloud is a SAAS platform and runs in the cloud to which customers can subscribe. This subscription makes it possible to use and, depending on the role of the user, manage an instance of this cloud. Managing the cloud is done via a localized Oracle Service Cloud client that is placed on a user's computer that is allowed to perform management tasks.

9.2.4 Extensions of Functionality

All components in the Oracle Service Cloud can be extended to include additional specialized functionality. This can include, for example, fields to the data model, the addition of rules, or the adjustment of the customer portal. The Oracle Service Cloud client enables configuration and extension of the application.

9.3 Oracle Service Cloud Usage Characteristics

The Oracle Service Cloud is a SAAS solution that enables interactions with customers around products and is aiming at delivering answers to questions or resolve product issues. These interactions are supported by a knowledge base delivering information through self-service interactions. Call center interactions with customers can be included when the customer requires more information. RightNow is targeted at delivering services for customers, based upon the service request classification, with a strong investigation focus through the knowledge base. Even though delivering support to product issues is named *incidents* in the Service Cloud, these interactions still follow the service request classification paradigm.

The product is delivered via a subscription model to customers and contains a full solution stack, with user interfaces delivered via a multitude of channels, processes, search functionality, call center support, and social media monitoring amongst others.

In Section 4.4, we introduced different ways companies can position themselves to meet the expectations of the customers. Three modus operandi are known in this area: *operational excellence, customer intimacy, and product leadership*. The Oracle Service Cloud aligns with the *product leadership* operating model and contains a state-of-the-art knowledge base enabling searching through the product catalog helping customers to understand the products. This helps the customer to make a measured decision before making a purchase and in the after sales support it helps the customer with queries and issues regarding the product.

The Oracle Service Cloud is a predefined product, with extension options in most functionality areas. Once delivered to the customers, the functionality cannot be changed at run-time, except for the continuous improvement of answers in the knowledge base and the adaption of rules through a rules modeler at run-time. The service request work is highly predictable, even though searching through the knowledge base can be complex. This makes the solution a production case management (PCM) type of case management.

Table 9.1 summarizes the usage characteristics of Oracle Service cloud.

Table 9.1 Service Cloud Usage Characteristics

Focus Area	*Product Characteristics*
Case management design area	Information and interaction design
Classification support	Two case management classifications are supported: service request supported via investigations
Delivery type: Full implementation or umbrella type	Full implementation
Product type	Cloud based (SAAS)
Agility at runtime: ACM or PCM	PCM type: Most of the functionality of the service request is defined upfront. The inclusion of Right Now policy automation (OPA) delivers flexibility at runtime. The continuous improvement of answers enhances the quality of the service request

9.4 Case Management Interaction Functionality with Oracle Service Cloud

Bringing service through all channels is the core competence of Oracle Service cloud and for this reason it excels in interaction functionality. In Chapter 3, we introduced the case management interaction design category, as shown in Figure 9.2.

9.4.1 Portal Design

The Oracle Service Cloud delivers support for the two main user groups, the customers and the contact center.

The *customers* are supported with a portal that contains all the aspects to get access to the specific product data, get in contact with support agents, and deliver feedback on the experiences:

- Self-service pages to raise questions and get automated answers, aimed at the ease of finding the right information
- Be able to engage with a contact center through different channels when more information is needed
- Show related information and experiences from other users
- Get in contact with communities to interact on product experiences
- Share experiences

A reference implementation is provided out of the box by the Oracle Service Cloud. This reference implementation shows the best practices for customer support and speeds up the case interaction design. The customer portal can be tailored toward the look-and-feel of the company and be personalized toward the needs of the customer, for which an example is provided in Figure 9.3.

The *contact center* is supported with a user agent desktop. This user agent desktop is aimed at delivering a full overview of the customer and the products in order to deliver a fast and good advice for the customer. Even though the service cloud itself is delivered through the cloud, the agents are supported with a client-based application. The user agent desktop can be configured

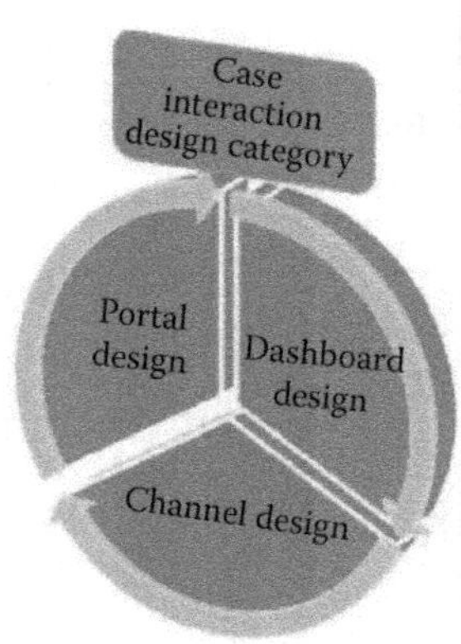

Figure 9.2 Case management interaction design category. The case Interaction design enables maximizing the support for the case work force. This design area contains three design parts: portal design, dashboard design, and channel design.

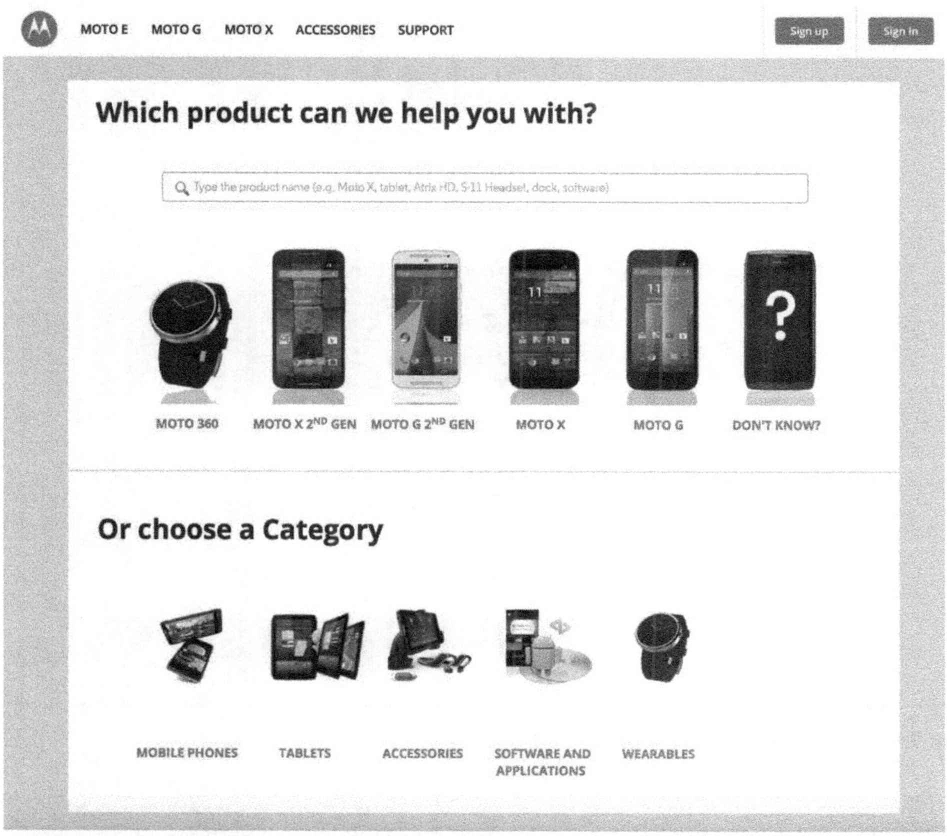

Figure 9.3 Customer portal based upon the Oracle Service Cloud.

toward the needs of the agent. Based upon the role of the agent, he/she gets access to certain functionality. The agent desktop contains features such as the following:

- The *workspace* is the view of the user agent in his/her daily work. Both the page layout and the content on the page, such as contacts, incidents, and answers can be adjusted to tailor for the agents' needs.
- *Workspace rules* help dynamically adjust the page display and behavior according to specific situations.
- *Agent scripts* and *desktop workflow* support the agents with a page flow to enter (and acquire) the information in the right order, enabling finding quickly a resolution for the customers' issues.

9.4.2 Channel Design

The Oracle Service cloud is designed to support a large variety of multichannel interactions with customers. This area is growing with new channels opening up:

- The *customer portal* can be accessed through a rich portal or a mobile customer portal
- Direct interaction between the customer and the contact center via chat, e-mail, or phone, for which an example is shown in Figure 9.4

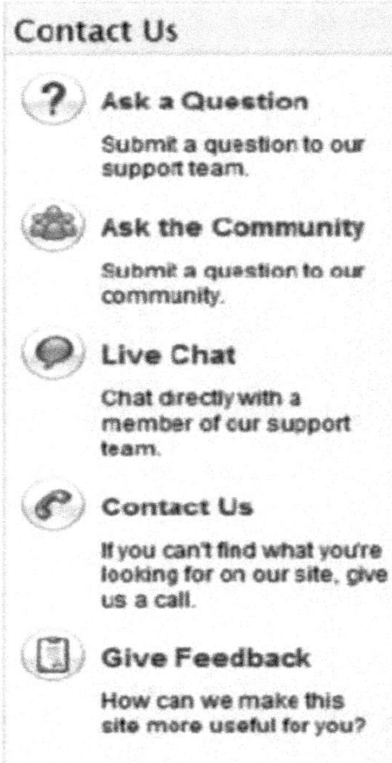

Figure 9.4 Channel option example—contact us.

- *Social experience* via a variety of communities, such as Facebook, Twitter, or Google
- *Broadcasting information* via campaigns, mailings, and feedback surveys

Everything is aimed in solving the incident or service request at low cost, favoring channels like self-service and through communities. But if one-to-one interaction is necessary, it offers e-mail support, chat, phone, and cobrowsing, a technology aimed at sharing the customer browser with the contact center. Everything is connected with the knowledge component that makes it possible to deliver the same answers through all channels.

9.4.3 Dashboard Design

The following aspects of the Service Cloud can be monitored:

Customer satisfaction and *workload of the customer agents* are provided in the *Oracle RightNow Analytics Cloud Service*. The quality of the knowledge base needs to be monitored in a continuous improvement loop, as will be described later in Section 9.7.1. The continuous improvement is supported with reporting of top-search keywords and customer reviews.

9.5 Case Management Information Functionality with the Oracle Service Cloud

The information design of the Oracle Service Cloud is aimed at delivering the customers the best answers and information for their question. The design components for the information design category are shown in Figure 9.5. For a full description of the case information design category, see Chapter 3.

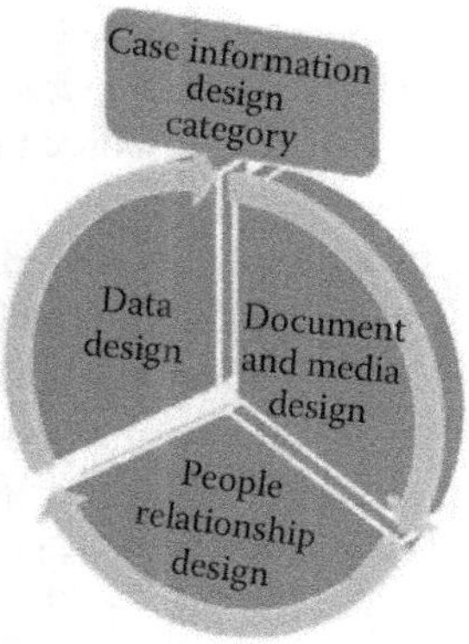

Figure 9.5 Case management information design category. The case information design deals with all sorts of data and documentation flowing through the case and maps the relationships between all persons and/or assets involved in the case. The case information design category contains three design components: data design, document and media design, and people relationship design.

Table 9.2 Information Design Support for Case Management with the Oracle Service Cloud

Information Design	*Functionality*	*Supported by Service Cloud*	*More Information in Section*
Data design	Case execution data	Yes	9.5.1
	Case supporting data	Yes	9.5.1
	Tactical-related information	Yes	9.5.1
Document and media design	Case input management	Yes	9.5.3
	Case output management	Yes	9.5.3
People relationship design	Internal stakeholders	Yes	9.5.2
	External stakeholders	Yes	9.5.2

The Service Cloud provides full support for all case management information design components as shown in Table 9.2.

9.5.1 Data Design

The basis for the Oracle Service Cloud is the knowledge base information model. This knowledge base model contains three main parts:

1. *Customer relationship model* (*CRM*) functionality, with information objects such as contacts, staff accounts, and organizations.
2. A product catalog where assets and products are stored.

3. A *service supporting part* that provides support for incidents, opportunities, and answers. An *incident* relates to a question or request for support. An *opportunity* contains the information about a possible sale with a customer. *Answers* are in response to questions raised by the customer.

The data model of the Oracle Service Cloud can be extended to tailor the application towards the specific needs of the business. This can include the addition of fields to the existing data model and the creation of custom objects. All new information types, both fields and objects, are available in all of the Oracle Service Cloud functionality, such as in workflows and workspaces.

Answering questions from customers based upon a set of search keywords is one of key capabilities of the Service Cloud. The management of answers in the Service Cloud, in the most basic form, is entering an *answer* and a *summary* of the answer. The Service Cloud uses the content of the answers to extract the search words that are used to provide the customer with the right response. As can be seen in Figure 9.6, the management of answers can contain more facets, such as combining the answer into product and categories, adding relationships with other answers, and the addition of attachments. The addition of keywords is only needed to put emphasis on specific words.

Managing the knowledge base is a continuous effort and is adjusted with improved knowledge from new customer–support interactions, as shown in Figure 9.7. The Service Cloud configuration starts with an initial seed of the knowledge with answers known to be important for customers. Once the Service Cloud is put into production, knowledge from the customer–support interactions can be used to add new answers, refine existing ones, and improve the organization of the knowledge base.

The management of the knowledge base contains the following activities:

- Defining and refining answers based upon customer interactions
- Organizing answers into categories
- Building relationships between answers to enable customers obtain quicker insight in product features
- Reporting on customer interactions and top-searches provides insight in the improvement areas for the knowledge base

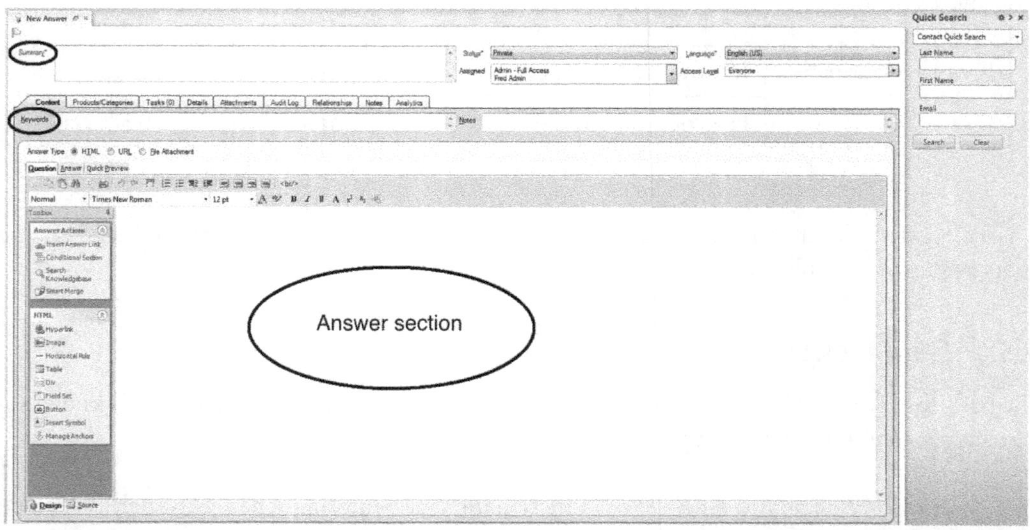

Figure 9.6 Management of answers.

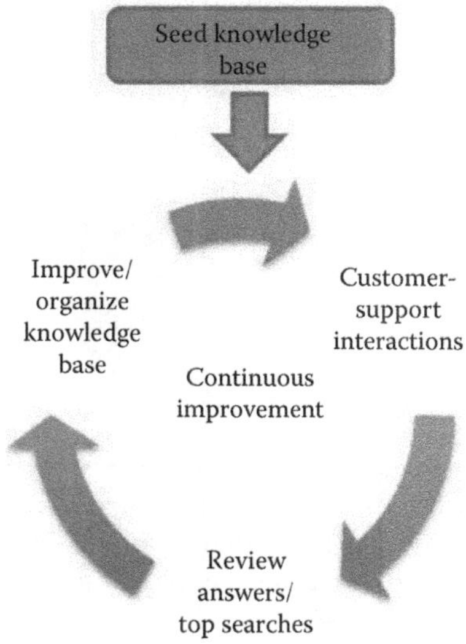

Figure 9.7 Knowledge base continuous improvement.

9.5.2 People Relationship Design

The Oracle Service Cloud CRM part is based upon two groups, *staff* and *contacts*.

The *staff* persons manage the Service Cloud and interact with the customers. *Contacts* are the customers asking information or services through the service requests. Both staff and contact can be organized into different organization levels. Additionally, the staff persons can be grouped into expertise areas such as products and level of expertise. This grouping is used for routing incident to the appropriate group.

A contact can be associated with assets; typically this is used to identify the products the customer has bought and provides the ability to deliver services and answers tailored for that product.

9.5.3 Document and Media Design

The document and media design for the Oracle Service Cloud relates to the product catalog and supports the customer with additional information about the products, such as demo videos, user guides, and product-specific images. These documents and media can be related to the answers as shown earlier in Figure 9.6.

9.6 Case Management Life Cycle Functionality with Oracle Service Cloud

In Chapter 3, we introduced the various aspects for the design of a case management solution. We will look at the case life cycle design category for the Service cloud, as shown in Figure 9.8.

Specifically, we will look at the way the Service Cloud supports the customer with self-service capabilities and, in situations where the question is too complex, provide additional contact center interaction support.

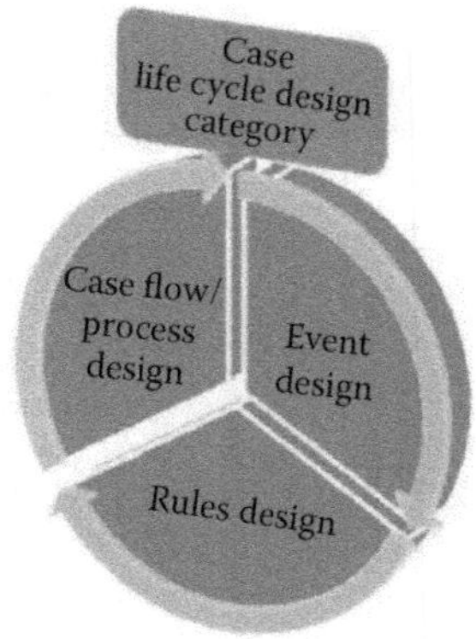

Figure 9.8 Case management life cycle design category. The case life cycle design category describes the coordination of activities in reaching one of the end goals and consists of three design components: case flow and process design, rules design, and event design.

9.6.1 Case Flow and Process Design

The Oracle Service Cloud aims to support the customers with the best answers for their questions. These answers help the customer to resolve an issue with a product or help them in making a thorough decision for purchasing the product. The Service Cloud delivers a customer interaction according to the service request classification. As described in Section 4.4, the service request case contains two main flows, a *triage* workflow and, where needed, a follow-up *service request case handling*. Both service request phases are supported by investigations. Figure 9.9 shows the service request phase in relation to the Oracle Service Cloud products.

The starting point for a customer, in the triage workflow, is the self-service web portal where the initial question is entered. With the support of the knowledge base, answers are provided to the customer. The customer finishes the interaction when the provided information is sufficient.

When the query turns out to be too complex to obtain a satisfying answer, additional support can be delivered in a direct interaction with the contact center. The service request case handling

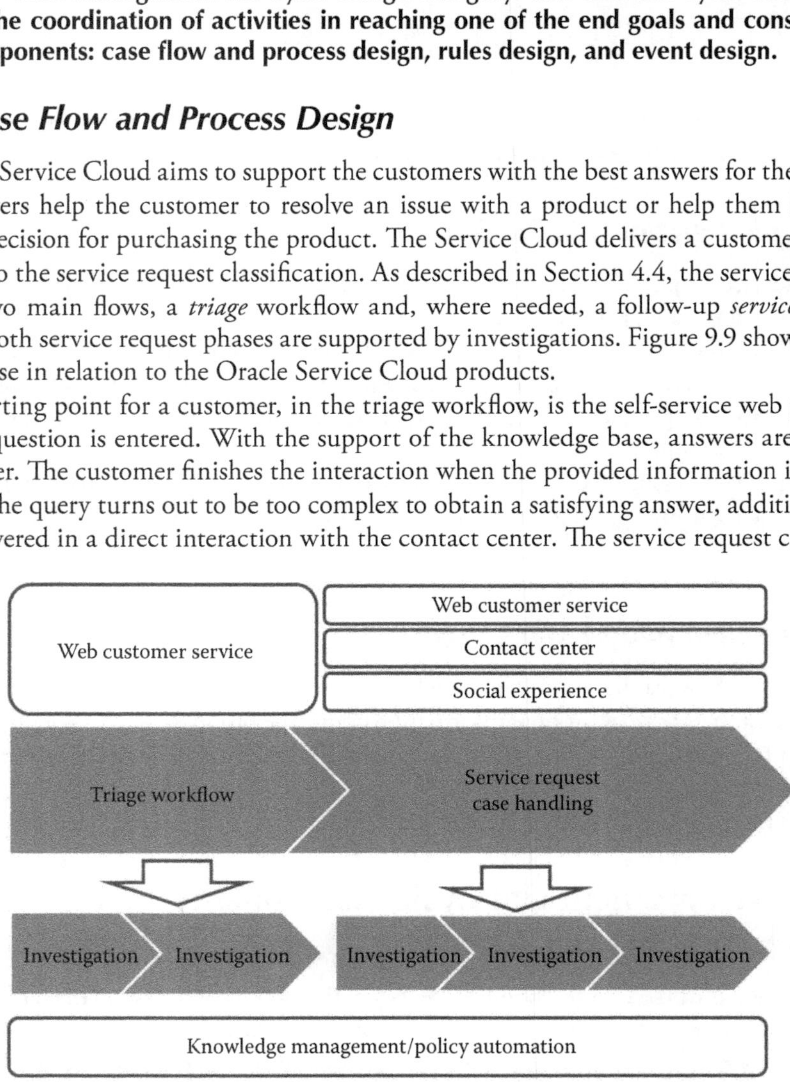

Figure 9.9 Oracle Service Cloud product usage in a service request.

is now started. At the same time, the customer can engage in discussions on different social media to get an answer. In this case handling, the customer is guided toward the appropriate answer to resolve his/her query or issue.

All information in the customer interaction, with the self-service pages, the contact center, and the social media, is stored for later usage. This information helps in improving the future customer interactions and can help to improve the answers in the knowledge base.

9.6.2 Rules Design

In Section 3.3.2.3.2, we discussed the different rules type that can support a case management solution. The Oracle Service Cloud delivers out-of-the-box support for two rules types, the *case life cycle decision-making* and the *entitlement determination*.

The *entitlement determination* will be handled in more detail in Chapter 10.

In order to support the *case life cycle decision-making*, a rules engine is available in the Oracle Service Cloud to automate the assignment of service requests (incident) from customers to specific contact center groups or persons. This assignment process can be based upon the characteristics of the service request, such as the source of entrance (for instance chat, portal, and e-mail), time created, product type, and the severity. Figure 9.10 shows an example of a rule based upon the *time-created* characteristic. In this assignment process, the rules engine can also update the service request state model to the next stage. Rules are organized in a rule base, which is a grouping of rules around data objects and can be applied to standard data objects such as contact, organization, task, incident, and answer.

9.6.3 Event Design

Events are raised in the Oracle Service Cloud based upon object event handlers. These handlers act upon a change happening in the data in one of the standard or custom objects in the database. When an event is raised, the object handlers can create or automate tasks based on the triggering event.

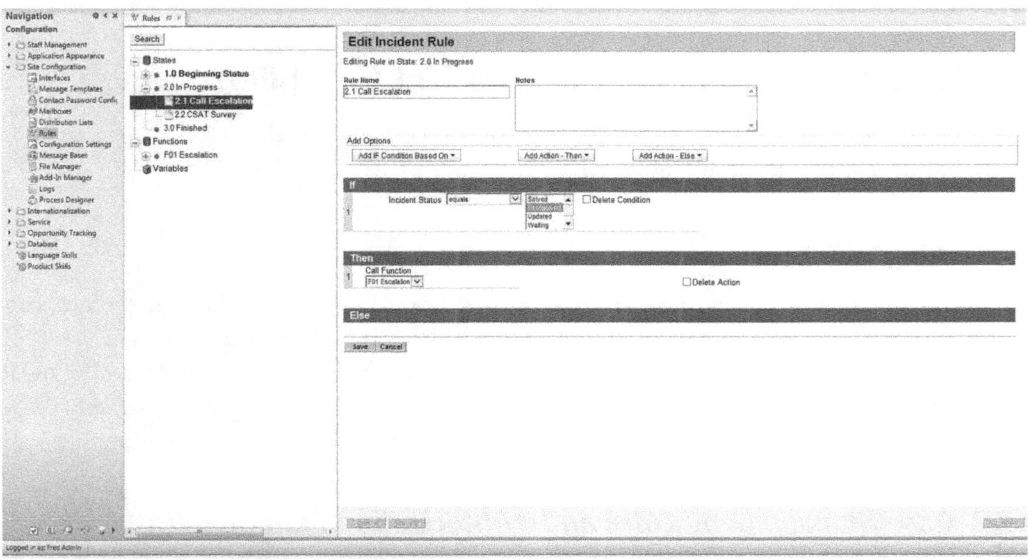

Figure 9.10 Oracle Service Cloud rules design.

For example, when an incident is updated an object event handler can invoke an external system service to update specific data, send an e-mail or notification to the customer, and create a manual task. The technology behind the object event handlers is the PHP scripting language.

9.6.4 Life Cycle Design Product Mapping to Oracle Service Cloud

We will summarize the life cycle design paragraph with a product mapping of the case management life cycle functionality toward the Oracle Service Cloud product components. This is based upon the drawing technique presented earlier in Chapter 5. Figure 9.11 summarizes the product functionalities part of the Oracle Service cloud.

On the left-hand side in Figure 9.11, the core case management capabilities are shown that are supported by the Oracle Service Cloud:

The *service-request* case flows and processes are supported by the Service Cloud functionalities *self-service flow* and the *contact center*. The overall flow supporting the case handling by the contact center is a simple milestone based *state model*.

Cloud integration and *channel integration* functionalities support the out-of-the-box integration with cloud products and all channels supported by the Oracle Service Cloud.

The *rules support* area contains three components:

1. *Business rules* support the assignment and routing of requests in the case life cycle decision-making.
2. *RightNow Policy Automation*, also known as *Oracle Policy Automation* (OPA), supports complex entitlement determinations, for example, guarantee-related determinations, is the problem covered by the guarantee policy?
3. *The knowledge base* is the core capability in the search functionality.

Event support is supported with the *object event handler* functionality that operates on top of the Service Cloud data model.

9.7 Cross-Functional Case Management Capabilities

Functionalities shared across all other functional areas is contained in the case management cross-functional category as shown in Figure 9.12.

9.7.1 Integration

The Oracle Service Cloud has an out-of-the-box integration channel and cloud integration capabilities. The Service Cloud interacts with all channels previously described in Section 9.4.2. The Service Cloud is also delivered with cloud integration capabilities with a number of standard Oracle applications, such as ATG, Sales Cloud, and Social Relationship Management. When more complex integration is required, the Oracle SOA Suite can be added to the solution.

9.7.2 Case Management Roles and Authorization Functionality

Profiles are the mechanism used in the Service Cloud to control which areas can be accessed with the Service Cloud. Profiles are created for customers and for internal personnel such as agents.

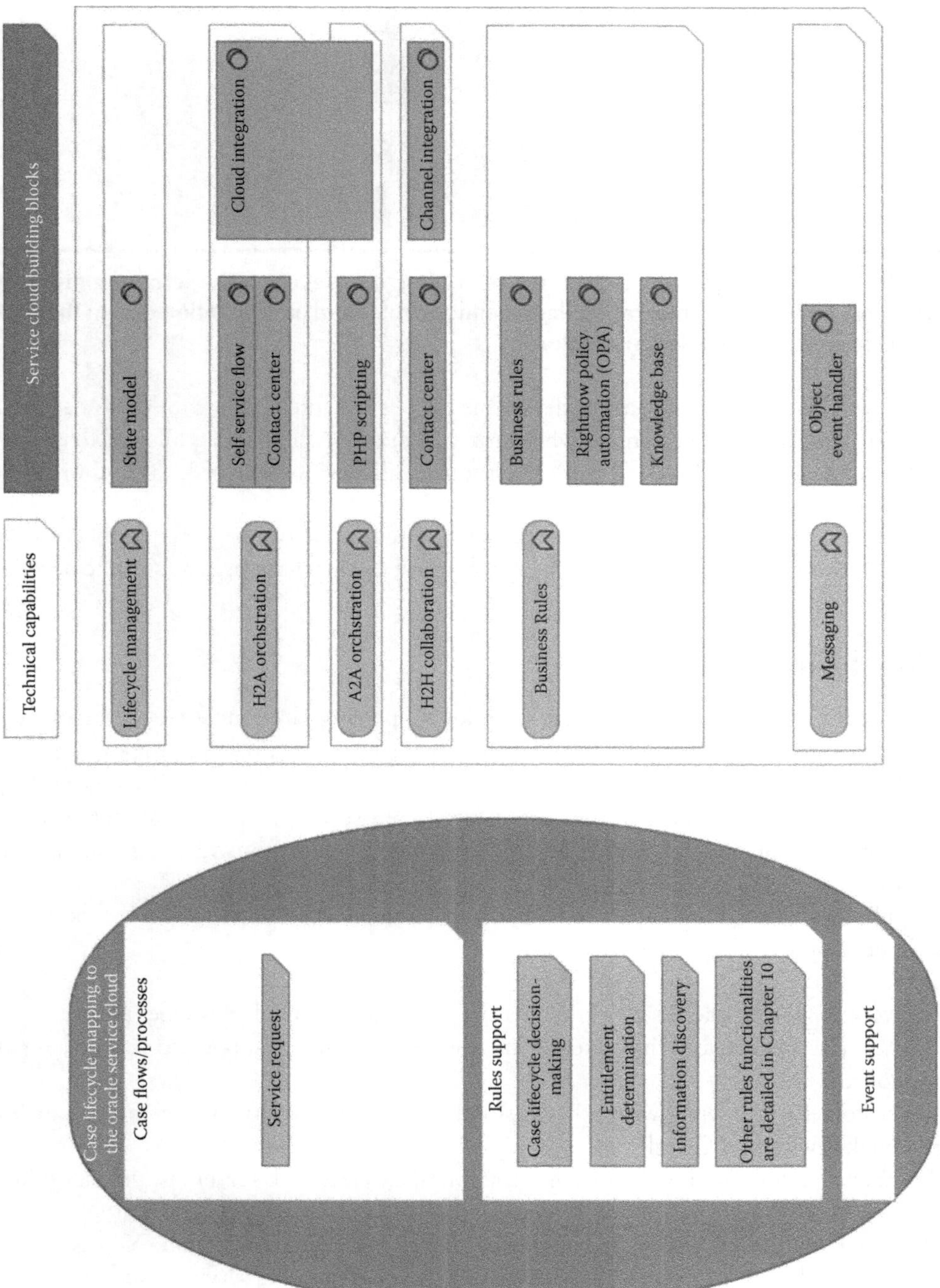

Figure 9.11 Life cycle management Oracle Service Cloud mapping.

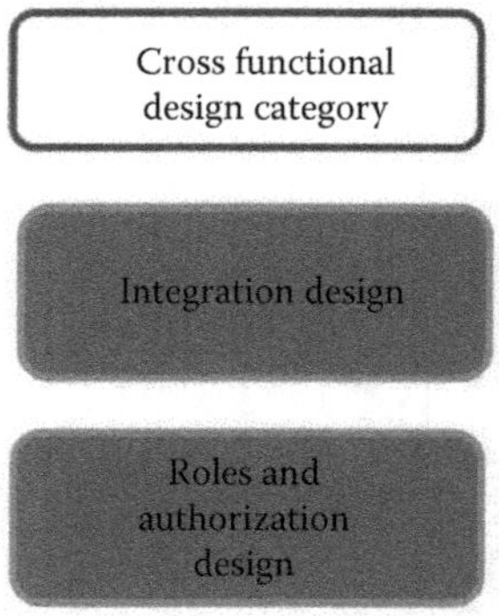

Figure 9.12 Case management cross-functional design category. The cross-functionality design category contains the integration design and the roles and authorization design that both support the other functional design categories.

Internal personnel profiles are used to determine the level of interaction with customers, such as who can engage with what customers, who can assign incidents, and who is allowed to perform chats with customers. Administrating type of personnel is allowed to create rules and administrate the knowledge base among other functionalities.

For *customers*, the profiles relate to the data security. Some data can be viewed publicly; other data is private, this data is only available for a customer when they have signed in to the portal.

9.8 Conclusion

The Oracle Service Cloud delivers an application for supporting all product-related interactions between the customer and a company. The Service Cloud enables organizations to position themselves in the area of product leadership. It contains a state-of-the-art knowledge base that helps customers understand the products. The customer uses self-service web pages to search for the answer they need. If the question is too complex, a contact center can provide additional interaction support.

The application has strong capabilities in the portal and channel capabilities. The Oracle Service Cloud supports a large variety of channels:

- The *customer portal* is accessible through a rich portal and a mobile customer portal.
- *Direct interaction* between the customer and the contact center is supported via chat, e-mail, or phone.
- The customer can interact with other customers through a variety of *communities*, such as Facebook, Twitter, or Google.
- *Broadcasting* information via campaigns, mailings, and feedback surveys is the last option.

Oracle Service Cloud is a SAAS platform and is enabled through subscription. No installation is required to use the product except for the software to configure the service cloud and for the contact center agent desktop.

The functionality of the Service Cloud contains predefined functionalities that can be extended in some areas. The main extension functionalities are in the data model, where additional custom fields and objects can be added and the customer portal that can be tailored toward the company website.

Chapter 10

Intelligence in Relation to the Case Execution

10.1 Introduction

In this chapter the usage of intelligence supporting case execution is described.

Intelligence supports the stakeholders with the information to make the right decisions during case activities. This intelligence can support the execution of a single case, relate to the governance of cases that currently are executed or to make forecasts and predictions based upon experiences with other cases.

In the previous chapters, we described the three Oracle case products, Oracle (Business Process Management (BPM)/Adaptive Case Management (ACM), Oracle Siebel, and Oracle Service Cloud. In this chapter we describe Oracle technologies that can support the intelligence needs of Oracle BPM/ACM, Oracle Siebel, and Oracle Service Cloud with functionalities that are not core for these products.

We start with summarizing the intelligence requirements needed in the case execution as defined earlier in Chapter 3, and map these toward a choice of Oracle products that are best suited for supporting the intelligence needs for the case execution.

10.2 Case Intelligence Design

In Chapter 3, we described the different categories of a case management design. The intelligence needs at run-time relate to the design areas life cycle, information and the interaction design categories, as shown in Figure 10.1.

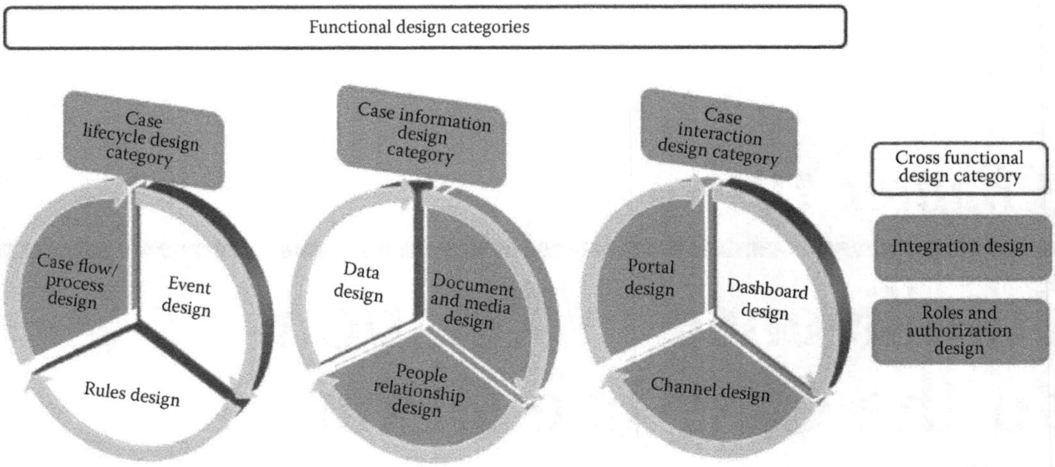

Figure 10.1 Case management design components that support intelligence design (in white).

10.2.1 Intelligence Determined by Rules Design

In the case life cycle design category, the rules design determines how decisions and checks are performed at operational level. A summary of the life cycle rule design functionalities is provided in the following:

- *Case life cycle decision-making*
  This relates to the life cycle management functionality determining the execution path of a case.
- *Entitlement determination*
  The entitlement decision entails the eligibility of the customer on a specific service or claim. This is typically guided by policies and regulations and can change on a regular basis.
- *Progress measurement*
  This relates to measuring the progress of a case. This involves measuring the case state against predefined progress indicators.
- *Data entry validation*
  Data entered into the case by any of the participants can have validation requirements attached to it, for instance, based upon regulations and policies.
- *Information discovery*
  Searching through structured and unstructured data that relate to the case execution can deliver some new or changed insights toward the output and behavior of a case.

10.2.2 Intelligence Determined by Event Design

The event design is used to determine how to handle special events. Specific attention will be given here to the monitoring of incident risk parameters, as described in detail in Section 4.5. This involves measuring case/process related data against predefined risk parameters, in order to predict the likelihood of an incident in the near future.

10.2.3 Intelligence Determined by Dashboard Design

In the case interaction design of a case, the dashboard design is the area where intelligence is delivered to manage the tactical and strategic information needed by the different stakeholders:

- Tactical dashboards support key performance indicators (KPI) management, workload management, and help in providing insight in customer satisfaction.
- Strategic dashboards are used for improvements in the area of case and process execution improvement, the case related products, and the decision support.

10.2.4 Intelligence Information Levels

In the case information design we presented following three information levels that determine the different intelligence needs by the different stakeholders:

- The *operational* level supports in real time the work on a single case.
- The *tactical* level is aimed at improving the efficiency, customer satisfaction, and controlling case-related KPIs.
- The *strategic* level enables looking back in time and investigating process and product improvements and forecasts.

10.3 Oracle Intelligence Products

Oracle technologies can support the intelligence functionalities that are described in the previous part in this chapter. In Table 10.1 the main Oracle technologies are mapped against these intelligence functionalities. In this table, several Oracle products are checked against the case management intelligence functionalities related to the different information levels, operational, tactical, and strategic.

The second column in this table shows where more detail related to the Oracle product can be found.

In the upcoming paragraphs we will look in more detail into the Oracle products that have not been described so far. We will look into the scope of the product, how the product relates to case management, and optionally the technical architecture.

We will not provide details for the Oracle Business Intelligence (BI) product in this book. Oracle BI is a product on its own and is distantly related to case management and many other books have been written already. The Oracle BI product delivers a rich set of functionalities such as ad hoc query and analysis, dashboards, enterprise reporting, scorecards, Online Analytical Processing (OLAP), and predictive analytics. In relation to case management, BI supports the stakeholders with case/process improvement, product improvement, forecasts, and trend analysis.

10.3.1 Oracle Business Analytic Monitoring

Oracle business activity monitoring (BAM) is a powerful business-friendly tool to support governance type of intelligence. Oracle acquired BAM as part of the PeopleSoft takeover in 2006. It was a hidden gem and came out as a surprise. Having its first implementation in .Net, it was

Table 10.1 Oracle Products Supporting Intelligence Needs

		Operational						Tactical			Strategic		
Oracle Product	*Where to Find More Details*	*Case Life Cycle Decision-Making*	*Entitlement Determination*	*Progress Measurement*	*Data Entry Validation*	*Information Discovery*	*Monitoring Risk Parameters*	*Workload, Efficiency Improvement*	*KPI*	*Customer Satisfaction*	*Case and Process Improvement*	*Product Improvement*	*Forecasts, Trend Analysis*
Oracle BPM/ ACM	Chapter 7	X	X	X				X					
Oracle Siebel	Chapter 8	X	X	X	X			X	X		X		
Oracle Service Cloud	Chapter 9	X	X	X	X			X	X	X	X	X	X
Oracle Business Rules	Chapter 7	X	X	X	X								
Oracle BAM	Section 10.2.1						X	X	X		X		
Oracle OEP	Section 10.2.2						X						
OPA	Section 10.2.3		X		X								
Oracle Endeca	Section 10.2.4					X							
Oracle BI											X	X	X
Oracle RTD	Section 10.3.5	X									X		

subsequently transferred to a Java implementation as part of the Oracle Fusion Middleware 11G. Now in the Oracle Fusion Middleware 12C version it is completely reengineered in order to be completely integrated with the BPM, Service Oriented Architecture (SOA), and BI products, and at the same time to be highly scalable and easily managed by means of the implementation on top of the Oracle WebLogic Server.

10.3.1.1 Functionality

BAM is aimed at providing real time insight in tactical and operational intelligence or "right" time intelligence as named by Oracle. Figure 10.2 provides an overview of the components that help deliver this real time insight:

In the *presentation* layer the following functional components are shown that deliver the insight to the end users:

- *Dashboards* deliver real time insight through a large variety of page compositions with different chart forms combined.
- *Alerts* are used to start follow up activities, such as starting a case or process, based upon a specific situation happening.
- *Reports* deliver insight via standardized reports delivered at specific times.

The *composition* layer combines together the information required by the functionality exposed in the presentation layer:

- *Workload insight* shows the case and process execution timings in order to deliver insight in the efficiency of the operation.

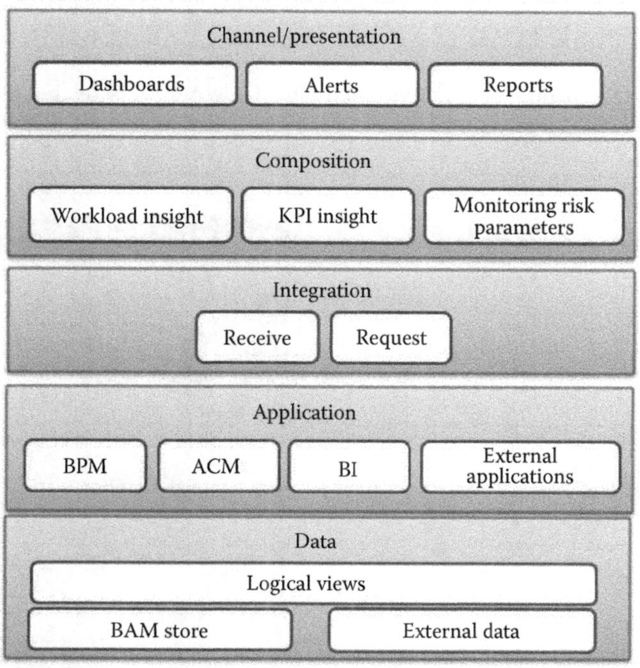

Figure 10.2 BAM functional components.

- *KPI insight* combines the real-time execution and content data and verifies these against predefined KPIs. These KPIs can be related to efficiency, regulatory, and/or customer-related parameters.
- The *monitoring risk parameters* relates to measuring case- and process-related data against predefined risk parameters (as described in Section 10.2.2).

The *integration* layer is used to receive or request information from the related applications placed in the application layer. This information is passed to the composition layer where the data composition takes place.

In the *application* layer, the application types are shown that deliver the information, the related BPM, ACM, and/or BI applications and external sources.

The *data* layer contains data storage and retrieval functionality. The data entered in the integration layer is stored in the BAM data store. BAM also offers the option to use data that is stored elsewhere in external data stores. A logical view delivers the option to combine both the BAM data store and the external view.

10.3.1.2 How Does BAM Relate to Case Management?

BAM mainly relates to the tactical type of information, as part of case management dashboard design, but also provides some aspects of operational and strategic information:

- The *tactical* information contains the main purpose for the BAM product where direct insight in KPIs and workload is provided through the BAM Dashboards. In the *operational* area, risk analysis provides functionality for monitoring risk areas.
  This relates to the description given in Section 10.2.2.
- BAM provides in the *strategic* area, insight where the handling of the cases and processes can be improved.

Figure 10.3 shows an example of a BAM dashboard showing KPIs related to the onboarding of partners.

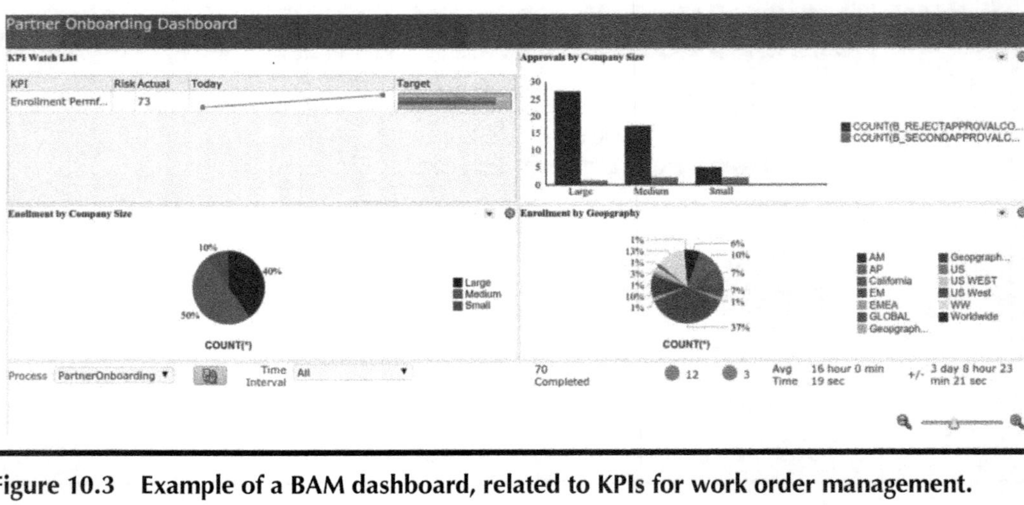

Figure 10.3 Example of a BAM dashboard, related to KPIs for work order management.

10.3.1.3 Technical Architecture

Oracle BAM is based upon already existing Oracle Fusion Middleware building blocks. The main technologies for BAM are as follows:

- Oracle Coherence, the in-memory grid database.
- Oracle Event Processing (OEP) aimed at listening at data streams and described in more detail in Section 10.3.2.
- Application Development Framework (ADF), the standard user interface across the complete Oracle Fusion Middleware and applications stack.
- The Oracle database is used to keep the meta data store (MDS), the repository where design and run-time artifacts are stored.

The BAM technical architecture, shown in Figure 10.4, contains two main parts, the *design* part and the *run-time* aspects.

The design time aspect supports the business with a browser-based solution to create the workload and KPI models, queries, dashboard, and alerts that are used in BAM to present the relevant information. These models and definitions are stored in the MDS, which is the shared repository for BPM, ACM, and BAM.

At run time, the data is delivered from both external data sources and the Fusion Middleware products BPM, SOA, and BI. The BPM, SOA, and BI data is delivered via native and predefined bindings. The external sources deliver their information via database adapters; web services calls or queues towards BAM. Data from both sources is picked up by (the Oracle coherence based) BAM persistence engine. The persistence engine then passes the information to the continuous query service (CQS), which is a query engine that has the ability to listen to a data stream, both parts of the persistence engine as well as already stored data. Every time a

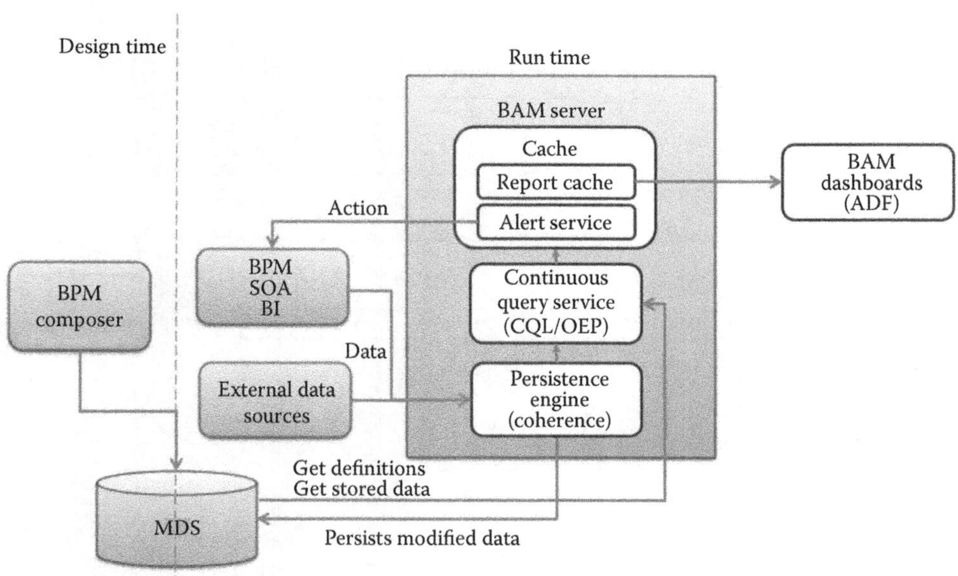

Figure 10.4 BAM technical architecture.

data change occurs, the CQS engine investigates which queries (and related dashboards) are affected by this change. The CQS engine subsequently forward this information to the report-caching engine, which pushes the result to all (open) dashboards. The CQS also pushes the changes to alert services related to the change and in turn initiates an action, for instance the start of a new process.

10.3.2 Oracle Event Processing

Oracle Event Processing (*OEP*) listens to data streams and filters out situations that require follow-up activities. These situations can be a unique event or a complex pattern of occurrences happening over a predefined timeframe originating from different sources. When OEP detects a specific situation, follow-up actions can be initiated, such as starting activities in ACM and BPM.

10.3.2.1 Functionality

Oracle OEP is based upon a four-step model, *listen*, *filter*, *compose*, and *send*. Figure 10.5 gives an overview of the different components involved:

- The four-step process *listen*, *filter*, *compose*, and *send* is part of the *composition layer*. The *listen* step receives data from different application sources, via the integration layer. These sources can be applications, social media, and also all connected devices (Internet of Things).
- In the *filter* step, the events are selected that are considered for follow up action.
- The *compose* step combines information together into a message.
- As a last step the messages are sent to applications that are interested in these events, via the channel layer.

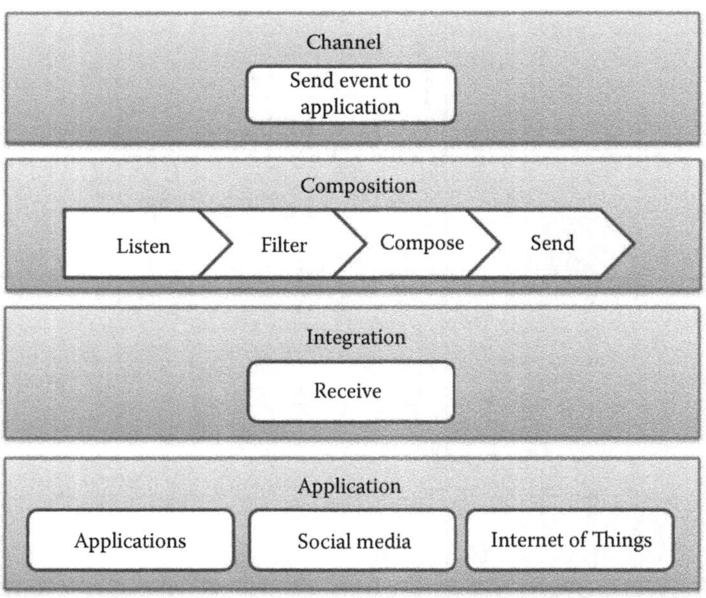

Figure 10.5 OEP functional components.

10.3.2.2 How Does OEP Relate to Case Management?

Oracle OEP is tailored at supporting the monitoring part in an incident type of case, as is described in Section 10.2.2.

This can range from offense of health and safety regulations, police-related incidents, to financial fraud–related incidents. Here, two examples from different markets where OEP listens to a data stream and filters out the situations that require further investigation are given.

Example 1: Off-loading products from a truck into a warehouse
In logistics, radio frequency identification (RFID) represents the new standard for the identification and tracking of products. Each product, for example, a box or a crate, is provided with an RFID tag containing a unique identification, which can be read by RFID portals or readers. The movement of the products can be measured by combining the data from the different RFID readers. These RFID tags help support to check the bill of lading against the actual products that are moved from the truck into the warehouse. Another application of RFID tracking is checking the expected off-loading zone against actual loading zone. If a case enters a wrong zone, then an alert, such as a text message to a manager, should be sent out directly. For instance, frozen meat should be in a low temperature zone, but when it is moved into a low temperature zone that is in maintenance, with a higher temperature than allowed according to regulations, an alert should be raised. This alert can be picked up by the OEP engine, which is listening to the RFID application. Since this is a health regulations violation, this might be a reason to start a case or to investigate the situation.

Example 2: Credit card fraud
This example is based upon personal experience of one of the authors. Some years ago, in 2003, at Oracle Open World in Paris, we went to a pizza restaurant at the Champs-Élysées to have some dinner after an exhausting day at the booth. I paid the bill for all the crew with my credit card. In the process of paying, the waiter walked with my credit card to the back and apparently copied my credit card. Two days later I received a phone call from my credit card company that the last 2 days my credit card had been spent at several locations across the globe, Paris, New York, Singapore, and others. The investigation team suspected fraud and wanted to verify if this behavior was correct. Since I did not travel around the world in those last days, my credit card was blocked and all false payments were returned. OEP listens here to the transaction data streams.

The OEP engine listened here to the credit card transaction stream. For this specific fraud example, the filtering part looks at the number of locations for every card ID over a period of, for instance, 24 h. When the number of locations is larger than one, a follow-up step is initiated that checks the locations involved and the feasibility of these locations happening within a certain timeframe. The filtering process can be enriched with complex rule facilities to verify the likelihood of fraud or credit card theft.

Technical Architecture
The main flow of a OEP architecture contains, as described earlier, four main parts, *listen*, *filter*, *compose*, and *send*.

The Oracle OEP implementation is based upon a flow diagram, the event processing network (EPN), in which stages, also named components, are assembled together. Every step in the EPN can receive events (event sink) or send events (event source), which means that at any stage in the flow, filtered events can be enriched and that information also can be sent out to related applications.

The implementation of the *listen* and *send* components is based upon adapters that have by default a queue based and web services type of implementation.

The *filter* and *compose* functionality is implemented in Oracle OEP as stages or components. For the *compose* functionality two options are available, the OEP channel functionality, which is a simple mapping of the received data in the right format or via specifically tailored Java beans.

The most exciting feature is the part of the *filter* functionality where with Oracle Continuous Query Language (CQL), querying of the data stream can be done. CQL is very much like the query language known from the database Sequential Query Language (SQL), with one very big difference, the ability to query data against the passage of time. With CQL we are able write code against time windows looking for an event that has specific properties or even more interesting for a combination of events that attracts our attention. This can be based upon a fixed time window, for example, by counting the amount of events coming in per time frame or starting the range-based query from the moment an event with certain specifics passes.

Here, an example of a query that could be used in the credit card fraud as described in the Oracle Open World at the Champs-Élysées example is given:

```
select distinct(cardId), count(distinct location)
from CreditCardTransaction [range 24 hours]
group by cardId
having count(distinct location)> 1
```

This query listens to a credit card data stream and looks for multiple locations over a range of 24 h.

10.3.3 Oracle Policy Automation

Oracle Policy Automation (OPA) is a business rules engine that is targeted at the handling of complex rules. OPA has its roots in the governmental market where it supports in transforming laws, regulations, and policies into rules in order to determine benefit entitlements and payment amounts. Later in the book, in Chapter 13, we provide an example around this topic. Even though OPA still is strong in the governmental market, the product can be used in any other markets.

10.3.3.1 Functionality

Figure 10.6 gives an overview of the main components of the OPA product, in relation to the products and application layers.

The heart of OPA is the *rules engine* known as Oracle Determinations Engine and is part of the composition layer. Both the design time and run time of OPA have some unique features:

- Design-time features:
  One of the key features of OPA is the way rules can be designed. Word and Excel can be used to transform the text-based laws, regulations, and policies into rules. A business analyst can do this activity and no support from developers is needed in this phase. A rules canonical data model ensures the uniqueness of the data definitions of the facts used in all the rule definitions.
- Run-time features:
  OPA often works in environments where both the rules and the customer situation are complex. The end goal of the rules execution is to determine a decision for the customer based upon the customer situation, such as the determination of an entitlement, defining of obligations with the customer, and/or determining a claim decision. The basis for the determination is a version of the laws, regulations, and policies and the customer situation, valid for a specific timeframe. When one of these variables changes, either the rules of the customer

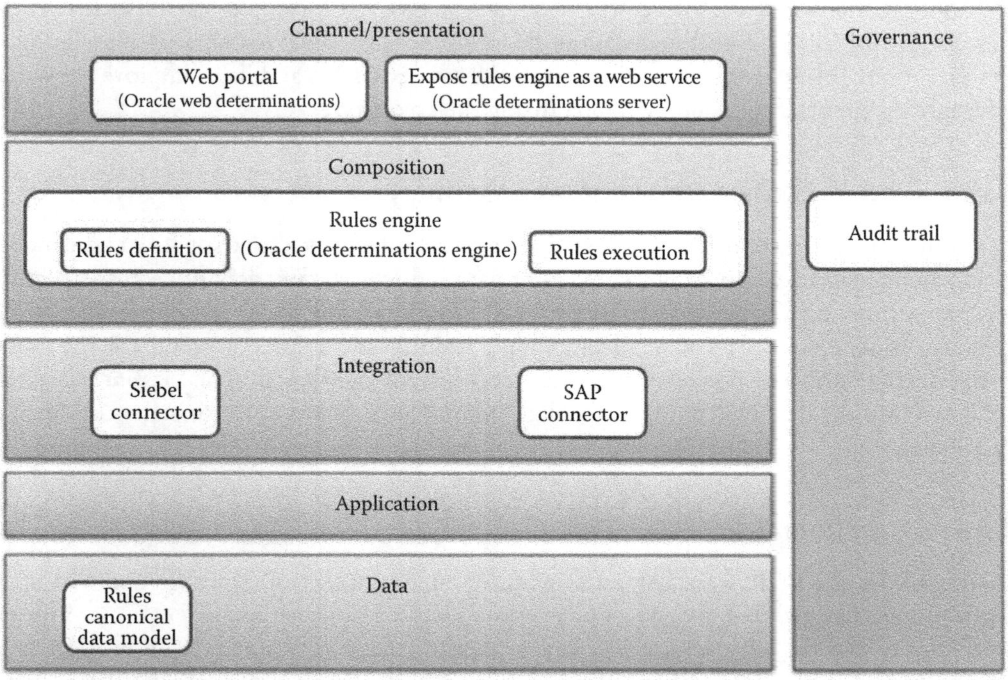

Figure 10.6 OPA functional components.

situation or a recalculation of the entitlement is required. *Temporal reasoning* enables a redetermination and a recalculation of the decision based upon the changed conditions in either the rules or the customer situation. OPA ensures that this redetermination is time aware, meaning that the recalculation is done for the timeframe where the change in rules or customer situation is applicable.

During the execution of the rules, different decisions are made. In some situations, due to compliance or contractual reasons, the decisions need to be stored. OPA enables audit trails containing the decisions on different levels, only the end decision, every in-between decision in the rule execution, or only specific in-between decisions.

OPA can be exposed via a web portal and as a web service. External applications, such as a case management system, usually include the rules execution via *web services* by means of Oracle Determinations Server.

Another way to use the OPA rules engine is as a *portal* through the Oracle Web Determinations product, part of the OPA product stack. This delivers a portal for assessing online a rule set by the customers. The customer is guided through the rules execution in an intelligent way: based upon the information they provide and the outcomes of the in-between results, rules are executed and a conclusion is presented in the portal.

10.3.3.2 How Does OPA Relate to Case Management?

As discussed in Chapter 4, both the *service request* and *incident management* case classifications include *investigative handling* cases in order to determine complex decisions to be made in a case.

Typically, functionalities such as *entitlements determination* are complex and require detailed investigation. OPA can off-load a part of the of *entitlements determination* work by automating the rules execution. This speeds up the efficiency of the case execution and helps improve the quality of the entitlement determination by standardizing the execution.

10.3.4 Oracle Endeca Information Discovery

Oracle Endeca is an e-commerce product that contains intelligence functionality and is beneficial in case management situations where information discovery functionality across structured and unstructured data is needed. Endeca specializes in analyzing and providing business intelligence for unstructured data. One of the unique features of the Endeca product is the guided search functionality, which enables users to access information based upon classifications, and drill down into the data by looking at the data from different views and using any combination of attributes.

10.3.4.1 Functionality

On a high level, the Endeca product contains three main functionalities: integration with structured and unstructured data sources, storage of the acquired information, and end-user information discovery functionality. Figure 10.7 summarizes the main functionalities in relation to the three main Endeca product components:

The *data integration* functionality is contained in the integration and application layers and is supported by the Oracle Endeca Information Discovery Integrator product component.

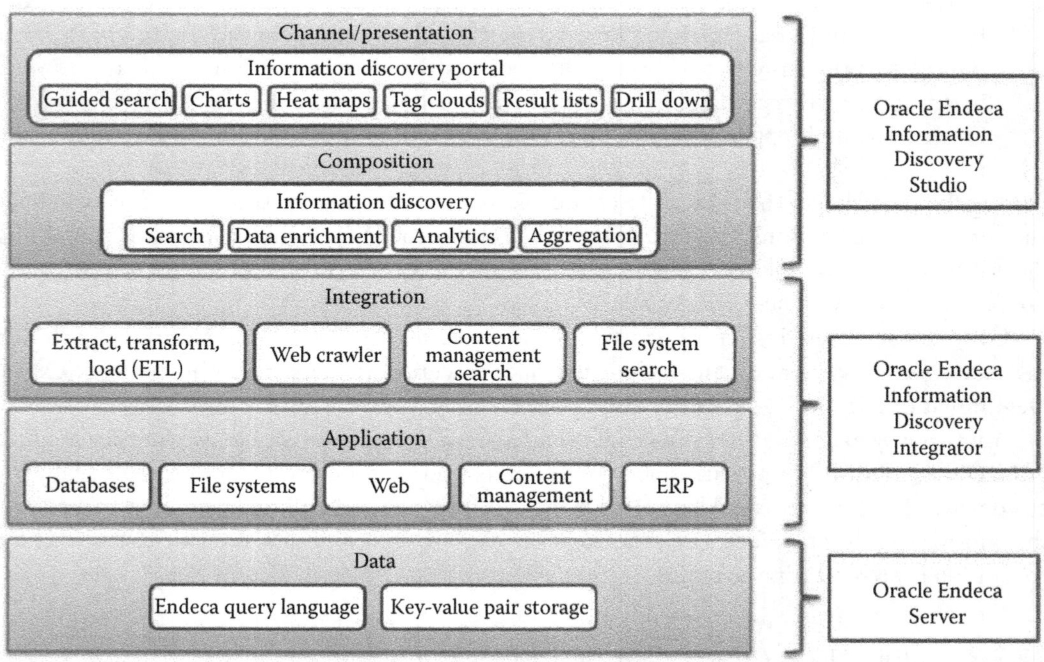

Figure 10.7 Endeca functional components.

The Integrator product is designed to load data into the Endeca server. The data stores that are fed into Endeca can be of any type, ranging from the database, Enterprise Resource Planning (ERP) systems, Microsoft Excel (XLS), Acrobat Portable Document Format (PDF), and unstructured data originating from Twitter and Facebook. One of the guiding principles of Endeca is "No data left behind," meaning we never know when we can use it, just store it.

The *data storage* functionality is part of the data layer and is supported by Endeca server. Endeca stores its data in a different paradigm than what is used in standard relational databases. In relational environments, predefined structures, such as tables, columns, and relationships determine a fix data model. Data that is entered into Endeca has all sorts of structure that can change over time. This can range from a simple record with attributes to EXtensible Markup Language (XML) structures containing a hierarchy. Upfront, not all (or no) relationships between the data objects are known. In order to challenge the data model knowledge gap, all data that enters the Endeca data is stored as records containing attributes that are simple key-value pairs. Endeca created a query language that enables searching through these key-value pair records and deliver the analytics needed for the end-user information discovery functionality.

The *end-user information discovery* functionality is part of the composition and channel and presentation layer, where Oracle Endeca Information Discovery Studio delivers this functionality. The power of Endeca is to combine all sorts of data across all records (vertical search), and at the same time enabling the enrichment of information by looking at the different data structures related to the queried objects. The Discovery Studio supports the end user with guided search functionalities and has capabilities to drill down and present the information in all sorts of formats.

10.3.4.2 How Does Endeca Information Discovery Relate to Case Management?

Endeca Information Discovery delivers intelligence that is useful in two case management classifications, service request and investigative management; see Chapter 4 for more details.

The *investigation* case management area is the obvious area where Endeca has added value. Specifically, when information is brought together from a large range of structured and unstructured sources, combinations can be made that were not clear before and can lead to new insights. A good example is a police investigation where a combination of police source information from a crime scene, a crime overview of the neighborhood, and social media information and can lead to a breakthrough in a case.

In the service request area, Endeca supports customers finding information in websites. Endeca helps narrowing down the information the customer is looking for with a guided filtering methodology.

This typically takes place in the triage part of a service request. The triage is the preparation phase of customer contact. This phase finishes with a decision whether to proceed with the request. This can lead into a case for further investigation. See Section 4.4.6.2 for more information.

Another example in the *service request* area is providing information about the customer to the company who are about to sell a product to the customer. When the product vendor is about to commit to an obligation that can span over multiple months or years, such as insurance, the company wants to know more about experiences with this customer, experiences that have the same customer profile or who live in the same neighborhood. For instance, if the potential customer wants to have a car insurance but lives in an area with exceeding car theft, the insurance can be denied or have a higher price attached to it.

10.3.5 Oracle Real-Time Decisions

Oracle Real-Time Decisions (RTD) is tailored for optimizing decision-making during customer interactions. RTD is not just a "static" rule engine but adds knowledge of all previous interactions to narrow down the choices that are available in that specific situation. Typical use cases for RTD include call center support, marketing improvement by learning, tailor campaigns on web pages for clients, and drill down toward product choices on the web based upon customer profiles and previous customer behaviors. The RTD base product is a marketing application, but this can be extended in any region.

10.3.5.1 Functionality

RTD enables business users to define performance goals, choices, and rules to support decision-making. RTD then adds predictive analytics on top to leverage previously encountered similar situations, and with that help narrow down the choices available for the client.

On a high level the RTD product contains functionalities as shown in Figure 10.8.

The decision engine is the main component of RTD. This is where information and decision components are brought together, based upon which a decision is made. The result of a decision is a weighted list of choices, which enable the customer and/or the business to make a justified decision.

The decision components, based upon which decisions are made, consists of performance goals, choices, rules, and models. As soon is the application is brought into production, the learning part starts and every decision is stored for later reference. The models "learn" from these decisions and customer behavior and take this information into account when the next decision is requested.

10.3.5.1.1 How Does RTD Relate to Case Management?

RTD is typically useful in service request type of cases. As described in Section 4.4, the service request case consist of two main flows, a triage workflow type of pattern and the service request case itself. The added value of RTD is in the triage part where there is intense communication between the first line of contact and the customer. In this area we need to be able to narrow down

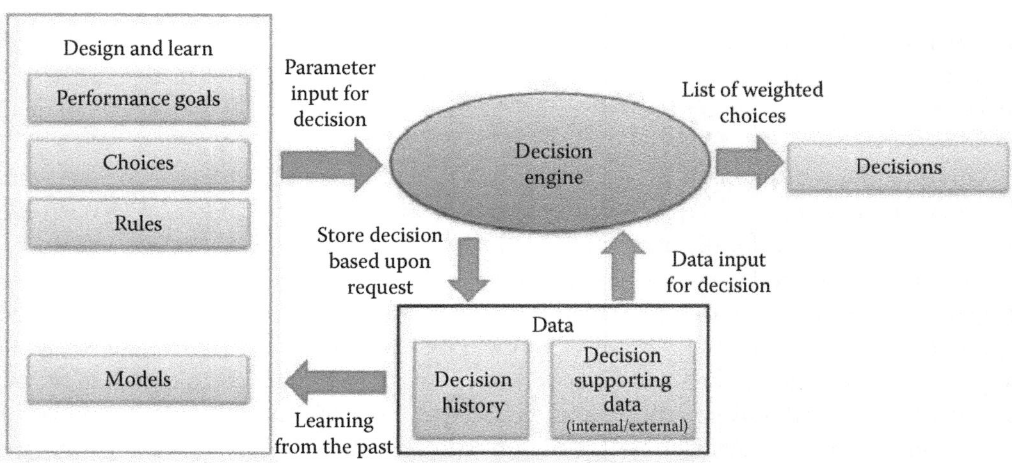

Figure 10.8 RTD high level overview.

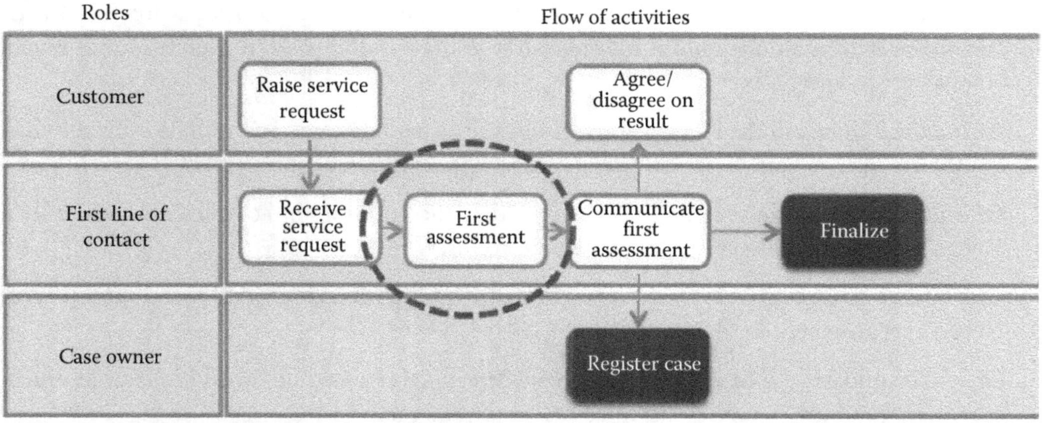

Figure 10.9 Usage of RTD in service request triage.

the choices for the customer. This in order to decide if the customer likes to proceed or that the response was adequate and no further activities need to be done. RTD and specifically the predictive analytics enable improving the efficiency in this area, providing a selected set of choices based upon which customers can make their decision. RTD also improves the quality of the choice by tailoring the choices for the client and learning from previous experiences with other clients. As a result, RTD helps lowering the initial costs during the initial customer service request stage and provides the customer with a better advice.

In Figure 10.9 encircled is the area in which RTD can support the assessment part.

10.4 Summary

In this chapter we focused on the usage of intelligence during the case execution and the implementation with Oracle products. The different stakeholders during the execution of a case use intelligence in order to make decisions. These decisions support the stakeholders on the following three levels:

1. To support the execution of a single case (operational information level)
2. To manage the governance of cases that currently are executed (tactical information level)
3. To make forecasts and predictions based upon experiences with cases (strategic information level)

The intelligence design is done in the three functional case design categories and specifically in the following design components:

1. The rules design component (life cycle design area)
2. The three information levels, operational, tactical, and strategic (information design category)
3. The dashboard design (interaction design categories)

We looked at different Oracle products that support the intelligence functionalities in the different intelligence-related design areas. The relation between the intelligence functionalities is summarized in Table 10.1.

Oracle BAM can be used in all three information areas, but the main focus for BAM is the governance-related functionality. In this area BAM delivers dashboards that give insight in workload management and KPIs.

Oracle OEP listens to data streams and filters out situations that require follow-up activities. OEP supports case management with the monitoring part in incident classifications.

OPA is a business rules engine that is targeted at the handling of complex rules in order to determine entitlements in service request classifications.

Oracle Endeca supports case investigations with information discovery functionality across structured and unstructured data.

Oracle BI supports the case stakeholders with strategic information aimed at case and process improvement, product improvement, forecasts, and trend analysis.

Oracle RTD supports service request classifications in the triage during the interaction with the customer. RTD supports the customer to narrow down the choices for the customer.

Chapter 11

Concluding Remarks

In this section we discussed the different Oracle technologies supporting case management, Oracle Business Processes Management (BPM)/Adaptive Case Management (ACM), Siebel, and the Oracle Service Cloud. Each of these products is tailored for different aspects of case management, when comparing the following usage characteristics:

- Main focus of functionality—What are the main case management design categories and classifications that the product relates to?
- Delivery type—Is the product delivered as a single entity or an umbrella type of solution?
- Product type—Is the product middleware, package based or cloud based?
- Agility at runtime—What agility does the product offer at runtime, does the product relate to ACM or production case management (PCM)?

Oracle ACM is part of the Oracle Service Oriented Architecture (SOA)/BPM suite and is based upon a middleware based product stack. Strong capabilities of Oracle BPM/ACM and SOA are supports for the event based lifecycle design and the integration capabilities. With these characteristics Oracle BPM/ACM is a good choice for an umbrella type of application used in an enterprise wide and cross application environment. This umbrella type of application takes responsibility for the end-to-end management and monitoring of all activities within the context of a case.

Oracle Siebel is a package based solution and is based upon customer relationship management (CRM) functionality. Key elements in the Siebel solution are the preconfigured CRM based data model and the extensibility of the solution. Siebel extended the CRM capabilities with case management functionality into different industries and cross-industry specific solutions. The Siebel product can be used in isolation, as a solution containing all case management functionality, and can be used in collaboration with other applications in a wider end-to-end scenario.

The *Oracle Service Cloud* is a cloud-based application aimed at delivering support for product related interactions with customers. Key element in the service cloud solution is the knowledge that supports both self-service search and customer contact center interactions. The product enables companies to position themselves in the area of product leadership.

The service cloud has strong capabilities in the portal and channel areas, where it enables the self-service portal through browsers and mobile, direct interaction with the contact center via a variety of channels and customer interactions with social communities.

Table 11.1 summarizes the characteristics of the Oracle case management product, as described earlier in this book.

All solutions based upon Oracle BPM/ACM, Siebel, and the Oracle service cloud require some level of intelligence at operational, tactical, and strategic level. Oracle BPM/ACM, Siebel and

Table 11.1 Usage Characteristics of Oracle Case Management Products

Focus Area	*Oracle BPM/ACM*	*Siebel*	*Oracle Service Cloud*
Case management design area	Life cycle design	Information and life cycle design	Information and Interaction design
Classification support	All three case management classifications are supported, service request, incident management, and/or investigative solution	All three case management classifications are supported: service request, incident management, and/or investigative solution	Two case management classifications are supported: service request supported via Iinvestigations.
Delivery type: Full implementation or umbrella type	Umbrella type	Full implementation	Full implementation
Product type	Middleware	Package based	Cloud based (SAAS)
Agility at runtime: ACM or PCM	ACM type: Ad-hoc processes as part of a case can be started Flexible stakeholder model Ability to add new event publishing sources	PCM type: The solution with all its aspects is defined upfront. Flexibility at run-time of the state-model is possible	PCM type: Most functionality of the service request is defined upfront. The inclusion of OPA (RightNow policy automation) delivers flexibility at run-time. The continuous improvement of answers improves the quality of the service request.

the Oracle Service Cloud all provide some level of support for intelligence functionality. When a specialized intelligence functionality is required (this is not the core of one of these products) additional products can be added to the solution. We looked at Oracle products that implement the case management intelligence functionalities:

- Support for the execution of a single case (operational information level) is provided by the products Oracle policy automation (OPA), Oracle business rules, Oracle Endeca and Oracle real time decisions (RTD).
- For managing the governance of cases that currently are executed (tactical information level) Oracle BAM is the de facto product in the Oracle landscape.
- To make forecasts and predictions based upon experiences with cases (strategic information level) is supported by Oracle business intelligence (BI).

CASE MANAGEMENT EXAMPLES

IV

Introduction

In this section, we provide four examples to explain how case management can support industry processes. The aim of these examples is to show the usage of the case management solution framework in practice, including the determination of classification type; discuss the specific design components; provide the technical solution mapping; and map their functionality toward Oracle products. The examples are simplified for the sake of brevity.

Each example chapter starts with a description of the specific industry process and the related business challenges. Then we look at the solution details to implement the example based upon the case management solution framework described earlier in (Section 2—Case Management Solution Framework). In the solution description, we start with the design aspects of a case management solution as described earlier in Section 2.

The design of a case management solution contains three main business design areas:

- The case life cycle design, which supports the coordination of activities in achieving the end goals
- The case information design, which deals with all sorts of data, documentation, and media flowing through the case
- The case user Interface design, which maximizes the support for the case work force via portals, dashboards, and a variety of channels

These three business areas are interrelated and supported by the cross-functional design areas integration and roles and authorization.

In every example description, we look at different design components for which the example provides specific characteristics. Figure S.1 gives an overview of the case management examples and the design components that are highlighted in the different chapters.

Each chapter concludes with a mapping toward Oracle Products that can be used to implement this specific example.

		Case Life Cycle Design			*Case Information Design*			*Case Interaction Design*		
Case Management Example	*Short Description*	*Case Flow/ Process*	*Rules*	*Events*	*Document/ Media*	*Data*	*People Relationship*	*Portal*	*Dashboard*	*Channel*
Mortgage request	A client requests a mortgage loan to finance the property he/she wants to buy									
Welfare request	Provisioning of welfare service to the citizens, such as child benefit and pensions									
Crime to court/ criminal investigation	The "crime to court" deals with all the activities from the moment that a crime has been committed until the moment somebody is brought to trial and is convicted									
Insurance (property) claim handling	Handling of a property claim entered by a customer									

Figure S.1 Case examples, design overview

Chapter 12

Mortgage Request Handling

12.1 Introduction

The goal of this chapter is to:

- Use the mortgage request process as an example of a case management solution based upon a service request classification in combination with some investigation cases
- Show how the mortgage request related business challenges *customer*, *regulations*, and *financial risk* impact the case management solution
- Show examples of the case management design components: lifecycle design, information design, people relationship design, and portal design
- Determine the solution for the mortgage request handling, and determine the Oracle products needed to implement the solution
- Show how the choice for a service request related operating model impacts the required functionality, technology choices, and supporting Oracle products.

12.2 Reading Guide

This chapter contains two main parts, the first part describes the mortgage request handling process including the main business challenges. The second part determines the solution for mortgages based upon the case management solution framework and contains a mapping towards Oracle products.

12.3 Mortgage Request and Business Challenges

12.3.1 Mortgage Request

The mortgage request handling process is used as an example of a predictable case management solution with a high level of customer/stakeholder interaction. This process is dominated by interactions between the customer, the mortgage provider, and other verification related stakeholders. These interactions are required to judge the customer situation, estimate the value of the property the customer likes to buy, evaluate what product options and variations are available, and check what is affordable for the customer. Even though the mortgage product itself can be complex, the process towards an agreement on a mortgage loan follows a sequential and predictable path containing sales, origination, and fulfillment. The mortgage provider starts a series of internal and external investigations in order to check the identity, solvability, and trust ability of the customer and the value of the property. After discussions with the customer are ended and the customer investigations turn out to be positive, a contract can be created and passed by the notary. After signing the contract, the funds can be made available.

Deviations in the standard flow may cause a cancelation of the process or a return to a previous process step. Nonpredictable events that impact the mortgage handling can originate from both the customer and the mortgage provider. The customer may for instance decide not to buy the house and stop the procedure. The mortgage provider can decide that a particular type of property ground leasehold is not allowed, and therefore the mortgage application will be terminated from the mortgage provider's side. Going back some steps in the mortgage a request process can be the result of incorrect entered data. A customer states at the start of the mortgage request that his salary is €35,000 annually. This amount is the basis for the proposed mortgage product types and variations. When during these discussions the employer income statement arrives and shows that the customer earns €34,500 annually this will not fundamentally change the proceedings. If however the statement shows that the customer's salary is €27,500 annually, the mortgage process will go one or several steps back, or go back to the initial advice stage.

12.3.2 Business Challenges

Three main areas pose business challenges for the mortgage institutes:

1. How are we going to serve our customers.
2. How to deal with new regulations imposed on the way mortgages are dealt with.
3. How to minimize the probability of default.

12.3.2.1 Serving the Customers

Mortgages always used to be a one-size-fits-all offering. The only difference between the mortgage providers was related to the interest rates. The last 10–20 years shows a shift towards three different ways of how customers want to be serviced, and how mortgage lenders position themselves to meet the customer needs:

- Should they go for *customer intimacy* and deliver customized products.
- Should they aim at *product leadership* in which they provide state-of-the art products.
- Should they focus on *operational excellence* and deliver a standardized product for a low price.

12.3.2.2 New Regulations

As a result of the financial crisis stricter regulations are imposed on the financial market. One of them being "Banks will be held accountable for making sure that borrowers have the ability to repay their loans, a sharp contrast from the previous housing bubble where some banks failed to check applicants' income or assets before they issued a loan." as is presented in an article in the MoneyNews website (http://www.moneynews.com/Personal-Finance/mortgage-banks-lender-regulations/2013/12/06/id/540393/).

Another regulation requirement is that end-to-end auditing is required. End-to-end auditing requires that every activity and decision in the mortgage request process needs to be recorded for future reference by authorities.

From a regulatory perspective the financial institutes are required to "know your customer." Knowing your customer, or verifying the identity of the customers, has a negative connotation. This verification includes checking the customer's involvement in criminal activities, such as fraud, money laundering, or terrorist financing.

12.3.2.3 Minimizing the Probability of Default

When a loan has been granted to a customer there is always a chance that this customer is not able to meet his/her debt obligation. In financial terms this is known as "probability of default." A financial risk profile of the customer gives an insight in the probability of a default. This risk profile is created in the mortgage origination phase of the mortgage request process.

12.4 Deriving a Solution Based upon the Case Management Solution Framework

12.4.1 Introduction

In Section II we presented the three steps leading toward a solution: determine the case management classification, the required functionality, and the required technical capabilities. We will focus specifically at the impact different operating models have on the solution. In addition we will provide a mapping towards Oracle products.

12.4.2 Determine Case Management Classification

The case structure for the mortgage request handling consists of multiple cases based upon two case management classifications, the *service request* and *investigations.*

1. *Service request*: A client requests a mortgage to finance the property he/she wants to buy, followed by interactions between the customer, the mortgage provider, and other related stakeholders to determine the outcome. In its simplest form, the outcome for a mortgage request by a customer is approved or denied. After approval different options arise relating to product varieties, duration of the mortgage, and payment schedules.
2. *Investigations*: As part of the origination and the fulfillment phase different investigations are started, such as the investigation of the customer financial risk profile. Each investigation is a separate case and connected to the service request case.

12.4.3 Determine Functional Components and Needs

Here we will focus on case management design components for which the mortgage request process provides good examples: the *case flow and process design*, *data design*, *people relationship design*, *portal design*, and *integration design* as shown in Figure 12.1.

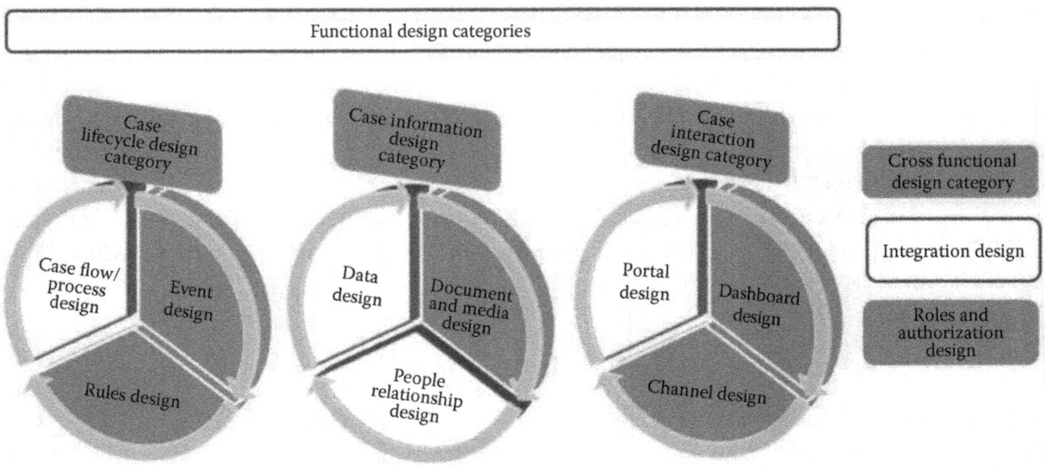

Figure 12.1 Solution topics (in white) discussed in this chapter.

The requirements for the mortgage lending process depend on the strategy that is chosen as to how to position the mortgage product in the market. In Section 4.4.4 we discussed the three strategy choices for market leadership: *customer centricity*, *product leadership*, and *operational excellence*. The choice for a specific strategy does not impact the mortgage process flow design, but impacts on how other design components are fulfilled. Table 12.1 shows the requirements related to the choice for a specific strategy and on which design component this has an impact.

12.4.3.1 Case Flow and Process Design

As is described in Section 3.3.1, the case lifecycle design category describes the coordination of activities in reaching one of the end goals and contains three design components, case flow and process design, rules design and event design.

On a high level the mortgage request process contains the following parts: Sales, origination, and fulfillment. The lifecycle of the mortgage request is dominated by a milestone based execution of activities. Prepopulating a list of activities per milestone enables the mortgage (case) workers to choose the most appropriate task/activity needed at a certain moment (Figure 12.2).

The *sales* phase in the mortgage lending process is the phase where the customer shows his interest in a mortgage and the first contact is made, even an early "no" might be given in this phase. This phase relates to the service request triage phase as presented in Figure 4.1, and is detailed further according to the triage model in Figure 4.2.

Origination is the process of creating the *mortgage*. During this process the customer delivers all information needed for the mortgage provider in order to make a decision, subject to proof of all required information by the client and other third parties in the next phase (e.g., income statements, valuation reports, etc.). During this phase additional investigations might be started in order to validate the request.

The *fulfillment* phase is the last phase in the mortgage process whereby the mortgage offer is finalized, all checks are verified, the customer signs the contract, and the money is released.

Both the origination and the fulfillment are milestones in the service request handling case flow and can be detailed according to the case flow and state model in Figures 4.2 and 4.4.

Table 12.1 Strategy Types and Impact on Solution

Strategy Choice	*Requirements*	*Impact on Mortgage Request Solution Requirements*	*Focus on Design Category/ Component*
Customer centricity	The customer wants a specialized offering, specifically tailored to his needs	Ensure that the involved sales person has all information of the customer available	Customer interaction/portal Cross functional/integration Customer information/data and PRM
		Give the customer insight in all proceedings of the case	Customer interaction/portal Cross functional/integration and security Customer information/data
		Include direct communication with the customer	Customer interaction/ channel
		Management steering via dashboards, KPIs related to: Mortgage process progress (minimize customer waiting time) Customer feedback (how are we doing)	Customer interaction/ dashboard
Product leadership	Responding rapidly to changing market situations and changing customer needs. For example, currently property values are lower than the mortgage amounts, therefore customers expect a new way of refinancing their mortgage	Be able to enter a broad range of products through a rich user interface	Customer interaction/portal Cross functional/integration Customer information/data

(*Continued*)

Table 12.1 (*Continued*) Strategy Types and Impact on Solution

Strategy Choice	*Requirements*	*Impact on Mortgage Request Solution Requirements*	*Focus on Design Category/ Component*
		Implement complex calculation models supporting customer wishes.	Customer lifecycle/rules design
		Fast support for new technologies	Cross functional/integration
		Management steering via dashboards, KPIs related to product type sales	Customer interaction/ dashboard
Operational excellence	Fast, cheap, and no hassle The McDonald's type of offering, which is completely predictable with no surprises and because of the scale of delivery it can be made cheap	Automate as much as possible.	Customer lifecycle/case flow process
		Automate rules	Customer lifecycle/rules design
		Minimize customer contact	Customer lifecycle/case flow process Customer interaction/portal and channel
		Management steering via dashboards, KPIs on: Amount of completely automated mortgage requests Amount of exception handlings and cost involved	Customer interaction/ dashboard

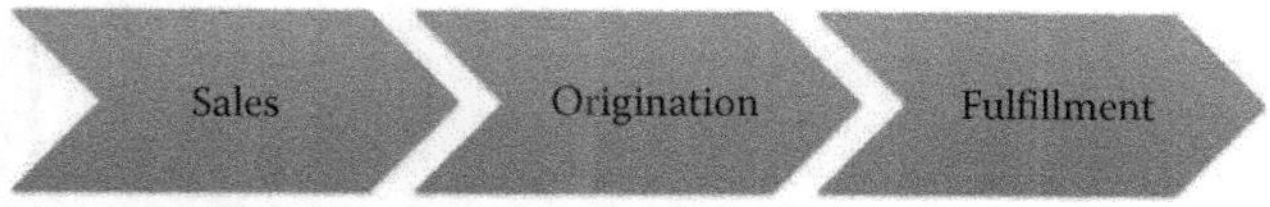

Figure 12.2 Mortgages request process flow—high level.

The process toward an agreement is highly predictable with a few exceptions originating from internal or external events:

- As described earlier in the *mortgage request* description there could be moments in the chain of activities where the process needs to go back one or more steps that can originate from both parties
- Fraud suspicion immediately stops the progress of the mortgage request process.

12.4.3.2 Case Information Design

As is described in Section 3.3.3, the case information design deals with all sorts of data and documentation flowing through the case, and maps the relationships between all persons and/or assets involved in the case. The case information design category contains three design components, data design, document and media design, and people relationship management design.

12.4.3.2.1 Data Design

During the mortgage lending request multiple persons can be working on the same mortgage request case. These persons originate from different departments and all have different views and activities. In order to be able to service the customer in a better way and at the same time also fulfill the compliance requirement a "one customer view" is required. This provides a complete overview of the customer including all products in use, know your customer, financial risk profile, and history of all activities and contacts. Providing a "one customer view" to all stakeholders ensures that no mistakes are made in the handling of the customer request. Another advantage is ensuring that questions are raised only once to the customer, this avoids irritation of the customer and reduces the risk of errors due to double entry of data. This data is provided to the stakeholders via a variety of channels.

Figure 12.3 provides an overview of the data objects needed when working with a mortgage request. These data objects are combined in folders related to the information needs of the mortgage workers:

- In the *"mortgage request"* area all the data related to the mortgage request are kept. This includes the involved persons, discussions, (intermediate) decisions, and delivered documents.
- The *"customer details"* area gives a full overview of the customer in relation to the mortgage request. It starts with the *accounts details* such as place of residence and (bank) account details. In *related parties* the persons or businesses, related to the mortgage request, are listed. The mortgage worker needs to have an overview of all products acquired at the mortgage provider that are currently used (*current "live products."*) During the mortgage request insight in the risk profile is needed, for instance to determine the chance of "default." This risk profile is updated on a continuous basis for instance with the payment behavior of the customer.

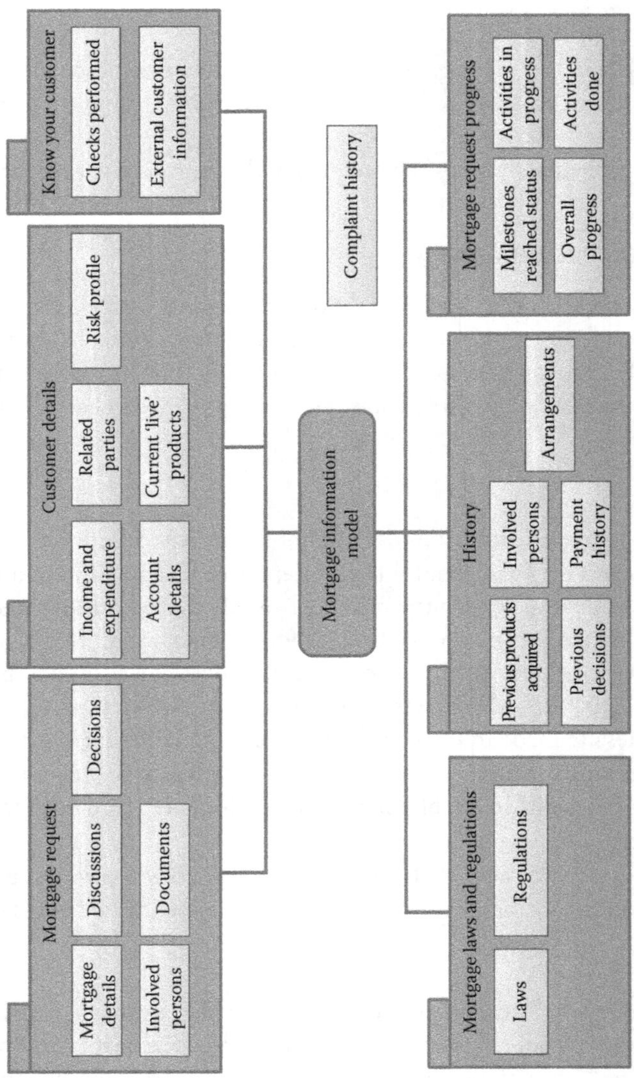

Figure 12.3 One customer view.

- The "*know your customer*" area contains all information related to possible criminal activities by the customer. This information is required by the regulator and gives an overview of the checks that are performed in the past including all external information that can point to criminal behavior.
- The "*mortgage request process*" area contains all information that gives a full overview of the current mortgage request process. It contains information about the current status of the request, outstanding actions by the stakeholders, lists the persons involved in this mortgage request, gives an overview of the discussions with the customer, and related documents.
- The "*history*" area contains all previous experiences with the customer. It provides an overview of the *previously acquired products* with the mortgage provider, what *decisions* are made in the relation with the customer, for instance was a request ever refused, and an overview of the *complaints* filed by the customer. It also contains an overview of all *arrangements* made with the customer. The *payment history* is an indicator for the risk profile of the customer. The *"involved persons"* area gives an overview of all persons working for the mortgage provider who were involved with this customer.
- The *"mortgage policies and regulations"* area is based upon the laws and regulations that the mortgage provider should abide by.

The *one customer view* is based upon data originating from a variety of data sources from within the system landscape or provided by external parties. The next step after the case management information design is the inclusion of the technical design areas "integration" and "security." Specifically related to the security design is that not everyone involved in the mortgage lending case is allowed to view and/or change the related data. Sensible information such as "know your customer" may only be viewed and/or changed by the mortgage owner.

12.4.3.2.2 People Relationship Design

The mortgage request process is a good example of a process with a complex people relationship design. During a mortgage request multiple persons are involved in the execution; the customer, persons who represent the customers (intermediaries), stakeholders within the mortgage provider, and external persons involved in investigations. Figure 12.4 shows the persons involved and the relationships between these persons. Three main stakeholders' groups can be distinguished; customer related, all stakeholders related to the mortgage provider, and external stakeholders.

The *customer* has direct contact with the mortgage provider or arranges an intermediary to execute all activities with the mortgage provider. When the contract is signed the customer has contact with a notary who legally witnesses the sign off. The customer also needs to contact an insurance company to arrange an insurance for the property.

At the *mortgage provider* two classes of employees are responsible for all interactions. The front office is responsible for all customer contact. The middle office is responsible for all internal contacts for arranging the mortgage and externally for acquiring services required for creating the mortgage loan.

The *external* stakeholders are external specialists who provide specific services that are needed during the mortgage loan request process, such as checking for fraud and estimating the actual value of the property.

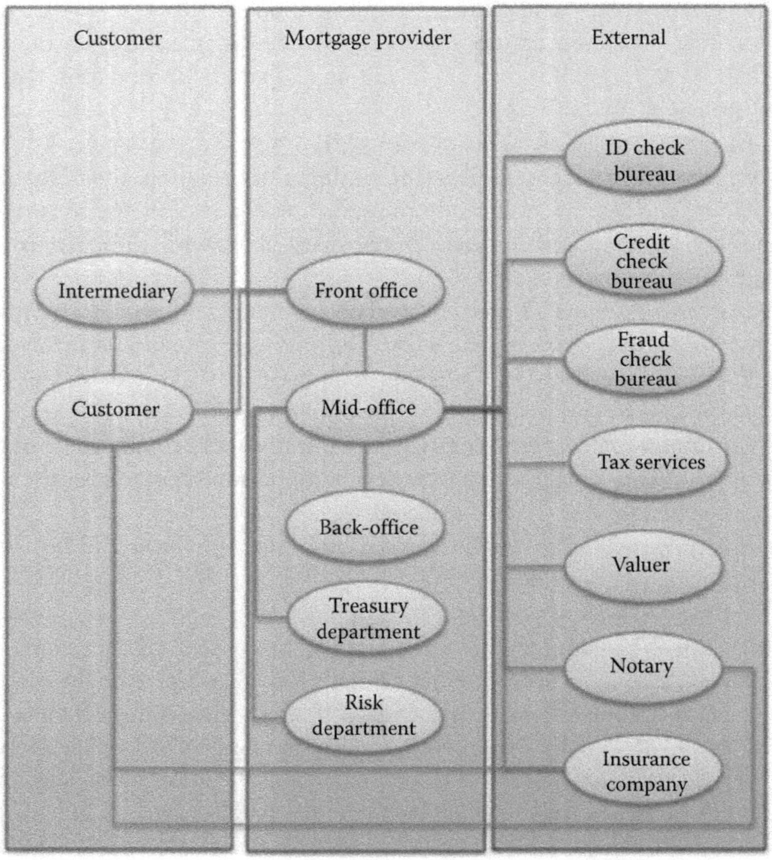

Figure 12.4 Mortgage stakeholders.

12.4.3.3 Case Interaction Design

As is described in Section 3.3.4, the case interaction design enables maximizing the support for the case work force and interactions with the customers. This design area contains three design parts, portal design, dashboard design, and channel design.

12.4.3.3.1 Portal Design

The portal design supporting the customer with the mortgage request depends on the choice for a strategy model as described in Table 12.1. The strategy choices *customer centricity*, *product leadership*, and *operational excellence* have different behaviors toward the interaction with the customer.

For *customer centricity* the portal design is focused at delivering insight in the progress of the mortgage request and share the in-between results with the customer. The portal (and the related channel) also needs to support direct interactions with the customer to enable a good relationship with the customer.

For the *product leadership* strategy the focus is at delivering a rich portal that enables the customer to make combinations of mortgage lending products and the customer situation with new innovative products. The portal should focus on delivering both content and calculation methods and must have the ability to include, in an agile way, new campaigns and products.

In the *operational excellence* situation the portal is aimed at providing the customer a simple means to run through the standardized mortgage request process. Even though this strategy is aimed at delivering low cost operations, the option to contact a service employee directly in the portal should be part of the process.

12.4.4 Determine Solution Mapping

12.4.4.1 Impact of a Mortgage Request Operating Model on Solution Capabilities

The main part of the solution for the mortgage request is to build the lifecycle and customer interaction design categories. For these two design categories the difference in the strategy models is most significant as can be seen in Figures 12.5 and 12.6.

In Figure 12.5 the lifecycle capability of a mortgage request is shown related to the three operating models. The strategy determines what orchestration capabilities should be used in the solution; direct human interaction (H2H), human-to-application interaction (H2A) or full-scale application-to-application interaction (A2A). In the *customer centricity* strategy there is a need for direct collaboration in the mortgage case that requires the need for a human to human (H2H) capability. The *product leadership* strategy requires interaction between the customer and case system; this relies on the human-to-application (H2A) capability. The *operational excellence* strategy on the other hand relies completely on an automated flow guided by application-to-application (A2A).

In Figure 12.6 the different capabilities are shown for the case interaction category. For two design components, the channel and the case portal, the choice for a strategy makes a difference.

All operating models require channel and presentation technical capabilities. First of all access to information is provided via a *web browser* and *electronic channels*. This information is provided via an overview with information coming from different sources such as customer information, case progress, and product information. This is supported by the *user interface integration capability*.

The *customer centricity strategy* requires support from the channel capabilities. In order to provide the customers with tools to enable direct contact at any time and any place, support for *mobile devices* and *apps* is needed.

The *product leadership strategy* additionally is supported by a *user interface* capability in the presentation design acting as an entry form for the mortgage request by the customer. The case request flow for the product leadership is supported by the lifecycle capability *human to application (H2A)*.

The *operational excellence* operating model in addition needs support for a standardized page flow (*user interface process*).

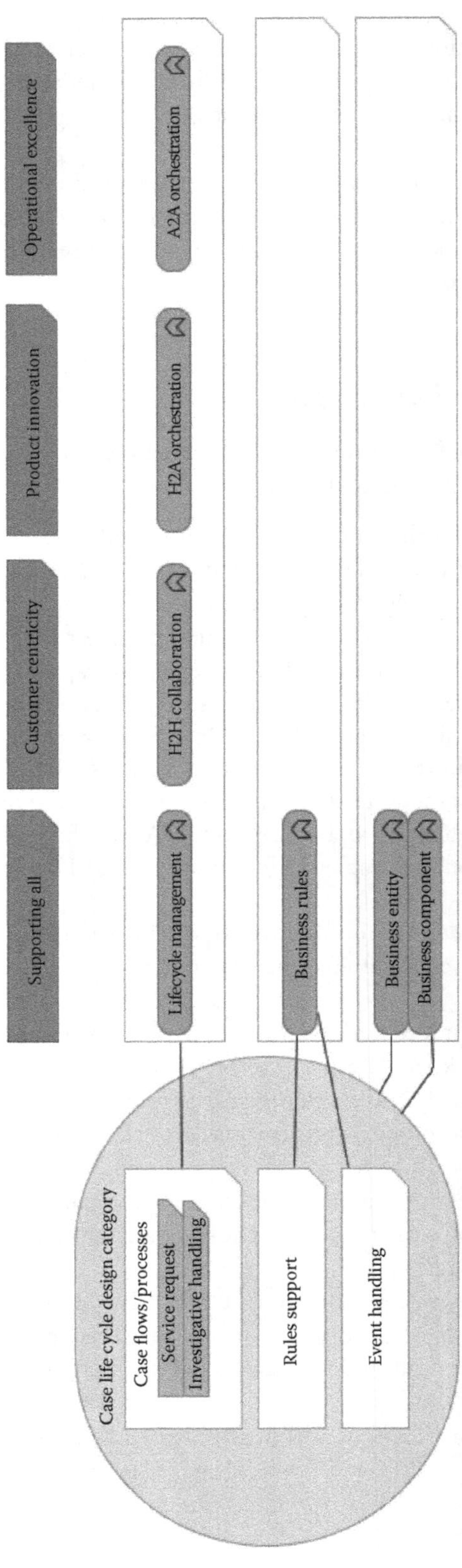

Figure 12.5 Operating model impact on mortgage lifecycle capabilities.

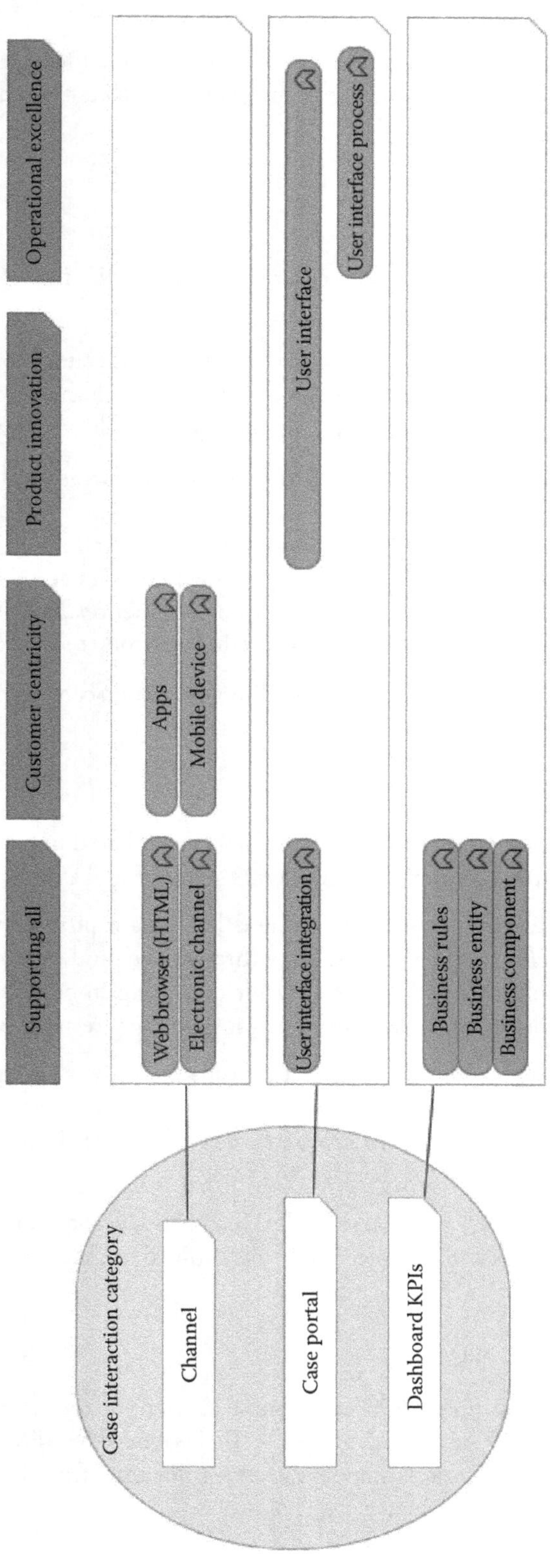

Figure 12.6 Operating model impact on mortgage interaction capabilities.

12.4.4.2 Mapping Mortgage Request Operating Models to Oracle Products

With the knowledge of the required capabilities for the mortgage lifecycle and the interaction design categories we are able to determine the main Oracle products that can support the mortgage request functionality.

12.4.4.2.1 Customer Centricity

In order to implement the mortgage customer centricity functionality three Oracle product suites are needed as is shown in Figure 12.7.

Oracle BPM/ACM: Oracle adaptive case management leads the execution of a mortgage request with the customer centricity model and guides the customer through the phases sales, origination, and fulfillment. BPM processes are used to support the case lifecycle with task execution.

Oracle SOA Suite: The Oracle SOA Suite delivers support in three areas—integration, portal, and dashboards.

The Oracle SOA Suite integration capabilities deliver support for all integration activities within the hybrid landscape where the mortgage request operates. Oracle application development framework (ADF) and Oracle WebCenter support the portal functionality. Business activity monitoring (BAM) supports the dashboard functionality, where customer satisfaction is measured.

Other Oracle products: Oracle communicator is used for direct interaction connectivity with the customer.

12.4.4.2.2 Product Leadership

The implementation of the operating model *product leadership* is based upon three Oracle product suites, of which Oracle customer experience (CX) is the main group, as is shown in Figure 12.8.

Oracle CX: Oracle CX delivers in this operating model the main product stack. Oracle service cloud is responsible for steering and content delivery through the product search by the customer. Oracle Endeca delivers sophisticated functionality for delivering information discovery type of functionality as is needed during the search for the best mortgage (related) product.

Oracle SOA Suite: The Oracle SOA Suite integration capabilities deliver support for all integration activities within the hybrid landscape where the mortgage request operates. The Oracle BAM functionality provides dashboard functionality where Key Performance Indicators (KPIs) related to product type sales can be measured.

Other Oracle products: Oracle policy automation (OPA) is an optional component for delivering functionality if complex calculations and rules need to be determined in the mortgage request process.

12.4.4.2.3 Operational Excellence

The product stack for *operational excellence* is the same as used for the *customer centricity* operational model as can be seen in Figures 12.7 and 12.9. The usage of the BPM/ACM suite products in the operational excellence operational model differs significantly from how these products are used in the customer centricity situation.

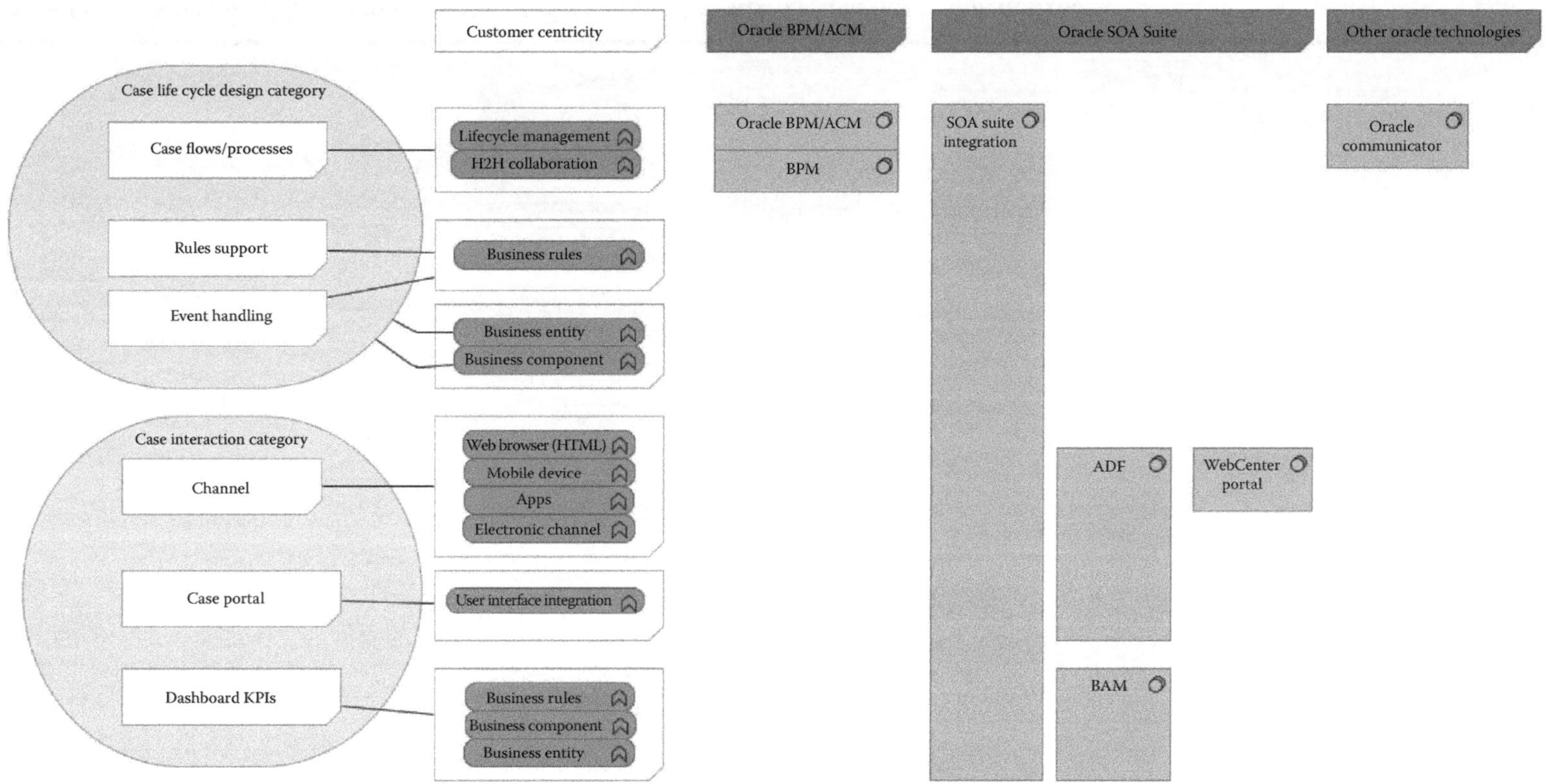

Figure 12.7 Oracle products supporting the customer centricity lifecycle and interaction design.

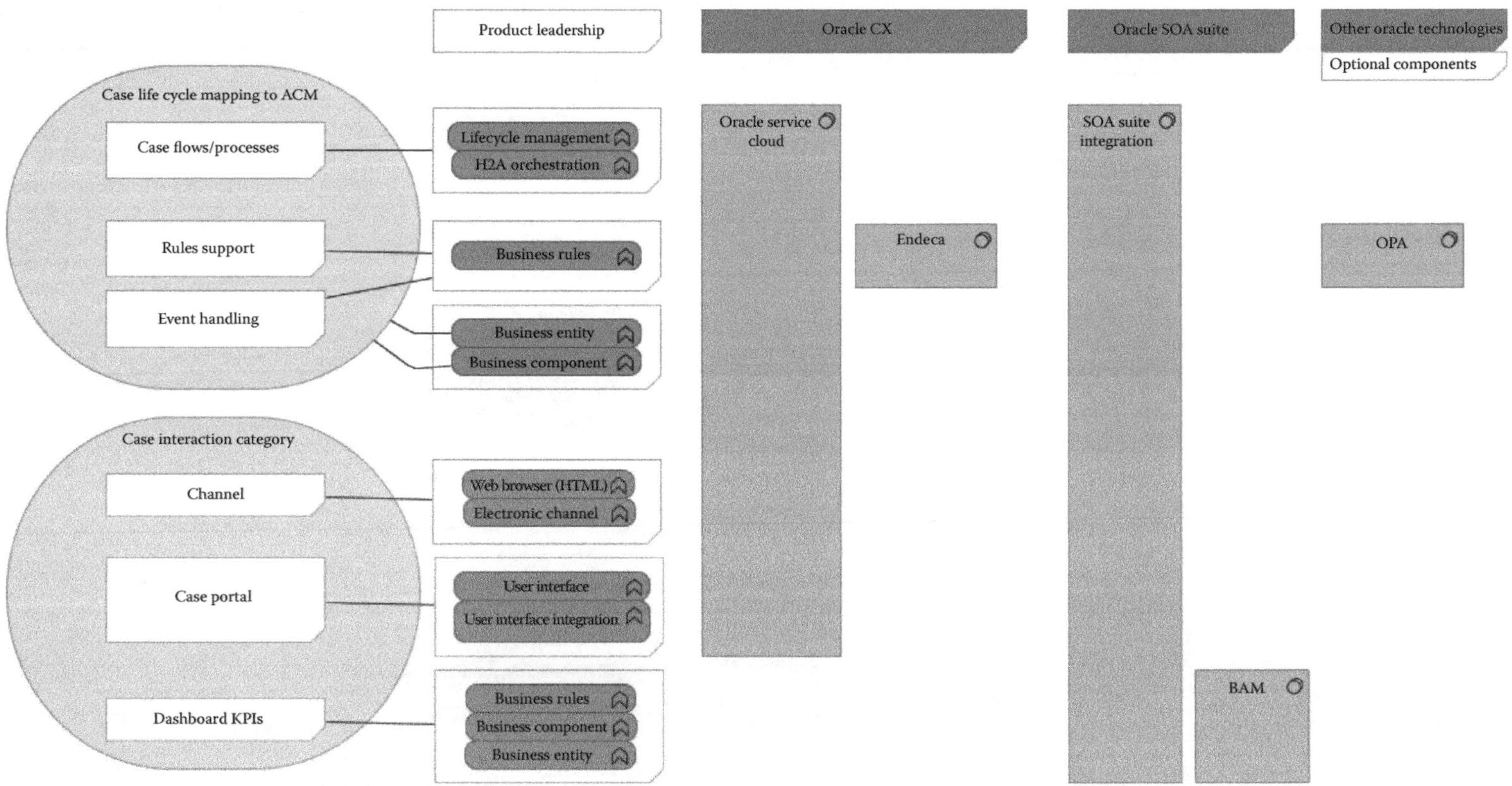

Figure 12.8 Oracle products supporting the product leadership lifecycle and interaction design.

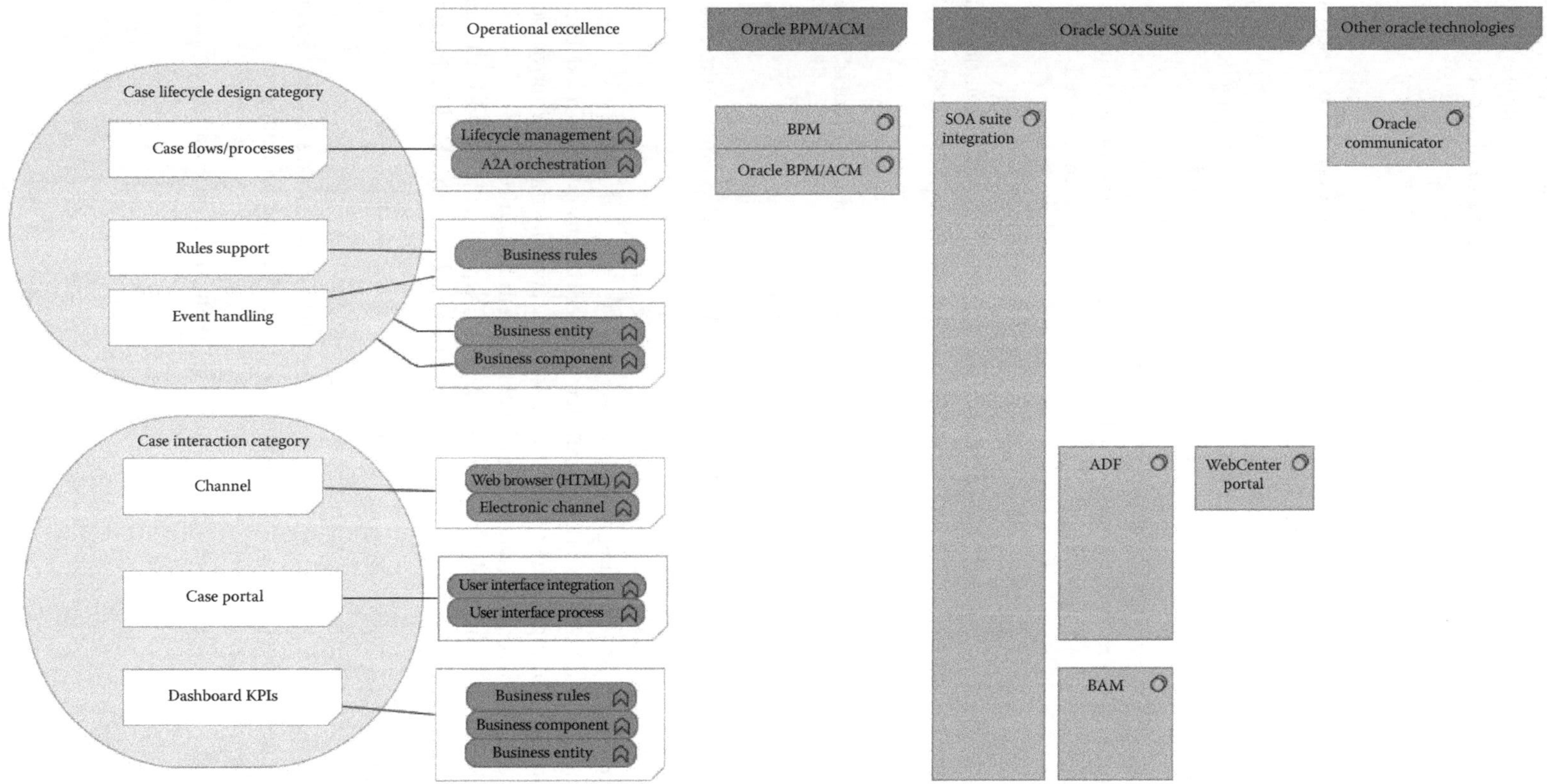

Figure 12.9 Oracle products supporting the operational excellence lifecycle and interaction design.

The operational excellence operating model is aimed at delivering a standardized model for a low price. This places BPM in the lead, aimed at delivering efficiency through a repeatable and automated workflow. ACM will only be included when an exception situation occurs that requires human intervention.

12.5 Conclusion

In this chapter the mortgage request handling process is used as an example of a service request with a high level of customer/stakeholder interaction.

The business challenges for mortgage request handling relate to *customer, regulations,* and *financial risk.* The customer related business challenge deals with how mortgage lenders position themselves, and determines the operating model that is going to be used:

- Should they go for *customer intimacy* and deliver customized products.
- Should they aim at *product leadership* in which they provide state-of-the art products.
- Should they focus on *operational excellence* and deliver a standardized product for a low price.

The impact of the three operating models on the design and technical solution mapping is investigated for the case lifecycle design category and case interaction design category. The following conclusions can be drawn for the operating models:

- For all three operating models the same high-level mortgage process models is used.
- The *customer intimacy* operating model:
  - Interaction with the customers is a key functionality.
  - Support for mobile devices and apps is needed.
  - The Oracle supporting platform is the Oracle BPM/ACM product suite and the SOA suite for integration.
  - Oracle ACM leads the execution of a mortgage request.
- The *product leadership* operating model:
  - The focus is at delivering a rich portal that enables the customer to make combinations of mortgage lending products and the customer situation with new innovative products.
  - Interaction between the customer and a case system is required.
  - The Oracle supporting platform is the Oracle CX product suite with the main products Oracle RightNow for the portal and content delivery and Endeca for information discovery.
- The operational excellence operating model:
  - Is aimed at delivering a standardized model for a low price.
  - Needs support for application to application orchestration and a standardized page flow.
  - The Oracle supporting platform is the Oracle BPM/ACM product suite and the SOA suite for integration.
  - Oracle BPM is in the lead, ACM will only be included when an exception situation occurs.

Chapter 13

Citizen Services in the Public Sector

13.1 Introduction

The goal of this chapter is to:

- Use the welfare request process as an example of a service request supported by complex rules management;
- Show how the welfare request related business challenges for the main three stakeholders, *government, citizens,* and *welfare organization* are *cost, quality, regulations,* and *flexibility* impact the case management solution;
- Focus on case management design components for which the welfare request process provides good examples: *case Flow/process design* and *rules design*;
- Determine the solution for the welfare request handling and show that the solution can be fully automated for the handling of high volume standard situations, and at the same time supports knowledge workers act upon complex nonstandard situations.
- Show how the combination of Oracle BPM/ACM and Oracle policy automation supports this solution.

13.2 Reading Guide

This chapter contains two main parts, the first deals with the welfare request process and gives an insight in the business challenges for the main stakeholders. The second part determines the solution for welfare request based upon the case management solution framework and contains a mapping toward Oracle products.

13.3 Welfare Request and Business Challenges

13.3.1 Welfare Request Handling

The handling of a welfare request deals with the provisioning of welfare service to the citizens, and involves products such as child benefits and pensions. Typically a welfare request process deals with a high volume of requests originating from a large customer base. In this process laws and regulations determine the end result, the entitlement. The customer expects to be serviced in the best way with no errors and limited contact.

Social welfare providers support a large customer base. Part of this work is done by hand, which impacts the speed of delivery of a request and can influence the quality of service. The service workers make decisions on "their best effort." Unfortunately this way of working might result in two welfare specialists dealing with the same type of request for two different customers come to a different conclusion, which can differ in the eligibility, duration, and height of the welfare benefit. In most service organizations working practice is silo based, meaning that only a select group of service workers have knowledge of one product, such as child benefit. Downside of this practice is that overlap in knowledge areas is not regular.

The functionality that is needed to support the welfare request is customer relationship management (CRM) in an extreme form. The welfare organization needs information about every citizen in a country or state, all their relationships, history of salaries, welfare schemes, and all decisions made related to the laws at the time the decision was made. This functionality puts a high demand on the system landscape, for instance the required storage needed to store all citizen information.

A functionality that will be described in detail later in this chapter is around "time travel." Decisions around providing welfare to a citizen are based upon information known at a certain moment in time. If it appears that the provided information, such as age, was not correct at that moment, whether caused by a data input error or fraud, the calculation of all welfare schemes for that person need to be recalculated. Needless to say that this is a complex job where all the information needs to be available and changes can be made in retrospect.

In order to fight against fraud and crime, systems of the welfare organization and other citizen providers need to be integrated, within a country but also across borders. For instance the integration between the welfare and the tax system provides an insight in a person's work history during the period he/she was also receiving welfare. This can lead to a renewed insight that the person was not entitled to receive welfare and might initiate a fraud investigation case against this person.

13.3.2 Business Challenges

The three main stakeholders in this area are *government and related politics* making the rules of engagement around the welfare services, the *welfare organization* providing the welfare services and, of course, the *citizens*. The operating model has been the same for decades, and is mainly based upon human activities executed by welfare case workers supported by some level of automation, and executed in segregation from other citizen service providers.

For the *government and related politics* the service operation needs to be more efficient, in control, adaptable to changes, and at the lowest costs. Especially the last reason, cost reduction, is an important driver for changes as a result of the financial crisis. One constraint towards cost reduction is that the service request handling needs to be done within the limits of the regulations.

Citizens request to be serviced better and faster, as they are used to in the current consumer-oriented society. As a result the relationship between the welfare service provider and the citizens is changing. Citizens demand online access to their own data and the ability to make changes to this data, through a variety of channels. Predictability of the delivered service is also high on the wish list of the citizens, which includes better upfront predictions of the expected result, timelines, in between updates, and minimum contact as possible. The Dutch Social Insurance Bank, the Sociale Verzekeringsbank (SVB), The Dutch welfare organization, even made their slogan based upon this dogma, "The best customer contact is no contact," meaning we know your situation, and are able to make the best decision with minimum contact.

The *welfare organizations* realize they need to adapt as a result of the changing environment. At the same time they need to deliver high quality work as people depend on the excellent operation of the citizen service providers. Reputation and trust of the citizens are therefore the key words for the operation of the citizen service organization.

13.4 Deriving a Solution Based upon the Case Management Solution Framework

13.4.1 Introduction

The business challenges for the welfare organizations, provided in Section 13.3.2 lead to a renewed solution in which automated case management will play a larger role. Here we provide an outline of the main parts forming the case management type of a solution and focus specifically on the case management design areas case flow/process design and rules design. The structure of this chapter is according the case management solution framework as presented in Section II. We will finish this chapter with a mapping towards Oracle products.

13.4.2 Determine Case Management Classification

The Welfare request can be classified as a *service request.* Citizens claim a welfare request via different channels such as on-line, via a letter or go to a welfare office. Once the request is entered the case manager will determine if the request is legitimate. This result is communicated with the customer. A negative result can turn into a discussion with the customers and a second intake investigation might take place. A positive decision will result into a follow-up *investigation cases* that lead to an entitlement decision. Input for the investigation of the welfare request is the citizen situation, which includes job(s) the customer has/had, the personal situation of the persons, owned assets, previous decisions, criminal records, laws applicable to the welfare request, etc.

13.4.3 Determine Functional Components/Needs

For this example we will focus on case management design components for which the welfare request process provides good examples: the *case flow/process design* and *rules* design as shown in Figure 13.1.

13.4.3.1 Case Life Cycle Design

As is described in Section 3.3.2, the case lifecycle design category describes the coordination of activities in reaching one of the end goals and consists of three design components, case flow and process design, rules design and event design.

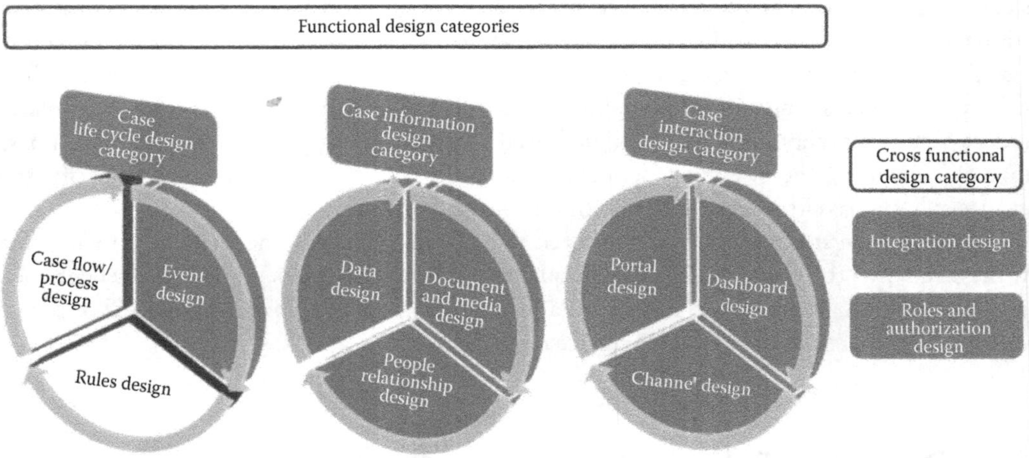

Figure 13.1 Solution topics (in white) discussed in this chapter.

13.4.3.1.1 Case Flow and Process Design

The first two processes in the welfare services value chain, *receive a customer event* and *determine entitlements*, as shown in Figure 13.2, cover the handling of a welfare request from a customer to the translation of this request in an entitlement. The last step in the value chain, *prepare financial consequences*, prepares the execution of the financial consequences as a result of this entitlement. The servicing is not part of the welfare request, and handles all arrangements made for a customer once the entitlement is in place.

Receive customer event: The receive customer event business process, as shown in Figure 13.3, describes receiving a benefit request via different channels and the actions taken by the case manager for the handling of the welfare request. In the first part of the process complexity and severity of the request are investigated resulting in follow up actions and priority of execution. This part is also known as triage as presented in Figure 4.2. The case manager registers the request and customer data as part of a task and checks if the data is complete. If not, the case manager contacts the customer for more information. Then the case manager creates a welfare request case and adds the task to the welfare request case. This is typically a workflow type operation and can be implemented as a process.

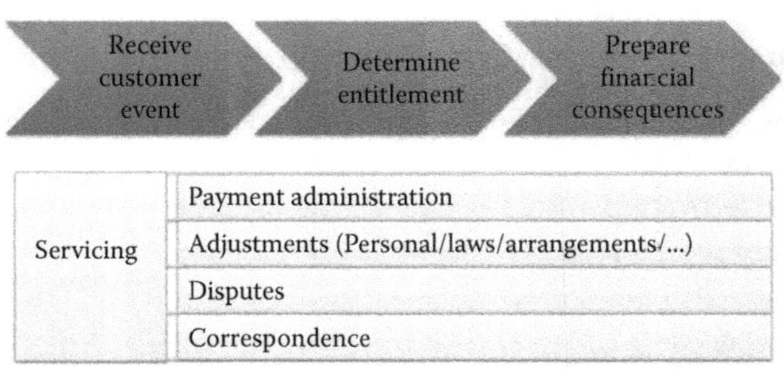

Figure 13.2 Welfare services value chain.

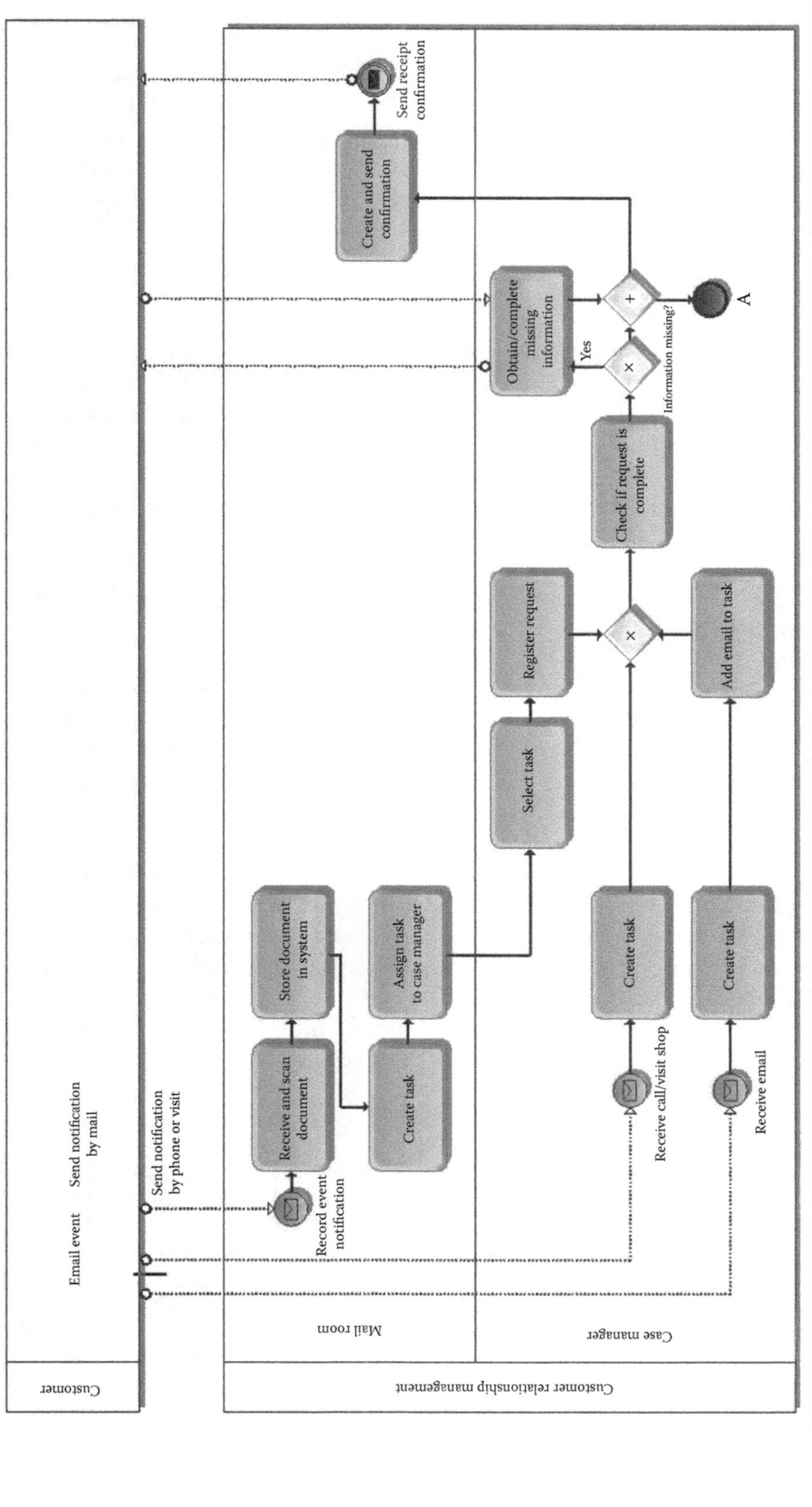

Figure 13.3 Receive customer event.

Determine entitlement: Both the determine entitlement and prepare financial consequences are milestones in the service request handling case flow, as presented in Figure 4.3. During the assessment of an entitlement, based upon the citizen request, the eligibility, duration, and height of a welfare benefit are determined by the case manager, as shown in Figure 13.4. If a review of a case is necessary, the case will be delegated to a reviewer (another case manager or a handler). Finally, the decision is sent to the customer and all relevant customer information and the decision on the entitlement is sent to the financial manager. After this activity the follow up step to prepare financial consequences can be started.

13.4.3.1.2 Rules Design

13.4.3.1.2.1 The Know is Separated from the Flow Decision management is related to laws and regulations and tends to change more frequently than the welfare entitlement process flow. The concept "the know is separated from the flow" relates to keeping the design and implementation of the process (the flow) and the rules (the know) separate. The rules for the entitlement decision process can be very complex. This complexity not only originates from the several laws related to the welfare request but also relates to the combination of information that impact the decision; such as current and historical personal situation, specific personal exceptions, the history of claim request, and previous decisions. Decision management needs to be supported by an engine that provides rules management in a business friendly way, but also enables "time-travel" related calculations (see Section 13.4.3.1.2.2).

13.4.3.1.2.2 Multireality and Temporal Reasoning or Time Travel As mentioned earlier, any decision made by the welfare provider is based upon the *reality* known to the provider at a certain moment of time. This reality is used as input for the welfare entitlement, and determines the amount of money to be paid to the customer within specific time intervals, as is shown in Figure 13.5. Multiple parties are involved in the determination of a welfare request: the citizen, the welfare provider, and official registration systems. All of these parties have their own view on the reality. Which reality is the correct one is the prime input for the decision making process. When during the process it becomes clear that the chosen reality was not the correct one, a decision can be made to change the reality to a different one and leads to a recalculation (or revoking) of the provided welfare scheme. Changing a reality as the basis for a welfare scheme can imply changing the past, the present, and the future.

The system needs to be able to store multiple versions of the reality, the source of the reality and an audit trail of the decisions made during the process.

Example

A citizen informs the welfare provider that he will move abroad from May 1 onward. This will impact his social services (products) he has been granted. His child welfare will stop and a "gap" will occur in his pension. The citizen request of the financial implications is calculated based on May 1st. For this, the system must be able do a provisional calculation based on the "truth" of the citizen. The final calculation only can take place when the official relocation message is received electronically from the municipality. The financial implications calculation will now be based on the "truth" of the municipality. When after six months it becomes clear that the citizen actually moved on June 15 instead of May 1, then a new reality based upon this delayed moving date should be calculated.

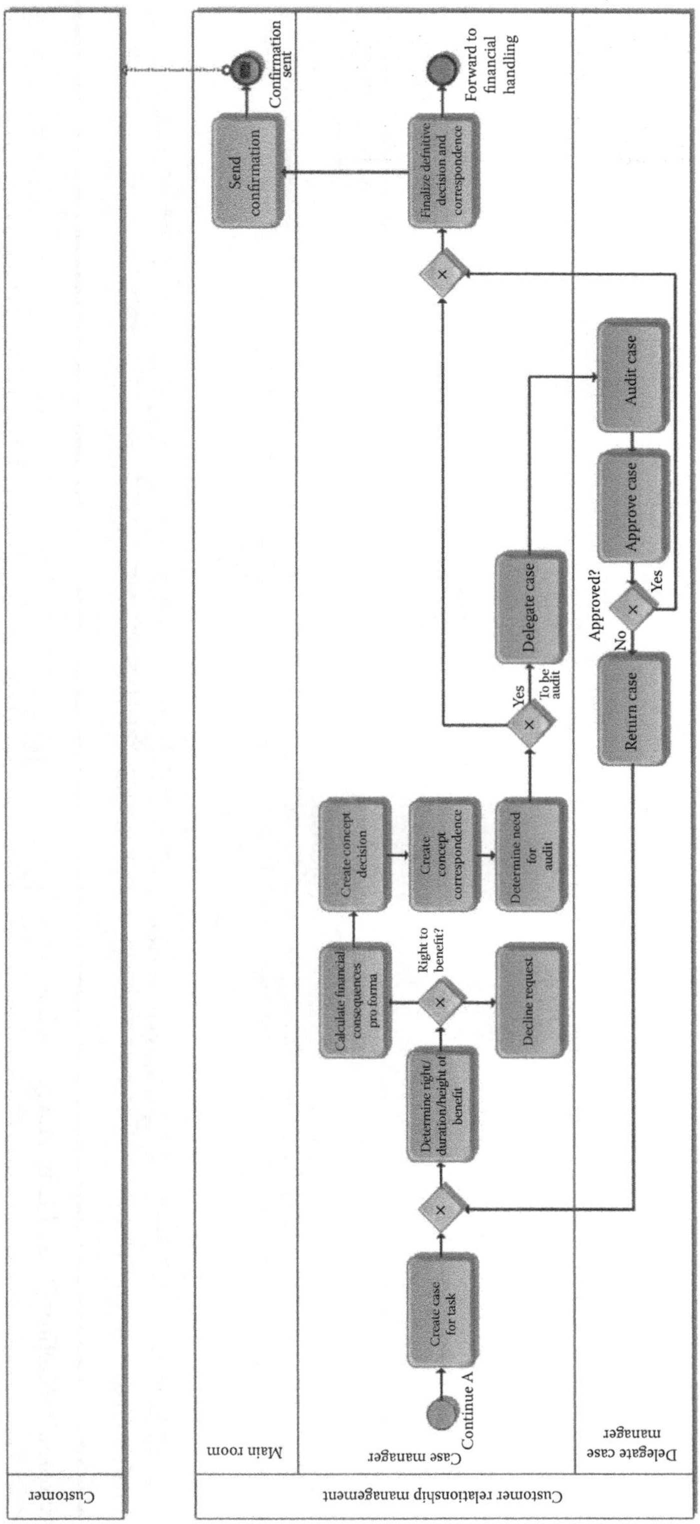

Figure 13.4 Determine entitlement.

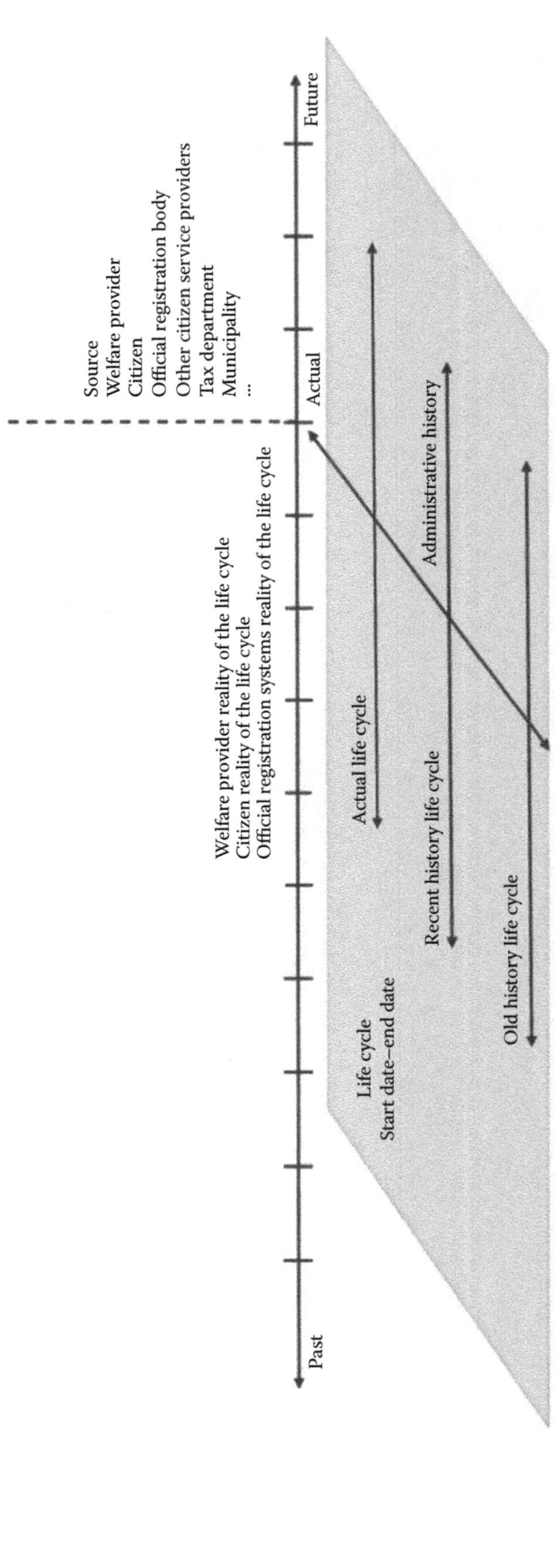

Figure 13.5 Multireality and temporal reasoning.

13.4.4 Determine Solution Mapping

As we have seen so far in the welfare request process overview and the business challenges for the solution, the case management solution should contain the following main characteristics:

- A predictable milestone based process model
- A high quality overview of the customer
- A complex rules engine, which enables business changes on a frequent basis and recalculation backward in time.

Another solution determining topic is the automation of the handling of high volume standard situations, and at the same time enabling knowledge workers to act upon complex nonstandard situations. One of the key characteristics of welfare request handling is the high volume of requests originating from the large customer base, including all citizens in a country or state. A large part of these welfare requests consists of predictable work that can be handled as straight through processing. Straight through processing or STP is the concept that a request can be handled without any human intervention. This will speed up the work and improve the predictability of the end result. Human intervention in the welfare request case handling is only needed in exceptional areas such as the questions stated as follows:

- Is the customer information complete? [No]
- Do fraud specific indicators provide an indication of a suspicion of fraud? [Yes]
- Do specific personal exceptions apply to the welfare rules? [Yes]
- Is the welfare request related to a change in an existing welfare request, for which the information base needs to be changed? [Yes]

The STP flow is responsible for orchestration of the execution. The actual functionality execution resides in the welfare systems, whether these are legacy (Cobol) systems or new Service Oriented Architecture (SOA) enabled systems. In order to be part of a STP flow, the welfare systems should be able to communicate with the STP flow in a standardized way. As more and more systems originating from other citizen service providers need to be connected to this STP flow an overall communication model needs to be agreed across all providers. This puts high demands on the integration capabilities of the landscape, with high requirements on availability and failover.

13.4.4.1 Determine Solution Capabilities

In the design paragraph Section 13.4.3 we looked at two design components, case flow/process flows and rules. We will determine the solution capabilities for these two design components in this paragraph.

In Figure 13.6 the solution mapping is shown for the case lifecycle design category containing the case flow/processes and rules support and specifically look at the difference between the *large volume STP handling* and the *complex nonstandard situations* handling.

The *large volume STP handling* is aimed at delivering a service with as less human intervention as possible, and contains a predictable execution path. Application to application (A2A) type of orchestration handling supports a process flow that does not require human intervention and

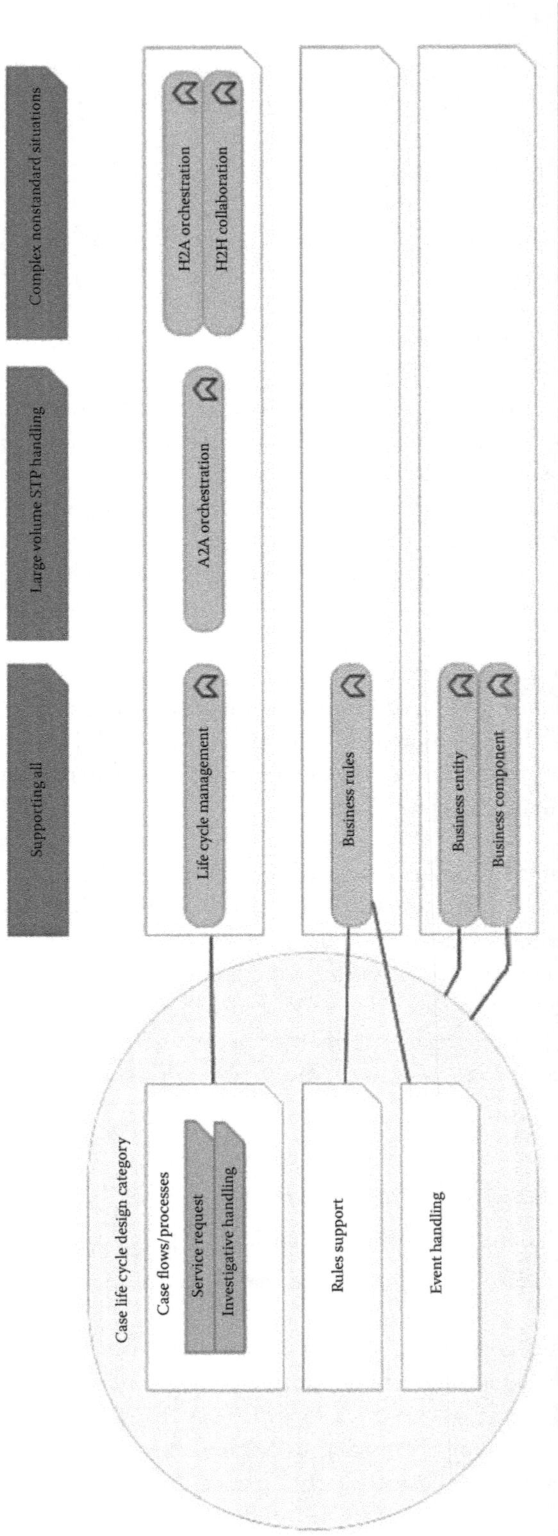

Figure 13.6 Welfare request solution mapping.

requires a predictable flow. Requesting child benefit is a highly standardized process, with predictable steps and activities executed automatically, and only in exception situations specific activities by welfare specialists. Figures 13.7 and 13.8 provide an overview of the Oracle products for the two scenarios. These figures are based upon the mapping structure as described in Section 5.5 and shown in Figure 5.11.

In the *complex nonstandard situations* the handling is executed by case workers, supported by system activities (human to application, H2A support) and contains direct interaction with the customers and other case workers (human to human, H2H support). These nonstandard situations can be determined directly at the start of a case or can be started as an exception flow from the STP process.

For both the STP and nonstandard situations business rules capabilities are crucial for determining the entitlement as discussed earlier in Section 13.4.3.1.2. This support is needed for both the entitlement determination and recalculations as a result of a change in the basis or reality of the entitlement.

13.4.4.2 Mapping the Welfare Request to Oracle Products

The *large volume STP handling* and the *complex nonstandard situations* have different solution characteristics as we have seen in the previous section. This has an impact on the choices for Oracle products to be used for these two scenarios.

13.4.4.2.1 Large Volume STP Handling

For the STP scenario the focus is on application to application (A2A) integration, and is implemented by Oracle BPM (and/or BPEL). Since we know nonstandard situations can be started directly at the start or as the result of an exception in the STP flow, the starting point for ACM is added in Figure 13.7.

A crucial part in this product overview is SOA suite integration part since multiple internal and external systems need to be integrated to deliver a complete customer and case overview enabling a correct entitlement decision.

Oracle policy automation (OPA) is the rules engine that enables the complex entitlement decision process, and also ensures support for time travel related functionality as described in paragraph Section 13.4.3.1.2.

13.4.4.2.2 Complex Nonstandard Situations

The same product stack is used as in the STP situation. For nonstandard situations ACM is in the lead, as opposed to the STP situation where BPM was in the lead. The SOA suite integration is again a crucial part for delivering all information from different internal and external systems (Figure 13.8).

The OPA product is here used for delivering the time-travel functionality (Section 13.4.3.1.2) for recalculation of entitlements, and investigating previous decisions.

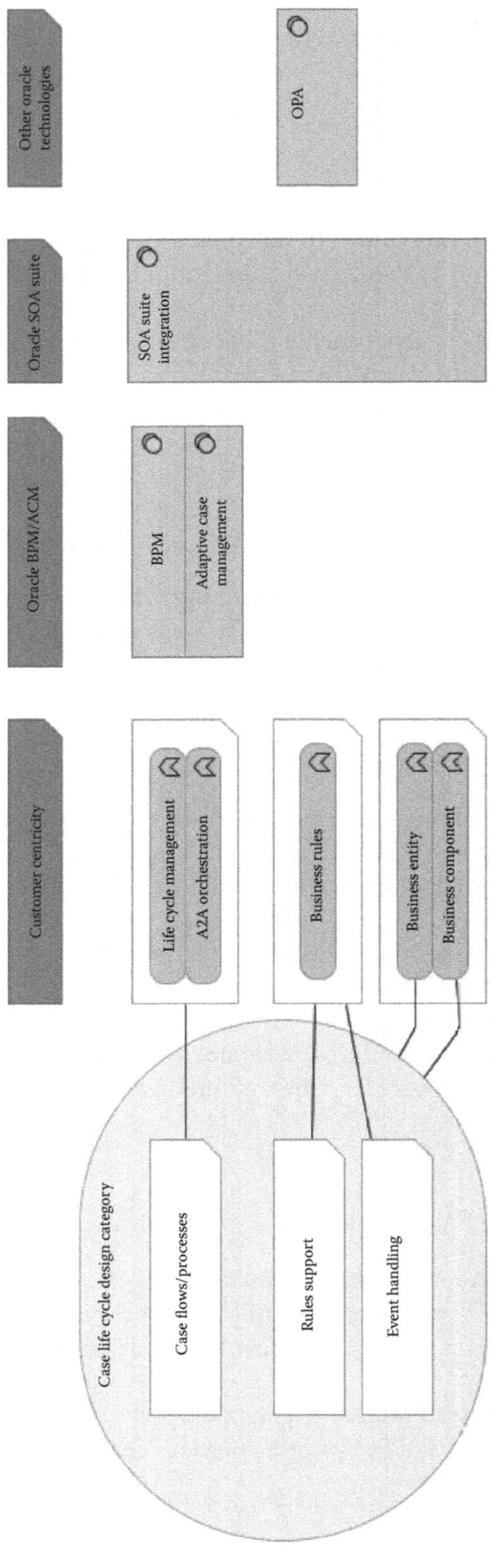

Figure 13.7 Oracle products supporting welfare request STP.

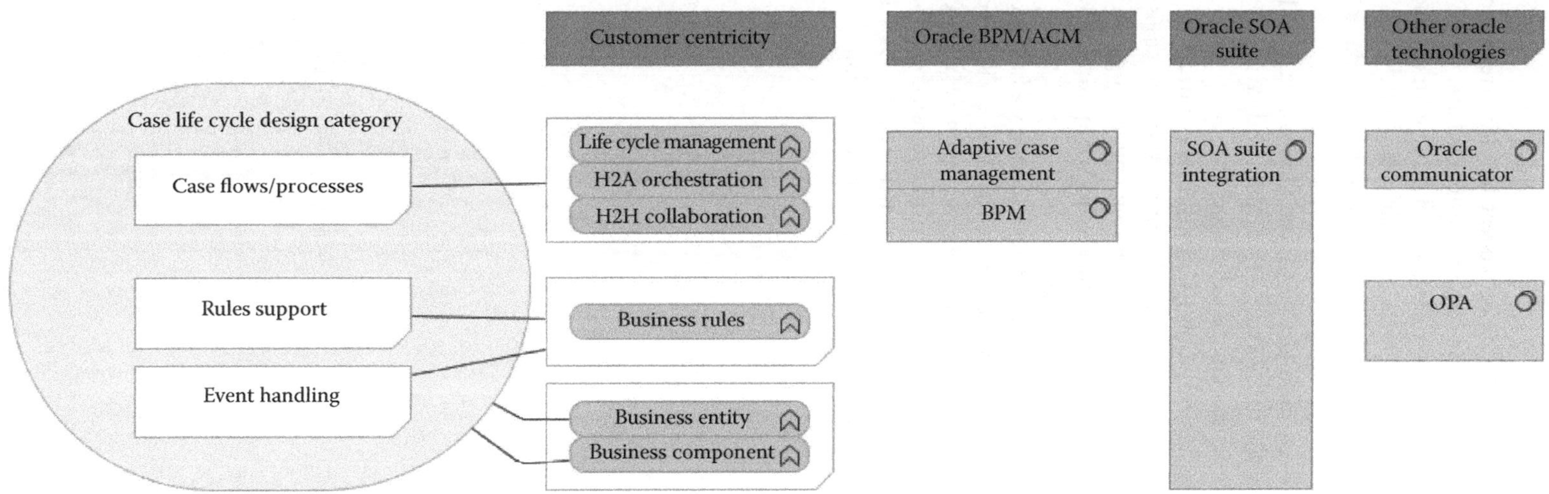

Figure 13.8 Oracle products supporting welfare request nonstandard situations.

13.5 Conclusion

In this chapter we have seen that the welfare request handling represents a case management example with a high volume of requests for a large customer base. These cases are based upon a predictable milestone process model and a rules engine dealing with complex regulations and laws. In order to ensure excellent delivery of services to their customers, the welfare provider needs to have access to customer information with a high degree of quality originating from both internal and external systems.

The welfare request related business challenges for the main stakeholders, government, citizens, and welfare organization, are *cost*, *quality*, *regulations*, and *flexibility*. Each of these business challenges has an impact on the case management solution.

The welfare request process case solution has different dynamics for the predictable requests and the complex nonstandard situations. The high volume standard cases are aimed at delivering a service with no human intervention via straight through processing (STP), ensuring lower costs. For the complex nonstandard situations the welfare request requires the work to be done by case workers in an adaptive case management manner.

In the solution mapping and Oracle product determination we have looked at the difference in implementation for the STP and the nonstandard scenarios. The STP scenario is fully automated with Oracle BPM. The nonstandard situations are based upon Oracle ACM. The solution relies heavily on the integration capabilities of the SOA suite integration components, ensuring the quality of information originating from internal and external systems. OPA is used for the complex determination of entitlements, or the even more complex recalculation of entitlements based upon the time-travel concept.

Chapter 14

From Crime to Court

14.1 Introduction

The goal of this chapter is to:

- Use the crime-to-court process as an example of a case management solution based upon an incident management case in combination with investigation cases and connected to many other cases.
- Show how the business challenges for the police force related to crime investigation, *globalization*, *effectiveness of the organization*, *technology*, *social values*, *crime patterns*, and *cost* impact the case management solution and IT landscape.
- Show examples for the case management design components for which the crime-to-court process provides good examples: *case flow and process design*, *event design*, *document and media design*, and *portal design*.
- Determine the solution for the police investigation handling and show the difference between the *full-blown* implementation scenario and the *umbrella* scenario; each scenario requires a different set of Oracle products.

14.2 Reading Guide

This chapter contains two main parts, the *police investigation and business challenges* and the *solution*. In the first part, an example of a police investigation is described and insight is given in the main business challenges. The second part determines the solution for a police investigation case based upon the case management solution framework and contains a mapping toward Oracle products.

14.3 Police Investigation and Business Challenges

14.3.1 Police Investigation

The crime-to-court process deals with all activities from the moment a law is broken until the conviction of a guilty person. Police investigation and court handling form the main parts of the crime-to-court process. The police investigation part contains unstructured processes and intensive interaction management with involved persons and is also event driven. The second part of the crime-to-court process, after hand over from the police to the prosecutor, deals with the court handling activities. This part is document driven, contains cross-departmental handling, and is a structured and predictable process. In this chapter, we will focus on the police investigation end-to-end process dealing with all the activities from the moment that a crime has been committed until the moment somebody is handed over to court.

The starting point for a police investigation is when the law has been broken or suspicion that a crime took place (or will take place in the near future). The term suspicion of a crime is also known as a lead. When an actual crime has been committed, a motive or reason is needed to create a police case, a prosecutor case, and court case. The lead is preliminarily investigated and if proof is found or more suspicion arises, follow-up investigations are needed. A police case is a container of multiple investigation cases and also can be linked to already existing police investigation cases. Each crime type will lead to a specific set of activities in the case, sometimes very predictable and predefined, but often depending on different circumstances and very unpredictable (led by cause and effect). When the police collect enough evidence, the case will be forwarded to the prosecutor, who will prepare a court case to prosecute the suspect. After preparing the case, the prosecutor will go to court, where the judge decides whether the suspect is guilty based upon the evidence of the prosecutor and the defense of the lawyer. This end-to-end process is simplified in Figure 14.1.

As an example, we will use a police case with the motive of a serious crime. It starts with a phone call of a citizen who reports a burglary at a warehouse. The call will be routed to the incident room (command control) of the police. The officer will open an *incident* to report the crime, circumstances, and location details. Then the officer determines the details of the incident and the priority based upon the provided information. The incident will be assigned to a patrol officer, who is briefed while he is driving to the crime scene. At the crime scene the officer does his investigation, collects more details like interviews with victims and/or witnesses, reports the stolen goods, the offences, suspect description, and the way the burglary took place. The incident level will be raised and automatically a crime case is created when the police officer locates a body on the crime scene. As this type of work is outside the responsibility of the patrol officer, he will hand over the responsibility of the investigations to other officers who also will be assigned to this incident and case. All information that is collected at the crime scene will be recorded as part of the incident, but now all the incident details also become part of the crime case. All collected

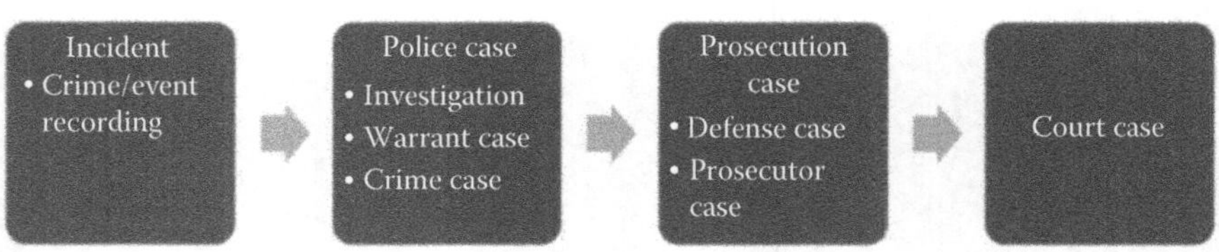

Figure 14.1 End-to-end crime-to-court process.

information that is found at the crime scene, such as property information and evidence, is stored properly, according to standard procedures and regulations. After the investigation is finished at the crime scene, the incident will be closed. All further investigations necessary to "build the case" will be part of the crime case. Often these kinds of cases cause an early involvement of the prosecutor, since decisions for further investigation or arrests need approvals from the district authority. After thorough investigations, a suspect is identified and can be arrested when enough evidence is available. This requires an arrest warrant and needs approval from a judge. To fulfill and administer this request, a warrant case is created and needs to be prepared, handled, and approved. This warrant case becomes part of the crime case. After arresting the suspect, the investigation officer will start the interrogation. Depending on the outcome, the officer can decide to proceed and hand over the case to the prosecutor. The investigation officer can also convince the suspect to cooperate with the police and offer him a possible reduction of his sentence. During the investigation of a case, a lot of events might impact this case. Media attention and public opinion can cause the police team to increase in size. There are also various time restrictions during a case, such as a suspect can only be held in custody for a predefined amount of time. When the police force has finished the investigation and plausible evidence is available against a suspect, the case can be forwarded to the prosecutor. The main goal for the prosecutor is to build a case that will hold in court and will prove that the suspect is guilty. In order to build the case, the prosecutor stays in contact with the police to obtain all the required evidence to prove the suspect is guilty. This can result in new research questions and possibly could lead to new arrests. When the prosecutor has finished the case, he is ready to go to court and present the case to the judge. At this time, the opposing lawyer starts preparing his defense for the suspect. He/she bases the defense on the information he gets from the prosecutor and the suspect. Based upon the information of the prosecutor and the defending lawyer, the judge will decide whether the suspect is guilty and pronounces the sentence.

We will finish with some observations that will be used later in the design paragraph (Section 14.4.3):

- Different police cases (with different case types) are linked together
- Involvement of multiple police officers require good hand over moments and communication
- The research is dominated by events altering the course of case
- Both structured and unstructured information can be brought into the case
- External communication to, for example, the press influences the research

14.3.2 Business Challenges for the Police Force Related to Crime Investigation

Police forces worldwide are facing increased difficulties in fighting crime as criminal organizations become advanced and work together on a larger scale. The following business challenges push police forces to evolve into a more effective and efficient organization.

14.3.2.1 Globalization

People are communicating more on a global level. The world market is changing into one marketplace and many people and companies are collaborating globally on a daily basis. Many police forces however are still focused on local level and do not have an extradition treaty with all countries. A criminal in one country can be a free man in another. In some cases this is even possible between states within a country. In order to fight criminals that work internationally police forces need to work together. Sharing information across police forces enable finding the culprits and the evidence needed to make the arrests. Combining shared information can also help to prevent crime. Using information on a global scale will allow police forces to detect patterns and detect criminal activities much faster. The business challenge around information sharing is the need for a trusted IT environment across departments and jurisdictions. Such a trusted IT environment increases the efficiency and effectiveness both locally and globally.

14.3.2.2 Effectiveness of the Police Organization

The challenges in the area of efficiency are mainly focused on the work that needs to be done in the office. A large part of an officer's working day is spent in the office doing administrative tasks. Most of these tasks require manual data input, which due to the lack of the ability to delegate work leads to higher execution times. Another fact attributing to the amount of work spent in the office is related to the usage of many systems required to find the right information needed in a specific case. This reduces the efficiency, but also the effectiveness as the right information is not always available at the right time and at the right place. Departments working in isolation are another cause for not having the right information. Not all departments want to share the information they have or the information of other departments is not easily accessible. In order to improve the success rate of court cases, the IT systems should be more supportive for the police officers. This can be done, for example, by making the police officers aware when new events happened in a case.

14.3.2.3 Technology

People are connected via social media on a larger scale and personal information is accessed easily via Internet. This increases the availability of privacy-related information for criminals. The vulnerability of people has also increased by the fact that most people cannot keep up with the latest technologies and the knowledge of how to protect themselves digitally. This creates opportunities for criminals and at the same time increases the work for the police. The opening of the digital world can also provide law enforcement with extra information to detect social patterns and prevent crime. As criminals adapt to these changes, this puts more pressure on the needs of the police and its partners.

14.3.2.4 Social Values Are Changing Rapidly

People around the world can share videos and images instantly; this changes social values faster than ever before. Ten years ago only journalists could publish information that was available for a big public; today an 8-year-old kid can put material online that can be viewed and shared around the world instantly. Companies are also using the availability of this information to improve their business. This does not always comply with privacy laws, in which area the police force also is involved to protect the larger audience.

14.3.2.5 Adaption to Social and Crime Patterns

Another driver is the current inability to analyze and act on criminal and emergency type of information. Due to the earlier described technological changes and the changes in society, more interesting data has become available to the police. This could drastically improve the ability to predict and prevent crime. The current IT systems landscape faces the challenge to include all new information sources such as social media and lacks the ability to identify trends and patterns to anticipate and prevent incidents.

14.3.2.6 National Budgets Are Being Reduced

Besides the previously described challenges, the current financial crisis pushes police forces to lower the cost of operation and increase the effectiveness of the systems. The police needs to become more effective in fighting crime and spend less time and money on administrative tasks. From prevention perspective, the police needs to be more visible in society, both on the streets and in the digital world.

14.4 Solution Design Aspects

14.4.1 Introduction

In Section 14.3.2, we described the current challenges the police forces are facing, and in which areas change is needed. Here we will address these challenges in the described solution, specifically tailored to the police investigation as part of the crime-to-court chain. We will use the case management solution framework as presented in Section II to describe the solution, and consequently will map the solution toward Oracle products.

14.4.2 Determine Case Management Classification

The police investigation process can be classified as a combination of *incident management* and *investigation* type of cases. As a result of an offense a police case is started and multiple investigations can be started. The targeted end result is an arrest with proven evidence for handing over to the prosecutor. The path toward this result is unpredictable in behavior and contains unstructured processes. Special events, such as new evidence or witnesses giving new information, can influence the course of the investigations. These special events can even have an impact after a person is convicted and the case is closed, which can lead to a release of the person and a reopening of the case.

The second part of the crime-to-court process starts after the police handed over the results of the investigation to the prosecutor. This process has the characteristics of a *service request* and is largely supported by additional *investigations*. The police force requests the prosecutor for a court case against a suspect. This court handling process is document workflow driven, guided by strict regulations, and largely predictable in the execution.

14.4.3 Determine Functional Components/Needs

In this design paragraph we will focus specifically on the design components *case flow and process design*, *event design*, *document and media design*, and *portal design* as shown in Figure 14.2. *In the design descriptions we will touch the integration and security design.*

14.4.3.1 Case Life Cycle Design

As is described in Section 3.3.2, *The case life cycle design category describes the coordination of activities in reaching one of the end goals and contains three design components, case flow and process design, rules design, and event design.*

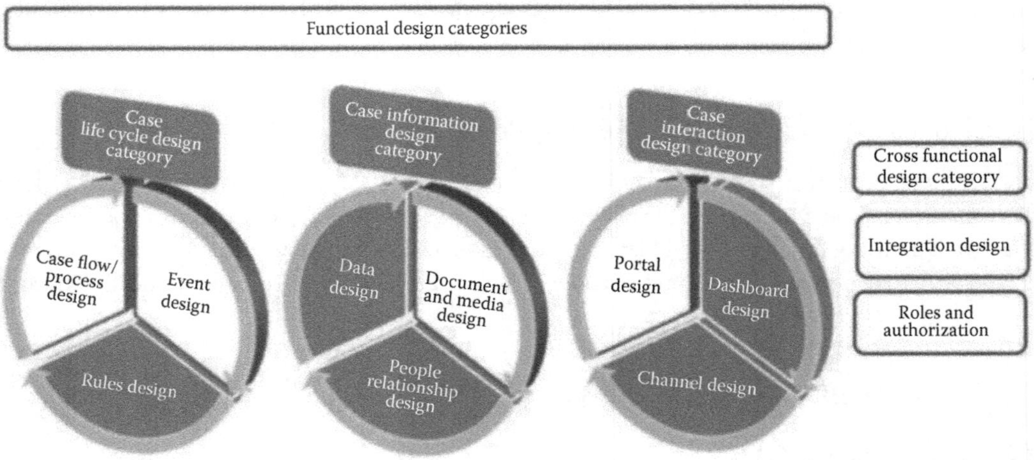

Figure 14.2 Solution topics (in white) discussed in this chapter.

14.4.3.1.1 Case Flow and Process Design

14.4.3.1.1.1 Police Investigation High-Level Flow In the flow diagram Figure 14.3, the different steps of a police investigation case are described. The high-level process flow is based upon a predictable milestone-based process. Three process phases, start, finalize, and close case, are highly predictable in execution; each phase is closed with a milestone. Each milestone can only be closed when the exit criteria are met and are driven by regulations. For instance, closing off the case can only be done when the handover of the case to the prosecutor was successful.

The second step in the process, investigate case, is dominated by a high degree of flexibility and unpredictability. In this phase, the police is trying the find enough information, which is the evidence for an arrest and to go to trial. These research events, such as new evidence or witnesses who testify, can lead to different insights and changed research directions.

14.4.3.1.1.2 Linking Police Cases Together Different types of cases exist in the context of a police investigation, which can be visualized in a hierarchy tree. As part of a police case, several case types can be created and connected together. Some cases can conditionally lead to another case and are connected together. In Figure 14.4, a partial overview of different police case types is shown. Some case types can be more administrative, while others have a primary focus on investigating in the field. Each of these case types has its own way of working, with data needed, roles attached, and activities that need to be done. On the left hand side of Figure 14.4,

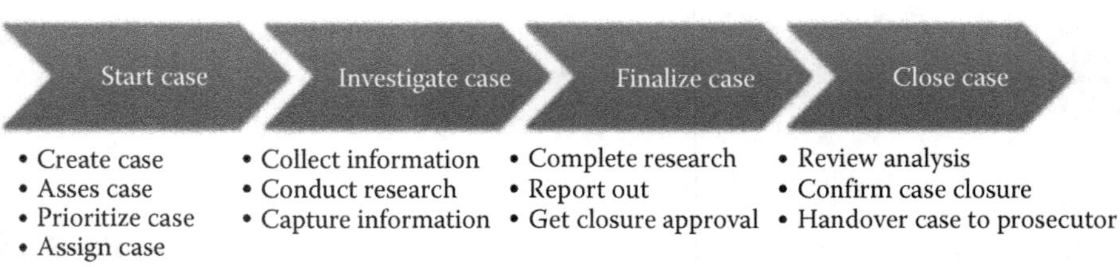

Figure 14.3 Police investigation main process.

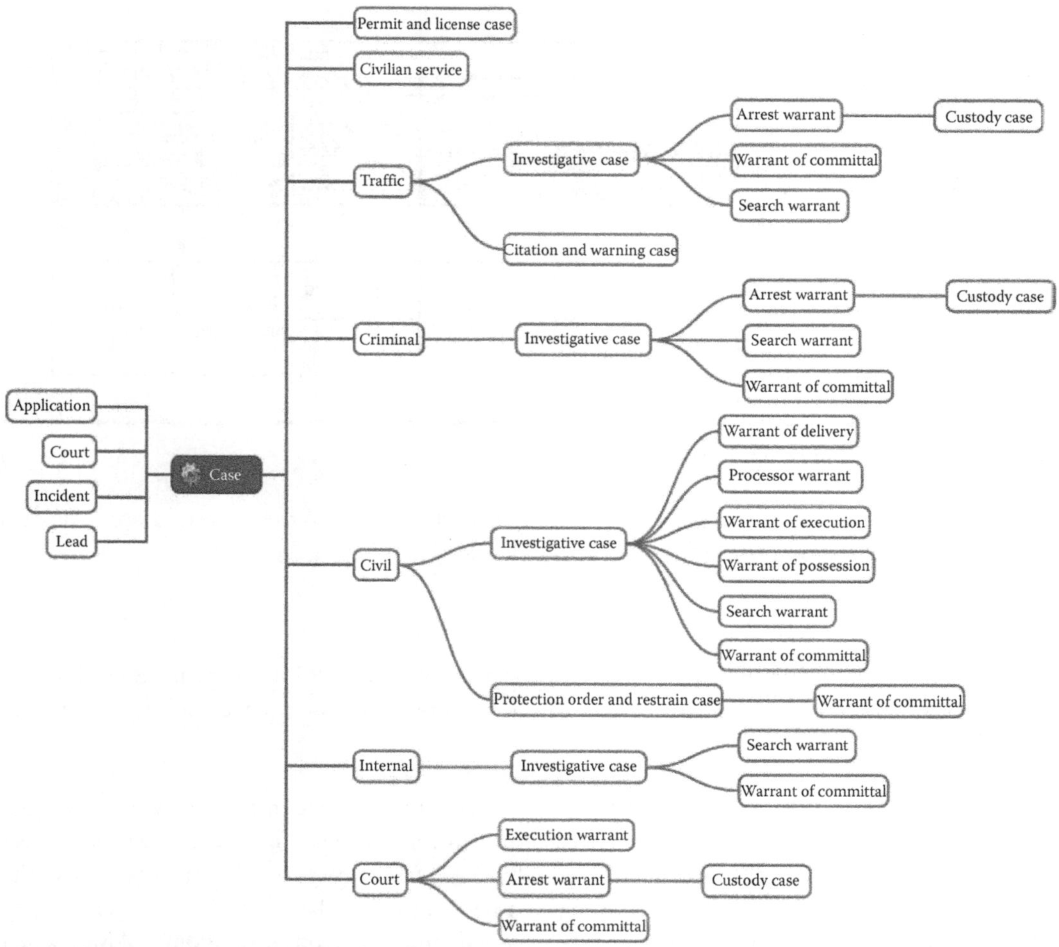

Figure 14.4 Police case type overview.

the "initiator types" of police cases are shown, which can be either automated via an application, an incident, a lead, or by the court.

In Section 14.3.1, we provided an example of a combination of multiple cases to support the burglary and homicide cases.

14.4.3.1.1.3 State Model One of the elements that support the predictable life cycle of a case is the state model. This model describes the states existing in the lifetime of a case, but also the possible transition between the different case states. The state model of a police investigation is a complex model with detailed sub–case states and state flows going back and forward, as shown in Figure 14.5. Each area in the model indicates a specific case status and substatus. When, for example, the case status is closed, the substatus is either "ready for prosecution" or "at prosecution". The status can only switch between statuses that are next to each other in the diagram. In the same example, when a case has the status "closed" and the substatus "ready for prosecution," the case can either be moved forward to "at prosecution" or moved back to "rejected". After that the case can be made active again and made ready for prosecution. The "happy flow" for a case would go from the case statuses "active" and "submitted" through the submitted substatuses

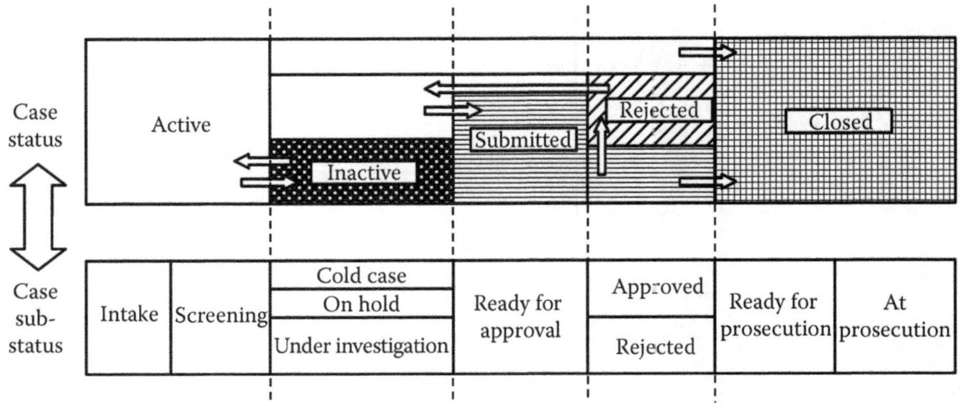

Figure 14.5 Police investigation state model.

"intake," "screening," "ready for approval," and "approved." Finally, in the "closed" status, the case will go through the substatuses of "ready for prosecution" and "at prosecution."

14.4.3.1.2 Event Design

The course of an investigation can be altered by events interfering with the police investigation. These events can originate by means of human intervention or via automated tooling monitoring (special) events.

14.4.3.1.2.1 Human Intervention

All police officers can intervene in the police investigation. The police officer owning the case can decide to terminate an investigation toward a specific suspect as a result of another suspect confessing to be guilty. The police officer owning the case is also the person to intervene in the police investigation as a result of time-related checks. A person is only allowed to be in custody for a certain amount of time, exceeding this time limit is only allowed when reasons are brought in and justified with the prosecutor. Police officers can bring in new evidence or gather new information via witnesses that can influence the flow of the investigation. Another type of intervention can be brought in via related cases. As discussed before, in Section 14.3.1, cases are linked together, a breakthrough in one of the cases can also invoke a change in other cases. A type of event that is not impacting the investigation flow is a request for update by one of the stakeholders and this only results in information handed over. For audit reasons, these requests are stored.

14.4.3.1.2.2 Automated Intervention

Automated monitoring of risk- and performance-related parameters could also impact the investigation flow. Monitoring of transactions on the stock market might at one point indicate fraudulent behavior of somebody who is already under investigation in other fraud investigation cases. Monitoring performance-related parameters might impact the team size and setup. When the progress of some police investigations is not high enough, police officers might be transferred to those cases to speed up the investigations.

14.4.3.2 Case Information Design

As is described in Section 3.3.3, *the case information design deals with all sorts of data and documentation flowing through the case and maps the relationships between all persons and/or assets involved in the case. The case information design category contains three design components, data design, document and media design, and people relationship management design.*

In a police investigation, all three topics in information design, document and media design, information design, and people relationship design, are important. We already highlighted the people relationship design and the data design in the example (Chapter 12) and will focus here briefly on one area, the document and media design.

14.4.3.2.1 Document and Media Design

In a police investigation, a distinction can be made between the input and output material.

The *input design* is a combination of both structured and unstructured data. This can be movies, interviews, sound tapes, social media information, and physical evidence, which all need further investigation on accurateness and validity for the investigation. The main purpose of this material is to build evidence for a specific case. For future reference this material also might be of interest. This requires an easy way of retrieving data related to the evidence material, such as creating adding tags or keywords to the material reference in a database.

The *output design* is focused on the deliverables that is needed during the handover toward the prosecutor. Since the handover deliverables are strictly guided by regulations, this process is highly structured.

14.4.3.3 Case Interaction Design

As is described in Section 3.3.4, *the case interaction design enables maximizing the support for the case work force and interactions with the customers. This design area contains three design parts, portal design, dashboard design, and channel design.*

We will use the police investigation process as an example to show examples of *portal design*.

14.4.3.3.1 Portal Design

During the police investigation multiple persons are involved, different cases are linked together, document and media are collected, and officers are working on activities. The police officers working on the case can originate from different departments, jurisdictions, and sometimes even across borders. Each stakeholder must have a view on the activities related to their responsibilities in the case.

In Section 14.3.1, we provided an example of a police case related to a burglary, which also turns out to be a homicide. In that example, the list of involved persons, cases linked together, documents and media, and activities is already growing:

- *Involved persons*: More than 10 different roles could be identified—citizens, incident room, police officer (triage), patrol officer, victims, witnesses, crime officers, crime agents, prosecutor, district authority, judge, suspects, and media.
- *Linked cases*: In the example, five cases are described—incident (burglary), crime case, search warrant, warrant case, and court case.
- *Documents and media*: Report crime scene, interrogation reports, and evidence as inputs for the case. After an arrest, the case file is handed over to the prosecutor.

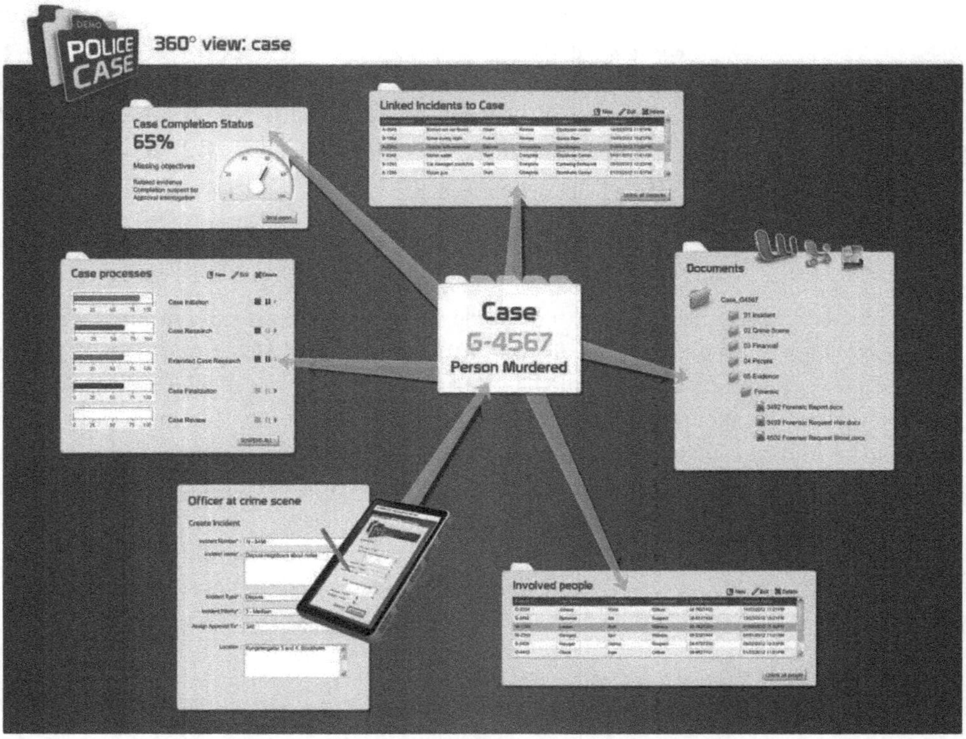

Figure 14.6 Police 360° case overview.

An overarching police portal is needed that provides insight and access to the different cases, based upon the roles of the police officers. On a case-by-case level, a holistic overview of the required functionality is shown in Figure 14.6.

All functionalities shown in Figure 14.6 have view–access functionality and provide functionality for making changes to the case. In Sections 14.4.3.1.1 and 14.4.3.2, we already discussed the *involved persons*, *documents and media*, and *linked incidents/cases*. Another functionality the portal should provide is direct access to a police officer at the crime scene via a variety of channels. The officer needs to be helped with all sorts of information related to the crime scene before he/she gets there. And once an officer arrives at the crime scene, he/she needs to able to send recorded material directly to the office and link the material to the case. The last functionality that the portal should provide is give insight in the progress of the cases and the related milestone and activities and also provide means to the police officer to intervene in the case. This functionality is crucial for the handover moment toward the prosecutor. A police case can be lost or withdrawn from court when the delivered information is not complete, inadequate, incorrect, or obtained in a nonlegal manner. The case/process completion status gives insight in activities that (still) need to be done.

Two fictitious examples of a police portal are shown in the following. First in Figure 14.7, the entry point for a police officer is shown and contains the cases he/she has access to, the outstanding tasks, and all sorts of news relevant to the police officer.

The next example in Figure 14.8 shows a view on a specific police case, containing all detailed information a police officer requires. On the right hand side of this portal, measurement information is shown that informs the police officer on the progress of the case. The *case completion*

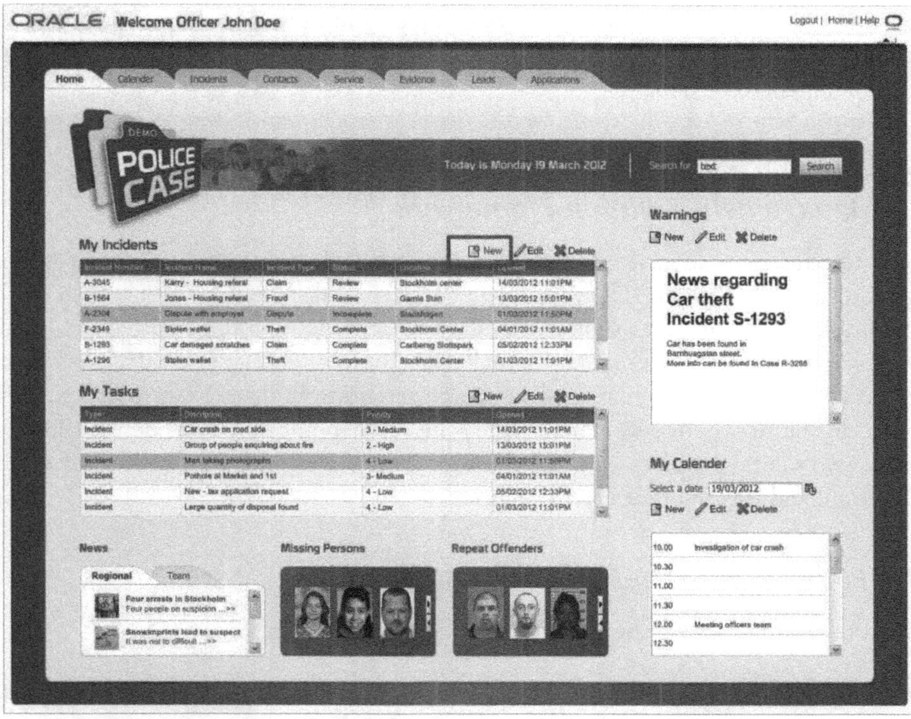

Figure 14.7 Police portal example.

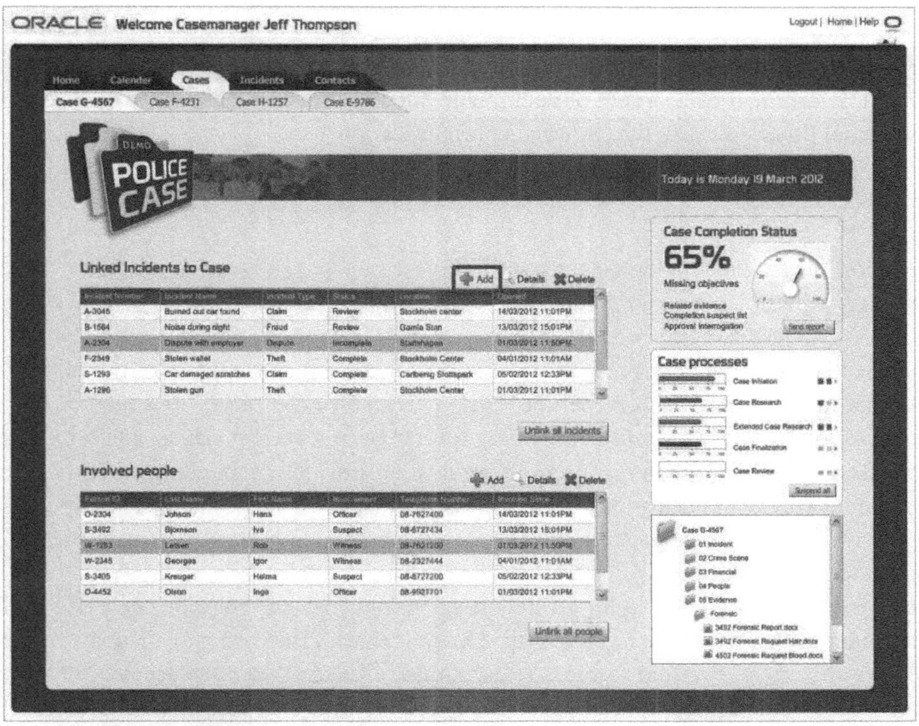

Figure 14.8 Police case view example.

status provides the officer with a percentage of completed material based upon predefined output parameters. The *case processes* part informs the officer of the processes that are finished, currently in progress, and still to be done.

14.4.4 Deriving a Solution Based upon the Case Management Solution Framework

In this solution mapping part we will look at two solution parts that are important for the police investigation solution, the case life cycle design supporting part and the part related to the case interaction design. The first area supports the flow of activities in all related police investigation cases and the second area supports the actual police officers on the ground with information, involved persons, documentation, related cases, and activities. Both areas are highly supported by integration capabilities. Before we describe the solution mappings for these design categories, we will discuss two solution choices for the inclusion of case management in the landscape, the full-blown solution, and the umbrella type of solution.

14.4.4.1 Full-Blown or Umbrella Type of Solution

In this chapter we have shown the complexity of a police investigation case:

- A large amount of police stakeholders originate from different departments, jurisdictions, and (international) organizations. Each stakeholder must have a view on the activities related to their responsibilities in the case.
- A complex case structure containing a hierarchy of investigation cases and linked to other police cases.
- Support from a variety of systems sometimes across organization borders.
- Input determined by a variety of documents, media, and physical evidence.
- Informal processes related to internal communication.

And (near) future needs

- Support for new technologies
- Ability to investigate social media

The current IT landscape does not entirely support all these requirements for the police force as stated earlier in Section 14.3.2. In the upcoming paragraphs, the capabilities required to build a renewed solution are presented, and a mapping toward what Oracle products could be used.

We will use the police Investigation example to show how to regain control over case supporting functionality in a complex and scattered landscape with two solution scenarios, the *full-blown solution* or the *umbrella type of solution*. These two extremes require different ways of delivery, product set, and timelines.

The *full-blown* solution includes all design categories into the solution, case life cycle, case information, and case interaction. In the full-blown scenario, the case management system takes control over all activities related to the case execution. This requires a replacement of the current case supporting systems and migration of all the data. In Figure 14.9, a simplified overview is given of the full-blown scenario. On the left hand side the starting point is shown before inclusion of

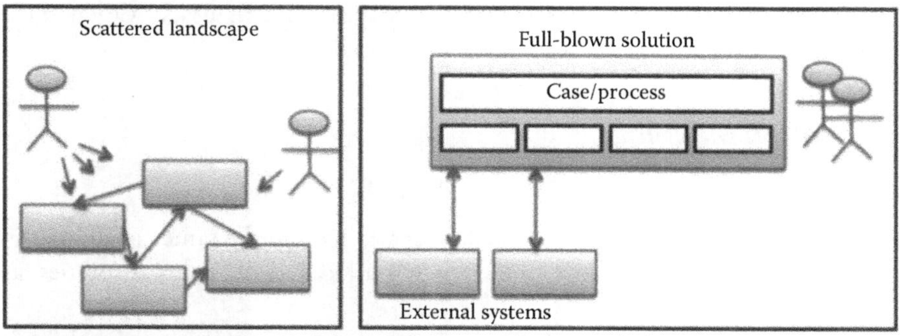

Figure 14.9 Full-blown scenario.

the solution. Even though in the full-blown scenario the solution takes responsibility for the entire case execution, the solution will not include all systems in the landscape, requiring some level of system integration with external systems.

The *umbrella* type of solution only includes the case life cycle category functionality into the solution. In this scenario, the case system takes responsibility for the end-to-end control of the case execution, and leaves the "low" level case activities in the existing systems. The data related to the case also stays in the existing systems. The data "flowing" through the case is the bare minimum required to be in control of the case and spawn off activities in the related systems. Optionally, also the case management portal and dashboard functionality can be included in the solution, when the functionality is not already available in the police investigation application landscape. The portal functionality is used to ensure a complete overview for all police officers. The dashboard functionality is required by management to get an understanding of the performance of the police force. Integration support is crucial for this scenario and all communication between the case umbrella system and the supporting internal and external systems needs to be ensured by integration. Figure 14.10 shows a simplified overview of the three phases for regaining control in the landscape. The first step is to get in control by means of an umbrella type of application on top of the existing applications and processes. This enables control in the landscape and adds capabilities to measure the performance of the overall process and singular activities. From the moment the end-to-end control via case management is in place, the improvement analysis can start. Already, during the control phase dashboards can be utilized for identifying bottlenecks and delays in the process, enabling for root cause analysis and eventually supporting process improvement.

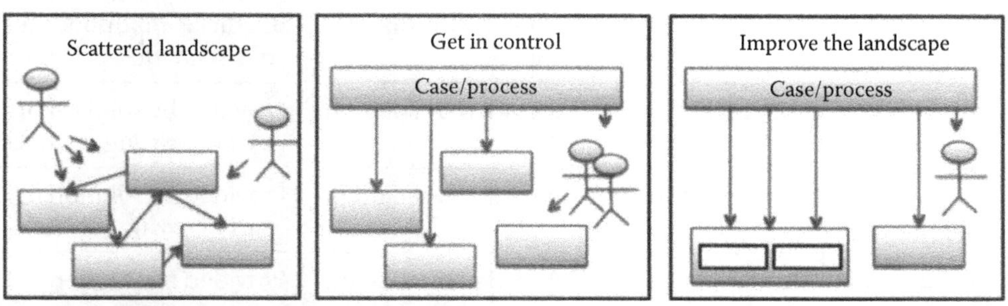

Figure 14.10 Umbrella scenario.

The full-blown and the umbrella scenario are not exclusive in usage. Often the umbrella scenario is used to rollout a full-blown scenario in a phased way.

14.4.4.2 Solution Mapping

14.4.4.2.1 Life Cycle Category Capability Mapping

Both the full-blown scenario and the umbrella scenario require the same capabilities in the life cycle category, but there is a difference in the execution location of these capabilities, as is summarized in Table 14.1.

The *full-blown scenario* provides all functionalities for the solution, except for the application-to-application (A2A) integration capabilities; this usually is provided by an external integration backbone and enables communication with external systems.

The *umbrella scenario* provides full support for the capabilities, life cycle management, A2A, and business rules supporting event handling. The other required capabilities, human to application (H2A), human to human (H2H), and business rules are either provided by the umbrella solution or part of the existing systems. As an example, checking evidence is part of the end-to-end police investigating. The umbrella application initiates the evidence validation at the forensic department; the workflow related to the evidence validation is executed by the forensic supporting applications, including all work related to the H2A, H2H, and business rules capabilities.

14.4.4.2.2 Case Interaction and Information Capabilities

The police investigation is a good example of the need for the interaction and information requirements. As stated earlier, a large amount of police officers from different departments, jurisdictions, and (international) organizations can work on the same case. During the execution of a police investigation, different media, documents, information, and knowledge around suspects and victims are

Table 14.1 Lifecycle Capabilities Usage by the Scenarios

Case Design Component	*Capability*	*Full-Blown Scenario*	*Umbrella Scenario*
Case flows and processes	Life cycle management	Provided by solution	Provided by solution
	A2A orchestration	Additional integration support needed	Provided by solution of crucial importance for this scenario
	H2A orchestration	Provided by solution	Provided by solution or part of existing systems
	H2H collaboration	Provided by solution	Provided by solution or part of existing systems
Rules support	Business rules	Provided by solution	Provided by solution or part of existing systems
Event handling	Business rules	Provided by solution	Provided by solution

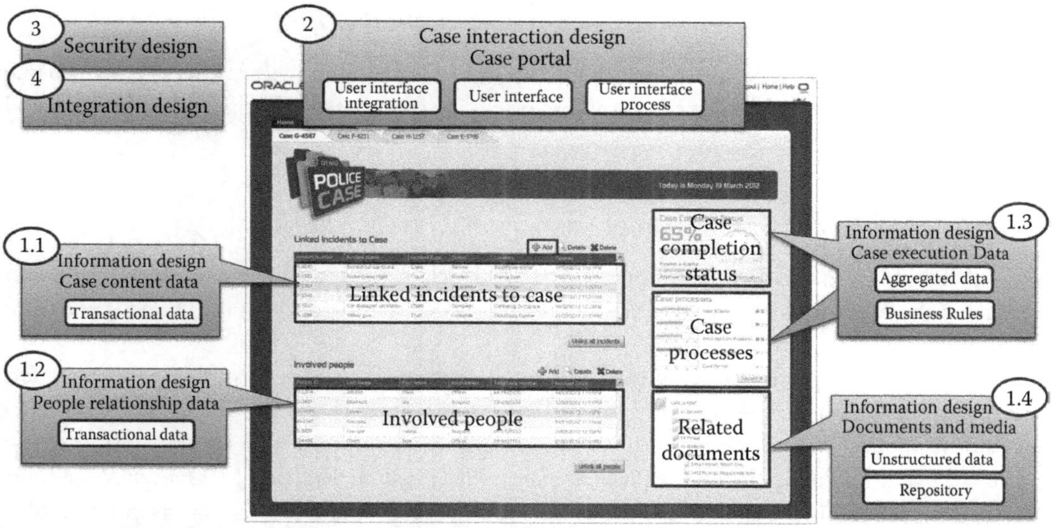

Figure 14.11 Police case overview required interaction and information capabilities.

shared. This needs to be presented to the police officers in a standardized way according to the roles and responsibilities. The full-blown scenario contains all functionality required in the interaction and information categories. For the umbrella scenario, the interaction and information functionality is optional, with the portal design component being the most likely functionality to be included.

In Figures 14.7 and 14.8, we provided portal examples for the police force showing a portal overview and a case-specific page. In Figure 14.11, the design components and required capabilities are mapped against the case-specific page.

Four design categories determine the portal solution as shown in Figure 14.11:

(1) The information design:
The page as designed in the Information design category
(1.1) Case content data delivers the specific-case data
(1.2) People relationship data gives insight in all persons involved and their relationships
(1.3) Case execution data is related to the progress of the case execution
(1.4) Documents and media provides insight in all documents and media objects or physical evidence brought into the cases
For the different information functionalities the technical capabilities are added, for example, the case execution data, showing progress bars, is determined based upon aggregated data.

(2) The case Interaction design:
The case portal page contains different user interfaces (user interface integration) and input functionalities for new and changed information via simple entry forms or more complex user interface orchestration (user interface process).

(3) Security design:
The functionality and information presented on a page is made available to the police officers according to their roles and responsibilities.

(4) Integration design:
The integration design relates to the provisioning of data to the portal and supports the channel communication. For the presentation of data on a portal additionally in the back-end, integration with different applications and the content management system needs to be ensured.

14.4.4.3 Mapping Police Investigation to Oracle Products

The full-blown and umbrella type of solutions have different characteristics and as a result also map to different Oracle products. The full-blown scenario is Siebel based and the umbrella scenario is Oracle ACM based.

14.4.4.3.1 Full-Blown Scenario Implementation with Oracle Siebel

The full-blown scenario is based upon a set of Siebel products and can optionally be supported by the WebCenter product Suite and the SOA Suite integration product as is shown in Figure 14.12.

The main Oracle product used in the full-blown scenario is the *Siebel case management product*, and specifically the police vertical, for which Capgemini created a specific implementation called "transform police" or "t-police" (http://www.capgemini.com/public-sector/transform-police-t-police, Capgemini Public Sector, 2015, Transform Police (t-Police)). *Siebel Customer Relationship Management (CRM)* is the choice for people relationship design and takes care of information of all involved persons in the case such as the police officers, victims, and suspects. The user interaction category is a discussion area for the Siebel implementation. *Siebel open User Interface (UI)* delivers a rich user interface and is tightly connected to Siebel. The integration capabilities with other

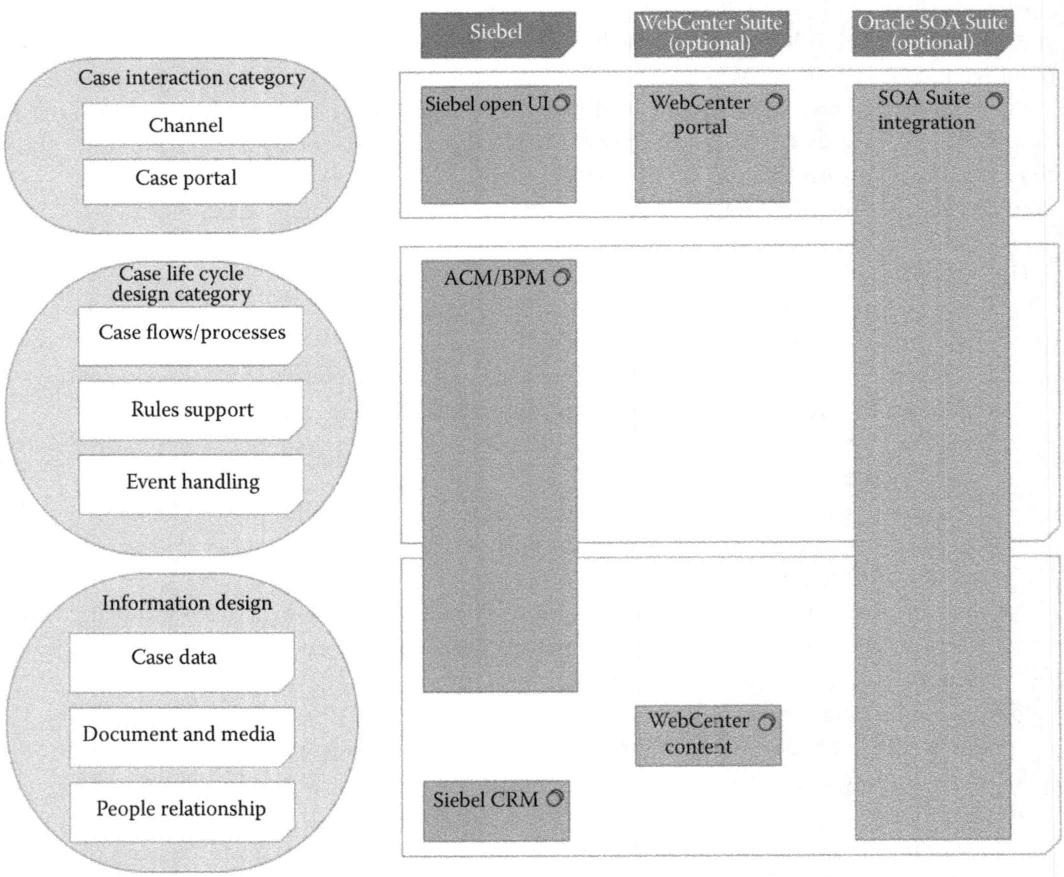

Figure 14.12 Full-blown scenario implementation with Oracle Siebel.

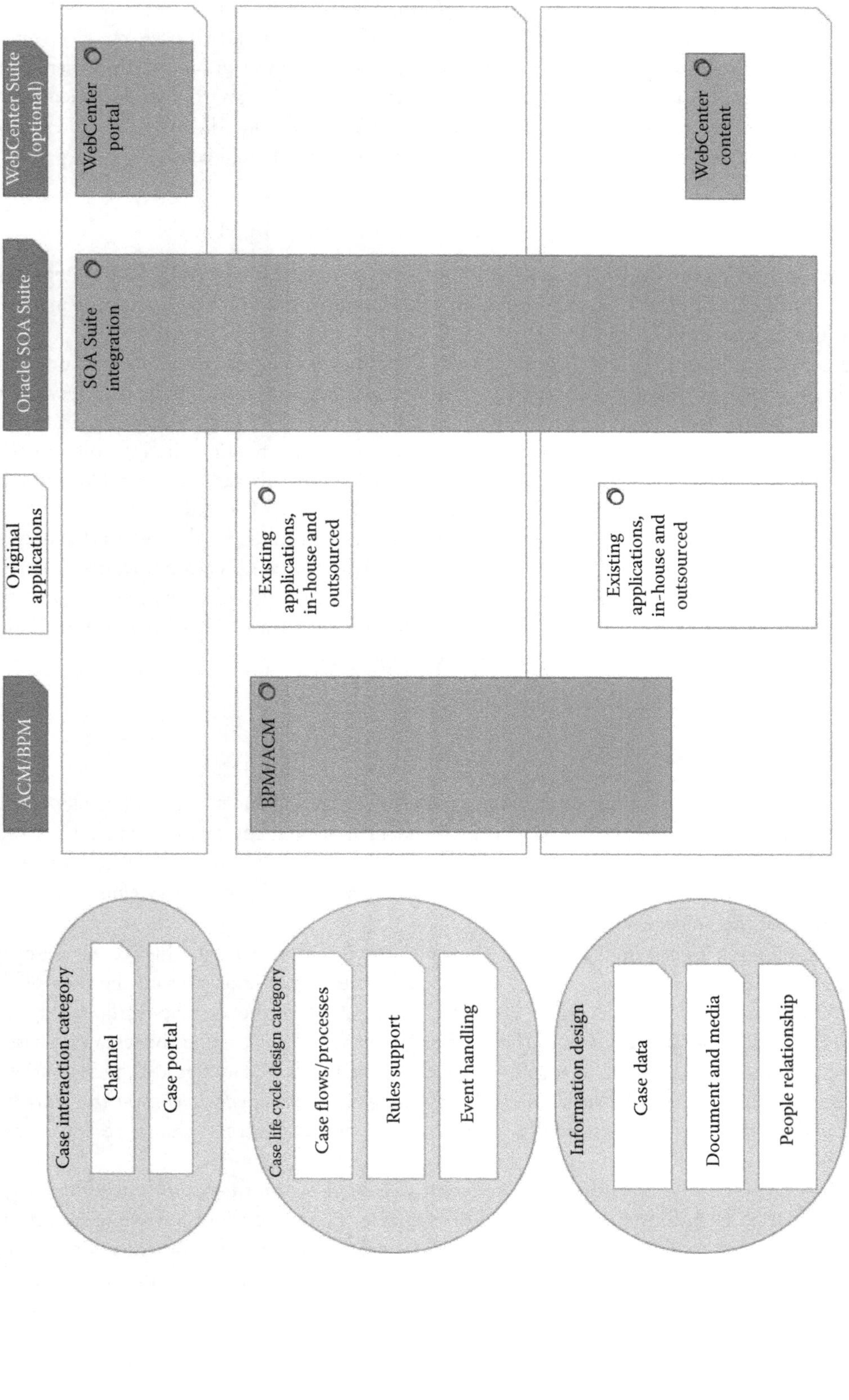

Figure 14.13 Umbrella scenario implementation with Oracle BPM/ACM.

applications, however, are minimal and as such can be used in a Siebel-only scenario. Nevertheless data that is available within Siebel based on integration can be visualized true the Siebel open UI. In situations where the portal needs to provide information from different sources, the *WebCenter portal* is a better choice, since this is tailored to deliver information in a rich user interface from a variety of data sources in a multichannel environment. Looking at the amount of documents and media information that needs to be stored in a police case environment, an external document management system is required and is implemented with *WebCenter Content*. The *SOA Suite* integration capabilities deliver the integration needed on all levels in the solution architecture.

14.4.3.3.2 Umbrella Scenario Implementation with Oracle BPM/ACM

This scenario is dominated by Oracle BPM/ACM, existing applications, SOA Suite integration software, and optionally the Oracle WebCenter Suite supporting portal and document management, as can be seen in Figure 14.13.

The combination of *Oracle ACM* and *Oracle BPM* delivers the backbone for the umbrella life cycle functionality and stores all the end-to-end case execution data. The *existing systems* are guided by BPM/ACM and execute the "low" level case activities and also take responsibility for storing all case content data, documents and media, and the people relationship information. The existing systems could be replaced over time with new application software, while still keeping the end-to-end process up-and-running with the overarching BPM/ACM solution.

The *SOA Suite integration* capabilities deliver the integration needed on all levels in the solution architecture and has an important role in the architecture enabling all communication between the BPM/ACM umbrella functionality and the existing systems. *WebCenter portal* delivers the 360° overview of the case across all systems in a rich user interface. *WebCenter Content* adds centralized document management capability to the landscape.

14.5 Conclusion

The crime to court process contains two parts, a police investigation and a court-handling process. The first process, the police investigation is an incident management classification and is supported by multilevel investigations; the second process, the court handling has the characteristics of a *service request* and is supported by additional *investigations*. In this chapter we have looked at the dynamics of the police investigation.

Specific attention is given to the research phase of the police investigation. This process is unpredictable as a result of events, such as new evidence added to the case or altering the flow of the process. During all phases, new cases can be started as a result of this police investigation and these cases are linked together in order to build the case to go to court. Even though the research phase is unpredictable, the overall police investigation process is milestone based and guided by regulations.

Police investigation–related business challenges are *globalization*, *effectiveness of the organization*, *technology*, *social values*, *crime pattern*, and *costs*. Each of these business challenges has impact on the case management solution.

During the police investigation, multiple persons are working on the case, all needing insight and access to the case information, according to their roles and responsibilities. We have seen the different aspects that need to be accessible via a police portal in order to support the police investigation: the involved persons, documents and media, linked incidents and cases, insight in the case progress, and the related security.

We have discussed the two scenarios for including case management in the landscape: *full-blown scenario* and the *umbrella scenario*, and looked at the respective implementation with Oracle products.

The *full-blown scenario* moves all new and existing functionality into one solution, with Oracle products as the Siebel police vertical and Siebel CRM as the base part of the solution.

The *umbrella scenario* provides support for end-to-end control across the landscape, but leaves the "low" level case activities in the existing applications. The Oracle BPM/ACM product, in combination with the Oracle SOA Integration, mainly supports the umbrella scenario.

Chapter 15

End-to-End Insurance Claim Management

15.1 Introduction

The goal of this chapter is to:

- Use the insurance claim management process, for property claims, as an example of a case management solution based upon an incident management case occasionally supported by some investigation cases.
- Show how the insurance claim–related business challenges on *financial, customer facing*, and *the supporting IT landscape* impact the case management solution.
- Show examples of the case management design components: case flow/process design, rules design, channel design, and dashboard design.
- Determine the solution for the end-to-end insurance claim case and show that end-to-end insurance claim case execution can be automated when it is supported by intelligence related to assessing the claim and fraud checks.
- Show that the overarching case flow is supported by Oracle BPM/ACM, and that the rules functionality is supported by Oracle Policy Automation (OPA) and Oracle Endeca Information Discovery.

15.2 Reading Guide

In the first part of this chapter, the insurance claim process and business challenges are summarized. The second part determines the solution for end-to-end insurance claim management based upon the *case management solution framework* and contains a mapping toward Oracle products.

15.3 Insurance Claims and Challenges

15.3.1 Insurance Claims

There are two categories of claims in general insurance: *property* claims and *injury* claims. Each type has its handling challenges, but for both claim types the claim handling is considered to be the "first moment of contact with the customer" and as such is the moment of truth for the relation between the insurance company and the customer.

Property or material claims like collision damages are typically straightforward. The loss can be determined fairly easy from a combination of a damage report, usually filled in by the involved persons, and a police report giving direct insight into whom to blame and liable to pay for the damages. The client can be offered an indemnity payment or can be serviced by a body shop paid for by the insurer. The time between filing and settling the claim is usually short and tends to vary from hours to a few days.

Injury related claims tend to be much more complex and less transparent. These claims have a higher level of sensitivity and deal with privacy of medical information and contain complex rules for determining the potential loss of claims. Injury claims are usually long-running claims: time between filing and closing a claim can be years. In case of disability, the claim can be open for a long period, often at least a year until finally the grade of permanent disability is determined.

In this chapter we focus on the property-related insurance claims.

The customer can enter a claim via different channels. Traditionally, the most common one used has been filling in a standard form that is sent via mail to the insurance company. Now, more channels are used such as filling in a form via the web or via a call center. A channel that is gaining popularity is the insurance app, which enables entering a claim at the scene where the incident happened. Once the claim is received, the incident is entered into the internal claim-related system and is handled via a combination of manual and automated activities. Based on the insurance agreement, a proposal is made that is communicated back to the customer. If the customer does not accept the offer, (new) discussions will start. These discussions continue up until the moment that both parties come to an agreement. Once the proposal is accepted, follow-up work can be started. When the insurance company offers end-to-end handling of car damages, the entire process of outsourced activities needs to be managed and monitored as part of the claim case.

15.3.2 Business Challenges Related to Insurance Claims

There are three main challenges insurance companies face in the insurance area, *financial*, *customer facing*, and the *supporting IT landscape*.

15.3.2.1 Financial

The insurance market has changed dramatically over the years. With the growth of Internet, all sorts of price-comparison tools introduce a decrease in price levels, which pushed the insurance companies into the red. The consumer loyalty is shrinking and as a result, customers are shopping around for a better-priced insurance contract. The financial crisis impacted both the property and casualty insurers like any other financial institutes and in some countries only government support prevented bankruptcy. In the *financial* area, the first and foremost challenge is lowering the operational costs. Claims management is one of the most important processes within an insurance company. Since the insurance price levels are at a low range, claims management is the place where money can be saved. Another financial challenge that needs to be challenged is claim fraud.

Insurance companies are looking for new ways to be more profitable. One of these ways is to develop new business models in the property claims area. These business models can be based upon a partner network where all the damages of the claim are being handled, such as repairing of the car in a garage that has a partnership with the insurance company. Another new topic in the insurance world is dealing with intelligence based upon "big data," for instance for the investigation of fraud trends. Since these data sets can contain all sorts of privacy-related data, this is a sensitive topic.

15.3.2.2 Customer Facing

The handling of claims is the moment of truth for the customer: it is where an insurer can retain or lose the client. The dilemma for insurance companies is looking for efficiency and driving down cost (operational excellence) while serving the customer in a way that he experiences as personal and fair. This is where social media can act as a big booster or a big crasher. Usually the extremes on both ends of the customer experience spectrum are posted on social media with the negative experiences taking up the majority of the reports. In order to collect and leverage these experiences, insurance companies need to monitor the social media and act directly when the claim experiences move toward the negative end.

15.3.2.3 Supporting IT Landscape

The previous business challenges pose challenges on the current IT landscape, in some cases still supported by old technologies in a scattered landscape. This makes it hard to provide the flexibility by the business and ensure stricter compliance rules defined by financial authorities.

15.4 Deriving a Solution Based upon the Case Management Solution Framework

15.4.1 Introduction

The solution description will be based upon the case management solution framework as described in Section 15.4.2, determining the case management classification, functionality, and the technical solution where we look specifically at the life cycle support, with the following topics:

- Fully automated support for the end-to-end claim handling and at the same time delivering support for knowledge workers in exception cases
- Inclusion of new business models in the end-to-end handling
- Different aspects of rule support for the insurance claim handling

We finish this chapter with a mapping toward Oracle products.

15.4.2 Case Management Classification

The claims request can be classified as an *incident management* type of case. It can be debated if the classification service request also fits, since the customer reports damage to his/her property and requests insurance claim compensation. The incident management process model relates more to

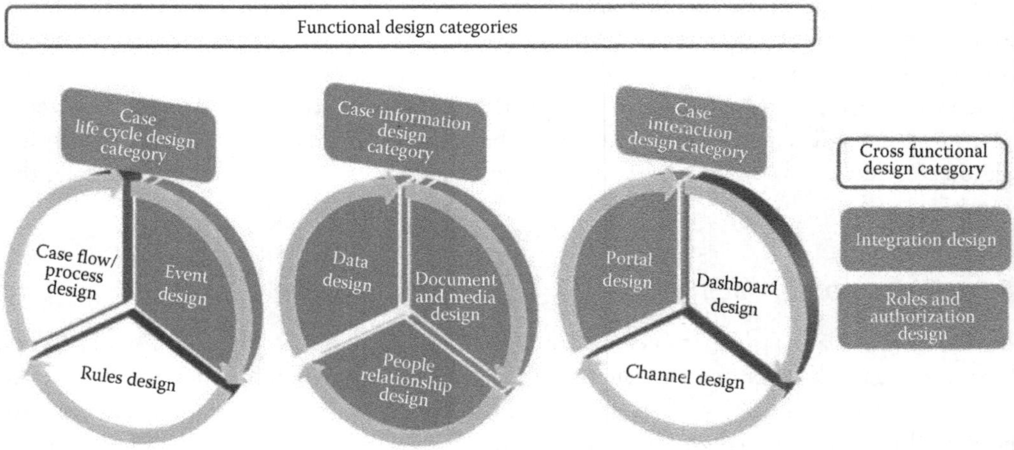

Figure 15.1 Solution topics (in white) discussed in this paragraph.

end-to-end claims management than the service request process model. The focus of the incident management process model is to solve the problem for the customer and detect who is guilty, resulting in a conclusion as to who has to pay the claim. For some of the property claims, inclusion of additional *investigations* might be needed, for instance, in case fraud is suspected.

15.4.3 Determine Functional Components and Needs

We will focus in this paragraph on the end-to-end claim management design components *case flow and process design, rules design, channel design, and dashboard design* as shown in Figure 15.1.

15.4.3.1 Case Life Cycle Design

As is described in Section 3.3.2, the case life cycle design category describes the coordination of activities in reaching one of the end goals and contains three design components, case flow and process design, rules design, and event design.

15.4.3.1.1 Case Flow and Process Design

On a high level, the insurance claim handling is a straightforward three-step process, and is executed in sequence. In Chapter 14 we showed a complex life cycle model for an incident management type of case. What makes the life cycle description for the end-to-end claim handling specific is that it should be able to include new business models and be fully automated with the inclusion of human interaction in deviating situations.

The high level structure of the insurance claim process contains three parts as presented in Figure 15.2:

- Record claim, where the customer files the claim through one of the channels
- Execute claim assessment, which consists of a fraud assessment, a value assessment, and a liability assessment among others
- Settle claim; in this phase an agreement between the involved parties is made and executed to settle the claim

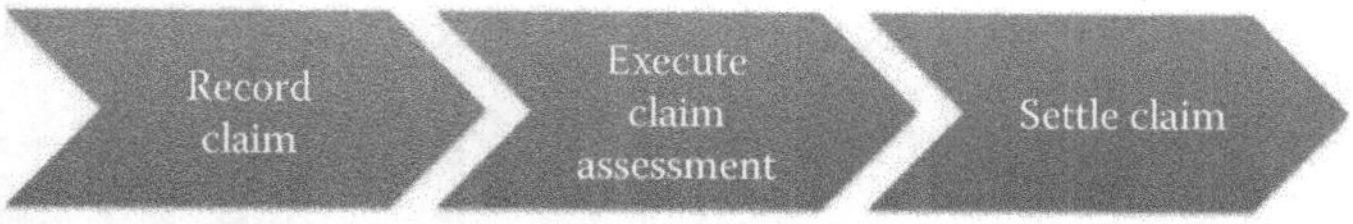

Figure 15.2 Claims management high-level process.

New business models help insurance companies with new means to be profitable. One of the new business models is expanding the chain of activities by including incident solving services via body shops paid for by the insurer.

For instance, a car insurer delivers additional services for settling damages as a result of accidents. For this service the insurer has included towing companies, garages, and rental companies in their network. When a customer reports a car incident via his mobile insurance app, the insurer directly arranges a towing company to tow the car to the nearest garage, arrange a rental car for the customer, and have the garage investigate the costs and do the repairs. The insurance company can also make an offer to the other party involved in the accident for servicing their damaged car.

The impact of the inclusion of such a business model into the offering is that the overarching claims case now should also include the management of all activities executed by the related companies.

15.4.3.2 Rules Design

Intelligence is needed in the claim assessment phase to decide the validity of the claim. As described in the previous paragraph, the aim is to automate the case as much as possible.
Two types of intelligence work can be distinguished:

1. Assessing the claim against policies:
   One part of the claim assessment is checking the claim against the policies, which is predictable work. This work includes activities such as checking that the terms and conditions are met, verifying that the amount equals the agreed amount, and validate that the claim data is not out of date.
2. Fraud checks:
   The key element in fighting fraud is getting an indication of fraud even before the claim is settled. The claim can be flagged ensuring the money should not be paid up until the fraud investigation is done and no problem is detected. Based on information from all claims, a scorecard can be derived that gives an indication of fraud. Such a scorecard is populated with information originating from the insurance company but can also be enriched from external sources. The scorecard indicators need to be renewed with new claims experiences on a regular basis, new fraud tricks, and social media–related discussions. These fraud checks can be automated with a combination of rules engines and information discovery type of applications and can be part of the straight-through processing (STP) processing. The challenge in this area is that the data used in these investigations can be privacy related and sensitive data. This might pose a reputation risk if this gets into the press.

15.4.3.3 Case User Interface Design

As is described in Section 3.3.4, *the case interaction design enables maximizing the support for the case work force. This design area contains three design parts: portal design, dashboard design, and channel design.*

We will use the insurance claim process as an example to show examples of *channel design* and *dashboard design*.

15.4.3.3.1 Customer Centricity Design—Channel Design

Channel support is important for both the insurer and the customer. For the insurer it is a means to cut down operating costs by simplifying and standardizing the access. For the customers, it gives access where and when they need it. Enabling entering the claim directly at the scene of the incident gives a head start in the claim execution process and the ability to engage with the customer in the earliest stage possible. As can be seen in Figure 15.3, the *record claim* process step is the area where the customer enters the claim. This area needs to be set up in such a way that claims can be entered via different channels without recreating different claim processes for every channel.

15.4.3.3.2 Dashboard Design

Three levels of information deliver intelligence across the lifespan of cases:

- At an *operational* level in real time supporting a (single) case with the right knowledge
- At a *tactical* level during "process alive" time aimed at improving the efficiency
- At a *strategic* level when looking back in time when investigating for process, product and knowledge improvement

Dashboards deliver information at real time on a *tactical* level related to the workload and key performance indicators (KPIs) of the insurance company stakeholders.

Workload information is crucial in the relation with the customers. As stated before, claim handling is the "first moment of contact" with the customer. The workload should be balanced with costs involved and allowed waiting time for the customer. A continuous investigation is needed to keep this balance in the right shape. Seasonal influences can have an impact on the amount of claims that are entered. This needs to be fed into the workload planning and be presented in the dashboards at real time.

All stakeholders have *KPIs* attached to the operation of the claim handling. This can be on a departmental micro level or related to the overall claim operation at macro level. KPIs on a departmental level are related to the efficiency of the operation. KPIs on the overall claim operation relate to effectiveness (customer satisfaction). Figure 15.4 shows a dashboard for work order

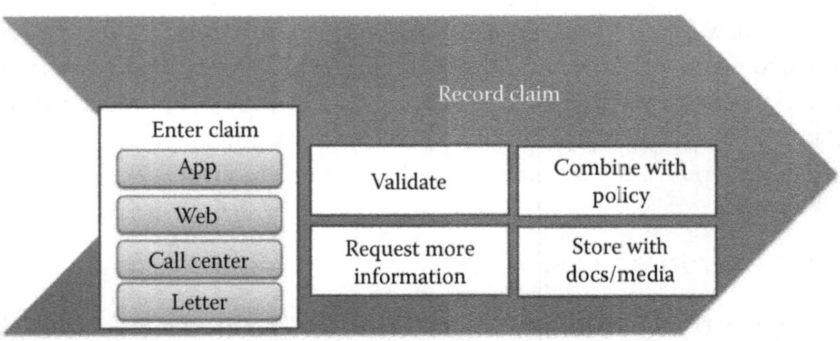

Figure 15.3 Channel access in record claim.

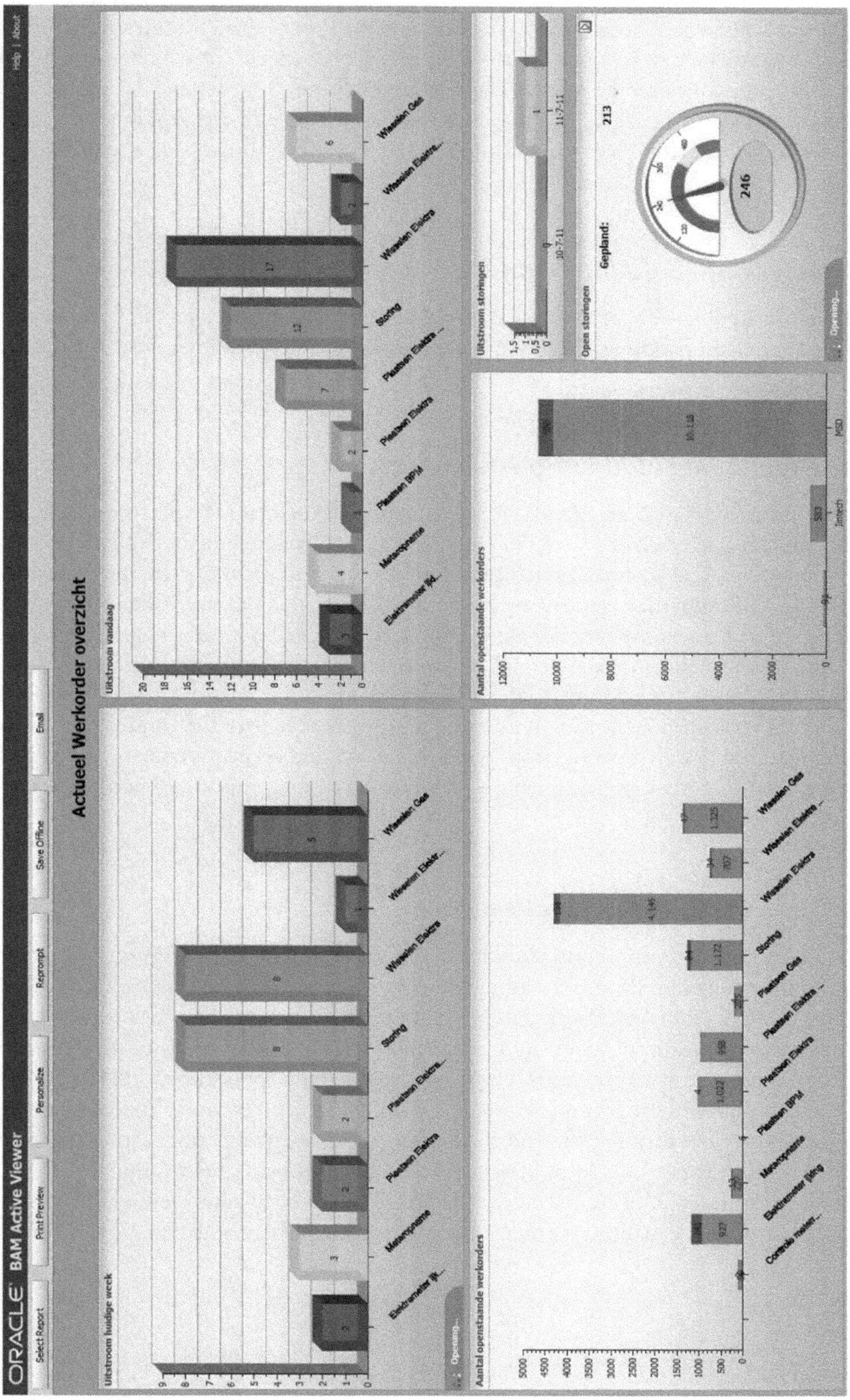

Figure 15.4 Governance with dashboards.

management from another market, but with the same characteristics as needed in the claims example. These work orders are related to the delivery of a service to a customer at their homes. The customer needs to stay at home for the delivery of the service, for which a time window is agreed. This process should be balanced against optimizing the costs and acting within the agreed time window. This dashboard shows the daily influx of work orders against the amount of finished work orders, and gives insight in the work orders that are outside one of the agreed parameters.

15.4.4 Determine Solution Mapping

In this solution mapping we simplify the case by only looking at the overarching flow of the end-to-end insurance claim handling, the related rules management and assume the existing systems stay in place.

15.4.4.1 Determine Solution Capabilities

Most of the property claims are standard claims and have predictable behavior and expected outcomes. These standard claims have the potential to be fully automated. This will help lower the cost of operation and increase the efficiency of the process execution. The prerequisites for moving the current claim management execution in an automated process is that the supporting applications are able to expose functionality as services via a well-defined integration backbone and that automated intelligence engines can be made part of the automated process. These intelligence engines support the assessment of the claim and check for possible fraud. When one of these checks shows suspicious behavior, knowledge workers take over the control of the execution of the claim and start investigations. Additional integration requirements are related to expanding the process with management and monitoring of new outsourced activities, such as car repairs.

15.4.4.1.1 Case Flows and Process Capabilities

The capabilities for the end-to-end insurance claim are summarized in Figure 15.5. The aim of the standard claim handling is to automate this fully, as described above. This requires application-to-application (A2A) capabilities that connect all functionalities exposed in the existing legacy application without any human intervention. When further investigation is needed, the knowledge workers needs access to the different applications guided by a case life cycle and is supported by human-to-application (H2A) interaction. The system should support flexibility for expanding the end-to-end claim management chain with new business models, where work is outsourced to other companies. This area needs to support both A2A integration capabilities and H2A. A2A capabilities are used for the activities in the end-to-end automated chain. H2A capabilities are needed in situations where additional approvals need to be given.

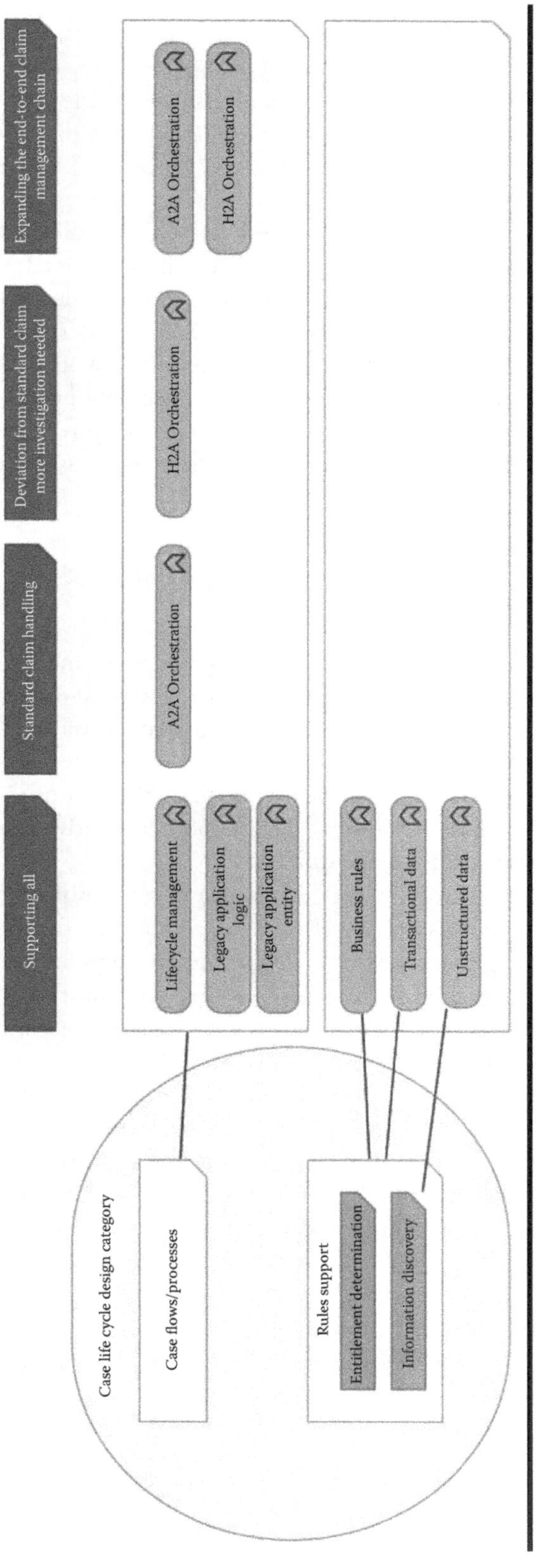

Figure 15.5 Insurance claim life cycle capabilities.

15.4.4.1.2 Rules Capabilities

Rules support is needed in two areas with different characteristics.

In the *entitlement determination* used for the assessment of the claim against policies, the rules validation is based upon transactional data, originating from the customer and the insurer. The business rules characteristics are based upon a predefined set of policies and regulations that can be complex.

In *information discovery*, used for fraud investigation, a business rules engine uses both transaction data and unstructured data to investigate indications of fraud. The business rule characteristics for fraud handling are based upon a scorecard that is derived from previous known fraud cases, new fraud tricks, and social media–related discussions. This scorecard is changed on a continuous basis and needs intelligence to be able to identify new trends.

Integration capabilities support all the application connectivity between the claims management overarching business process management (BPM) and adaptive case management (ACM) processes and the existing landscape including new outsourced activities and connectivity with social media.

15.4.4.2 Mapping the End-to-End Insurance Claim Handling to Oracle Products

Three main Oracle product groups support the end-to-end claims management solution, Oracle BPM/ACM, Oracle rules-centric products, and the Oracle service-oriented architecture (SOA) integration product stack, as shown in Figure 15.6. The products on the right, in white, are the solution-supporting systems.

The case flows and processes are supported by the combination of Oracle BPM and ACM. BPM supports the standard claim handling; ACM supports the activities required when a claim needs further investigation by a knowledge worker.

For the rules support, two products are used supporting the different requirements. Oracle Policy Automation (OPA) supports *assessing the claim against policies* functionality. OPA delivers a business-friendly rules management tool for complex rules management.

The fraud analysis is executed by the Endeca Information Discovery product. Endeca Information Discovery is used for storing and retrieving unstructured information and contains analysis functionality that is optimized for data discovery. The input for fraud analysis is a scorecard that is compiled together from a combination of different sources such as:

- Transactional claim data delivered by the customer and the insurer
- Unstructured data that originates from different sources such as social media
- Customer related data, such an area and age
- Insured product data

Oracle SOA suite integration supports all the application connectivity within the solution. In this solution, the aim is to automate the claims management as much as possible. This requires an integration backbone that should be robust and reliable.

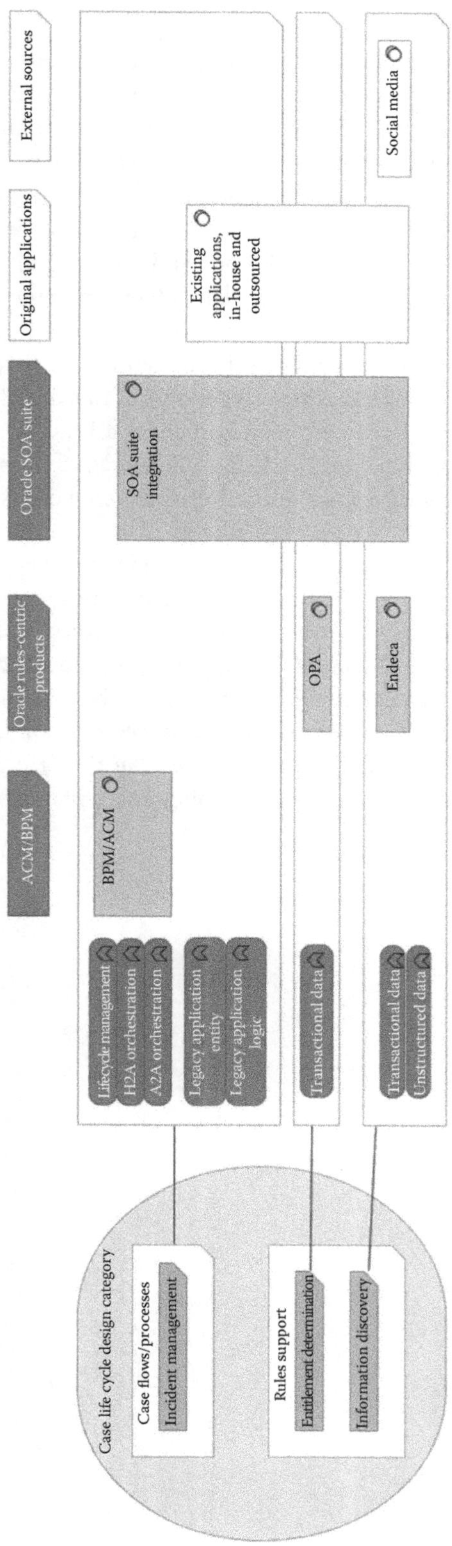

Figure 15.6 Insurance claim Oracle product mapping.

15.5 Conclusion

In this chapter, we looked into the management of insurance property claims. This is an example of a predictable case management solution, with an intake via different channels. The majority of cases can be handled fully automated. During the automated execution, intelligence helps assessing the claim and looks at possible suspicion of fraud. When these intelligence checks indicate a suspicion of fraud, insurance knowledge workers perform further investigation.

The case structure of the property claims is based upon the incident management classification. In situations in which the claim is not valid or fraud is suspected, investigations are started.

The inclusion of new business models in the claims handling process can help the insurance companies to be more profitable. We have seen an example of such a new business model in the property claim area, with the inclusion of services in the claim process that help solve the incident damage, such as making a car repair handling. The impact of this diversification of services is that the incident case handling is expanded with management of all these activities.

The insurance claims–related business challenges are related to the areas of *financial, customer facing, and the supporting IT landscape*. Each of these business challenges has an impact on the case management solution.

In the solution part, we looked at automating the claims management as much as possible in order to improve cost effectiveness and increase the efficiency. In situations where more investigation is required, knowledge workers take over control over the execution of the claim. Oracle BPM supports the automated part and Oracle ACM supports the knowledge worker part. The automated handling of claim management could be extended by the inclusion of outsourced activities supporting new business models. Another typical part of the solution is the inclusion of two different types of rules engines, one supporting the *assessment of the claim against policies* functionality and the other *fraud analysis*. OPA supports the policy assessment whereas the fraud analysis is supported by Oracle Endeca.

Chapter 16

Concluding Remarks

We provided four examples in this part to show how the case management solution framework is used and under what conditions the different case management-supporting Oracle products can be used in the solution.

The first two examples are of the service request classification and the other two examples are incident management–based case management classifications.

The first example of a service request is the *mortgage handling* in which a client requests a mortgage loan to finance the property he/she wants to buy. This process is dominated by interactions between the customer, the mortgage provider, and other verification-related stakeholders. Even though the mortgage product can be complex, the process toward an agreement on a mortgage loan follows a sequential and predictable path from sales to origination and ends with fulfillment. During this process the mortgage (case) worker sometimes needs to choose the most appropriate task/activity from a preset list. The Oracle products supporting the solution depend on the operating model that is chosen:

- The *customer intimacy* operating model:
  - Interaction with the customers is a key functionality
  - Oracle Adaptive Case Management leads the execution of a mortgage request
- The *product leadership* operating model:
  - The focus is at delivering a rich portal that enables the customer to make combinations of mortgage lending products and the customer situation with new innovative products
  - The Oracle supporting platform is the Oracle Customer Experience (CX) product suite with the main products Oracle Service Cloud for the portal and content delivery and Endeca for information discovery
- The *operational excellence* operating model:
  - This is aimed at delivering a standardized model for a low price
  - The Oracle supporting platform is the Oracle BPM/ACM product suite and the service-oriented architecture (SOA) suite for integration

The second example of a service request is the handling of a *welfare request* in the public sector, for instance, the handling of child benefit or pensions. The customer expects to be serviced in the best way with no errors and limited contact. The prerequisite for dealing with this type of requests is that the welfare provider needs to have a complete insight and understanding of the situation of the customer. The execution path of the entitlement process is sequential and can be automated for most situations. Rules management can support the determination of the eligibility, duration, and amount of an entitlement in this automated process. Welfare (case) workers can choose the appropriate tasks from a preset list where the process is nonautomated.

The automated part of the solution can be filled in with Oracle BPM. The nonstandard situations are based upon Oracle ACM. The solution relies on the integration capabilities of the SOA suite integration components. Oracle Policy Automation (OPA) is used for the complex determination of entitlements.

The first incident management example is the *crime-to-court* process. This process contains two main parts, which have completely different dynamics. The first part is the police investigation, and is unpredictable in behavior. In this police investigation part, a lot of investigations may be initiated to reach a successful end. Special events, such as new evidence or witnesses giving new information, can influence the course of the investigations. The second part of the crime-to-court process is when the police has handed over the results of the investigation to the prosecutor. The court handling process is document workflow driven and largely predictable in the execution.

We discussed two implementation types for the solution. The *full-blown scenario* moves all new and existing functionality into one solution, this could be implemented perfectly with the Siebel police vertical, containing all functionality to support the police investigation. The *umbrella scenario* provides support for end-to-end control across the landscape, but leaves the "low" level case activities in the existing applications. The Oracle ACM/BPM product, in combination with the Oracle SOA integration, is a good choice for this umbrella scenario.

The second incident related example is "insurance claim handling." Insurance claim handling is considered to be the "first moment of contact" with the customer, and as such is the moment of truth for the relation between the insurance company and the customer. The flexibility that is needed in the end-to-end claim handling is the inclusion of new business models, such as including servicing the repair of the car, via body shops and garages, paid for by the insurer as part of the claim handling. As a consequence of the large volume of claim requests and the focus on operating costs, a large amount of these types of claims is executed in an automated way. Even though the process is highly automated, the focus should stay on the customer, timely delivery of results, and meeting (or exceeding) expectations. In this automated process, different parameters are checked that might indicate fraud. Oracle BPM supports the highly automated part and Oracle ACM supports the knowledge worker part. Rules engines such as OPA support the policy assessment. For fraud assessment, Oracle Endeca could be used.

TUTORIAL V

Introduction

In this section, we provide two tutorials for case management products: Oracle BPM/ACM and Oracle Siebel.

In the tutorial for Oracle BPM/ACM, we provide a deep insight into the Oracle adaptive case management (ACM) product with a hands-on tutorial. This hands-on tutorial is based on a credit card charge dispute scenario.

The tutorial for Oracle Siebel is related to an approach of how to design and implement a package-based case management solution using the Siebel application. The way the application is used will be shown based upon a police investigation example implemented with the *Law Enforcement and Policing Operations* extension.

Chapter 17

Oracle BPM/ACM Tutorial

17.1 Introduction

In the previous chapters we showed the different aspects of case management, some examples of where it is applicable and also how to design and architect a case management solution, and looked at Oracle case management technologies. Let us make it a bit more real through a hands-on tutorial using a credit card charge dispute scenario, that a quite a few of us who use credit cards have gone through at least once in his or her life.

The goals of this chapter are as follows:

- Do a deep dive into the Oracle Adaptive Case Management (ACM) product
- Provide a hands-on experience with Oracle ACM
- Focus on the case management life cycle design category to show the strength of Oracle ACM

17.2 Credit Card Charge Dispute: Use Case

17.2.1 Use Case Design Topics

In Chapter 3 we introduced the design components needed to describe the case management functionality. In this chapter we will use a simplified credit card charge dispute case where some case management design areas are highlighted as shown in Figure 17.1. In order to get a good understanding of the Oracle ACM product, we will focus mainly on the case life cycle design category and will touch upon the case information design category topics.

17.2.2 Use Case Description

You receive your monthly credit card statement, open it, and realize the balance due is not what you were expecting. An amount is charged that does not match with the price of the product you recently purchased. There are a couple of choices on how to report this issue—report it directly from the credit card company's website or just pick up the phone and call their customer care number. In either case they register your complaint and temporarily remove the charge from your credit card until they investigate why this happened. After a few weeks, you get a letter letting you know that the charge was indeed a wrong charge made by the merchant and that it has been corrected and that the issue has been resolved in your favor.

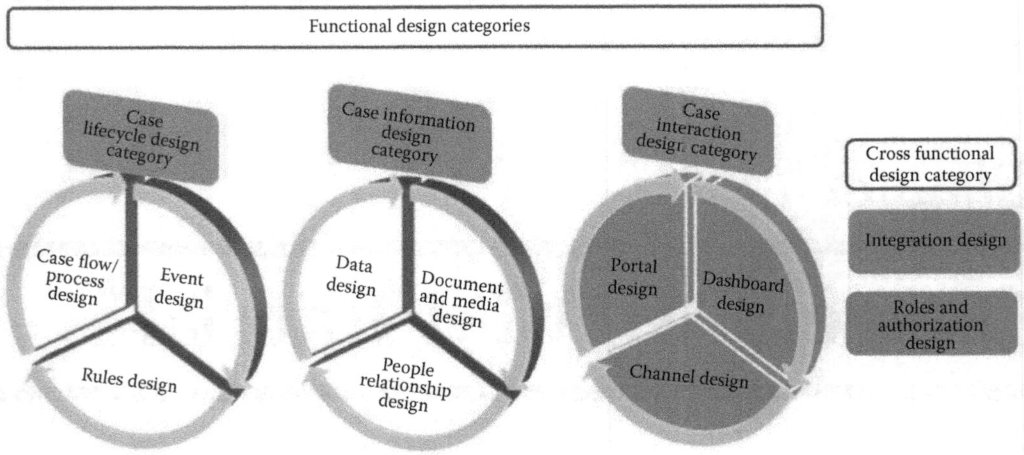

Figure 17.1 Case management design categories and components used in the ACM tutorial.

What you were involved in was a typical case management scenario that can be classified as an *incident management case* as described in Chapter 4. You as the *subject* of the case were the one that initiated the case. To resolve your case, a number of persons, participants that have a stake in resolving the case in the most effective manner (stakeholders), performed different actions (activities) to progress the case from its start until its closure. This will involve collaboration with departments within the company as well as with external entities, such as the merchant whose charge is under dispute. Let's take a behind-the-scenes look at how this case was processed. Since the objective of this tutorial is to give you a hands-on experience with Oracle ACM and not a lesson in credit card dispute handling we will keep the process simple.

Let us look at the steps that describe our example use case.

1. Based on the complaint, a case is opened by the customer service representative (CSR).
2. The CSR reviews the case and prepares it for processing by adding relevant information. She requests a signed letter from the customer declaring that the charge being disputed was not made by him and also asks for the copy of the invoice.
3. Once the letter is received from the customer, the CSR updates the case by adding the document to the case.
4. If the amount disputed is less than $25 and the CSR concludes, based on the documents and information received from the customer, that this charge is in fact not valid, she has the authority to write-off the charge.
5. Up until now the case has been in its initial phase. With the receipt of the letter, it can now move to the next phase. The next, *analysis*, phase is where an analyst is assigned to review and investigate the disputed charge.
6. As part of his review the analyst reviews the transactions on the customer's credit card.
7. Once satisfied he has all the information, he requests the merchant to provide a copy of the sales draft for the charge.
8. The analyst receives the copy of the sales draft that he adds to the case.
9. Based on the sales draft and the documents provided by the customer, the analyst concludes that the charge indeed is wrong.
10. The analyst initiates a chargeback on the merchant for the extra amount charged and gives the merchant 30 days to contest the chargeback.

11. The merchant does not contest the chargeback.
12. The case is closed in favor of the customer and he is informed about the final outcome.
13. During the process, the customer may call to get an update on the dispute.
14. During the process fraud may be detected and a follow up fraud case is opened.

In Section 4.5, we presented the standard flow for the incident management classification. The characteristics of the *credit card dispute* align with an incident *management* as shown in Table 17.1.

In Figure 17.2 we added the roles *customer* and *shop owner* and simplified the model toward the current *credit card dispute* case.

Table 17.1 Alignment of the Credit Card Dispute with Incident Management

Alignment	*Incident Management Characteristics*	*Specific Alignment Details for Credit Card Dispute Case*
✓	Incident handling is aimed at solving the problem and finding the root cause	The credit card dispute process is aimed at solving a balance due misalignment and communicates with the customer and shop owner to identify who is to blame, the customer, the shop owner, or the credit card company
✓	Initiation of an incident may be unpredictable	The customer discovers an error in his credit card statement and reports this at the credit card company. An incident like this can happen, but not on a regular basis
✓	The high level execution of an incident is predictable, but certain parts of the execution are highly influenced by events	The process follows a standard flow containing assessment, investigation, and communication with the customer and the shop owner
		Events, like fraud, can happen during the case execution, but have a low probability
✓	Both internal and external communication is key	External communication with the customer and the shop owner are key in the process
		Internal communication between the analysts can help finding the root cause quicker
✓	Data related to an incident is of both structured and unstructured in nature	The input for the data is structured. Receipts or other proof can be unstructured data
✓	Intelligence is needed to solve the case	Combining customer and shop owner information helps to solve the case. Monitoring intelligence provides information for possible fraud
✓	(Optionally) incident may be started by a customer	The incident is started by a customer
✓	(Optionally) regulatory requirements are often important	Regulatory requirements are not described in this case, but in a "real" credit card dispute it is important

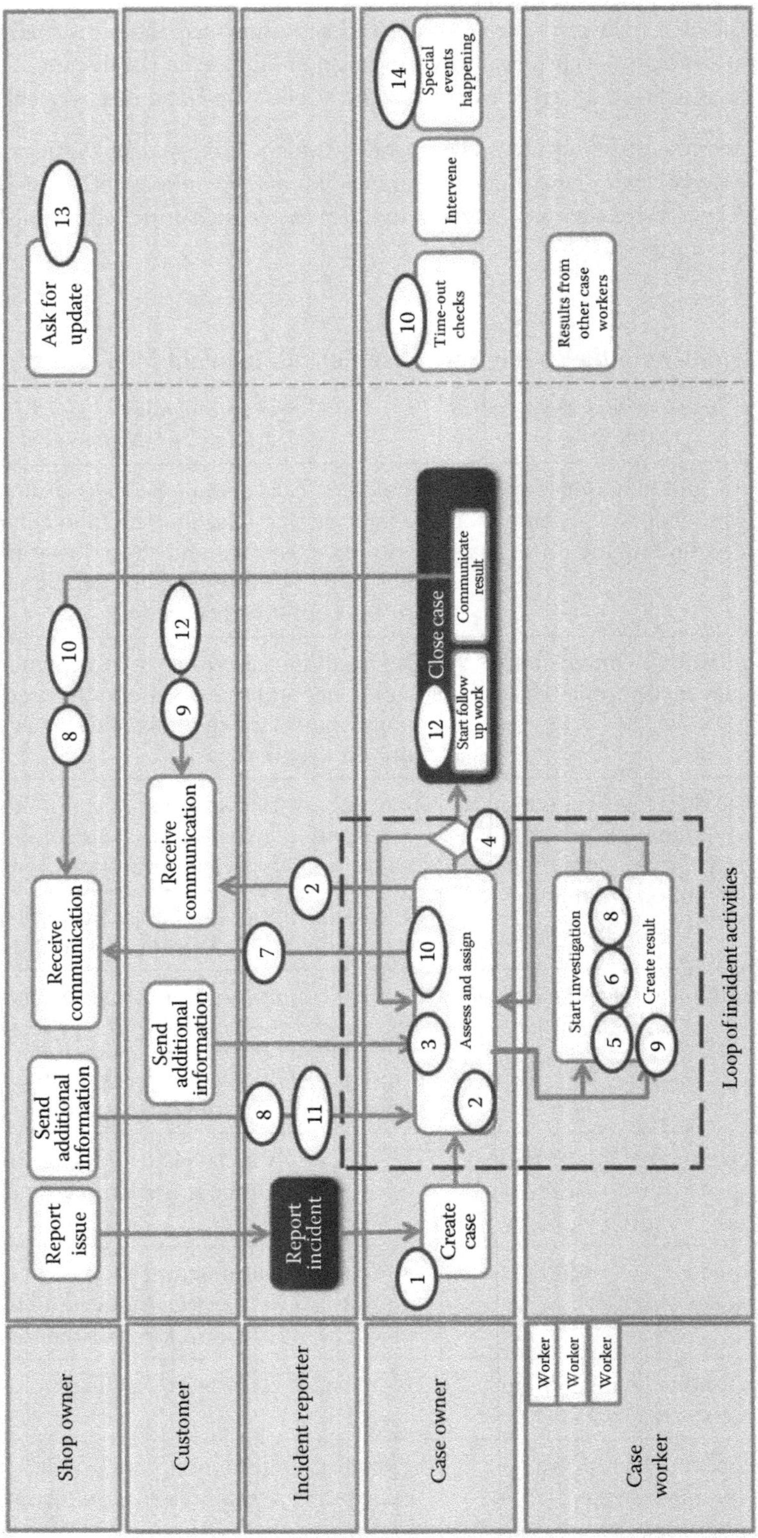

Figure 17.2 Mapping the credit card dispute activities on the incident management case flow.

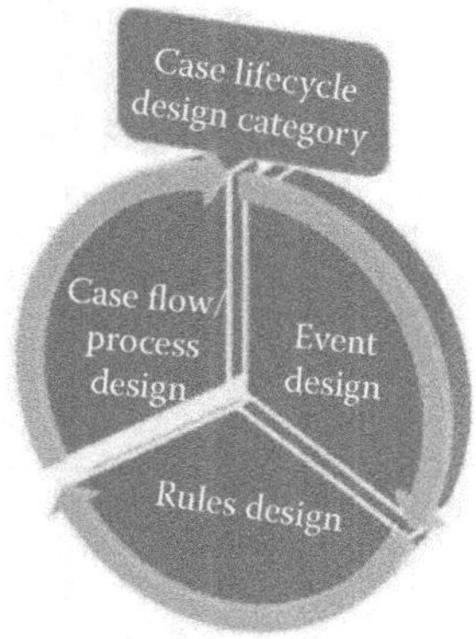

Figure 17.3 Case management life cycle design category.

17.2.3 Credit Card Charge Dispute Life Cycle Design

In Chapter 3 we introduced the various aspects for the design of a case management solution. We will look here at the case life cycle design category for the credit card charge dispute as shown in Figure 17.3. The case life cycle design category describes the coordination of activities in reaching one of the end goals and consists of three design components: case flow and process design, rules design, and event design.

17.2.3.1 Case Flow and Process Design

A typical unstructured process does not follow any predefined path and therefore, using any type of flow diagram during analysis may not be very useful. In our use case, the unstructured part relates to the sequence (or lack thereof) of activities performed within a high-level structured sequence of milestones. A mind map can help to graphically capture these requirements.

For the purpose of this hands-on tutorial a mind map is used to capture the requirements of the use case.

Let us begin by answering some questions.

What activities are being performed?
The first things you need to identify are all the different activities that are being performed throughout the life of the case. Here the key activities (not in any particular order):

- Prepare case—Initialization activity for setting up the case for processing.
- Review charge dispute—Review the details of the dispute to ensure all required information is provided for further processing.
- Request documents from customer—Request customer to send one or more supporting documents necessary for resolving the dispute.
- Write-off charge—Initiated by the case owner to accept the dispute and write-off the charge without having to go through detailed investigation. Typically allowed only for disputed amounts less than $25.
- Investigate charge—Initiate an investigation to resolve the dispute.
- Request document from merchant—Request the merchant to submit supporting documents required to resolve the case.

- Initiate chargeback—Initiate the process to charge the merchant for the disputed charge if the investigation shows that it was the merchant's fault.
- Notify customer—Send customer various notifications regarding the dispute case.
- Notify merchant—Send merchant various notifications regarding the dispute case.

These activities are shown in the figure below:

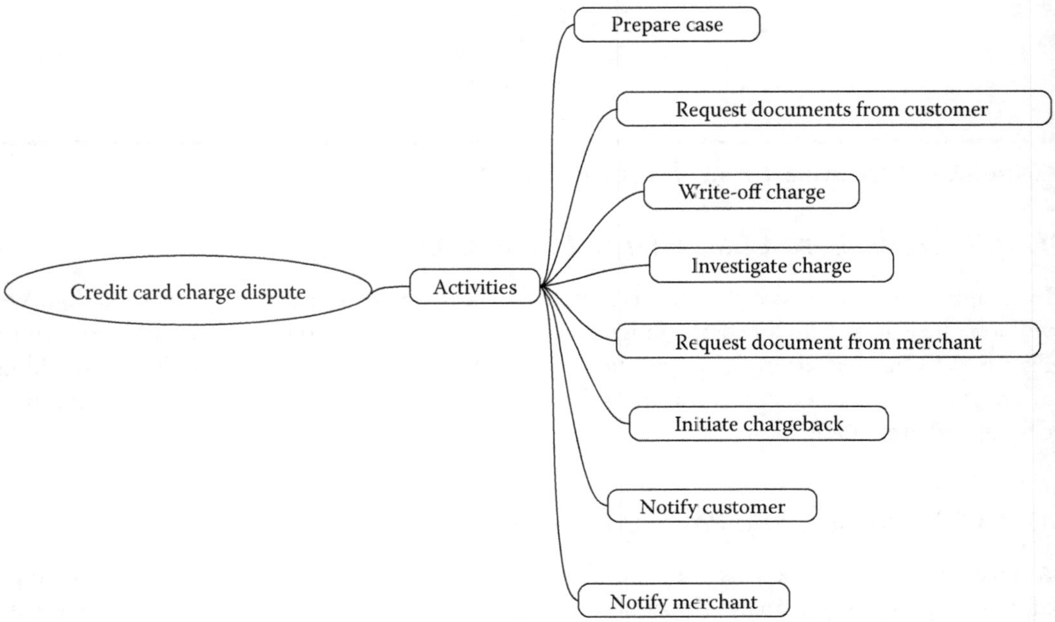

What are the important milestones to track?
It is important to identify milestones in the case life cycle that can be used to assess how the case is progressing. In our use case scenario, the following milestones seem to be important to track:

- Initial case review completed
- Analysis started
- Merchant interaction initiated
- Analysis completed

At this point we have identified what actions need to be performed, and what important milestones will help us track the case.

Adding the milestones to the mind map, we see the following in the figure below:

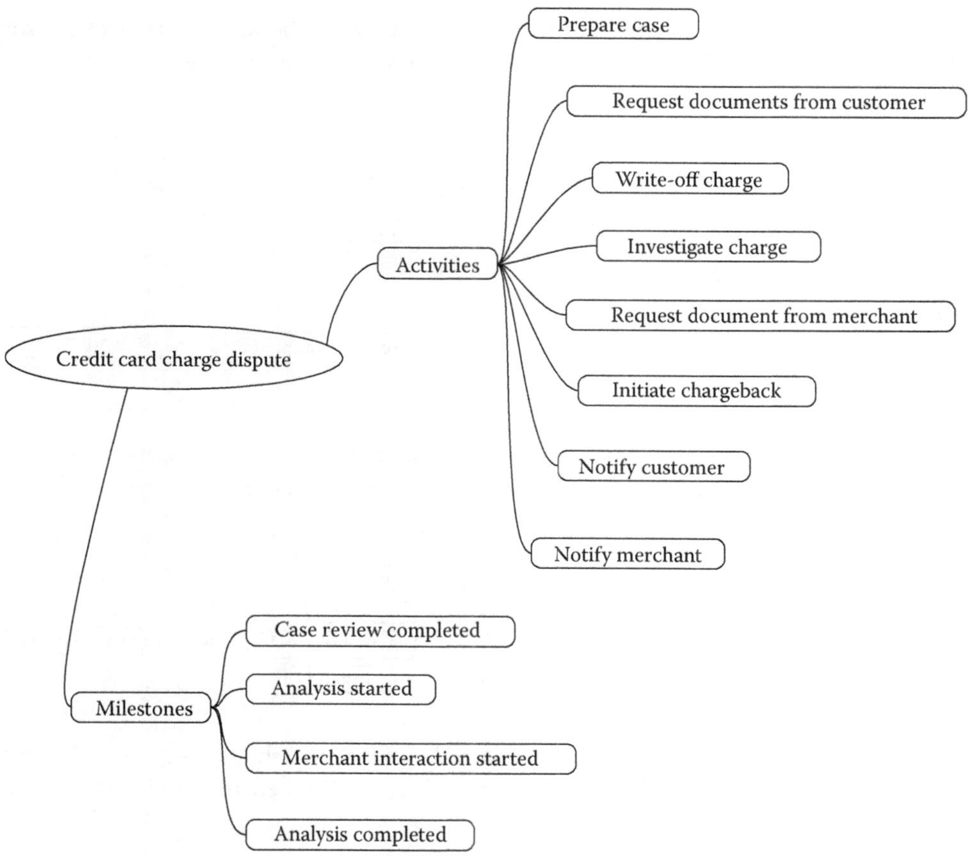

17.2.3.2 Rules Design

What policies govern the case?

We now have a good idea of the different activities that may be performed to progress the case from start to finish. We also know which milestones are important to us. Although case work tends to be lot less structured and a bit more ad hoc as compared to a traditional process, it is not completely without controls. There are rules and policies that control which activities are more appropriate given the state of the case at any point in time.

For instance, the activity to write-off a charge should only be available if the amount being disputed is less that a specific amount and if the charge falls under specific types of charge. Similarly, there are dependencies between activities. For example, "request documents from merchant" should be available only after the "merchant interaction" milestone has been reached.

For our example, here are the set of rules that need to be applied to this case:

1. Activity "review charge dispute" is repeatable and is required to be done at least once and should be available only after the case initialization is complete as shown in the following figure:

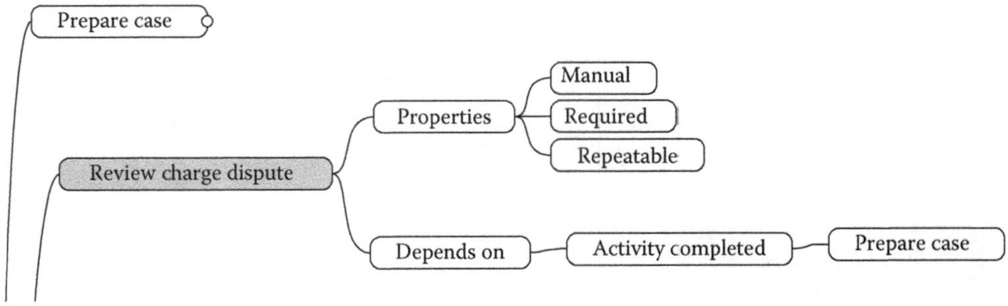

2. Activity "request documents from customer" is optional and can be repeatable. It depends on the activity "review charge dispute" being started as depicted in the following figure:

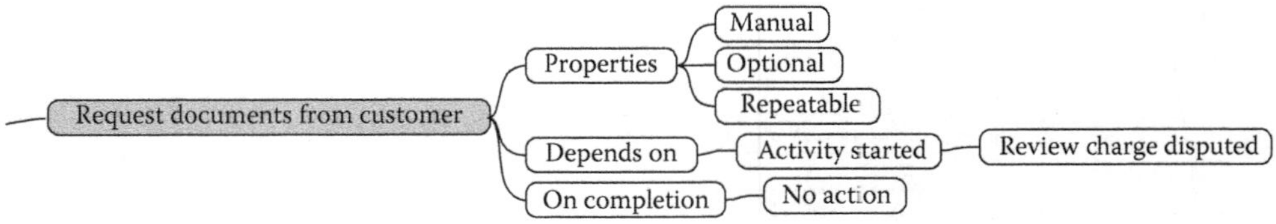

3. Activity "write-off charge" is nonrepeatable and optional and should only be available after "review charge dispute" is completed and only when the disputed amount is less than $25 as shown below:

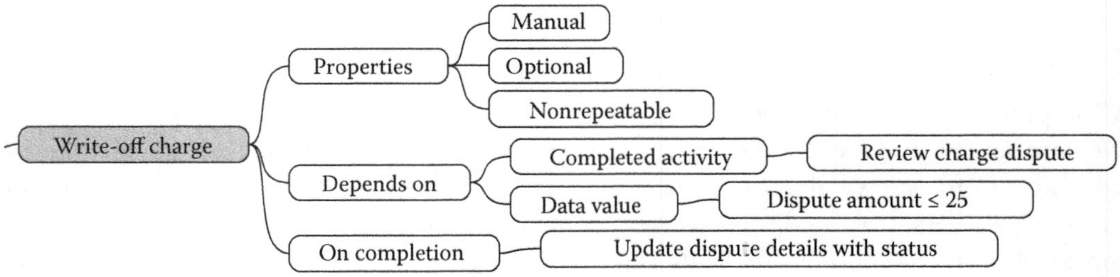

4. Activity "investigate charge" shown below is optional and can only be done once. It should only be available after analysis has started.

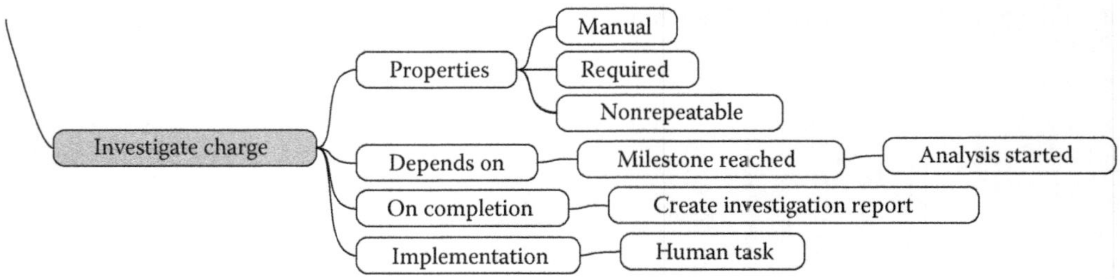

5. Activity "initiate chargeback" shown below is optional and nonrepeatable and should only be available once analysis is complete and the result of the investigation indicates it was the merchant who was at fault.

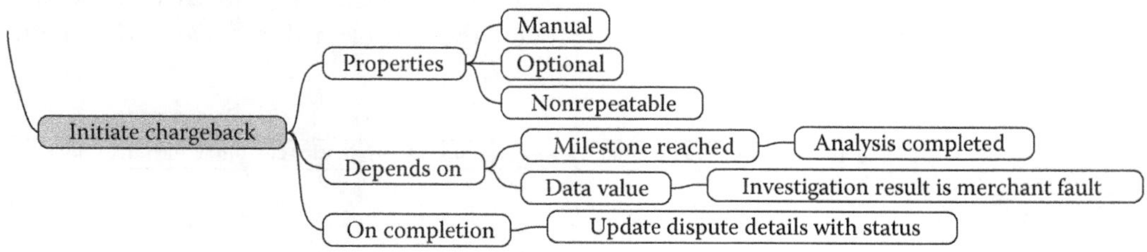

6. Activity "notify customer" shown below is optional and repeatable and has no dependencies.

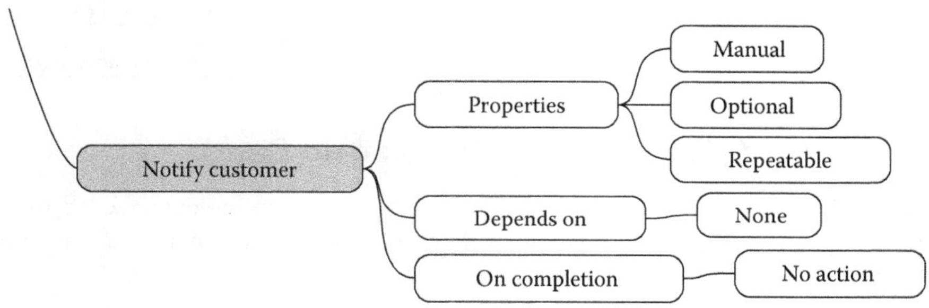

7. Activity "notify merchant" shown below is optional and repeatable and has the same dependencies as "initiate chargeback".

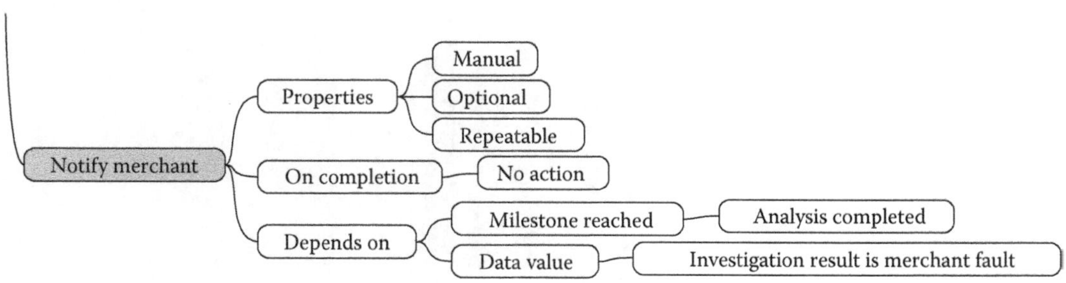

17.2.3.3 Event Design

What external events can affect the case progression?

Events drive how a case progresses. Events can be both internal events as well as external events. Internal events are those that are raised because of actions being performed on the case. For instance, uploading a supporting document is an event, which may result in an action being taken to review the uploaded document. Similarly, the completion of an activity raises an event that in turn could cause a milestone to be reached. We have already addressed which internal events are of interest to us and how they should be handled. We did this by analyzing dependencies between activities, milestones, etc.

External events on the other hand are the ones that occur outside the control of the case engine. In our use case, we have one external event that needs to be handled as part of the case processing; the event is that of a customer calling to get an update on the dispute. This would typically result in the case owner communicating the status of the case via an email.

Another event that can occur outside of the case that will impact the case is when a possible fraud is detected. Fraud detection will typically happen in different systems altogether and this needs to be communicated to the case so that appropriate actions are taken. In our use case, if a possible fraud is detected, a new case should be started for the fraud and the current case should be suspended until a decision is made regarding the fraud. This is explained in the following figure:

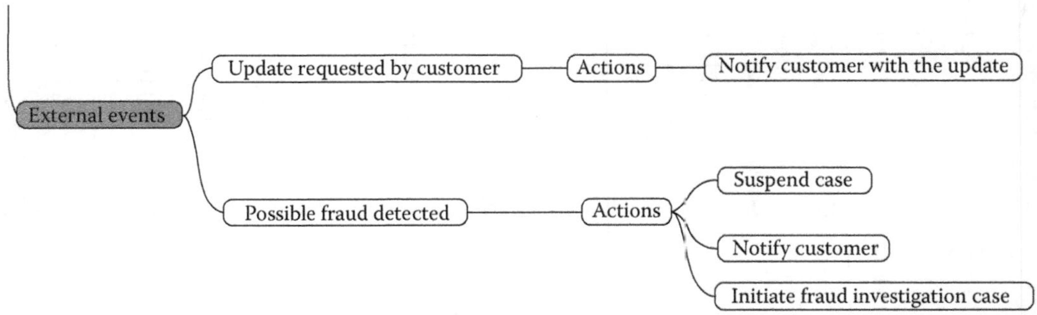

17.2.4 Credit Card Charge Dispute Information Design

In this paragraph we will look at a high level of information requirements needed to create the Oracle ACM implementation for the credit card charge dispute. Case management information design category is shown in the following figure:

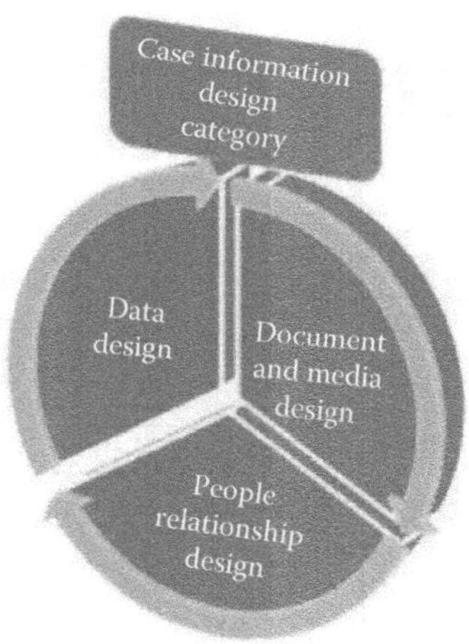

The case information design deals with all sorts of data and documentation flowing through the case and maps the relationships between all persons and/or assets involved in the case. The case information design category contains three design components, data design, document, and media design and people relationship design.

17.2.4.1 People Relationship Design

Who will be participating in the case?
In the simplified scenario, we have three main stakeholders—the CSR who handles the service call and creates the case, the analyst who works on the case to resolve it, and a case manager who

oversees dispute management cases. Each of these stakeholders may also have different levels of privileges. For instance the case manager will have full access to the case, whereas the CSR may only be granted view-only access to the case. There will be other people who will be indirectly participating for performing specific tasks assigned to them. But they typically will not have access to the case itself as explained in the following figure:

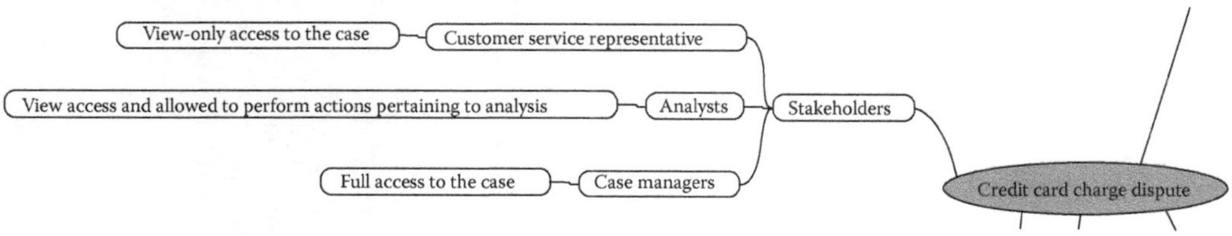

17.2.4.2 Data Design and Document Management Design

What information does the case require and how is it used?

Case processing is information-centric. Source of information can be structured data, typically provided by applications and databases, and unstructured data such as documents, images, videos, etc.

In our simplified use case, the following data items will be needed:

- Dispute—Provides details of the dispute registered, such as the customer ID, disputed transaction details, the date the dispute was registered, credit card number associated with the transaction, status of the dispute, resolution of the dispute, etc.
- Customer—Customer account details
- Credit card account—Credit card information including transaction history
- Investigation report—Details of the dispute investigation outcome

The data can be categorized based on its usage as follows:

- Reference only—Used only as reference by case workers and stakeholders
- Read-only case data—Used in the case as part of rules and policies, data expressions, input to activities, etc., and is not updated by the case engine
- Case data—Same as read-only case data but it gets updated by the case engine as the case progresses

Our use case data can be defined using the categorization shown in the figure below:

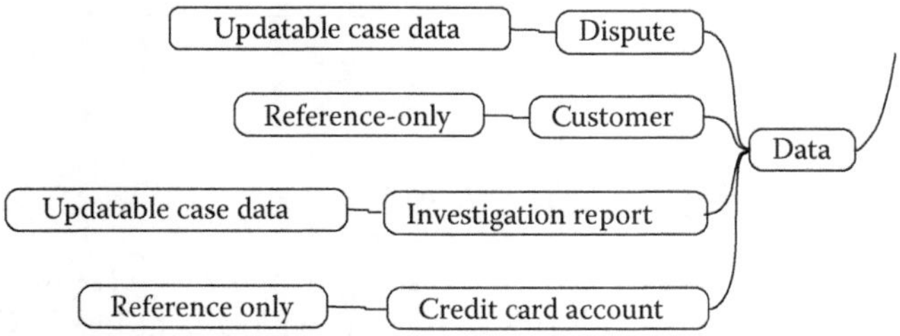

NOTE: Read-only case data can be marked as "external," which results in the case calling a user-defined handler to fetch the data from an external source as and when needed. The details of this are beyond the scope of this book.

The completed mind map, shown in the figure below, captures the analysis. We will use this in the next chapter as the input for our design.

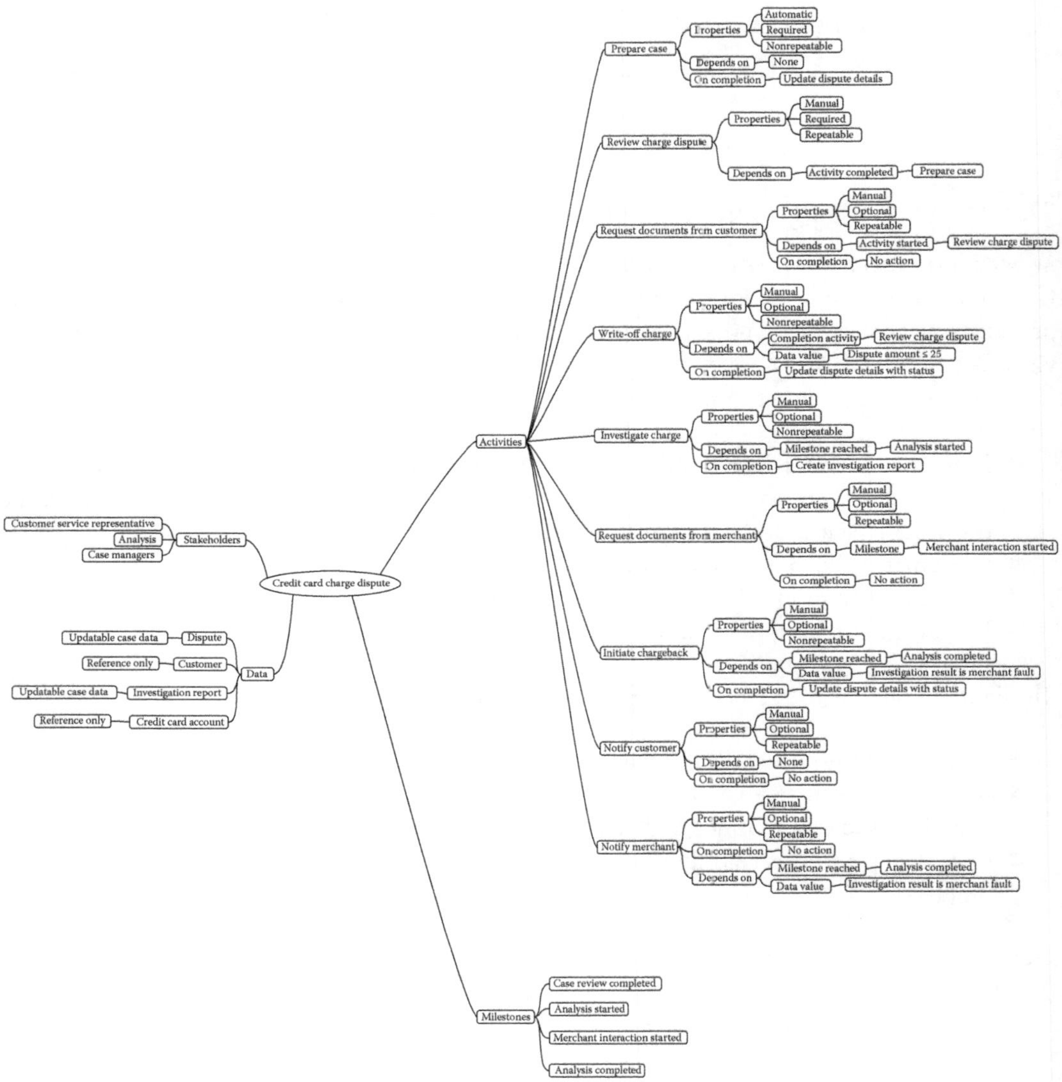

17.3 Installation and Tutorial Files

In this section you will implement the credit card charge dispute use case we analyzed in the previous paragraph. Before beginning with this tutorial, download and install Oracle BPM 12.1.3. This software is available on http://www.oracle.com/technetwork/middleware/bpm/downloads/

index.html. This is a "quickstart" installer, which allows you to run business process management (BPM) and adaptive case management (ACM) from within the Oracle JDeveloper, without having to do a separate server installation. Follow the instructions from the installation guide available at http://docs.oracle.com/middleware/1213/core/SOAQS/index.html.

All tutorial material needed in this chapter, the data definitions in XSD and test XML files, are presented in Appendix 17.A. These files and a resulting complete set of tutorial files are also available on the following website: http://oraclecasemanagementsolutions.com/.

17.4 Key Elements of Oracle Adaptive Case Management

We have introduced Oracle ACM already in Chapter 7. This chapter goes one level deeper and describes the details of all ACM-related functionalities. Oracle ACM provides a comprehensive framework for building highly flexible and dynamic business process applications. It extends Oracle BPM Suite's scope to address unstructured ad hoc processes by introducing the notion of a *case* as shown in the following figure:

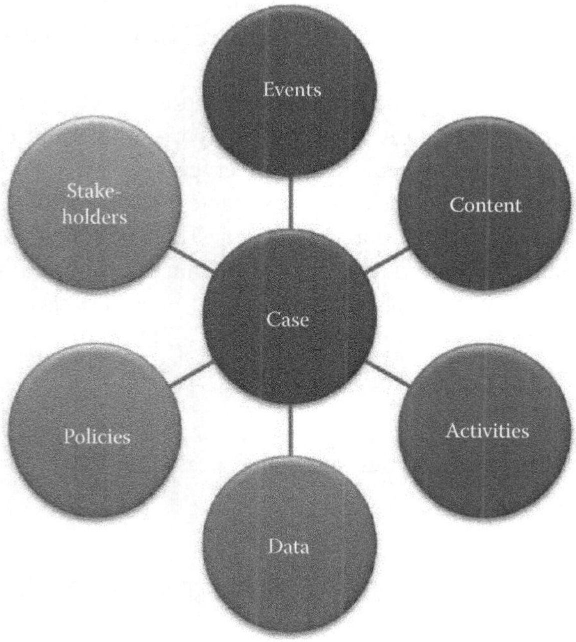

17.4.1 Case

A case is a container that holds the state of the case and includes the following:

- The overall state, such as whether the case is active, suspended, or closed
- The current state of the milestones
- Data needed for progressing the case
- Documents and other content
- Case Stakeholders and their access privileges
- Details about relationships with other cases

The case engine in Oracle BPM Suite is responsible for the life cycle of all cases. The state of the case changes when participants in the case perform activities relevant to the case. Internal and external events also can cause changes in the case state.

Designing and implementing a case, therefore, involves identifying these various elements of the case and defining the details for each. Before we start designing the case model for our "credit card charge dispute" use case, let us take a deeper look at these key elements.

17.4.2 Case Activities

Activities are actions performed on the case by either the user or the system with a goal to progress the case to its completion. These actions may be performed by the case participants or by the system itself.

17.4.2.1 Activity Implementation

Activities in Oracle ACM can be implemented using any of the following:

- Business process model and notation (BPMN)—Activities can be implemented as structured BPMN processes. These can use the full set of BPMN activities to model the activity implementation.
- Human tasks—Human tasks, one of the core components of Oracle BPM, can be used as an activity implementation and is suitable for activities that require work assignment and tracking. A BPM process is not required for this type of activity.
- Custom—If BPM and human task are not suitable implementation options, Oracle ACM allows adding a custom activity implementation. This implementation is a Java class that implements a specific Java interface. This allows you to provide any kind of activity. An example of such an activity implementation could be a Java class that creates a calendar invite using one of the calendar protocols such as CalDAV.

17.4.2.2 Activity Properties

Table 17.2 describes the various properties that define a case activity.

17.4.3 Case Data

Case data refers to data that is needed by the case for the following functionalities:

- Rules conditions used in the case life cycle determination
- Expression evaluation—To determine various case property values such as case title, case category, stakeholder members, and folder names for content storage

All instances of case data objects, by default, are stored as part of the case (internal case data) and managed by Oracle ACM.

17.4.3.1 Data Definition

Case data can be of simple types such as string, integer, and date. In most situations, the case data will be a complex type, with its own structure.

Table 17.2 Activity Properties

Property	*Description*
Name	Name of the activity
Manual	The user will initiate the activity from the case workspace. The case workspace is described in more detail in Section 17.6.4.1
Automatic	The case engine will initiate the activity whenever the activity is available for use
Required	When this property is set, the activity is required to be initiated and completed
	The result of this setting is that the case cannot be closed normally; it can only be force-closed
Repeatable	When this property is set, the activity can be initiated any number of times with an instance of a case. Without this property being set, an activity can be initiated only once during the case's lifetime
Conditional	If this property is set, the activity will have to be explicitly made available. Typically, this is done with the support of rules actions. If the activity is marked as unconditional, it is available as soon as the case is started. As a result, the case engine initiates automatic and unconditional activities as soon as the case starts
Input	Defines the data items that will be passed as input to the activity implementation. The input can either come from one or more of the *case data* items or can be captured from the user using an *activity form*
Output	Defines the data items returned by the activity implementation after successful completion. One or more of these data items can be configured to update the corresponding *case data*

Case data structure can be defined in two ways:

- Using the BPM business components catalog—you can use existing business objects or define new ones and use them as types for the case data
- Using XML Schema definitions

17.4.3.2 External Case Data

Some data, used in the case, originates from external sources, such as an ERP application. This data is not stored in the internal case data store, but is only referenced. This is in order to avoid the data getting stale or out of sync with the actual data. For example, a case data object may refer to a service request created in the CRM application. When the service request is updated via the CRM application, the corresponding case data object needs to be refreshed with the changes.

This can be a challenge to implement, since the CRM application will typically be unaware of the case.

Oracle ACM provides the ability to mark case data items as being external. Whenever the case needs the data, for example, to evaluate a rule, it will call a registered Java class that implements a specific interface. The implementation of this Java class is up to the case developer and will typically handle getting the data from appropriate sources. So for our service request example, you would declare the case data to be external. During case processing, every time the case needs any data from the service request, it will call the Java class, which in turn will fetch the data from the CRM application. This way, there is no danger of keeping two copies of data in sync.

17.4.4 Case Stakeholders

A case can have different groups of people working on it at various points in time during its lifetime. These groups of people are called stakeholders. Oracle ACM provides a flexible stakeholder model that allows you to define the different stakeholders at design time. It also allows changing of the model at runtime. This runtime change to the stakeholder model is limited to the particular instance of a case.

Stakeholder membership can be a combination of individuals, groups, application roles, and even BPM process roles. Stakeholder member definitions can be either named or dynamic. There are following three ways a member can be added dynamically to the stakeholder:

- Using an expression—you can specify an XPATH expression on a case data item that will evaluate to a valid member (individual and group role, or process role)
- Programmatically, at startup—you can add members to one or more stakeholders during startup by setting up the case parameters appropriately
- At runtime, using the case workspace

17.4.5 Case Documents

Content such as Word files, PDF files, images, and videos is a key part of any case. Case progression can be influenced by content operations such as upload, delete, and update.

Oracle ACM provides basic content operations that include file *upload*, *file check-out*, *file check-in*, and *deletion* of a file. It integrates with a content management system (CMS) for managing the document storage. By default, the documents are stored in the same database as the ACM persistent store. This mode is useful during initial development only. It is recommended to configure a CMS—either the preintegrated Oracle WebCenter Content or any CMIS (content management interoperability services) compliant CMS, such as Alfresco.

17.4.6 Rules and Policies

With Oracle ACM, it is possible to model a case without any rules and policies. In such cases, all activities are made available to all stakeholders at any time during the case. This may be fine where the nature of the work is truly ad hoc and where full flexibility is required. But in most use cases there is a need for some control and governance and the ability to guide the case workers through the case processing.

This is where rules and policies help by controlling which activities to make available at what point in time. Rules can also be based on the state of one or more milestones, changes in state of the case, changes to data, contents of the data, etc. Using a combination of conditions, one can put meaningful controls in the case without constraining the case workers' ability to use their knowledge and best judgment to process the case.

Oracle ACM uses the Oracle Business Rules engine as the rules engine and automatically creates a rules dictionary appropriately seeded with case functions, case metadata, and case data as fact types.

Most of the rules you define will make use of the different events that the case engine raises to determine the actions to take.

17.4.7 Case Events

The Oracle Adaptive Case engine at its core is driven by events. Events can be either internal or external. Internal events are generated as a result of changes to the case. The case engine generates the following types of events:

- Life cycle events
- Activity events
- Milestone events
- Document events
- Data events
- User events

Most of these events further define subtypes that indicate the specific event that has occurred. Table 17.3 lists all the events and their subtypes.

17.5 Implement the Case with Oracle ACM

Now that you have a good overview of the key case elements in Oracle ACM, let us identify these elements in our use case and use them to define our "credit card charge dispute" case model. We will use the following series of steps to design, deploy, and test a case management solution based upon Oracle BPM/ACM:

- Design the case management solution
  - Create case project
  - Configure case properties
  - Create case data model
  - Set up content configuration
  - Define user events
  - Define stakeholders and permissions
  - Define case activities
  - Define case life cycle decision-making rules
- Deploy
- Test

Table 17.3 Case Events List

Event Type	*Subtype*	*Event Raised When ...*
Life cycle	STARTED	Case is created
	COMPLETED	Case is completed
	UPDATED	Case header is updated (typically via API)
	DUEDATE_REACHED	Case due date is reached
	SUSPENDED	Case is suspended, either manually or automatically via rules
	RESUMED	Case is resumed from its suspended state
	REOPENED	A closed case reopened
	ABORTED	Case is aborted
Activity	ACTIVATED	An activity is marked as being available for instantiation either by the user or via rules
	COMPLETED	An instantiated activity completes successfully
	FAULTED	An instantiated activity aborts due to an exception
Milestone	REACHED	Milestone is marked as having been reached, either by the user or via rules
	REVOKED	A milestone that was previously marked as having been reached is now set to be open again
	DEADLINE_REACHED	Due date associated with the milestone is reached
Document	ADDED	A document is added to the case
	DELETED	A document is deleted from the case
	MODIFIED	A checked-out document is checked-in
Data	*No subtype*	Case data is modified
User	*No subtype*	A user event is raised

17.5.1 Create the Case Management Project

Start JDeveloper 12.1.3 that you installed as per instructions at the beginning of this chapter:

1. Create a new application workspace by selecting *File→New→Application*.
2. In the *New Gallery* window shown below, select BPM application

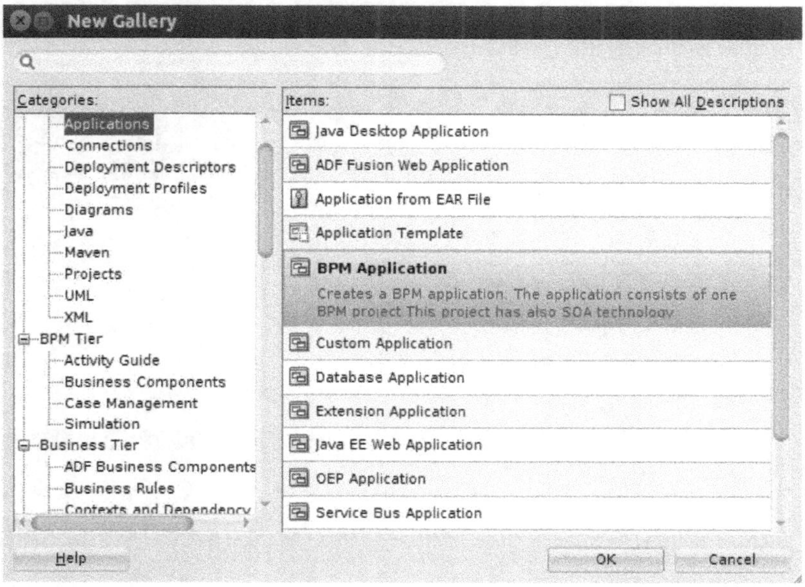

3. Name the application "CCDApplication" (CCD being short for credit card dispute) and choose the appropriate directory for the application. Use *acmbook.tutorial.ccd* as the *application package prefix*. This is shown in the figure below.

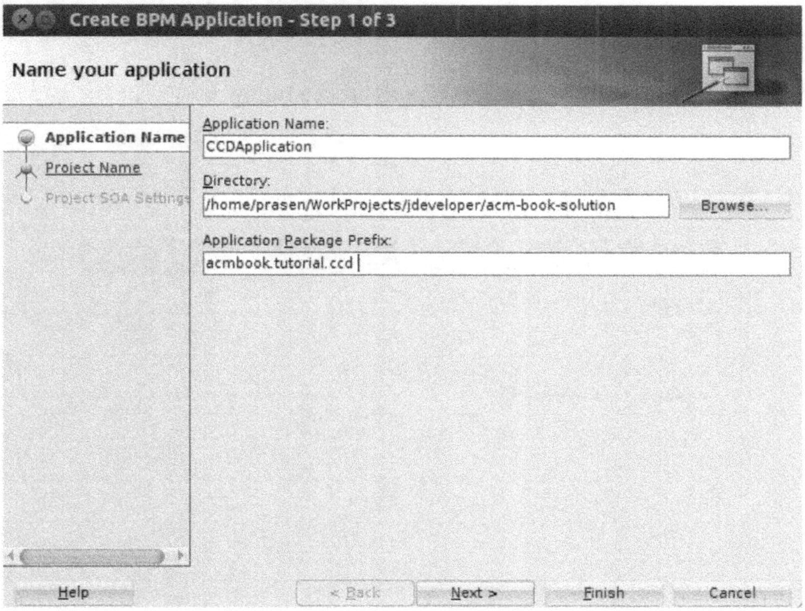

In step 2 of the *Create BPM Application* wizard, enter project name as ***CCDCase*** and click on *Next*. Make sure you select "BPM" from the "Project Features" list.

4. In step 3 of the wizard, keep the default composite name and select *Composite with Case Management* and click *Finish* as shown below.

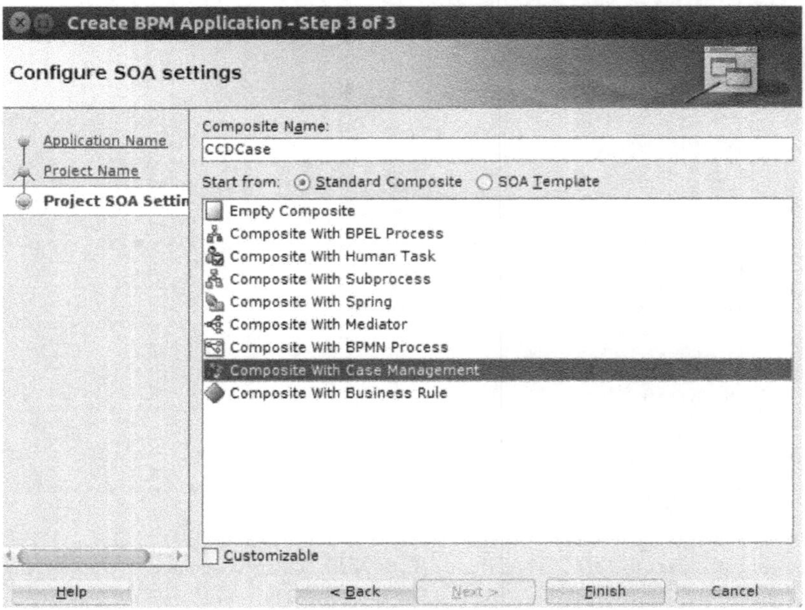

5. Accept the default in the *Create Case Management* window shown below and Click *OK*.

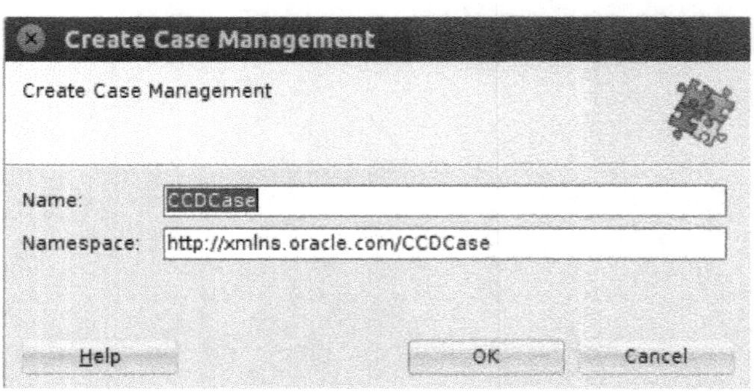

This will create a new case project and open the case management definition page shown below for editing.

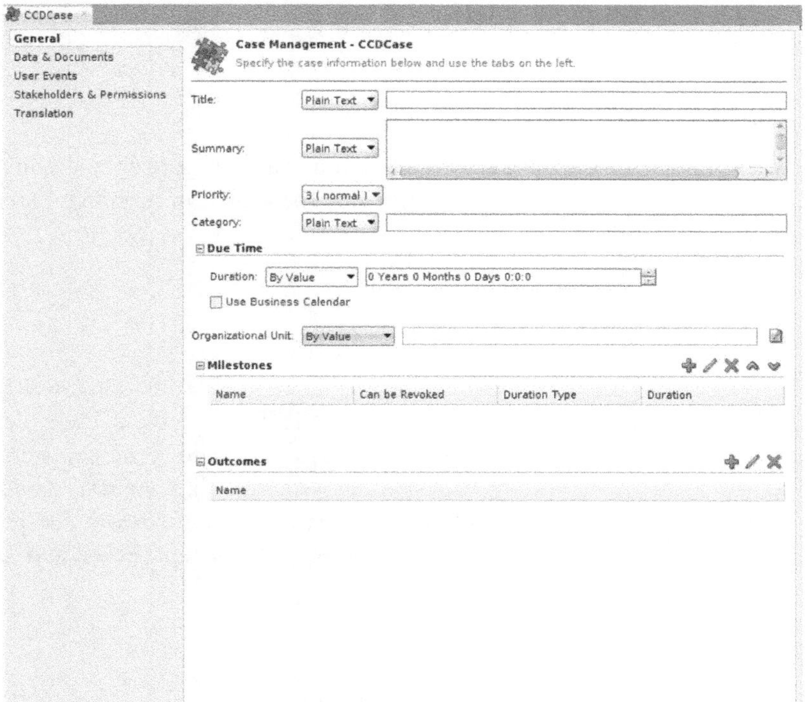

17.5.2 Define the Case Properties

The case management definition page has multiple tabs, each for defining different properties and elements of the case. Let us start with the *General* tab.

17.5.2.1 Title

This defines the title that will be displayed in the case UI for a given case instance. The title can be a simple string value or a translation. Translations can be parameterized, which means not only can you create a translation table for multiple languages but you can also create dynamic text that is evaluated at runtime. This allows you to define meaningful titles such as "Credit Charge Dispute Case for John Doe," where the "John Doe" part is inserted at runtime based on an XPATH expression.

For now, select *Plaint Text* and type in "Credit Card Charge Dispute Case." Once you have defined the case data we will update this to use a translation.

17.5.2.2 Summary

This defines a brief summary of the case. This can be plain text or can be a parameterized translation just like the title, described previously.

For this tutorial, leave the summary blank.

17.5.2.3 Priority

Defines the case priority ranging from 1 (highest) to 5 (lowest) and is useful in querying cases. It can also be useful in defining rules based on the case priority.

Set the priority to 3.

17.5.2.4 Category

This can be used to categorize the case. For example, you could categorize the dispute cases based on the card holder's status such as gold, platinum, etc. The value can be either a literal string or can be a parameterized translation.

For now, leave this field empty.

17.5.2.5 Due Time

You can define when a case becomes due by defining the duration. The duration can either be a fixed value or can be derived at runtime from case data using an XPATH expression. The expression should result in a valid XML duration format. The due time is calculated based on the case start time. If *Use Business Calendar* is checked and an *Organization Unit* is chosen, then the time computation will consider appropriate business holidays defined for that organization unit, to arrive at the due time.

Set the duration to 7 days and keep the *Use Business Calendar* unchecked and *Organization Unit* empty.

17.5.2.6 Milestones

Milestones help to track the progression of the case. We identified the following milestones in our analysis in the previous chapter:

- Initial case review completed
- Analysis started
- Merchant interaction initiated
- Analysis completed

Add an entry for each milestone by clicking on the ✚ icon and name them as per Table 17.4. Each of the columns is explained here:

- *Name*: This is the internal name for the milestone. This name is used in rules for managing the state of the milestone. If you need to see the milestones in a particular order in the Case UI, you need to ensure they are appropriately named. The case UI sorts milestones alphabetically. For our use case, prefix each name with A01, A02, etc., to ensure the milestones are displayed in the desired order.
- *Display Name*: This is displayed in the case UI.
- *Can be Revoked*: If checked, the user can reopen a milestone that has been completed.
- *Duration*: If set, this marks the milestone as being overdue when the specified duration is complete (Table 17.4).

17.5.2.7 Outcomes

Outcomes are predefined set of possible outcomes of the case. These are used while closing the case indicating how the case was closed.

Table 17.4 Milestones Definition

Internal Name	*Display Name*	*Can Be Revoked*	*Duration*
A01_InitialCase ReviewCompleted	Initial case review completed	No	3 days
A02_AnalysisStarted	Analysis started	No	No duration keep the default values 0 years, 0 months, 0 days
A03_Merchant InteractionStarted	Merchant interaction started	No	No duration
A04_Analysis Completed	Analysis completed	Yes	5 Days

Table 17.5 Outcomes Definition

Outcome	*Display Name*
CaseResolvedNoDispute	Case Resolved—charge is valid
CaseResolvedMerchantAtFault	Case Resolved—merchant at fault
CaseResolvedOurFault	Case Resolved—our fault

Add the following outcomes (Table 17.5):

Once you have completed the outcome definitions, you are done with general case properties and your *General* tab should be like the figure below:

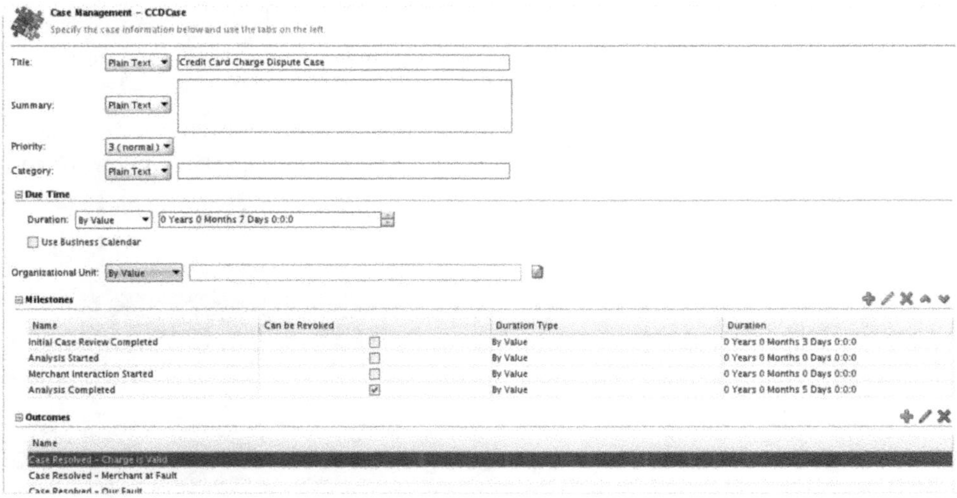

17.5.3 Define the Data Model

17.5.3.1 Identify the Case Data Objects

During the analysis of the use case, we identified the different data elements that will be needed during the processing of the case as shown in the following figure:

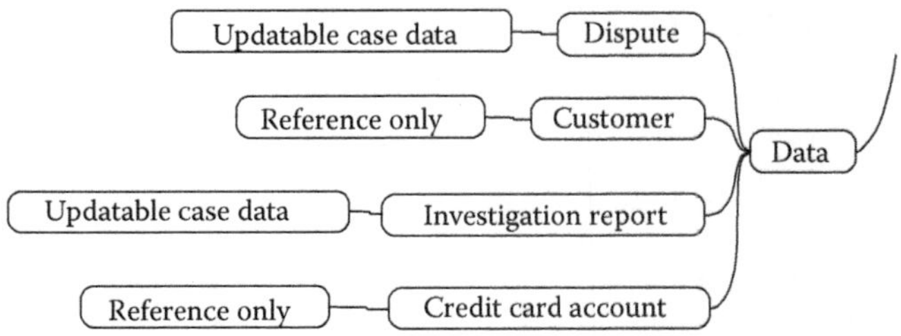

You can use this analysis to further determine data elements that need to be defined in the case. Let us start with the obvious ones—*dispute* and *investigation report* are definitely required to be defined in the case as they will be updated during the case processing.

You also have *customer* and *credit card account*, which are primarily reference data that will be displayed on the user interface to give the case worker the appropriate contextual information about the case. *Credit card account* data need not be defined as case data since it is not referred directly in the case. On the other hand, the *customer* data may be required as case data since attributes from it may be used in the case. For example, you can define the case title to include the name of the customer in the title. This means that you will need to provide an XPATH expression that evaluates to the name of the customer. Another example would be the need to categorize the case based on the status of the customer. Both of these attributes will typically be available in the *customer* data.

This narrows down the list of case data objects to include in the case definition

- Dispute
- Investigation report
- Customer

The following sections describe the definition of these data objects with Oracle ACM.

17.5.3.2 Define the Case Data Objects

To create the case data definitions, switch to the *Data & Documents* tab from the *General* tab that you have been working on until now. Clicking on the ✚ icon will open the window for adding a new case data definition.

Table 17.6 describes this pop-up window:

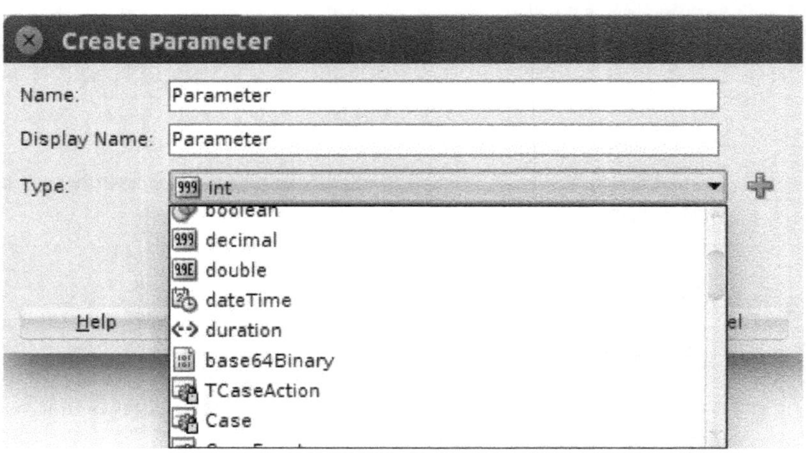

Table 17.6 Description of New Case Data Creation Pop-Up

Field	*Description*
Name	Name of the case data. This name is used in your expressions and as fact names in Oracle Business Rules
Display Name	This will be used to label the data in the user interface
Type	Defines the type of the case data. The type can be any of the basic types such as *string*, *int*, and *date*. Complex types can also be used. When using complex types, there are three options 1. Use existing business object from the business components in the project 2. Create a new business object based on an existing XML Schema 3. Create a new business object from scratch In the case of options 2 and 3, the object definition ends up being stored in the business components library

17.5.3.2.1 Dispute Data Definition

Create the dispute data object using option 3 (from scratch) described earlier. Use the following values (Table 17.7):

1. Click on the ✚ icon, that is alongside the *Type* field, to open the *Create Business Object* window. Name the object as *DisputeBO*.
2. Click on the *Search* icon 🔍 to open the *Browse Modules* window. This will show all the different modules available in the business catalog.
3. Click on the *New* icon to create a new module named *CCDBusinessObjects*.

The data object creation process so far looks like presented in the following figure:

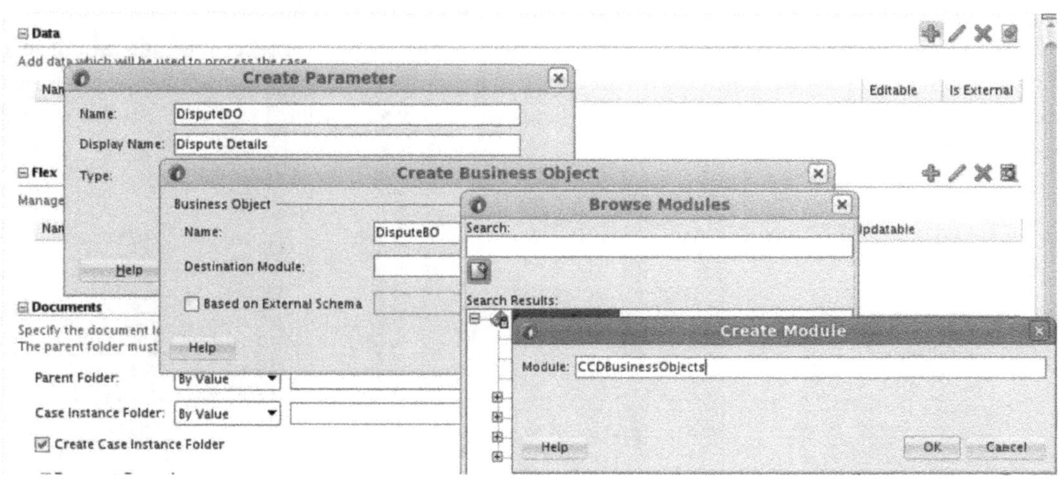

4. Select this new module and click on *OK*.
5. Click on *OK* to close the window and click *OK* again to complete.
6. At this point you have defined a new case data called *DisputeDO* but have not yet defined the structure of this object. You do that in the following steps.

Table 17.7 Values for Dispute Data Object Creation

Field	*Value*
Name	DisputeDO
Display Name	Dispute details
Editable	Yes
Is External	No (unchecked)

7. Expand the *Business Components* folder in the *Projects* panel shown below. Within it you should see the *CCDBusinessObjects* module you just created. Expand this folder to see the *DisputeBO* object. Click on the *Refresh* icon if you do not see the business object.

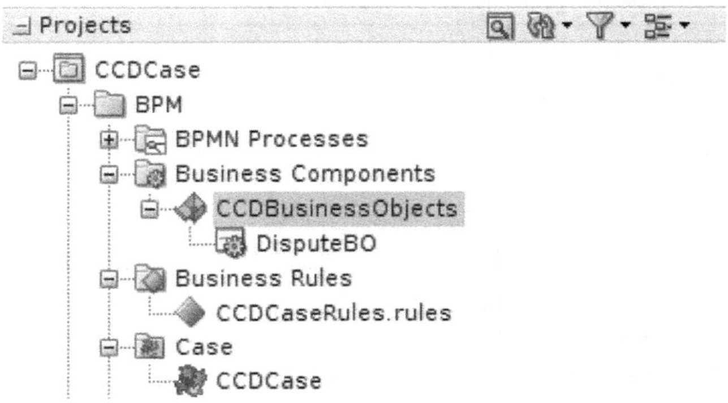

Double-click on the *DisputeBO* object to open it. Oracle BPM allows you to define complex data models and provides features such as the ability to define abstract data definitions and use object inheritance. It also allows you to define methods in the object using Groovy scripts; this is outside the scope of this tutorial. For this tutorial you will define a concrete object without inheritance and without any methods. Click on the *Add* icon ✚ to add new attributes as defined in the figure below. The arrows ⇧ ⇩ help to arrange the fields in the correct order. Press the *Save* button after finishing the work.

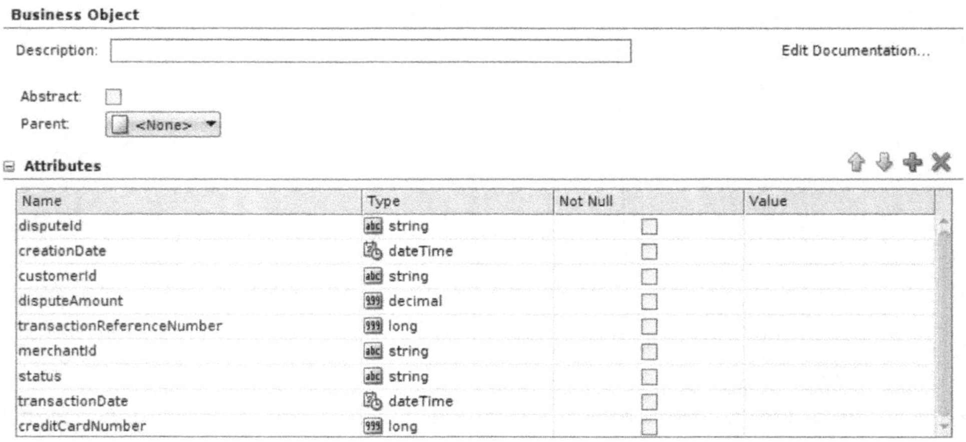

17.5.3.2.2 Investigation Report Data Definition

Create the investigation report data object just as you created the dispute data object. Name the case data object *InvestigationReportDO* and provide the display name as *Investigation Report.*

For the type of this object, create a new type names *InvestigationReportBO* under the *CCDBusinessObject* module. The following figure shows the structure of this data object.

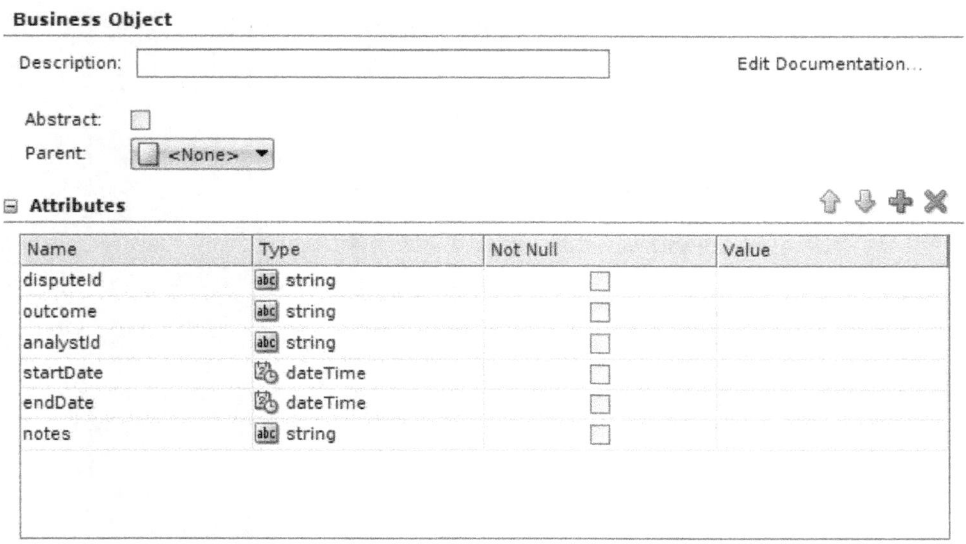

Press the Save button after finishing the work.

17.5.3.2.3 Customer Data Definition

Customer data is a good candidate for being defined as an external data. Any changes to the customer details in the database that is the source of truth for customer information should be available to the case. If the data is not defined to be external then the copy of the customer data in the Case will quickly become stale depending on the duration of the case and the frequency of changes to the customer information.

Implementing external data handler is an advanced topic and beyond the scope of this book, so, for this tutorial, you define the data as being internal; same as the previous two objects. For this object, instead of creating the data definition from scratch, you use a predefined schema (customer.xsd). See Section 17.3 for the locations from where this schema can be obtained.

1. Add a new case data with the name *CustomerDO* and display name as *Customer Details*.
2. When defining the type, click on the *Add* icon.
3. Name the business object as *CustomerBO* in the *Create Business Object* window.
4. Select the destination module to be *CCDBusinessObjects*.
5. Select based on external schema. This will enable the *Search* icon for loading the XSD.
6. Click on the *Search* icon to open the *Type Chooser* window.
7. Click on the *Import Schema File* icon to open the file browser window. Browse to the location where you downloaded the customer.xsd file and select it.

8. In the *Localize Files* pop-up window shown below, keep the default options and click *OK*. You should see the customer.xsd under the *Project Schema Files* tree in the type explorer.

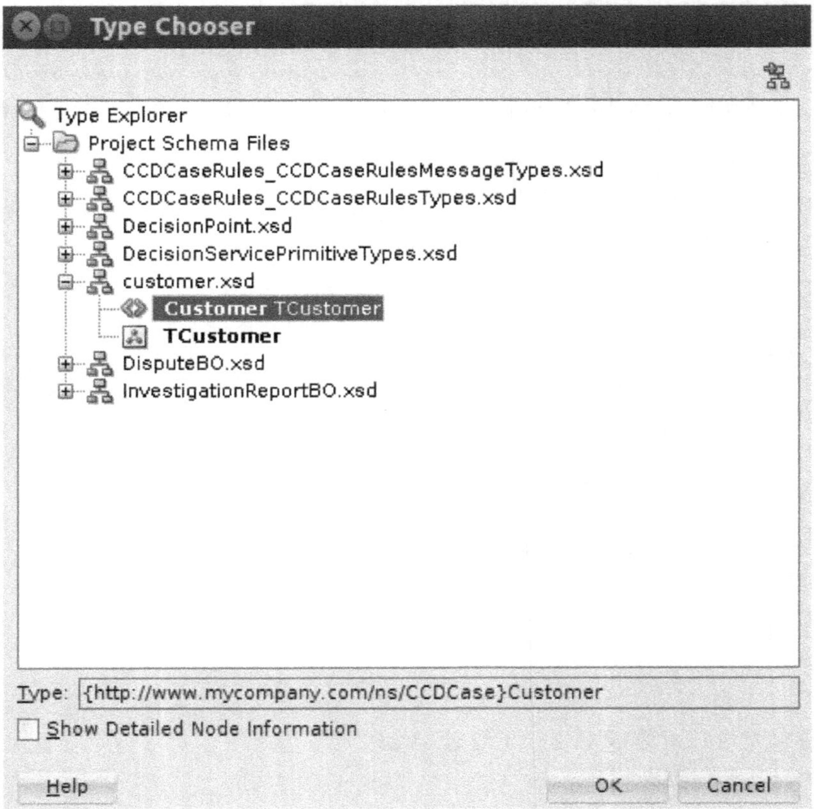

9. Select the first node, *Customer*, under the customer.xsd as shown in the figure above. Click *OK* on the open windows to complete the case data creation. Make sure you leave the *Is External* checkbox unchecked.

Press the *Save* button after finishing the work.

You now have the case data defined and it can be used in expressions and rules in the following parts of the tutorial.

17.5.3.3 Create Data Forms

The case data objects you defined can be viewed and updated at runtime from the BPM Workspace. This is possible by creating data forms. Data forms are autogenerated ADF applications that are embedded in the BPM Workspace. Oracle Application Development Framework (ADF) is the facto user interface standard within the Oracle Fusion Middleware and is based upon the J2EE Java Server Faces standard.

The following steps walk you through creating a single data form application that will have a page (and an ADF task flow) for each case data object:

1. Select the *Data & Documents* tab in the case definition page.
2. Select *Dispute Details* data object and click on the create form icon and select *NewProject*. Name the project *CCDCaseDataForms* and click *OK* to complete. This will create a new project that contains an ADF task flow with a single ADF page called *DisputeDO.jspx*. You can modify the layout and add other UI controls, validations, etc., to your specific requirements. For the purpose of this tutorial, the default form layout is used. Save all projects and close the *DisputeDO.jspx*, *DisputeDO.xml*, and *DataControls.dcx* files.
3. Navigate back to the *CCDCase* definition, select the *Investigation Report* object and click on the *Create Form* icon. This time around, select *Select Existing Project*. In the pop-up that opens, select the *CCDCaseDataForms* project and click *OK* to complete.
4. Modify the generated *InvestigationReportDO.jspx* ADF page to remove the *Save* and *Reset* buttons by selecting the button and deleting it. This will disable updating the data from the workspace. This way you can enforce that the investigation report is only updated via an activity. There are a number of more elegant options for doing the same, such as making all fields read-only and conditionally disabling the *Save* and *Restore* buttons based on logged in user. But for this exercise, let us keep it simple.
5. Repeat steps 3 and 4 for the *Customer Details* data object. This form should also disallow updates.

17.5.3.4 Define Flex Fields

The case engine stores all the case data objects as XML in the case database along with other case instance metadata. This makes it difficult for queries that require attributes from these data objects as part of the query criteria. For example, if you wanted to find all *CLOSED* cases for **CustomerDO.customerId** equal to ***110220*** and **InvestigationReportDO.outcome** equal to ***VALID_CHARGE***, you would have to first fetch all cases with status equal to ***CLOSED*** and then for each case, inspect the XML for the corresponding data object to find the required cases. This is obviously not a very efficient way of querying cases. Oracle ACM provides a way to map XML elements in the Case data to user-defined fields, called **Flex Fields**.

Flex fields are a mechanism by which you can expose selected data from the case data objects as named fields in the case. These can then be used in the query criteria when fetching cases. The case engine provides support for defining 20 such fields for each string, number, and date types with a maximum of 60 such fields across these types. The values for these fields are provided via XPATH expressions using the appropriate case data objects.

Although querying cases using the Case API is beyond the scope of this book, we will add a couple of Flex Fields to see how to define them. In the following steps you add two flex fields—one for the customer ID and another for the investigation report outcome.

1. Click the add icon for *Flex Fields* in the *Data & Documents* tab.
2. In the *Create Flex Field* window, enter the name of the flex field as ***CustomerId***, choose the type as *String* and leave the *Column Name* to the default selected.
3. For the source file, click on the *Express Builder* icon to open the expression builder.

4. Expand the *CustomerDO* node in the *Variables* panel, select *CustomerId* and click on *Insert into Expression* to copy it into the expression panel as shown in the figure below.

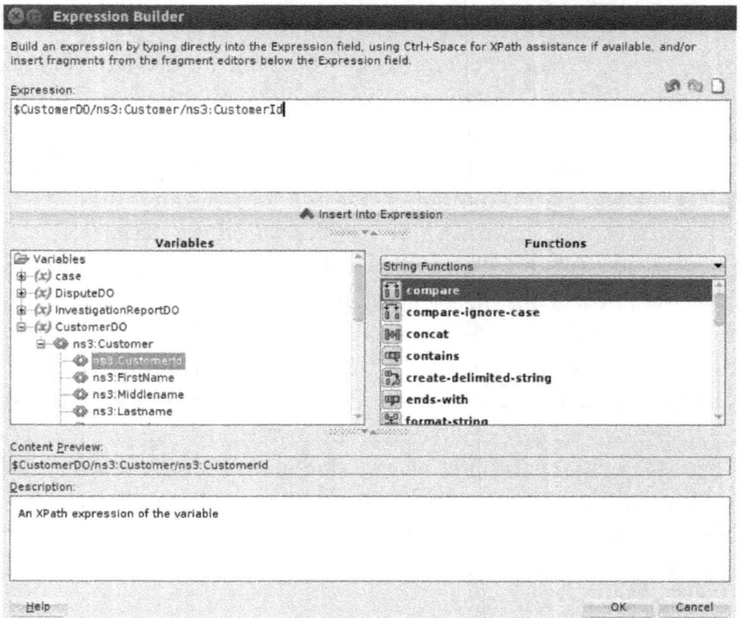

Click on *OK* to close the window and click *OK* again to complete.

Note: The namespace prefix (ns3) may be different in your project.

5. Repeat the steps for defining a flex field named *InvestigationOutome*. Define the type as *String* and for the expression, select the *outcome* attribute from the *InvestigationReportDO* variable.

Press the *Save* button after finishing the work.
This completes your data definition. At this stage your *Data & Documents* tab should look something like this as shown in the figure below:

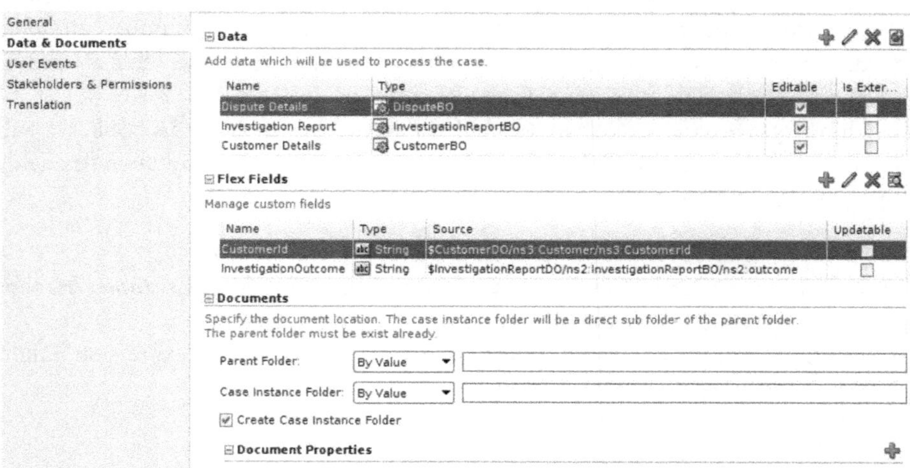

17.5.4 Content Configuration

Oracle ACM provides out-of-the-box integration with Oracle WebCenter Content, a Content Management System (CMS) for managing content acquired, generated, or used as reference by a case. For development purposes, a built-in database-based content storage is provided with the Oracle BPM/ACM product. This content storage does not have CMS features such as check-in and check-out and is only meant to be used as a development configuration. In this tutorial, we will use this integrated content server in JDeveloper. If you do have an instance of Webcenter Content that you can use, you can configure the BPM server to use that. Please refer to https://docs.oracle.com/middleware/1213/bpm/bpm-develop/case_mgmt_bpmpd.htm#CIHJBCAB for steps to configure CMS integration for ACM.

In case you plan to use a CMS such as Oracle WebCenter Content, follow these steps to set up your case.

1. In the *Data & Documents* tab, enter a name for the parent folder under which all the content for this case type will be stored. Use the name ***CCD Case Content***.
2. Select *Create Case Instance Folder*. This will store content to the named instance-specific folder. If this is not checked, content for all instances will be stored under the parent folder.
3. For the *Case Instance Folder*, select *By Expression* and click on the *Expression Builder* icon to define the expression that will evaluate to a value that will be used to create the instance-specific folder.
4. Use the value of ***disputeId*** as the name of the instance folder as shown in the figure below.

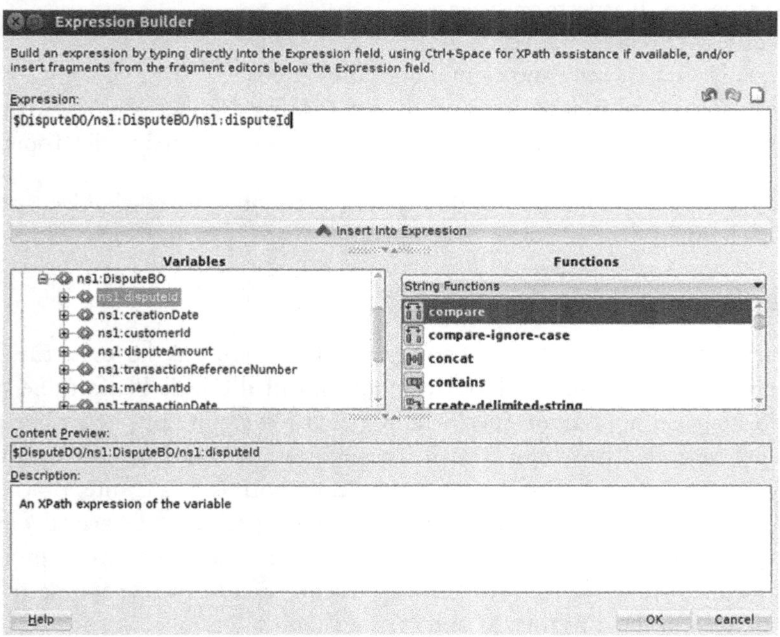

Note: If you use WebCenter Content as the CMS, you need to enable the *Framework Folders* feature in it. The parent folder should be relative to the root folder.

Table 17.8 User Events

Name	Display Name
ProbableFraudDetected	Probable fraud detected
CustomerRequestsUpdate	Update requested by customer

17.5.5 Define User Events

For this use case, there are two predefined user events that the user can raise via the BPM Workspace:

- A probable fraud is detected while investigating the case
- Customer requests an update on his case

You define these two events in the *User Events* tab. Add the two events given in Table 17.8 by clicking on the *Add* icon.

17.5.6 Define the Stakeholders and Permissions

We have identified following three main stakeholders in this use case:

- Case manager—person (or persons) responsible for the overall progress of the case
  - Has access to all aspects of the case
- Customer service representatives
  - Can only view the case and cannot take any actions
- Dispute analysts—persons responsible for investigating disputes
  - Can view the case and can perform activities relevant to solving the dispute

Before you define the stakeholders, let us do a quick primer on how stakeholders and permissions are used in Oracle ACM.

17.5.6.1 Application Roles

Oracle ACM leverages the same roles and permission infrastructure as the rest of the Oracle Fusion Middleware stack and that is handled by a component called Oracle Platform Security Services (OPSS). OPSS manages application-specific and global role definitions and corresponding permissions in a policy store. These roles are called application roles and are used by all components such as J2EE applications, ADF applications, WebCenter portals, SOA Suite, BPM Suite, and, of course, ACM. Application roles allow creating user groups specific to the needs of an application without having to make changes to the configured lightweight directory access protocol (LDAP) directory such as MS Active Directory. These application roles can be comprised of individual users, groups defined in the directory, as well as other application roles.

17.5.6.2 Application Policies

Application policies define authorization policies that control access to resources in an application. Authorization policies define the resource to be controlled, the action(s) to be authorized, and the Java class that implements the permission implementation. Policies are typically granted to application roles. These can also be granted to individual users or groups defined in the directory such as LDAP.

17.5.6.3 Stakeholders

Stakeholders in a case are created as application roles and are associated with a special J2EE application called *OracleBPMProcessRolesApp*. These roles are created in the same way the process roles corresponding to the swim lanes in a BPMN process are created. Stakeholders can have any combination of user, groups, application roles, and process roles as members. An important difference between stakeholder roles and other application roles such as process roles is that the membership for stakeholders is defined in the case database and not the OPSS policy store. This is to allow runtime and instance-specific changes to the stakeholder model. If you do define members to a stakeholder via OPSS, the case engine will not obey it. Stakeholder roles are created as application roles primarily to allow access control using permissions.

17.5.6.4 Permission Labels

Oracle ACM provides access control to various aspects of the case using the notion of a permission label. Permission labels are strings and denote the type of permission such as "Highly Confidential" and "Public—Read-Only." These can be any arbitrary labels. These labels can then be attached to various elements in the case. In version 12.1.3 (the version used in this book), only activities can have a label attached at design time. For all other elements, the case API can be used to attach labels at runtime.

For each label, three application roles are created—one for each action (READ, UDPATE, and INVOKE). For example, if you have label called "CONFIDENTIAL," then the three roles will be CONFIDENTIAL.READ.Role, CONFIDENTIAL.UPDATE.Role, and CONFIDENTIAL.INVOKE.Role. To associate permission labels with stakeholders, you add the appropriate role, group, or user to appropriate permission label role.

The following sections describe the steps to define the stakeholders and permission for our use case.

17.5.6.5 Define Roles

Before you create the stakeholders, application roles need to be created that will define the memberships. These roles can then be used to define stakeholder members, for assigning tasks, and for defining swim lanes in BPMN processes.

1. From your *Applications* tab in JDeveloper, open the *Organization* node under *BPM* as defined below.

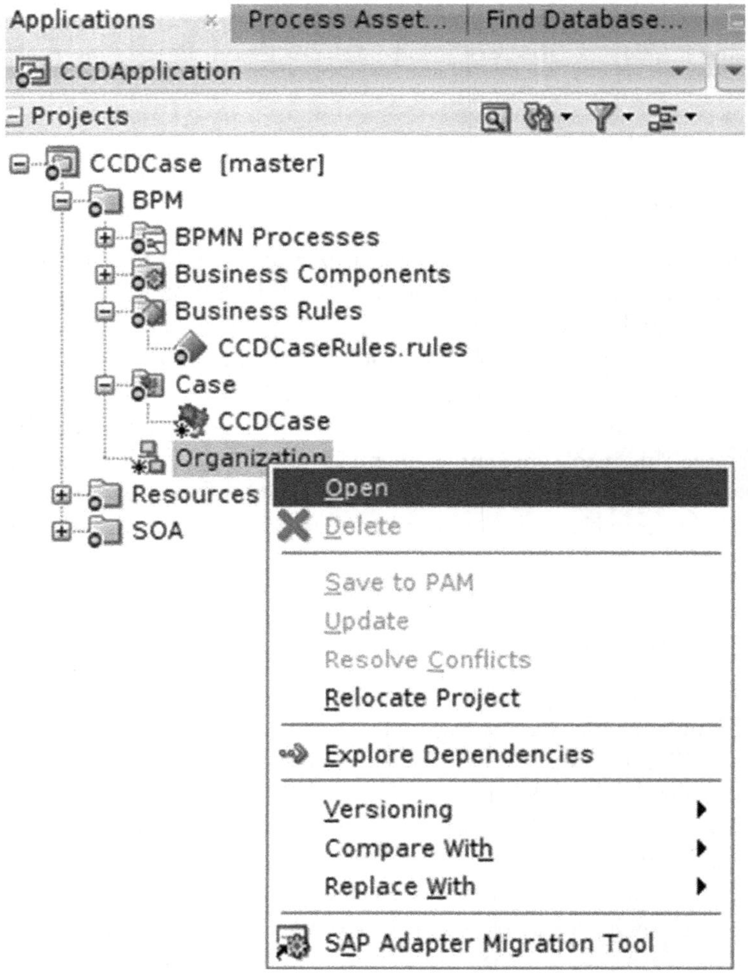

2. Click on the *Add* icon to open the dialog for the *Role* name.
3. Enter the value for *Name* of the role as *Analysts.*
4. Repeat steps 2 and 3 for adding the *CSR* role.

Note: As a best practice, role memberships should not be done at design time. You will do that once we deploy the application.

17.5.6.6 Define Stakeholders

1. Open the CCDCase case definition and select the *Stakeholders & Permissions* tab.
2. Add the following stakeholders by clicking on the *Add* icon for *Stakeholders* (Table 17.9):
3. Click on the *Add* icon next to *Dispute Analysts* stakeholder and select *Add Process Role.*

Table 17.9 Stakeholder Definition

Name	*Display Name*
Stakeholder_DisputeAnalysts	Dispute analysts
Stakeholder_CSR	Customer service representatives
Stakeholder_CaseManager	Case manager

4. You now see a new member with type *Process Role* added in the table as shown below. Click in the *Value* column and then on the icon at the right in the column to select the *Analysts* process role you defined earlier.

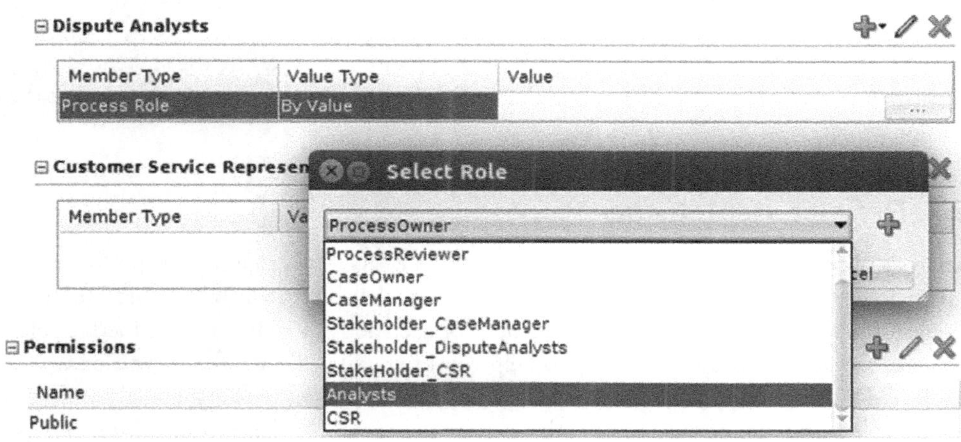

5. Repeat step 4 for customer service representatives. This time select the *CSR* role.
6. For the case manager role select *Add User* rather than *Add Process Role* like you did in the previous steps. In the *Value* column enter *weblogic*.

This completes the stakeholder definition.

Note: You can assign a case manager dynamically at runtime when you start the case. The WebLogic user is only used as the default case manager. This is explained in Section 17.6 in the later part of this chapter.

17.5.6.7 Define Permissions

All Oracle ACM projects, when created, are seeded with two default permission labels:

- Public
- Restricted

Table 17.10 Permission Definition

Name	*Display Name*
PublicRO	Public read-only
FullAccess	Full access
InvestigatorsAccess	Restricted access—investigators

As discussed earlier, these labels can be arbitrarily named and can be anything you want them to be. You define your own after removing the default labels.

1. Select the *Public* permission and delete it. Repeat that for *Restricted.*
2. Click on the *Add* icon to add the following new permissions (Table 17.10):

This completes your design time definition of the permissions. You define the stakeholder permissions using the Oracle Enterprise Manager Fusion Middleware Control, after you deploy the case application project.

17.5.7 Define Case Activities

The analysis in the previous chapter identified a number of activities that may be performed on the case. Along with the activities, their properties were also identified. This will be used to define the activities in the case. Refer to the analysis chapter for each activity that was identified. Table 17.11 summarizes the activity properties and will help you in creating the activity definitions.

Table 17.11 contains a property and type, which was not discussed in the analysis. This indicates the implementation of the activity. This can be either a *BPMN* process or a *human task.* The decision on whether to use BPMN instead of human task in case of work assignment activities depends on the following:

- Need for pre- and/or postprocessing in regards to the task.
- Need for handling human task outcomes. In the 12.1.3 version, the outcome from task-based activities cannot be saved to case data. You need to wrap that in a BPMN process so that the outcome can be processed in BPMN.
- Need to sequence tasks—task leads to another task or tasks in a predetermined sequence (structured flow).

The column *Conditional* is set to *Yes* if the analysis determined that this activity depends on one or more events.

The following sections describe the definition and implementation of the activities listed in Table 17.11. In order to keep the tutorial simple but still show all the important aspects of ACM, you will be creating very simple implementations of these activities. We will provide in the following paragraphs an example for a BPMN and a human task activity type.

Table 17.11 Case Activities and Their Properties

Activity Name	*Type*	*Auto/Manual*	*Reqd.?*	*Conditional?*	*Repeat*	*Input Types*	*Output Types*	*Save Output?*
PrepareCase	BPMN	Auto	Yes	No	No	DisputeBO	DisputeBO, InvestigationReportBO	Yes
ReviewChargeDispute	HT	Manual	Yes	Yes	Yes	DisputeBO	DisputeBO	Yes
RequestDocumentsFromCustomer	BPMN	Manual	No	Yes	Yes	DisputeBO, CustomerBO	None	No
WriteOffCharge	BPMN	Manual	No	Yes	No	DisputeBO	DisputeBO	Yes
InvestigateCharge	HT	Manual	Yes	Yes	No	DisputeBO, InvestigationReportBO	InvestigationReportBO	Yes
RequestDocumentsFromMerchant	BPMN	Manual	No	Yes	Yes	DisputeBO	None	No
InitiateChargeBack	BPMN	Manual	No	Yes	No	DisputeBO	None	No
NotifyCustomer	BPMN	Manual	No	No	Yes	DisputeBO CustomerBO	None	No
Notify Merchant	BPMN	Manual	No	Yes	Yes	DisputeBO	None	No

17.5.7.1 Create a BPMN-Based Activity

Start with the *PrepareCase* activity implementation. This activity is automatic and unconditional, which means it will be activated as soon as the case starts. And since it is unconditional, it will be initiated as soon as it is activated. Activities like these are useful for doing any initial processing before the case workers start working on the case. It is also a good way to update or initialize one or more case data objects. In your simplified implementation, you do the following:

- Update the status of the dispute to "*ASSIGNED*."
- Initialize the investigation report to be returned to the case.

To create a BPMN-based case activity, you need to first create a BPMN process and then create an activity from this process. The following section describes the steps using *PrepareCase* as an example.

Create PrepareCase BPMN process:

1. In the *Projects* browser, right-click on *BPM→BPMN Processes* and select *New→BPMN 2.0 Process…* as shown in the following figure:

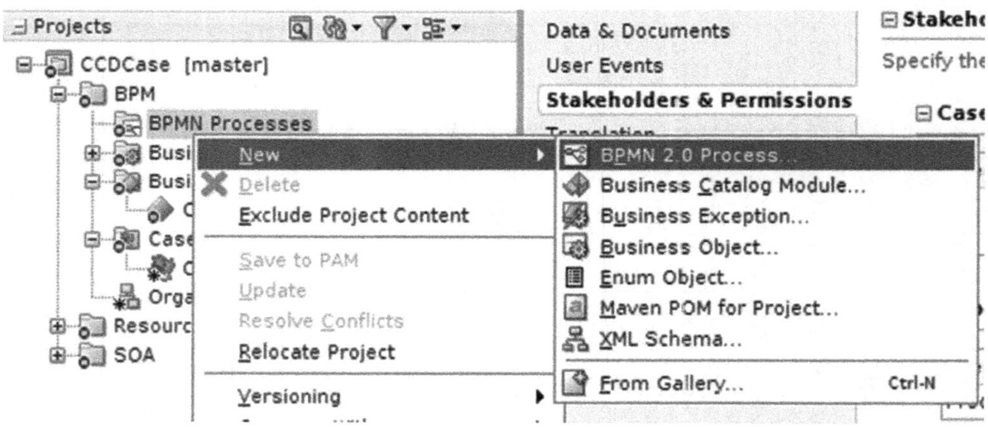

2. Name the process *PrepareCaseProcess* and accept the other defaults and click on *Next.*

Case activities implemented as BPMN processes can be either synchronous or asynchronous. If a process is modeled as an asynchronous process, make sure the process has an end message event (that is, it is not a one-way asynchronous process); otherwise the activity will be treated by the case as "active" perpetually.

3. The process you are creating should take dispute details as an input and return the updated dispute details back to the case.

At the *Arguments* step in the *BPMN 2.0 Process Wizard* window, click on the *Add* icon to add an input argument. Enter the argument name as *disputeDetails* and select *Browse...* in the *Type* dropdown list.

4. Select *DisputeBO* from the list shown below.

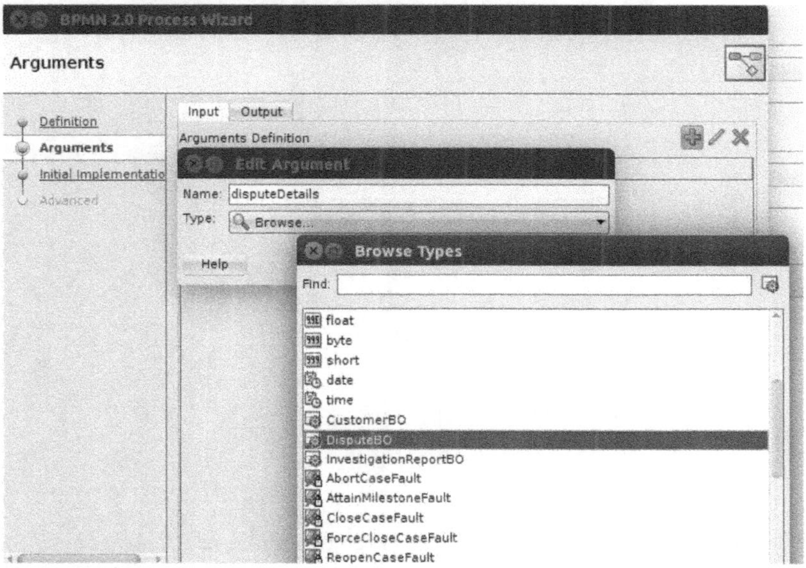

5. Switch to the *Output* tab and repeat the above steps. Name the argument *updatedDisputeDetails*. Add another argument and name it *investigationReport* and for the type, chose *InvestigationReportBO* from the type *List of Values*.
6. Click on *Finish* to create the BPMN process. You should see a simple process with a start and end message event.

In the following steps you add a process data object to hold the dispute details received as input and then update status attribute in the object.

7. In the *PrepareCaseProcess* structure panel, right-click on the *Process Data Object* and select *New*.
8. In the *Create Data Object* pop-up, enter the name as *disputeDetailsDO* and select *DisputBO* as the type (select *Browse* to show the type *Browser*). Keep other defaults and click *OK* to complete.
9. Repeat step 8 for *investigationReportDO* of type *InvestigationReportBO*.
10. Right-click on the *Start* node and select *Properties* to open the properties window. Switch to the *Implementation* tab.
11. Click on *Data Associations* and drag *disputeDetails* from under *Arguments* to *disputeDetailsDO* under *Data Objects*. Click *OK* to complete.

12. Drag and drop the *Script* task from the component ribbon above the process model to the process between the *Start* and the *End* nodes as shown below.

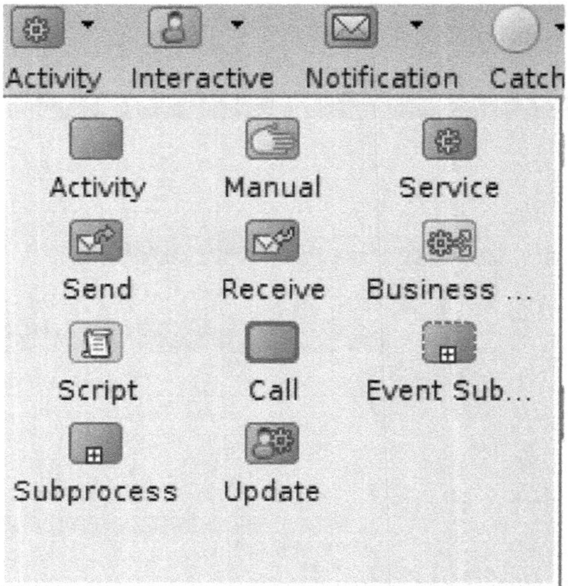

13. In the properties window for the Script, enter the name as *Update Data*. Switch to the *Implementation* tab and click on *Data Association*. In the *Data Association* window, expand the *disputeDetailsDO*. Right-click on the attribute named *status* under *disputeDetailsDO* and select *Expression*, to open the *Expression Builder*. Type in "ASSIGNED" (including the enclosing quotes) in the *Expression:* field. Click *OK*.
14. Drag *PrepareCaseProcess→Data Objects→disputeDetailsDO→disputeId* from the left-hand side to *PrepareCaseProcess→Data Objects→investigationReportDO→disputeId* on the right-hand side as shown below.

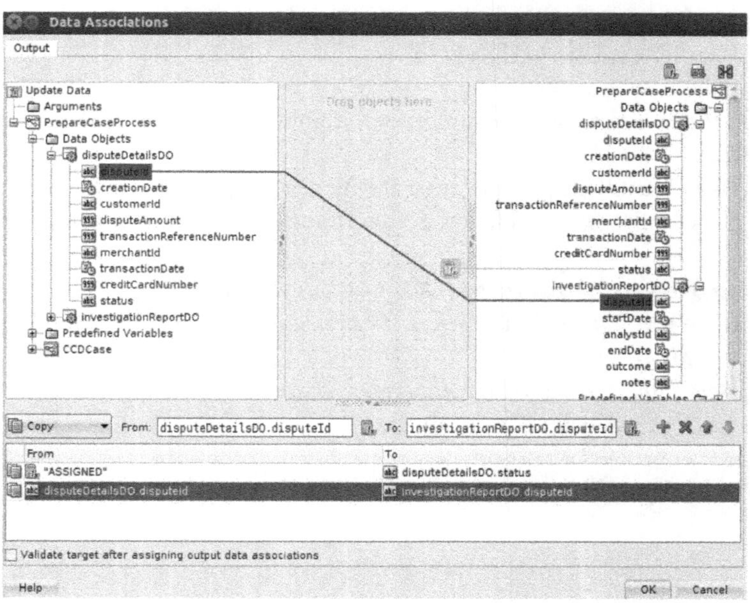

15. Click *OK* to complete. Your process should look like this:

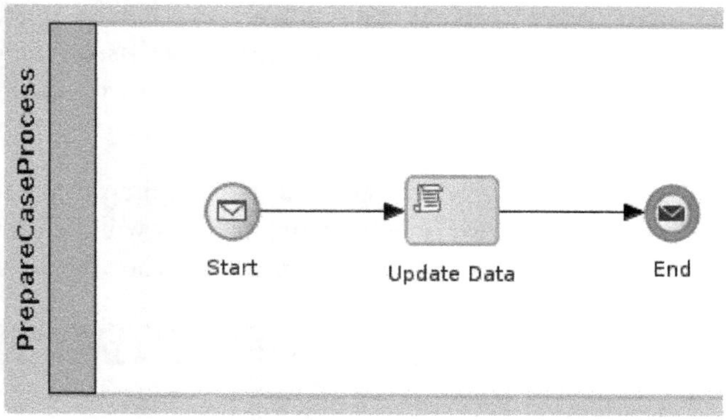

16. The last step copies the data to the output so that it can be returned to case. Right-click on the *End* node and select *Properties*. Switch to *Implementation* tab and click on *Data Associations*. In the *Data Associations* window, drag *disputeDetailsDO* from under *Data Objects* to *udpatedDisputeDetails* under *Arguments*. Similarly drag *investigationReportDO* to *investigationReport*.
17. Click *OK* to complete and click on *Save All* to save the project.

Create PrepareCase Activity:
Now that the BPMN process for PrepareCase is complete, you can define the activity for it.

1. Right-click on the *PrepareCaseProcess* under *CCDCase→BPM→BPMN Processes* in the *Projects* browser panel. In the pop-up menu, select *Promote as Case Activity*. Enter the name as *PrepareCase* and display name as *Prepare Case*. This will open the PrepareCase activity page.
2. Refer to Table 17.11 and complete the definition.
3. Make sure you check *Save Output as case data* for both output parameters. Your completed activity definition should look like this:

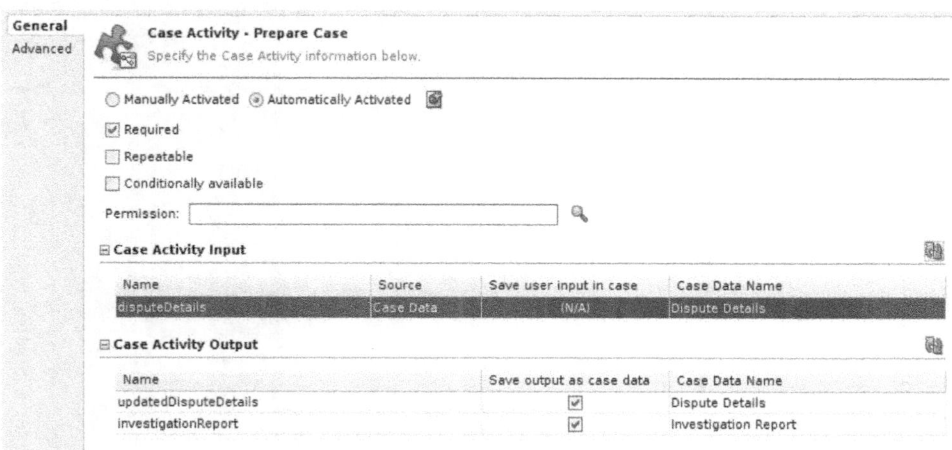

This completes the definition for the PrepareCase activity. Similarly, using Table 17.11, create activities that are of type BPMN.

17.5.7.2 Create a Human Task–Based Case Activity

We have identified two activities that are based on human task. The following steps describe, using the InvestigateCharge as an example, how to create a human task–based activity. A human task is comprised of two parts: a task definition and a task form. You start with the task definition. *Create InvestigateChargeTask human task*:

1. Make sure *CCDCase* in the *Projects* browser is selected and press CTRL+N to open the *New Gallery* window. In the search box, type in "Human." This will filter down the list to two items. Select the *Human Task (Service Components)* item as shown below.

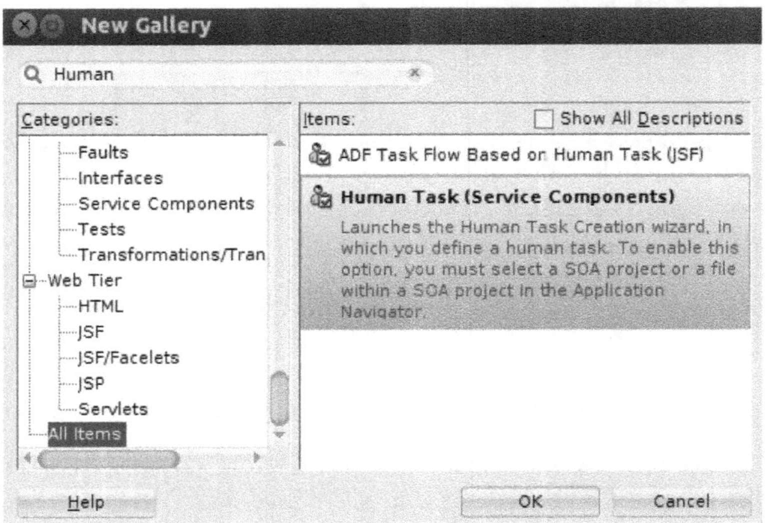

2. This will open the *Create Human Task* pop-up window. Enter the name of the task as *InvestigateChargeTask*. Keep other defaults and click *OK* to complete. This will open the *InvestigateChargeTask* task definition.
3. Select the *Assignment* tab and drag the *SingleParticipant* component from the *WorkflowEditor* palette into *Stage1* box as shown below.

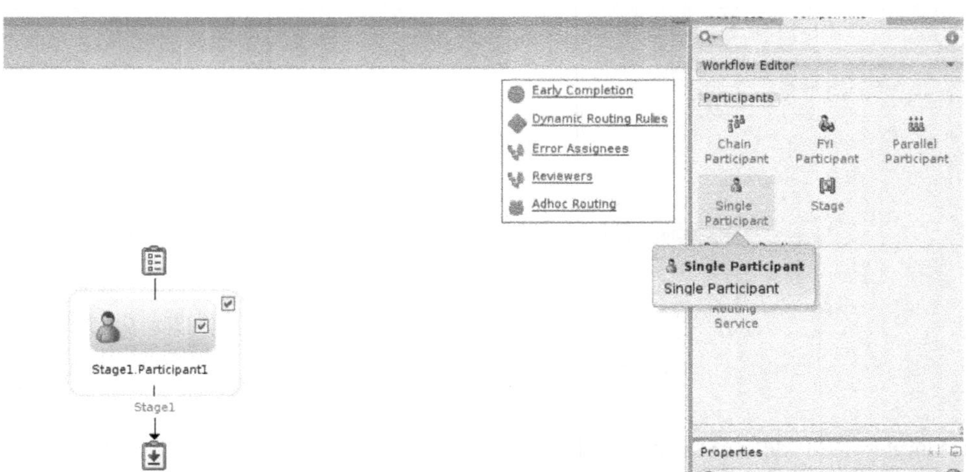

4. Double-click on the *Stage1.Participant1* to open the *Edit Participant Type* window.
5. Click on the *Add* button and select *Add Application Role*. In the value column type in *CCDCase.Analysts* as shown below.

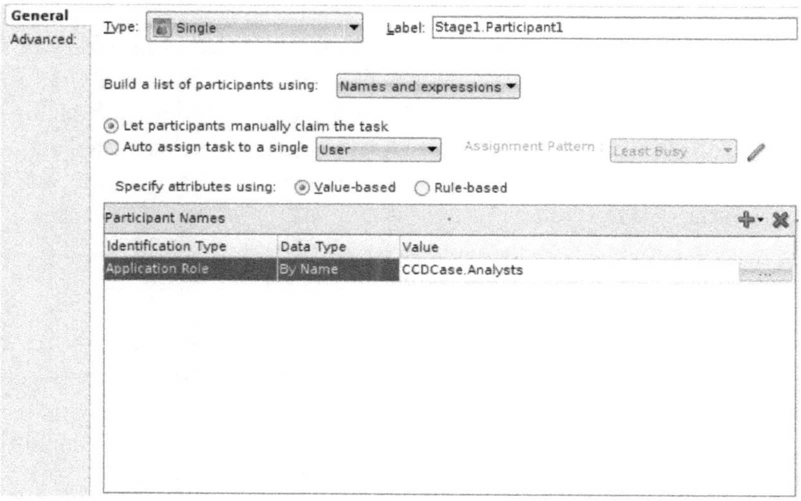

6. Click *OK* to complete and *Save All* to save.
7. In the following steps you define the data elements that will be used by the task. Refer to Table 17.11 for the input parameters for the *InvestigateCharge* activity.
8. Select the *Data* tab and click the *Add* icon and select *Add other parameter* from the list to open the *Add Task Parameter* window. Make sure *Variable* is selected and select *Element*. Click on the search corresponding to the element field to open the *Type Chooser* window.
9. Select *Project Schema Files →DisputeBO.xsd→DisputeBO* and click *OK*. Back in the *Add Task Parameter* window, select *Editable via Worklist* and click *OK* to complete.
10. Repeat steps 8 and 9 and this time select *Project Schema Files→InvestigationReportBO.xsd→InvestigationReportBO*.
11. Select the *General* tab to define the task properties. For *Task Title*, enter *Investigate Charge Dispute #* and then select the *Expression Editor* icon to open the *Expression Builder* window. In the expression builder, select *task:task→task:payload→ns1:DisputeBO→ns1:disputeId* and click on *Insert Into Expression* to copy the expression. Click *OK* to complete.

Note: The name space ***ns1*** may be different in your project.

12. Enter *Investigate Credit Card Charge* for *Description*.
13. Click on the *Search* icon for *Outcomes* and unselect *APPROVE* and *REJECT* and select *OK* from the list of outcomes. Click on *OK* to close the *Outcomes Dialog* window.
14. In the *Application Context* enter *OracleBPMProcessRolesApp*. This defines the application stripe to use for application roles. This is the default application stripe for all BPM roles. Make sure the name is correctly entered; otherwise your task will not get assigned correctly.
15. Your task definition is complete at this point.

Create Task Form for InvestigateCharge Task:
Most tasks require some form to be presented to the assignee to be completed as part of the task. You can create these forms in a number of ways—autogenerate, use task-form wizard, build from scratch or use web forms in the browser-based BPM composer. For the purpose of this tutorial you will use the autogenerate option.

In the *InvestigateChargeTask.task* page, click on *Form* and select *Auto-Generate Task Form* to open the *Create Project* window. Enter the name of the project as *InvestigateChargeTaskForm* and click *OK* to complete. This will create a new ADF project that will contain the autogenerated task form and associated artifacts. Wait for the taskDetails1.jspx page to be created and click *Save All* to save all the projects. Typically you would rearrange the fields in the page to be more presentable. For now, you keep the default layout.

17.5.7.2.1 Create Investigate Charge Activity

1. In the *Projects* browser select *CCDCase→BPM→Human Tasks→InvestigateChargeTask.task*, then right-click and *Promote as Case Activity*. Enter the *Name* as *InvestigateCharge* and *Display Name* as *Investigate Charge.*
2. In the InvestigateCharge activity definition page, select *Required*. Change the source of disputeBO and investigationReportBO case activity input to case data.
3. Click on the *Search* icon for the *Permission* and select InvestigatorAccess permission. This will restrict this activity to only those users that have InvestigatorAccess permission granted. You will be setting this up later in the exercise using the Fusion Middleware Control.
4. Select *Save output as case data* for both the case activity output parameters. Your completed definition should look like this:

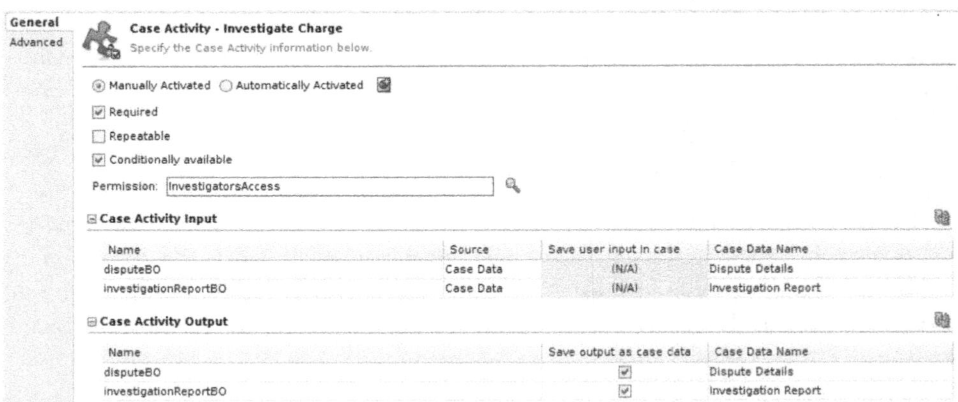

This completes the definition for the *InvestigateCharge* activity. Similarly, create *ReviewChargeDispute* Human Task activity by referring to the Table 7.11 and following the same steps as for *InvestigateCharge* task. For task participant use the Application Role *CCDCase.CSR.*

17.5.8 Define the Rules

Your case definition at this point in the exercise is essentially complete. The case can be deployed now and used. But you will only see activities that you have defined as being unconditional. All conditional activities will require rules to be defined that will enable (activate) these activities so that they can be executed (either manually or automatically). If you would like to see the case in action, without the conditional activities, you can follow the instructions in Section 17.6.

In the following sections you define the rules for activating activities as well as changing the milestone status based on the analysis done in the previous chapter. One of the ways to be productive with defining rules is to tabulate all the different dependencies in a spreadsheet. You start with the mind map and look at all the "Depends on" nodes. Create separate tables for each type of event. For example, in the following figure, *Review Charge Dispute* activity depends on an activity to be completed.

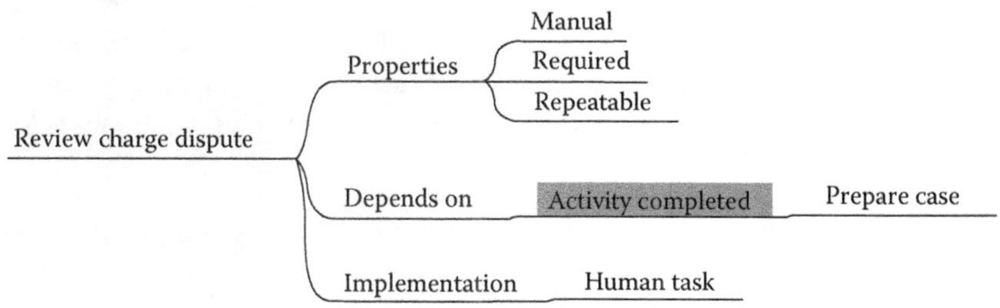

As shown below, in this case it is an activity event, whereas it is a milestone event for *the Investigate Charge* activity.

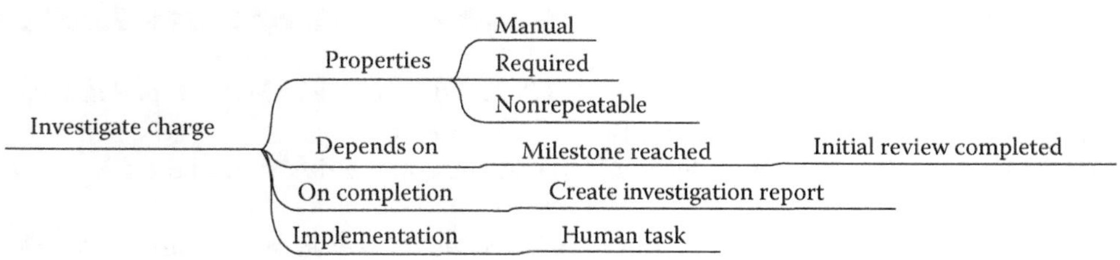

By using this method, you can create tables such as these. Table 17.12 captures all actions to be taken when specific activity events occur.

Start with defining rules for the activity events and then move to milestone and user events.

Table 17.12 Activity Event Actions

Activity Event	*Activity Name*	*Additional Condition*	*Action*	*Name*
Completed	Prepare case	–	Activate	Review charge dispute
Completed	Review charge dispute	Dispute amount ≤ 25	Activate	Write-off charge
Completed	Review charge dispute	–	Reach milestone	Initial review completed (A01)
Activated	Review charge dispute	–	Activate	Request document from customer
Activated	Investigate charge	–	Reach milestone	Analysis started
Activated	Initiate chargeback	–	Reach milestone	Merchant interaction started
Completed	Investigate charge	–	Reach milestone	Analysis completed

17.5.8.1 Activity Event Rules

The Table 17.12 is best defined using a decision table in Oracle Business Rules. Following steps guide you through defining this decision table.

1. Before you begin, you need to make sure the rules dictionary is updated with the names of activities and milestones.

> There is an issue with the 12.1.3 release where the dictionary is updated only when changes to case data are made. So to force a dictionary update, add a dummy case data, save the project, delete the dummy case data, and then save the project again as shown below.

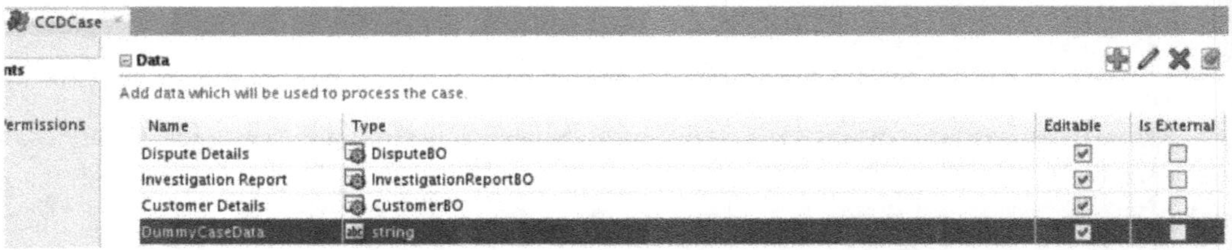

2. From the *Projects* browser select *CCDCase→BPM→Business Rules→CCDCaseRules.rules* and double-click to open it in the Oracle Business Rules editor.
3. Click on the *CCDCaseRules* under *Rule Sets* and click on the *Add* icon in the *Decision Tables* column.
4. Click on *Decision Table 1*, change the name to *Activity Event Rules*, and press *ENTER*. The following describes the rule for the first row in Table 17.12.
5. Click on *Add* icon and select *Condition*. This will add a row for the new condition. Double-click in the ***C1*** cell under *Conditions* column heading to open a drop-down with a list of *Value Options*. In the text field, enter *CaseActivityEvent*. This will filter the list to show the *CaseActivityEvent* fact. Select *CaseActivityEvent→activityName*.
6. Click on the "?" in the *R1* column, select *COMPLETED*, and click *OK*.
7. Click on the *Add* icon and select *Condition*. Double-click on *C2* and select *CaseActivityEvent→activityName*.
8. Select *Activities* from the *Value Set* drop-down list as shown below.

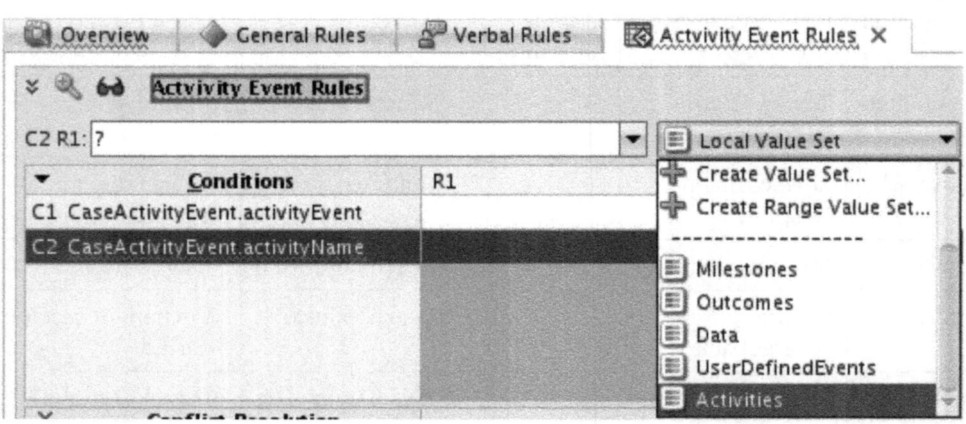

Click on the "?" under *R1* and select *PrepareCase* as shown below.

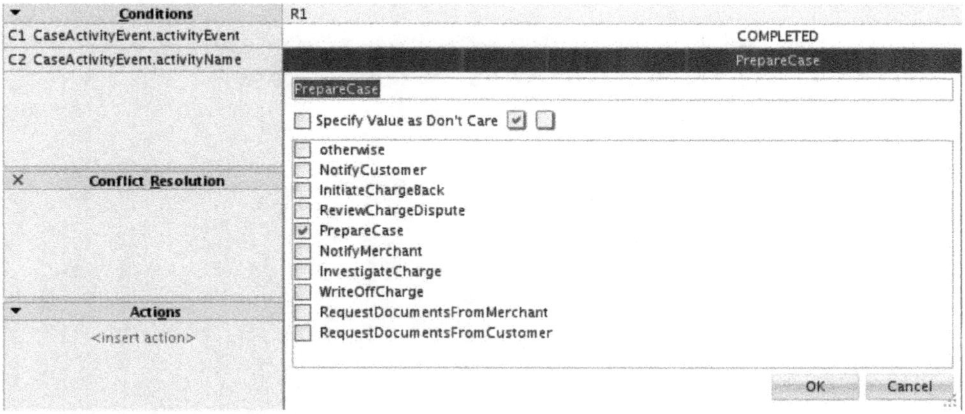

9. Click on the *Add* icon and select *Action→call*. This will add a new row under the *Actions* column on the bottom half of the table.
10. Double-click on *A1* under *Actions* and select *activateActivity*. In the *Arguments* table, click in the *Value* column select *Activity.ReviewChargeDispute* from the drop-down list as shown below. Go to the bottom-end of the drop-down list to locate the *Activities* object.

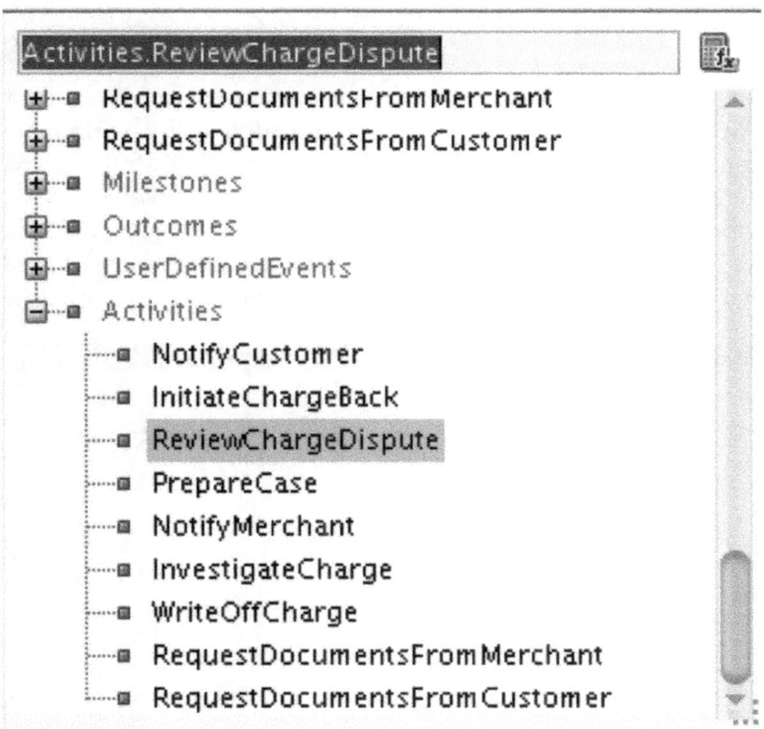

Select the *Parameterized* option.

11. Unselect *Always Selected.*
12. Back in the decision table, select *A1-R1* cell.

13. Your first rule, “activate *ReviewChargeDispute* when *PrepareCase* completes”, shown below, is now defined.

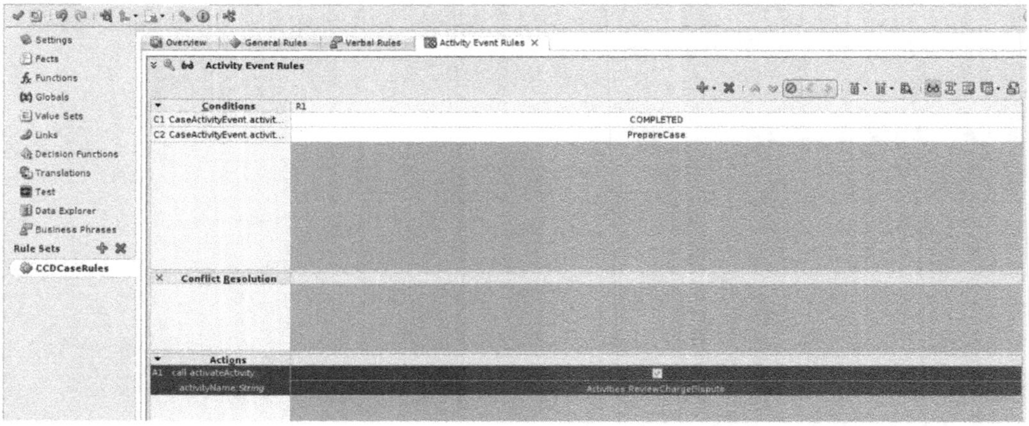

14. Now define the rule for the second row in the *Activity Event* table, which is “Activate WriteOff Charge when ReviewChargeDispute is completed and if dispute amount is < = 25.”

Click on the *Add* icon and select *Rule*.

15. It is a good practice to use a value set for ranges such as “more than 10 but less than 25.” Moreover, when using *Decision Tables*, value sets are required for selecting values in the rules column. Select *Value Sets* in the sidebar of the rules editor. Click on the *Add* icon and select *Range Value Set*. This will create a new value set named “Value Set 1.” Select this value set and edit it by clicking on the *Edit* icon to open the *Edit Range Value Set* window.
16. Change the *Name* to *WriteOffRange*. Click on the *Add* icon to insert a row in the *Range Values* table. This will add a row with endpoint as 0; change the value from 0 to *1*. Add another row and change the value of the first endpoint to *26*. You now have the range defined:

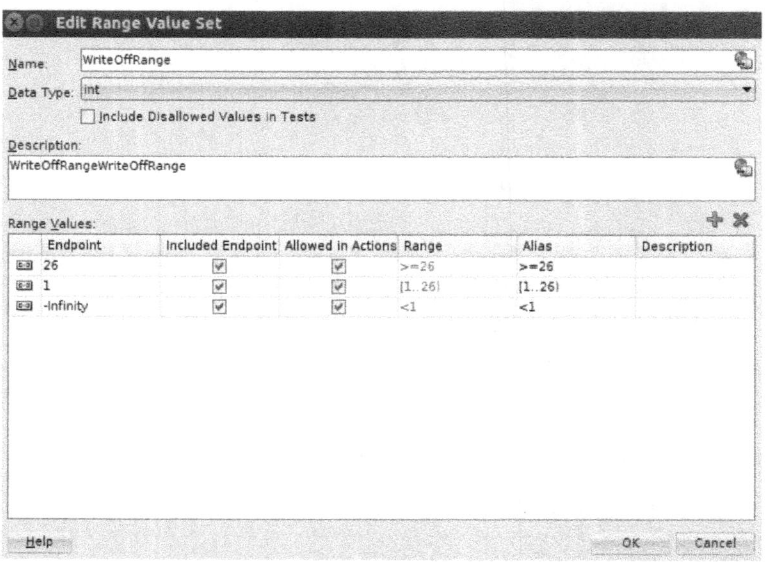

17. Select the *CCDCaseRules* under *Rule Sets* and you should see the decision table you have been working on. Since we already have conditions defined for *activityEvent* and *activityName*, you do not need to add new conditions. All you need to do is add a new rule that checks for the activity name to be *ReviewChargeDispute*. To do that, click on the *Add* button at the top and select *Rule*. This will add a new column *R2*. Select the cell *C1-R2* and it should open a drop-down list with activity event types. Select *COMPLETED*. In the *C2-R2* cell, select *ReviewChargeDispute*.
18. Now you need to define the action to be taken for this new rule. Since you already defined an action for activating an activity (*A1*), you change the value for this rule without having to add a new action. Click the cell *A1-R2* and select *Activities→WriteOffCharge*. Make sure you select the A1-R2 row so that it has a check marked for the cell.
19. This rule is still missing one condition. Writing off a charge is only allowed if the disputed amount is less than or equal to 25. So you need to add a new condition for this. Click on the *Add* icon and select *Condition*. In the new *C3* row, double-click to open the drop-down and select *DisputBOType→disputeAmount*. From the drop-down list for value sets, select the *WriteOffRange*. Click in the *C3-R1* cell and select *Specify Value as Don't Care*, since this particular condition is not relevant for the *R1* rule. In the *C3-R2* cell, select the *[1..26)*range (which is greater than or equal to 1 and less than or equal to 25). This completes the rule definition for the second dependency.

Repeat this for the remaining rows in the *Activity Events* table. Once you have completed all the rules for the activity events, your decision table should look as shown in the figure below.

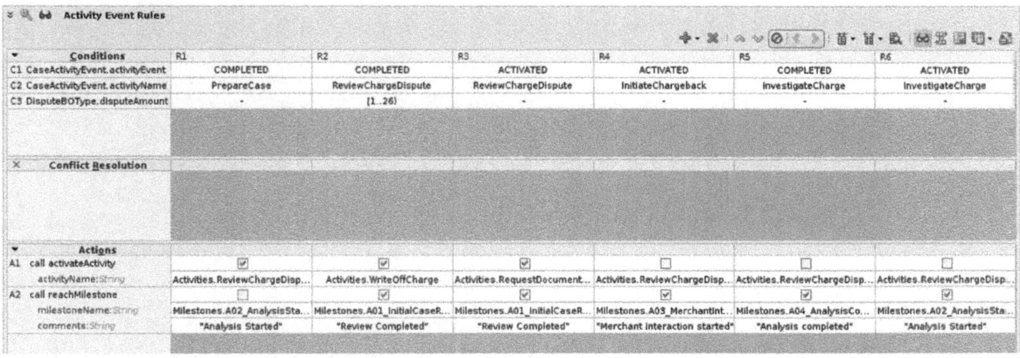

17.5.8.2 Milestone Event Rules

Following the same instructions as those for activity event rules, create a new decision named *Milestone Event Rules*. Use Table 17.13 to define your rules.

Here are some hints to help you with the creating these rules.

1. Use the fact named *CaseMilestoneEvent*. The relevant attributes in this fact are *milestoneEvent* for the event raised (*REACHED*, *REVOKED*, etc.) and *milestone*, which contains the name of the milestone.
2. For milestone names, make sure you select the *Milestone* value set.
3. Create a value set called *InvestigationReportOutcomes* that has the following values: *MerchantFault*, *OurFault*, and *CustomerFault*.

Table 17.13 Milestone Events

Milestone Event	*Milestone*	*Additional Condition*	*Action*	*Name*
Reached	Initial review completed	—	Activate	Investigate charge
Reached	Merchant interaction started	—	Activate	Request documents from merchant
Reached	Analysis complete	Result = Merchant fault	Activate	Initiate chargeback
Reached	Analysis complete	Result = Merchant fault	Activate	Notify merchant

4. For the additional condition (result = merchant fault), use the fact *InvestigationReportBOType.outcome*. Make sure you select the *InvestigationReportOutcomes* as the value set for this condition.
5. You will need to add more than one action for activating activities.

Once you complete your rules definition for the milestone events, your decision tables should look like this:

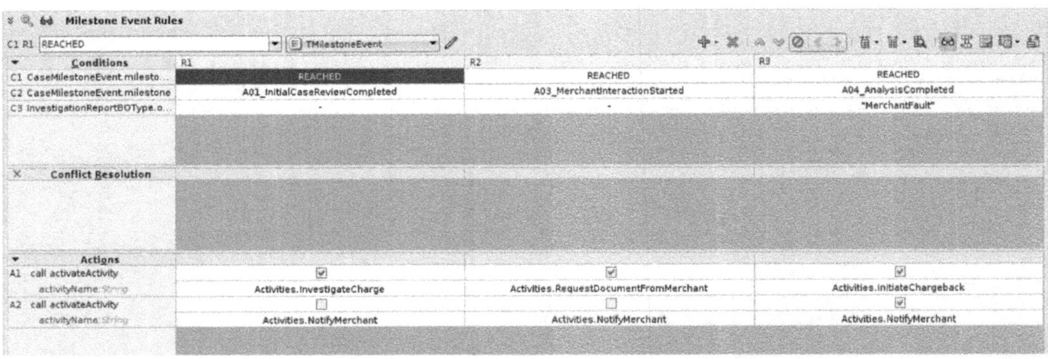

17.5.8.3 User Event Rules

We identified two user events that the user can raise while processing the case. The actions that need to be taken are defined in Table 17.14.

Define the rules for these two events by creating another decision table. This time, name it *User Event Rules*. Use the *fact UserDefinedEvent.eventName* in the conditions and make sure you select *UserDefinedEvents* as the value set for the rules.

Table 17.14 User Event Actions

Event Name	*Conditions*	*Actions*
Update requested by customer	—	Notify customer with updates
Probable fraud detected	—	Suspend case Notify customer Initiate fraud case

Note: For the purpose of this use case, you need to only define the rule for "Notify Customer."

Once you are done with defining the rules, you are ready for deploying and testing your first case-based application.

17.5.9 Resulting Application

The architecture of the Oracle SOA Suite is based upon the service composite architecture (SCA). Every SOA, BPM, and ACM application is combined together in SOA composites, based upon SCA. These composites are composed together with the different Oracle SOA-based technologies, such as BPMN activities, human tasks, rules, BPEL, events, adapters, and (of course) ACM. The resulting application is packaged and installed on the Oracle SOA Suite on top of the WebLogic Server.

The resulting composite for the CCDCase application is shown in the figure below.

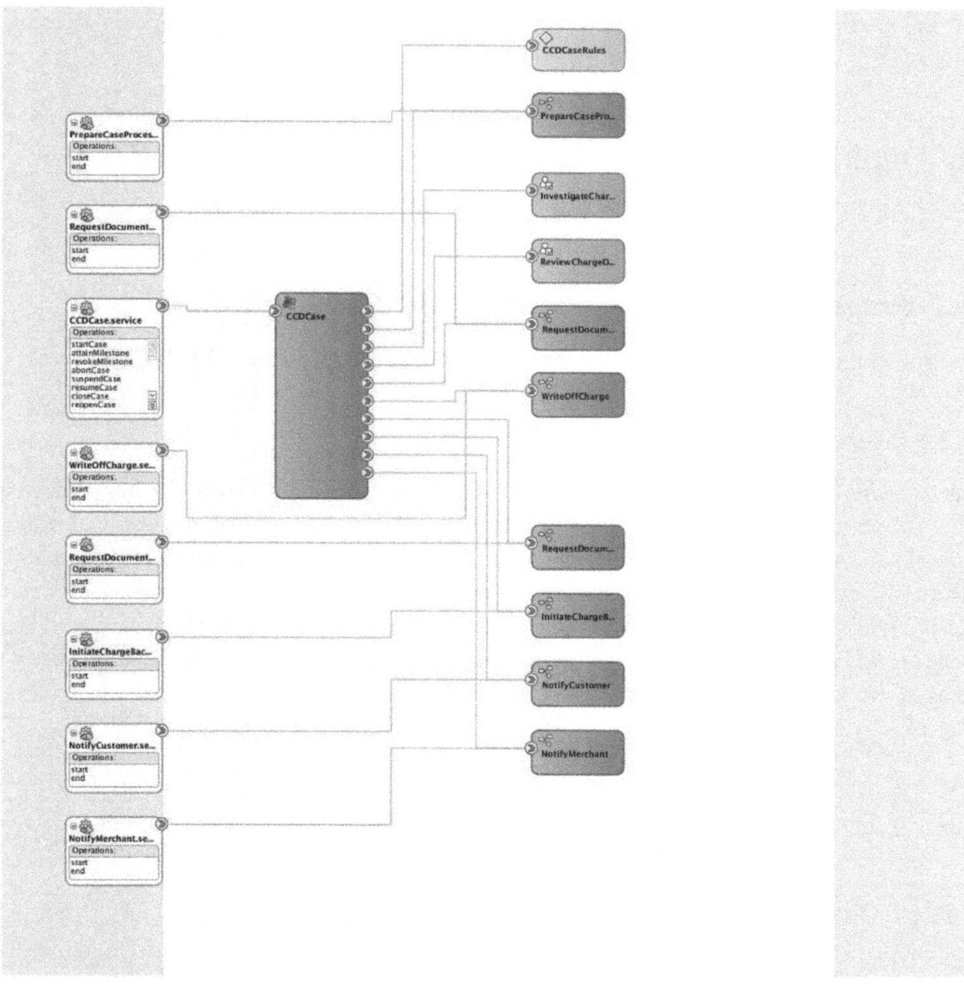

Every Oracle ACM application is exposed via web services containing a standard set of operations that can be used to control the case execution, such as startCase, closeCase, and attainMilestone, as shown in the figure below.

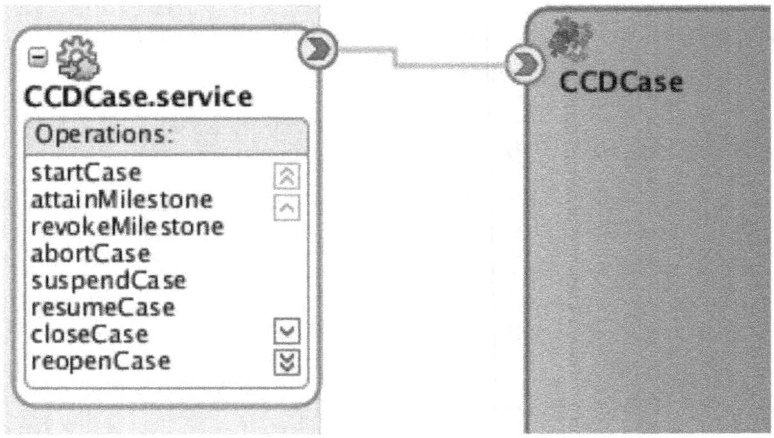

In the next chapter we will use this service to start the CCDCase and work on a credit card dispute case.

17.6 Deploy and Test

This section describes the steps for deploying the application and then using it.

17.6.1 Prepare Server for Deployment and Test

Before you can deploy your application, you need to start the integrated WebLogic Server.

17.6.1.1 Start the Integrated WebLogic Server

Navigate to *Run→Start Server* instance from the JDeveloper menu. If this is the first time you are starting the server, you will be prompted to provide the administrator name, password, and the port number for the server. Keep the default port number (*7101*) and enter the user name as *weblogic* and password as *welcome1*. The server should start in about 5–8 minutes (the first time it will take a lot longer as it will create a new domain first and then start the server). Once it starts up, you should see the message *SOA Platform is running and accepting requests* in the *Running: IntegratedWeblogicServer – Log* panel as shown below.

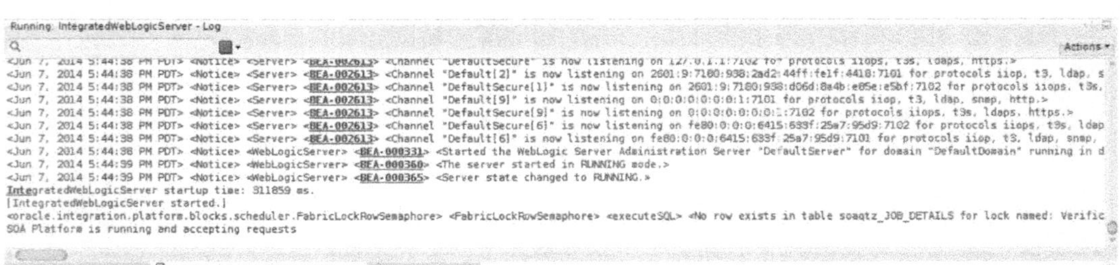

Note: If you do not see the panel, press <Control+Shift+L>

17.6.1.2 Enable Development Mode

The default audit-level setting for the SOA infrastructure server is production, which reduces the amount of information logged as part of the instance audit trail. This is optimal for most production deployments but is not very useful during development. Change the audit level to development so that you can get detail audit trail for the case instances you create.

1. Using your web browser, login to http://localhost:7101/em as *weblogic* user with *welcome1* as the password
2. In the *Target Navigation* panel on the left, expand the *SOA* folder and select *soa-infra (DefaultServer).* On the *soa-infra* page, click on the *SOA Insfrastructure* drop-down list and select *SOA Administration→Common Properties* as shown in the figure below.

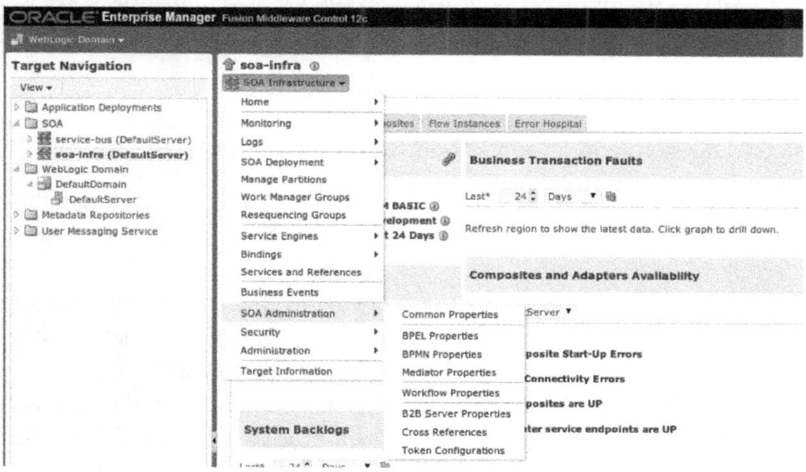

3. In the SOA infrastructure common properties page, select *Development* from the *Audit Level* drop-down list and click the *Apply* button on the top right of the page.

17.6.1.3 Create Test Users

When the integrated server is installed, three users are created, one of them being WebLogic—the administrator. To test your case application, you need a few users that will be added to the different process roles you defined while modeling the case. You create the users at this time and add them to the appropriate process roles after the case application is deployed.

1. In the *Target Navigation* panel, select *WebLogic Domain→DefaultDomain.*
2. In the *DefaultDomain* page that is displayed, select *Security→Users and Groups* from the *WebLogic Domain* drop-down list.
3. Make sure you have the *Users* tab selected and click on the *Create* button to open the *Create A New User* form. Use the following values to create the users (Table 17.15):

Table 17.15 Test Users

Name	*Description*	*Provider*	*Password*
jcooper	James Cooper	DefaultAuthenticator	welcome1
jstein	John Steinbeck	DefaultAuthenticator	welcome1
wshake	William Shakespeare	DefaultAuthenticator	welcome1

17.6.2 Deploy Case Application

Now that the server is running and configured, you can deploy the case application. There are following four different deployments that you need to do, though the order in which they are done is not important:

- CCD case—case composite project
- CCD case data forms—the J2EE application that contains the data forms
- Review charge dispute task form—the J2EE application that contains the form for the review charge dispute task
- Investigate charge task form—the J2EE application that contains the form for the investigate charge task

17.6.2.1 Deploy the Case Composite

To deploy the CCDCase composite application, follow these steps:

1. In the *Projects* browser in JDeveloper, select the *CCDCase* project and right-click. In the pop-up menu, select *Deploy→CCDCase ....*
2. Select *Deploy to Application Server* and click on *Next.*
3. Set the *New Revision ID* to *1.0* and select *Overwrite any existing composites with the same revision ID* and uncheck *Keep running instances after redeployment.* Click on *Next* to continue.
4. Click *Next* in the *Task flow Deployment* step without selecting anything.
5. Select *IntegratedWebLogicServer* and click *Next* and then *Finish* on the next step.
6. As shown below this will initiate the deployment process. Watch the *Deployment* tab in the log window to see the deployment process. Once the deployment is complete you should see the *Deployment finished* message.

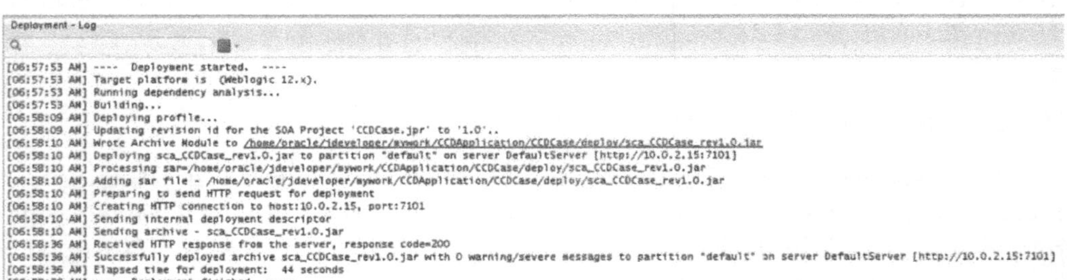

17.6.2.2 Deploy Case Data Forms Application

The case data form application is a J2EE application and should be deployed from the *Application* menu.

1. Select *Application→Deploy→CCDCaseDataForms...*
2. Select *Deploy to Application Server* and click on *Next.*

3. Select *IntegratedWebLogicServer* and click on *Next* and then click on *Finish* to begin deployment. If you see the *Oracle Deployment Configuration* pop-up show up, click on *Deploy* to continue as shown below.

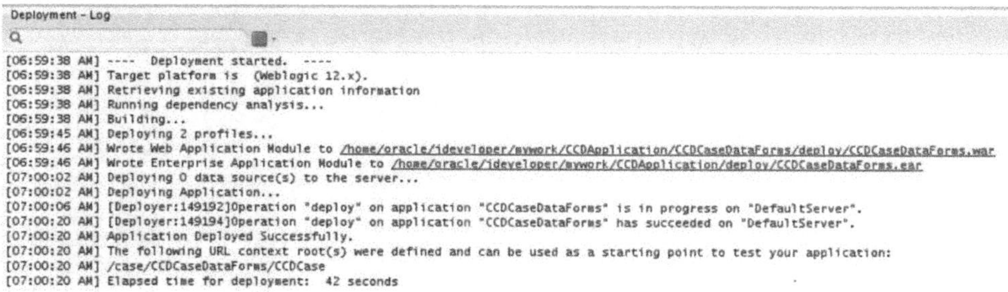

17.6.2.3 Deploy Task Form Applications

The last part of the deployment is the deploying of the task forms you generated. The process for deploying these is the same as that for the case data forms since these forms are also standard J2EE applications based on ADF.

Follow the instruction in the previous section to deploy the following:

- Review charge dispute task form
- Investigate charge task form

17.6.3 Create a Case Instance

You now have everything deployed and are now ready to test the application.

As described in Section 17.5.9, every Oracle ACM application is controlled via a standard set of web service operations. A new case is created by invoking the `startCase` operation on the case service. Any web service client, such as SOAPUI (http://www.soapui.org/), can be used to initiate a case. Your WebLogic Server also provides a simple web service test client that can be used to invoke web services. You use this client for your case.

The `startCase` operation takes one parameter—`startCaseInputMessage`, which in turn contains the full case object. All elements in the case object are optional. You can call `startCase` with an empty case object by just passing in`<ns:case/>` and a case will still be created. For your first test, you use an XML document defined in Appendix 17.A. See Section 17.3 for the locations where to obtain this schema.

There are two important parts of the case in this test data:

- The stakeholder member—this is one of the many ways to add one or more stakeholders and members at runtime. The test XML is adding *jcooper* as the case manager. The name `Stakeholder _ CaseManager` corresponds to the name that you gave the case manager stakeholder in the case model.
- Case data—this is how you can create instance of one or more case object on case startup. In this test, you see that there are two data objects. The first is the dispute details and the second is the corresponding customer details.

This is not the only way to create a case. Typically you would either have a mediator, a BPMN, or a BPEL component in the composite wired to the case component. This component would capture basic required information for creating a case and in turn will build the case object using an XSLT and then call the `startCase` method in the case service.

The following steps describe how to create a new case instance:

1. Using your web browser open the URL http://localhost:7101/soa-infra. You should see a page that looks something like the figure below:

2. Select the link *TestCCDCase.service*. This will open the *Web Services Test Client* page and you should see the different operations provided by the case service such as `startCase`, `attainMilestone`, and `revokeMilestone`.
3. Click on the *Test* button for the `startCase` operation to navigate to the test page for this operation. The default view is a form-based view. Since you are going to use a precreated XML input, click on the *Raw Message* button to switch to XML mode.
4. Clear the XML in the text box and copy and paste the XML from the test XML document, presented in Section 17.A.2 and click on *Invoke* to call the service.
5. Once the call returns successfully, you should see the response from the case that will contain the case ID assigned to the new case as shown below.

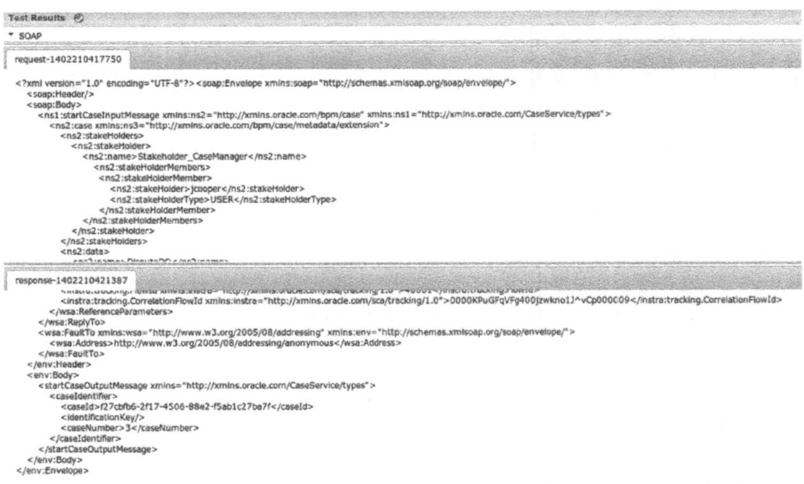

17.6.4 Working on the Case

Once a case is created, case participants use the BPM Workspace application to work on their cases. The BPM Workspace out of the box available with Oracle BPM, is a browser-based application that provides all the functions required to participate in business processes—either structured on unstructured. It provides the following key functions:

- Case workspace
- Comprehensive worklist
- Process tracking
- Process dashboard
- Administration

For your use case, you will primarily be using the case workspace. Before you start working on the case, let us take a quick tour of the case workspace. You can find more detailed information on using the BPM Workspace in the Oracle BPM 12.1.3 documentation (https://docs.oracle.com/middleware/1213/bpm/bpm-user/bpmug_ws_gt_strt.htm#BPMUG115).

17.6.4.1 Case Workspace

Oracle ACM provides a web-based user interface, the case workspace, which provides an overview on the complete state of the case and enables executing activities on the case. The figure below shows an example of the case workspace. The areas highlighted and numbered are described in the following:

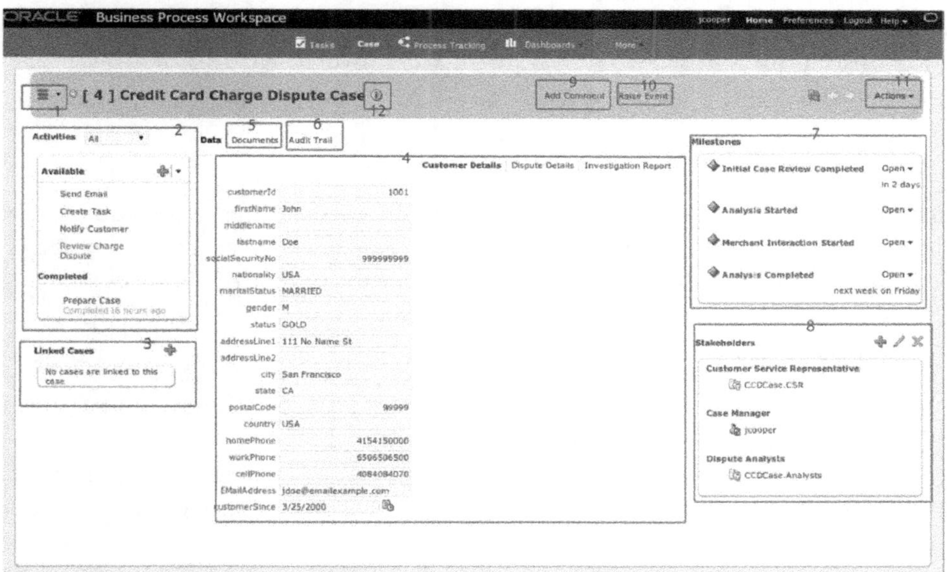

1. Clicking on this opens the case list view where you can see all the cases that you are a participant in. You can also search for cases using different case attributes and metadata.
2. It is the activity panel and shows all available, running, and completed activities. Highlighted activities indicate required activities. The *Add* icon allows case participants to add activities to the list of available activities.
3. The *Linked Cases* panel shows all the cases that are linked to this case. You can also create new links using the *Add* button. Links can define one of four predefined relationships; related-to, depends-on, duplicate-of, and subcase. All of these except the subcase can be defined at runtime only. Subcase relationships can be defined either at runtime or design time. Subcases are beyond the scope of this book and hence have not been discussed.
4. The center panel is a tabbed panel and shows the details of the different case data. There will be one link for each case data object that has been instantiated. If an instance of a case data

object is not created, there will not be a link for it. For the details to show up, you need to build and deploy a data form, which you have done already.

5. Switching the tab to *Documents* allows you to add, update, and download documents from the configured CMS.
6. The *Audit Trail* shows a trail of all the events that have occurred since the start of the case.
7. The *Milestones* panel shows all the milestones defined for the case. The case worker can manually update the state of the milestone by switching the *Open* state to *Completed*. If a milestone has a deadline defined, you will see when it is due. For example, in the figure it shows that the *Initial Case Review Completed* milestone is due in 2 days.
8. Stakeholders can be managed in the workspace using this panel. Selecting the stakeholder and clicking on the *Edit* button allows you to add new members to the case. Clicking on the *Add* button allows you to add a new stakeholder and the members. Note that any changes done to the stakeholder model at runtime are specific to that case only.
9. The *Add Comment* link allows case participants to insert comments in the audit trail. This is very useful to document the progress or any information pertinent to the case.
10. The *Raise Event* link allows case participants to raise user-defined events. These events have to be defined in the case model.
11. The *Actions* drop-down list allows case workers to close, suspend, resume, or abort the case.
12. Clicking on this icon shows the case instance information such as priority, category, start date, and due date.

17.6.4.2 Update Process Roles

You defined two process roles in your case project—`CCDCase.CSR` and `CCDCase.Analysts`. But these did not specify the members. Although you can define the membership at design time, it is better to manage roles using the BPM Workspace. Before you work on the case, add members to these roles. The following steps describe how to do that.

1. Open the URL http://localhost:7101/bpm/workspace. This is the URL for the BPM Workspace. Log-in as *weblogic* with password as *welcome1*. Make sure you started the integrated WebLogic Server, as described in Section 17.6.1.1
2. Once you have successfully logged in to the workspace, click on the *Administration* link at the top of the page. Click on the *Roles* link, if it is not already selected. You should see the roles administration page:

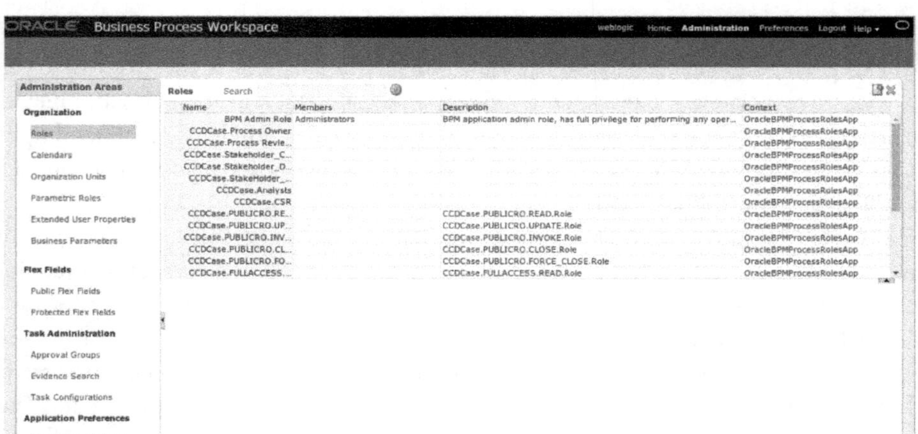

3. Click on the *CCDCase.Analysts* in the *Roles* table. This will open up the *Details: CCDCase. Analysts* panel.
4. Click on the *Create* icon in the *Members* table to open the identity browser where you can search for roles, groups, and users to add.
5. Change the selection from *All* to *Users* and enter *jstein* in the search field and click on *search*. You should see the user jstein that you added earlier. Select the row and click on *OK* to add.
6. Click on *Save* to save the changes.
7. Repeat steps 3 through 6. This time, choose *CCDCase.CSR* and add the user *wshake* to it. Make sure you click on *Save* when done.
8. Log-out of the workspace.

17.6.4.3 Grant Investigator Access Permission

Earlier in the exercise you associated the permission *InvestigatorsAccess* to the *Investigate Charge* activity so that only appropriately privileged users can initiate this activity. You define the users that have this privilege using the Fusion Middleware Control.

1. Open the Fusion Middleware Control in the browser by navigating to http://localhost:7101/em.
2. Login as *weblogic* with password as *welcome1*.
3. Open *Application Deployments→OracleBPMProcessRolesApp→OracleBPMProcessRolesApp(DefaultServer)*.
4. Right-click and select *Security→Application Roles* shown below.

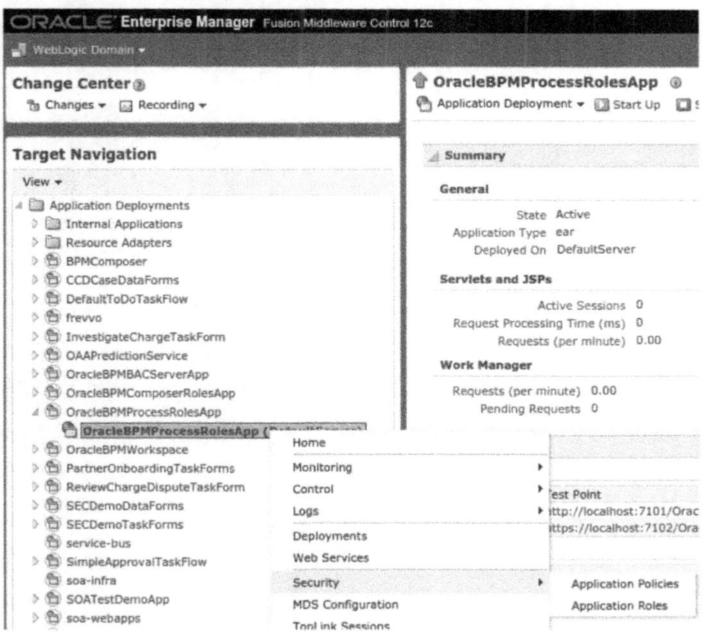

5. In the *Search* panel, enter the string *CCDCase.INVEST* and click to search. This should show you the different application roles as shown in the following figure that were automatically created for each of your permissions defined in the case. Each of these roles is used to control different operations such as READ (read document, read data, read audit trail, etc.), UPDATE (update any of the case elements), CLOSE (close case), FORCE_CLOSE (force close a case when there are required activities open), and INVOKE (invoke an activity or raise an event).

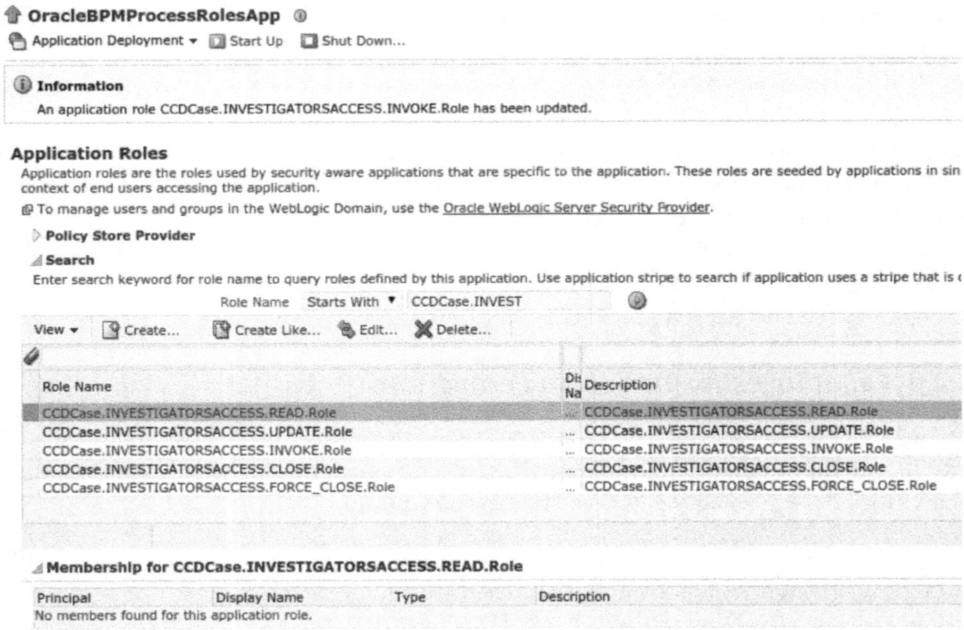

6. Select the *CCDCase.INVESTIGATORACCESS.INVOKE.Role* role and click on *Edit.*
7. In the *Add Principal* pop-up, select *Type* as *User*, and enter *Principal Name* as *jcooper* and click to search.
8. As shown below, select the listed user and click *OK* to add it to the invoke role.

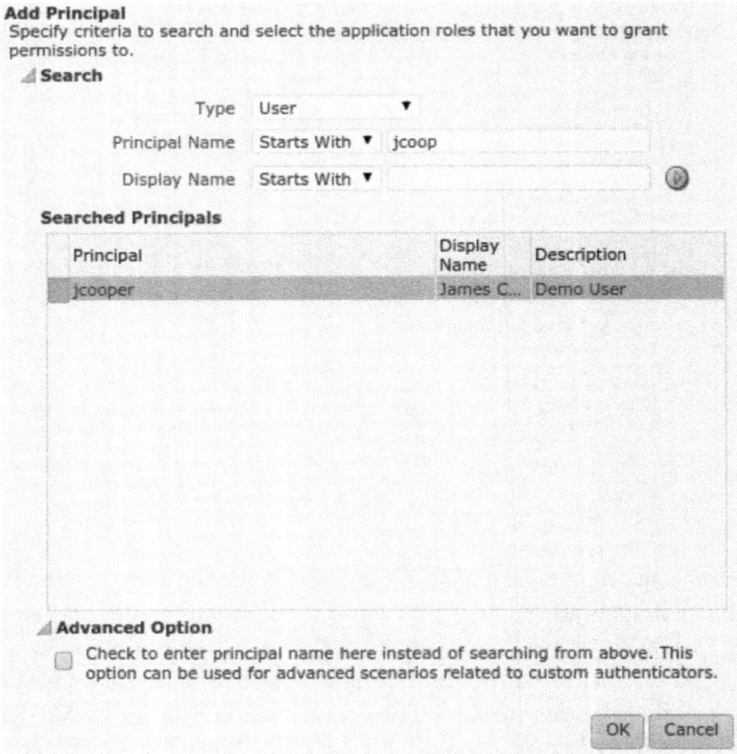

17.6.4.4 Scenario #1

You use two scenarios to test the application. In the first scenario, a charge of $34.56 is disputed by John Doe. The case was created using this information in the previous section. James Cooper is the case manager for this case. Here is how the case gets processed.

1. James Cooper logs in to the BPM Workspace using his user ID *jcooper* and password as *welcome1*.
2. He clicks on the *Case* link to navigate to the case workspace. He sees John Doe's dispute case. He looks at the case details clicking on the *Dispute Details* link. In the dispute details, he changes the status from *ASSIGNED* to *IN PROCESS* and saves it.
3. He clicks on the *Audit Trail* link to look at all that has happened to this case since it was created.
4. He decides to inform the customer about the case status and initiates the *Notify Customer* activity. Since we have only created dummy processed for these activities, the *NotifyCustomer* finishes immediately. He still sees the *Notify Customer* activity in the list of available activities since this is a repeatable activity and can be initiated any number of times.
5. Next he notices a required activity—*Review Charge Details*. As shown below, he initiates this activity and waits for the activity to complete. This activity results in a task being assigned to the CSR role. If notifications were configured for this task, the CSRs would get an email informing them of this new task.

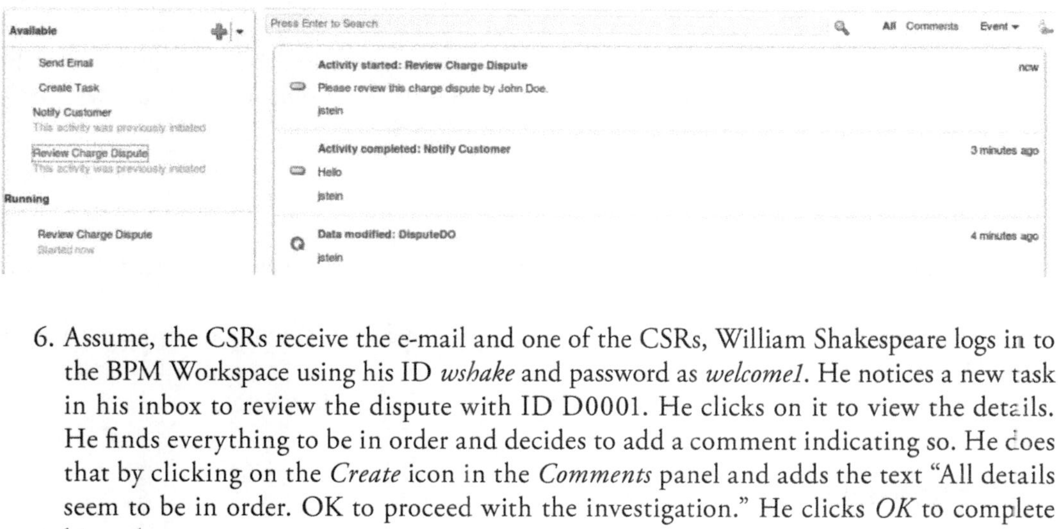

6. Assume, the CSRs receive the e-mail and one of the CSRs, William Shakespeare logs in to the BPM Workspace using his ID *wshake* and password as *welcome1*. He notices a new task in his inbox to review the dispute with ID D0001. He clicks on it to view the details. He finds everything to be in order and decides to add a comment indicating so. He does that by clicking on the *Create* icon in the *Comments* panel and adds the text "All details seem to be in order. OK to proceed with the investigation." He clicks *OK* to complete his task.
7. James Cooper checks back on the case to see if the review is completed. He refreshes the case workspace by clicking on the refresh icon and notices that the review has been completed. He clicks on the *Audit Trail* to view the events. He then clicks on the *Comments* link to see if there were any comments added by the CSR and notices William's comment.
8. James also notices that the first milestone, *Initial Review Completed*, has been achieved. Since the case has now progressed to the next part of the processing, he also sees a couple of more activities, namely, *Investigate Charge* and *Request Documents from Customer*, are now available.

Note: If you have setup your permissions properly as described earlier, only James should have access to the *Investigate Charge* activity. To test this, log-out and log-in as wshake or as jstein. They should not be seeing this activity at all.

9. Since James is satisfied with the information available, he initiates the investigation by clicking on the *Investigate Charge* link. This causes a task being assigned to the analysts to complete the investigation. This also marks the start of the analysis and the *Analysis Started* milestone is marked as having been reached.
10. John Steinbeck, one of the analysts, logs in to the BPM Workspace using his ID as *jstein* and password as *welcome1*. He notices the new task for investigating the charge dispute case with ID D0001. He clicks on the task to show the task details. He conducts his investigation and once done he opens the task and sets the *Outcome* to *MerchantFault* (this is case sensitive) in the *Investigation Report BO* section of the task form. He clicks *OK* to complete the investigation task.
11. Assume that James receives a notification when the investigation is complete. He checks in on the case clicks on *the Investigation Report* and sees the outcome was that the merchant is at fault. He also notices that since it is a merchant fault, activities for communicating with the merchant and initiating chargeback are now available. He also notices the *Analysis Completed* milestone has been automatically marked as *Completed.*
12. James initiates the chargeback process by clicking on the *Initiate Charge-back* activity link.
13. Once the chargeback process is complete, he decides to close the case by clicking on the *Action* drop-down list and selecting *Close Case.* He selects the outcome as "Case Resolved – Merchant at Fault" and clicks *Close Case* to complete the case.

17.6.4.5 Scenario #2

In the second scenario, the amount of dispute is $20 and the case owner decides to write-off the charge.

Use the same test XML as for scenario #1 but change the dispute amount to 20 and the dispute ID to D0002.

Run through this scenario by yourself using scenario #1 as a reference.

17.7 Summary

In the first part you learned how to analyze a case using a mind map diagram by identifying all the different activities that may be required to process the case. The mind map serves the purpose of graphically showing all the related elements of case and their dependencies.

In the second part you saw how to convert the mind map into an implementation design using simple tools such as XSL tables for tabulating all events and corresponding actions. You used these tables later on to create rules using Oracle Business Rules. You built the complete case application by creating activities based on BPMN process and human tasks and deployed and tested it all from within Oracle JDeveloper.

17.A Appendix

17.A.1 customer.xsd

```
<?xml version = '1.0' encoding = 'UTF-8' ?>
<schema xmlns = "http://www.w3.org/2001/XMLSchema"
xmlns:xsd = "http://www.w3.org/2001/XMLSchema"
     xmlns:tns = "http://www.mycompany.com/ns/CCDCase"
targetNamespace = "http://www.mycompany.com/ns/CCDCase"
     elementFormDefault = "qualified">
<element name = "Customer" type = "tns:TCustomer"/>
<complexType name = "TCustomer">
<sequence>
<element name = "CustomerId" type = "xsd:integer"/>
<element name = "FirstName" type = "xsd:string"/>
<element name = "Middlename" type = "xsd:string"/>
<element name = "Lastname" type = "xsd:string"/>
<element name = "SocialSecurityNo" type = "xsd:integer"/>
<element name = "Nationality" type = "xsd:string"/>
<element name = "MaritalStatus" type = "xsd:string"/>
<element name = "Gender" type = "xsd:string"/>
<element name = "Status" type = "xsd:string"/>
<element name = "AddressLine1" type = "xsd:string"/>
<element name = "AddressLine2" type = "xsd:string"/>
<element name = "City" type = "xsd:string"/>
<element name = "State" type = "xsd:string"/>
<element name = "PostalCode" type = "xsd:integer"/>
<element name = "Country" type = "xsd:string"/>
<element name = "HomePhone" type = "xsd:integer"/>
<element name = "WorkPhone" type = "xsd:integer"/>
<element name = "CellPhone" type = "xsd:integer"/>
<element name = "EMailAddress" type = "xsd:string"/>
<element name = "CustomerSince" type = "xsd:dateTime"/>
</sequence>
</complexType>
</schema>
```

17.A.2 test-startcase-input.xml

```
<soap:Envelope xmlns:soap = "http://schemas.xmlsoap.org/soap/envelope/">
<soap:Body>
<ns1:startCaseInputMessage
          xmlns:ns1 =http://xmlns.oracle.com/CaseService/types
          xmlns:ns2 = "http://xmlns.oracle.com/bpm/case">
<ns2:case xmlns:ns3 = "http://xmlns.oracle.com/bpm/case/metadata/
extension">
<ns2:stakeHolders>
<ns2:stakeHolder>
<ns2:name>Stakeholder_CaseManager</ns2:name>
<ns2:displayName>Case Manager</ns2:displayName>
```

```
<ns2:stakeHolderMembers>
<ns2:stakeHolderMember>
<ns2:stakeHolder>jcooper</ns2:stakeHolder>
<ns2:stakeHolderType>USER</
ns2:stakeHolderType><ns2:applicationContext>OracleBPMProcessRolesApp</
ns2:applicationContext>
</ns2:stakeHolderMember>
</ns2:stakeHolderMembers>
</ns2:stakeHolder>
</ns2:stakeHolders>
<ns2:data>
<ns2:name>DisputeDO</ns2:name>
<ns2:data>
<DisputeBO xmlns:xsi =http://www.w3.org/2001/XMLSchema-instance

xmlns = “http://xmlns.oracle.com/bpm/bpmobject/CCDBusinessObjects/
DisputeBO”>
<disputeId>D0001</disputeId>
<creationDate>2014-01-01T00:00:00</creationDate>
<customerId>1001</customerId>
<disputeAmount>34.56</disputeAmount>
<transactionReferenceNumber>2234</transactionReferenceNumber>
<merchantId>BB1134</merchantId>
<transactionDate>2013-12-20T00:00:00</transactionDate>
<creditCardNumber>4444555566667777</creditCardNumber>
<status>NEW</status>
</DisputeBO>
</ns2:data>
</ns2:data>
<ns2:data>
<ns2:name>CustomerDO</ns2:name>
<ns2:data>
<Customer xmlns:xsi =http://www.w3.org/2001/XMLSchema-instance

xmlns = “http://www.mycompany.com/ns/CCDCase”>
<CustomerId>1001</CustomerId>
<FirstName>John</FirstName>
<Middlename></Middlename>
<Lastname>Doe</Lastname>
<SocialSecurityNo>999999999</SocialSecurityNo>
<Nationality>USA</Nationality>
<MaritalStatus>MARRIED</MaritalStatus>
<Gender>M</Gender>
<Status>GOLD</Status>
<AddressLine1>111 No Name St</AddressLine1>
<AddressLine2></AddressLine2>
<City>San Francisco</City>
<State>CA</State>
<PostalCode>99999</PostalCode>
<Country>USA</Country>
<HomePhone>4154150000</HomePhone>
<WorkPhone>6506506500</WorkPhone>
<CellPhone>4084084070</CellPhone>
<EMailAddress>jdoe@emailexample.com</EMailAddress>
<CustomerSince>2000-03-25T00:00:00</CustomerSince>
```

```
</Customer>
</ns2:data>
</ns2:data>
</ns2:case>
</ns1:startCaseInputMessage>
</soap:Body>
</soap:Envelope>
```

Chapter 18

Siebel Tutorial

18.1 Introduction

Siebel is a package-based solution that contains out-of-the-box case management solutions for specific use cases in different industry domains. Once a decision is made to implement a case management solution with Siebel, different activities need to be done to implement the solution. We will look at two aspects of a Siebel-based implementation scenario; the approach on how to design and implement a package-based case management solution and to use the package. In this chapter we will use a police investigation example implemented with the *law enforcement and policing operations* extension, as described in Chapter 8.

The goals of this chapter are as follows:

- Give a high level overview of the Siebel implementation approach
- Show how the implemented solution is used by the end user
- Provide usage details of the Siebel extension for the law enforcement and policing operations solution

18.2 Siebel Implementation Approach

The Siebel implementation approach is based upon following four phases:

- Choosing the Siebel functionality
- Familiarization
- Design
- Implementation

These phases align with the case management solution framework as presented earlier in Section II. The relation between the Siebel implementation approach and the case management solution framework is shown in Figure 18.1. In the first phase, *choosing the Siebel functionality,* the *case management classification* and the Siebel product type is determined. The *case management functional design* is done in the phases, *familiarization* and *design*. After the case

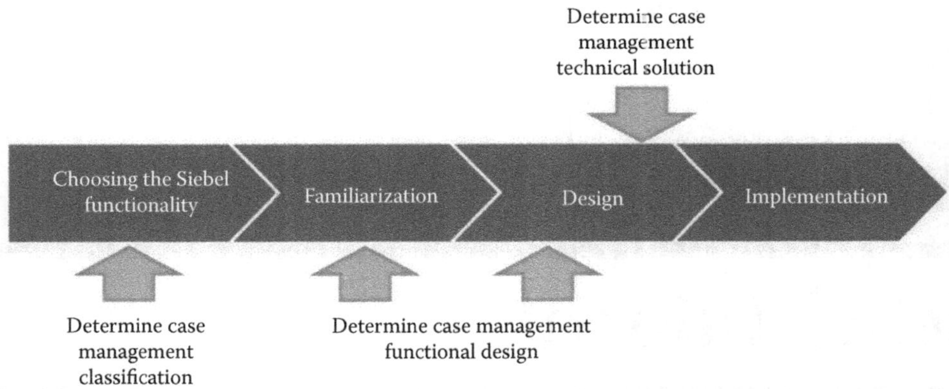

Figure 18.1 The Siebel implementation approach.

management functional design is finished, the *solution mapping* can be determined as part of the design phase. In the last phase the implementation of the Siebel-based case management application can take place.

18.2.1 Choosing the Siebel Solution Type

In Chapter 8 we discussed the different functionalities Siebel provides. The base functionality is a CRM-based application extended with case management capabilities. Siebel extended the case management functionalities toward different industry and cross-industry-specific solutions, known as verticals and horizontals. The first step in the Siebel implementation approach is to determine which Siebel functionality is going to be used as the basis for the solution. In this stage, the following characteristics are used:

- Related industry domain
- Required processes and case high level definition
- The case management classification, service request, incident management, and/or investigation
- Fit–gap with existing base product, verticals, or horizontals

In this chapter we will look at the Siebel *law enforcement and policing operations* extension to fulfill the requirements of the police force in order to be able to fight criminality more effectively.

The classification of the case management to be used in the solution is of the type incident management. This classification impacts the life cycle and the need for intelligence on different levels. This classification was discussed in more detail in Section 4.5.

18.2.2 Familiarization

The core users, process owners and change champions are acquainted with the case management functionality during the familiarization phase. This helps them to understand, absorb, and document the impact of the changes to existing processes and ways of working. This phase provides the foundation for change management, solution realization, and deployment. Typically this phase has a short duration.

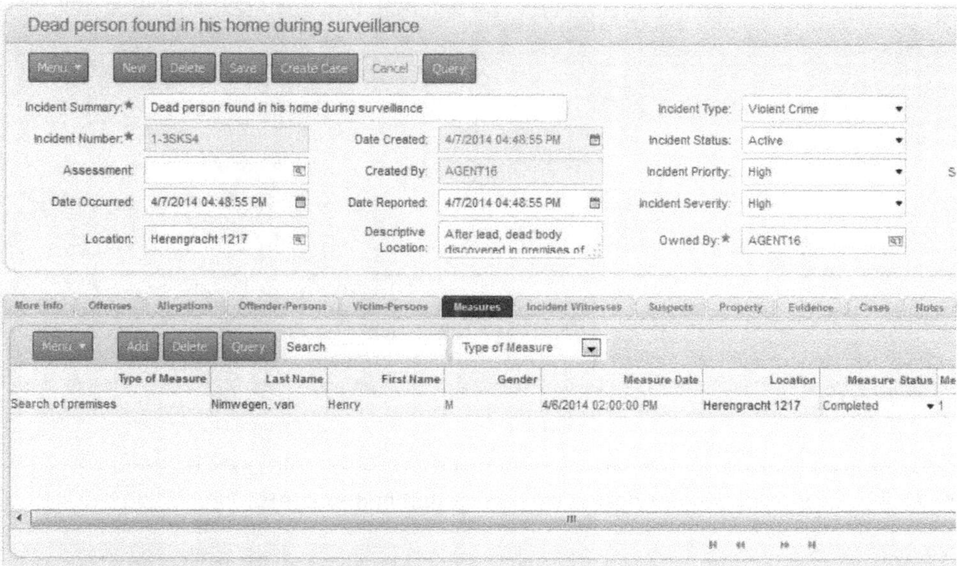

Figure 18.2 Screen design for coercive measures within an incident used for PWT and CRP.

The deliverables of this phase are as follows:

- Business vision, including the scope of the project
- The main requirements for the system
- An overview of the to-be processes and a gap analysis with the current processes
- A first draft of the to-be application architecture
- Insight in a data migration plan outlines the data migration needs, phasing, and approach

Two of the most used types of workshops within the familiarization phase are the *package walk through* (*PWT*) and the *conference room pilot* (*CRP*) with the different stakeholders. Both deliver an innovative contribution to this phase. In the *PWT* sessions, the desired functionality is compared with the standard available functionality in the Siebel product. The outcome of the PWT sessions is used to create a first draft of the system. In the *CRP* sessions, this predefined system is evaluated in a more detailed manner and adjusted in an iterative and interactive way.

These sessions are supported by the user interfaces to visualize the way the system supports the functionality. An example of such visualization is shown in Figure 18.2 that supports the sessions used to determine the police investigation functionality.

18.2.3 Design

The design aims at delivering two case management solution framework artifacts, the case management functional design, shown in Figure 18.3, and the solution mapping.

18.2.3.1 Functional Design

Every functional category will be investigated with the stakeholders; this will be used as input for the configuration and customization part in the implementation phase.

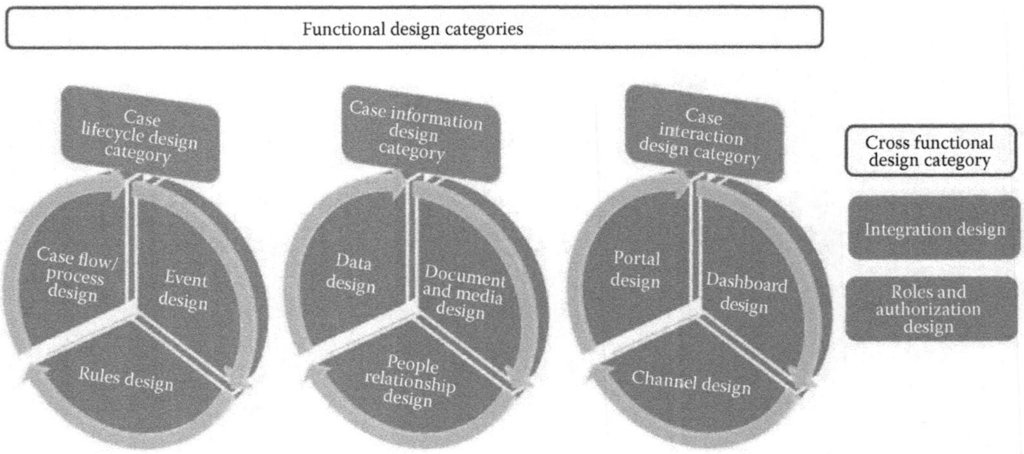

Figure 18.3 Case management design categories and components.

For the police investigation, case-specific attention will be given to the following areas:
Case life cycle design category—As we have seen in Chapter 14, the life cycle management for the police investigation is complex:

- Many investigation types exist.
- Complex state models describe the execution of each investigation type.
  Figure 18.4 shows an example of a complex state model for a lead investigation.
- Different processes support the execution of (allowed) activities during specific states in the state model. Figure 18.5 shows an example of a process around coercive measures against a suspect.
- Both human and automated activities support the process workflows.

All these design aspects need to be designed in relation to the capabilities of the Siebel *law enforcement and policing operations* extension.

Case information design category—The Siebel *law enforcement and policing operations* extension data model already contains information entities that support the work of police investigations, as described earlier in Chapter 8. The main information entities are combined in *incidents*, *leads*, and *cases*. During the design, these information entities are checked against the needs of the police force and related to the current information sources.

Case interaction design categories—Out of the box Siebel delivers standard portal views for the different stakeholders in the police investigations. The police force needs to have the ability to visualize the relations between persons, cases, activities, documentation, and media. All police stakeholders have different requirements what information they need to have access to and how this should be visualized. In this design, the user interface design is shaped toward the needs of the end users in iterative workshops. Another aspect in this design is investigating the channel types the police need to work with the application. Besides, the out-of-the-box browser-based portal new media are entering the police force, such as mobility and connecting to different social media.

Cross-functional design category—In police investigations, often sensitive information is used that should not be made available to everyone in the police force. The Siebel functionalities, *user interfaces*

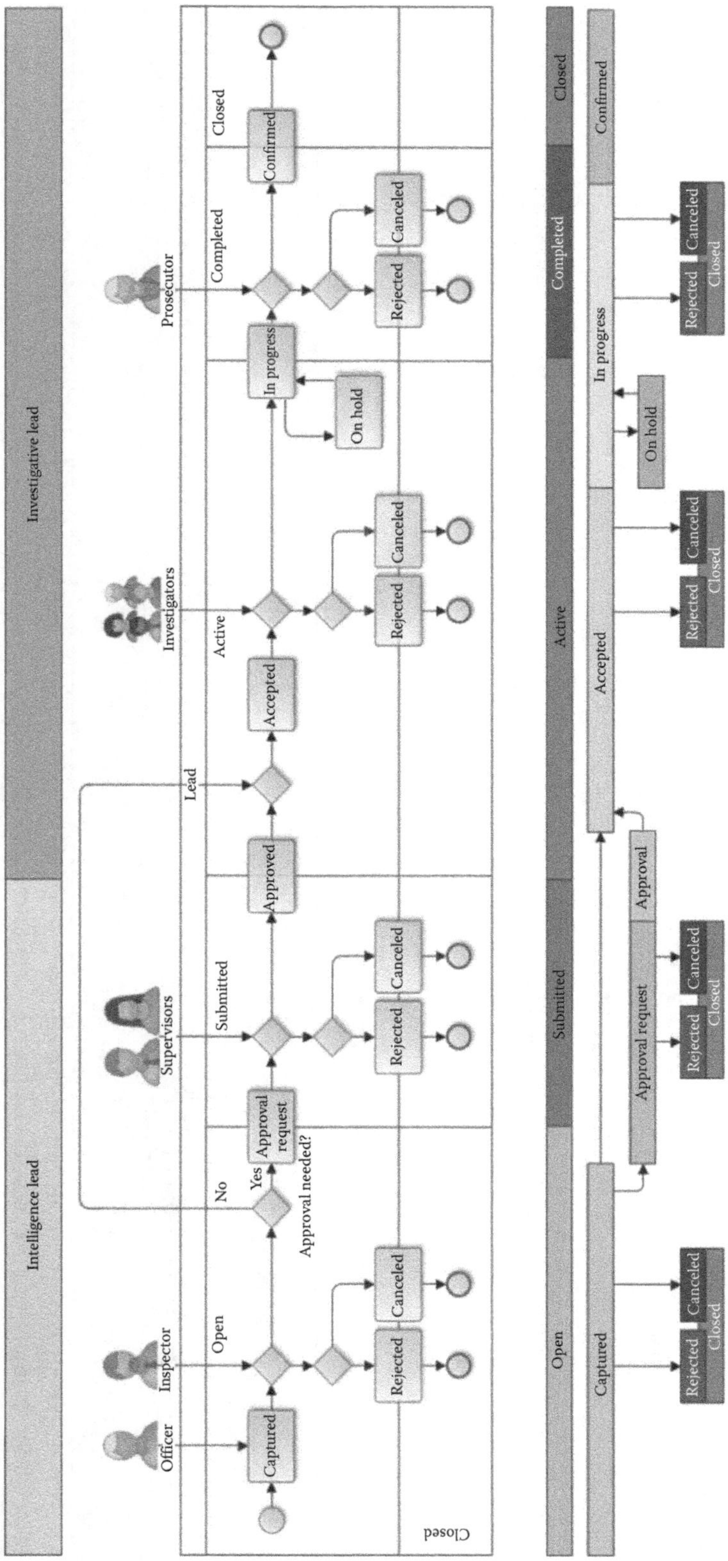

Figure 18.4 Complex state model of a lead to support its full life cycle.

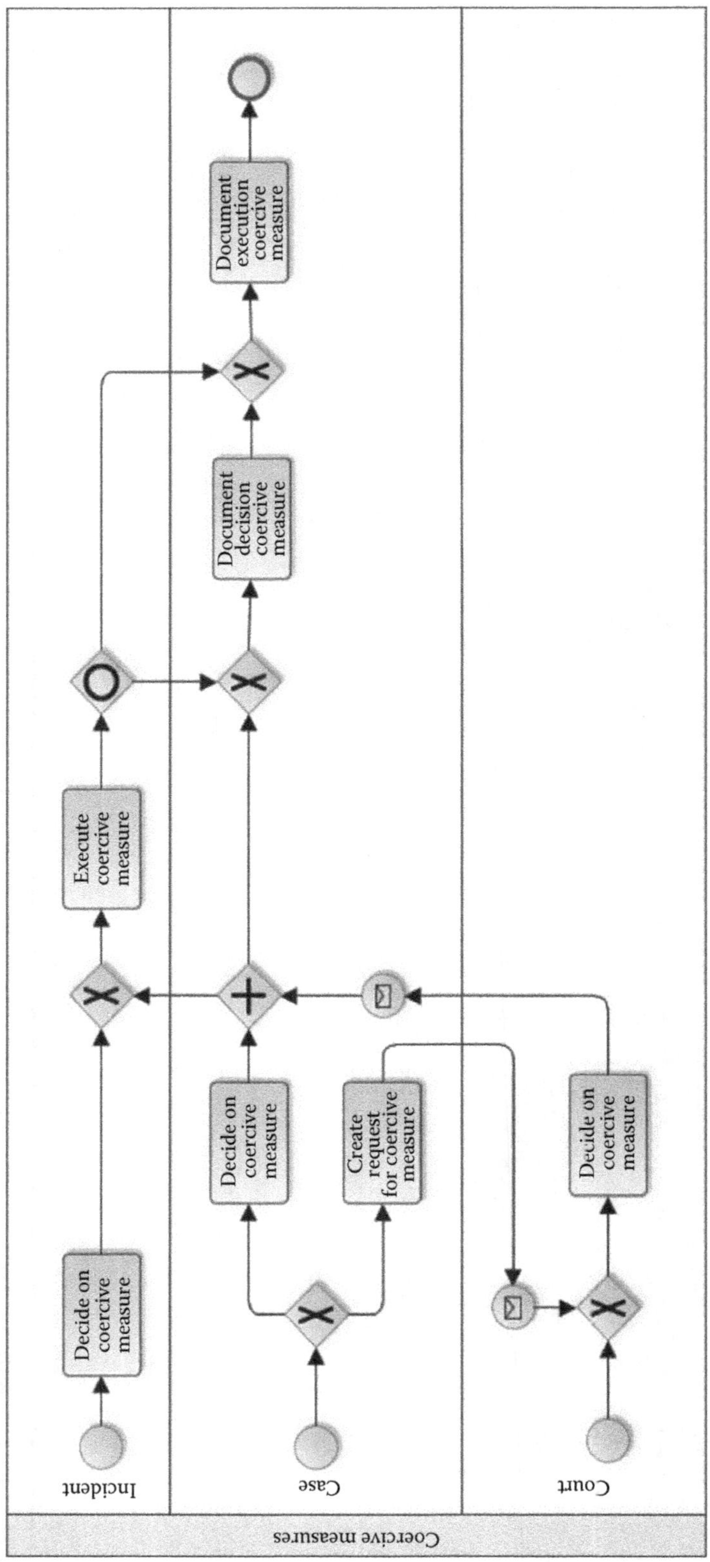

Figure 18.5 Example of a process around coercive measures against a suspect.

access management and responsibilities and *Data related record level access management* enable designing *roles and authorization* functionality on both user interface and on data level.

The Siebel application is going to be placed in an already existing complex police application landscape where information needs to be exchanged between the different applications. In this, the design investigation is done around data ownership, related applications, and the way information is shared between Siebel and the other applications.

18.2.3.2 Solution Mapping

As discussed in Chapter 8, two scenarios exist for implementing Siebel in an already existing landscape, the "Siebel single entity" scenario and the "Siebel in a wider application landscape" scenario.

In the "Siebel single entity," all functionality required by the police force for police investigation is contained in the Siebel *law enforcement and policing operations* extension.

In the second scenario "Siebel in a wider application landscape," the Siebel application is only responsible for a part of the end-to-end police investigation and/or additional support is needed in areas where Siebel does not deliver the needed functionality.

Both scenarios have implications on required functionality in related applications, data migration, and the already mentioned integration capabilities of the application.

18.2.4 Implementation

In the implementation phase, the standard application is configured as specified and custom components such as interfaces and data conversion scripts are built. The objective is to deliver the application as intended by the design and ready for testing and validation. Unit testing is an integral part of the implementation process and is carried out by the developers within the development environment. In this phase, test preparation takes place by establishing the various test plans for system test, integration test, and user acceptance test. The test scenarios are created based on the defined functionality during the design phase often captured in use cases.

During the realization of the application, feedback loops are established to involve the police organization early in the process of reviewing the solution. These feedback session aid the adoption process in the organization and enable necessary changes where needed in the application.

The setup of the application is done on two levels: at the business administration level and the technical administration level:

Business Administration level: Within this level the business logic and user access of the application is managed. The business administrators require a good understanding of the business functionalities. The following (noncomplete) list shows examples of topics that are administrated at this level:

- *State model*: State models determine the lifecycle of the entities in the application. It controls the status change, what statuses are available, who can change them, and when it can be changed. An example of setting up a state model is shown in Figure 18.6.
- *Assignment manager*: These rules can be managed at business administration level. These rules determine what user is assigned to cases and tasks. Due to its complexity and impact, the assignment rules are often managed at technical administration level.

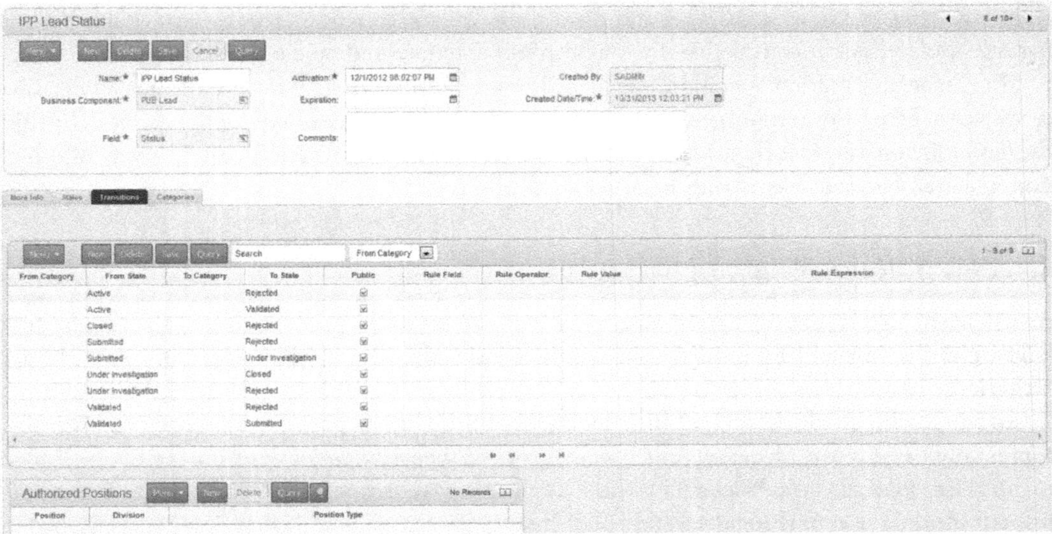

Figure 18.6 Setup screen for state models.

- *Responsibilities and positions*: A user can have one or more responsibilities and usually one position. A responsibility determines what functionality the user can access and the position determines what data the user can access. The access to screens, views, and applets is managed in the responsibilities assigned to the users.
- *List of values*: For speeding up the end-user work and data quality, purposed pick lists are defined in the system. The values of the pick lists are managed in one big table called the list of values (LOV). Dependency of combined pick lists is also managed in the LOV.

Technical Administration Level: This level of administration and setup is related to the IT side of the application. This level requires an understanding of the system architecture and technical functionalities of the application and the interfaces. Within this level, the application software, databases, and interfaces are managed:

- *Workflows and business services*: Within Siebel business processes can be automated using workflow and business services. Workflow to control the processes within the application and business services to control the processes outside the application.
- *Integration and data migration*: Integration with other applications and databases as well as migrating data from external sources into the application database is managed in the technical administration level.

18.3 Using the Police Investigation Application

When the police investigation application is delivered to the police organization, the end users need to be trained into using the application. Here we will show, based upon a police investigation in a murder case, the different steps how the application is used to support the police officers. We use a simplified detective story to show the different activities for which the police case management is used and will show how a lead, an incident, and a case are created within Siebel and how these are linked together.

The implementation we use for this police investigation example is based on a position and role set up specifically defined to fit this story and can be adjusted to other needs and requirements.

18.3.1 Storyline

The storyline is taken from one episode of a famous Dutch detective TV series by Baantjer (http://en.wikipedia.org/wiki/A._C._Baantjer). The author Baantjer used to be a police officer himself and brought knowledge from his own field work into the novels.

In this series, the senior police officer de Cock and his junior sidekick Vledder solve cases with a typical sense of humor known in Amsterdam. The episode we use here is "Healing Masters" (http://www.baantjer.org/). The plot in this episode takes place in a cosmetic surgery clinic and in short deals with tense business relations, a love affair, and a badly treated customer resulting in three homicides. The timeline in Figure 18.7 shows the different activities and events taking place from the moment one of the surgeons has been found murdered. In this picture the three main police case types, the lead, the incident, and the case are plotted. The case starts with the intake of a lead indicating a missing person. When the police officers go to the house of the missing person, they find the body. All information at the crime scene is captured as an incident. The severity of the incidents leads to the creation of the case and is used to store all activities related to the investigation, such as witness statements. The case is also linked to the lead and all Incidents captured during the investigation.

18.3.2 Recording a Lead

The story starts with capturing the information of the interview with the woman that warned the police. This will be captured as a lead *Henry van Nimwegen missing*. This process is called the (easy) intake of a lead. The recording of a lead is a sequential process during which the following information is entered:

- Generic information
- Person, object location, and event (POLE) information
- Operational details
- Lead details

Once the lead is entered, the lead can be further worked on and/or viewed by all authorized personnel in a lead 360° overview. The lead can also be shared with other agencies or organizations via the lead export.

18.3.2.1 Creating the Lead and Entering the Generic Lead Information

The starting point for entering a lead is the lead page as shown in Figure 18.8. From this page, new leads can be created, existing leads can be searched, and the lead can be linked to a case or shared with other agencies or organizations (lead export).

The intake of the lead, shown in Figure 18.9, starts with entering the lead name, which is a short recognizable label. An extensive description of the lead will take place at a later moment.

The date field will be prefilled and cannot be overwritten by the actor. The lead ID is fixed by the system and the actor will also be automatically recorded as the creator of the lead. Lead assignment

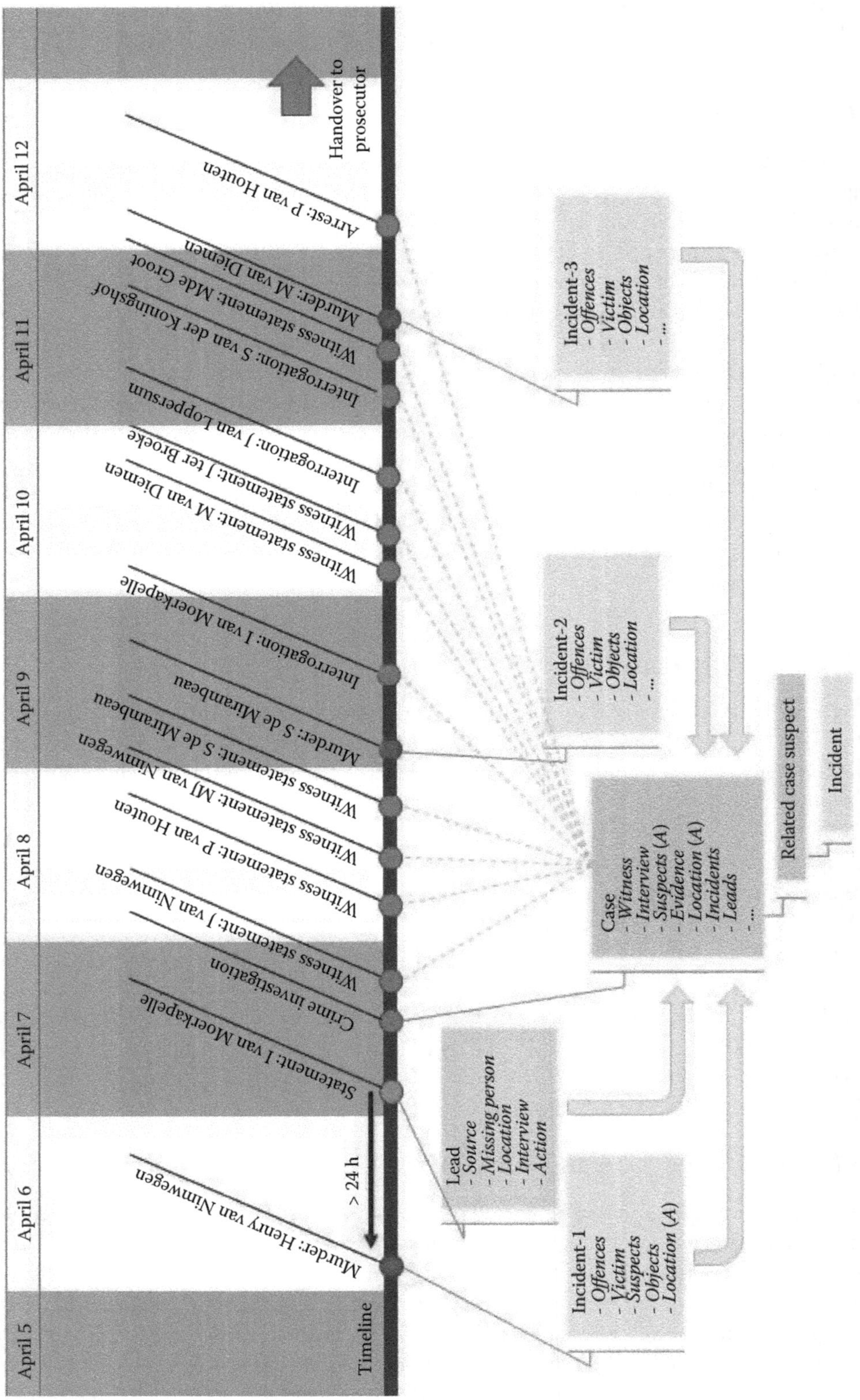

Figure 18.7 Timeline for the "Healing Masters" murder case.

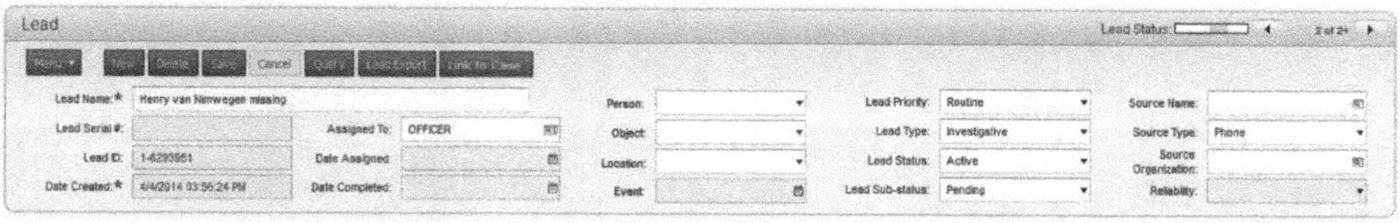

Figure 18.8 The lead page.

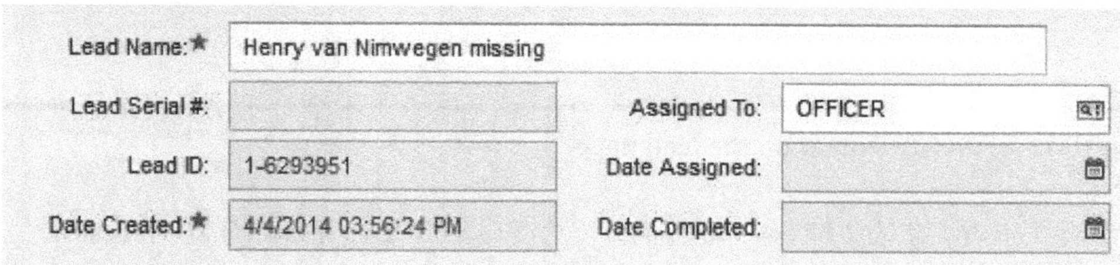

Figure 18.9 Intake of the lead.

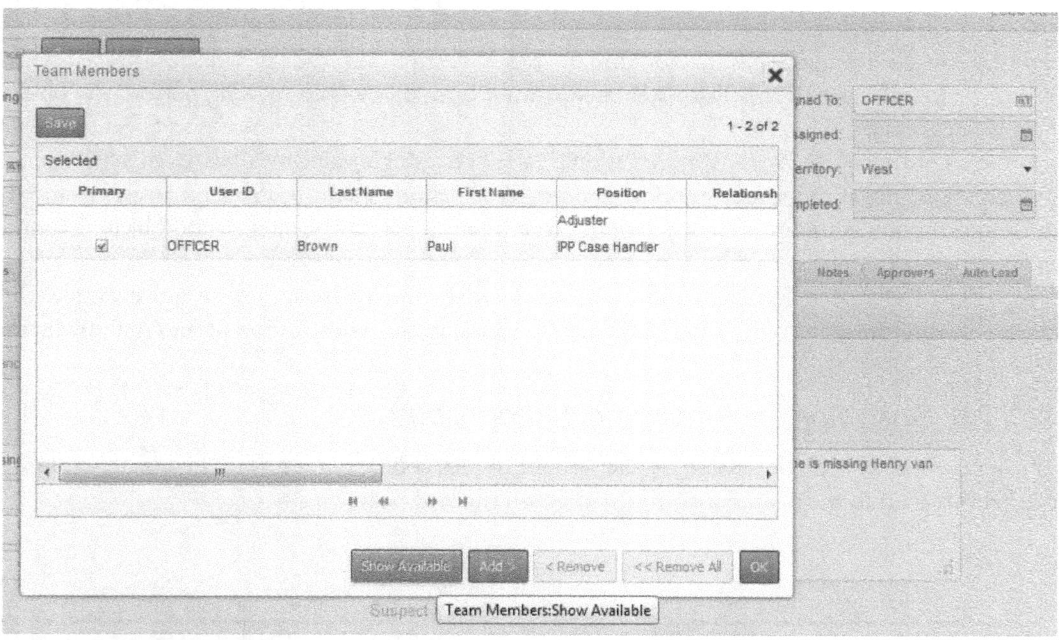

Figure 18.10 Multivalue pick list.

will take place manually based on a multivalue pick list capability (), as shown in Figure 18.10. It is possible to assign multiple persons (team) to a lead. One of the assigned officers will be the prime and final responsible person (primary).

Assignments can be done manually, automatically, and semiautomatically. Often the assignment rules are based and set up on specific needs and requirements that fits best to a police force and can be changed or adjusted at any time.

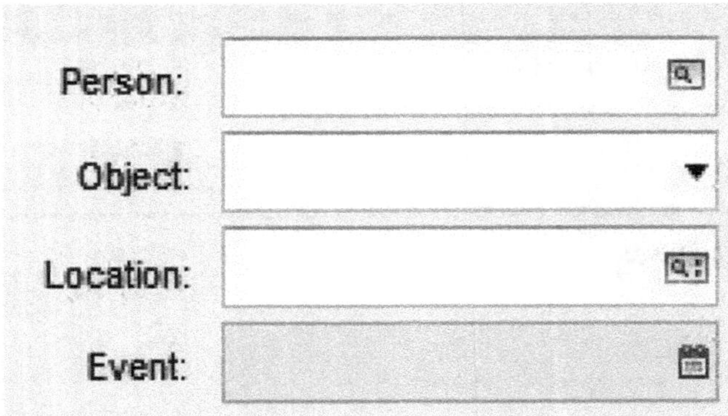

Figure 18.11 POLE fragment on the lead page.

18.3.2.2 Entering the Person, Object Location, and Event Information

The person, object location, and event (POLE) information is the basic information that is needed during the initial information gathering, as shown in the POLE fragment on the lead overview page in Figure 18.11.

The *person* can be selected via a single-value pick list. When the person does not exist in the system, a new person can be created.

In the *object* field describes the nonhuman object related to the lead. When the lead deals with a "lost or found" object, this field is entered. In our example, with a missing person, the object field is left empty.

The recording of the *location* information is based on a single value pick list. In this field information about the address, area and Geographic information system (GIS) details can be stored. Area information is useful when a proximity to a location is known, such as and object is found in a public park or near to a lake.

The last POLE detail is *event* and is related to a data and a description. In our example, the event relates to the date Henry van Nimwegen was missing and a description of the circumstances.

18.3.2.3 Recording the Operational Information

The operational information relates to the way the police will handle this lead. Figure 18.12 shows the fields related to the operational information on the lead page.

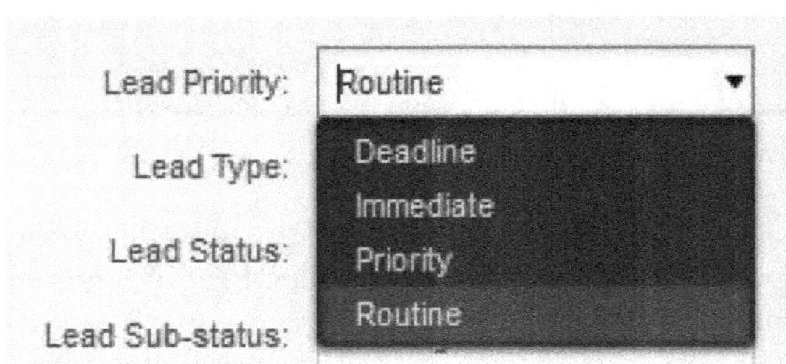

Figure 18.12 Examples of lead priority values.

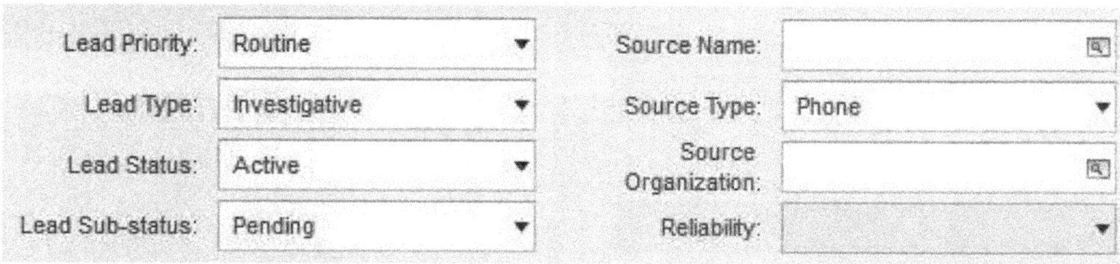

Figure 18.13 Operational fragment on the lead page.

Most of the operation information can be stored by making use of the LOV capability. This will speed up the intake and store information in a consistent way. All these LOVs are maintained at run-time via the business administration page "administration-data."

- The *lead priority* gives an indication when the lead will be acted upon.
- The *lead Type* determines who will be assigned to the lead.
- In Figure 18.4, an example of a state model for a lead is shown. The *lead (sub) status* gives detailed information of the whereabouts of the lead in the state model.
- The source information relates to the origination of the lead as shown in Figure 18.13.

18.3.2.4 Adding More Lead Details

During the investigation on the lead, information becomes available that needs to be attached to the lead investigation. The Siebel police application offers support for linking *attachments, note*, and more *POLE* information to the lead. Incidents and cases, as will be described later in this chapter, can also be linked to the lead. In Figure 18.14, an example of an attachment, the recorded *"Interview with Irene van Moerkapelle,"* is shown.

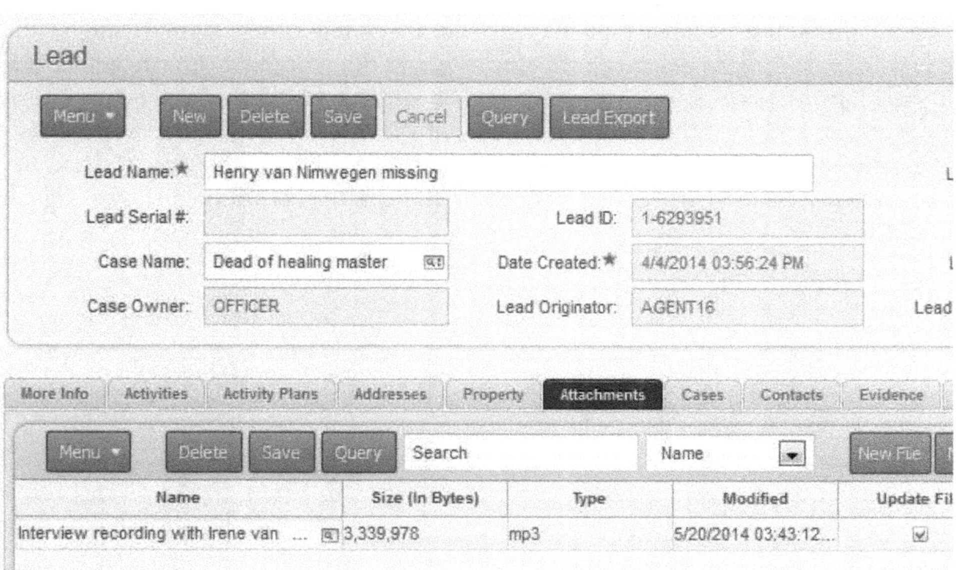

Figure 18.14 Adding an interview in MP3 format to the lead.

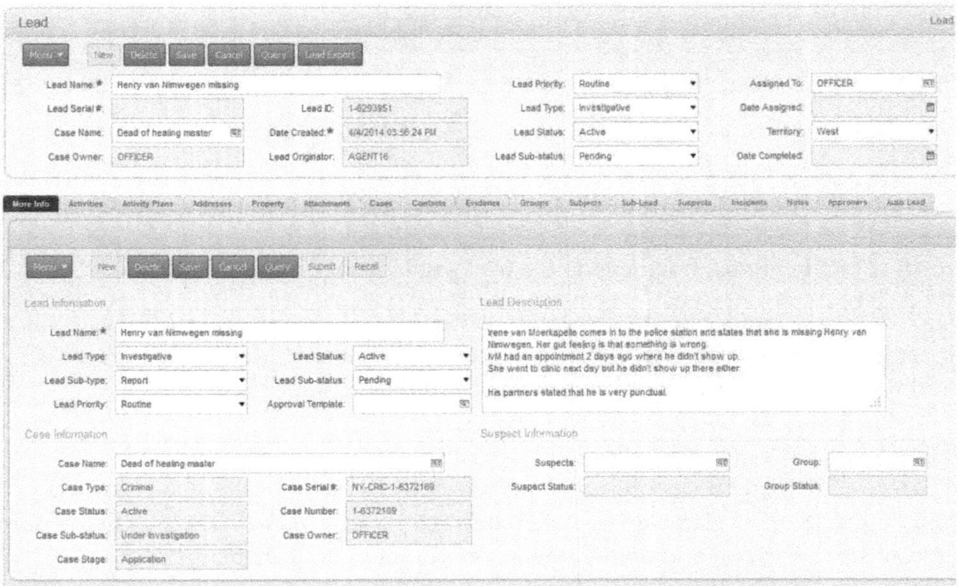

Figure 18.15 Providing a 360° overview in the lead overview page.

18.3.2.5 Provide All Relevant Lead Information in the Lead 360° Overview

A complete overview of the lead and all related attachments, notes, lead details, and relations to incidents and cases is available in the lead 360° overview as is shown in Figure 18.15. This view is available to all authorized personnel who need to work on this specific lead or work on related leads, incidents, and/or cases and are searching for commonalities.

18.3.2.6 Sharing the Lead Information via Lead Export

Another important feature is the capability to share a lead and its related information with other agencies and organizations, where police officers are working on other investigations and looking for relations between police investigations. The lead can be shared in different formats like mail, document, and file. The outcome (answer) of the information request normally is stored as an attachment to the lead. The lead export can also be used to hand-over the lead information to intelligence and analytic tools of specialized departments within the own organization (Figure 18.16).

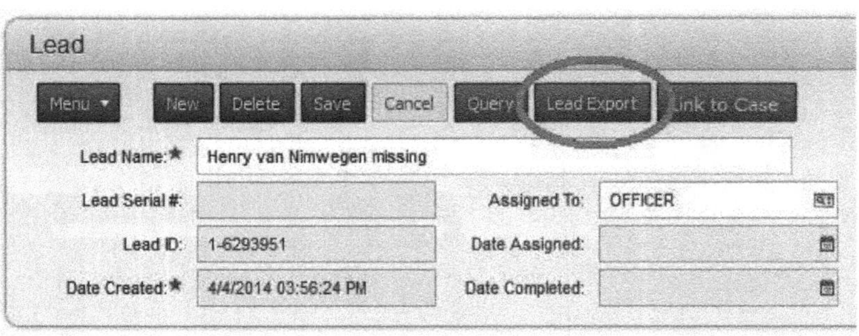

Figure 18.16 The lead export.

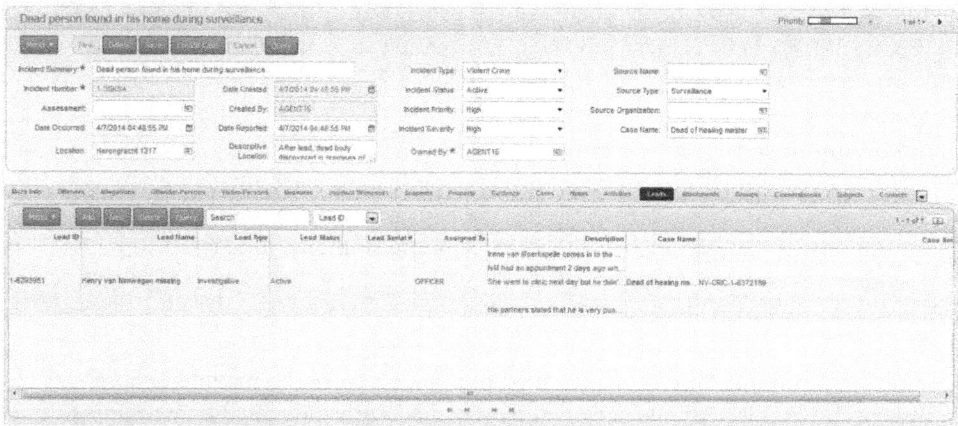

Figure 18.17 The incident creation page.

18.3.3 Recording an Incident

In the crime story example, a surveillance car is sent to the home of Henry van Nimwegen after the lead intake. The police officers discover in the home the dead body of Henry van Nimwegen and results in the creation of an incident "Dead person found in his home during surveillance." The original lead is automatically linked and related to the incident. Figure 18.17 shows the incident information on the top part of the incident creation page and the relation with the lead in the lower part of the page.

In the following we explain some standard capabilities around incident management, creating and working on an Incident, offense management, and coercive measures related to the Incident.

18.3.3.1 Creating an Incident

The creation of an incident starts with entering generic information around the incident and contains the following base information:

- Incident summary
- Dates (occurred, created, and reported)
- Location
- Operational information (type, status, priority, severity, and owner)
- Source (name, type, and organization)

This information is typically entered in the system by a police officer at the scene or at the control room as shown in Figure 18.17. Assessment functionality can be used to determine the incident type, priority, and severity. Eventually the Incident will be assigned to an individual officer, a team, or patrol car.

18.3.3.2 Working on an Incident

The various persons working on the incident will capture more details. These persons are the patrol officers at the crime scene and when a more serious crime took place, the detectives and investigators. All information stored at the crime scene will be in real time available to all users who have access (rights) to this incident. The incident page offers functionality to store all sorts of detailed information related to the incident. A series of tab pages, shown in the middle part of the incident page in Figure 18.17, offer the means to enter information such as the following:

- Offenses
- Person information
- Relations between persons (offender–person, victim–persons), incident witnesses, suspects, and contacts
- Physical related material such as property, evidence, and attachments
- Activities
- Relations with leads and cases

Additionally, it allows you to create a detailed profile of a potential offender whose real identity is not known. This subject profile can then be matched with the actual contact record once the identity is discovered

18.3.3.3 Offence Management

Offence management provides the capability to track and cross reference criminal offences as part of the incident. Offences can be logged as part of the incident and used for reporting purposes and further analysis. The tab page offenses on the incident page provide the offense management functionality as shown in Figure 18.18.

Data about the offenders, victims, force used, and assets can be captured quickly and easily. Officers can follow up on the offence by adding notes or related documents to the record to provide a comprehensive picture of the offence. All of the necessary information for reporting, tracking, and managing offences is easily entered and readily available to officers. The offence management capability enables officers to track alleged offenders and associated offences that arise as part of an incident and record associated arrests, manage property, and file evidence. Officers can capture structured information about the circumstances surrounding the incident using specific categories such as suspicious death, serious assault, robbery, or sexual assault, along

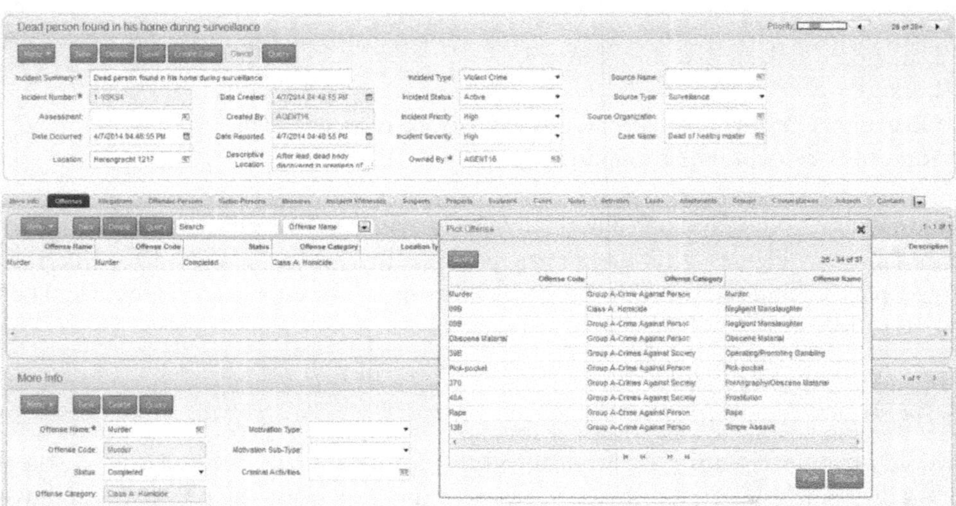

Figure 18.18 Incident offense management.

with descriptive text, to allow detailed information to be captured, and yet still provide for ease in reporting and analyzing crime trends. Additionally, offence management allows officers to track the use of drugs or alcohol related to the offence and record any use of force during the offence, including the use of any weapons.

18.3.3.4 Coercive Measures

Coercive measures functionality is used to ensure that the criminal investigation procedure is not disturbed and prevent the continuance of criminal activity. This functionality is used in both incident and case management. Examples of coercive measures are arrest, detention, seizure, and search of premises and covert coercive measures are telecommunications interception and technical surveillance. The decision to detain a suspect is always made by a competent court of law at the request of the police. Nobody may be detained if this would be unreasonable on account of the nature of the case. The coercive measures management can be found on the incident page as part of the tab page measures as shown in Figure 18.19.

Coercive measures give the police the power to apprehend and arrest suspects but also to submit their cases to a prosecutor for decision. Coercive measures may be used only if this is justifiable in view of the severity of the offence under investigation, the importance of solving the case, and the infringement of the rights of the suspect or others that the usage of coercive measures would entail.

18.3.3.5 Incident Overview

A last feature we would like to mention is the *More Info* feature. The feature shows all relevant information of the incident that a user would like to see in one view. This view is also known as the incident 360° overview, as part of the *More Info* tab page shown in Figure 18.20.

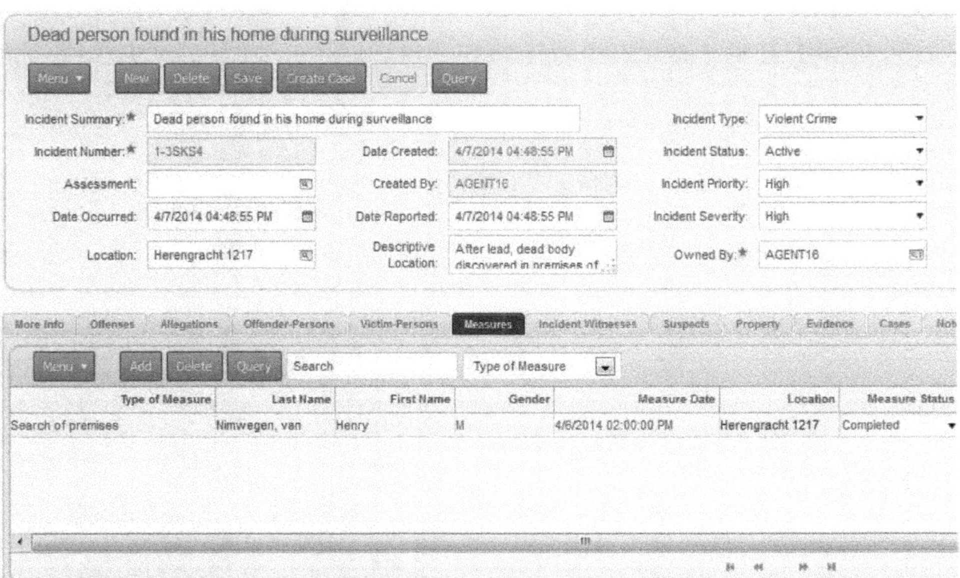

Figure 18.19 Coercive measures.

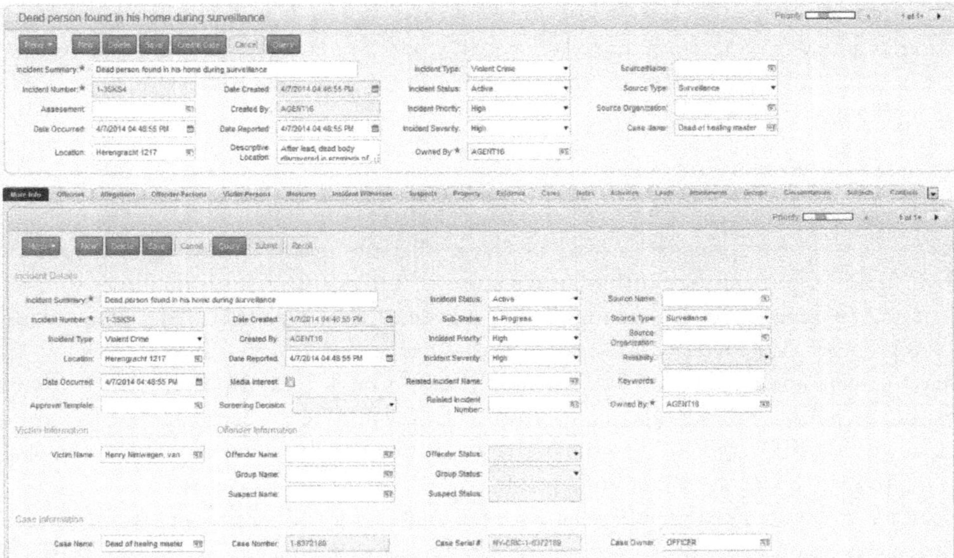

Figure 18.20 Incident 360° overview.

18.3.4 Recording a Case

We started the police investigation example with the creation of a lead. The discovery of the dead body of Henry van Nimwegen leads to the creation of an incident. From the incident a case can be created, as is shown in Figure 18.21. A case deals with the investigation related to a crime that has been committed.

The Siebel *law enforcement and policing operations* provides a secure electronic case file that is used by officers to manage a crime investigation. It provides a team-based investigation for the case and allows the various tasks to be assigned to the members of the team. A security model ensures that only specified officers, detective, and investigators can access a case. The investigation case

Figure 18.21 Creating a case from an incident.

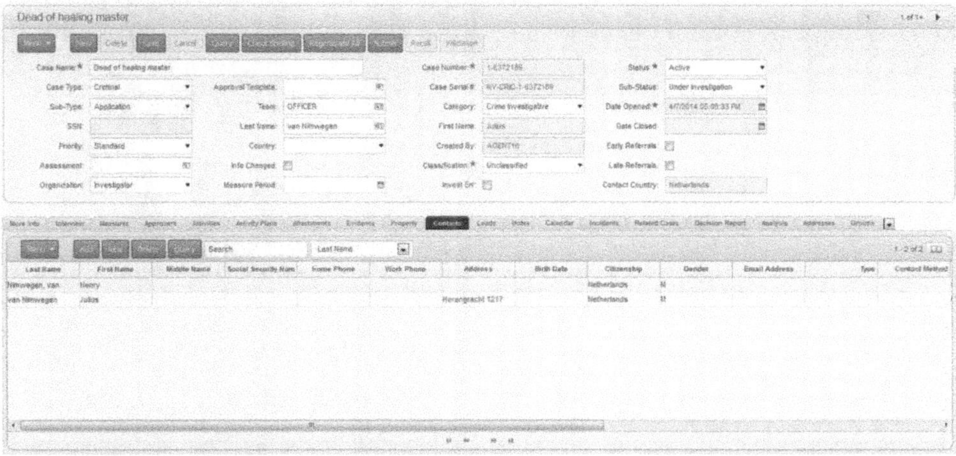

Figure 18.22 The case overview.

is linked to all of the necessary objects to hold the full set of crime information in one integrated place, thus, making it quicker and easier for officers to find and share information. Figure 18.22 shows an example of the case for the police investigation example we use in this chapter.

In the following we explain some standard capabilities around the case handling, the information held as part of the case file, assignment of work, case serialization, evidence management, involved persons, and the report out.

18.3.4.1 Information Held as Part of the Case File

Similar to the incident management, the case page offers functionality to store all sorts of detailed information related to the case. Tab pages, as shown in the middle part of the case overview in Figure 18.22, provide different pages to enter case related information, such as the following:

- Collected case information
- Interviews, assets, quotes, evidence, property, notes, assessments, and circumstances
- Activities
- Plans, activity plans, arrests, assessments, and approvals
- Persons
- Involved organizations, case team members, identities, and identification Info
- Related information
- Leads and incidents

18.3.4.2 Assignment of Cases and Ownership

By default, cases are assigned to the user who creates the case. Cases can be assigned to one or more employees. Assignment of cases can occur automatically, based on geographic location, availability, or other criteria. Administrators can set up assignment rules based on various criteria of the case record. Case ownership can also be adjusted manually by adding employees to the case team. The police investigation is strictly guided by laws and needs strict approval functionality for instance with arrests and coercive measures. The application offers dotted line, or

Figure 18.23 Case approval overview.

cross-department, approvers to model organizational approval workflows. A case approver list can be established to obtain approvals from various people from different departments. For example, both the case supervisor and the finance manager can be designated to approve before a payment will be issued. Additionally, it allows substituting or additional approvers to be added to a case as needed. A case agent, with the correct assigned approval roles, can manually add an approver to the list in addition to the predefined approvers already in the system. Figure 18.23 shows an example of an approval list for our police investigation example.

18.3.4.3 Case Serialization

Case serialization provides the ability to standardize case numbering across the agency by generating unique, custom-defined serial numbers for cases and related leads and evidence. When a case record is created in the solution database, a unique serial number is automatically generated and stamped on the record, as shown in Figure 18.24.

In many agencies, the case numbering system is a standard employed to track case files and all related material. Using case serialization, administrators can set the case serial number to include a combination of multiple fields so that the composite number is meaningful to an investigator. For example, case serial numbers can be generated from a combination of fields unique to the case and combined with either a local counter, based on the number of cases in the system, or a universal counter that numbers every record individually. When related records are created, such as leads or evidence that is related to the case, serial numbers will automatically be created in the proper format, utilizing the unique numbering methodology defined by the agency.

Figure 18.24 Case serialization.

18.3.4.4 Evidence Management

Evidence management enables agencies to track and manage evidence associated with the cases they are managing. Evidence management supports a two-tier evidence model, on a single case level and across multiple cases. This model enables agencies to track unique physical items in addition to managing these items as evidence in the context of one or more cases. It provides the capability to consolidate evidentiary items across an agency, yet still manage evidence in the context of each individual case. During an investigation, evidence collected at a crime scene, such as a weapon, can be logged as a unique item in the application, and later linked as evidence in multiple cases. Figure 18.25 shows an example of evidence, a bullet found at the crime scene, logged as part of our police investigation example.

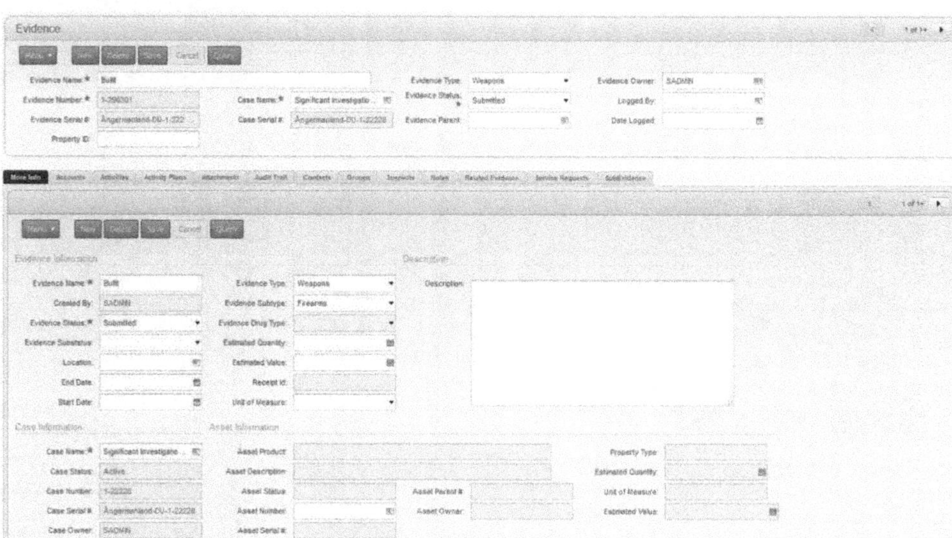

Figure 18.25 Evidence management in the context of a case.

For each evidence record, different activities and documents can be tracked, in accordance with the specific requirements of each case. The application enables agencies to manage the history of activities or actions specific to each case and each piece of evidence. All activities associated with a piece of evidence, such as entry into a property store, submission for forensic tests, or transfer to court during a trial, are securely logged against the evidence. This ensures that its history is known and therefore, the admissibility of the evidence is not compromised.

Agencies can also establish start and end dates for each evidence item and serialize evidence as part of a case and manage the disposal process once the items of evidence no longer need to be held.

18.3.4.5 Involved Persons

A person within a case (or incident) can be a suspect, a victim, an offender, a witness, but also a lawyer or a family member. Within the police investigation, it is important to store all relevant information of a person and visualize it based on the "role" of the person. The person information is available in the *Identification Info* tab page in the case overview, as shown in Figure 18.26.

18.3.4.6 Report Out

When the case is solved and needs to be handed over to the prosecutor, a report out needs to be created of the case content. It is possible to produce a report using different templates, customize the name of the report, change the type (PDF, Doc, RTF, mail or fax) or use other languages (Figure 18.27).

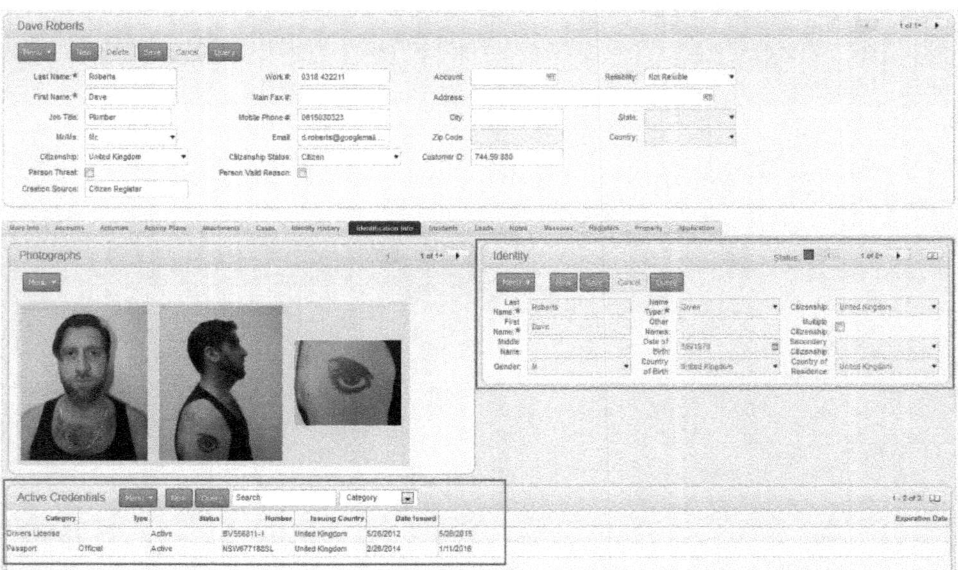

Figure 18.26 Involved persons in the case.

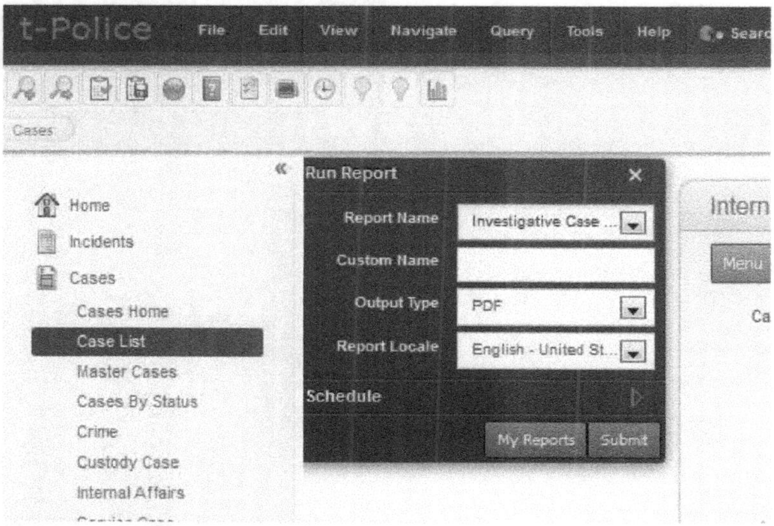

Figure 18.27 Report out of the case.

18.4 Conclusion

In this chapter we have provided a tutorial for a Siebel-based case management solution on two aspects, the Siebel implementation approach and the usage of the application.
The Siebel implementation approach contains four phases:

- Choosing the Siebel functionality
- Familiarization
- Design
- Implementation

We aligned these phases with the case management solution framework (CMSF) as presented earlier in Section II.

The CMSF supports the Siebel approach as follows:

- The first step in the Siebel implementation approach is to determine which Siebel functionality is going to be used as the basis for the solution. The CMSF case management classification supports the determination of the Siebel industry solution as required for the solution.
- In the familiarization (PWT workshops) and the design (CRP workshops) the functionality required for the solution is determined. The CMSF case management design categories and components support the determination of the required functionality.

In the second part we looked at the usage of an implementation of the Siebel law enforcement and policing operations solution. In this example we used a detective story to show how a Siebel application in real life is used. The basis for the Siebel law enforcement and policing operations solution is the lead, incident, and case functionality. We provided examples for all three functionalities in the police investigation example provided in the detective story.

Chapter 19

Concluding Remarks

Dear reader, if you are here after having gone through most of the chapters of this book in some detail, then congratulations for having completed the journey and thanks for your time and interest. We, the authors, have put in significant effort and burnt plenty of midnight oil to put together the content that benefits from our extensive work in this and related areas as well as from a lot of specific research that we undertook in support of this book. In spite of all the hard work that goes into writing a book like this, we thoroughly enjoyed the process; we do sincerely hope that you enjoyed reading the book and found the content useful.

When you reflect on the essentials of case management, especially the adaptive version, you will find that this approach of organizing and executing business activities is possibly the closest we can get to the way we, the humans, solve nontrivial problems. Most of human actions are event driven and so is case management. When we are in trouble trying to solve a difficult problem we naturally consult others who may help us or we seek alternate approaches to attack the problem; you have seen in the solution architecture and implementation chapters that case management applications facilitate collaboration among stakeholders and allow new activities or participants to be added during the case progression. We make decisions based on our knowledge and experience keeping within applicable norms of interaction and behavior; these are also the guiding principles of case management application architecture and usage. We are usually goal oriented in a problem-solving situation and consider the details of the fine-grained actions secondary to finding the final solution; goal orientation is also a fundamental aspect of case management. Since case management can handle knowledge work needed to solve difficult business problems not amenable to traditional business process management (BPM), and since the supporting technologies necessary to design and implement case management are available at a high level maturity, it is not a surprise that there is currently a high level of interest in case management; a quick search on the Internet will rapidly establish this observation. Software vendors have, of course, taken this growing interest seriously. While early stage solutions for case management technology platforms were usually from smaller and niche vendors, in recent years larger ISVs such as Oracle have made case management technology one of their key offerings; many System Integrator (SI) firms like eProseed and Capgemini now include case management consulting as part of their core competency; these trends are further pushing broader adoption of case management (Figure 19.1).

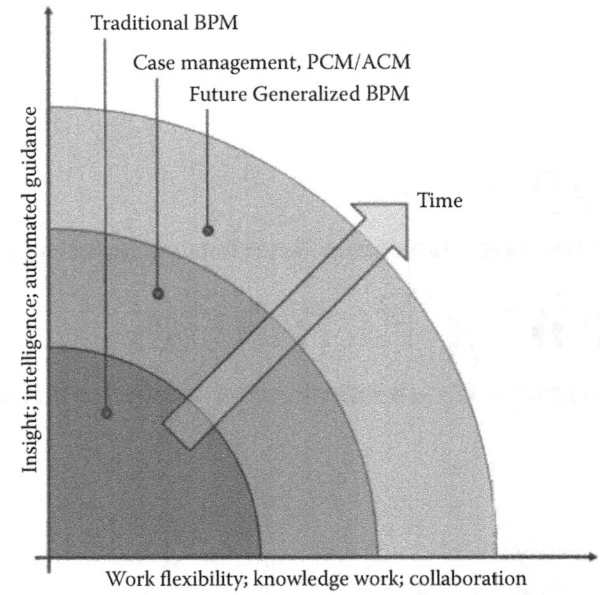

Figure 19.1 Expected evolution of traditional BPM and ACM into Generalized BPM.

So, what does future hold for case management? Besides deeper and wider adoption across industries, we expect to see the following:

1. A stronger movement toward hybrid solutions, that is, combination of traditional BPM and case management in the same solution balancing efficacy and efficiency; we termed this as "Generalized BPM" approach in this book
2. Integrated tooling support from independent software vendors (ISVs) for Generalized BPM solutions, as Oracle has already done in their BPM suite product, and many others are starting to offer similar capabilities
3. Tighter integration of content and portal technologies with case management technology platforms for still better handling of structured and unstructured content and for facilitating easier and more productive human interactions
4. Inclusion of more analytics of all varieties in case management solutions such as historic trends and real-time and predictive analytics that could provide timely and helpful insights to knowledge workers trying to resolve cases
5. More progress toward simplified yet powerful case worker interfaces that mimic natural description of tasks and team interactions
6. Better harnessing of knowledge from records of cases solved that could be packaged as assisting modules to inspire and guide knowledge workers.

An interesting thing to note here is perhaps the emerging *battle* between the proponents of adaptive case management (ACM) and BPM. A few years ago there were predictions by the pundits that the market size of ACM will be significantly larger than that of BPM, some going as far as stating that it will be an order of magnitude larger. Also, some of these industry watchers had claimed that ACM will subsume BPM. ACM will provide additional capabilities for managing business activities, thus, substantially increasing the proportion of all business activities that would be digitized—we do not, however, believe that there is enough evidence yet to reasonably predict if ACM market would be order(s) of magnitude larger than BPM or that it will engulf the traditional BPM discipline. ACM solution construction, as we have explained in several ways so far, is event driven. It is technically possible to recreate a process graph (as in traditional BPM) using appropriate event generation and event handling. In other words, it is possible to use ACM technology platform to replicate traditional BPM processes—we do not think this is necessarily a smart idea since wherever traditional BPM processes do a good job, there is no real benefit of introducing ACM. Lately, we are noticing suggestions that BPM will absorb ACM—we do not think this is a useful debate either since ACM characteristics have many differences when compared to traditional BPM. Of course, we could extend the definition of what BPM encompasses, for example, as we have done in defining "Generalized BPM" that essentially combines traditional BPM and ACM leveraging the commonalities while recognizing the difference. And, yes, we do predict that something like Generalized BPM will subsume traditional BPM and ACM in forthcoming years.

As we have remarked earlier in the book, a large portion of business activities contain elements of unpredictability and much of high-value work require nonroutine knowledge work—case management's goal is to deliver solutions to these types of business activities. Hence, it is safe to assume that the popularity of case management will continue to rise for a while and it will eventually become a mainstream strategy for solving business problems. Along with you, dear reader, we are eagerly waiting to participate in this evolution.

We provided two tutorials in this part to show how a case management solution is designed, implemented, and used with the products Oracle BPM/ACM and Oracle Siebel.

In the Oracle BPM/ACM tutorial, we introduced a mind-mapping technique to identify the different activities part of the case. Based upon a credit card charge dispute scenario we showed how to create and test a BPM/ACM application in JDeveloper.

In the Oracle Siebel tutorial we provided an alignment between the case management solution framework and the Siebel implementation approach. In the second part of this tutorial we showed the usage characteristics of the Siebel law enforcement and policing operations solution. We used a police investigation to show the main police supporting functionalities *lead*, *incident*, and *case* are used.

Appendix A: CORA Model Capabilities*

Layer	*Cluster*	*Capability*	*Description*
Channel access	Ultra thin client	Ultra thin client	Capability to access an application by only delivering presentation data to the client and sending user actions (i.e., server-based computing)
	Thin client	Web browser (HTML)	Capability to access an application through a web browser using plain HTML
	Thin client	Mobile device	Capability to access an application installed on a mobile device. (apps)
	Rich client	Web browser (RIA)	Capability to access an application through a web browser providing a desktop-like user interface (rich Internet application)
	Rich client	Workstation	Capability to access an application through a client installed on a work station
	–	Electronic channel	Capability to provide inbound and outbound electronic data exchange from and texternal actors (B2B and B2C)
Presentation	–	User interface	Capability to validate user input and render and format presentation data output
		User interface process	Capability to orchestrate user interactions in a one-time execution span
		User interface integration	Capability to integrate different user interfaces in one view

(*Continued*)

* The definition of the layers and capabilities described in this chapter are obtained from the CORA model (www.coramodel.com).

Layer	*Cluster*	*Capability*	*Description*
Composition	Orchestration	Human to human	Capability to collaboratively use the same resource, which can consist of multiple actors and multiple time execution spans
	Orchestration	Human to application	Capability to allocate tasks tusers and control the required routing of these tasks
	Orchestration	Application to application	Capability to allocate tasks to applications within an organization and control the required routing of these tasks
	Orchestration	Business to business	Capability to allocate tasks to applications between organizations and control the required routing of these tasks
	Composition	Business component	Capability to compose reuse business logic from one or more IT systems and add (often cross domain) business logic
	Composition	Business entity	Capability to compose business specific cross-domain data objects (i.e., employee, invoice, etc.)
	Composition	Business rules	Capability to compose and execute cross-domain and cross-application business rules
	Composition	Life cycle management	Capability to manage the end-to-end management of all activities in a business process or case
Integration	Synchronous communication	Service mediation	Capability to provide a standard way of describing and calling a function synchronously
	Asynchronous communication	Messaging	Capability to provide a standard way texchange messages asynchronously
	Asynchronous communication	File transfer	Capability to provide a way to exchange (large) messages made up of files asynchronously
	Common	Integration core	Capability to provide core functionality for exchanging data, like transformation, enriching, filter, etc., including capabilities for loading and extracting data and data quality management (e.g., cleansing)

(Continued)

Layer	*Cluster*	*Capability*	*Description*
	Common	Integration metadata	Capability to provide metadata functionality for use during the exchange of data
Application	Make	Make application logic	Capability to provide a set of specific coherent business logic
	Make	Make application entity	Capability to provide (application specific) data objects (i.e., customer and order)
	Buy	Buy application logic	Capability to provide a set of specific coherent business logic
	Buy	Buy application entity	Capability to provide (application specific) data objects (i.e., customer and order)
	Legacy	Legacy application logic	Capability to provide a set of specific coherent business logic
	Legacy	Legacy application entity	Capability to provide (application specific) data objects (i.e., customer and order)
Data	Data access	Data access	Capability to perform operations on data resources, for example, CRUD (as a minimal set)
	Data storage	Master data	Capability to store master data
	Data storage	Transactional data	Capability to store transactional data
	Data storage	Unstructured data	Capability to store unstructured data
	Data storage	Aggregated data	Capability to store aggregated data
	Data storage	Canonical data	Capability to store canonical data
Security	—	Authentication	Capability to check if a user (human or system) is the one it indicates it is by various (combined) means like username and password, chip card, finger print, etc.

(*Continued*)

Layer	*Cluster*	*Capability*	*Description*
	—	Principal propagation	Capability to forward the user credentials throughout the landscape
	—	Compliancy	Capability to pre- and post-assess the compliancy of activities performed in a system against organizational policies, industry standards, and regulations
	—	Encryption (data at rest)	Capability to encrypt data stored in databases, files, and/or messages
	—	Authorization	Capability to authorize the use of functionality and data, preferably based on role-based access and managed from a life cycle perspective
	—	Single sign-on	Capability to log in one system and then reuse the authentication data to log in into another system automatically
	—	User management	Capability to manage users, groups, authentication details, and authorizations
	—	Logging	Capability to log all kinds of system activities
	—	Archiving	Capability to move data, which is no longer actively used, to separate data storage device for long-term retention
	—	Auditing	Capability to establish whether information systems maintain the integrity of stored and communicated data
IT governance	Service-oriented architecture (SOA) governance	SOA governance	Capability to provide service policies, a service repository, and a service registry. The registry capability facilitates the publication, discovery, and consumption of services. The repository capability provides a broader view that allows tracking of services and maintains its relationships tother assets types

(*Continued*)

Layer	*Cluster*	*Capability*	*Description*
	—	System management	Capability to manage individual system software assets
	—	System monitoring	Capability to monitor system assets, ranging from database growth to server temperature
	—	Business activity monitoring	Capability to monitor the performance of business processes supported by automation from the level of activities tprocesses
	—	Configuration management	Capability to manage versions of individual software components and documents and their composition intreleases
	—	Change management	Capability to support the submission of a change request, the definition of solutions, change impact analysis, decision process, and implementation, including software transport
	—	Repository management	Capability to store and query metadata, including software versions
	—	Test management	Capability to perform automatic testing
	—	Batch management	Capability to define, schedule, execute, and monitor jobs
	—	Incident management	Capability to restore a normal service operation as quickly as possible and to minimize the impact on business operations

Appendix B: A Solution Characteristic

Industry Sector	CM Application	"I" T	"IM" T	"S" T	Automated Tasks	Human Interactions	Integration (EAI, B2B)	Business Rules/Expert System Help	Regulations/ Statutes	Structured Content	Unstructured Content	Special Event Handling/ CEP	Special Security Considerations	Customer Facing	Communication External
Horizontal/Common															
	Employee onboarding	N	N	H	M	M	M	N	L	M	L	N	L	H	L
	Customer onboarding	N	N	H	M	M	M	L	L	M	L	N	L	H	L
	AP and AR processing	L	N	H	L	M	M	L	L	H	L	N	L	L	L
	Facilities management	L	N	H	L	H	L	N	M	M	L	N	N	L	L
	Order/Complaint/ service exception management	L	N	H	L	H	M	M	L	M	M	N	N	H	M
	Proposal and bid management	H	N	L	L	H	L	L	L	H	M	N	N	L	M
	Trade and contracts management	L	N	H	M	M	M	L	L	H	L	L	M	L	M
	GRC (Compliance tracking and reporting)	H	M	M	M	M	H	H	H	H	H	L	L	L	M
	Complaints	L	N	H	L	H	M	M	M	M	M	L	L	H	L
PS + Social Services															
	Benefits eligibility	M	N	H	M	M	M	H	H	L	L	N	N	H	L
	Grants management	M	N	H	M	H	L	M	M	H	L	N	N	H	L
	Tax returns processing	H	N	L	H	L	M	H	H	H	L	N	N	M	L
	Unemployment/ Welfare services	M	N	H	M	H	M	M	M	L	H	N	N	H	L

(Continued)

Industry Sector	CM Application	"I"	"IM"	"S"	Automated Tasks	Human Interactions	Integration (EAI, B2B)	Business Rules/Expert System Help	Regulations/ Statutes	Structured Content	Unstructured Content	Special Event Handling/ CEP	Special Security Considerations	Customer Facing	Communication External
		T	T	T											
	Information request processing	H	N	L	L	H	L	M	H	H	M	N	N	H	L
	Patent application processing	H	N	H	L	H	L	H	H	H	M	N	N	H	H
	Permits & operator licenses	M	N	H	L	H	M	H	H	H	M	N	N	H	H
	Environmental safety monitoring	H	H	M	M	H	L	H	H	L	H	H	L	L	H
	Child protection/ Substance Abuser Help/HIV Advisory	M	M	H	L	H	L	H	H	L	H	N	N	H	H
	Disaster relief	M	H	H	H	H	H	M	M	M	H	H	N	H	H
	Terror/Epidemic threat handling	H	H	L	H	H	H	H	H	L	H	H	H	H	H
	Adverse incident tracking in clinical trials	H	M	L	H	H	M	H	H	H	H	M	H	H	H
Financial Services															
	New account opening	L	N	H	H	L	M	M	H	H	M	L	H	H	L
	Loan origination	M		H	H	H	M	M	H	H	M	L	H	H	L
	Investor servicing	H	L	H	L	H	L	L	H	M	M	L	H	H	L
	Dispute resolution	M	H		L	H	L	M	M	M	M	L	L	H	M
	Wealth management	H		M	L	H	M	L	H	M	L	M	H	H	L

(Continued)

Industry Sector	*CM Application*	*"I"*	*"IM"*	*"S"*	*Automated Tasks*	*Human Interactions*	*Integration (EAI, B2B)*	*Business Rules/Expert System Help*	*Regulations/ Statutes*	*Structured Content*	*Unstructured Content*	*Special Event Handling/ CEP*	*Special Security Considerations*	*Customer Facing*	*Communication External*
		T	*T*	*T*											
	Corporate communications	M	H	N	H	L	L	L	L	H	L	L	M	L	H
	Regulatory reporting	M	N	H	M	M	H	L	H	H	L	L	M	L	H
	Fraud and money laundering investigations	H	H	N	L	H	M	M	H	H	M	M	H	L	H
	M&A services	H	N	M										L	H
	Stock market listing	H	L	M	L	H	L	H	H	H	L	M	H	L	H
	Fraud management	H	M	L	L	H	M	H	H	M	H	H	H	L	H
Insurance															
	P&C claims processing	M	H											H	L
	Underwriting & risk management	H	N	M	M	M	M	H	H	M	L	L	M	L	L
	New account opening	L	N	H	H	L	M	M	H	H	M	L	H	H	L
	Policy management	L	N	H	M	M	M	H	H	M	L	L	H	L	M
Healthcare															
	Member enrollment	L	N	H	M	M	M	L	H	H	L	L	H	H	L
	Payer claims processing	H	M	N	H	M	M	H	H	H	M	L	H	H	L

(Continued)

Industry Sector	CM Application	"I"	"IM"	"S"	Automated Tasks	Human Interactions	Integration (EAI, B2B)	Business Rules/Expert System Help	Regulations/ Statutes	Structured Content	Unstructured Content	Special Event Handling/ CEP	Special Security Considerations	Customer Facing	Communication External
		T	*T*	*T*											
	"Continuum of care" coordination	M	H	N	M	H	H	M	H	H	M	M	H	H	M
	Legal contracts management	L	H	N	M	M	M	L	H	H	L	L	H	H	L
	Policy and procedure management	M	N	H	M	M	M	H	H	M	L	L	H	M	L
Legal + Police															
	Legal practice management, time tracking and billing	L	N	H	H	M	H	H	H	H	L	L	H	L	L
	eDiscovery and case information management	H	M	N	H	M	H	H	H	H	L	M	H	L	L
	Docketing and court proceedings coordination	M	N	H	H	H	M	M	H	H	L	L	H	L	L
	Criminal investigation	H	H	L	M	H	M	M	H	L	H	H	H	L	H
	Mandatory information collection (e.g., biometrics)	H	N	H	H	M	H	H	H	L	H	L	H	L	L

(Continued)

Industry Sector	*CM Application*	*"I"*	*"IM"*	*"S"*	*Automated Tasks*	*Human Interactions*	*Integration (EAI, B2B)*	*Business Rules/Expert System Help*	*Regulations/ Statutes*	*Structured Content*	*Unstructured Content*	*Special Event Handling/ CEP*	*Special Security Considerations*	*Customer Facing*	*Communication External*
		T	*T*	*T*											
Energy & Utlities															
	Process safety management	M	H	N	M	H	M	H	H	L	M	M	H	M	M
	FERC eTariff (US)	N	N	H	H	N	M	M	H	H	N	N	L	N	M
	Project and transmittals management	L	N	H	M	M	M	L	L	H	L	L	L	M	M

"I" - Investigative; "IM" - Incident Mgmt; "S" - Service Request or Offer

Index

A

Activity governance, 86, 88
Adaptive case management (ACM), 407–409
 agile adaptivity, 49
 BPM suite
  audit trail, 188–189
  BPMN 2.0 compliant process, 178
  case flow and process design, 180–182
  characteristics, 179
  cross-functional design category, 189–191
  document and media design, 189
  event design, 182
  features, 180–182
  interaction design category, 185–187
  product mapping, 183–185
  rules design, 182–183
  stakeholder, 190
  variations and unpredictability, 178
 business agility, 16–17
  adaptive planning, 41, 43
  business capabilities, 38
  range and time, 38–39
  solution component granularity, 44
  solution management complexity, 44
  system-theoretic approach, 43
  working styles, 44–45
 business case
  business needs and financial benefits, 94–95
  cost–benefit-risk, 94
  costs, 95–96
  dominant forces, 92–93
  format, 93
  risks, 96–97
 CAS (*see* Complex adaptive systems (CAS))
 case activities
  BPMN (*see* Business process modelling notation (BPMN))
  human task (*see* Human task–based case activity)
  implementation, 326, 348–349
  properties, 326–327
 case elements, 324–326
 case management project
  CCDApplication, 331
  composite selection, 332
  editing page, 333
  gallery, 331
 CCDCase application, 363–365
 content configuration, 343–344
 credit card charge dispute (*see* Credit card charge dispute)
 customer.xsd, 379
 data definition, 326–327
 data objects
  customer data, 339–340
  data forms, 340–341
  definitions, 336
  dispute data, 337–338
  flex fields, 341–342
  identification, 336–337
  investigation report, 339
 DCM and PCM, 48
  characteristics, 67–68
  competing design, 62
  cost-quality-time, 69
  definition, 66
  deterministic *vs*. nondeterministic, 67–69
  Google's search engine, 66
  Holy Triangle, 61
  Iron Triangle, 61
  load and deformation characteristics, 65
  pure play vendors, 62
  purpose case management, 63
  quality-cost-time, 63
  system classifications, 64–65
  traditional ERP, 67
 definition, 21–24, 67
 deployment and testing
  case workspace, 369–370
  CCDCase composite application, 366
  CCDCaseDataForms, 366–367
  CSR, 373
  dispute details, 373
  enable development mode, 365
  instance, 367–368
  Investigate Charge activity, 374

investigator access permission, 371–372
Notify Customer activity, 373–374
roles administration, 370–371
task form, 367
test users, 365–366
WebLogic Server, 364
documents, 328
event design, 329
external case data, 327–328
interactionism, 47
midsize insurance company, Europe
adoption plan, 90–91
BPM model, 89
handling claims, 88
maturity, 91–92
Nile crocodiles and cuttlefish, 48–49
open and adaptive system, 50
vs. PCM
collaboration, 73
dimensions, 74–75
event-driven paradigm, 73
features and capabilities, 75
high-quality user interfaces, 76
journey, 70–71
National Defense Executive Reserve Conference, 71
radar chart, 74
record applications, 76
TEI formula, 73
permissions
application policies, 345
application roles, 344
definition, 348
labels, 348
properties
category, 334
duration, 334
milestones, 334
outcomes, 334
priority, 334
summary, 333
title, 333
rules design
activity event actions, 357
Add icon, 360
definition, 356–357
dummy case data, 358
investigate charge activity, 356
milestone events, 361–362
Parameterized option, 359–360
and policies, 328–329
PrepareCase activity, 359–360
review charge dispute, 356, 359–360
user events, 362–363
value set, 358
WriteOffRange, 360
SR-CAS, 50–51
Four-Cs (*see* Four-Cs principles)
hybrid nature, 60–61
KPIs, 61
relevance of elements, 55–56
stakeholders
application roles, 345–346
definition, 344–348
OracleBPMProcessRolesApp, 344
program, 328
runtime, 327–328
XPATH expression, 328
target adaptive system, 52
test-startcase-input.xml, 380–381
tutorial files installation, 324–325
usage characteristics, 239, 241
user events, 344
AIIM, *see* Association for Information and Image Management (AIIM)
Application Development Framework (ADF), 186–187, 340–341, 344, 355, 367
Application layer
BAM, 228
CORA model
cross-functional design areas, 162, 164
design categories and components, 157, 159
high-level mapping, 158–159
information design mapping, 162–163
interaction design, 161–162
lifecycle design, 159–161
Endeca Information Discovery, 234–235
OPA product, 232
Association for Information and Image Management (AIIM), 22

B

BAM, *see* Business analytic monitoring (BAM)
BPMN, *see* Business process modelling notation (BPMN)
BPM suite, *see* Business process management (BPM) suite
Business agility, 38
adaptive planning, 41, 43
business capabilities, 38
range and time, 38–39
solution component granularity, 44
solution management complexity, 44
system-theoretic approach, 43
working styles, 44–45
Business analytic monitoring (BAM)
application layer, 228
composition layer, 227–228
dashboard, 228
data layer, 228
implementation, 225, 227
integration layer, 228
presentation layer, 227
technical architecture, 229–230

Business case
costs, 94–96
dominant forces, 92–93
format, 93
needs and financial benefits, 94–95
risks, 96–97
Business Process Execution Language (BPEL), 180, 185
Business process management (BPM) suite; *see also* Adaptive case management (ACM)
BPMN 2.0 compliant process, 178
case flow and process design, 180–182
characteristics, 179
cross-functional design, 189–191
event design, 182
features, 180–182
information design, 187–188
audit trail, 188–189
document and media design, 189
interaction design, 185–186
channel design, 187
portal design, 186–187
maturity model
architecture, 84, 87
business and strategy, 84
capability domains, 83–84
governance, 88
information, 88
infrastructure, 87
OA&M, 88
organization, 88
projects, portfolios, and services, 88
product mapping, 183–185
rules design, 182–183
stakeholder, 190
variations and unpredictability, 178
Business process modelling notation (BPMN)
case activities and properties, 348, 349
creation, 350, 352
credit card rewards dispute resolution, 15, 40–41
data association, 352–353
definition, 353–354
implementation, 348
input type, 350–351
Start and End nodes, 351
Business-to-business (B2B) orchestration, 185

C

Capability maturity model (CMM), 18, 23, 34, 79, 106
BPM (*see* Business process management (BPM) suite)
CMMi, 80
generalized BPM, 80–81
maturity levels, 81–82
SOA, 80
Capability maturity model integration (CMMi), 80–81
CAS, *see* Complex adaptive systems (CAS)
Case management (CM), 14, 16
ACM (*see* Adaptive case management (ACM))
application of solution, 28
Broker model, 25
delivers value, 24
Forrester's classification, 26–27
knowledge-oriented, 24
self-service models, 24
BPM suite (*see* Business process management (BPM) suite)
British sitcom, 4–5
business dictionary, 5
classifications
Forrester case management, 119–120
incident management case (*see* Incident management case classification)
investigative case (*see* Investigative case classification)
principles, 120–121
service request (*see* Service request classification)
CORA model (*see* Common reference architecture (CORA) model)
creating solutions
ACM solutions, 27–30
agile methods, 33–34
build/buy, 30, 32–33
case data, 37
case documents, 37
CMMN standard, 34
credit card rewards dispute resolution, 36, 38–41
customer/internal supporting systems, 34
levels, 34–36
credit card rewards disputes
BPMN, 11
CSR ticket, 10
real-life variations, 11, 13
traditional BPM model, 11–12, 14
crime-to-court process (*see* Crime-to-court process)
criminal investigation, 7–9
DCM (*see* Dynamic case management (DCM))
doctor and patient, 5
ecosystem, 18–20
functional design
design components (*see* Case management design components)
design template, 116–117
principles, 101–102
goal-driven, 9–10
history, 20–21
knowledge work freedom, 9–10, 17–18
Nordstrom, 4
on-demand collaboration, 9–10
PCM (*see* Production case management (PCM))
solution framework, 171
uncertainty, 3
WF and BPM, 3

Case management design components
cross-functional design
aim, 114
integration, 115–116
principles, 114
roles and authorization, 114–115
information design
aim, 108
document and media design, 112
operational level, 108–109
people relationship design, 112
principles, 108
strategic level, 110–111
tactical level, 109–110
interaction design, 113
aim, 112
channel functionality, 113–114
dashboard functionality, 113
portal functionality, 113
principles, 112
lifecycle design, 104
aim, 103
case/process flows design, 104–107
event design, 106, 108
principles, 104
rules design, 106
Case management model and notation (CMMN), 23, 34, 106
Case Management Society of America (CMSA), 22
Case management solution framework (CMSF), 99
CBD, *see* Component based development (CBD)
CEP, *see* Complex event processing (CEP)
Channel access layer, 156
Clinical case management, 25
CM, *see* Case management (CM)
CMM, *see* Capability maturity model (CMM)
CMMN, *see* Case management model and notation (CMMN)
CMS, *see* Content management system (CMS)
CMSA, *see* Case Management Society of America (CMSA)
Common reference architecture (CORA) model, 411–414
business rules capabilities, 165, 169
case flows and processes capabilities, 165, 167–168, 170
event handling capabilities, 165
functional decomposition
cross-functional design areas, 162, 164
design categories and components, 157, 159
high-level mapping, 158–159
information design mapping, 162–163
interaction design, 161–162
lifecycle design, 159–161
IT landscape, impact of
business functionalities, 156
methodological input, 157–158
risk identification, 155
solution architecture, mapping, 157–158
stacked solution layer, 156
technical capability mapping, 156–157, 166, 168
Competitiveness of firms, 5–6
Complex adaptive systems (CAS)
characteristics, 54
complicated systems, 53
components, 54–55
individual parts, 52
intentionality and purposefulness, 56
schematic of, 52–53
sense-and-respond manner, 56
subsystems, 54
Complex event processing (CEP), 30, 418–422
Component based development (CBD), 44
Composition layer, 156, 227–228
Content management system (CMS), 20, 328, 343, 369
Continuous Query Language (CQL), 232
CORA model, *see* Common reference architecture (CORA) model
Credit card charge dispute
case flow and process design, 317–318
description, 313–316
event design, 321–322
incident management, 315
information design
data design, 323–324
document management, 323–324
implementation, 321
people relationship design, 322–323
rules design
initiate chargeback, 321
investigate charge, 320–321
milestones, 319–320
notify customer, 321
notify merchant, 321
request documents, 319
review charge dispute, 320
write-off charge, 320
Credit card rewards disputes
BPMN, 11
CSR ticket, 10
real-life variations, 11, 13
resolution, 36, 38–41
traditional BPM model, 11–12, 14
Crime-to-court process
business challenges
crime patterns, 282–283
globalization, 281–282
national budgets, 283
police organization, 282
social values, 282
technology, 282
police investigation (*see* Police investigations)
Criminal investigation, 7–9, 134, 399, 421
CSR, *see* Customer service representative (CSR)
Customer capital, 5–6
Customer centricity, 256–257, 260–261, 302
Customer relationship management (CRM), *see* Siebel
Customer service representative (CSR), 314, 322, 373

D

Data integration, 234–235
Data layer, 156, 162, 228
Data objects
  customer data, 339–340
  data form creation, 340–341
  definitions, 336
  dispute data, 337–338
  flex fields, 341–342
  identification, 335–336
  investigation report, 339
Data storage, 156, 235
Diamond Credit Card Company, 10–11
Dynamic case management (DCM), 22, 48
  characteristics, 67–68
  competing design, 62
  cost-quality-time, 69
  definition, 66
  deterministic *vs*. nondeterministic, 67–69
  Google's search engine, 66
  Holy Triangle, 61
  Iron Triangle, 61
  load and deformation characteristics, 65
  pure play vendors, 62
  purpose case management, 63
  quality-cost-time, 63
  system classifications, 64–65
  traditional ERP, 67

E

Endeca Information Discovery, 306
  components, 234
  data integration, 234–235
  data storage, 235
  end-user information, 235
  investigation area, 235
  service request area, 235
End-user information discovery, 235
Enterprise Resource Planning (ERP), 57–58, 67, 76, 235
Event delivery network (EDN), 185
Event-driven architecture (EDA), 177

F

Flex fields, 341–342
Forrester's classification, 26–27, 119–120
Four-Cs principles
  capabilities, 58–59
  collaboration, 59
  context, 57–58
  coordination, 59–60
Functional decomposition
  cross-functional design areas, 162, 164
  design categories and components, 157, 159
  high-level mapping, 158–159
  information design mapping, 162–163
  interaction design, 161–162
  lifecycle design, 159–161

H

Holy triangle, 61
Human task–based case activity
  creation, 354–356
  definition, 356
  task form, 356
Human-to-human (H2H) collaboration, 185

I

Incident management case classification
  business challenges, 134
  context, 133
  crime-to-court process (*see* Crime-to-court process)
  design components, 136–138
    case flow model, 139–142
    case state model, 143–145
    phases, 135, 139
  determination, 134
  industry processes, 134
  principles, 135
Insurance claim management, 312
  case flow and process design, 300–301
  case management classification, 299–300
  customer facing, 299
  financial, 298–299
  injury claims, 298
  IT landscape, 299
  property claims, 298
  rules design, 301
  solution mapping
    case flows and process capabilities, 304–305
    entitlement determination, 306
    information discovery, 306
    integration capabilities, 306
    Oracle product, 306–307
  user interface design
    channel design, 302
    dashboard design, 302–304
Integration layer, 156, 162–163, 228
Intelligence design
  BAM
    application layer, 228
    composition layer, 227–228
    dashboard, 228
    data layer, 228
    implementation, 225, 227
    integration layer, 228
    presentation layer, 227
    technical architecture, 229–230
  components, 223–224
  dashboard design, 225
  Endeca Information Discovery, 234–235

event design, 224
information levels, 225–226
OEP
credit card fraud, 231
functionality, 230
off-loading products, RFID, 231–232
OPA, 232–234
RTD, 236–237
rules design, 224
InvestigateCharge activity
creation, 354–356
definition, 356–357
task form, 356
Investigative case classification
business challenges, 145
context, 143, 145
design components, 148–150
case flow model, 146–147
case handling work, 151
case state model, 151–153
loosely coupled interactions, 146
determination, 145
industry processes, 145
principles, 145
Iron triangle, 61

J

Java server faces (JSF), 187, 340

K

Key performance indicators (KPIs), 302
BAM dashboard, 228
case management information levels, 109
case owners and departmental stakeholders, 110
claim handling, 302
operating model, 260
Oracle SOA suite, 261
product leadership lifecycle, 26, 263
tactical dashboards, 113
Knowledge governance, 88

L

Law enforcement and policing operations solution, 195

M

Mobile application framework (MAF), 187
Mortgage request handling
business challenges
customer service, 248
probability of default, 249
regulations, 248–249
case flow and process design, 250, 253
customer intimacy, 311
information design
document and media, 253
one customer view, 253–255
people relationship, 255–256
interaction design
customer centricity, 256
operational excellence, 257
product leadership, 257
investigations, 249
operating model
customer centricity, 257, 260–261
lifecycle capability, 257–258
operational excellence, 257, 261, 263–264
product leadership, 257, 261–262
product leadership, 311
service request, 249

N

Nordstrom, 4

O

Object Management Group (OMG), 18, 23
OEP, *see* Oracle Event Processing (OEP)
OOTB case management, *see* Out-of-the-box (OOTB) case management
OPA, *see* Oracle policy automation (OPA)
Operational excellence, 257, 261, 263–264, 311
Operations, administration, and management (OA&M), 83, 88
OPSS, *see* Oracle Platform Security Services (OPSS)
Oracle business intelligence, 110, 139, 225
Oracle Event Processing (OEP)
credit card fraud, 231
functionality, 230
off-loading products, RFID, 231–232
Oracle Platform Security Services (OPSS), 344
Oracle policy automation (OPA)
design and run time features, 232–233
entitlements determination, 233–234
insurance claim, 306–307
product leadership, 261–262
STP, 275–277
Oracle service cloud
cross-functional design
integration, 220
roles and authorization functionality, 220, 222
functionality, 210
history, 209
information design
components, 214–215
data design, 215–217

document and media design, 216–217
people relationship design, 217
interaction design
channel design, 213–214
dashboard, 214
portal design, 212–213
life cycle design
case flow and process design, 218–219
event design, 219–220
product mapping, 220–221
rules design, 219
usage characteristics, 210–211, 239–241
Out-of-the-box (OOTB) case management, 30

P

PCM, *see* Production case management (PCM)
Person, object location, and event (POLE) information, 394–395
Police information model, 199–200
Police investigations
case flow and process design
high-level process, 284
police case type, 284–285
state model, 285–286
case recording
evidence management, 403–404
incident, 400
information, 401
involved persons, 404
ownership assignment, 401–402
report out, 404–405
security model, 400–401
serialization, 402–403
classification, 283
end-to-end process, 280–281
event design, 286
full-blown scenario, 312
external systems, 290–291
implementation, 294, 296
interaction and information capabilities, 292–293
lifecycle capabilities usage, 292
incident recording
coercive measures, 399
creation, 397
More Info feature, 399–400
offence management, 398–399
persons working, 397–398
information design, 286–287
interaction design
completion status, 290
documents and media, 287
functionality, 288
involved persons, 287
linked cases, 287
police case, 288–289
police portal, 288–289
lead recording
generic information, 391, 393
interview recording, 395
lead export, 396
operational information, 394–395
POLE, 394
360° overview, 396
storyline, 391–392
umbrella scenario, 312
dashboard functionality, 291
implementation, 295–296
interaction and information capabilities, 292–293
lifecycle capabilities usage, 292
phases, 291
portal functionality, 291
Policy governance, 86, 88
PrepareCase activity
creation, 348, 350
data association, 351
definition, 353
implementation, 348
input type, 351–353
Start and End nodes, 352
Presentation layer, 156, 227
Production case management (PCM), 22, 48
characteristics, 67–68
competing design, 62
cost-quality-time, 69
definition, 66
deterministic *vs*. nondeterministic, 67–69
Google's search engine, 66
Holy Triangle, 61
Iron Triangle, 61
load and deformation characteristics, 65
pure play vendors, 62
purpose case management, 63
quality-cost-time, 63
system classifications, 64–65
traditional ERP, 67
Product leadership, 250–251, 257, 261–262, 264, 311

R

Radio frequency identification (RFID), 231
Range agility, 38–39
Real-Time Decisions (RTD), 236–237
Record-level access, 207
RFID, *see* Radio frequency identification (RFID)
RTD, *see* Real-Time Decisions (RTD)

S

SAAS, *see* Software-as-a-service (SAAS)
Sense-and-respond complex adaptive systems (SR-CAS)
Four-Cs principles
capabilities, 58–59
collaboration, 59

context, 57–58
coordination, 59–60
hybrid nature, 60–61
KPIs, 61
relevance of elements, 55–56
Service cloud, *see* Oracle Service cloud
Service-oriented architecture (SOA) suite; *see also* Adaptive case management (ACM)
agile adaptivity, 178
CCD case, 363–364
channel design, 187
customer centricity, 260
customer intimacy, 264
EDA, 177
full-blown scenario, 294
Fusion Middleware, 178
generalized BPM, 86
information support, 188
infrastructure, 366, 368
insurance claim, 306
integration capabilities, 179
integration functionality, 190, 206
interaction design, 260, 262–263
lifecycle management Siebel mapping, 204
operational excellence, 263
Oracle lifecycle mapping, 184
portal design, 186–187
principle, 178
product integration, 190
product leadership lifecycle, 262
umbrella scenario, 295–296
welfare request
nonstandard situations, 275, 277
STP, 275–276
Service request classification
business challenges, 122–123
context, 120
design components, 125–127
case flow model, 124, 128–129
case handling work, 128, 130–131
case-state model, 132–133
design template, 124
determination, 120–121
industry processes, 121–122
principles, 123
Siebel, 239, 409
building blocks, 194, 197
case flow and process design
assignment management, 201–202
law enforcement and policing operations, 202–203
state model, 201–203
workflow management, 201
characteristics, 195–197
configuration *vs.* customization, 194
CRM, 193
cross functional category, 206–207
extensions function, 194–195
familiarization, 384–385
functional design
complex state model, 386–387
cross-functional design, 386, 389
information design, 386
interaction design, 386
life cycle management, 385–386
process around coercive measures, 386, 388
function integration, 206
horizontal and verticals, 194
implementation, 383–384
business administration level, 389–390
technical administration level, 390
information design
document and media design, 200
people relationship and data designs, 198–200
interaction design, 205–206
lifecycle design, 204
case flow and process design, 200–203
event design, 203
product mapping, 203–205
rules design, 203
police investigation (*see* Police investigations)
portal and channel design, 205–206
roles and authorization, 206–207
solution mapping, 389
terminology, 194, 196–197
usage characteristics, 239, 241
SOA suite, *see* Service-oriented architecture (SOA) suite
Software-as-a-service (SAAS), 209–211
Solution characteristics, 418–422
SR-CAS, *see* Sense-and-respond complex adaptive systems (SR-CAS)
Stakeholder governance, 86, 88
Straight through processing (STP)
application-to-application, 185
welfare request, 273, 275–276
Strength-based case management, 25

T

Time agility, 39, 44
Total Elemental Interactions (TEI), 73

W

Welfare request process, 311–312
investigation cases, 267
life cycle design
decision management, 270
determine entitlement, 270–271
multireality system, 270, 272
receive customer event, 268–269
nonstandard situations, 275, 277
organizations and citizens, 266–267
service request, 267
STP, 273, 275–276
Work flow (WF), 3, 74